A HISTORY OF
AMERICAN MAGAZINES
VOLUME III: 1865–1885

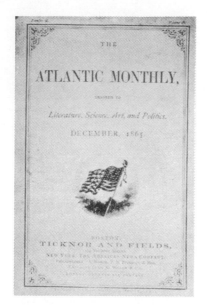

COVERS OF FOUR LEADING MAGAZINES OF THE
POSTWAR PERIOD

The flag on the *Atlantic Monthly* cover was a Civil War feature and disappeared in the latter sixties. The *Harper's* cover shown here was retained for many years. The *Galaxy* cover is the third one used by that magazine. The *Scribner's Monthly* cover was designed by C. H. Jenckes.

A History of

AMERICAN MAGAZINES

1865–1885

BY

FRANK   LUTHER   MOTT

THE BELKNAP PRESS OF

HARVARD UNIVERSITY PRESS

Cambridge, Massachusetts

1967

THE FIRST PRINTING OF THIS BOOK WAS PUBLISHED BY THE
HARVARD UNIVERSITY PRESS IN COÖPERATION WITH THE
MODERN LANGUAGE ASSOCIATION OF AMERICA, WITH
THE ASSISTANCE OF A GRANT AWARDED BY THE AMERICAN
COUNCIL OF LEARNED SOCIETIES FROM A FUND PROVIDED
BY THE CARNEGIE CORPORATION OF NEW YORK

LIBRARY OF CONGRESS CATALOG CARD NUMBER 39–2823
PRINTED IN THE UNITED STATES OF AMERICA

To

ARTHUR MEIER SCHLESINGER

"HE WAS A SCHOLAR, AND A RIPE AND GOOD ONE,
EXCEEDING WISE, FAIR SPOKEN, AND PERSUADING."

PREFACE

THE method of presentation of materials employed in the preceding volumes of this series has been continued in the following pages. A full explanation of that method will be found in the Preface of Volume II, dealing with the period of 1850–65. Two more volumes, which will bring the history down to the present, are in preparation.

I wish to acknowledge here my special obligation to Mr. Willard Church, of Montclair, New Jersey, for the loan of valuable documents relating to the *Galaxy*; to Mr. Ernest W. Clement, of Buffalo, New York, for similar materials relating to the *Western Literary Messenger*; to Mr. Francis H. Bangs, of Haverford, Pennsylvania, for details of the many periodical connections of his father, John Kendrick Bangs; to Mr. Franklin J. Meine, of Chicago, for the privilege of examining his collection of comic periodicals; to hundreds of men and women with special knowledge of various details of magazine history who have taken time to answer inquiries; and to the many editors and publishers of current periodicals who have furnished me with material, sometimes at the cost of no little labor.

Moreover, it is a pleasure to repeat my thanks to Professors Jones, Foerster, Clark, Paine, Schlesinger, and Thornton for their valued help with this, as well as with the preceding volume. I wish to acknowledge also the help in publication of the Modern Language Association of America, exerted through its secretary, Professor Long, its Committee on Research Activities, and its delegates to the American Council of Learned Societies.

I am much indebted to Miss Mildred Mott and Mrs. Vera I. Mott for the preparation of the indexes to Volumes II and III.

FRANK LUTHER MOTT

State University of Iowa
Iowa City, Iowa
June 1, 1938

CONTENTS

CHAPTER IV

WOMEN AND THEIR MAGAZINES

CHAPTER V

SCIENTIFIC, TECHNICAL, AND TRADE JOURNALS

CHAPTER VI

MEDICINE, LAW, FINANCE, AND AGRICULTURE

CONTENTS

CHAPTER VII

EDUCATION AND ART

CHAPTER VIII

MUSIC, THE THEATER, AND SPORTS

CHAPTER IX

LITERARY PHASES OF POSTBELLUM MAGAZINES

CHAPTER X

POLITICS AND ECONOMICS

CHAPTER XI

A POSTSCRIPT ON SOME FEATURES OF THE PERIOD

CONTENTS

SUPPLEMENT

SKETCHES OF CERTAIN IMPORTANT MAGAZINES
WHICH FLOURISHED 1865–1885

ILLUSTRATIONS

A HISTORY OF
AMERICAN MAGAZINES
1865–1885

CHAPTER I

MAGAZINE PUBLISHING AS A BUSINESS

THE twenty years after the Civil War were filled with problems of extraordinary difficulty. In spite of their variety, nearly all of these problems may be said to have arisen from troubles in assimilation: it was as if the nation had eaten a tremendously big meal and was suffering from a painful indigestion.

TROUBLES OF THE GREAT AMERICAN DIGESTION

It had, for example, taken in the Great West, and the difficulties attending the assimilation of that region were many and various. The Union Pacific had to be built, and the Crédit Mobilier scandals grew out of the financing of that gigantic project; the wars against the Indians and the slaughter of the buffalo are ruthless episodes of this absorption of the West into the nation. The Union had also, after four years of conflict, enforced its claim to sovereignty over the southern states, and here again were acute pains of indigestion: it is unnecessary to itemize the political, industrial, and social trials of a tragic "reconstruction." That whilom frontier, the Mississippi Valley, was also presenting difficulties of assimilation. Having won, almost overnight, the agricultural dominance of the nation, it became quite as suddenly the seat of a dangerous agrarian discontent.

Another kind of gorging had added to the nation's troubles. The tremendous expansion of currency during the war and even after its close, coupled with the continued postponement of the resumption of specie payments by the government, created a speculator's market. It was a great feast while it lasted; and even after Jay Cooke's failure in September 1873, with all the disasters that followed on its heels, speculation in railroad stocks and Wall Street gambling in its most audacious forms continued on the basis of an inflated currency. Men who had come up quickly from poverty to wealth and had acquired no notion of the social responsibilities of financial power found themselves in the saddle: Drew had begun as a cattle drover, Vanderbilt as a ferryman, Gould as clerk in a country store, Fisk as a peddler. The very novelty of wealth bred unscrupulousness.

It was much the same in the matter of governmental corruption. Here the failure to assimilate foreign elements, particularly the Irish, had some part in the debacle; but in the main, the trouble lay in the ease with which untrained men could vault into power. Tweed, Sweeny, Connolly, Hall, and the others who robbed the city of New York worked with Fisk and Gould. Gambling and corruption were in the air. Getting rich was too easy. Members of Congress, of the President's cabinet, caught the contagion; and the Whiskey Ring scandal involved, in its aftermath, the President himself.

To cure the national dyspepsia resulting from this high living — even to come through it alive — was as much of a test as the Civil War itself. Reconstruction was in some way accomplished; the West was built up; the Middle West went forward in spite of its aches and pains; the worst of the rascals were driven out; national credit was restored; the financial crisis of 1873–78 was passed.

Another general observation must be made about the period as a whole. More than most periods, it was a time of new growths. Whether the war was responsible, or whether it was merely the yeasty state of the public mind in these years, the fact is that the old sanctions — ecclesiastical, educational, social — were breaking down. The moral conventions maintained so long under the vague name of "puritanism" were losing their old power. The public attitude toward churches was changing. The ideal of classical education was losing its position. Frontier manners were being mellowed and refined. The hundredth anniversary of our nationality marked an era in our national mind and spirit as well as in our chronology. And emerging from the economic and social thought of the time were such movements as the antitrust crusade, labor unionism, humanitarian organization, the single-tax enthusiasm, and bimetallism.

The two decades are clearly a unit in magazine history. Beginning with the exuberance of the years immediately following Appomattox, passing through the trial by depression of the seventies, the magazines came up to 1885 gradually gaining in prestige and prosperity but functioning along much the same lines that had been laid down shortly after the war. No break came until the founding of a group of such innovators as the *Forum*, the *Arena*, the *Cosmopolitan*, *Munsey's*, and *Scribner's Magazine* in 1886–89.

"A MANIA OF MAGAZINE-STARTING"

In the period of expansion immediately following the war, when money was plentiful, when improvements in presses, stereotyping, and engraving encouraged periodical publication, and when a spirit of optimism was abroad in the entire North and West, a boom in magazines set in. The *Round Table* was fearful lest what it called "a mania of magazine-starting" should "spend itself by every successful writer becoming possessed of a magazine of his own." [1]

A calculation based on census figures and the advertising directories of the period gives a scant 700 periodicals for 1865, somewhat over 1,200 for 1870, twice that many for 1880, and some 3,300 for 1885.[2] This means that in the two decades the number of periodicals multiplied more than four and a half times — increases of somewhat over 100 each year, speeded up toward the end of the period to 150 more each year. Allowance for an average life, within the period, of four years (a liberal estimate), gives some eight or nine thousand periodical publications not newspapers issued in the years 1865–85.

[1] *Round Table*, VI, 337 (November 23, 1867).

[2] The Census Bureau's failure to distinguish sharply between newspapers and periodicals, and its changes in categories from decade to decade, make comparisons difficult. The figure given for 1865 takes the 1860 census enumeration of 532 "literary and miscellaneous" periodicals (excepting those classified as political and religious, which were chiefly newspapers), adds one-third of the religious category for reviews and miscellanies, and makes allowance for an increase over 1860 of about 125. (See footnote, vol. II, p. 4.) Most of the increase of the 1870 census must be credited to the years 1865–70. The figure for 1870 is reached by the same method, using the census enumeration of 1,131 as a basis. By 1880 the religious newspapers had changed their status and should be classified as periodicals, so the total is made up for that year of all classes except that called "news, politics and family reading," which evidently designates newspapers. Ayer's *American Newspaper Annual* began in 1880, and it carried an annual tabulation by states and by frequency of publication; the variation in the figure for monthlies is a good barometer for the total for periodicals.

CIRCULATIONS

A discussion of circulations during any period before the days of circulation auditing must be prefaced by the statement that there is no more than a relative significance in the available figures. George P. Rowell, publisher of the first annual collections of newspaper circulation statistics, tells in his recollections how much difficulty he had in getting magazine publishers to set down their circulation figures. He tells how the Harpers were so offended by his inquiry into the circulation of the *Weekly* that they broke off a business connection with the Rowell advertising agency that had brought them several thousand dollars a year, and how Bowen, of the *Independent*, made a great mystery of the business of furnishing a statement.[3] There was something sacrosanct about circulation figures. The fact is that there was so much dishonesty in the statements before the days of circulation auditing that even honest publishers were supersensitive in the matter. Again and again one finds a contradiction between the statement in Rowell's *Directory* and an editor's statement, or between the statements of editor and publisher.[4]

But circulations were undoubtedly growing. By 1874 the *New York Weekly*, a cheap story-paper, was advertising 350,-000 — which it thought "the largest circulation in the world." [5] But it went down a bit by the eighties, as its prototype the *New York Ledger* had; and the *Youth's Companion* went up, achieving by 1885 the largest circulation of the period outside of the group of mail-order papers — 385,000. The House of Harper had two periodicals with lists running over 100,000 — the *Monthly* and the *Weekly*. *Scribner's Monthly* was also in that class; by 1885 (as the *Century Magazine*) it had reached 200,000. *Godey's* had over 100,000 in 1865, but twenty years later it was down to one-fourth of that of its rival; *Peterson's* exceeded 150,000 in the early seventies, but declined consider-

[3] *Printer's Ink*, November 22, 1905, p. 8. Rowell's reminiscences were also published in book form: George Presbury Rowell, *Forty Years an Advertising Agent* (New York, 1906).

[4] See *Christian Register*, C, 391 (April 28, 1921) for a story illustrating this point.

[5] Advertisement in *Scientific American*, XXI, 413 (December 26, 1874).

ably in the next decade. Both of them were far behind the newer *Ladies' Home Journal*, with its 270,000, by the end of our period, and even behind the *Delineator's* 165,000. *Frank Leslie's Popular Monthly* reached 100,000 by 1884. The *People's Literary Companion*, of Augusta, Maine, pioneer mail-order paper, claimed half a million by 1871. The *Police Gazette*, *Texas Siftings*, and half a dozen cheap story-papers had their hundred thousands by the end of our period. Among the agricultural papers, the *American Agriculturist* led with 160,000 at the end of the sixties but declined during the following decade; while *Home and Farm*, of Louisville, Kentucky, and *Farm and Fireside*, of Springfield, Ohio, passed the 100,000 mark soon after their beginning in 1877. Beecher's *Christian Union*, begun in 1870, was the only religious publication to get into this class, if we except the Sunday school and tract society papers. Altogether there were more than thirty periodicals which were quoted at 100,000 circulation or over between 1865 and 1885.[6]

The outstanding success in this list — the *Youth's Companion* — made its gains by means of premiums, as did many of the others. Premiums were given to new subscribers, to old subscribers for renewals, to clubs of old or new subscribers. Every imaginable article of art or utility — and some of neither — were used: books, pictures, clothes, tools, sewing machines, church bells, pianos, and so on. Probably "chromos" were most popular. The *Literary World* advised young men who intended marrying that they could furnish their houses cheaply if only they would take enough magazines:

By subscribing for the *Family Philosopher* he will obtain a commodious cookstove; a year's tolerance (paid for in advance) of the *Prophylactic Prognosticator* will be rewarded by the gift of a black

[6] Sources for circulation figures in this period, besides publishers' claims in their own periodicals and in advertising, are George P. Rowell's *American Newspaper Directory*, published annually in New York 1869–1908 (except 1878–79 and 1897–1901, when it was published quarterly; and 1902, when it was a semiannual); *N. W. Ayer & Son's Newspaper Annual*, now more properly called *Directory of Newspapers and Periodicals*, published since 1880 in Philadelphia; and *Pettengill's Newspaper Directory for 1878*, New York, S. M. Pettengill & Company. It should be remembered that circulations are for the year of the date of the directory until 1893. In addition to the periodicals mentioned above, the following had 100,000 circulation in our period: *Ledger*, *Fireside Companion*, *Young Men of America*, *Pomeroy's Democrat*, *Style*, and *Wood's Household*

walnut bedstead; and the subscription price of the *Epizootic Essayist* will be returned to him a hundred fold in the shape of a set of parlor furniture. . . . This premium business is being run into the ground. Thousands of periodicals are alluring subscribers by the promise of what seems to be three or four times their money's worth. . . . We believe in chromos; they do much to refine our homes, and to encourage a love for the beautiful, but under the present system of wholesale gratuitous distribution, their office will be degraded and they will take rank as Sunday School picture cards.[7]

It was, and they did. The premium system, begun long before, reached its highest development in the early seventies, but by the end of our period it was rather well worked out and was thrown aside so far as its use in any large or conspicuous way was concerned. The *Youth's Companion* was one of few periodicals which continued to use premiums effectively for many years.

The system of club or combination rates grew up in the seventies, injuring the business of the news dealers.[8] The American News Company prospered, however, establishing a branch called the Western News Company at Chicago in 1866. The prices it charged news dealers allowed them five to ten cents on thirty-five-cent magazines like *Harper's* and *Scribner's* and three cents on ten-cent weeklies like *Appleton's* and *Harper's Weekly*.[9] The Central News Company, of Philadelphia, also did a big business. As the newsstand business increased, periodicals came more and more to date their numbers ahead so they could be on the stands on the dates printed on the covers or even before: this was an adopted custom by 1870.[10] The news companies shipped by express rather than by the mails.

Magazine, New York; *Saturday Night*, Philadelphia; *Our Fireside Friend* and *Health and Home*, Chicago; *Sunny South*, Atlanta, Georgia; American Tract Society's *American Messenger* and *Child's Paper*; the Presbyterian Board's *Sabbath School Visitor* and *Westminster Lesson Leaf*; the Sunday School Union's *Child's World*, Philadelphia; *Sunday School Journal*, New York; *Youth's Temperance Banner*, New York. Four or five of these were circulated gratis.

[7] *Literary World*, III, 104 (December 1, 1872).

[8] *Publishers' Weekly*, IX, 82 (January 22, 1876); XV, 235 (February 22, 1879).

[9] *Ibid.*, VII, 152 (February 6, 1875), and XVI, 832 (December 13, 1879).

[10] *National Quarterly Review*, XVIII, 136 (December 1868); *Punchinello*, I, 77 (April 30, 1870).

A news depot in the seventies did not present the bright colors that came to be characteristic of such places in the following period. The standard magazines had no pictures on their gray or brown or buff covers. The story-papers, however, made up for the pictorial shortcomings of the exteriors of general magazines, for the front page of each, small folio in size, was decorated with a slashing woodcut depicting some sensational scene of action — a burning house with fireman rescuing heroine, a duel, a locomotive plunging to destruction. But these were not commonly displayed alongside the buff *Atlantic*, the brown and gilt *Galaxy*, or the gray *Scribner's*.

ADVERTISING

With increasing circulations, advertising began to be attracted to the magazines. There is a common misconception to the effect that *Scribner's Monthly* originated magazine advertising. This probably had its beginning in a remark of George P. Rowell's in his autobiography: "It was the success of *Scribner's* . . . that first gave magazine advertising the impetus that has grown to be so great." This is doubtless true enough, but it does not carry with it the absurd corollary that there was no magazine advertising before *Scribner's*.[11] *Scribner's* was the first high-class general magazine to offer large circulation to advertisers, but the results it obtained were not impressive until just before it gave place to the *Century*. Its best advertising business was in its last Christmas number, December 1880: in that issue it carried forty-nine pages of advertising, of which seven were for the Scribner Company's books and magazines. But the most remarkable thing about this showing was that it included twenty pages of "miscellaneous advertising," as everything not under the head of publishers' announcements was called.

The *Galaxy* was the first high-grade magazine to carry any considerable variety of "miscellaneous advertising." It tried the scheme, not unknown before, of inserting colored advertising pages, first for a favored advertiser or two, and then for the whole advertising section. It also followed for several years the

[11] See *Printer's Ink*, December 13, 1905, p. 6, for Rowell statement; but see also vol. II, pp. 13–14; and Mott, *A History of American Magazines, 1741–1850*, pp. 34, 200, 516.

reprehensible practice of inserting a leaf of advertising between its engraved frontispiece and the first page of reading matter. Through 1868–70, when the *Galaxy* was using colored inserts, its advertising ran to about twenty-four pages monthly; but it dropped off later.

Lippincott's was *Scribner's* nearest competitor in quantity of advertising through most of the seventies, but at a lower rate befitting its smaller circulation.[12] Twenty-four pages was a high figure for it ordinarily. In its earlier years it carried several pages of small "cards" of the leading business houses of Philadelphia.

The *Atlantic* carried from ten to fifteen pages of advertising throughout the period. The *Overland*, courting advertising from the first, was similarly supported. Frank Leslie's publications, especially the *Popular Monthly* and the *Illustrated Weekly*, did a good advertising business. Nearly all the weeklies carried advertising; and with such religious periodicals as the *Independent* and the *Christian Union*, income from that source was very important.

Harper's Weekly was one of the best advertising media of the country; but the *Monthly* was reserved, until 1882, solely for the use of the firm's own book advertising. It had been started with that in mind, and its publishers did not propose to surrender its space to strangers or rivals. The Howe Sewing Machine Company offered $18,000 for the fourth cover page of *Harper's Monthly* for one year in the early seventies and was amazed to receive a polite refusal.[13]

The financial crisis of 1873–78 brought precarious times for magazines. Nearly all of them made desperate efforts to build up advertising business; in the main, those that succeeded weathered the storm and those that failed went under. Advertising played a big part in commercial rehabilitation in the early eighties. In those years it demonstrated its value and established its place in the general magazine.

Advertising rates at the beginning of the period were often inconsistent with circulations, but by 1885 they had settled to

---

[12] According to *Ayer's Directory* of 1880, *Lippincott's* charged thirty cents a line and *Scribner's* $1.25.

[13] *Printer's Ink*, December 13, 1905, p. 6.

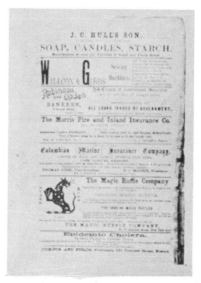

ADVERTISING PAGES FROM MAGAZINES OF THE SIXTIES
AND SEVENTIES

Upper left: *Scribner's Monthly*, December 1874. Upper right: *Lakeside Monthly*, January 1872. Lower left: *Galaxy*, December 1867. Lower right: *Atlantic Monthly*, December 1865.

figures more or less adjusted to size and quality of subscription lists. For example, the *Saturday Evening Post*, which asked thirty cents an agate line in 1865 on the basis of 20,000 circulation, was quoting five cents less on twice as many subscribers in 1885. The *Spirit of the Times*, with 20,000, was asking the same price in 1869 that was quoted by *Pomeroy's Democrat*, with 275,000, i.e., fifty cents; by 1885 the *Spirit*, though showing a slight increase in circulation, was down to thirty cents. By 1885 the *Youth's Companion* was getting $2.25, *Harper's Monthly* $2.00, the *Century* $1.75, and *Leslie's Popular Monthly*, the *Ladies' Home Journal*, and *Godey's* each $1.00. The *New York Weekly*, high in quantity but low in quality of circulation, received $1.25 a line, and the *Police Gazette* $1.00. The *Atlantic*, alas, refused to quote circulation figures and could ask only seventy-five cents per line for advertising.[14]

Among the chief abuses of advertising in the postbellum period were the "reading notices" — advertisements which were passed off as regular reading matter. The religious papers were not exempt from this kind of dishonesty. Washington Gladden is said to have left the *Independent*, of which he was religious editor, because the departments of financial and insurance notes were made up chiefly of this veiled advertising. In 1874 the trustee in bankruptcy for Jay Cooke & Company brought an action against Henry C. Bowen, publisher of the *Independent*, to set aside as contrary to public policy a contract by which Bowen was to lend the use of his editorial columns to sell the bonds of the Northern Pacific Railroad. Bowen was to get a percentage on all bonds sold and had actually received $50,000 in bonds and $460,000 in stock.[15]

A pioneer in the protection of readers against advertising swindlers was the Philadelphia *Farm Journal*, which began to guarantee its advertising in 1880. Wilmer Atkinson, its publisher, promised his subscribers that he would make good any losses they sustained by trusting *Farm Journal* advertisers who proved to be "deliberate swindlers," and in the advertising

---

[14] Rates for English reviews were not over £5 a page (about twenty-five cents an agate line), and half of that for the monthlies. See John Oldcastle, *Journals and Journalism* (London, 1880), p. 41.

[15] *Nation*, XVIII, 233 (November 8, 1874).

directories he warned all comers that "only a select class of advertisements are received."

Some great advertising agencies [16] were organized shortly after the war, and typographical display began to be developed. John E. Powers, advertising manager for the *Nation* in the seventies, was a great influence in the development of the art in that decade.[17] It was the *Nation* that suggested in 1875 that artistic values were being worked out in advertising:

> The elements of decorative design are all employed, though crudely. The preparation and placing of advertisements of all sorts have assumed the proportions of a business to which the entire time and thought of a number of men are devoted.

In this same article is recorded what appears to be the very beginning of "the Great White Way," with its infinitely various flashing signs:

> There appears nightly upon the roof of a building on Broadway a large circular spot of greenish light thrown on a screen, and looking like a disabled moon that has drifted too low and got caught among the chimneys, on the luminous disc of which appear alternately pictures of a simple kind, adapted to the gaze of a mixed crowd, and advertisements of various desirable goods for sale.[18]

One can but wonder who the enterprising advertiser was who used illuminated advertising on Broadway before the days of electric light.

PAYMENTS TO CONTRIBUTORS

The payment of editors and contributors is to be considered in relation to contemporary prices and salaries. An investigation made in 1866 showed an increase of nearly 90 per cent in the prices of necessities over the figures that had prevailed before the war and in its early stages.[19] The wages of laborers

---

[16] S. M. Pettengill & Company, Peaslee & Company, George P. Rowell & Company, and Carlton & Smith. See Frank Presbrey, *The History and Development of Advertising* (Garden City, 1929), pp. 261–275.

[17] Presbrey, *op. cit.*, p. 302.

[18] *Nation*, XX, 342 (May 20, 1875).

[19] Report of David A. Wells, Special Commissioner of Revenue (*Senate Executive Documents*, 39th Congress, 2d Session, No. 2). Includes a comparison of prices in 1860 and in 1866.

had not increased in proportion, but they showed advances in the various fields varying from 25 to 100 per cent. And prices went on rising. "Many sorts of goods and labor are to be had," said a *Galaxy* writer in 1868, "not at fifty per cent above the old prices, but at two hundred per cent. Mechanics quadruple their old charges, and grumble at that." [20]

Magazine rates of payment did not increase proportionately. The *Atlantic's* rate rose in these years from its former $6.00 a page to $10.00,[21] and more for favored contributors, though the "tyro rate" was about half that for many years. True, Fields, Osgood & Company did pay Bret Harte $10,000 to write "not less than twelve pieces" for their publications in 1871; but this was a unique generosity indulged on the top wave of Harte's popularity. Out of it the *Atlantic* got four short stories and five poems, and *Every Saturday* one poem and a "condensed novel" — a return which rather disappointed the publishers.[22] To its most famous contributors the *Atlantic* was inclined to be liberal: it would pay Lowell $300 for a long poem.[23]

The *Galaxy*, never a financial success, had a variable rate, which ranged from two cents a word to Mark Twain and Justin McCarthy to one-third of a cent a word to less prominent writers.[24] On the whole, its scale was about that of the *Atlantic*;

[20] *Galaxy*, VI, 274 (August 1868).

[21] This conclusion is derived chiefly from letters in the *Galaxy* collection of Mr. Willard Church, Montclair, New Jersey. Edward Everett Hale, George C. Eggleston, and J. W. DeForest received this rate from the *Atlantic*, according to their letters.

[22] *Every Saturday's* part in this arrangement has not been commonly recognized, but its own advertising at the time emphasized its expectations vigorously. See p. 358. See also Geoffrey Bret Harte, ed., *The Letters of Bret Harte* (Boston, 1926), p. 13, for itemized account.

[23] C. E. Norton, ed., *Letters of James Russell Lowell* (New York, 1894), I, 353. Lowell received the same amount from the *Nation:* see Rollo Ogden, *Life and Letters of Edwin Lawrence Godkin* (New York, 1907), II, 73.

[24] These conclusions are reached from an examination of Mr. Willard Church's collection of *Galaxy* correspondence, in which more than fifty references to specific payments to authors, are made, e.g.: Richard Grant White, $225 a month for 10,000 to 13,500 words in editorial departments; Charles Astor Bristed, $25 for 3500 words; John Esten Cooke, $4.00 per page; Caroline Chesebrough, $4.00 per page; Maria Louise Pool (1866), $3.00 per page; James Franklin Fitts, about $4.00 per page; Jane G. Austin's serial *Cypher*, $2.66 per 500-word page, or about half a cent a word; "H. H.," $10 per short poem; John S. Dwight, translations of German poems, $10 each; Charles Godfrey Leland, $15 per poem; W. D. Howells, $50 for a long poem; Richard Henry Stoddard, $10 a poem;

it bought many of the same authors and used much the same class of material.

The new *Putnam's* did not do quite so well, averaging about $7.00 a page, according to figures given in the valedictory in its last number. Major Putnam, in his life of his father, says that the competition of *Lippincott's*, the *Galaxy*, and *Scribner's* had the effect of raising the prices demanded by contributors from the older rates of $3.00 or $5.00 to $10 or $20.[25] Perhaps the increased cost of potatoes had something to do with the matter. At any rate *Lippincott's* and *Scribner's Monthly* helped to fix the price to contributors during these days of the early seventies at about $10 a page for magazines of the higher class.[26]

The conclusion is plain that magazine writers were not paid a living wage in our period. To provide $2,000 as a minimum income for moderate comfort, a magazine author had to write and sell an article a week; and certainly few could do that. Richard Grant White wrote in 1866 in the *Galaxy*:

A man who undertakes to live by occasional contributions to weekly or daily papers, for which he receives five to fifteen dollars, or to the magazines, for which he gets five dollars a page . . . will soon find himself a fit subject for the poor-house. . . . There are hundreds, almost thousands, of bookkeepers and salesmen in the city of New York whose salaries are three or four times as large as the incomes of hard-working men of letters whose reputations extend the country over and to Europe. . . . I have known the conductor of a periodical publication send an author of established repute ten dollars for a piece of work corresponding in time and thought expended upon it to

Edward Rowland Sill, ditto; Julia Ward Howe, $10 to $20 each for her poems; Phoebe Cary, $10 to $25 per poem; William Winter, $15 to $40 per poem (the latter 48 lines long); Bayard Taylor, $50. ("The remuneration I now receive from other magazines is fifty dollars on acceptance," wrote Taylor, May 10, 1869.)

[25] George Haven Putnam, *George Palmer Putnam: A Memoir* (New York, 1912), p. 362.

[26] The *Independent* was paying good prices for poetry; see Laura Stedman and G. M. Gould, *Life and Letters of Edmund Clarence Stedman* (New York, 1910), I, 439. The Harpers came into the American market more and more during this period, though they still adhered to their English serials. In 1871 they paid John Hay $50 for "Banty Tim." See W. R. Thayer, *Life and Letters of John Hay* (Boston, 1915), p. 359. But a struggling magazine like the *Overland Monthly* paid only $25 a story and $15 a poem. See "Overland Monthly: Moneys Paid Contributors," a manuscript in the University of California Library.

that for which any one of five hundred lawyers of respectable ability and corresponding reputation in New York would have refused to accept less than fifty dollars as a retaining fee.[27]

A better-considered statement is that written by Charles Astor Bristed in behalf of the International Copyright Association, and signed by him, with S. Irenaeus Prime, James Parton, Richard Grant White, G. P. Putnam, and Henry Holt. It says:

> If the average magazine writer could readily place all that he can conscientiously write, then with three hundred working days in the year, he could make fair clerk's wages, say from fifteen to eighteen hundred dollars; in fact he is able to place one-third or less of his writing, and his gains are as likely to fall below as to exceed three hundred dollars. . . . Dr. Holland, . . . while admitting that he has received more money for copyright than the great majority of American authors, declares that the product of his literary labors would not support his family. . . . The tax returns of the literary men in and about Cambridge are very instructive in this connection. Only one of them has even a *comfortable* prosperity, and he (though one of the most popular of living poets) does not owe it to his pen.[28]

There were many statements of a similar tenor. Dr. Holland asserted in *Scribner's* that "the brightest author in America, though he produce books of universal acceptation, can never get rich," and added later: "Not one author in twenty can live on his authorial earnings." [29]

The magazine pay of the postbellum period may be considered also in its relation to that of the palmy *Graham* days.[30] On the basis of *Graham's* $800 a number, it was paying what would correspond to $13 a *Putnam* page. But the cost of living had tripled, and *Putnam* and its confreres should have paid close to $40 to equal *Graham's* figure in 1842. A fairer comparison is that afforded by the old and new series of *Putnam's*, which underpaid its writers at $3.00 in 1853, and underpaid them still more at $7.00 in 1870. But, as Grant White says in what appears to be an editorially inspired note to his article quoted

---

[27] *Galaxy*, II, 543, 545 (November 15, 1866).

[28] *Ibid.*, X, 812 (December 1870). The poet referred to was doubtless Longfellow.

[29] *Scribner's Monthly*, V, 637 (March 1873); VIII, 748 (October 1874).

[30] See Mott, *op. cit.*, p. 506.

above, "According to my observation and experience, they generally pay as well as they can afford." [31]

For this state of affairs the Bristed declaration gives a large share of the blame to the lack of international copyright agreements, and doubtless some of the onus belongs there; though it must be remembered that authorship, save in exceptional cases, is an ill-paid vocation, and that complaints such as those we have been quoting are to be met in all periods and countries. *Harper's* was roundly abused on all sides for its use of English material; yet *Harper's* paid more for advance sheets of English serials than it would have had to pay for the work, it is safe to say, of any living American writer. [32] Certainly not all the troubles of American authorship can be blamed upon the lack of international copyright.

Prices remained about the same throughout the panic years and increased somewhat in the early eighties. Howells, James, and Cable each got $5,000 a serial by the end of our period. [33] The *Century* paid General Grant $50 apiece for his four Civil War articles, but such was their success upon publication that Roswell Smith, the publisher, sent Grant a second check for the same amount as the first. [34] Some of the story weeklies were good paymasters: Mayne Reid received $8,000 for a serial in *Leslie's Weekly* and $5,000 from the *Fireside Companion*, [35] and Mary Jane Holmes is said to have received from $4,000 to $6,000 for each of the many serials she wrote for the *New York Weekly*, and "Ned Buntline" even more than that. [36] But on the other hand, some high-class magazines paid little or nothing to contributors, thus promoting a scandalous liaison between lofty aims and insubstantial rewards. Brander Matthews called upon the editor of the *International Review* about pay for an article, one day in the early eighties, only to be told that

[31] *Galaxy*, II, 545 (November 15, 1866).

[32] The price of the sheets of *Great Expectations* was at the rate of $20 a page of magazine size, but that included the rights to book publication also.

[33] *Critic*, IV, 307 (June 28, 1884).

[34] W. W. Ellsworth, *A Golden Age of Authors* (Boston, 1919), p. 108.

[35] Charles F. Lummis, *Mesa, Canon and Pueblo* (New York, 1925), p. 19.

[36] See J. C. Derby, *Fifty Years Among Authors, Books and Publishers* (New York, 1884), p. 572, for Mary Jane Holmes; and Fred E. Pond, *Life and Adventures of Ned Buntline* (New York, 1919), p. 93, for the assertion that "Ned" got $20,000 a year from Street & Smith.

the contributors to his magazine received a two-fold reward: first, the signal honor of appearing in its pages; and second, an honorarium in money, the exiguity of the latter being proportioned to the altitude of the former.[37]

RECOGNITION OF THE MAGAZINIST

About 1865–70 came a change in the accepted style for magazine writing, and with it more or less recognition of the arrival of a new group of writers. It should be noted that the ponderous eighteenth-century sentence was still the best form in many American periodicals — especially the reviews — throughout the fifties. The first sentence in an article about O. A. Brownson and the Catholics in the *Democratic Review* of 1852 contained no less than 521 words.[38] Heaviness was in high repute. True, Willis and his kind had made a brilliant success in the forties by writing brightly of inconsequentialities; but to write with spirit or even gaiety about important matters — ah, that was not done! Godkin said in 1865, regarding the first few numbers of the *Nation*:

It has been so far rather heavy, and I find it difficult to lighten it. . . . It is very difficult to find a man to do the work of gossiping agreeably on manners, lager beer, etc., who will bind himself to do it whether he feels like it or not. In fact, it is very difficult to get men of education in America to handle any subject with a light touch. They all want to write ponderous essays if they write at all.[39]

"Probably," said the *Independent* in the following year, "there are not enough first-class magazinists in all America to fill the *Atlantic* alone, even if they did nothing but write for it." [40] But writing improved, largely through the influence of magazines like the *Nation*, *Putnam's*, the *Galaxy*, and the *Atlantic*. By 1872 the *Literary World* was pointing out that "compactness of structure and crispness of style" were "the most characteristic features of the model magazine article." [41] And in 1877 the *National Republic* declared that "writing for the magazines has become a profession, employing a considerable number of

---

[37] *Outlook*, CVII, 51 (September 12, 1917).
[38] *Democratic Review*, XXXI, 601 (November–December 1852).
[39] Ogden, *op. cit.*, I, 240.
[40] *Independent*, April 26, 1866, editorial page.
[41] *Literary World*, III, 56 (September 1, 1872).

trained experts." [42] The *North American Review* had been less stodgy under Norton and Lowell and Henry Adams; but when Rice got it in 1878 and made it a monthly and moved it to New York, it unmistakably joined the procession which was playing the livelier tune. Thus the old Johnsonian style was resigned to a few theological quarterlies whose specific gravity must have been high in any case, and the new writing and the new writers for magazines triumphed.

Many of the most prominent among the magazinists of this period are now quite forgotten except by the grimy rummagers in attics and bespectacled investigators of long shelves of bound files in libraries. Eugene Benson, unless he is remembered as a painter, is not remembered at all; yet he was a very brilliant critic and causeur in the *Galaxy* and *Atlantic*. That incisive and graceful essayist, David A. Wasson, who contributed frequently to the best magazines, lives in few if any memories today, though John Burroughs wrote of him in 1862: "With the exception of Emerson (whom he excels in finish if not in calm dignity) I know of no writer so original, so profound." [43] Charles Astor Bristed, scion of wealth and culture, who wrote so provocatively for the *Galaxy* and so entertainingly for the *Spirit of the Times*, usually under the name of "Carl Benson," has joined his fellow magazinists in the limbo of the forgotten. Junius Henri Browne's versatile work in many magazines over a long period of time purchased no remembrance for him. Frederic Beecher Perkins, famous librarian, whom Tilton called "a born magazine writer," [44] is forgotten outside of libraries. The name of Richard B. Kimball, lawyer and railroad builder, is perpetuated not by his voluminous magazine contributions but by the name of a town in Texas which he founded. The medical and travel articles of Dr. Titus M. Coan are known only to the explorers of old files; even the *Dictionary of American Biography* relegates him to oblivion. And the work of two consuls, both of whom contributed much to periodicals in America and Europe — Albert Rhodes and George M. Towle — has enforced but little more claim upon remembrance. And so it goes. The magazines are shifting sands.

[42] *National Republic*, I, 574 (June 1877).
[43] Clara Barrus, *Life and Letters of John Burroughs* (Boston, 1925), I, 65.
[44] *Independent*, June 6, 1866.

Anonymity in magazine authorship continued to decline; when the *North American Review* began publishing the names of its authors in 1868, it delivered a staggering blow to the ancient tradition of the anonymous review. The *Nation* was the chief bulwark of the unsigned article in the seventies. Its editor wrote in 1866:

> An article of which the author is known is hardly ever judged on its merits. If he is still obscure, most people will not take the trouble to read what he says; if he is famous, they will devour the veriest twaddle that comes from his pen, and insist on new supplies every day.[45]

But the chief reason for the *Nation's* anonymity was, of course, a desire to assimilate all the contents to the journal's common policy and style. A member of its staff, writing many years later, remarked:

> To submit to being an anonymous contributor to the *Nation* required a good deal of self-sacrifice. The ideas governing the conduct of the paper were essentially those of the editor; the style, by a constant influence and association, more and more his; and the editorial contributor had to learn to write under him, . . . sometimes galling for such as actually had made names for themselves.[46]

W. C. Brownell, in some recollections of the days when he served with Godkin and Garrison on the editorial staff of the *Nation*, tells how

> we all three proof-read the entire paper, and each "corrected" on occasion the editorial as well as the contributed material in ultra-democratic fashion. . . . I remember witnessing with joy his [Godkin's] reducing by half one of [Fitzedward] Hall's interminable and intricately correct articles, out of sheer exasperation. Garrison, who was never exasperated, looked at the proof rather ruefully. He probably had to explain to Hall.[47]

One of the "principles of editing observed by Dr. Holland on *Scribner's*," according to an assistant, "was respect for the

[45] *Nation*, II, 822 (June 28, 1866).
[46] *Nation*, CI, 55 (July 8, 1915).
[47] *Ibid.*, pp. 42, 43.

opinions of contributors, which in all our laborious editing were never altered." [48] An inspired editorial suggestion by Will Carey, of *Scribner's*, occasioned the change of the title of Stockton's now famous story "The Lady or the Tiger?" which the author had originally called "The King's Arena." [49] Holland was very careful not to suggest unchaste ideas to his readers, as George T. Lanigan, a writer of light verse, learned when he submitted to him the following idea for a poem:

A young lady at Saratoga, who, after the hop in the evening, retires to her room, puts on a loose wrapper, and makes herself comfortable. As she sits in her chair, she thinks over her evening — what this man said and that one whispered, how this girl was dressed and that one had her hair arranged, her triumphs and her disappointments.

F. S. Church was to illustrate the poem; but Dr. Holland objected, saying, "How is it possible for the readers of this magazine to imagine Mr. Church, who, I understand, is a bachelor, in the young lady's room at such an hour as he would have to sketch her?" He had the happy idea, however, of making the poem say that the girl was the artist's wife, until Lanigan, now much amused, raised a further difficulty. "How is it possible," he asked, "to suppose *me* in *Mrs. Church's bedroom?*" And since the good doctor couldn't see his way clear to marrying the girl to both the artist and the poet, *Scribner's* readers never made the belle's acquaintance. [50]

The traditions of *Scribner's* remained unaltered when the name was changed to the *Century* and Gilder succeeded to the editorship. Gilder admitted it might be true that America was, as an English critic had said, "a nation of prudes," but "if so, we can only say that this is the price we pay for being, on the whole, the decentest nation on the face of the globe." [51]

Fields, the successor of Lowell on the *Atlantic's* tripod, was an indulgent editor; but Howells was again somewhat the

[48] R. U. Johnson, *Remembered Yesterdays* (Boston, 1923), p. 113.

[49] Ellsworth, *op. cit.*, p. 31. For the history of this story, see also Stockton's "How I Wrote 'The Lady or the Tiger?'" in *Ladies' Home Journal*, November 1893, pp. 1–2; Walter L. Pforzheimer's "The Lady, the Tiger and the Author" in *Colophon*, N.S., I, 261–270.

[50] *Critic*, I, 196 (September 1888).

[51] Johnson, *op. cit.*, p. 125.

"academic taskmaster freely blue-penciling the essays of his unhappy pupils." [52] Howells himself says that his proofreading "sometimes well-nigh took the character of original work, in that liberal *Atlantic* tradition of bettering the authors by editorial transposition and paraphrase, either in the form of suggestion or of absolute correction." [53] Some contributors objected — Stedman, for example — and this "bettering" was on at least one occasion called "pulverizing." [54]

Stedman also suffered at the hands of the *North American* editors. Lowell, then one of the editors of that review, wrote to him in 1866 anent a critical article:

> I shall take the liberty to make a verbal change here and there, such as I am sure you would agree to could we talk the matter over. I think, for example, you speak rather too well of young Lytton, whom I regard as both an impostor and as an antinomian heretic. Swinburne I must modify a little, as you will see, to make the *Review* consistent with itself. But you need not be afraid of not knowing your own child again. [55]

That at least one successor of Lowell in the editorship of the *North American* was dictatorial we have Henry Cabot Lodge's testimony to show. When Lodge became Henry Adams' assistant editor, Adams one day handed him an article by "an eminent local historian and antiquary, saying, 'We shall print this article, of course, but I wish you to go over it and strike out all superfluous words, and especially all needless adjectives.'" Which the young authority did. [56]

William Conant Church and his brother Francis, editors of the *Galaxy*, also wielded large powers over their contributors. They forced Rebecca Harding Davis, much against her will, to permit the cutting of large portions of her serial, *Waiting for the Verdict*; and they once brought Richard Grant White, their contributing editor, to the point of resigning by what he considered the mishandling of his work. The title of James T.

---

[52] L. Frank Tooker, *The Joys and Tribulations of an Editor* (New York, 1924), p. 118. The phrase is applied to Lowell.
[53] *Atlantic Monthly*, C, 597 (November 1907).
[54] Stedman and Gould, *op. cit.*, I, 536.
[55] *Ibid.*, I, 375.
[56] H. C. Lodge, *Early Memories* (New York, 1913), p. 244.

McKay's story, "A Five-Handed Game," was changed to "Carol Clyde" because the original name seemed irreverent: the implication was that God held the fifth hand of the game in question. A letter of the popular authoress Jane G. Austin in regard to her novel *Cypher* may be quoted practically in full:

My dear Mr. Church

It is hardly to be expected that you should understand "the feelings of a mother" but without them you cannot in the least appreciate the horrible sacrifice you have asked of me. My poor Cypher! That babe of my brain over whose long pages I have wrought so lovingly and lingered so delightedly and now my own hands have dismembered it — dragged it page from page — drained out its life blood and shorn it of every redundant beauty — Behold it — shaven, shorn, trimmed down from its native luxuriance to a mere bean-pole — every superfluous word cropped away — hardly a musical phrase left to poor Gillies or a sunset reflection to Neria — even pouts [?] reduced to "time" as inexorably as a pugilist's breath.

Well — I have taken out 108 pps. . . . And Obi has been pruned of all his tenors and the fisherman's ball which is the delight of my heart is gone altogether.

I hope you will be pleased — *I* am not. . . .

Yours very truly

Jane G. Austin [57]

GREAT EDITORS OF THE PERIOD

A dozen or more editors were outstanding in these two decades. There was Edwin Lawrence Godkin, incisive thinker, bold writer, idealist; such an intellectual aristocrat was not equipped to direct the fortunes of a popular magazine, and the *Nation* was for the few from the first. There was George William Curtis, another aristocrat, another critic of his times, but a gentler personality. An editorial essayist for the Harper periodicals, he touched politics, society, and literature; but Curtis, like Godkin, was not of the stuff of which great popular editors are made.

[57] The letter is dated March 23, 1868, and refers to Miss Austin's serial, *Cypher*. This letter and the other facts about the *Galaxy* given here are derived from the collection of *Galaxy* material in the hands of Mr. Willard Church, Montclair, New Jersey.

It was Dr. Josiah G. Holland, of *Scribner's Monthly*, who filled that bill. Dr. Holland fitted in with his times; he was intensely sympathetic with that upper middle class for which the great general magazines were made. Himself an important sentimental poet, every inch a moralist, he had an inquiring journalistic mind and wide interests. Industry, geniality, and enough literary discrimination to satisfy his public made him, given a good publisher, the most successful editor of his era. After his death in 1881, a man he had trained in editorship, Richard Watson Gilder, continued the tradition of success on the *Century*.

William Dean Howells was perhaps a better editor than Holland. As director of a magazine of the highest literary prestige he had a great opportunity; but in spite of the real enterprise he displayed, the *Atlantic* was not a financial success. In some respects Howells was a greater editor than Lowell had been: he had wider geographical sympathies, and he was a better worker. His delightful personality and his ability as a reviewer were helpful in his task.

Henry Ward Beecher, of the *Christian Union*, was a great contributing editor, but not an office worker; and Henry C. Bowen, of the *Independent*, was a great publisher-editor. Atwater, Whedon, Bellows, and Bledsoe were able editors in the limited field of the religious review. The *North American Review* had some great men for editors in the years 1865–77 — but they were not great editors, which is another thing. Lowell was really an editorial contributor, in the main; Charles Eliot Norton, Henry Adams, and others did good work; but it took the editorial boldness and originality of Allen Thorndike Rice to lift the review out of its rut in 1878. Rice was of the later type of "hustling" editor.

Henry Mills Alden was a successful editor, though one cannot but think that Fletcher Harper, his publisher, had much to do with the prosperity and adequacy in its field of *Harper's Monthly*. Bret Harte made a great hit in his short editorship of the *Overland*, but it was largely through his contributions to the magazine. Some of the agricultural journals had able editors — Wilmer Atkinson, Orange Judd, Donald G. Mitchell, and D. D. T. Moore.

Lastly, it should be noted that certain editors who had already established themselves firmly continued that success from the former period into the years following the war: the cheerful Godey, the shrewd and literary Peterson, the enterprising Leslie and Bonner, the hard-hitting Sears, and the moral Arthur.

CHAPTER II

MAGAZINES NORTH, SOUTH, EAST, AND WEST

THE whole geographical aspect of America changed in the sixties. "So rapid has been the development," said a writer in the *Atlantic*, "that maps of 1864 are obsolete in 1866." [1] And Francis Vinton, writing in *Appleton's Journal*, added: "The strides of our country outstrip the pen of the ready writer, while Terminus, the god of landmarks, sits in despair, not knowing where to inscribe our boundaries." [2] The westward movement, invited by the Union Pacific, led by thousands of discharged soldiers and their families, and protected by the United States army, was opening up a new empire. The Middle West, with its new agricultural dominance; the South, in the throes of rehabilitation; New England, recently urbanized and industrialized — all presented new aspects and spoke with new voices. "As soon as the country began to feel its life in every limb with the coming of peace," wrote Howells, "it began to speak in the varying accents of all the sections." [3]

These "varying accents," so far as they were uttered by the periodicals, may be considered separately: first, the old "East," including both New England and the Middle Atlantic states; second, the South; third, the Middle West, comprising the basins of the Ohio and the upper Mississippi; and fourth, the western frontier country — plains, Rockies, and coast.

NEW YORK, BOSTON, AND PHILADELPHIA

By 1865 New York was doing far more publishing than her two ancient rivals, Boston and Philadelphia, together. The Harpers, Appleton, Putnam, Scribner, Wiley, Carleton, and other book houses were in full course of production; and the tendency after the war was for each book publisher to equip himself with a general literary magazine, in the British fashion.

---

[1] *Atlantic Monthly*, XVII, 333 (March 1866).
[2] *Appleton's Journal*, IV, 522 (October 29, 1870).
[3] W. D. Howells, *Literature and Life* (New York, 1902), p. 175.

At any rate, a fourth of the country's monthly periodicals came from New York in 1880, as the census showed. Of periodicals in the hundred-thousand circulation class during some part of the period 1865–85, New York had two-thirds, Philadelphia one-fifth, and Boston one-thirtieth.

No other American city was given half the attention in the magazines that New York received. Not only was she described by her own periodicals; but those of other cities, recognizing in her picturesqueness a source of "good copy," printed occasional articles about her development and the life of her people. Thus H. T. Tuckerman, writing of Broadway in the *Atlantic*:

> Despite its dead horses and vehicular entanglements, its vile concert saloons, the alternate meanness and magnificence of its architecture, the fragile character of its theatrical structures and their limited, hazardous means of exit, — despite falling walls and the necessity of police guardianship at the crossings, the reckless driving of butcher-boys and the dexterity of pick-pockets, — despite the slippery pavement and the chronic cry for "relief," — Broadway is a spectacle and an experience worth patient study, and wonderfully prolific of life pictures.[4]

Another great New York street, the Bowery, was the subject of an even more entertaining article in the same magazine a little later.[5]

New York's incredibly bad government was a frequent theme, and the fight against its corrupt political machine furnished one of the liveliest episodes of the period.[6] Its inefficient transportation and dangerous streets were inexhaustible topics. The horsecars were "crowded to the utmost discomfort . . . still the throng increases," said *Harper's Weekly*. "The project which is at this moment most widely discussed is an underground railroad." [7] But this plan, which was worked out as the "Arcade System," found opposition at Albany; and Baltimore had the first subway in America.[8] In the meantime a primitive elevated railroad was erected, and a pneumatic trans-

---

[4] *Atlantic Monthly*, XVIII, 717 (December 1866).
[5] *Ibid.*, XX, 602 (November 1867).
[6] For *Harper's Weekly* see vol. II, sketch 28.
[7] *Harper's Weekly*, X, 3 (January 6, 1866).
[8] *Scientific American*, XXIX, 32 (July 9, 1873).

portation plan discussed.[9] *Appleton's* tells how the first elevated (in Greenwich Street) was rescued from failure by a timely change in method of operation:

Instead of the endless rope, driven by stationary engines placed at regular intervals, which was first employed, the cars are now run by small dummy engines on the track. . . . The engines are compact, make but little noise, consume their own smoke, and do not seem to unduly excite the horses in the street below. The speed is about twice as fast as that of the surface street-cars drawn by horses.[10]

That New York's vice and crime excited great interest is evidenced not only in the cheaper sensational journals, but also in the more staid reviews. Without doubt a study of metropolitan life on its lower levels is essential to an understanding of the times. Flamboyant vice was one of the corollaries of postbellum expansiveness, and the growing magnetism of the city to attract rural youth made the sins of the great metropolis a matter of importance to the whole country. When, in 1885, Denman Thompson gave lovers of melodrama a picture of the country boy who had been lured by the bright gaslights of the city into "dens of iniquity" in his popular play, "The Old Homestead," he was really dealing with a common occurrence and one which caused much anxiety. "When I see a young man coming from the tame life of the country and going down in city ruin, I am not surprised," declared the Reverend T. DeWitt Talmage in one of his Brooklyn Tabernacle sermons. "My only surprise is that any escape, considering the allurements." [11]

And certainly the same was true for the country girl, if we may believe even a small part of the writings of the time. The streets of New York were clearly unsafe for women without dependable escorts after dark. The *Nation* estimated the number of streetwalkers at six thousand and "criminal women" at twice that figure, with 773 houses of ill fame, in 1867, when

[9] See vol. II, pp. 320–21. See also *Punchinello*, I, 53 (April 23, 1870) ; I, 107 (May 14, 1870) ; *Scientific American, passim* for 1870.
[10] *Appleton's Journal*, V, 658 (June 3, 1871).
[11] *Christian Herald*, I, 5 (October 24, 1878). The Y. M. C. A. was founded chiefly to protect such young men. See *Granite Monthly*, VII, 250 (April 1884) and IX, 17 (January 1886).

the city was under a million and a half in population.[12] In the same year *Harper's Weekly* reported 9,250 saloons and practically no enforcement of Sunday closing laws.[13] The *Galaxy* published a series of articles on "The Nether Life of New York" by Edward Crapsey in 1871 and 1872, and *Appleton's Journal* had a series called "The Dangerous Classes of New York" by C. L. Brace, a famous social worker, in the same year. With due allowance for the exaggerations of sensationalism, the accounts of New York night life found in such articles and published currently in papers like the *National Police Gazette* and *Frank Leslie's Illustrated*, in Talmage's sermons on "The Night Side of New York" as printed by the *Christian Herald* and many other papers, and in a host of pamphlets, books, plays,[14] and periodicals of the day, are significant indices of an important phase of American society in the postbellum period.

And in spite of its large publishing business, its lively journalism, its Bohemian Pfaff's cellar, and a literary salon or two, New York was accused of having no real literary life. "It was an excellent school for me — to get out of!" exclaimed Thomas Bailey Aldrich after he had escaped to Boston and *Every Saturday*. Then he added an observation in an accent beautifully Bostonian: "I wonder that I got out of it with my English tolerably correct." [15] The *Nation*, welcoming the *Galaxy* in 1866, remarked with discouragement, "Literature is not in any great favor here, and literary men do not abound," [16] and in a famous article by Dennett it pronounced "Knickerbocker literature" to be "essentially imitative and colonial." [17]

"As to authorship in New York, it has never had the respect

[12] *Nation*, IV, 153 (February 21, 1867). See also Herbert Asbury, *The Gangs of New York* (New York, 1928), p. 175. *Woodhull & Claflin's Weekly* often discussed this matter more picturesquely than reliably.

[13] *Harper's Weekly*, XI, 34 (January 19, 1867).

[14] George G. Foster's *New York by Gas Light* (New York, 1850) and Solon Robinson's *Hot Corn* (New York, 1854) both had plays founded on them. For notes on several plays of this type, see A. H. Quinn, *A History of the American Drama from the Beginning to the Civil War* (New York, 1923), pp. 304–308. See also the good bibliography in Alvin H. Harlow's *Old Bowery Days* (New York, 1931), and Chapter IX of Asbury, *op. cit.*

[15] Ferris Greenslet, *Life of Thomas Bailey Aldrich* (Boston, 1908), p. 102.

[16] *Nation*, II, 534 (April 26, 1866).

[17] *Ibid.*, V, 459 (December 5, 1867).

and affection here that Boston accords it. New York gives us a
market — a valuable gift — but relegates to New England and
the interior the task of reading our works." [18] Thus wrote Edmund Clarence Stedman in 1882. Boston was still commonly
believed to be the cultural capital of the country. She had only
one periodical in the hundred thousand class — the *Youth's
Companion* — but she had the *Atlantic Monthly*, declining in
circulation, to be sure, but still maintaining an assured pre-
eminence in literature. New Yorker John Bigelow wrote on
Christmas Day, 1876: "*Putnam* redivivus is out. It . . . falls
short of the *Atlantic* standard. It looks as if we should have to
get New England to do our writing for some time yet." [19] And
Charles Godfrey Leland, traveled student and New York and
Philadelphia magazinist, could not but remark in Boston "the
very general respect manifested in all circles for culture and
knowledge in any form, in which respect it is certainly equalled
by no city on earth." [20] The New York *Critic*, admitting that
its own city was deficient in a "reverence for the best in thought,
for the inspiration of fine sentiment," and therefore could produce Vanderbilts but not Emersons, adds the declaration of a
"profound thinker" that "he could almost see the fine essence
of inspiration steaming upward as a visible vapor from the
scalps" of the members of one of the Boston culture clubs.[21]
Such soft impeachments Bostonians were in the habit of accepting without argument, but Holmes wrote with characteristic
acuteness to Lowell in 1876:

We Boston people are so bright and wide-awake and have really
been so much in advance of our fellow-barbarians with our *Monthly
Anthologies* and *Atlantic Monthlies* and *North American Reviews*,
that we have been in danger of thinking our local scale was the absolute one of excellence — forgetting that 212 Fahrenheit is but 100
Centigrade.[22]

[18] Laura Stedman and G. M. Gould, *Life and Letters of Edmund Clarence
Stedman* (New York, 1910), II, 73. See also I, 489.
  [19] John Bigelow, *Retrospections of an Active Life* (New York, 1909), IV, 156.
See also W. B. Parker, *Edward Rowland Sill* (Boston, 1915), p. 182.
  [20] C. G. Leland, *Memoirs* (London, 1893), II, 38.
  [21] *Critic*, I, 278 (October 8, 1881).
  [22] John T. Morse, *Life and Letters of Oliver Wendell Holmes* (Boston, 1896),
II, 116.

It was a proper reminder. Boston had fallen far behind as a commercial center. She had lacked industrial vision, wrote Charles Francis Adams in the *North American* in 1868. She had,

in spite of her wealth and prestige, her intrinsic worth and deserved reputation, her superficial conceit and real cultivation, failed to solve the enigma, — had not risen to the height of the argument. The new era found her wedded to the old; and her eyes, dimmed with experiences of the past, could not credit the brilliant visions of the future. . . . She has lost much of her influence and all of her prestige.[23]

The census of 1870 ranked Boston as the sixth city, St. Louis and Chicago having crowded in ahead of her since 1860. And in the postbellum period she lost two of the proudest badges of her intellectual superiority: in 1866 the *Christian Examiner* was removed to New York, to be followed a dozen years later by the revered *North American Review*, thus raising the cultural balance of that arrogant city of which Adams had said Boston was only a satellite.

Philadelphia strove throughout this period to maintain her place as the third periodical publishing center of the country, though hard pressed by Chicago.[24] Two good general magazines did much for her literary reputation—*Lippincott's* and the *Penn Monthly*. She was still thought of as the fashion-magazine city, with *Peterson's* and *Godey's* and the new and booming *Ladies' Home Journal*; and in class magazines — especially the legal, medical, and religious journals — she was prolific. At the very middle of our period all eyes were turned Philadelphia-ward, and thither the steps of the nation moved in 1876 when the great Centennial Exposition opened its doors.

The chief general periodicals of the East, located for the most part in these three cities of New York, Philadelphia, and Boston, may now be passed in the rapid review of a comprehensive survey.

[23] *North American Review*, CVI, 10 (January 1868).
[24] See *Compendium* of Tenth Census, Tables 131–134.

GENERAL QUARTERLIES IN THE EAST

The two general quarterlies which were in course of publication in 1865 were the *North American Review*,[25] which celebrated its semicentennial in that year, and the *National Quarterly Review*,[26] then five years old. Charles Eliot Norton and James Russell Lowell had been editors of the *North American* since 1863; Norton gave place to Professor E. W. Gurney after five years' service, and he to Henry Adams in 1871. The next year Lowell went abroad, and Adams took Henry Cabot Lodge as his assistant. But it was when Allen Thorndike Rice bought the *Review* in 1877 that the great break with its sanctified traditions occurred. Rice changed it from a quarterly to a bimonthly, and later to a monthly; he became editor himself and took his journal down off its pedestal and into the sweaty arena of popular disputation; and then — climacteric vandalism! — he swept off its Harvard robes and transported it bodily to New York. In that new Babel it found itself neighboring with the *National Quarterly*, edited by Edward I. Sears until the centennial year, when he was succeeded by Dr. David A. Gorton.

Except for a few shorter-lived reviews scattered over the country,[27] these two were the only general secular quarterlies of the period. Perhaps Tucker's *Radical Review*, of New Bedford, Massachusetts, should be mentioned here, though it was of a somewhat specialized sort.[28] Other quarterlies of a more theological cast will be considered in connection with religious periodicals.

There was a marked tendency to abandon quarterly publication. In 1864 Lowell, who had just undertaken his editorial work on the *North American*, had written to Motley that "perhaps the day of the quarterlies is gone by, and those megatheria of letters may be in the mere course of nature withdrawing to

[25] Treated more fully in vol. II, sketch 1.
[26] Treated more fully in vol. II, sketch 34.
[27] *Harkness' Magazine* was a dollar quarterly of miscellany published by John C. Harkness at Wilmington, Delaware, 1872–77. An attempt was made to revive it as a "booster" magazine in 1888 and again in 1892. The *Pittsburgh Quarterly Magazine* (1867–68) was of the same type; it was succeeded by the monthly *Leisure Hours* (1868–70), William O'Dwyer editor and publisher.
[28] See p. 301.

the swamps to die." [29] Some years later the *Citizen and Round Table* observed:

Men at the present date live too fast for the slow-going quarterlies. Questions that excite our utmost interest die away and are forgotten by the time the quarterly review is ready to discuss them.[30]

EASTERN LITERARY MONTHLIES

Chief of all the monthlies which held over from antebellum days were *Harper's* [31] and the *Atlantic*.[32] James T. Fields, senior member of the firm which owned the *Atlantic*, was its editor from July 1861 to July 1871, though from the beginning of our period he was frequently an absentee editor. Young William Dean Howells, of Ohio, just returned from a consulship in Venice, became virtual editor in 1866 and titular editor in 1871. The *Atlantic* was not a money-maker, but *Harper's* was flourishing like the green bay tree. Its managing editor during the first four years of our period was Alfred H. Guernsey, a Hebrew scholar who had become an invaluable part of the Harper organization, though as a matter of fact, Fletcher Harper himself was the controlling personality in the *Monthly's* destinies. In 1869 Guernsey was succeeded by Henry Mills Alden, who was to see a half-century of service in this capacity.

The bells celebrating Lee's surrender had scarcely ceased ringing when Charles Scribner & Company issued the first number of a new literary monthly called *Hours at Home*.[33] The

[29] C. E. Norton, ed., *Letters of James Russell Lowell* (New York, 1894), I, 335. The *Independent* said much the same thing on April 26, 1866.

[30] *Citizen and Round Table*, VII, 521 (March 25, 1871). See also the statement in the *Annual American Cyclopaedia* for 1878, p. 484, that "the quarterly review may be said to have disappeared." This was after the *North American's* change to monthly publication.

[31] Treated more fully in vol. II, sketch 16.

[32] Treated more fully in vol. II, sketch 30.

[33] May 1865–October 1870, in eleven semiannual volumes. Editors were James Manning Sherwood, 1867–69, and Richard Watson Gilder, 1869–70. Sherwood, an indefatigable worker, was at the same time joint editor of the *Presbyterian Review* and associate editor of the *Eclectic Magazine*, and at various times edited half a dozen other religious magazines. Among the contributors were many prominent clerical writers, as well as laymen like J. G. Holland, R. G. White, W. G. Simms, and H. T. Tuckerman. Some material from English periodicals was used. Among its serials were such diverse works as Horace Bushnell's *Moral Uses of Dark Things*, Tolstoy's *Sevastopol*, and Charlotte Yonge's

first few volumes were definitely religious in tone, and the editor was a Presbyterian clergyman; but the evangelical motive gradually became less pronounced. The magazine was discontinued in 1870 to make room for a new venture by the same house — *Scribner's Monthly*.

Two new literary monthlies were begun in 1866 — *Beadle's Monthly* [34] and the *Galaxy*.[35] The former was modeled upon Harper's and was a handsome and acceptable magazine throughout its eighteen numbers; it represented the second (and, from the literary point of view, more successful) attempt of the dime-novel publishers in the magazine field. The *Galaxy* was one of the more important magazines of the period, a New York rival of the *Atlantic*, with which it was combined when it gave up the struggle in its twelfth year. The brothers W. C. and F. P. Church were its editors.

The *Northern Magazine*, founded in May 1867, by the New Jersey State Literary Union at Newark, with Captain Allen Lee Bassett as editor, printed some contributions by well-known magazinists before it was merged into *Putnam's* in July 1868.[36]

In 1868 two of the best-known magazines of the time were founded — *Lippincott's*,[37] of Philadelphia, and the second *Putnam's*,[38] of New York. *Lippincott's* was to have a varied career, but throughout the period under consideration it was a high-class general magazine, rather conservative, beautifully printed, and blessed with a fine group of contributors. John F. Kirk,

---

Heir of Redclyffe. There was considerable criticism of books, and some of art and music. Tracts and sermons were frequent in the earlier volumes. In its number for July 1865, it quoted with approval a comment probably written by Holland and printed in the *Springfield Republican*: "It is avowedly 'evangelical' in its tendencies; it is varied in contents, chaste in style, liberal in tone." Holland was later offered the editorship, but refused because he thought the magazine "moribund" (*Scribner's*, XXII, 302; June 1881).

[34] Treated more fully in vol. II, sketch 27.

[35] Treated more fully in the present volume, sketch 6.

[36] It was called the *New Jersey Magazine* for its first two issues. It was a rather amusing periodical, though badly edited and containing some "booster" material. It printed serials by Harriet Prescott Spofford and James Parton, and theatrical articles by Olive Logan. The editorship was declined by Gilder and Holland, both contributors (Rosamund Gilder, ed., *Letters of Richard Watson Gilder*, Boston, 1916, p. 43)

[37] Treated more fully in the present volume, sketch 11.

[38] Treated more fully in vol. II, sketch 21.

the historian, was editor. *Putnam's*, too, was a magazine of high grade, but it soon succumbed to the very lively competition which it had to meet.

The year 1870 is a notable date in the founding of periodicals. The most important magazine begun in that year was *Scribner's Monthly*,[39] later to be called the *Century*. Under the editorship of Dr. Josiah G. Holland, it came very soon to share with *Harper's* the most advantageous position among American literary magazines. The *Atlantic*, the *Galaxy*, *Lippincott's*, and *Putnam's* used pictures sparingly or not at all; they left to *Scribner's* and *Harper's* the development of high-class illustration in copious quantity — a characteristic which eventually became the distinction of the American general magazine that made it, by the end of our period, the superior in attractiveness of anything else of its kind in the world. *Scribner's* Presbyterianism was somewhat more conspicuous than *Harper's* Methodism; and the younger magazine was less English than its rival, Dr. Holland's own novels being perhaps as successful for serial use as available British productions would have been. In biography and travel the two magazines pursued much the same policy.

Old and New[40] began in Boston in the same year and month as *Scribner's* in New York; when it decided to quit, in 1875, it was merged in *Scribner's*. Edward Everett Hale was editor. Perhaps *Old and New* should be classified among religious periodicals, for it was definitely a Unitarian organ and a successor of the more formal *Christian Examiner*; but it was a magazine of general literature as well.

The *Penn Monthly*[41] was also begun in January 1870. It was

[39] Treated more fully in the present volume, sketch 21.

[40] Treated more fully in sketch 17.

[41] January 1870–July 1882. William W. Newton and Otis H. Kendall were joint editors with Thompson. "It aims to be a magazine for all, discussing questions of public interest in literature, science, art and philosophy in a thoughtful way." Social science, education, and art were outstanding topics in the *Penn*. It was an organ for the Philadelphia Social Science Association. In its later numbers it carried a department of University of Pennsylvania news appealing to alumni. It published the Dresser art lectures in 1877 and a series on ceramics by J. J. Talbot the following year. There were some travel articles, and Henry Coppee's "Conquest of Spain by the Arab Moors" was a serial in 1873. H. W. Furness, Henry C. Carey, Henry C. Lea, and S. Weir Mitchell were contributors. Barker later claimed to have had a chief part in the editorship.

founded by Wharton Barker, publisher, and Professor Robert Ellis Thompson, of the University of Pennsylvania, editor, and had a rather close connection with that institution. It published some poetry, but no fiction, devoting itself to serious discussions of sociology, politics and art. It was not unlike the *International Review*,[42] which was founded four years later in New York, though the *International* had better-known contributors from at home and abroad and dealt more with foreign questions. Rice very probably got his idea of making the *North American* a monthly from these two reviews.

Baldwin's Monthly[43] was another 1870 birth — a curious magazine which mingled literature with the retail clothing business. Baldwin the clothier published Walt Whitman and many other notables, and distributed 50,000 free copies of his magazine each month. He was a typical New Yorker with the New York view of literature as the handmaid of commerce. *Potter's American Monthly*[44] was also allied to other fields; it grew out of the *American Historical Record* and blossomed into a general magazine with historical interests during the years 1875–82.

In the centennial year of 1876 Frank Leslie founded one more of his numerous family of periodicals and christened it

[42] January 1874–June 1883. It was founded as a bimonthly by John McD. Leavitt, who edited it for five years. A. S. Barnes & Company, the publishers, then made it a monthly, and John T. Morse, Jr., and Henry Cabot Lodge became editors. Robert P. Porter was editor in 1882, for the first eight months with Henry Gannett; and William R. Balch edited the last five numbers. The contents were varied, with good articles on literature and art, and some belles-lettres. Book reviews were given special attention; and there was an attempt to live up to the title by enlisting foreign contributors and following foreign literatures. P. G. Hamerton had a series on art beginning in the second volume; E. A. Freeman was a frequent contributor; and Karl Blind, Sir Edwin Arnold, Justin McCarthy, and J. A. Froude were also familiar names in the table of contents. But American names were far more frequent: John Fiske, Henry James, Jr., Brander Matthews, Holmes, Higginson, Whittier, Bryant, Wasson, and many others who were well known. Lounsbury's "English Language in America" was published serially, and Arnold's translation of the *Mahabharata*.

[43] An eight-page quarto by O. C. Baldwin. In the beginning it was highly eclectic and fragmentary, though amusing; but by 1875 Baldwin began to buy good names — William Winter, Paul H. Hayne, Thomas B. Thorpe, Elizabeth Oakes Smith, and so on. It "was conducted in a fine, manly way by Mr. Baldwin, who paid reasonable prices for articles," wrote Mrs. Smith in her autobiography. See Mary A. Wyman, *Two American Pioneers* (New York, 1927), p. 224. *Baldwin's* seems to have ended in 1886.

[44] See p. 260.

optimistically *Frank Leslie's Popular Monthly.*[45] Cheaper in price and of lower literary grade than *Harper's* and *Scribner's*, but well illustrated, it quickly built up a large circulation which compensated for some of the Leslie failures. In spite of his ups and downs and his bankruptcy in 1878, Frank Leslie, with his score or so of periodicals, was one of the most prominent publishers of these years. He died in 1880, but his wife ably carried on his business.

A few other more or less general magazines were founded in the seventies: the *Granite Monthly*,[46] "a New Hampshire magazine devoted to history, biography, literature, and state progress," which began its long career at Concord in 1877; *Donahoe's Magazine*,[47] which published "tales, biography, episodes in Irish and American history, poetry, miscellany, etc.," under Catholic auspices from 1879 to 1908; *Rideout's Monthly Magazine* (1878–83), New York, a cheap publication which accumulated a considerable circulation before its owner failed in 1883.

[45] Treated more fully in sketch 28. Another monthly of the Leslie tribe was *Frank Leslie's Ten-Cent Monthly*, which began in August 1863 and became *Frank Leslie's New Monthly* in June 1865. In the following year this periodical gave place to *Frank Leslie's Pleasant Hours*, a fifteen-cent illustrated monthly "devoted to light and entertaining literature," which lasted until 1896.

[46] Founded by H. H. Metcalf, April 1877, and edited by him in 1877–79, 1892–93, 1900–03, 1906–18, and again in 1927. John N. McClintock was editor from December 1879 to December 1890; he had been publisher of the first volume. The Republican Press Association owned it in 1894, later selling it to the Rumford Printing Company; Metcalf was publisher as well as editor, 1906–18. Many other persons have been associated in the editorship. The file is very irregular, with many omissions and double numbers. It changed its name in 1929 to *New Hampshire: the Granite State Monthly;* then it changed back to the old name four months before it perished, December 1930. It was always distinctively a state magazine, with emphasis on contemporary biography and state history. It carried a monthly portrait engraved on steel until 1890, when half-tones were substituted. Professor Edwin D. Sanborn, of Dartmouth, author of a *History of New Hampshire*, and Silas Ketcham, author of a *Dictionary of New Hampshire Biography*, were copious contributions in the magazine's earlier years. Frank B. Sanborn's illustrated autobiography in 1904 was a good feature. In its last years the *Monthly* was a "booster" magazine.

[47] Founded and conducted until his death in 1901 by Patrick Donahoe, editor of the famous Catholic and Irish weekly, the *Pilot*. Publishers were T. B. Noonan & Company, Boston. It was very Irish, its green cover being decorated with pictures of a harp, St. Patrick, etc. It became less Irish-minded and rather more Catholic in the nineties. In its earlier years it depended much on clipped "selections," but it later became more original and contained better illustration.

In 1883 John W. Orr, a leading New York commercial engraver on wood, established the *Manhattan* [48] as a fully illustrated standard magazine publishing the best authors. Though Orr and his backers are said to have spent $100,000 on it, the venture was abandoned in less than two years. The *Brooklyn Magazine* [49] (1884–88), another ambitious monthly, lasted but little longer.

It is plain that in the field of the general literary monthly, the East produced but few successful new magazines after the prolific years of 1865–70. Only two of first-rate importance appeared between 1870 and 1885 — the *International Review* and *Leslie's Popular Monthly*. As will be seen later, the West also produced two in this class during those years. [50]

THE TRIUMPHS OF AUGUSTA, MAINE

But if we turn to the field of the story-paper, we find the enterprising publishers of such cheap products extremely active in the monthly field. It was in 1869 that the mother of the whole brood of mail-order papers, the *People's Literary Companion*, [51] appeared in Augusta, Maine. This group of periodicals, which for forty years was to blacken thousands of tons of cheap print paper annually, began with one E. C. Allen. Allen had a good washing-powder recipe, which could be de-

[48] Published January 1883–September 1884. It began as an Odd Fellows' journal, its publisher being a leader in that society and a former proprietor of the *American Odd Fellow*. It was designed to aid and abet also the Knights of Pythias, Red Men, etc.; but after a few numbers it dropped its secret society affiliations and came out as a standard magazine much like *Lippincott's* in appearance. It ran serials by Edgar Fawcett and Julian Hawthorne, poetry by Whittier and Stedman and Stoddard, good travel articles and book reviews, and an excellent department of Table Talk. H. C. Bunner, Brander Matthews, Junius Henri Browne, Joel Benton, Julia Ward Howe, Louise Chandler Moulton, and Kate Field were among the contributors. It was an excellent magazine in its last sixteen months. The remark about its finances was made by John Brisben Walker in the *Cosmopolitan Magazine*, XIV, 261 (January 1893).

[49] To be treated in a separate sketch in the succeeding volume.

[50] The *Lakeside Monthly*, Chicago, and the *Overland Monthly*, San Francisco, qq.v.

[51] September 1869–November 1907. It was a weekly by the middle seventies, with a much reduced circulation, but a monthly again in 1882. It became a part of "Lane's List," successor to E. C. Allen & Company, in 1895. Shortly before the postal law of 1907 put an end to it and its fellows, it was selling at ten cents for fifteen months.

pended upon to make dishwashing a pleasure and house clean-
ing one long holiday; his problem was to get agents to sell it —
not the powder, but the printed formula. The ingredients were
simple and cheap and could be bought at any drugstore. Allen
had the forty-word formula printed on slips which bore also
the legend "Price $1.00" and which he sold to his agents at $10
a hundred or $25 a thousand; the housewife could buy one
only upon her express agreement not to reveal the secret formula
to anyone. It seems incredible, but the system worked. We
must remember that the years immediately following the war
were easy-money years.

Allen advertised modestly for agents who wished to multiply
their investment by ten, and got some replies. He put his remittances into more advertisements, and more remittances began to flood his makeshift office. One day he appeared before
the desk of George P. Rowell, the great New York advertising
agent, and said he wished to buy $30,000 worth of advertising.
Rowell demanded a deposit of one-third on the spot, and Allen
pulled it out of his coat pocket and paid it over; then Allen
asked if he might have a discount for cash in advance on the
remainder, and Rowell offered him 5 per cent. "Well," remarked Allen, as he abstracted another $19,000 from the same
pocket, "that is worth saving." This, let us remember, was in
the infancy of advertising, and the whole proceeding seems to
have been rather a shock to the good Mr. Rowell.[52]

It was shortly after this that Allen decided to start a periodical of his own to carry his advertising. He was branching out
into engravings and chromolithographs and other lines. He
founded the *Companion*, a sixteen-page small folio devoted to
stories, household helps, fashions, poetry, and humor, priced
at fifty cents a year but sold for less in clubs. In fact, it was
in large part distributed free, and it reached a circulation of
half a million in its second year.[53] Allen's prosperity did not go
unnoted in Augusta, and in 1874 P. O. Vickery established in
the same city and on much the same plan *Vickery's Fireside
Visitor*, which lasted for a third of a century. In the following

[52] George P. Rowell, *Forty Years an Advertising Agent* (New York, 1906),
p. 194.
[53] *Printer's Circular*, V, 467 (January 1870).

year True & Company began *Our Fireside Journal* in Augusta, to run five years. These papers were all forerunners of groups each of which was later listed together for the benefit of advertisers. They were all published with a view to attracting the advertising of concerns which sold by the direct-mail method, and they came to be called "mail-order papers." By the late seventies their business had grown so that most of them were issued weekly. Though Augusta always retained the doubtful glory of being the home of the mail-order paper, publishers in many other cities imitated her successes;[54] and eventually such story-papers as the *Fireside Companion*, of New York, the *New York Weekly*, the *Chicago Ledger*, and the *Chicago Fireside Friend* came to depend chiefly or wholly upon mail-order advertising.

There were many other monthlies scattered through the East which were neither mail-order papers nor standard literary monthlies.[55] Some were eclectics, some were local literary mis-

[54] Portland, Maine, was only a little behind Augusta in this type of periodical. There George Stimson began his *Centennial Record* (1876–79) as an illustrated folio telling all about the great exposition, but the next year turned it into a cheap story-paper with mail-order advertising; he also published the longer-lived *People's Journal* (1877–91). H. Hallett & Company, Portland, published *Our Home and Fireside Magazine* (1873–88). There was another *People's Journal* published in Philadelphia by Zeigler, McCurdie & Company, 1867–75; beginning at fifty cents, it was later sold for a dollar a year. *Leisure Hours* (1877–82), of New York, was followed by a weekly *Leisure* (1882–83). The *Cherub* (1870–79) was devoted at first not to mail-order advertising, but to a patent medicine; it was published by J. Latham & Company, proprietors of a cathartic extract. In 1876, under the name of *Illustrated Home Guest*, it went over to the mail-order houses.

[55] The *American Miscellany* (1865–74), edited in Boston by James H. Brigham, was devoted to "entertaining literature." *Ballou's Dollar Monthly* continued in Boston (see vol. II, p. 31). *Beecher's Illustrated Magazine* (1870–72) was a respectable attempt by J. A. Beecher at Trenton, New Jersey. *Drake's Magazine* (1882–93) was a dollar monthly with an excellent humor department founded in New York by John N. Drake. Frank Leslie had two cheaper monthlies — *Frank Leslie's Budget* (1878–96), at twenty cents and later ten cents, and *Frank Leslie's Pleasant Hours* (1866–96) at fifteen cents. *Gleason's Monthly Companion* (1872–87) was a late sequel to that Boston publisher's weekly of similar name. The *Modern Age* was a Buffalo foreign eclectic of 1883. *Sunday Afternoon* (1878–81) was a high-grade magazine of entertaining reading, chiefly fiction, published by E. F. Merriam at Springfield, Massachusetts. Washington Gladden was editor during its first year and continued as an associate when Merriam took over the editorship. The name was changed to *Good Company*, October 1879. The magazine had an excellent corps of contributors. *Zell's Monthly Magazine* (1872–73) was a Philadelphia miscellany in folio.

cellanies, and some aspired to compete with the bigger magazines and failed. Monthlies designed for women and the home must be considered in another chapter.[56]

MORE OR LESS LITERARY WEEKLIES IN THE EAST

Perhaps the most important American weekly in existence at the beginning of 1865 was the one for which the Harpers furnished the management, George William Curtis most of the editorials, and Thomas Nast many of the news pictures and cartoons. These three elements, with serial fiction and news articles, combined to make *Harper's Weekly* [57] popular and powerful. Quite as fully illustrated and somewhat more sprightly was *Frank Leslie's Illustrated Newspaper*;[58] but there was less character in its editorship, and it went down in circulation during the war while *Harper's Weekly* was going up. It suffered, too, from the panic, and was published by a receiver for a time after Leslie's bankruptcy of 1878.

July 6, 1865, the *Nation* [59] published its first number. Under the editorship of Edwin L. Godkin, and with the coöperation of the ablest publicists of the country, the *Nation* furnished the American people throughout our period the best journal of opinion they had ever known. In politics, economics, science, the arts, and literature, authoritative writers presented clear and forceful views. Heaviness, which had been the bane of most serious writing in America, found little place in the pages of Godkin's weekly. The *Nation* did not build up a large circulation, having only 8,000 subscribers by 1880, but it exerted a strong influence upon thinking people.

Two months after the appearance of the *Nation*, the *Round Table* [60] resumed publication. It had been started during the war, but after a seven months' struggle had decided to await more peaceful times. It called itself "A Saturday Review of Politics, Finance, Literature, Science, and Art." It was trenchant and aggressive and a very good influence in the journalism of the period. Perhaps it scolded too much and made friends

[56] See pp. 98–101.
[57] Treated more fully in vol. II, sketch 28.
[58] Treated more fully in vol. II, sketch 26.
[59] Treated more fully in the present volume, sketch 4.
[60] Treated more fully in the present volume, sketch 1.

too rarely. It was forced to suspend, or rather to merge with a newspaper, in 1869.

The *Round Table* and the *Nation* were primarily journals of opinion; while *Harper's Weekly* and *Leslie's Illustrated*, though they too had strong opinions, were popular illustrated miscellanies with strong emphasis on current events. Into this latter class in 1869 came *Appleton's Journal*.[61] It was exceptionally well illustrated, with both woodcuts and steel plates. It seems now, in its bound files, most interesting and attractive; but it lacked that slashing boldness in picture and in opinion which its rivals possessed. In 1876 it became a monthly, and its quality declined until it died in 1881. The *Golden Age*,[62] founded by Theodore Tilton after he left the *Independent* in 1870, was of a similar type, though wanting in illustration.

After the panic, came two Philadelphia weeklies of opinion of the *Nation* type. *Forney's Progress* [63] was attractively printed and possessed great variety but no literary brilliance; it was conducted by John W. Forney, a famous Philadelphia politician and newspaper editor. The *American* [64] was an offshoot of the *Penn Monthly*, begun in 1880 under the editorial supervision of William R. Balch and Robert Ellis Thompson. It had some excellent contributors, including Walt Whitman, H. H. Boyesen, H. C. Bunner, and Paul Hamilton Hayne. In 1882 it took over *Stoddart's Review*,[65] continuing it as the

[61] Treated more fully in the present volume, sketch 15.

[62] Published March 4, 1871–September 25, 1875. William T. Clarke succeeded Tilton as editor and publisher in 1874, and the paper was then changed from small folio to quarto in size. Tilton welcomed all types of opinion, declaring "no idea will be too radical" for presentation in his paper. There was much brief bright comment. A serial story by Amelia E. Barr was published in 1873, and one by Tilton himself called "Tempest-Tossed: A Love Story" in 1873–74.

[63] Published November 6, 1878–September 12, 1885. It was strongly Republican in politics. Finance, drama, clubs, science, law, chess, and books were among its interests. C. G. Leland was its London correspondent, and there were also regular letters from Paris and New York. Its price was reduced from $5.00 to half that after 1880, and the size and quality declined.

[64] Wharton Barker was publisher, and after a suspension, 1891–94, he was both editor and publisher until the end in 1900. It always carried news of books and art. In politics it was mildly Republican in its earlier volumes, but strongly antitrust. Later it was independent, with an inclination toward Populism.

[65] Begun as a weekly by J. M. Stoddart & Company, March 3, 1880, chiefly to advertise that firm's reprint of the *Encyclopaedia Britannica*, it was devoted to "the graver aspects of thought." It became a monthly in June 1880.

monthly edition of the *American*. It specialized in "temperate but earnest" discussion of politics and literature. A brilliant and ambitious attempt was Albion W. Tourgée's *Continent*,[66] on which its vigorous proprietor lavished $100,000 in his three years' effort to set it up as a going concern. It was of the *Harper's Weekly* kind of combined miscellany and opinion. An undistinguished Washington venture of these same years was the *American Register* (1881–84), a democratic "journal of politics, literature, science and news."

STORY-PAPERS AND CHEAP MISCELLANIES

Besides the higher-class journals of opinion and miscellany, there were in the weekly field many story-papers and cheaply printed periodicals designed, for the most part, for week-end reading. A considerable number of these were continued from the preceding period,[67] and some were half a century old at the end of our period. By the eighties many of them had come over into the mail-order class, which had originally been composed of monthlies. A few of those started in the larger eastern centers between 1865 and 1885 may be mentioned here.

The indefatigable Leslie began his copiously illustrated *Frank Leslie's Chimney Corner* June 6, 1865. It was very successful for several years, but fell off in the later seventies; in December 1884 it was succeeded by a kind of postscript called *Frank Leslie's Fact and Fiction for the Chimney Corner*, which for six months tried adulterating the familiar diet of fiction with more serious matters. But the effort was useless. The same year in which the *Chimney Corner* was set alight saw the beginning of James Elverson's Philadelphia *Saturday Night* (1865–1902), which consistently maintained one of the big circulations of our period. Another paper designed for Sunday reading was the *Boston Budget* (1879–1918), which, though it grew rather slowly, lived to enjoy a distinguished position in its class.[68]

---

[66] Treated more fully in sketch 37.   [67] See vol. II, pp. 34–43.

[68] It was a Sunday paper in our period, but it became primarily a woman's home journal in the late eighties and nineties, and, after it absorbed the *Beacon* in 1905, a society and amusement paper. William Grant James, who had been managing editor for some years, became editor in 1899, succeeding Charles Emerson Cook. Lilian Whiting was an assistant editor in the nineties. The *Budget* absorbed the veteran *Saturday Evening Gazette* in 1906.

Keppler and Schwartzmann, publishers of *Puck*, issued a handsome weekly filled with cheap stories and called *Fiction* for seven or eight months in 1881–82.

The dime-novel publishers did well with this type of periodical.[69] George Munro's New York *Fireside Companion* (1866–1907) was long a successful paper. Munro had been a bookkeeper for Erastus Beadle, but left him to form a partnership in 1866 with Irwin Beadle and publish the *Companion* and a series of dime novels. This was the house that made "Old Cap Collier" and "Old Sleuth" famous. Beadle & Adams published their *Star Journal* (1870–81) somewhat less successfully, calling it latterly the *Saturday Journal*; and then they followed it with *Beadle's Weekly* (1882–97), the name of which was changed in 1886 to *Banner Weekly*. This latter paper was a famous one in its class. It published such good old thriller-authors as Colonel Prentiss Ingraham, Captain Mayne Reid, "Ned Buntline," Albert W. Aiken, and Professor Edward S. Ellis; and it never succumbed to the lure of mail-order advertising.

Other weeklies of the cheaper sort were specifically designed for women and the home, and will be considered in connection with women's interests,[70] while still another group must be placed among the juveniles.[71]

If these periodicals were sub-literary, what shall we say of another class — the sex-and-crime sensation mongers? Let us allow a magazine critic of their own times to characterize them:

Vilest among those that are vile, very Arch-Bestials in a carnival of bestiality are the latest born among them . . . they have the same debauched features, the same imbecility — leave nothing more to be desired by the Low-Priests of Depravity . . . veritable Bibles of Damnation.[72]

[69] The "Libraries" of Beadle and other dime-novel publishers may sometimes be called magazines, since some of them carried not only serial numbers but dates. Beadle dated the weekly issues of his *Dime Library* (1878–97) and *Half-Dime Library* (1877–98) beginning in 1879. Edmund Pearson refers to these as magazines in his *Dime Novels* (Boston, 1929), p. 54. But *Old Sleuth Library* and some others were undated.

[70] See pp. 98–101.

[71] See pp. 174–80.

[72] *Land We Love*, V, 81 (May 1868).

Rather strong language, but deserved. It was directed especially at two New York papers started early in 1868, neither of which, apparently, outlasted the year — *Stetson's Dime Illustrated* and Joseph Carter's *Last Sensation*. They were imitators of the police gazettes,[73] but they out-Heroded their Herod and played up the sex angle in crime beyond anything that had been done before. Then *Day's Doings* was founded June 6, 1868, ostensibly to be devoted to "current events of romance, police reports, important trials, and sporting news." It began with a history of the prize ring, but its real reliance was upon sensational sex stories culled from the newspapers and from reports of trials; "Free Love; or Wedded to Death" and "A Maiden's Perils" were typical headings. The woodcuts which occupied nearly half its space were as sensational as the articles. "The prudish censors," said the editor in 1871, "who have endeavored to associate its name with the idea of immorality, have been rebuked by the extraordinary popularity which has attended this journal from its birth." [74]   James Watts & Company, the founders, sold the paper to Frank Leslie in 1873, and he toned it down and made a family paper of it before merging it with one of his own periodicals in 1876. But as if to compensate for this loss to moronic literature, Richard K. Fox, who bought the *Police Gazette* [75] in 1877, immediately began his "Vice's Varieties" and such sensational features. That sort of crudity paid, and in 1883 Fox began a new paper recalling in its title the old sheet that had scandalized the censors. He named it *Fox's Illustrated Week's Doings*, "the spiciest dramatic and best story paper in America," and began in its first number a series on "The Prettiest Women in Paris." This paper he suspended at the end of the following year in order to start the *Illustrated Day's Doings and Sporting World* (1885–90). One standing head in the new paper ran "This Wicked World — Samples of Man's Duplicity and Women's Worse Than Weakness." "Frisky females" and "fly Gothamites" abound in these columns, depicted by slangy writers and by artists who tried to be shocking. Meantime the Boston *Police News* [76] was keeping up

[73] See vol. II, p. 187.

[74] *Day's Doings*, VII, 2 (June 3, 1871).

[75] Treated more fully in vol. II, sketch 9.   [76] See vol. II, p. 187.

with the procession. Its specialty was horrors: one of its masterpieces was the story of a woman buried alive who gave birth to a child in her coffin.[77]

That any magazines should have been published in the South in the years immediately following the war seems remarkable. "We know the impoverished condition of our people, and that some of them find it inconvenient to pay even a small amount," [78] said *Scott's Monthly* in appealing for funds. But at least a score of southern magazines of literary intention were issued, most of them ephemerally, within four years after the end of the war;[79] and among religious and other class journals there was much activity.

New Orleans, Atlanta, Baltimore, Richmond, and Louisville were the important southern centers in the publication of periodicals. At New Orleans, for the most part, *De Bow's Review* published its "After the War Series" irregularly from 1866 to 1880.[80] Daniel K. Whitaker's *New Orleans Monthly Review* was published irregularly 1874–76, followed by a number or two of a *New Orleans Quarterly Review* in 1878. Whitaker republished these in 1880 as a "New Series" of the old *Southern Quarterly Review*, of two numbers. James E. Waldo's *Present Age* (1870–72), a quarterly miscellany at a dollar a year, was published in New Orleans; and such weekly miscellanies as the political and theatrical *Figaro* (1883–84), James H. Hummell's *Weekly Budget* (1875–76), and a waspish, reformatory *Mascot* (1882–95). William Evelyn and William B. Smith published *Crescent Monthly*, 1866–67.

Atlanta was the home of one of the most important southern magazines of the period — *Scott's Monthly*.[81] It published

[77] *Illustrated Police News*, January 6, 1883, p. 2.

[78] *Scott's Monthly Magazine*, III, 324 (April 1867).

[79] See Frank McLean, "Periodicals Published in the South before 1880" (University of Virginia thesis, 1928), p. 49.

[80] Treated more fully in vol. II, sketch 10.

[81] *Scott's Monthly Magazine* was published December 1865–December 1869. W. J. Scott, the founder and editor, was an Atlanta bookseller. W. H. Wylly edited the final number. About one-fourth of the contents were "selected." There were many accounts of war incidents and campaigns, including Major B. W. Frobel's "Field and Camp" serial. A few portraits were published, includ-

early work of Lanier, Hayne, and Maurice Thompson, but survived only four years. The *Sunny South* [82] was a family weekly of miscellaneous contents published for many years in Atlanta. It and the Louisville *Home and Farm* were the only southern periodicals to reach 100,000 circulation before 1885. The *Sunday Gazette* (1878–81) was the most literary of a series of Atlanta Sunday papers.

The *Richmond Eclectic* was a monthly which began in November 1866, with Moses D. Hodge and William Hand Browne as conductors. In January 1868 Lawrence and H. C. Turnbull and Fridge Murdoch took it over and moved it to Baltimore, calling it the *New Eclectic.* Then in April of the next year it absorbed the *Land We Love* [83] and published an increasing number of good original articles and stories, including Richard Malcolm Johnston's "Dukesborough Tales," and work by Simms, Cooke, Gildersleeve, and Margaret J. Preston. In 1871 the magazine abandoned eclecticism and became the *Southern Magazine*,[84] under William Hand Browne's editor-

ing those of Lee and Davis by George E. Perine of New York. The subscription price was $5.00, or $4.00 in advance; and it claimed "upwards of five thousand circulation," chiefly in five southern states, in November 1867.

[82] Published 1875–1907. J. H. Seals was publisher in the eighties. It printed Sylvanus Cobb, Will Allen Dromgoole, etc. The latter was connected with the paper editorially for a time, and Henry Clay Fairman was editor in the nineties. It was succeeded by the *Uncle Remus Magazine.*

[83] Founded and conducted by General Daniel H. Hill, May 1866 to March 1869. Its love for the Southland entailed not only a recounting of the South's story of the war, but also a hatred of the North. Much of it was written by the editor; but Margaret J. Preston, John R. Thompson, P. H. Hayne, and Dr. F. O. Ticknor, besides the writers mentioned above, were contributors. James P. Irwin and J. G. Morrison were partners in the publication. Histories of campaigns, tales of heroism, and the humor of the camp vied with agricultural and literary articles, poetry, and travel in its pages. In spite of the fact that it claimed twelve thousand subscribers in 1867 (see cover of April number), it complained of nonpayment of accounts "owing probably to the extreme poverty of the South."

[84] The proprietors after the merger were Murdoch, Browne, and W. L. Hill, who sold to the Turnbulls in 1873. Besides those mentioned as *New Eclectic* contributors, the *Southern Magazine* enlisted Lanier, Hayne, Longstreet, and Bagby. It was the official organ of the Southern Historical Society in its last year or two. In some ways it partook of the nature of a review, and it was always a bit heavy. Mrs. Preston, who contributed to it gratis, wrote to Hayne in 1869: "The Turnbulls have been men of means (they have lost heavily lately), and during the first year of their connection with the magazine sunk five thousand dollars in endeavoring to maintain it." See Elizabeth Preston Allan, *Life and Letters of Margaret Junkin Preston* (Boston, 1903), p. 250.

ship. But its publishers failed, and it was suspended in 1875. Among other Baltimore ventures were the monthly *South Atlantic* (1877–82), by Carrie Jenkins Harris, which had been transplanted from Wilmington, North Carolina; *Southern Society* (1867–68), with a list of superior contributors; and another brief eclectic — A. C. Meyer's *Continental Magazine* (1883).

Richmond, where the *New Eclectic* had its beginnings, was also the home of W. M. Hazlewood's literary and educational *Seminary Magazine* (1863–73). Its scope was broadened and its name altered in 1870 to the *Old Dominion*, but such changes did not stay its dissolution in the panic year.

Louisville was a publishing center of some importance. Besides notable class publications, it had Porter Thompson's *Twelve Times a Year* (1867–71), a miscellany in octavo; the *Louisville Monthly Magazine* (1879–80); and — much the most important of all — the *Southern Bivouac*.[85] The *Bivouac* was the project of the Southern Historical Association and was devoted in its earlier years chiefly to the publication of papers on the Civil War; but when General Basil W. Duke and R. W. Knott became editors in 1885 they broadened it considerably. Paul Hayne, Maurice Thompson, John Esten Cooke, and Lafcadio Hearn were among its writers.

THE SOUTH IN NORTHERN MAGAZINES

Of course all magazines that discussed politics were interested in reconstruction as a problem, but the sympathetic interpretation of the South was a different matter. That began with the *Nation's* series "The South as It Is," by J. R. Dennett — an extremely valuable sequence of descriptive and analytical articles. The *Galaxy* and *Lippincott's* printed many sketches of southern

[85] Subtitle: A Monthly Literary and Historical Magazine. Issued September 1882–May 1887. The Association was publisher until August 1883, when E. H. and W. N. McDonald took it over and broadened its scope. William M. Marriner and W. N. McDonald were the chief editors. Then in June 1885 B. F. Avery & Sons, publishers of *Home and Farm*, bought it and began a new series with Duke and Knott as editors. The magazine was now much improved in every way, though still more or less devoted to war papers. Its war songs and the humor of the camp were notable. The magazine is said to have grown out of a department in a local newspaper called "The Bivouac." It was finally merged in the *Century*, which, said a later southern magazine, wanted a clear field in the publication of war papers. See Fetter's *Southern Magazine*, V, 58 (August 1894).

conditions in the late sixties and early seventies, and they also opened their pages to such southern writers as Lanier, Hayne, Cooke, Mrs. Preston, and Simms. *Lippincott's*, indeed, came to be considered as in some degree a spokesman for the South. There was a concerted effort to encourage settlement from the North. *Harper's Weekly* announced in 1866:

> We propose to publish a series of carefully prepared maps of the Southern States, beginning with Mississippi in this number of the *Weekly*, accompanied by concise and complete industrial statistics, that the general character and special advantages of the Southern part of the country may be understood by those who are thinking of settling there.[86]

Every Saturday, Appleton's Journal, and *Frank Leslie's Illustrated* also published attractive series of articles and pictures of the South in the late sixties and early seventies.

But the magazine series about the South which attracted the greatest attention was the one written by Edward S. King for *Scribner's Monhly* in 1873–74. It was entitled "The Great South" and was brilliantly and copiously illustrated. In 1874 *Harper's Monthly* followed this lead with an illustrated series by "Porte Crayon" called "The New South." George Cary Eggleston's "A Rebel's Recollections" made the *Atlantic's* gesture of conciliation to the South in the same year.

In the later seventies southern writers made what seems almost a concerted advance upon northern literary strongholds. Lee and Johnston and Early had been defeated in the conflict of '61–'65, but Cable, Craddock, Page, and their cohorts won a complete victory a decade later when they established themselves in the northern magazines. Edward King discovered George W. Cable in a New Orleans countingroom and persuaded him to submit one of his Creole stories to *Scribner's*: it was the premonitor of a southern local color boom which was really launched by Miss Murfree's "The Dancin' Party at Harrison's Cove" in the *Atlantic* for May 1878. Three years later *Scribner's* said:

> Attention has recently been called to the large number of southern contributions to the magazines. No less than seven articles con-

[86] *Harper's Weekly*, X, 3 (January 6, 1866).

tributed by southern writers appeared in a recent number of *Scribner's*, and we are glad to recognize the fact of a permanent productive force in literature in the southern states. . . . New England is no longer king. Her great literary school is dying out. . . . The South and West are hereafter to be reckoned upon.[87]

THE VOICE OF THE WEST

Yes, the West, too, was clamoring at the gates. How could it be otherwise? The West had gained tremendously in population, in transportation, in industries, in political power, and in culture; and it was not in the nature of a region famed for "tall talk" and "boring with a big auger" to keep quiet for long.

The discovery that the Middle West and the Far West were already more or less settled and powerful seems to have come with a shock to the American people as a whole in the late sixties. Over and over again the phenomenon is described and wondered at and philosophized upon. "America has moved west of late," observed the *Nation* in 1868;[88] while C. C. Coffin states the fact more vividly in the *Atlantic*: "Civilization at a stride has moved a thousand miles, and taken possession of the home of the buffalo."[89] More philosophical is a remark by an observer in the *Journal of the American Geographical Society*, a remark which voices a doctrine to be held by many historians a decade or two later: "The recession of our frontier is the most important and the most interesting fact of our national history."[90] The East, which had been accustomed to think of everything on the sunset side of Pittsburgh as "the West," was surprised to discover that there was a great Middle West, now the center of the nation's agriculture and netted with railroads; that the plains were being cleared of Indians and buffalo together; that the Rocky Mountains were no longer a barrier;

[87] *Scribner's Monthly*, XXII, 786 (September 1881). See also, for similar comment from a similar source, *Southern Bivouac*, N.S., I, 351 (November 1885), and N.S., II, 773 (May 1887).

[88] *Nation*, VII, 528 (December 24, 1868).

[89] *Atlantic Monthly*, XVII, 333 (March 1866).

[90] *Journal of the American Geographical Society of New York*, XIV, 166–204 (1882), General Egbert L. Viele's article on "The Frontiers of the United States." F. J. Turner's address to the American Historical Association on "The Significance of the American Frontier" was delivered in 1893.

and that the Pacific Coast was already the seat of a vital and challenging civilization.

Following the depression of the seventies, there was an increasing westward movement of population — what the *Century* called "a renewal of the western furore." The editor wrote in December 1882:

> The western migration of 1881 was regarded as phenomenal, but it has probably been exceeded in volume by that of the season just closed. It is hardly an exaggerated estimate to say that a million of people have transferred themselves, during the past eight months, from the Atlantic seaboard states and from the older states of the Mississippi Valley, and from the perennially swarming hive of Europe, to the prairies of Dakota, Nebraska, Kansas, and Texas, the valleys of the Rocky Mountain System, and to the farther regions of the Pacific slope.[91]

THE AMBITION OF ST. LOUIS

Of the Middle West much was heard in both praise and blame. In finance and commerce it had its fierce rivalries with the East. But its greatness was undeniable. It was "the natural and inevitable seat of empire," [92] declared *Harper's Weekly*. An *Atlantic* writer pointed out that its progress "in all the range from the most stupendous to the most delicate manufactures" enabled it to stand alone.[93] The *Nation* noted that "the subject of removing the Federal Capital to some place in the West is undergoing vigorous agitation, St. Louis being at present the principal competitor for the honor of succeeding Washington." [94]

In 1870 St. Louis, having doubled its population in the preceding decade, was the third city in the United States. A reporter for the *Atlantic Monthly* said it was the "center and natural metropolis of the Mississippi River Valley." [95] In addition to these material things, it had a brave faith in its literary future and its leading magazine declared: "It is the belief of those interested in the *Western* that St. Louis may be a not in-

[91] *Century*, XXV, 301 (December 1882).
[92] *Harper's Weekly*, XI, 450 (July 20, 1867).
[93] *Atlantic Monthly*, XXIII, 444 (April 1869).
[94] *Nation*, IX, 183 (September 2, 1869).
[95] *Atlantic Monthly*, XIX, 666 (June 1867).

considerable literary center." [96] Its German population may have been responsible to some degree for the interest in German philosophy which formed the basis for what was called "the St. Louis Movement," headed by William T. Harris, Denton J. Snider, and others.[97] Out of this activity came the *Journal of Speculative Philosophy*,[98] which, as one informed critic later said, "made St. Louis famous throughout the civilized world." [99]

Aside from the *Journal*, the young metropolis was chiefly notable, in publishing activity, for certain women's magazines,[100] and for its legal, medical, and other class periodicals, rather than for magazines of general literary appeal. In this latter field its only important bid for favor was the *Western* (1866–81), edited by H. H. Morgan. This began as the *Western Educational Review*, Thomas Davidson editor, but in 1872 its scope was broadened at the same time that its name was shortened; and thereafter it spoke for its region on literary, artistic, and educational matters.[101] *Ware's Valley Monthly*, which published three volumes 1875–76, was subtitled *A Journal of Western Thought and Life*.

GROWING CHICAGO

Chicago, thought the editor of *Appleton's Journal*, was "crowded with a population that 'carries more steam,' perhaps, than any other on the face of the earth." [102] Chicago's population had tripled in the decade preceding 1860; it tripled again in the following decade; and its failure to repeat the feat in

[96] *Western*, IV, 239 (March 1878).

[97] See Charles M. Perry, *The St. Louis Movement in Philosophy* (Norman, Oklahoma, 1930).

[98] Treated more fully in sketch 8.

[99] *Educational Review*, XXXIX, 132 (February 1910).

[100] See p. 101.

[101] January 1875–November 1881, form a New Series I–VII. For its last four years (1878–81) it was a bimonthly. Among its contributors were W. T. Harris, William M. Bryant, Lewis J. Block, James K. Hosmer, and (less frequently) Elizabeth P. Peabody, Edgar Fawcett, and G. P. Lathrop. Octave Thanet's first story appeared here in 1880. There were considerable Shakespeariana, much art criticism, and notices of the St. Louis learned societies. The magazine was always somewhat schoolmasterish, an inheritance from its original purpose; but it contained some good articles and is a landmark of western culture.

[102] *Appleton's Journal*, I, 250 (May 22, 1869).

the seventies was largely owing to the great fire of 1871. "Chicago," said *Harper's Weekly* in 1868, "is the great western city. Her grain and her cattle and pork not only inundate our eastern markets, but there is left a large margin for exportation." [103] James Parton studied the city for the *Atlantic*: he told how it had become a greater "porkopolis" than Cincinnati, gave statistics of its amazing exports of wheat, cattle, and lumber, and related the means by which it had literally lifted itself out of the mud of its original site.[104] Its position as the center of a great railway network made it the transportation capital of the country, and most of the railroad journals were published there.[105]

But it had been too busy doing all these things to give much attention to literature before the war. "It may be as well to admit," wrote the editor of its leading magazine in 1869, "that, as a literary center, Chicago has not hitherto enjoyed as high a rank as has been universally conceded to her in respect of commerce." [106] But by 1870 there were some literary interests in this city of "hustle." In that year the Lakeside Publishing Company was issuing no less than nineteen periodicals in various fields. The leading historian of Chicago magazines has counted nearly a hundred periodicals "with some sort of literary interest dominant in their pages" published in Chicago in the sixties and seventies.[107]

The *Western Soldiers' Friend* [108] was a curious miscellany whose editors, Mr. and Mrs. C. Augustus Haviland, liked dialect stories and the humor of the times. The *Lyceum Banner* (1867–72) was a bimonthly by Mrs. H. M. F. Smith and Mrs. Lou H. Kimball. The *Chicagoan* (1868–69), a weekly of much higher grade than these, was edited and published by H. N. F. Lewis; and Robert Collyer and Robert Dale Owen were contributors.

[103] *Harper's Weekly*, XI, 702 (October 31, 1868).

[104] *Atlantic Monthly*, XIX, 325 (March 1867).

[105] See p. 125.

[106] *Lakeside Monthly*, II, 434 (December 1869).

[107] Herbert E. Fleming, *Magazines of a Market-Metropolis* (Chicago, 1906), p. 112. This is a reprint of Fleming's two-part paper, "The Literary Interests of Chicago," in the *American Journal of Sociology*, XI, 377, 499, 784, and XII, 68.

[108] Begun as a weekly in 1867, with the purpose of advocating soldiers' pensions, it carried much reprint material and some that was original. In 1870 it became a monthly and changed its name to *Gem of the West and Soldiers' Friend*. Apparently it ended in 1874.

In 1869 it absorbed two other weeklies and changed its name to the *Universe*, but it had taken in too much territory and did not outlive the year. The *Illustrated Chicago News* was a well-intentioned weekly of 1868.[109]

Most important of the Chicago magazines of the time was the *Lakeside Monthly*,[110] which began in 1869 as the *Western Monthly*. Under the editorship of the talented and scholarly F. F. Browne, it deserved and achieved a high reputation before the hard times put an end to it in 1874. The *Western Magazine*[111] began as a "booster" periodical for western cities, with headquarters in Omaha, in 1876; three years later it was moved to Chicago, and Mrs. Helen Elkin Starrett, lecturer and journalist, edited it with special attention to women's clubs. Then in 1882 it absorbed the *Alliance*,[112] a first-class religious paper, and became the *Weekly Magazine*, with financial support from such local magnates as George M. Pullman and Marshall Field. David Swing wrote weekly essays for it, and William A. Starrett did political reviews. The business manager was blamed for its failure in 1884. A third monthly of some distinction was the *United States Monthly Magazine*, edited and published for two and a half years from July 1881, by Willys S. Abbot. It was also called *Abbot's Monthly*, was well printed, and published writers like Ella Wheeler and Jane Grey Swisshelm.

There were many weeklies of the story-paper type, of which a few may be named here. The *Evening Lamp* was lighted in 1869 and burned steadily for forty years. A. N. Kellogg, its founder, was the originator of "ready-prints" for country weeklies — a device by which four pages of a newspaper were printed with miscellany in Chicago and sent out to local papers all over the Middle West for inclusion with their regular issues. The *Lamp* was supplied with this "boiler plate," prepared primarily for country papers. The *Chicago Ledger*,[113] founded by Samuel

---

[109] A. M. Farnum and C. A. Church, publishers. Thomas Nast drew pictures for it, and J. T. Trowbridge contributed a serial. It lasted only a few months.

[110] Treated more fully in sketch 14.

[111] See Fleming, *op. cit.*, p. 508.

[112] See p. 83.

[113] See Fleming, *op. cit.*, p. 501. Begun in 1872, it was merged with the *Toledo Blade* in 1924 under the name *Blade and Ledger*, Chicago. After the death of W. D. Boyce in 1929, the company was bought by George W. Weatherby and others. The paper was suspended 1933-36.

H. Williams and long edited by him, had a similar origin: it was at first filled with "plate" designed for newspaper miscellany. Later it became a mail-order paper, passing into the hands of W. D. Boyce in 1891, and gaining a large circulation as a cheap story and sensation paper. The *Novelist* was an illustrated weekly story-paper edited by George E. Blakely, 1874–81, and the *Chicago Index* (1875–91) was a similar periodical conducted in our period by C. E. Tues.

Excepting only the critical *Dial*,[114] the *Current* was the most important venture of literary Chicago in the early eighties. Founded by the brilliant journalist Edgar L. Wakeman in 1883, the *Current* presented its readers weekly comment on public affairs, serial fiction by Joaquin Miller, Lucy H. Hooper, and E. P. Roe, nature essays by John Burroughs and Ernest Ingersoll, poetry by Hayne, Scollard, and Riley, short fiction by Opie Read, Edgar Fawcett, and Dan DeQuille, and so on. Altogether it marshaled the most brilliant array of contributors that had ever appeared in the pages of a Chicago periodical. But Wakeman got into a financial tangle and took French leave in 1885, abandoning the weekly to straits that it escaped only by its death in 1888.[115]

Chicago's fecundity in "home" magazines and in class journals in many categories[116] was a feature of the city's development throughout the period.

[114] The *Dial* and *Literary Life* must be classified with the periodicals of literary criticism, p. 234. The *Dial* is treated more fully in sketch 33.

[115] Published December 22, 1883–October 13, 1888; merged with *America*. Subtitle: The Weekly Literary, News, and Family Journal of Our Time. Wakeman was assisted by G. C. Cochran and G. C. Matthews as associate editors, John McGovern succeeding Cochran in July 1884. After Wakeman's departure, the two associate editors conducted the paper for a short time; then McGovern was sole editor for a few months. A. H. Harryman was editor during the final year. The *Current* was changed from a sixteen-page quarto to a thirty-two page octavo in 1887. A. E. Davis was the financial savior of the paper after Wakeman's defection: for the latter incident, see *Current*, IV, 145 (September 5, 1885) and *New York Tribune*, December 14, 1885, p. 1. Under Wakeman, the *Current* had an extraordinary amount of brief comment on a great variety of affairs, critical in point of view and fairly dull. It inclined to Republicanism, favored free silver, scolded the Mormons. David Swing was an editorial contributor for six months in 1885. A notable Easter number was issued April 24, 1886. Under Harryman there was less general comment and more literary miscellany.

[116] These are treated in Chapters IX and X. See a list (1865–79) in F. W. Scott, *Newspapers and Periodicals of Illinois, 1814–79* (Springfield, 1910), pp. 82–149.

OTHER MIDWESTERN CENTERS

Cincinnati also had class periodicals in considerable numbers, as well as the story and miscellany papers belonging to a city of her size, e.g., the *Saturday Night* (1872–85), the monthly *Golden Hours* (1869–81), and the widely distributed weekly *Cincinnati Times* (1832–1901). The *Ladies' Repository*,[117] whose Methodistic tales and engraved landscapes had once been so popular, declined toward its end in 1880. The *Present* (1884–86) was a cheaper monthly. But the glory of Cincinnati as one of the chief magazine centers had departed: the shift of population and the rise of Chicago had left her far behind. Parton, looking Cincinnati over for the readers of the *Atlantic*, found it at the beginning of our period a city of wealth, dirt, and a great unassimilated foreign element, whose chief distinction lay in its ability to turn out "three finished hogs a minute." [118] *Harper's Weekly*, however, praised the city for its great library — "the largest, best-arranged, and only fire-proof library building in the country." [119]

Toledo, Ohio, had several interesting periodicals — among them the famous weekly *Blade* (1847–1924), edited at one time by "Petroleum V. Nasby." *Whittaker's Milwaukee Magazine* (1871–77) contained some interesting western material. *Gregg's Dollar Monthly and Old Settler's Memorial* (1873–77), of Hamilton, Illinois, is valuable for its historical articles. Like so many others listed here, it was highly miscellaneous in character. Thomas Gregg, its editor and owner, conducted eight other local papers and magazines for short periods and at various towns.[120] The *Kansas Magazine* (1872–73) was a briefer though more ambitious venture at Topeka; its name was used in 1886–87 for a Kansas City, Kansas, attempt, and again at Wichita, 1909–12.[121] E. V. Smalley's *Northwest Magazine* (1883–1903) at St. Paul was a "booster" monthly.

[117] Treated more fully in vol. II, sketch 5.
[118] *Atlantic Monthly*, XX, 229–246 (August 1867).
[119] *Harper's Weekly*, XVIII, 265 (March 21, 1874).
[120] The name was changed to *Dollar Rural Messenger* in 1876. See article on Gregg by David C. Mott in *Annals of Iowa*, Third Series, XIV, 263 (April 1924); also *ibid.*, XII, 622, and frontispiece (April 1921).
[121] See J. P. Callahan's "Kansas Magazines," in a revival, as an annual publication, called *Kansas Magazine 1933*, p. 56.

THE GOLDEN WEST

San Francisco was a publishing center of real importance in the postwar period. The *Golden Era*,[122] originally wild and woolly enough, had by this time been ruined, as one of its original editors remarked, by "namby-pamby schoolgirl trash." [123] It continued, however, under various ownerships. There was an unusually exuberant crop of the cheap and short-lived weekly and monthly miscellanies in San Francisco.

But the great California magazine of the times was the *Overland Monthly*.[124] The work of Bret Harte, its editor during its first years, brought fame to the *Overland*; but after he left it at the end of 1870, it fared badly until its suspension in 1875.

The monthly *California Mail-Bag* (1871–78), a booster magazine with spicy résumés of news, was conducted by Frederick A. Marriott, who was also publisher of the *News-Letter*.[125] The latter was edited from 1868 to 1872 by Ambrose Bierce, whose "Town Crier" papers therein made a wide reputation. The *Wasp* was founded by the Korbel brothers in 1876, and it published Harte, Mark Twain, and Bierce in its early years. It was distinguished for its colored cartoons, as well as for its sharp commentary on California politics and affairs. In 1877 Frank M. Pixley, a well-known California character, a man of wealth, and a vigorous journalist, founded the *Argonaut*. He had for junior partner for three years Fred M. Somers, who later founded, with Anton Roman, the monthly *Californian* [126] (1880–82), which prepared the way for the New Series of the suspended *Overland*. But the *Argonaut* proved to be a success. Ambrose Bierce's column of "Prattle" lent brilliance to a paper

[122] See vol. II, p. 117.
[123] Ella Sterling Cummins [Mighels], *The Story of the Files* (San Francisco, 1893), p. 17.
[124] Treated more fully in sketch 12.
[125] See vol. II, p. 118, footnote. Cummins, *op. cit.*, pp. 187–189.
[126] The first volume was published by the *Overland* publisher, Anton Roman, but a new company was organized before the end of the first year. Charles H. Phelps was editor after Somers retired in May 1880 until August 1882, when Warren Cheney succeeded him. Among contributors were E. R. Sill, Joaquin Miller, Ambrose Bierce, John Muir, Ina D. Coolbrith, and Charles H. and Milicent W. Shinn. Not all contributors and not all material were Californian. It was a well printed and creditable magazine, but it gave way to the New Series of the *Overland*, begun in 1883.

which was far from dull in any respect. "It is my intention," wrote Bierce at the inauguration of his *Argonaut* column, "to purify journalism in this town by instructing such writers as it is worth while to instruct, and assassinating those that it is not." [127] But Pixley parted company with Bierce in 1879, under circumstances which gained him Bierce's undying hatred [128] — and how Bierce could hate! The *Wasp* was the gainer by the transaction, for it was the *Wasp* which took Bierce on, soon to make him editor. For five years his vitriolic wit, his prejudices, and his brilliant writing not only made the *Wasp*: they were the *Wasp*. It stung busily here, there, and everywhere. It delighted in publishing epitaphs of its enemies: the one for Pixley began, "Here lies Frank Pixley, as usual." It printed pages of "Prattle" and "The Devil's Dictionary." Bierce, says one of his victims, was "Public Executioner and Tormentor." [129] In the midst of a picturesque and turbulent society, the *Wasp* and the *Argonaut* were as colorful weeklies as any in our history.[130]

A few periodicals of general interest in other far western cities may be mentioned. The *Utah Magazine* (1867–69) was a literary weekly founded by Mormons at Salt Lake City, chiefly to oppose Brigham Young's policies.[131] The *West Shore* (1875–91), of Portland, Oregon, an illustrated monthly, and the *North Pacific Coast* (1879–81), of New Tacoma, Washington Territory, a bimonthly, were designed largely to exploit the advantages of the new Northwest.[132]

---

[127] *Argonaut*, March 25, 1877.

[128] See, for this incident and for many facts about the early *Argonaut*, Jerome A. Hart, *In Our Second Century* (San Francisco, 1931), especially Chapters VIII–XI. Also Carey McWilliams, *Ambrose Bierce* (New York, 1929), pp. 122–144; and Cummins, *op. cit.*, pp. 190–233.

[129] Charlotte Perkins Gilman: see McWilliams, *op. cit.*, p. 156.

[130] The latter survives as an urban weekly of society and the arts. Jerome A. Hart became joint owner of the *Argonaut* with Pixley in 1880; Pixley died in 1895, and Alfred Holman and Edward R. Morphy were later editors. The *Wasp* and *News-Letter* were merged under the name *Wasp News-Letter* in 1928 and it was in turn merged with the *Argonaut* in 1935.

[131] Founders were E. L. T. Harrison, William S. Godbe, and Henry W. Lawrence. It became the *Mormon Tribune*, a newspaper, in 1870.

[132] Two Alaskan periodicals were printed in San Francisco in the late sixties: Svoboda's *Alaskan Herald* (1868–76); and the *Esquimaux* (1866–67), edited by John J. Harrington by and for the Russian extension of the Western Union

Of all these western ventures, the only one which attracted eastern attention was the *Overland*, though it was hazily understood that somewhere in that wild western outland there were periodicals for which men like Ambrose Bierce and Joaquin Miller wrote. But eastern magazines themselves gave many hundreds of pages to western matters, and at least one eastern magazine was begun to exploit the West — *Gazlay's Pacific Monthly* (1865), of New York.

The inveterate American traveler, turned away from Europe in the early seventies by the Franco-Prussian War, found the West, newly opened to sight-seers by the Union Pacific, an attractive goal for his vacation trip. "We are all on our way to California now," wrote a correspondent to *Punchinello* a year or two after the transcontinental road was opened.[133] This new travel interest was reflected at once in magazine articles, which ranged from rather naïve narratives like "A Lone Woman's Trip to Omaha and Beyond," with its connotation of a terrifying hinterland,[134] to such an extensive illustrated series on the West as that by J. Ross Browne in *Harper's*. Some of these articles were definitely guidebookish, like Samuel Bowles' three-part description of the Pacific railroad in the *Atlantic* of 1869 and Susan Coolidge's article in *Scribner's* for May 1873 on California.

Western-born William Dean Howells, who came to the staff of the *Atlantic* in 1866, did much to call attention to both the Middle West and the Far West; he welcomed Bret Harte and allied himself with Mark Twain. The *Galaxy*, begun in 1866, showed an interest in the West from its first number. Mark Twain conducted a humorous department in the *Galaxy* in 1870–71, at the same time that J. W. DeForest's serial "Overland" was running; Custer's "Life on the Plains" was cut short in 1876 by the author's death in the famous massacre. *Scrib-*

Telegrapn expedition. The later was originally printed at Port Clarence, Russian America, as a monthly quarto of four pages, but was later reprinted at San Francisco for more general circulation.

[133] *Punchinello*, II, 116 (November 19, 1870).
[134] *Atlantic Monthly*, XXIV, 327 (September 1869).

ner's Monthly, like *Harper's*, made much of illustrated articles
on western scenery; and *Putnam's*, *Lippincott's* and *Appleton's*
were not far behind.

Nevertheless, there was a fundamental antagonism between
East and West which showed itself again and again. The western influence, said the *Nation*, as exerted

> on our literature, oratory and manners, has not been elevating or
> refining, and it would have been vastly better for the country had
> circumstances made the growth of these communities slower, and
> thus allowed women to take a more prominent part in the building
> them up, and the ideas and manners of the older states to retain a
> stronger hold on them.[135]

This is an almost perfect statement of the natural antipathy
involved, and of the shock produced by western realism on
aesthetic tenderness in the East. The man who did more than
any other to bring the West to Easterners and make them like
it was Mark Twain. But even he sometimes failed in the effort,
as when, on the occasion of the Whittier birthday dinner at
which Mark was introduced to the *Atlantic Monthly* group, his
satire of the gods of the New England literary Pantheon horri-
fied his hearers. The wild man from the West had devised a
comic story caricaturing Emerson, Holmes, and Longfellow in
a mining-camp setting:

> They were a rough lot. . . . Mr. Emerson was a seedy little bit
> of a chap, red-headed. Mr. Holmes was fat as a balloon; he weighed
> as much as three hundred and had double chins all the way down to
> his stomach. Mr. Longfellow was built like a prize-fighter. His head
> was cropped and bristly, like as if he had a wig made of hairbrushes.

All this was received in absolute and unsmiling silence. Mark
had expected roars of laughter; but having started on his *jeu
d'esprit*, he could not stop, and had to continue to the end of
what was probably one of the flattest failures in the long history
of unsuccessful after-dinner speech making. The faces of his
audience "turned to stone with horror," wrote Mark many years
later. "It was the sort of expression those faces would have
worn if I had been making these remarks about the Deity and

[135] *Nation*, II, 51 (January 10, 1866).

the rest of the Trinity." Both the humorist and his host felt very sick about it all, and Mark wrote letters of abject apology the next day to each of the caricatured trinity.[136] What Mark Twain did not know, and what he never could have understood, was that he was guilty of real sacrilege in making free with these great men; what his audience could never see was that Mark and his fellow Westerners were interested in men as men, and not at all in the fine notions they had built up about one another.

WESTERN PROBLEMS

The *Nation* and *Harper's Weekly* frequently discussed the Indian question. The latter periodical, with *Leslie's Illustrated*, contained many spirited drawings depicting the Indian fighting. The *Weekly* summed the matter up effectively when it observed: "The Indians were, unfortunately, located on the Great Highway of the West." [137]

The destruction of the buffalo was a spectacular phenomenon of the times. The *American Sportsman* pointed out that a hundred thousand of them were killed in the region about Dodge City, Kansas, in the season of 1872–73. Its editor wrote:

> The buffalo is subserving a great purpose in the social economy of the nation, if that is any satisfaction to him. The tide of emigration that has set into the Arkansas valley have a subsistence until they can open and improve their farms, and by the time the last buffalo has disappeared from Kansas the frontier will be subdued to civilization, and be self-supporting. The buffalo will in this, or at the furthest, the next, generation, take its place in the natural history books along with the dodo.[138]

Three years later a writer in the *Penn Monthly* said that the "Southern Herd" was then "a mere remnant" in northern Texas, and the "Northern Herd" was restricted chiefly to the Yellowstone Basin. He further asserted that the average annual slaughter for the preceding thirty or forty years had been three to four million animals.[139]

[136] *North American Review*, CLXXXVI, 482 (December 1907).
[137] *Harper's Weekly*, XI, 371 (June 15, 1867).
[138] *American Sportsman*, II, 88 (March 1873).
[139] J. A. Allen in *Penn Monthly*, VII, 214–224 (March 1876).

Harper's Weekly called attention to the fact that thousands of prairie chickens were shot in the trans-Mississippi states and shipped in barrels to the eastern markets in the late sixties.[140] The *American Sportsman* records the industry of two Iowa boys who, after two days' shoting, brought to market "a wagon-bed even full" of ducks, geese, quail, and prairie chickens.[141]

The most important phase of western history during this period was homesteading, by which some fifty million acres were taken up by settlers in the decade and a half which followed the passing of the Homestead Act. H. H. Boyesen wrote brilliantly of Kansas homesteading in *Scribner's Monthly* for November 1879. The hegira which was a part of this development, the railroad building which was at once cause and effect of it, and the social life which was an accompaniment of it were paramount forces in the molding of the America of the seventies. A writer in *Appleton's Journal* describes the Northern Pacific's new "immigration department" founded by Jay Cooke, and declares that it is the truest philanthropy to bring in these families,

furnish them with land and implements of culture, and even houses to live in, and set them at work on the rich soil which borders the railroad; so that, in one or two years, they shall raise wheat for the market, providing tolls for the road, and wealth for themselves.[142]

Harper's Weekly made much of a picturesque incident in which Asa S. Mercer, president of Washington Territory University, was the Moses who led a troop of four hundred women into the Northwest to furnish an ameliorating feminine influence in the too masculine wilderness.[143]

The plains, said Fitz Hugh Ludlow, in a brilliant prophetic article in the *Atlantic*, seem "inevitably set apart for the one sole business of cattle-raising." [144] That was in 1864; within a few years the great business of cattle-shipping from Abilene, Wichita, and Dodge City, and the life of the cowboy had caught

---

[140] *Harper's Weekly*, XI, 801 (December 21, 1867).
[141] *American Sportsman*, II, 101 (April 1873).
[142] *Appleton's Journal*, IV, 523 (October 29, 1870).
[143] *Harper's Weekly*, X, 8–9 (January 6, 1866).
[144] *Atlantic Monthly*, XIV, 613 (November 1864).

the public imagination and were being pictured in the illustrated magazines.[145]

Western outlawry was also of great public interest, though the matter was not often treated seriously. The sensation papers throve upon it, and the comics had their fun with it. *Texas Siftings* thought it was no wonder Jesse James died poor: he had run through so much property during his life — mostly real estate.[146] *Judge* satirized the courteous treatment accorded Frank James when he surrendered to Governor Chittenden amid congratulatory speeches and resolutions.[147] The *Police Gazette*, which boasted Jesse James as a subscriber, seemed to take a delight in his successive escapes from his pursuers. "It is plain," said that recorder of sensation, "that he is the most knowing person in Missouri as far as we've got." [148]

Nor had the story of mining lost its fascination, though now it was silver mining which attracted the greater attention.[149] *Appleton's Journal*, speaking of the need of certain legislation for the mining interest, said in 1871:

> In nineteen years it [mining] has reclaimed over one-third of our entire territory from the savage, and now promises to be the largest contributor of all interests to our national wealth. . . . Let but science and philosophy, statesmanship and capital, be once fairly interested in developing its resources, and the results will be glorious not only to our national power and wealth, but to the interest of art, literature, trade, and science, throughout the civilized world.[150]

The *Nation*, too, was impressed by the commanding position of the mining industry in America:

> Its importance has been already recognized by Congress in the introduction of a bill for the establishment of a much-needed Mining Bureau, and by several of our principal colleges in the establishment of schools of mines.[151]

[145] See, for example, *Frank Leslie's Illustrated Newspaper*, XXXII, 385 (August 19, 1871).

[146] *Texas Siftings*, I, 20 (November 24, 1877).

[147] *Judge*, October 21, 1882, p. 2.

[148] *National Police Gazette*, April 1, 1882.

[149] For mining periodicals, see pp. 114–15.

[150] *Appleton's Journal*, VI, 491 (October 28, 1871).

[151] *Nation*, II, 38 (January 11, 1866).

A TYPICAL *HARPER'S WEEKLY* WAR SKETCH

A drawing by Theodore R. Davis in the issue of January 14, 1865, entitled "Kilpatrick's Last Charge at Waynesboro, Georgia, December 4, 1864."

RAILWAY STATION AT CHICAGO IN 1870

From *Appleton's Journal*, April 2, 1870. The original "cartoon" measures 13 x 19 inches, and the sheet upon which it was printed was folded in. The drawing is by Thomas Hogan.

CHAPTER III

RELIGIOUS PERIODICALS AFTER THE WAR

RELIGIOUS journals in the postbellum period were of two kinds — the reviews, monthly or quarterly, devoted largely to theology and scholarship; and the weeklies, which gave some attention to general news.

The lives of the reviews were commonly filled with disappointments. The writers for them, though seldom gifted with the ability to be interesting, were utterly sincere. They wrote as teachers — sometimes as prophets even. Yet one is often moved to almost as much admiration for the readers as for the writers; they, too, were earnest, and they had an appetite for solid food that seems extraordinary in this light-minded generation. What shelvesful, what libraries of learning — theology, metaphysics, philosophy, philology, exegesis!

ACRIMONIOUS WEEKLIES

If there was less of weight in the religious weeklies, there was more of liveliness. The reviews were the heavy artillery, the papers the musketry and bayonet brigade. They put spirit into their charges — too much spirit, thought the critics. The *Round Table*, which dealt much in criticism of its religious contemporaries, said in 1864:

Not many years ago the House of Bishops of the Protestant Episcopal Church issued a pastoral letter specially rebuking the contentious and mischievous spirit of the religious press of their church. The General Association of Connecticut, made up of Congregational ministers, at one of its annual sessions, unanimously passed censure upon the too-common asperity of religious newspapers, especially in the matter of a controversy.[1]

Not the least of the offenders in this regard was Theodore Tilton, editor (1863–70) of the *Independent*, whose style was that of a poet, full of fire and fancy, but who dipped his pen in

[1] *Round Table*, I, 132 (February 13, 1864).

vitriol as unhesitatingly as in ink. The New York *Evangelist*, an excellent paper of its kind, was thus described by Tilton:

Take a man who can neither write nor preach nor keep his temper nor mind his own business; thrill his bosom day by day with twenty years of dyspepsia; flush his brain with the hallucination that his bookkeeping mind is competent to religious journalism; put a pen in his hand wherewith to write himself down a Pecksniff; set him like a dog in his kennel, to make a pastime of snapping at the respectable people of the neighborhood; and then, gentle reader, you have a specimen copy of the *Evangelist*.[2]

This may be clever, but it is scarcely respectable, and it is a kind of exercise that is not very difficult. But in the sixties it was a very general opinion in the journalistic profession (if profession it could be called) that caustic personalities were necessary in order to give spirit to a journal and keep up its circulation. They were a convention of the art.

But there were those who objected even then to what Hudson euphemistically calls "this robust Christianity." [3] In the *Life and Letters of Edwin Lawrence Godkin* may be found a letter Godkin wrote privately to the *Independent* in 1868 after his ancestry and antecedents had been reviewed in connection with opinions he had expressed in the *Nation*. Three sentences will give the gist of it:

We have endeavored in the *Nation*, and successfully endeavored, in the interest of reason as well as decency, to make discussion impersonal. If I were to make your birth or education a means of exciting a prejudice against you personally, or of weakening the effects of your arguments, I should consider myself a very base and malignant person. . . . It seems to me that you should be amongst the last to encourage a tendency which is the curse of the press of the country.[4]

Ten days after the date of this letter there appeared in the *Independent*, evidently in direct reply to it, an editorial entitled

[2] Quoted from the *Independent* in Frederic Hudson's *Journalism in the United States from 1690 to 1872* (New York, 1873), p. 298, and Lyman Abbott's *Reminiscences* (Boston, 1915), p. 329.

[3] Hudson, *op. cit.*, p. 300.

[4] Rollo Ogden, *Life and Letters of Edwin Lawrence Godkin* (New York, 1907), II, 53. Letter dated September 7, 1868.

"Personal Journalism," from which it will be sufficient to quote the following:

> As to personalities, they are the very life and support of journalism; and without them no periodical for the people could hope for a prosperous existence. . . . Calling names, to be sure, is low and puerile and unworthy of decent journalism, but to allude to the personal antecedents or characteristics of public writers or public men whose principles or actions are in question is not only proper but necessary in journalistic discussions.[5]

Godkin's words, "you should be amongst the last to encourage" the tendency, indicate a feeling common to the secular press, that the religious papers were false to a standard of journalistic ethics which should be, even if it actually was not, higher than that of the average newspaper. The *Round Table's* first volume is full of this assumption. With it was associated a natural antagonism between the journalist trained in the newspaper office and the clergyman who thought he could be an editor. Frederic Hudson's *Journalism in the United States*, published in 1873, itself highly journalistic, exhibits this viewpoint: Hudson discusses the religious papers in a facetious tone, not untouched with gentle scorn. Eugene Benson in the *Galaxy* argued that journalism and religion were incompatible,[6] and disapproved the whole institution of the "pious press." Lowell, when the *Atlantic's* theology was attacked, called the religious press "a true sour-cider press, with belly-ache privileges attached."[7] The mixture of "dry-goods and religion," as the *World* called it, was constantly under fire; and since the religious editors themselves were not inclined to be gentle with each other, their lot was not, on the whole, a quiet one.

But it should not be understood that the religious papers were filled habitually with personalities. Even for the *Independent* under Tilton, the quoted attack on the *Evangelist* is extreme in its scurrility. The *Christian Union* was distressed by what it called "the perpetual war-whoop" of its exchanges, and itself abstained from personalities; and although there was plenty of

---

[5] *Independent*, September 17, 1868.

[6] *Galaxy*, VII, 356 (September 1869).

[7] Charles Eliot Norton, ed., *Letters of James Russell Lowell* (New York, 1894), I, 289. Letter dated December 19, 1858.

sharpness and recrimination, and a never-ending theological quarrel, there was, in most of the religious papers, comparatively little real mudslinging.

RELIGIOUS NEWSPAPERS

In the period under consideration, the religious weeklies suffered an important change. Since the first popularity of this type of periodical in the twenties,[8] they had been newspapers — with a special interest in religious affairs, indeed, but still weekly news sheets in competition with the secular press. In the seventies a divergence developed which tended to lead them away from the general news field. The chief factor in this development was the great success of the *Christian Union*, founded in 1870, and devoted to religious reading.

Further, Beecher's periodical was a quarto which gave little attention to secular news. Following its example, the religious weeklies one after another cut down their folio sheets, and in doing so seemed to renounce their newspaper pretensions. "A proper newspaper," as the elder Willis had written, "is in the folio form." [9]

The rise of the great dailies had gradually crowded the religious weekly out of the news field; its fate was apparent enough by the end of the Civil War, after the people had been educated to a demand for "spot news," and few could be content with weekly résumés industriously garnered from the dailies, or correspondence sent from news centers by mail. The religious papers were still journals of opinion, and at times, as Bryce pointed out a little later, of very influential opinion;[10] they still purveyed the church reports and religious news; but they went further than they had before in furnishing miscellaneous family reading.

STATISTICS OF RELIGIOUS PERIODICALS

The total number of religious journals virtually doubled between 1865 and 1885. From about 350 in 1865, it rose to over 650 at the end of our period.[11] Nearly half the aggregate

[8] See Mott, *A History of American Magazines, 1741–1850*, pp. 136–139.
[9] Hudson, *op. cit.*, p. 293.
[10] James Bryce, *The American Commonwealth* (New York, 1910), II, 278.
[11] The census of 1870 set the total at 408, and that of 1880 at 556. Ayer's annual, omitting many of the periodicals which did not accept advertising, listed

circulation, however, belonged to a comparatively small group of Sunday school papers. A few Sunday school teachers' papers — the *Sunday School Times*, the *Sunday School Journal*, and the *Baptist Teacher* — ran to over 50,000 circulation each. None of the reviews went much beyond 10,000, and most of them had much less. Beecher's *Christian Union* soared well above 100,000 for a few years, but it was fixed at a fifth of that at the end of our period. The *Independent* likewise declined in these years. On the other hand, several Catholic papers, notably the Boston *Pilot*, steadily increased in circulation. Four of the Methodist *Christian Advocates* kept among the leaders, the one located at New York doubling its list in the course of the two decades.

The total of religious weeklies was surprisingly large. The census gave 208 as the number of them in 1870. A sect, schism, or school too small to support a review might have several weekly papers. "The first measure after secession," the *American Quarterly Observer* had once remarked, "is to establish a periodical." [12] Most large cities had several of these papers; by 1869 fourteen cities had three or more apiece.[13] Though in both aggregate number and total circulation they fell far below the secular newspaper press, they did not, as a rule, fall below it in ability; and they possessed a formidable power.

CATHOLIC PERIODICALS

The growth of the Catholic church in the United States was an outstanding phenomenon of the times. Its membership doubled in our period. Its activity in establishing parochial schools and its attack upon the public school system in 1867 drew the fire of the *Nation, Harper's Weekly*, and other journals.[14] In the latter periodical Thomas Nast drew some strong anti-Catholic cartoons. There was a widespread fear of the

---

555 religious journals for 1885. The Ayer list in 1880 was about 20 per cent below census figures; this doubtless represents nearly enough the proportion of religious periodicals to be added to the Ayer total for 1885.

[12] *American Quarterly Observer*, III, 142 (July 1834).

[13] See Rowell's *American Newspaper Directory*, 1869, List III. Rowell's list, which cannot be depended upon to be complete, shows New York to have 54, Philadelphia 22, Boston 19, Chicago 15, Cincinnati 11, San Francisco 10.

[14] *Nation*, IV, 151 (February 21, 1867); *Harper's Weekly*, XI, 194 (March 30, 1867).

Catholic power, which was evidenced most emphatically by articles in the *Galaxy, Appleton's Journal,* and *Puck* — all bitterly anti-Catholic. Nearly all the evangelical journals engaged in the pastime of Catholic-baiting now and then, and a few were wholly devoted to it. The *Converted Catholic* (1883–1928) was founded, and for more than a quarter of a century edited, by a renegade priest, James A. O'Connor; and the *American Protestant* was published 1870–88, first in New York and then in Washington.

In the face of this opposition, and in some degree because of it, the number of Catholic periodicals grew steadily until at the end of the period under consideration it equaled that of the most prolific of the Protestant denominations — the Methodists. Indeed, the Ayer list for 1885 enumerates seventy-four Catholic and seventy-three Methodist periodicals,[15] while in aggregate circulation the Catholic journals were far ahead.[16]

The *Catholic World,*[17] in many respects the foremost of American Catholic periodicals, began its career in 1865 under the care of Father Isaac T. Hecker. In the same year the *Ave Maria* was founded at Notre Dame University by Father Granger and has continued as a monthly magazine of general literature. The next year the monthly *Messenger of the Sacred Heart* was begun by Jesuits at Woodstock, Maryland, later to move to New York.[18] The *De la Salle Monthly* (1869–77) was published by the New York Catholic Protectory, being called *Manhattan Monthly* in its last three years. *Brownson's Quarterly Review* [19] finished its last series in 1875 and was succeeded in the following year by the more representative *American Catholic Quarterly Review,* edited in Philadelphia by James A. Corcoran and supported by the pens of the leading church dig-

---

[15] See list of religious periodicals in Ayer's *American Newspaper Annual* of 1886.

[16] The census for 1880 gives an aggregate circulation of 450,752 for 70 Catholic journals and 375,461 for 75 Methodist journals.

[17] Treated more fully in sketch 3.

[18] In 1902 it shortened its title to *Messenger.* After March 1909 it was followed by the weekly *America,* and the original title was renewed for a supplement to *America.* A supplement, 1884–96, to *Messenger of the Sacred Heart* was called *Pilgrim of Our Lady of Martyrs;* it was continued separately, 1897–1926.

[19] See Mott, *op. cit.,* p. 685.

nitaries.[20] *Donahoe's Magazine* was a general monthly of Irish Catholic inspiration.[21]

Besides these quarterlies and monthlies, there was a long list of weeklies. A number held over from the preceding period [22] — Donahoe's Boston *Pilot* with a circulation which had reached 72,000 by 1885, and the New York *Tablet* with a list which, though much smaller, made it the second Catholic weekly. The *Catholic Standard* was founded in Philadelphia in 1866 with James Keogh as editor, and has long held a high position, latterly as the *Catholic Standard and Times* by reason of its merger with L. A. Lambert's *Catholic Times* (1893–95).

The Second Plenary Council, of 1869, extended much encouragement to the Catholic press, and it was followed by the establishment of a multitude of diocesan journals.[23] Some week-

[20] Published January 1876–January 1924. A *General Index 1876–1900* was issued. Corcoran had been editor of the *United States Catholic Miscellany*. He was followed in the editorship of the *Quarterly Review* by Archbishop Patrick John Ryan, 1890–1911. To use an advertising phrase of the publishers, this journal presents "a complete Catholic chronicle" of half a century. Religion and ecclesiastical policy were prominent in its contents; but literature, education, art, science, history, and philosophy were not neglected. Among extensive contributors were Cardinals Manning and Gibbons, Archbishops Seghers, Keane, and Lynch, Bishops O'Conor, Becker, Spalding, Chatard, and Lynch. O. A. Brownson, John Gilmary Shea, Brother Azarias, George Parsons Lathrop, John Boyle O'Reilly, and T. P. O'Connor were occasionally in its tables of contents.

[21] See p. 36.   [22] See vol. II, pp. 76–77.

[23] See Apollinaris W. Baumgartner, *Catholic Journalism* (New York, 1931), pp. 22–32, for a list which is helpful, though often unsatisfactory. Some of the more important are *Western Watchman* (1865–1934), St. Louis; *Northwestern Chronicle* (1866–1936), established in St. Paul but moved to Minneapolis in the seventies; *Catholic Herald-Citizen* (1870–current), Milwaukee, which began *Catholic Vindicator*, became *Citizen* in 1878, absorbed *Catholic Herald* in 1935; *Catholic Union* (1872–current), Buffalo, which became *Catholic Union and Times* by the absorption of *Catholic Times* (1877–81), Rochester; *Catholic Universe* (1874–current), Cleveland, founded by Bishop Gilmour, which became the *Catholic Universe-Bulletin* by the absorption of the Cleveland *Catholic Bulletin* (1911–27); *Catholic Transcript* (1876–current), Hartford, which was called the *Connecticut Catholic* until 1898; *McGee's Illustrated Weekly* (1867–82), New York, Maurice Francis Egan, editor; *Catholic World* (1881–1929), St. Louis, which absorbed *Church Progress* (1878–84), Marshall, Illinois, and became *Church Progress and Catholic World*; *Catholic Journal of the New South* (1882–1936), which began at Memphis under the title *Adam*, changed to the longer name in 1888 and, though still dated at Memphis, was added in 1912 to the chain of Catholic papers headed by the *Catholic Citizen*, Milwaukee.

lies of wider circulation were also launched. The New York *Catholic Review* (1872–98) was "looked upon as the standard Catholic paper of the United States" during most of its existence.[24] It was founded by Patrick V. Hickey, a trained journalist, who edited it until his death in 1889, when he was succeeded by J. Talbot Smith, the church's historian. Hickey was also the founder and editor of the *Illustrated Catholic American* (1880–96), a New York family weekly. *Catholic Book News at Home and Abroad* (1879–1909?) was mainly a house organ for Benziger Brothers, New York booksellers. The chief juveniles were Father Hecker's *Young Catholic* (1870–1905) and the *Guardian Angel* (1867–1909), long published by Daniel F. Gillin.

METHODIST JOURNALS

The *Methodist Review*[25] was under the control, during the postbellum period, of one of the greatest of Methodist editors, Daniel D. Whedon. The *Southern Review*,[26] though begun not as a religious journal but as an apologia for the Confederate States of America, was adopted in 1871 by the Methodist Church South, whose own review had been suspended since 1861. Its editor, Albert T. Bledsoe, was a good writer and a powerful polemic. The *Ladies' Repository*[27] changed its name in 1877 to *National Repository*, but its broader policy kept it alive only three years longer. The *Heathen Woman's Friend*, of Boston, was begun in 1869, to change its title in 1896 to *Woman's Missionary Friend;* and the *Sunday School Journal* (1868–1926) was a prosperous monthly for teachers.

Of the weeklies in the Methodist denomination, the *Christian Advocate* of New York continued to hold the leadership, reaching its high point of circulation with 70,000 in 1879. Next to it, but with less than half its distribution, were the *Western, Northwestern*, and *Central Christian Advocates*, located respectively

[24] *Chautauquan*, XX, 716 (March 1895). Article, "Journalism of the Catholic Church in the United States," by James J. Dunn. The *Review* was absorbed into the Milwaukee *Catholic Citizen* chain in 1898 and discontinued.

[25] See Mott, *op. cit.*, p. 299.

[26] Treated more fully in sketch 7.

[27] Treated more fully in vol. II, sketch 5.

at Cincinnati, Chicago, and St. Louis.[28] The leading weekly for the Methodist Church South continued to be the *Christian Advocate* of Nashville.[29] Comparatively few important Methodist journals were founded in the postbellum period,[30] those which were already under way serving the church's membership in the various regions. Perhaps the most important of those established in the period were the *Michigan Christian Advocate* (1875–current), Detroit, for the northern church; and the *Central Methodist* (1869–1931), founded as the *Christian Observer* at Catlettsburg, Kentucky, but finally located, after various removes, at Louisville.

There were several Methodist journals founded by and for Negroes. Most important were the *A. M. E. Church Review,*[31] the quarterly of the African Methodist church; the *Southwestern Christian Advocate,*[32] of New Orleans, allied with the northern Methodist body; and the *Star of Zion* (1867–current), published in various North Carolina cities as the organ of the Zion Methodists.

The *Free Methodist* began in New York in 1868; moved to Aurora, Illinois, four years later; sojourned in Sycamore, Illi-

[28] See vol. II, pp. 65–68, for these and for other Methodist weeklies which survived from the preceding period.

[29] See vol. II, p. 68, footnote.

[30] Besides those mentioned above, there were: *Pennsylvania Methodist* (1874–1906), Harrisburg, called *Conference News* 1874–94; *Peninsula Methodist* (1875–1910), Wilmington, Delaware; *Rocky Mountain Christian Advocate* (1876–83), Salt Lake City; *Philadelphia Methodist* (1879–1914); *Kansas Methodist* (1879–88), Topeka; *American Methodist* (1881–94), a subsidiary of the *Michigan Christian Advocate; Montana Christian Advocate* (1882–89), Helena. Among weeklies of the Methodist Church South: *Episcopal Methodist* (1866–94), Baltimore; *Methodist Advocate* (1869–1931), published in succession at Chattanooga, Knoxville, and Jackson, Tennessee; *Arkansas Methodist* (1882–current), Little Rock, called *Western Methodist* 1907–16. The leading Sunday School teachers' journal of the Methodist Church South was *Sunday School Magazine* (1871–current), Nashville, now the *Church School Magazine.*

[31] Founded at Philadelphia, July 1884, by the A. M. E. Publishing House, with B. T. Tanner as editor. Tanner had been the editor of the *Christian Recorder,* his church's weekly, for sixteen years. Reverdy C. Ransom, who became editor in 1917, moved it to Nashville shortly after his election. It ended in 1936.

[32] Founded as *New Orleans Advocate* in 1866, and officially adopted by the General Conference two years later. It was suspended 1870–72, but after its revival it was again made official in 1876 and has remained so. It is now published as the "Southwestern Edition" of the church's *Christian Advocate.*

nois, 1876–80; and then lived till its end in 1935 in Chicago. The *Christian Standard and Home Journal* (1867–1906), edited by E. I. D. Pepper, was a Methodist holiness weekly. The *Living Epistle* (1866–1909) was an Evangelical monthly.

BAPTIST PERIODICALS

The Baptists had more periodicals in the postbellum period than any other denomination; but since many of their papers were short-lived, the total at any one time fell below those of the Catholic and Methodist journals. The *Baptist Quarterly* (1867–77), edited by H. G. Weston and issued by the church's Publication Society in Philadelphia, was succeeded in 1879 by the more important *Baptist Review*,[33] conducted in Cincinnati by J. R. Baumes. With their traditional activity in missions, the Baptists maintained several monthlies devoted to that interest, most of them being veterans.[34] Two periodicals exploiting home missions were added to the list during the postbellum period — the *Baptist Home Mission Monthly* (1878–1909) in New York and *Tidings* (1881–1911) in Chicago. The *Baptist Teacher* (1870–1916), of Philadelphia, had a large circulation.

The New York *Examiner and Chronicle*, under Edward Bright's strong editorship, was the great Baptist weekly of the times; second only to it in circulation and influence was the Boston *Watchman and Reflector*. The *National Baptist* (1865–94) was the chief Philadelphia spokesman. In December 1867 an important merger of several middlewestern Baptist papers resulted in the Chicago *Standard* (1867–1920), which became the leading journal of the denomination in the northwestern country. The *Baptist Beacon* was founded at Oregon City in 1877, to become the *Pacific Baptist* at Portland and later at McMinnville, and to absorb most of the Baptist papers on the coast before being itself received into the broad bosom of the *Standard* in 1920.

[33] The title was changed in 1882 to *Baptist Quarterly Review*. Three years later it was moved to New York, where Robert Stuart MacArthur, the famous preacher, and H. C. Vedder, the literary critic, became its editors. MacArthur retired at the end of 1889, leaving the control to Vedder. Prominent contributors were David Jayne Hill, E. Benjamin Andrews, Daniel Coit Gilman, J. F. Genung, D. D. Thompson, Albion W. Small. The contents were varied, and Vedder's comment on contemporary literature was notable. The end came in 1890.　　　　　　　　　　　　　　　[34] See vol. II, p. 63.

There were many other periodicals of this denomination in the North and West;[35] but when we turn to the Southern Convention, we find that the torrent has become a flood.[36] The two most famous southern Baptist papers founded in our period were both born in 1874 — the *Baptist Reflector*[37] and the *Texas Baptist*.[38] Of several Negro Baptist papers, the *Christian Index* (1867–1937), of Jackson, Tennessee, and the *Georgia Baptist* (1880–1934), of Augusta and Macon, have been the most successful. The Primitive Baptists began the *Gospel Messenger* (1878–1923) in this period and published it in various North Carolina and Georgia cities.

PRESBYTERIAN PERIODICALS

The Presbyterians had not only the *Princeton Review*,[39] still under Hodge until 1871, but also the *American Presbyterian Review*,[40] which had been founded to represent New England

[35] For those founded in the preceding period, see vol. II, pp. 63–64. Founded after the war were, among others: *Christian Herald* (1870–1910), Detroit, called in its last nine years *Michigan Christian Herald; Indiana Baptist* (1881–1902), Indianapolis, which became *Baptist Outlook* in 1889, and *Indiana Baptist Outlook* the next year; *Baptist Commonwealth* (1882–1917), Philadelphia, which was founded as *Baptist Exponent; Free Baptist* (1882–1904), Minneapolis. See Chapter XVIII of A. H. Newman's *A Century of Baptist Achievement* (Philadelphia, 1901).

[36] See vol. II, pp. 63–65, for southern Baptist papers founded in the preceding period. Among those founded after the war were: *Central Baptist* (1866–1913), which began at Palmyra, Missouri, under the name *Missouri Baptist*, but changed title and moved to Kansas City after its merger with *Baptist Record* (1866–68), of St. Louis; *Baptist Visitor* (1866–78), Baltimore, etc.; *Baptist Courier* (1869–current), founded at Yorkville, South Carolina, as *Working Christian*, moved to Charleston, Columbia, Greenville, taking its present title in 1878; *Alabama Baptist* (1874–current), Birmingham; *Baptist Flag* (1875–1925), Fulton, Kentucky; *Baptist Record* (1877–current), founded at Clinton, Mississippi, but later moved to Jackson; *Florida Baptist Witness* (1884–current), which was founded at DeLand, but absorbed *Florida Baptist* (1883–87) and moved to Ocala, Arcadia, Jacksonville. See Gaines S. Dobbins, "Southern Baptist Journalism" (Thesis, 1914, Southern Baptist Seminary).

[37] Founded at Morristown, Tennessee, by O. C. Pope in 1874 as *Baptist Reflector*. It was moved to Nashville in 1878 and four years later was merged with *American Baptist* (1876–82), Chattanooga, with the name *American Baptist Reflector*, which it retained until its end in a merger with the *Tennessee Baptist* in 1888.

[38] Began at Paris, Texas, as *Baptist Messenger* in 1874, but changed title on its removal to Dallas five years later. It absorbed *Texas Baptist Herald* (1865–86), becoming *Baptist and Herald*, to end in 1900.

[39] See Mott, *op. cit.*, p. 529.   [40] Treated more fully in vol. II, sketch 31.

Calvinism but was abducted by New Yorkers; in 1871 it died in that city after bequeathing its list to its rival. There was also the *Presbyterian Review* (1880–89), a New York quarterly edited by Charles A. Briggs, of Union Theological Seminary. Briggs had, as successive co-editors, A. A. Hodge, son of the famous editor of the Princeton *Review;* F. L. Patton, and B. B. Warfield. In the South, the *Cumberland Presbyterian Review* and the *Southern Presbyterian Review* still held forth.

Among the monthlies, Charles F. Beach's *National Presbyterian* (1873–1902), of Indianapolis, was outstanding. A religious and literary octavo called *Our Monthly* (1870–74) had a varied career, being moved from Cincinnati, city of its nativity, to Philadelphia after its second year.[41] A new monthly devoted to missions appeared at Richmond — the *Missionary* (1872–89), — and the *Presbyterian Home Missionary* was published in New York 1881–86. *Our Banner* (1873–94) was a Reformed Presbyterian monthly.

The New York *Observer* had the largest circulation among Presbyterian weeklies. It represented the conservative part of the church, though by the eighties it was practically undenominational. The New York *Evangelist*, livelier and quite as earnest, spoke for the New School Presbyterians. The three most prominent weeklies begun in the postwar period were the *Occident* (1868–1900), of San Francisco; the great middlewestern paper, the *Interior* (1870–1926), of Chicago, backed by Philip Armour, the packer, and Cyrus H. McCormick, inventor of the reaper;[42] and the *Presbyterian Journal* (1875–1910), of Philadelphia, which became the *Westminster* in 1904 and was finally merged with the *Interior*. Other weeklies were distributed among the various states.[43]

[41] Another *Our Monthly* was published by Presbyterians at Clinton, South Carolina, beginning in 1867, to represent the Thornville Orphanage, William P. Jacobs editor. It is still current.

[42] Founded by R. B. Mason; William C. Gray, backed by McCormick, rescued it after its collapse in the Chicago fire and edited it for thirty years. It absorbed the *Western Presbyterian* (1866–69), of Danville, Kentucky, and the *Occident*, changing title to *Continent* in 1910, when it absorbed the *Westminster*. For its history, see *Journal of Presbyterian Historical Society*, X, 36 (March 1919).

[43] For Presbyterian weeklies from earlier periods, see vol. II, pp. 62–63. Among others begun between 1865 and 1885 were: St. Louis *Presbyterian* (1866–94);

PROTESTANT EPISCOPAL JOURNALS

The *American Church Review*,[44] now published in New York, continued to be the quarterly of the Protestant Episcopal church. The *Church Monthly*,[45] of Boston, became in 1870 the *Church Weekly*, of New York, but survived only another year. W. T. Gibson's *Church Eclectic* was published in Utica, New York, during our period;[46] and the *American Literary Churchman* (1881–85) had a brief life in Baltimore.

Some of the church's weeklies were well known, as the New York *Churchman* and the Philadelphia *Episcopal Recorder;*[47] but both were exceeded in circulation by the end of our period by a newcomer from the West — the *Living Church* (1878– current), of Chicago,[48] edited and published by C. W. Leffingwell. The Church looked to the West for many of its newer journals.[49] L. H. Morehouse's *Young Churchman* (1870–1922), of Milwaukee, was a widely circulated juvenile with both weekly and monthly editions.

Southwestern Presbyterian (1868–1908), New Orleans; *Rocky Mountain Presbyterian* (1872–80), Denver; *Presbyterian at Work* (1873–78), Philadelphia; *Christian Herald* (1882–87), Omaha; *Northwestern Presbyterian* (1884–90), Minneapolis. The *Afric-American Presbyterian* was published at Wilmington, North Carolina, 1879–91. The Cumberland Presbyterians had the St. Louis *Observer*, 1875–1900.

[44] Treated more fully in vol. II, sketch 13.

[45] See vol. II, p. 69.

[46] Taken over by the Young Churchman Company, of Milwaukee, and conducted separately in that city during the nineties. In 1900 Arthur Lowndes became editor, in New York City.

[47] See vol. II, p. 70.

[48] Purchased by the Young Churchman Company, of Milwaukee, in 1892 and made a quarterly, but resumed weekly publication in 1900.

[49] Among the longer-lived Episcopal papers, chiefly weeklies, founded in this period were: *Pacific Churchman* (1866–current), San Francisco; *Church* (1870–86), Philadelphia; *Oregon Churchman* (1871–current), founded at Vancouver, Washington, as *Columbia Churchman*, but moved to Portland in 1887, there to be called for a few years *Oregon and Washington Churchman;* the monthly *Church News* (1871–1936), St. Louis; *Kansas Churchman* (1872–1918?), Topeka; the monthly *North East* (1872–89), Portland, Maine; the monthly *Kentucky Church Chronicle* (1875–89), Louisville; *Iowa Churchman* (1877–1923), Davenport; *Church Kalendar* (1879–90), Westfield, New York; *Montana Churchman* (1883–current), founded at Virginia City, but moved to Deer Lodge 1890, Butte 1900, Helena 1902.

The list of Congregational periodicals for the years 1865–85 is comparatively short, but it contains the names of several really important journals. To begin with the quarterlies, the *Bibliotheca Sacra* [50] was under the charge of Edwards A. Park, and the *New Englander* [51] was under equally distinguished editorship. The *Boston Review* [52] became the *Congregational Review* when it was taken to Chicago in 1870; it perished in the great fire. The *Congregational Quarterly* [53] was done to death in the house of its friends in 1878. The monthly *Andover Review* [54] (1884–93) began an important career immediately after the *Bibliotheca Sacra* was removed to the West in 1883. The *Church Building Quarterly* (1882–1909), New York, was a valuable periodical in its specialized field.

Among the weeklies there were also some outstanding journals of Congregational faith or flavor. The old *Boston Recorder* was merged in the *Congregationalist*, of the same city, in 1867.[55] The famous *Independent*,[56] whose editorship passed in 1870 from Theodore Tilton to H. C. Bowen, the publisher, became less a sectarian newspaper and more an undenominational religious journal. The two newcomers of importance in the postbellum period were the New York *Christian Union* [57] and the Chicago *Advance*. The former, founded by (or at least *for*) Henry Ward Beecher in 1870, was the great success among religious periodicals of the period until the Beecher-Tilden scandal dimmed its luster. It had little more than a tinge of Congregationalism and called itself undenominational. As for the *Advance*,[58] it was founded in 1867 by William Weston Pat-

---

[50] See Mott, *op. cit.*, p. 739.

[51] Treated more fully in vol. II, sketch 7.

[52] Treated more fully in vol. II, sketch 32.

[53] See vol. II, p. 71.

[54] To be treated more fully in a separate sketch in the succeeding volume.

[55] For these two papers, see vol. II, p. 71.

[56] Treated more fully in vol. II, sketch 14.

[57] Treated more fully in the present volume, sketch 16.

[58] Apparently the circulation never got above 25,000. Among contributors were Lyman Abbott, David Swing, General O. O. Howard, E. P. Roe, J. S. C. Abbott, and R. S. Storrs. It serialized that chief of best-sellers, *In His Steps*, but it was devoted largely to missionary activities in the late seventies. J. T. B. Marsh and H. L. Turner were editors 1873–74 (between Patton and Howard),

ton as a result of dissatisfaction with the *Independent's* want of religion,[59] and soon became the leading spokesman of western Congregationalism. In 1873 Charles H. Howard became its editor and publisher, the size was reduced to quarto, and the contents were raised to a somewhat higher literary level. A scheme of publication in both New York and Chicago, with T. DeWitt Talmage as eastern editor, was attempted without success in 1876–77. There were a few other Congregational weeklies and some missionary monthlies.[60]

UNITARIAN JOURNALS

The most distinguished Unitarian journal, the *Christian Examiner*,[61] joined the *Monthly Journal of the Unitarian Association*[62] in making way for the new nonsectarian magazine to be published under Unitarian auspices in 1869 — *Old and New*[63] — which had, however, only a little over five years of life. The *Monthly Religious Magazine*[64] continued until 1874, when it was combined with the new *Unitarian Review*,[65] a quarterly with a remarkable list of contributors but an uninspired editorship. The great Unitarian weeklies were the New York *Liberal Christian*,[66] which absorbed the *Christian Inquirer*[67] in 1866, but itself perished in 1877; and the Boston *Christian Register*.

---

and after Howard's retirement the following editors served: Robert West, 1882–86; F. A. Noble, 1886–88; Simeon Gilbert, C. F. Thwing, and J. A. Adams, 1888–89; J. A. Adams and H. S. Harrison, 1889–1913. It was merged in the *Congregationalist* in 1917.

[59] See vol. II, pp. 373–74.

[60] Among the weeklies were: *Plymouth Pulpit* (1868–86), New York; *New Hampshire Journal* (1881–98), published by W. W. Prescott at Montpelier, Vermont, but dated at Concord, New Hampshire; *Congregational Iowa* (1882–1928), Oskaloosa, Grinnell. Among state monthlies: *Kansas Telephone* (1880–94), Manhattan; *Nebraska Congregational News* (1880–1910), Lincoln; *Pilgrim* (1881–90), Minneapolis. Leader of the missionary journals was the *Missionary Herald* (see Mott, *op. cit.*, p. 134). Two missionary magazines founded in this period were *Life and Light for Heathen Women* (1869–1922), Boston, a quarterly 1869–72, and afterwards a monthly including home missions and dropping *Heathen* from the title; and *Mission Dayspring* (1882–1913), Boston.

[61] See Mott, *op. cit.*, p. 284.

[62] See vol. II, p. 72.

[63] Treated more fully in sketch 17.

[64] See vol. II, p. 72.

[65] Treated more fully in sketch 26.

[66] See Mott, *op. cit.*, p. 373.

[67] *Ibid.*, p. 374.

Differences between liberals and conservatives in the Unitarian Association led in 1867 to the formation of the Free Religious Association, and two or three periodicals of importance were allied more or less definitely with this group. Theodore Parker had died in 1860, but his spirit and principles lived on in the men who edited and contributed to these journals. For example, the *Radical*, a Boston monthly of 1865–72, had for its chief contributors during its first few years John Weiss, Samuel Johnson, and David A. Wasson — three brilliant disciples of Parker. Samuel H. Morse was editor and publisher, and he enlisted such able writers as Moncure D. Conway, O. B. Frothingham, T. W. Higginson, the elder Henry James, Edward Rowland Sill, and Bronson Alcott. While the first half of the file was specifically labeled "Devoted to Religion," it was fairly broad in scope, and increasingly so toward the end.[68] A weekly of similar affiliations was the *Index* (1870–86), founded and for ten years edited by Francis Ellingwood Abbot. It was begun at Toledo, Ohio, where Abbot was minister of an "independent" society. David R. Locke, far better known as "Petroleum V. Nasby," was a member of Abbot's congregation, and not only suggested the paper but advanced the money for the first year or two of its publication. The *Index* printed contributions from many of the writers for the *Radical*, though its tone was not always so lofty or its attitude so philosophical. It moved to Boston in 1873 and seven years later was made over to the Free Religious Association, B. F. Underwood being editor for the last few years.[69] The western representative of this movement of radical Unitarianism was *Unity* (1878–current), of Chicago, edited for nearly forty years by Jenkin Lloyd Jones. It was a semimonthly at first, but became a weekly in 1885. Robert Collyer, David Starr Jordan, and George Willis Cooke were prominent contributors; and well-known eastern Uni-

---

[68] Joseph B. Marvin was co-editor, 1866–67. Publication was omitted July 1870–January 1871; otherwise the file runs regularly, September 1865–June 1872. See Clarence L. F. Gohdes, *The Periodicals of American Transcendentalism* (Durham, North Carolina, 1931), Chapter X.

[69] It was supplanted by *Open Court*. An Index Association, of which T. W. Higginson was president for a time, published the paper after Locke's support ceased and until it was taken over by the Free Religious Association. See Gohdes, *op. cit.*, Chapter XI.

tarians were also represented. A considerable list of other periodicals, religious and secular, was merged in *Unity*.[70]

PERIODICALS OF THE SMALLER DENOMINATIONS

But it was the Universalist denomination which made the greatest progress in amalgamation of periodicals in the years 1865–85. By the latter date the Boston *Universalist Leader* [71] had absorbed all the weeklies of that faith except the *Gospel Banner*, which came in later, and the *Universalist Herald*.[72] *Manford's Magazine* [73] was published at Chicago throughout the period, and the *Universalist Quarterly* [74] continued as the church's review.

The leading Lutheran journals of the preceding periods [75] were continued after the war. The *Lutheran Church Review* (1882–1927) was begun in Philadelphia, while in the South *Our Church Paper* (1873–1907) was published at New Market, Virginia, and in the West the *Lutheran Witness* (1882–current) held forth at St. Louis. The *Evangelical Review* [76] became the *Quarterly Review of the Evangelical Lutheran Church* in 1878.

The *Mercersburg Review*,[77] important in the history of the promulgation of German theological ideas in this country, became the *Reformed Quarterly Review* in 1879. The German Reformed Church also published the *Mission Gleaner* (1883–1917) at New York.

The Disciples of Christ had a review called the *Christian*

[70] *Unity* was issued for its first few months under the name *Pamphlet Mission*. J. T. Sunderland was edtior, 1878–79, and John Haynes Holmes has been editor since Jones' retirement in 1918. See Fiftieth Anniversary Number, March 5, 1928.

[71] The *Leader* is the direct descendant of the *Universalist Magazine*, a weekly paper begun in 1819. It was called *Universalist* from 1862 until its merger with the *Christian Leader*, which was the successor of the *Utica Evangelical Magazine* (1827–43) and other periodicals. Thereafter it was entitled *Universalist Leader* until 1926, when it reverted to the title *Christian Leader*. It is sometimes said to have begun in 1898 (see *Union List of Serials*) because it began new numbering on its consolidation in that year with *Gospel Banner*. For papers absorbed, see vol. II, p. 72.

[72] See vol. II, p. 73, footnote.

[73] See vol. II, p. 73, footnote.

[74] See vol. II, p. 72.

[75] See vol. II, p. 73.

[76] See vol. II, p. 73.

[77] Treated more fully in vol. II, sketch 15.

Quarterly, published in Cincinnati, through the years 1869–76.[78] It was followed by the *Christian Quarterly Review* (1882–89), conducted by E. W. Herndon at Columbia, Missouri. The *Millennial Harbinger*[79] continued until 1870, when it was succeeded by the *Watchman* (1870–86), of Washington, North Carolina. In 1868 the *Herald of Gospel Liberty*,[80] of Newburyport, Massachusetts, then sixty years old and the veteran of religious weeklies in America, absorbed the *Gospel Herald* (1843–68), of Dayton, Ohio, and removed to the latter city. To the already considerable list of Christian papers,[81] there were added in our period the Nashville *Gospel Advocate* (1866–current); the Louisville *Christian Guide* (1867–1902), founded *Apostolic Guide* at Covington; and the monthly *Missionary Tidings* (1883–1918), Indianapolis. The merger of the St. Louis *Christian* (1864–82, begun in Kansas City) and the Chicago *Evangelist* (1865–82, begun in Oskaloosa, Iowa) formed the *Christian-Evangelist*, still issued in St. Louis.

For the Jews, Julius Silversmith's Chicago *Occident* (1873–95) a radical Reformed Judaism journal, exceeded the several papers which continued from the preceding years[82] in circulation by the end of the postbellum period. Of several New York Jewish periodicals begun after the war,[83] the *American Hebrew* (1879–current) was the most important. The *Jewish Voice*, which began in the same year at St. Louis, ended in 1933, and the San Francisco *Jewish Progress* lasted for a quarter of a century, 1875–1900. In the same city was the *Jewish Times*

---

[78] Published in eight regular volumes by R. W. Carroll & Company, 1869–71, and W. T. Moore, 1872–76. Its editor throughout was W. T. Moore, pastor of the Central Christian Church, Cincinnati. Among the associate editors were President W. K. Pendleton, of Bethany College, and President Isaac Errett, of Alliance College, later editor of the *Christian Standard*. Others prominent in the church's educational, missionary, and pastoral activities were associate editors and contributors. The articles practically all deal directly with religious questions, but the viewpoint of the quarterly was, in general, liberal and comparatively unsectarian.

[79] See vol. II, p. 74.

[80] See vol. II, p. 74.

[81] See vol. II, p. 74.

[82] See vol. II, pp. 77–78.

[83] Other New York Jewish periodicals of importance founded in this period: *New Era* (1870–76), the monthly *Jewish Advocate* (1878–87), *Hebrew Standard* (1882–1922), and a Christian paper with racial loyalty — *Christian Hebrew* (1883–96).

(1879–1924) called *Jewish Times and Observer* after it had absorbed the *Hebrew Observer* (1856–90).

The Friends, or Quakers, had three new journals,[84] representing different branches of their society — the *Christian Worker* (1871–94), of New Vienna, Ohio; the Philadelphia *Journal* (1873–85); and the *Western Friend* (1879–90), at Baxter Springs, Kansas. The *Herald of Truth* (1864–1908) was a Mennonite organ at Elkhart, Indiana.

For the United Brethren, there were the *Brethren Evangelist* (1879–89) at Ashland, Ohio; the *Woman's Evangel* (1881–1931), at Dayton, Ohio, called *Evangel* after 1919; and the *Gospel Messenger* (1883–current), begun at Mount Morris, Illinois, but now published from Elgin. The *Religious Telescope* continued at Dayton.

Zion's Hope (1869–current) and the *Saints' Herald*[85] at Lamoni, Iowa, represented the Latter-day Saints, or Mormons. The *Shaker* (1871–99), which later became the *Shaker and Shakeress* and then the *Manifesto*, was printed first at Shakers, New York, and then at East Canterbury, New Hampshire. The Second Adventists published *Our Rest and Signs of the Times* (1873–91) in Chicago. The *Advocate of Christian Holiness* (1870–1909) was published at Boston; it was called the *Christian Witness* after 1881. The *Gospel Trumpet* (1881–1903), of Moundsville, West Virginia, was also a Holiness periodical. The Covenanters issued the *Christian Nation* in New York 1884–1929.

PERIODICALS DEVOTED TO SPIRITUALISM

Spiritualist societies and their leaders were very active in publication. The Boston *Banner of Light* was the only one of the several journals in this field in the fifties [86] to survive to our period, but more than a dozen were presently published to give it company. The first of the newcomers and one of the most important was Thomas G. Newman's folio *Religio-Philosophical Journal* (1865–1905), begun in Chicago, but in 1895 moved to San Francisco, where it became *Philosophical Journal*. An-

---

[84] For those continuing from the preceding period, see vol. II, p. 74.
[85] See vol. II, p. 74. Both are now published at Independence, Missouri.
[86] See vol. II, pp. 209–10.

other folio was the Chicago *Present Age* (1868–72), by Colonel Dorus M. Fox, which was published also in New York. The *Voice of Angels* (1875–87) was a semimonthly from Somerville, Massachusetts, while the *World's Advance-Thought* (1876–1918) came from Salem, Oregon, later to move to Portland and go over to Ethical Culture. Utica, New York, contributed the *Olive Branch* (1876–89). The editor of the Chicago *Watchman* (1880–91) was announced as "Watchman," H[attie] A. Cate, amanuensis. The *Carrier Dove* (1884–93), of Oakland, California, was edited by Elizabeth Lowe Watson, medium; and, like most of the other periodicals of its class, it was devoted largely to "mediumistic experiences." There were several others of shorter life.[87]

The Swedenborgians, from whom the Spiritualists drew much inspiration, added to their existing quota of magazines several new ventures, of which *New-Church Life* (1881–current), a Philadelphia monthly, was the most successful.

UNDENOMINATIONAL JOURNALS

Church union continued to·be a lively topic of discussion among the religious periodicals, and the number of interdenominational journals increased. A paper called *Church Union* (1867–69) formed the basis for Beecher's *Christian Union*; another of the same name was published in New York from 1873 to 1899, and the *Christian Witness* (1866–86), of Columbus, was devoted to that cause.

A few religious family weeklies attained considerable circulations outside of the denominations. The *Christian at Work*, later *Christian Work* (1866–1926), was edited for a time by T. DeWitt Talmage and contained good reading of an evangeli-

[87] Among them: *Spiritual Republic* (1867–?), by F. L. Wadsworth and J. C. Barrett, Chicago (a file for the first six months of 1867 is in the Houdini Collection in the Library of Congress, and it is mentioned in the Chicago City Directory for 1869); *News from the Spirit World* (1868–70), by Mrs. A. Buffum, Chicago; *Western Star* (1872), by Emma Hardinge Britten, Boston; *Brittan's Journal of Spiritual Science, Literature, Art, and Inspiration* (1873–74), a quarterly in octavo by Dr. S. B. Brittan, New York; *Crucible* (1873–77), Moses Hull's New York monthly devoted to spiritualism and free love; *Spiritual Record* (1879–80), by the First Society of Spiritualists, Chicago, Cora L. V. Richmond, medium; *Light for Thinkers* (1881–86), Atlanta, Georgia; and *Facts* (1882–87), a monthly by L. L. Whitlock, Boston.

cal cast.[88] Talmage was also editor throughout most of its life of *Frank Leslie's Sunday Magazine* (1877–89), of New York.[89] John Dougall's New York *Witness* (1871–1920) attained 100,-000 circulation shortly after 1880. *Zion's Watchman,* of Albany, was founded by John Lemley in 1878 and published for over a third of a century.[90]

The Chicago *Alliance* (1873–83), founded by David Swing, Robert Collyer, and others, combined religious news with essays which possessed some literary excellence. Francis F. Browne was its literary editor for a time. But it was always indigent, and its business management was unskillful, to say the least. "Gail Hamilton" once wrote a letter to its editor refusing to contribute without remuneration. "So long as you cultivate literature on a little oatmeal," she said characteristically, "bless you, my children, bless you; but leave me my fatted calf!" [91]

The *Christian Herald* (1878–current) was begun as the New York edition of a London journal which was issued chiefly in order to promulgate the sermons of C. H. Spurgeon. It also published Talmage's sermons and some religious fiction, anecdotes, and miscellany; and it soon gained that reputation for a kind of freshness of religious experience which it has since maintained.

This fashion of issuing periodicals devoted to the publication of sermons spread rather widely in the seventies, in spite of a noticeable falling off in pulpit influence.[92] The *National Preacher* (1826–66) ended early in the period; and the *Metropolitan Pulpit* began ten years later in the same city, to be-

[88] It originated in the Y.M.C.A. movement and was later taken over by the Remingtons of the Remington Arms Company. Joseph Newton Hallock and his son W. W. had editorial charge, 1874–1923; then Frederick Lynch bought it, with the help of Andrew Carnegie. International peace, Christian unity, and liberty in the pulpit were its "causes." See *Christian Century,* XLIII, 409 (April 1, 1926).

[89] This was a monthly, in spite of the weekly connotation of its title. Charles Force Deems was editor, 1877–79.

[90] See Lemley's *Personal Recollections* (Albany, 1901). Lemley also founded the *Golden Censer* (1868–80). A son, Walter H., continued the *Watchman* after the father's death and until 1913.

[91] See Herbert E. Fleming, *Magazines of a Market-Metropolis* (Chicago, 1906), p. 507 for the *Alliance*; and for "Gail's" letter, see Augusta Dodge, *Gail Hamilton's Life in Letters* (Boston, 1901), II, 790. Letter, September 7, 1877.

[92] See p. 86.

come, after sundry changes of name and alterations of editorial policy, the current *Homiletic and Pastoral Review*. Chief cities had their sermon repositories for brief periods — *Boston Pulpit* (1872), *Chicago Pulpit* (1871–73), and so on. The New York *Pulpit Treasury* (1883–1907) was more longevous. The publication of sermons in both religious and secular journals was not uncommon, especially those of the more sensational preachers of the period. Talmage claimed in 1878 that three million readers followed his sermons weekly.[93]

Three nonsectarian journals of Biblical learning began in the early eighties — the *Oriental and Biblical Journal*, edited by Stephen D. Peet, which published only three quarterly numbers in 1880; the Germanic *Journal of the Society of Biblical Literature and Exegesis* (1881–current), Middletown, Connecticut, which was only an annual in our period;[94] and the *Hebrew Student* (1882–1920), of Chicago, President Harper's journal, later famous as the *Biblical World*.[95]

An interdenominational missionary journal was established by Royal G. Wilder at Princeton, New Jersey, in 1878 with the title *Missionary Review of the World*. It was edited by Wilder for ten years and then for nearly a quarter of a century by Arthur T. Pierson. Added to the brief list of undenominational journals for Sunday school teachers [96] was the *National Sunday School Teacher* (1866–82), Chicago.

Periodicals were issued in several cities by the Young Men's

[93] *Christian Herald*, I, 4 (October 24, 1878).

[94] Published semiannually 1886–1911, and then quarterly. Its name became *Journal of Biblical Literature* in 1890. Always close to German scholarship, many of the *Journal's* articles have been in the German language. The Society was founded by Philip Schaff and others in 1880. The *Journal* was moved to Boston in 1884 and has since been published in Norwood, Massachusetts, New York, and New Haven.

[95] After the first year the title was changed to *Old Testament Student*, and in 1889 to *Old and New Testament Student*. The *Biblical World* began a new series, January 1893. Editors: William Rainey Harper, 1893–1906; Ernest DeWitt Burton, 1906–12; Shailer Mathews, 1913–20. Members of the faculty of the Divinity School at the University of Chicago were associate editors. It was bimonthly for the last two and a half years. Largely philological at the beginning, the journal broadened in the nineties to include social questions, the science-and-religion discussion, Sunday school reform, and so on; but it was always a "higher criticism" bulwark.

[96] See vol. II, p. 101.

Christian Association, which made a conspicuous growth after the war. Of these, the most important were the *Association News* (1879–91) in Philadelphia and the *Y.M.C.A. Watchman* (1876–1932) in Chicago. The latter, after moves to Cleveland and New York and several changes of name, was published for the entire organization as *Association Men*. The Salvation Army's *War Cry* was begun in New York in 1882. The American Tract Society followed its *Christian Banner* [97] with a more brilliant periodical — the *Illustrated Christian Weekly* (1871–92), edited in the early seventies by Lyman Abbott and illustrated by Timothy Cole's woodcuts. Other tract societies and religious propagandists were active in the interdenominational field.[98]

RELIGIOUS ISSUES

The chief religious and theological topics of the times were discussed by the general magazines as well as by the church periodicals. The debate on the evolutionary hypothesis, for example, with its inescapable theological phases, filled many pages in magazines that were designed for popular reading.[99] The question of future punishment suddenly became a matter of great public interest in 1877–78. "There has been nothing more curious of late," observed the *Nation* in January 1878, "than the amount of interest excited by, and discussion expended on, the question of the existence or non-existence of Hell, and on its nature." [100] The *North American Review*, which just then had a penchant for symposia, carried one on Hell in March 1878 to which Noah Porter, O. B. Frothingham, H. W. Bellows, and three others contributed learned disquisitions.

Doubtless the stimulus for this popular interest in Sheol

[97] See vol. II, p. 75.

[98] The *Outlook* (1882–93), later called *Sabbath Quarterly*, of Alfred Center, New York, was the journal of the American Sabbath Tract Society; and *Zion's Watch Tower and Herald of Christ's Presence* (1879–current), later *Watch Tower*, was published in Pittsburgh, Brooklyn, and other cities by a millenarian tract society. Besides these journals of tract societies, there were such interdenominational papers as L. H. Earle's *Boston Contributor* (1872–1906) and the Boston *Watchword* (1878–1921). The latter was called *Watchword and Truth* after its merger with St. Louis *Truth* (1874–97).

[99] See pp. 106–07.

[100] *Nation*, XXVI, 50 (January 24, 1878).

arose from the preaching of Dwight L. Moody, whose great religious revivals, following on the heels of the financial panic, reached their height in the middle seventies. "All Brooklyn is reported as crazy over Moody and Sankey," we learn from *Potter's American Monthly*. "These that have turned the world upside down are come hither also," it quotes, and adds, "Their success everywhere is one of the marvels of our day." [101] *Harper's Weekly* followed the Brooklyn meetings, showing the immense crowds in illustration; it had done the same for the Philadelphia meetings, at the first of which ten thousand people were said to have been in the audience.[102] *Harper's Weekly* was strongly Methodistic in trend;[103] many other journals — including the Congregational *Advance*, for example — were far less enthusiastic about Moody.[104] The Moody periodical — the *Record of Christian Work* — was begun in 1881 at East Northfield, Massachusetts, and published for over half a century.

But there can be no doubt that, on the whole, the churches were losing some of their influence; certainly religious sanctions were declining from their ancient strength. Indeed, Noah Porter went so far as to speak in the *Princeton Review* of "the more or less settled and prevailing conviction that faith is not only failing, but that it is doomed to a slow but certain dissolution." [105] It was a sign of the times that church attendance was no longer a solemn obligation upon all properly behaved persons. The *Nation* pointed out the "relative diminution of the power exerted by the pulpit over the popular mind," and added that on Sundays many men and women "crave the quiet and silence of home." [106] The *North American Review* returned to this subject again and again. It reiterated Leonard Bacon's dictum: "Rest is the primary and fundamental idea of the Sabbath," [107]

[101] *Potter's American Monthly*, VI, 73 (January 1876).

[102] *Harper's Weekly*, XIX, 918 (November 13, 1875); XIX, 1000 (December 11, 1875); etc.

[103] *Ibid.*, X, 625, 626, 632–634 (October 6, 1866). This is an account of the centenary of American Methodism occupying a large part of the issue and showing the paper's tendency.

[104] *Advance*, VIII, 990 (October 14, 1875).

[105] *Princeton Review*, 4th ser., IX, 165 (March 1882).

[106] *Nation*, IV, 390 (May 16, 1867).

[107] *North American Review*, CXXXI, 323 (October 1880).

and it repeatedly commented on the failure of the American pulpit.

> It is a generally admitted fact [wrote an anonymous observer] that in these days only a small proportion, even of intelligent and eminently respectable people, are regular attendants on religious services every Sunday. . . . The pulpit is behind the age. . . . Science is today doing more for morals than the church. Churches, at least in large cities, are for the rich.[108]

The bicycle craze was blamed for the falling off in church attendance in some quarters, but the attempt to turn the new sport to churchly use by organizing the practice of riding the wheel to church was frowned upon by the strait-laced. The bicycle could not "be used on the Sabbath, even for church-going, without exciting prejudice and having 'the appearance of evil.' "[109]

In spite of critics, there were famous preachers in those days. Beecher, Talmage, Moody, Chapin, Bellows, and Phillips Brooks were before the public. These men, however, were not held sacrosanct as the old New England ministers had been, and they were often criticized. Beecher was long under fire on the matter of personal immorality. "Dr. Talmage is the clown of the ecclesiastical arena, and wherever he is there is a circus," declared *Life*.[110] Talmage's sensational methods and his passionate sermons about night life in New York were frequently attacked by *Puck*, which pictured him all mouth.

The difficulty was not wholly with the pulpit, however. The older theology was breaking down. The *Manhattan* called attention to "the present popular confusion of religious belief." It heard on all sides, "from press, pulpit and platform, the most contradictory statements, explaining the old theology in a way which would have made Calvin and Jonathan Edwards start with horror."[111] But while leaders like Moody pointed the way back to old beliefs, others saw the need for revision of creeds. "It is not to be denied," admitted Beecher in the *North American*, "that in every community where the intellect has been

---

[108] *Ibid.*, CXXXVII, 76–79 (July 1883).
[109] *Wheelman*, II, 369 (August 1883).
[110] *Life*, V, 32 (January 15, 1885).
[111] *Manhattan*, I, 503 (June 1883).

aroused, good men have become dissatisfied with the old and prevalent creeds." [112]   And Oliver Wendell Holmes declared: "Creeds imperatively demand revision, and the pews which call for it must be listened to, or the preacher will by and by find himself speaking to a congregation of bodiless echoes." [113]

Indeed a revision of the Bible did arrive in the eighties — the Revised Version of the New Testament in 1881, and that of the Old Testament in 1885. But the *Nation's* reviewer insisted that "the new translation has been either sternly rejected or received with apology and resignation by orthodox denominations." [114]

Enter "Bob" Ingersoll, bringing with him the smell of brimstone. The revivified *North American* was the arena of his most brilliant exploits in journalism. There he held a debate with Jeremiah S. Black in 1881, in which he declared that "a profound change has taken place in the world of thought. . . . The pulpit is losing because the people are growing." [115]   All of which his opponent and fellow lawyer denied categorically. Ingersoll soon became a tradition, his head unbowed under churchly anathema. Most periodicals joined in the attack on the great agnostic. "Bob Ingersoll," said *Life* in 1885, "is now lecturing on blasphemy, about which he probably knows more than any man now living." [116]   But he was allowed to return to the charge in the *North American* a few years later, with the Reverend Henry M. Field as an opponent. This debate was entered by a man who perhaps carried more prestige in utterance than any other personage in the English-speaking world — William E. Gladstone.[117]   But Ingersoll had the last word.

There were a few "freethinker's" journals. The Boston *Investigator*,[118] still edited by Horace Seaver, was frankly atheis-

---

[112] *North American Review*, CXXXVI, 1 (January 1883).

[113] *Ibid.*, CXXXII, 138 (February 1881).

[114] *Nation*, XXXII, 401 (June 9, 1881).

[115] *North American Review*, CXXXIII, 109 (August 1881).

[116] *Life*, V, 186 (April 2, 1885).

[117] See vol. II, pp. 252–53.

[118] Founded in 1831 by Abner Kneeland, famous "free enquirer," who was convicted of blasphemy on account of the publication. Horace Seaver was editor, 1845–90, and was succeeded by L. K. Washburn, who remained in control until the end of the paper in 1904. Josiah P. Mendum was publisher for half a century.

tic. Dr. J. R. Monroe's *Iron-Clad Age* (1855–98) was an agnostic weekly from Indianapolis. The Reverend E. C. Towne's Chicago monthly *Examiner* (1870–71), which published five numbers, and E. M. McDonald's New York *Truth-Seeker* (1873–current) were radicals. The San Francisco *Universe* (1882–93) was another agnostic.

PHILOSOPHICAL JOURNALS

There was a small group of journals devoted to philosophy. Of these, far the most important — and in some respects one of the greatest journals of the whole period — was William T. Harris' St. Louis *Journal of Speculative Philosophy* (1867–93).[119] A pseudophilosophical phenomenon was *Wilford's Microcosm* (1881–93), of New York; in 1885 the name was shortened to the *Microcosm*. A. Wilford Hall was editor and publisher, and he described his erratic periodical as "a religio-scientific monthly magazine devoted to the discoveries, theories and investigations of modern science in their bearing on the religious thought of the age," and later as "the organ of the substantial philosophy." The *Platonist* (1881–88) was a little monthly edited and published with some irregularity by Thomas M. Johnson at Osceola, Missouri. It reprinted many minor works in the field of Platonism. It was continued by the *Bibliotheca Platonica* (1889–90) under the same auspices.

[119] Treated more fully in sketch 8.

CHAPTER IV

WOMEN AND THEIR MAGAZINES

I F THERE is any matter emphatically entitled to be considered 'a thing of the day,' it is this 'Woman Question,' " [1]
wrote Charles Astor Bristed in the *Galaxy* in 1870. Accordingly, women's rights — and wrongs — received much consideration in the general magazines. "Having been idolized,
sung and flattered through all the moods and tenses of poet's
feeling, it seems at last woman's destiny to be soberly *considered*," [2] observed *Appleton's Journal*.

EQUAL SUFFRAGE

General magazines, as the *Nation* noted at the very beginning of the postbellum period, were greatly influenced by "the
preponderance of female names on the subscription lists." [3]
This petticoat rule was particularly noticeable in *Appleton's
Journal, Harper's*, and *Scribner's;* and it was only a little less
evident in such magazines as the *Atlantic*, the *Galaxy*, and
Lippincott's. In view of this state of affairs, the suffragists
would doubtless have had virtually all the magazines on their
side if the women themselves had favored the reform with
any show of unanimity. As it was, though most periodicals
debated the matter at length, comment was predominantly
hostile.

One of the most notable discussions of equal suffrage was
published in the *North American Review* in 1879–80. It grew
out of a frightened protest by Francis Parkman called "The
Woman Question," in which he prayed God to deliver America
from "the most reckless of experiments" toward which he saw
"a few agitators" driving the country. [4] To this article five
suffragists — Julia Ward Howe, Thomas Wentworth Higginson,
Lucy Stone, Elizabeth Cady Stanton, and Wendell Phillips —

---

[1] *Galaxy*, IX, 841 (June 1870).
[2] *Appleton's Journal*, I, 89 (April 17, 1869).
[3] *Nation*, III, 169 (August 30, 1866).
[4] *North American Review*, CXXIX, 321 (September 1879).

replied in a symposium two months later. A rejoinder by Parkman followed, but the reformers seemed to have rather the better of it.[5] Another flare-up of the controversy in the *North
American* came in 1883, when Dr. William A. Hammond asserted that there were "grave anatomical and physiological
reasons" against women in politics. "In the first place, the brain
of man is larger than that of woman," and besides, "a peculiar
neurotic condition called the hysterical is grafted on the organ
of woman."[6] To this there were replies aplenty, as there
were also to "Ouida's" article against "Female Suffrage" in
1886.

The *Atlantic Monthly* showed itself friendly to the "cause"
more than once: Higginson, Mrs. Howe, and "Gail Hamilton"
were a powerful trio of its advocates among *Atlantic* contributors. John Weiss, Mrs. Stanton, and others advocated woman
suffrage in the *Radical*, and the Boston *Index* was also committed to the reform. "Gail Hamilton's" articles in the *Independent* of 1871, containing some frank criticisms of family
life, were commended by Higginson in the *Woman's Journal*,
and some of them were reprinted there.[7]

The comic papers satirized the suffrage movement unmerci-
fully. *Punchinello* was an inveterate enemy of the "strong-
minded woman," and its wit at their expense was often
indelicate. It called the 1870 convention of the Equal Suffrage
Association "the annual Hen Convention of Antediluvian Fos-
sils";[8] and Sorosis, pioneer of the woman's club movement, was
as subtly nicknamed "Sore-eye Sissies" on more than one occasion. *Puck*, at the time of one of the periodical advances
of the crusaders upon Congress, satirized the suffragists in a
double-page cartoon: Lucy Stone, Susan B. Anthony, Elizabeth
Cady Stanton, Anna Dickinson, Mary Walker, Isabelle Beecher
Hooker, and others were represented as geese flocking about the
Capitol, which reared itself in the background. "Flocking for
Freedom," the picture was entitled, with the motto: "They

[5] *Ibid.*, CXXIX, 413 (November 1879). For Parkman's reply, *ibid.*, CXXX,
16 (January 1880).
[6] *Ibid.*, CXXXVII, 137 ff. (August 1883).
[7] *Woman's Journal*, II, 97 (April 1, 1871).
[8] *Punchinello*, I, 347 (August 27, 1870).

saved the ancient Capitol; they besiege the modern." Accompanying the cartoon was the following sonnet:

> Shame unto womanhood! The common scold
> Stands railing foul-mouthed in the public street;
> And in the mart and 'fore the justice seat
> Her shallow tale of fancied wrongs is told.
> No woman these such as our hearts enfold,
> Held of all men desirable and sweet,
> Who have our love and service at their feet;
> Mothers and wives are cast not in this mold,
> Nor of this likeness. Rather such are meet
> To herd with them whose love is bought and sold,
> Whose passionless pulses to no purpose beat:
> For these have hearts as empty and as cold,
> And all their lives are like them; incomplete,
> Unfruitful and unbeautiful and bold.[9]

Harper's Weekly had a running commentary in opposition to suffrage for women, and once a full-page drawing by Charles G. Bush called "Sorosis 1869," which showed a satiric conception of a women's political convention: tea drinking is mingled with speech making; and the men, sitting on the steps leading to the convention hall, are caring for the babies.[10] But the *Weekly* quoted good Bishop Simpson's observation (as behooved its Methodistic loyalties) to the effect that "God is evidently intending that women shall do more than they have done in the past." [11] At least, that was a concession. *Harper's Monthly* printed the dictum of Catherine E. Beecher, elder sister of Henry Ward Beecher and Mrs. Stowe, delivered with the customary Beecher air of making the divine will manifest to docile readers:

Woman's *distinctive profession* includes three departments — the training of the mind in childhood, the nursing of infants and of the sick, and all the handicrafts and management of the family state.[12]

The economic phase of the problem underwent a change in our period, and women invaded fields unknown to them before.

[9] *Puck*, II, 8–9 (January 23, 1878).
[10] *Harper's Weekly*, XIII, 312 (May 15, 1869).
[11] *Ibid.*, XIV, 770 (December 3, 1870).
[12] *Harper's Monthly*, XXXI, 710 (November 1865).

"It is curious to note," said the *Critic* in 1883, "how the question of the employment or advancement of women floats to the surface in current literature." [13] The *Printers' Circular*, which was especially interested in the activity of women in the printing trades, quoted some figures in 1869 to the effect that 75,000 women in New York and its suburbs were dependent on their own labor at wages half those of men in the same occupations — ranging from $4.50 a week for seamstresses to $18 a week for editors. There were ten practicing "doctoresses" in the city.[14] But the good old argument against such doings was that which Frederick Sheldon restated in the *Atlantic* — the folly of abdicating the throne of beauty to plunge into economic and political life.[15] This was the general position taken by the older women's magazines, which, in the main, eschewed the controversy.

Reformers had a natural affinity for the lecture platform, and audiences were easy for the leading suffragists to find. Anna Dickinson, Mrs. Stanton, Mrs. Woodhull, Mrs. Livermore, Susan B. Anthony, Olive Logan, and many another advocate of women's rights spent some months out of each year following the lyceums and lecture courses. Miss Dickinson, said *Punchinello*, was "incessantly and frantically roaming from one end of the country to the other." [16] The *Nation* had an editorial about the dress, manners, and behavior suitable and unsuitable to the female lecturer. She should sit while speaking, as Kate Field did, for

the world is not yet ready to see her, with any pleasure or profit, attempt anything approaching energy of manner in public. . . . The declamatory and passionate style of oratory is not suited to her voice or to her upper limbs.

Moreover, the *Nation's* writer advised that "to wear pantaloons, or purely 'sensible clothes,' on the rostrum" was a mistake.[17]

[13] *Critic*, III, 357 (September 8, 1883).
[14] *Printers' Circular*, IV, 124 (June 1869).
[15] *Atlantic Monthly*, XVIII, 425 (October 1866).
[16] *Punchinello*, II, 23 (October 8, 1870).
[17] *Nation*, VIII, 371 (May 13, 1869).

The *Revolution*,[18] begun with high hopes by Susan B. Anthony as publisher and Elizabeth Cady Stanton and Parker Pillsbury as editors in 1868, met with financial difficulties and was abandoned by its original projectors before its end in 1872. Mary A. Livermore published her Chicago *Agitator* briefly in 1869 and then merged it in the Boston *Woman's Journal* [19] of which she became editor for three years (1870–73). After Mrs. Livermore's retirement the *Journal* was conducted for more than twenty years by Lucy Stone and her husband, Henry B. Blackwell. Higginson, Garrison, and Mrs. Howe were associate editors at various times. According to its own statement, it was "not the organ of any association, but it is thoroughly identified with the interests and in harmony with the principles of the American Woman Suffrage Association." Mrs. Stanton thought it was not belligerent enough,[20] but among those who were less extreme the *Woman's Journal* won many friends.

The *Woman's Campaign* was published in New York during the presidential canvass of 1872 by Mrs. Helen Barnard; Miss Anthony tried to finance a continuation of it, but failed.[21] She had better luck with the *Ballot Box* (1876–81), of which she and Mrs. Stanton were associate editors. This journal was founded in Toledo, Ohio, by Sarah Langdon Williams, who had been editor of a woman's department in the *Toledo Blade*. After two years, Mrs. Williams turned the paper over to Matilda Joslyn Gage, a leading suffragist, who moved it to Syracuse, New York, and called it the *National Citizen and Ballot Box*. Another Ohio venture was the Cincinnati monthly *Aegis* 1880–86).

[18] Treated more fully in sketch 10.

[19] Published 1870–1931. Lucy Stone raised most of the $10,000 used to found the paper. Alice Stone Blackwell was editor after the deaths of her parents; she had been an assistant before. The *Journal* became the *Woman Citizen* in 1917, but later resumed the older name. In that year it was moved to New York and Virginia Roderick became editor. For a statement of principles, see II, 4 (January 7, 1871); and for historical articles, N.S., XVI, June 1931, p. 25 and N.S., XIV, December 1929, p. 9.

[20] *Woman's Journal*, IV, 84 (March 15, 1873).

[21] See Ida Husted Harper, *Life and Work of Susan B. Anthony* (Indianapolis, 1898), I, 509.

COMPLETION OF THE RAILROAD TO THE PACIFIC

The road was completed May 10, 1869; this woodcut (drawn from a photograph) appeared in *Harper's Weekly*, June 5, with the title: "Completion of the Pacific Railroad — Meeting of Locomotives of the Union and Central Pacific Lines: The Engineers Shake Hands." Note the imperfect joints of the separately engraved blocks which show the sky in this picture.

FLOCKING FOR FREEDOM.

SUFFRAGE ADVOCATES AS GEESE

This cartoon appeared in *Puck*, January 23, 1878, as a double-page colored lithograph. It was drawn by Joseph Keppler, *Puck's* famous part-owner and artist. The portraits represent, from left to right: Lucy Stone, Susan B. Anthony, Elizabeth Cady Stanton, Mrs. Cozzens (neck and head only), Anna Dickinson, Dr. Mary Walker (rear view), Isabel Hooker (wings outspread), and Elizabeth Tilton.

Still further west there were four suffrage journals of considerable importance. The Chicago *Sorosis* (1868–69), by Mrs. M. L. Walker, was the least of them. Clara Bewick Colby's *Woman's Tribune* (1883–1909), begun as a monthly in folio at Beatrice, Nebraska, came to have a national influence. It was moved in 1889 to Washington. The *New Northwest* (1871–90) was Abigail Scott Dunning's radical weekly at Portland, Oregon. Mrs. C. M. Churchill edited the monthly *Queen Bee* in Denver, 1879–96.

But the most spectacular advocate of suffrage in the period was *Woodhull & Claflin's Weekly*,[22] that strange and incongruous periodical edited and published by "the terrible siren," Victoria Woodhull, and her sister, Tennie C. Claflin, and conducted more or less irregularly by them and their aids and parasites for about six years in the early seventies. The irregularity was occasioned chiefly by jail sentences for obscenity and by lecture tours. The *Weekly's* advocacy of woman's rights, spiritualism, free love, and "the Woodhull's" candidacy for president of the United States; its exposé of the Beecher-Tilton case, and its occasionally scandalous plain speaking, give its columns more than their share of excitement and place it among the most important of the curiosa of American periodicals.

Another group of women's magazines is less important for its advocacy of women's rights, but peculiarly interesting because they were published, edited, and sometimes set in type and printed, by women for women. The *Chicago Magazine of Fashion, Music and Home Reading* (1870–76) was a rather amateurish production by Mrs. M. L. Rayne, a woman of high standing in Chicago social circles. In St. Louis three other enterprising women were active in magazine work: Julia M. Purington began in 1871 the *St. Louis Ladies' Magazine*, which dropped the word *Ladies'* from its title in 1874, and then continued obscurely until 1892 at least; Charlotte Smith issued the *Inland Monthly Magazine*, 1872–76; and Mary Nolan published in 1872–75 the *Central Magazine*, which was written, set in type, printed, and mailed out entirely by women. It printed pictures of its composing rooms, showing women workers, to prove its complete feminization. The *Ladies' Own Magazine*

[22] Treated more fully in sketch 19.

(1869–74) was edited and published by Mrs. M. Cora Bland in Indianapolis; and *Woman's Words: An Original Review of What Women Are Doing* (1877–81) was edited by Mrs. Juan Lewis in Philadelphia.

All this activity on the part of "editresses" met with severe censure from certain arbiters of manners and morals. The New York *Citizen* voiced a not uncommon opinion when it asserted that "for total disregard of all the restraints of propriety," there was nothing quite so shamefully disregardful as the journals edited by "strong-minded women." [23] But this was only crying against the wind.

One antisuffrage periodical raised its standard — the *True Woman* (1870–73), a monthly edited by Mrs. Charlotte E. McKay. It was begun in Baltimore, but moved to Washington for its last number or two.

WOMAN'S DRESS AGAIN

The perennial topic of woman's dress was, of course, occasionally discussed in the general magazines. There were two phases of the matter — the debate on the "hygienic dress" ideas of such reformers as Mrs. Bloomer and Dr. Walker, and the comment upon the widespread extravagance in styles and in expenditure for dress immediately after the war. Criticism of both extremes was common. Dress reform was discussed somewhat more calmly than in the preceding period; [24] the *North American Review* devoted one of its symposia to the subject in 1885. Extravagance in dress was a lively topic somewhat earlier. "There is no sign of the times so full of dread omen to the nation," said the *Round Table* in 1865, "than the unbounded extravagance of the women." [25] When the reader finds, in a neighboring column, the advertisement of "J. W. Bradley's New Patent Duplex Elliptic (or Double) Spring Skirt," he decides that the editor may be right.

A full-dressed Girl of the Period [said one of *Punchinello's* comic writers], as she sails out for an afternoon airin, looks like somethin

[23] Quoted in *Printers' Circular*, IV, 330 (November 1869).
[24] See vol. II, pp. 50–56. In 1870 E. D. Draper, one of the founders of the *Woman's Journal*, was offering silk for bloomers to all who would wear them.
[25] *Round Table*, II, 2 (September 30, 1865).

as I imagine the north pole would, with a ½ dozen rainbows rapt about it . . . there's more flummy-diddles and mushroom attachments to a woman's toggery nowadays than there is honest men in Wall Street. Durin the past season, overskirts and panears have been looped up, makin the fair secks look as if she was gettin her garments in trim to leap over some frog-pond. . . . Long trailin dresses are agin comin into fashin, to the great detriment of the legitimate okerpashon of street-sweepin.[26]

Chic was much alarmed about the fashion of bare arms. "In the name of all that men have hitherto held sacred in clothing, let us ask where this thing is to end," it wailed.[27] Bangs received no little attention in various journals when they became the mode in 1880.[28]

Fashion magazines flourished as never before. Most of the women's periodicals dealt with fashions to some extent, but many new monthlies devoted chiefly to the styles were begun in the postbellum period — nearly all of them in New York and Philadelphia. Ayer lists eighteen fashion magazines in New York alone in 1880. William Jennings Demorest, publisher of several periodicals, including a *Mirror of Fashion* since 1860, founded *Demorest's Monthly Magazine*[29] in 1865 and with the help of "Madame" Demorest and "Jennie June" made it a pronounced success. It was in 1868 that Ebenezer Butterick began his modest *Metropolitan* to advertise the paper dress patterns which he had invented. Paper patterns, by the way, when used in connection with the newly popular sewing machines, revolutionized home dressmaking. Butterick in 1873 started the lower-priced *Delineator*,[30] which rapidly gained popularity. Meantime *Demorest's* had become a competitor in patterns, and gave them away with each issue of the magazine as Frank Leslie had done in his *Ladies' Gazette* as early as 1855. But the most successful purveyor of styles in our period was *Harper's Bazar*,[31] founded in 1867 and published weekly for a third of a century before it also turned to monthly issue. The *Bazar*,

[26] *Punchinello*, II, 187 (December 17, 1870).
[27] *Chic*, March 1, 1881, p. 2.
[28] *Ibid.*, September 15, 1880, p. 7.
[29] Treated more fully in sketch 2.
[30] Treated more fully in sketch 22.
[31] Treated more fully in sketch 9.

though it adopted the practice of enclosing tracing patterns, was from the first much more than a fashion magazine: it was a woman's *Harper's Weekly*.

Somewhat less important among fashion periodicals was *Frank Leslie's Ladies' Journal* (1871–81), the early numbers of which were called *Once a Week*, and which was the weekly associate of the monthly *Frank Leslie's Lady's Magazine*.[32] George Munro, also a publisher of a string of periodicals, issued the monthly *Fashion Bazar* in 1879–89. One of several advertising journals devoted to dressmaking and fashions was the widely distributed *Style* (1880–94), published by the Domestic Sewing Machine Company. *Toilettes* (1881–1914) was called the *Criterion of Fashion* in its last year. All of these and more [33] were issued from New York.

MAGAZINES FOR WOMEN AND THE HOME

Harper's Bazar, Frank Leslie's Ladies' Journal, and *Demorest's* might well be classed with that larger group of magazines which took some thought of literature as well as of styles in dress, and which upon occasion followed women into the kitchen and the nursery. Of this group, the old Philadelphia leaders — *Godey's, Peterson's*, and *Arthur's* — and *Frank Leslie's Lady's Magazine* in New York — continued along paths already laid out.[34] Boston's *Ladies' Repository*[35] ended with 1873, and Cincinnati's magazine of the same name changed to *National Repository*[36] in 1877 for its last few years of existence.

New York established its preëminence as the publication center for "home" magazines in the seventies. *Wood's Household Magazine* (1867–81) was moved there from Newburgh, New York, where S. S. Wood had established it and where

---

[32] Treated more fully in vol. II, sketch 23.

[33] Among the others were *Ehrick's Fashion Quarterly* (1867–87), a *Delineator* subsidiary called *Metropolitan Fashions* (1873–88), *Andrew's Bazar* (1874–83) moved from Cincinnati to New York in 1879, *Lady's Bazar* (1877–86), *Benedict's Fashion Journal* (1878–87) of Philadelphia, the quarterly *Ridley's Fashion Magazine* (1880–90), *Season* (1882–96). Except as stated, the above were all New York monthlies.

[34] For *Godey's* see Mott, *History of American Magazines, 1741–1850*, pp. 580–594; for the others, see vol. II, sketches 6, 20, and 23, respectively.

[35] See vol. II, p. 57.

[36] Treated more fully in vol. II, sketch 5.

"Gail Hamilton" was its "editor for a year" [37] about 1870. The more important weekly magazine *Hearth and Home* was founded by the advertising firm of Pettengill, Bates & Company in 1868 "for the farm, garden and fireside." Donald G. Mitchell and Harriet Beecher Stowe were editors, and Mary Mapes Dodge and Joseph B. Lyman associates, at the start; but Lyman and Mrs. Stowe left the staff after the first year. Edward and George Cary Eggleston and Frank R. Stockton were later associate editors. At first the new journal was carefully balanced between agriculture on one side and literature and the home on the other, but it gradually abandoned the farm and became a home literary miscellany. Its tables of contents listed many well-known names, and two notable serials appeared in it — E. P. Roe's *A Chestnut Burr* (later famous under its book title, *The Opening of a Chestnut Burr*) and Edward Eggleston's *The Hoosier Schoolmaster*. But *Hearth and Home* lasted only seven years.[38]

The *Domestic Monthly* (1873–95), "an illustrated magazine of fashions, literature, and the domestic arts," was edited in New York by H. C. Faulkner and attained a considerable circulation. In the same city the *Ladies' Illustrated Newspaper* was published monthly, 1874–86. S. H. Moore's *Fireside at Home* (1879–1918) was a monthly which sold for fifty cents a year and throve upon mail-order advertising; it changed its name to *Ladies' World* in 1887. Another New York monthly of the same kind and price was the *Housewife* (1882–1917). The *Brooklyn Advance* (1877–86) was a monthly home journal published first as *Our Neighborhood*.

Turning to Philadelphia, we find two or three distinctive new

[37] Augusta Dodge, *Gail Hamilton's Life in Letters* (Boston, 1901), II, 653.

[38] December 26, 1868–December 25, 1875. Holmes, Bryant, Trowbridge, and Grace Greenwood were all in the first number, and Nast drew the paper's first picture. Andrew S. Fuller and W. C. Flagg of Alton, Illinois, joined the staff in the second year. The paper "lost a fortune to its proprietors" in its first two years. It was sold to Orange Judd & Company, publishers of the *American Agriculturist*, in October 1870, and David W. Judd took charge, though Mrs. Dodge remained on the staff until she became editor of *St. Nicholas* in 1873. For a time the literary quality declined, and then fiction increased. Departments of household hints, juvenile reading, and current events were retained; and there was copious illustration. Among contributors were E. E. Hale, Mrs. R. H. Davis, Rose Terry Cooke, Harriet P. Spofford, Louisa M. Alcott, Elizabeth S. Phelps.

women's journals, one of which was to develop in later years an outstanding success. This was the *Ladies' Home Journal*,[39] founded in 1883 by Cyrus H. K. Curtis. It was edited by Mrs. Curtis, who hid her identity more or less effectually under the pen name of "Mrs. Louisa Knapp." At first it was a cheaply printed eight-page small folio at fifty cents a year, and its first serial was a sentimental Ella Wheeler tale. But it continually enlisted more and better writers, it enlarged its size, its publisher developed a genius for promotion, and by the end of our period it was claiming a quarter of a million circulation. The *Caterer and Household Magazine* (1882–87), also of Philadelphia, had a literary and gustatory flavor all its own. James W. Parkinson, its editor for the first two years, claimed "some little judgment as a gourmet," and his "Cat Club Papers," articles on dining, and selected recipes and verse made a pleasing menu. The name was changed to *Cheer* for the last six months. *Our Second Century* was a family weekly of eight folio pages published in Philadelphia, 1876–86.

Two women's magazines of long life appeared in Boston in the seventies — the cheap *Woman's Home Journal* (1878–1909), and D. L. Milliken's more distinguished *Cottage Hearth* (1874–94). To the latter such writers as Edward Everett Hale, Joaquin Miller, Susan Warner, Lucy Larcom, and Rose Terry Cooke contributed. An equally distinguished group of contributors appeared in the *Woman's Century* (1877–90), published at Brattleboro, Vermont, by Frank E. Housh and edited by his wife, Esther T. It changed its title in December 1884 to the *Woman's Magazine*. At New Haven, E. C. Baldwin published the *Home World*, 1880–88.

Out in Cleveland, Ohio, the *Home Companion* began in 1873 as a small monthly juvenile. Eleven years later it was purchased by the successful publishers of *Farm and Fireside* at Springfield, Ohio, and made a semimonthly women's periodical, later to attain success as the *Woman's Home Companion*.[40]

There was much reliance on chromo premiums in the early seventies. The New York Graphic Company bought the paper in June 1874, reducing the size. See George Cary Eggleston, *Recollections of a Varied Life* (New York, 1910).

[39] To be treated more fully in a separate sketch in the succeeding volume of this work.

[40] To be treated more fully in a separate sketch in the succeeding volume of this work.

Chicago was prolific in magazines designed for women and the home, but most of them were of brief duration. The most important was Edward P. Fenn's *Western Home* (1868–71), which was aided by the pens of Mrs. Stowe and Robert Collyer. It perished in the great fire, though a revival was attempted 1874–75. One of the biggest of Chicago circulations was that of *Our Fireside Friend* (1872–75), which boomed its list to 100,000 in order to attract mail-order advertising that did not come in sufficient quantities to pay the printer and paper maker.

At Minneapolis was the *Housekeeper* (1877–1913), which was climbing toward high circulation at the close of our period. San Francisco had a *Ladies' Home Journal*, 1877–87.

Magazines designed for women, the home, the fireside, and so on were often infected with the virus of mail-order advertising,[41] which inevitably had a cheapening effect upon paper stock, presswork, and contents.

SOCIETY JOURNALS

A type of urban and urbane weekly grew up in the years after the war which was comparatively new to American journalism. Its prototype, perhaps, was the New York *Home Journal*.[42] It was smart, clever, literary, and interested in art and in amusements. It devoted many of its columns to society chat. It flourished only in large cities, and in most of them its proper development came very late in our period. Certain literary weeklies, such as the *Wasp* and *News-Letter* in San Francisco,[43] fell in with this trend only late in the eighties or nineties.

Such weeklies seemed to flourish best in Boston. The *Suffolk County Journal*, begun in 1846 as a community newspaper at Roxbury, came to the city in the seventies and changed its name to *Boston Home Journal*, devoting itself to society and travel until its end in 1905. The *Saturday Evening Herald* (1874–1908) was "devoted to literature, art, music, and society": in its later years "society" should have been placed first in the list. John M. Dandy was an editor for over twenty years, and Lyman B. Glover, an accomplished writer and dramatic

---

[41] See pp. 37–39.
[42] Treated more fully in vol. II, sketch 11.   [43] See p. 56.

critic, for more than a decade. The *Boston Beacon* (1884–1904) was likewise devoted to literature and society.[44]

George Pope Morris died in 1864, and Nathaniel Parker Willis three years later; but Morris Phillips, the adopted son of General Morris, carried on the *Home Journal*[45] in New York, making it more and more a social reporter. The *Fifth Avenue Journal* (1872–73), brief though it was, had the distinction of a series of *portraits chargés* by Frank Bellew. In 1879 W. R. Andrew came to New York from Cincinnati, where he had been publishing a fashion journal, and founded *Andrew's American Queen* as a society paper: it was later to become the famous (and occasionally infamous) *Town Topics.*[46]

In Baltimore, the *Telegram* (1862–1907), which had formerly been a Sunday-reading paper, turned to society and drama. The *World Magazine* (1870–93) in Chicago specialized in society, the drama, and fiction.

EDUCATION OF WOMEN

While the periodicals that have just been discussed devoted themselves to increasingly specialized fields within women's interests, the general magazines continued their debates upon various phases of the "woman question." One of those phases was education.

Vassar Female College had been opened in 1865, and nearly every periodical in the country made its comment on the event. There had been "female seminaries" before, as well as some examples of coeducation, but Vassar was the first conspicuous women's college. The *Round Table*, in the following rather ill-written remarks, was in agreement with most of the editors:

> To compel the female brain to do the work of the male brain is just as much as to unsex the fair sex as to make her arms or her back perform masculine labor. . . . Drag not "the young girl put into your hands" into the wide orbit of Jupiter, where she must tire and droop in the extended course; but lead her in the narrower and more

[44] Cyrus A. Page was its editor until 1898, being succeeded by Huntington Smith. It was merged in M. M. Ballou's *Boston Budget* (1879–1918) in 1905.
[45] See separate sketch 11, vol. II.
[46] The history of *Town Topics* belongs to a later period; it will be detailed in the next volume of this series.

befitting sphere in which moves the "silvery car" of Venus. . . .
Banish the barbarous curriculum proposed by your committee —
dead languages, higher mathematics, metaphysics, and similar un-
feminine studies. . . . Substitute belles lettres. . . . This is the
appropriate field for the well-educated woman.[47]

Better comment on the education of women is to be found in
several articles in *Scribner's Monthly*. The *National Quarterly
Review* claimed that a very severe article in which it called Vassar "a third-rate boarding school" brought it five hundred commendatory letters and many new subscriptions.[48]

The question of women's participation in sports was another
difficult question. *Appleton's Journal*, while approving plenty
of outdoor exercise for women, condemned public display, declaring that "the competition of women with each other in
swimming or rowing matches is intensely repugnant to every
conception we have of the sex." [49]

[47] *Round Table*, I, 164–165 (February 27, 1864). The *Round Table* relents
somewhat in III, 345 (June 2, 1866).
[48] *National Quarterly Review*, XVII, 294 (September 1868); XIX, 124 (June
1869); XIX, 381 (September 1869).
[49] *Appleton's Journal*, IV, 438 (October 8, 1870).

CHAPTER V

SCIENTIFIC, TECHNICAL, AND TRADE JOURNALS

SPECIALIZATION was the trend of the era. "No one who watches the growth and progress of journalism," observed the *Scientific American* in 1870, "can fail to mark the tendency of the age toward the establishment and support of publications devoted to specialties." [1] This tendency was progressively strengthened throughout the postbellum period, until by 1885 there were few occupations, activities, or interests which did not have their own groups of periodicals. To consider certain of these specialized groups — commonly called "class periodicals" — in the years of 1865–85 is the purpose of this chapter.

It will be wise, however, in order to afford some perspective for a survey of technological journals, to examine briefly the advancement of science in the period as reflected in more general magazines.

POPULAR INTEREST IN SCIENCE

The extraordinary growth of American interest in scientific matters in the sixties and seventies was attested on every hand, but nowhere more markedly than in the magazines and newspapers. In beginning the *American Naturalist*, its editors spoke of "the rapidly increasing interest in the various departments of natural history";[2] while the founders of the *Popular Science Monthly* in 1872 and of the *Western Review of Science and Industry* (Kansas City, 1877) insisted in their salutatories upon "increasing interest in science" as the reason for their ventures.[3] Simon Newcomb wrote in the *North American Review* in 1874:

Within the past three or four years there has been a large increase in the amount of popular science publication in this country, which is seen in the establishment of a scientific magazine and in the appear-

---

[1] *Scientific American*, XXII, 47 (January 15, 1870).
[2] *American Naturalist*, I, 1 (March 1867).
[3] *Popular Science Monthly*, I, 113 (May 1872); *Western Review of Science and Industry*, I, 1 (February 1877).

ance of "scientific columns" and "scientific departments" in many of our newspapers and magazines.

Professor Newcomb condemned the inaccuracy of many of these "scientific" notes, but added:

The most notable exceptions have been the "Scientific Department" of the *Atlantic Monthly* while it lasted, the "Editor's Table" of the *Popular Science Monthly*, and of late the "Scientific Record" of *Harper's Magazine.*

Silliman's *Journal of Science* he named as the "solitary periodical of the first rank" in science.[4]

The *Atlantic* added the word "Science" to its subtitle in 1868. Nearly all the magazines established departments of scientific notes. *Appleton's Journal*, edited at first by E. L. Youmans, gave considerable attention to such matters. Science ranked next before fiction, travel, and history-biography in number of pages in the *Galaxy* file, and that standing may be taken as typical of the general magazines for this period.

Scribner's reported a significant observation made by Whitelaw Reid in an address in 1873 at Dartmouth College:

Ten or fifteen years ago, the staple subject here for reading and talk, outside study hours, was English poetry and fiction. Now it is English science. Herbert Spencer, John Stuart Mill, Huxley, Darwin, Tyndall, have usurped the places of Tennyson and Browning, and Matthew Arnold and Dickens.[5]

Another sign of this trend is found in the statistics kept by the Astor Library, in New York, which show that by 1872 scientific works had advanced to a popularity equal to that of books of general literature among the Astor's readers.[6]

Scientific education in the schools was making a notable advance. D. C. Gilman pointed out in the *North American* in 1867 that the newly organized land-grant colleges were "national schools of science."[7] C. W. Eliot, writing in the *Atlantic*

---

[4] *North American Review*, CXIX, 286 (October 1874). See also, to the same effect, the *Annual American Cyclopaedia* for 1873, p. 410.

[5] *Scribner's Monthly*, VI, 608 (September 1873).

[6] *Ibid.*, VI, 381 (July 1873).

[7] *North American Review*, CV, 495 (October 1867). But see also article by Professor F. W. Clarke on "American Colleges vs. American Science," *Popular Science Monthly*, IX, 467 (August 1876), in which the scientific scholarship of these colleges is criticized.

two years later, reviewed the scientific and technological courses available in higher education: there were the Sheffield Scientific School at Yale, the Lawrence Scientific School at Harvard, the School of Mines at Columbia, the Rensselaer Polytechnic Institute at Troy, New York, the Massachusetts Institute of Technology at Boston, and scientific courses paralleling the classical courses at Brown University, Union College, and the University of Michigan.[8] German influence became paramount in scientific study. "As students once gathered in Paris, so now they flock to Germany," observed *Science* in 1883.[9]

Of course, a part of the interest in science which distinguished the period was technological: an unusual number of important inventions, keeping pace with rapidly developing industries, caught the popular imagination. "The leading feature of American science," pronounced one observer, "is its utilitarianism." [10] Another incentive to scientific interest was the spread of the contagion for "collecting." This may be traced back to the stimulation of the lyceums in collecting geological specimens before the war,[11] but the work of Agassiz and Audubon and the organization of societies bearing their names and devoted largely to collecting natural history specimens carried the fever on. Interest in the new science of microscopy brought about the organization of other clubs to buy expensive instruments to be used in common.

So far as pure science was concerned, it received general attention through one phase — the acrimonious and universal discussion of a single theory in the field of biology. George E. Pond stated the matter without exaggeration in the *Galaxy:*

The Taine of the twentieth century who shall study the literature of the nineteenth will note an epochal earmark. He will discover a universal drenching of *belles-lettres* with science and sociology, while the ultimate dominant tinge in our era he will observe to be Darwinism. Not only does all physical research take color from the new theory, but the doctrine sends its pervasive lines through poetry, novels, history. A brisk reaction betrays its disturbing presence in

[8] *Atlantic Monthly*, XXIII, 203 (February 1869).
[9] *Science*, II, 455 (October 5, 1883).
[10] *Ibid.*, I, 1 (February 9, 1883).
[11] See Mott, *A History of American Magazines, 1741–1850*, pp. 446, 489.

theology. Journalism is dyed so deep with it that the favorite logic of the leading article is "survival of the fittest," and the favorite jest is "sexual selection." In the last new book, in the next new book, you will detect it.[12]

The omnipresent evolutionary hypothesis was most prominent in the religious and scientific journals and in such general magazines as gave special attention to science or religion or both. At least one periodical was published largely to exploit the theory — *Evolution*, issued from Boston from 1877 to 1880 under the successive editorships of J. D. Bell and Asa K. Butts. It was not a scientific periodical, but a journal of liberal opinion, with contributions from such writers as George Willis Cooke, B. F. Underwood, and T. W. Higginson. But the opposition to evolutionary ideas was very strong, and a writer in the *Critic* pointed out as late as 1882 that, excepting only Harvard and Cornell, no college in America permitted its faculty to speak out in favor of the doctrine.[13]

Another evidence of great popular interest in matters scientific was the amazing success of John Tyndall's lectures on physics delivered in New York in the winter of 1872–73. They were given with illustrative demonstrations, drew great crowds, and aroused intense interest. Newspapers, as well as such periodicals as the *Scientific American*, reported them fully. The Chicago *Advance* noted that

the *New York Tribune* sold over fifty thousand copies of its special sheet containing full reports of Professor Tyndall's lectures, and this besides an enormous extra sale of the regular issues in which the lectures were first reported. The people have a wonderful appetite for science just now.[14]

JOURNALS DEVOTED TO GENERAL SCIENCE

It is impossible to divide the journals devoted to pure science from those given over to various fields of applied science; nor is it easy to separate technological publications from mere trade magazines and papers. Nearly all the periodicals broke out of

[12] *Galaxy*, XV, 695 (May 1873).
[13] *Critic*, II, 268 (October 7, 1882).
[14] *Advance*, VI, 11 (January 30, 1873).

their prescribed limits more or less: the *Scientific American*, for example, which followed applied science and technology, was frequently concerned with pure science on the one side, and had an alliance with the patent business on the other.

Of journals devoted to general science, there were but two at the beginning of our period — Silliman's *Journal of Science*,[15] then under the care of Benjamin Silliman, Jr., and James Dwight Dana; and the *Scientific American*,[16] interested chiefly in mechanics. There were, of course, occasional publications of state or local scientific organizations, usually of annual, or quarterly, or irregular issue, and made up of official proceedings.

But several general science magazines were founded during the fifteen years after the close of the Civil War. Only one of these belongs to the sixties — the *American Naturalist*, begun in 1867 under an endowment in the will of George Peabody for the advancement of the natural sciences. It was at first published by the Essex Institute, primarily a lyceum, at Salem, Massachusetts, as "a popular illustrated magazine of natural history." But the word "popular" was dropped in the fifth year, and the periodical in time came into other hands, continuing its usefulness particularly in the biological sciences.[17] E. L. Youmans' *Popular Science Monthly* [18] was founded chiefly to speak for Herbert Spencer in America, but its editor's own ability soon made of it an influential and successful popular magazine. Near the end of our period a group of prominent scientists established the weekly *Science* in Cambridge. D. C. Gilman was president and Alexander Graham Bell vice-president of the supporting association, and Samuel H. Scudder was treasurer and editor. It was an immediate success; and although it had its

[15] See Mott, *op. cit.*, p. 302. Ownership of the *Journal* passed to Yale University in 1926 by gift from Edward S. Dana, and it is now endowed. At that time Ernest Howe became editor, and upon his death in 1933 Richard S. Lull succeeded him.

[16] Treated more fully in vol. II, sketch 8.

[17] It was moved to Philadelphia in 1878, but returned to Boston in 1898, where Ginn & Company were publishers. In 1908 the Science Press, New York, took it over, changing the subtitle to indicate a change in policy: "a monthly journal devoted to the advancement of the biological sciences with special reference to the factors of evolution." Leading editors have been A. S. Packard, E. D. Cope, F. C. Kenyon, J. McKeen Cattell (since 1908).

[18] Treated more fully in sketch 24.

difficulties in the later eighties, it regained prestige a few years later.[19]

Some western ventures were less important. S. A. Miller's *Cincinnati Quarterly Journal of Science* (1874–75) was mainly devoted to local conchology and ichthyology. E. H. Fitch's *Scientific Monthly* (1875–76), of Toledo, Ohio, became the *Journal of Science* (1876–82) and was eventually moved to Chicago, where it came into various hands. Theodore S. Case's *Kansas City Review of Science and Industry* (1877–85) dealt with the natural sciences, defended evolution, and "boosted" the West.[20] C. R. Orcutt's *West American Scientist* (1884–1919) was the organ of the San Diego (California) Society of Natural History.

There were other short-lived periodicals devoted to science in its more general aspects, chiefly illustrated weeklies; and there were some advertising journals for collectors of natural history specimens.[21]

JOURNALS OF THE VARIOUS SCIENCES

But many of the sciences had special periodicals of their own long before the end of the postbellum period, and some had half a dozen or more each. Most of these journals were not highly technical, as were the great scholarly reviews that grew up later, but more popular. Chemistry, however, had its *American Chemical Journal* [22] (1879–1913), edited at Johns Hopkins by Ira Remsen; after a long and distinguished life, it was absorbed by a periodical which had begun in the year of its own birth — ·

[19] To be treated more fully in a separate sketch in the succeeding volume of this work.

[20] Until August 1878 it was called *Western Review of Science and Industry*. Warren Watson was editor of the last two numbers.

[21] *Science News* (1878–79) and *Naturalist Advertiser* (1871–75), both of Salem, Massachusetts; *Scientific Man* (1878–82), the monthly *Young Scientist* (1878–87), D. J. Tapley's monthly *American Progress* (1873–91), and *Illustrated Scientific News* (1878–81), all of New York; *Scientific Observer* (1877–87), by the Boston Scientific Society; *Scientific Commercial* (1875–76), Buffalo; *Scientific Record* (1879–81), Washington; *Naturalist and Fancier* (1877–79), Grand Rapids, Michigan; the fortnightly *Bowdoin Scientific Review* (1870–72), Brunswick, Maine; A. E. Foote's *Naturalists' Leisure Hour* (1877–95), Philadelphia, called during its first year *Naturalists' Agency Monthly Bulletin*.

[22] It was published irregularly but with bimonthly intention until 1898, when it became a monthly. C. A. Rouiller was co-editor the last three years. General indexes were published in 1890, 1899, and 1914.

the *Journal of the American Chemical Society*.[23] The *American Chemist* (1870–77) was the New York successor to the American edition of the *Scientific News*. The *American Chemical Review* (1882–87) was a Chicago monthly. Cheaper and more popular in design were the *Journal of Applied Chemistry* [24] and the widely circulated *Boston Journal of Chemistry*.[25] The *American Laboratory* (1874–77), of Boston, was devoted chiefly to chemical experimentation.

Another Johns Hopkins publication was the quarterly *American Journal of Mathematics* (1878–current), edited and published by J. J. Sylvester until 1884, when Simon Newcomb and Thomas Craig took charge of it.[26] J. E. Hendricks' *Analyst* (1874–83), of Des Moines, was a "journal of pure and applied mathematics"; it finally made over its subscription list to Ormond Stone, of the University of Virginia, who began the *Annals of Mathematics* [27] in 1884, making it a bimonthly as the *Analyst* had been. The *Mathematical Magazine* (1882–1910) was "a journal of elementary mathematics" by Artemas Martin; it was issued quarterly in Washington at a dollar a year.[28] For astronomy, the *Sidereal Messenger* (1882–91) was conducted at

[23] Properly dated numbers do not begin until 1893. Edward Hart was editor, 1893–1901; William A. Noyes, 1902–17; Arthur B. Lamb, 1918–current. It has been published from New York, Washington, Cambridge, etc.

[24] "Devoted to chemistry as applied to the arts, manufactures, metallurgy, and agriculture." It was a monthly of sixteen pages, published January 1866 to May 1875; it was issued simultaneously in New York, Philadelphia, and Boston, at $1.50 a year.

[25] It was moved to New York and the name changed to *Popular Science*, later *Popular Science News*, in 1883. It was a monthly "devoted to the science of home life, the arts, agriculture, and medicine." Dr. James R. Nichols and William J. Rolfe were proprietors in Boston, and Benjamin Lillard was the New York owner. It was easily confused with Youmans' *Popular Science Monthly*, which was often called *Appleton's Popular Science Monthly* to make the distinction. It is complete in thirty-six volumes, July 1866 to December 1902.

[26] Called *American Journal of Mathematics Pure and Applied* for its first two years. Frank Morley was editor, 1900–28, and it has since been edited by a board. There were general indexes in 1889 and 1929.

[27] A new series was begun when the magazine was transferred to Harvard University and edited by a board of which Stone was the head; the same board edited it when it was moved to Princeton in 1911. It is still published at Princeton.

[28] This magazine fell as much as three years behind its publishing schedule, its 1884 numbers being issued as late as 1887. It was suspended 1885–89 to catch up, and issued irregularly thereafter.

Northfield, Minnesota, by William W. Payne, of the Goodsell Observatory, Carleton College. It was of high grade and had the general support of scholars in its field.[29]

John M. Coulter began his *Botanical Gazette* in Crawfordsville, Indiana, in 1876,[30] later publishing it in Bloomington, where he had become a professor in the University of Indiana, and at Madison, Wisconsin; in 1896, when he was president of Lake Forest Academy, it was taken into the fold of the University of Chicago Press. *L. B. Case's Botanical Index* (1877–81), of Richmond, Indiana, was less important.

Psyche has been published by the Cambridge Entomological Club since 1874, and *Auk* by the American Ornithological Union since 1876. The latter was the *Bulletin of the Nuttall Ornithological Club*, of Cambridge, for its first seven years. Frank H. Lattin founded the current *Oölogist* at Albion, New York, in 1884, for collectors of birds' eggs, calling it the *Young Oölogist* for two years. Another *Oölogist* (1875–93) was begun by Frank B. Webster at the village of Rockville, Rhode Island; but after moving about and changing its name to *Ornithologist and Oölogist*, it settled in Boston. Of briefer life was the little *New York Aquarium Journal* (1876–77). The *American Journal of Conchology* (1865–72) was edited by George W. Tryon, Jr., and published by the Philadelphia Academy of Natural Sciences.

Amateur interest in science was also reflected in the many microscopists' clubs and periodicals. The first periodical of this type was the *American Journal of Microscopy and Popular Science* (1875–81), of New York. It was followed by the *American Quarterly Microscopical Journal* in 1878, an organ of the New York Microscopical Society, edited by Romyn Hitchcock. This was made a monthly in 1880 and seven years later was taken

[29] In 1892 it was enlarged to include attention to the new discoveries in spectroscopy, and the name was changed to *Astronomy and Astro-Physics*. George E. Hale, of the Kenwood Physical Observatory, Chicago, became joint editor to care for this new phase. It was sold, December 1894, to the University of Chicago Press, which founded its *Astrophysical Journal* as a successor. See *Popular Astronomy*, XI, 593 (December 1932). This journal had no connection with O. M. Mitchel's Cincinnati *Sidereal Messenger* (1846–48).

[30] It was preceded by the *Botanical Bulletin* in 1875. Henry Chandler Cowles became editor in 1929.

over by Charles W. Smiley and moved to Washington, where it was published until 1902. The *Microscope* (1881–97) was founded at Ann Arbor by Charles H. and Louisa Reed Stowell, who gave particular attention to the application of microscopy to the study of medicine. Smiley purchased it in 1892, moving it to Washington, and finally merging it with his *Journal*. The bimonthly *Microscopical Bulletin and Science News* (1883–1902) was published by James W. Queen & Company, of Philadelphia, manufacturers of scientific instruments.

Meteorology had long been a subject of popular interest, occupying a place even in the general magazines: now it had its special periodicals. The *American Meteorologist* was published in St. Louis 1875–77. The government's weather bureau at Washington issued a *Weekly Weather Chronicle*, 1872–81, and its *Bulletin of International Meteorological Observations*, 1875–89.[31] The *American Meteorological Journal* (1884–96) was published at Ann Arbor by Mark W. Harrison, director of the astronomical observatory at the University of Michigan, with editions for Boston, New York, and Chicago.

Geology was represented by the *School of Mines Quarterly* (1879–1915), of New York, the *Paleontological Bulletin* (1872–85), of Philadelphia, and U. P. James's *Paleontologist* (1878–83), of Cincinnati.

The *American Antiquarian and Oriental Journal* (1878–1914), by Stephen D. Peet, was primarily a journal of American archaeology, but included much of ethnology and of Egyptian and classical archaeology.[32] It was published in Chicago.

---

[31] See Henry Carrington Bolton, *A Catalogue of Scientific and Technical Periodicals, 1865–1895* (Washington, Second Edition, 1897), for additional data on this publication and on many others referred to in this chapter.

[32] This was a learned quarterly, the "direct outgrowth of the interest created in American antiquities by the Centennial Exposition in 1876" (XXXIII, 5, January 1911). It began as *American Antiquarian*. In 1881 Peet merged his *Oriental and Biblical Journal* (see p. 84) in it and added *Oriental Journal* to the title. Peet was elected secretary of the American Anthropological Association shortly after he started his journal, and many prominent ethnologists and archaeologists were contributors. He moved the *Antiquarian* to Salem, Massachusetts, in 1909, but relinquished it to J. O. Kinnaman, of Benton Harbor College, in 1911. It was published at Benton Harbor, Michigan, 1911–12, and then for its last two years at Toledo, Ohio. There was considerable illustration of a somewhat inferior grade.

More or less scientific were the journals of numismatics and philately [33] published for collectors; pseudoscientific were the astrological guides.[34]

ENGINEERING AND MINING

In the various technological fields, periodicals sprouted in large numbers, reflecting the rapid progress of a machine age. The two best-known general engineering journals of the post-bellum period were *Van Nostrand's Eclectic Engineering Magazine*,[35] of New York, and George H. Frost's *Engineering News*,[36] of Chicago, which moved to New York in 1879. After Frost's journal deserted the city of its birth, Merrick Cowles and John W. Weston started the *American Engineer* (1880–92) there; in its later years it was devoted chiefly to mechanical engineering. Two famous engineering societies undertook the periodical publication of proceedings in the seventies — the American Society of Civil Engineers and the Engineers' Club of Philadelphia [37] —

[33] These were published for amateur collectors of coins and stamps. Those of longer lives were *American Journal of Numismatics* (1866–1919), Boston; *American Journal of Philately* (1868–1906), *Philatelic Monthly* (1875–99), and *Philatelic World* (1880–91), New York; *Mason's Coin and Stamp Collectors' Journal* (1867–82) and *Coin Collector* (1880–86), Philadelphia. The quarterly *American Antiquarian* (1870–89), New York, was for collectors of autographs, paper money, etc.

[34] The chief astrological journals were *Broughton's Monthly Planet Reader* (1860–67) and *Astrological Journal* (1860–69), Philadelphia; and *American Horological Journal* (1869–73), New York.

[35] The word *Eclectic* was dropped from the title in 1879, and the magazine became original in contents. It was published monthly in New York from 1869. David Van Nostrand was editor and publisher until his death in 1886. Merger with the *American Railroad Journal* took place in 1887.

[36] Founded as a monthly journal of civil engineering in April 1874, it became a weekly with its third volume. The title varies somewhat, beginning as *Engineer and Surveyor*. In April 1917 it was consolidated with the McGraw Publishing Company's *Engineering Record*, which had been founded in New York by Henry C. Meyer, December 1877, as *Plumber and Sanitary Engineer*, called in 1880 *Sanitary Engineer*. The name of the combined journal became *Engineering News-Record*, its present title. General indexes were published in 1890, 1899, 1904, 1909, and 1917. For a list of its many supplements, see *Periodicals*, I, 25–27 (January–March 1918). For historical articles, see *Engineering News*, LXXVIII, 2, 5, 6 (April 5, 1917).

[37] The former society began its monthly *Proceedings* in November 1873. The Philadelphia club began its quarterly *Proceedings* in 1879, making them monthly in 1916, and changing their title in 1922 to *Engineers and Engineering*, which ended in 1932.

and the *Journal of the Association of Engineering Societies* was published monthly in various cities to present the proceedings of clubs in Boston, St. Louis, Chicago, and other engineering centers, 1881–1915. There were a few other engineering periodicals of a general nature,[38] but most of such journals were more or less specialized.

Mining, for example, had a large quota of periodicals. In 1880 Ayer's *Annual* listed fifty-three periodicals devoted to that field.[39] Chief among those surviving in our period from earlier years were the *California Mining and Scientific Press* and the Michigan *Mining Journal.*[40] In the year after the war two prominent papers in this class were begun — the *Chicago Mining Review* (1866–1907), by Edward A. Taft, which changed its name in the nineties to *Mining Review and Metallurgist;* and the *American Journal of Mining*, of New York, which in its fourth year became *Engineering and Mining Journal* and has lived to absorb all the mining periodicals mentioned above and half a dozen more.[41] A famous Colorado journal was the *Mining Review* (1872–77), of Georgetown, which was moved to Denver in 1875 and was later supplanted there by the *Mining and Scientific Review* (1878–95).

Charles W. Eliot once wrote in the *Atlantic Monthly* of "the periodical hot turns of the intermittent mining fever to which the American people is subject." [42] One of these "hot turns" occurred in 1877–79; and it resulted in another crop of mining journals, including the *New York Mining Record* (1877–92), the San Francisco (later New York) *Mining and Metallurgical*

[38] Three others may be mentioned: *Technologist* (1870–77), New York; *Engineer of the Pacific* (1877–80), San Francisco; *Stevens Indicator* (1884–current), of the Stevens Institute of Technology, Hoboken, oldest of alumni journals in this field.

[39] Few of these were really engineering journals, however. Many were investment journals, and some were little more than newspapers of mining fields.

[40] See vol. II, pp. 80–81.

[41] G. F. Dawson was the first editor. He was succeeded by R. W. Raymond in 1867. R. P. Rothwell was editor, 1874–1901, for the first fifteen years of that period jointly with Raymond. It was weekly, 1866–1929, and then became semimonthly. In 1906 it was purchased by the Hill Publishing Company, McGraw-Hill since 1917. For a list of supplements and plates, see *Periodicals*, I, 13–14 (October–December 1917).

[42] *Atlantic Monthly*, XXIII, 212 (February 1869).

Journal (1878–1901), the much more general *School of Mines Quarterly* (1879–1915), of Columbia University, and others.[43]

MECHANICS AND INVENTION

Indeed nothing can be more obvious to the student of the class magazines than the fact that each group, and in a smaller degree each individual periodical, possesses a historical significance which is not limited to its own narrow field. Each group interprets a phase of social, economic, or intellectual activity; each magazine helps to give the reader of the dusty files an understanding of a special aspect of its times.

So it is with the mechanical journals. Not the least interesting phase of the various and exciting postbellum period was the activity of inventors. "Mechanical ingenuity," said Tyndall, lately returned from America, in an address to the Royal Society, "engages a greater number of minds in the United States than in any other nation in the world." [44] Accordingly, there were a score or more of periodicals devoted to patents, and others devoted to the more scientific aspects of mechanics. Chief of the publications which gave special attention to the interests of inventors were the old *Journal of the Franklin Institute*,[45] which began its fortieth year in 1865, and the *Scientific American*,[46] which was half that age. Growing up in New York during this period were the *American Artisan and Patent Record*,[47] the *American Machinist*,[48] *Steam*,[49] and the *Mechanical*

[43] Including also the *Maine Mining Journal* (1880–1918), which became *Industrial Journal* in 1883, of Bangor and Portland; *Ohio Mining Journal* (1882–98), Columbus; *Colliery Engineer* (1881–1915), which began as *Mining Herald*, Pottsville, Scranton; and many which lasted only a year or two.

[44] *Popular Science Monthly*, XIV, 569 (March 1879).

[45] See Mott, *op. cit.*, p. 556.

[46] Treated more fully in vol. II, sketch 8.

[47] Published May 11, 1864–December 1865. It dropped the second part of its title in 1869, but in 1872 added another: an *Illustrated Journal of Popular Science*. H. T. Brown was the chief editor. It was a weekly until its last year, when it changed to monthly publication. It is not to be confused with S. Fleet's *American Artisan* of 1848.

[48] Published since November 1877. It began as a monthly, but adopted weekly publication in July 1879. Jackson Bailey was editor until 1888, and Horace B. Miller was the first publisher. John A. Hill became publisher in 1896, and the McGraw-Hill Publishing Company in 1917. Early numbers dealt much with

Engineer [50] — all important journals. *Mechanics* (1882–99), in Philadelphia, was a cheaper monthly by John M. Davis; it broadened its field when it became *Engineering-Mechanics* in 1892. The Boston *Inventor's and Manufacturer's Gazette* was published from 1866 to 1886. Ohio had several periodicals of this class. *Leffel's Illustrated Mechanical News* [51] was published at Springfield; the *Scientific Machinist* (1882–98) was begun as *Western Machinist* at Cleveland; and in Cincinnati the *Artisan* (1878–87) and the *American Inventor* (1878–98), called *World's Progress* after 1889, were low-priced periodicals.

One of the period's chief incentives to invention was the great Centennial Exposition in Philadelphia in 1876. The Centennial's object lesson in American mechanical progress was a matter of national pride. "The world has never seen such a display of machinery," said *Arthur's Home Magazine*.[52] Magazines generally gave a considerable share of attention to the great fair,

---

steam power and foundries; later there was more of welding, press working, machine design, metal cutting, and management. In the nineties it protested against neglect of the human element in scientific management. It took a leading part in founding the American Society of Mechanical Engineers. See "Fifty Years of the *American Machinist*" by James H. McGraw, LXVI, 824 (May 19, 1927).

[49] *Steam* was founded in 1880 as a monthly. *Power* was begun in September 1884, also as a monthly, by H. L. Swetland. In November 1884 Swetland took over *Steam* and incorporated it into his new periodical, calling it *Power-Steam*. For a few months he carried the numbering of both papers, but later he adopted that of *Steam*. In 1892 the name reverted to *Power*, though for about three years after the absorption of the Chicago *Engineer* in 1908 it was called *Power and the Engineer*. In 1904 it was purchased by the Hill Publishing Company, which became McGraw-Hill Publishing Company in the merger of 1917. It adopted weekly publication in 1908. It has been devoted to the "generation and transmission of power," and its file is almost a textbook and history for this field. It has been well illustrated. For list of supplements, see *Periodicals*, I, 20 (January–March 1918).

[50] Founded in 1881 by Egbert P. Watson; broadened in scope in 1888 with change of title to *Engineer*. In 1898 it absorbed *Scientific Machinist*, of Cleveland, and moved to that city, devoting itself to power plant engineering, Arthur L. Rice, editor. Five years later it moved to Chicago, ending in 1908.

[51] Published March 1871–February 1894. It was originally a monthly small folio of eight pages selling for fifty cents a year. It gained a circulation of twenty thousand; and then James Leffel, publisher, moved it to New York in 1881, publishing it bimonthly at a dollar and a half under the title *Mechanical News*. While at Springfield it specialized in milling, bearing the title for a time of *Leffel's Illustrated Milling and Mechanical News*.

[52] *Arthur's Home Magazine*, XLIV, 232 (April 1876).

and the pictorials often played up its show of mechanics and invention. Several periodicals were founded solely to describe the Centennial; of these the most important was the *Scientific American Supplement* (1876–1919), later continued as a monthly somewhat more technical in nature than its weekly parent. The world's fair at Vienna in 1873 also excited much attention in American magazines.

One of the most important mechanical developments of the times was that of the sewing machine. Though actually invented in the forties, it was not until after the war that it was widely manufactured and exploited. James Parton, writing in the *Atlantic Monthly* in 1867, estimated that "we are now producing the astounding and almost incredible number of one thousand sewing machines every working day, at an average cost to the purchaser of sixty dollars each." [53] The leading manufacturers combined to keep the price up and asked Congress to renew the patents in 1873 — to the indignation of the *Scientific American*, which claimed that the cost of manufacture was $5.00 to $7.00, while the prices at retail at that time ranged from $60 to $125.[54] There were several periodicals devoted to the industry, of which the *Sewing Machine Journal* (1873–93) and the *Sewing Machine News* (1877–93), both of New York, and the Chicago *Sewing Machine Advocate* (1879–1913), were the leaders.

Great improvements were made in printing presses. A Walter press, of the type that was working "a revolution in newspaper printing" by impressing the stereotyped forms on a continuous roll and delivering twelve thousand eight-page papers an hour, was installed in the office of the *New York Times* in 1873.[55] The interested reader may follow various improvements connected with printing in the weekly numbers of the *Scientific American:* Andrew Campbell's perfecting press and folder, Benjamin C. Tilghman's development of chemical pulp in paper making, diverse experiments in typesetting machines. Such developments were occasionally noticed in the printers' journals, though these were mainly concerned with the art of typography and the business of printing and publishing.[56]

[53] *Atlantic Monthly*, XIX, 540 (May 1867).
[54] *Scientific American*, XXVIII, 49 (January 25, 1873).
[55] *Ibid.*, XXVIII, 21 (January 1, 1873); XXIX, 321 (November 22, 1873).
[56] See pp. 131–32.

Another invention of great importance to journalism was that of the typewriter. The work of Sholes and Densmore and the manufacture of their machine by the Remington Arms Company received some notice. A revolution in the mechanics of literary composition was heralded by this advertisement:

Literati: Men of Letters may now dispense with amanuenses. A flow of thought may be transcribed by the use of the Type Writer as swiftly as it can be uttered and with a far greater degree of legibility than by the old process of dictation and transcription with the pen.[57]

The perfection of fire-fighting equipment, improvement of fireproofing, and the study of the causes of fires were matters of great concern in our period. Periodicals dealing with mechanical invention, civil engineering, construction, and insurance devoted many pages to the fire problem. The Portland fire in 1866, the terrible Chicago conflagration of 1871, the great fire in Boston in 1872, and the destructive forest fires in Michigan and Wisconsin furnished the chief reasons for these discussions. The great fires "have filled the country with alarm," said *Harper's Weekly*.[58] The illustrated journals printed many pictures of conflagrations; full-page woodcuts of flaming buildings and rescues by firemen were long a staple of such journals. There were several firemen's periodicals, the two most important of which were the *National Fireman's Journal*[59] and the *Fireman's Herald*,[60] both of New York.

Inventions related to transportation and farming will be referred to in the sections devoted to the periodicals of those industries.[61]

WIZARDRY OF ELECTRICITY

But the field of invention which really caught the popular imagination was electricity; and the inventor whose name stands out clearly above all others in that field was Thomas A. Edison,

---

[57] *Life*, December 11, 1884.

[58] *Harper's Weekly*, XI, 131 (March 2, 1867).

[59] Founded by Clifford Thomson and P. Y. Everett in 1877, the latter soon retiring. It dropped the word *National* from its title after the second annual volume. It was the official organ of state and national organizations of firemen. Later titles have been *Fire and Water* and *Fire Engineering*.

[60] Founded in 1881; name changed to *Fire Service* in 1921; discontinued in 1927.

[61] For applications of electricity to transportation, see p. 126; for new agricultural implements, see pp. 150–51.

whose "seemingly inexhaustible store of wonders," said a writer in *Scribner's Monthly*, "has made him the theme of every tongue." [62]

There were, however, plenty of doubters when Edison first announced his invention of an electric light practicable for house lighting. Electricity had already been used, at great expense, for illumination in lighthouses, and much had been written of experiments in the general field.

> Just now [wrote Professor Youmans in his *Popular Science Monthly* at the end of 1878] a revolution in illumination is widely anticipated. . . . In this state of the public mind, the announcement of Mr. Edison that he had actually solved the problem which would make electrical illumination available for common household uses was generally accepted, as a matter of course, and sent a tremor through the gas-stocks of the world. Nevertheless, the desideratum has not been reached, and, for aught that actually appears, we are no nearer this important consummation than we were twenty years ago.

Then he pointed out that thirty or forty years before, the economical use of electric light had been thought practicable; and he reprinted a contemporary article from the *New York Sun* which declared that "the panic in gas stocks is premature." [63] It was not until February 1880 that *Scribner's Monthly* printed what Edison himself declared to be "the first correct and authoritative account of my invention of the electric light" in an article by his assistant Francis R. Upton.[64] Two months later the *Journal of Science* contained a statement by two well-known professors of physics of tests to which they had subjected the invention in Edison's own laboratories. They testified that they had made this test "in view of the great interest which is now being felt throughout the civilized world in the success of the various attempts to light houses by electricity, together with the contradictory statements made with respect to Mr. Edison's method"; and they concluded that if the lamp itself could be made cheap and durable enough, there was "no reasonable doubt of the success of the light." [65] The ensuing contest between gas

[62] *Scribner's Monthly*, XVIII, 297 (June 1879).
[63] *Popular Science Monthly*, XIV, 234 (December 1878).
[64] *Scribner's Monthly*, XIX, 531 (February 1880).
[65] *American Journal of Science*, CXIX, 337 (April 1880).

and electric lighting belongs to commercial history. It was long drawn out, but its result was never doubtful. In 1883 the *Electrical World* had this news note:

The installation of two hundred Edison lamps in the offices of the *New York Sun* is a notable victory for the Edison company, as one of the principal owners of that journal is a heavy owner of gas stocks. . . . It has had an article this very month insisting that electric lighting was a failure.[66]

Second only to interest in the incandescent lamp was that manifested in one of Edison's inventions which was outside the electrical field — the phonograph, or, as a writer in *Popular Science Monthly* more properly called it, the "speaking phonograph." [67] It was, said this commentator, "the acoustic marvel of the century"; and Edison himself, telling of it in the *North American Review* shortly before his greater invention was announced, declared: "Of all the writer's inventions, none has commanded such profound and earnest attention throughout the civilized world as the phonograph." [68] He then went on to name some of the uses to which it could be put, such as giving dictation, furnishing music, preserving the speeches of orators, and aiding in education. Other ideas for its future have proved less practicable or have, at least, been less used: Edison suggested that the records should be used in place of letters so that correspondence would be spoken as well as written; that books for the blind and invalids be recorded for the phonograph; that relatives preserve the sayings and the voices of loved ones and "the last words of the dying" in this permanent form; that telephone conversations be so recorded; and that a phonographic clock be devised to "tell you the hours of the day, call you to lunch, send your lover home at ten, etc." Apparently a sequel to this article was *Puck's* happy suggestion that irate wives accustomed to wait up for the return of roystering husbands should confide their curtain lectures to the phonograph and themselves seek slumber.[69]

[66] *Electrical World*, I, 263 (April 28, 1883).
[67] *Popular Science Monthly*, XII, 719 (April 1878).
[68] *North American Review*, CXXVI, 527 (May–June 1878).
[69] *Puck*, April 24, 1878, p. 4.

Edison had been working on the telephone when Alexander Graham Bell anticipated him, but the former made an extremely important contribution to the instrument in his carbon receiver. Bell's invention was one of the sensations of the Centennial of 1876, and the next year

during the month of April "telephone concerts," at which large audiences were present, were given in Boston and Washington, through musical instruments played in Philadelphia. At both, the music, though rather feeble in tone, was distinctly heard by the audience in all parts of the hall.[70]

Six years later the *Electrical World* was able to report a capitalization of telephone companies aggregating over a hundred million dollars.[71]

Work on the electric dynamo by the French Gramme, the German Siemens, the English Wheatstone, and the American Weston was duly chronicled in the *Scientific American*, the *Franklin Journal*, and other periodicals; but until about 1880 it was generally thought that the dynamo was not very practical and that electric power could never be made cheap enough to compete with that derivable from steam.[72]

The earliest electrical journals were those devoted to the telegraph.[73] Two newcomers of this group in the years after the war were the Western Union's *Journal of the Telegraph* (1867–1914) and the *Operator* (1874–85), both of New York. The *Journal of the American Electrical Society* was published in Chicago from 1875 to 1880. Then, with the invention of the incandescent light and the improvement of the dynamo, came a dozen or so of electrical journals,[74] of which the most important

[70] *American Journal of Science*, CXIII, 402 (May 1877).

[71] *Electrical World*, I, 502 (August 11, 1883).

[72] See *Scientific American*, XXIX, 352 (December 6, 1873), and *Popular Science Monthly*, XIV, 235 (December 1878).

[73] See vol. II, p. 92.

[74] Besides those mentioned above, there were *Pacific Electrician* (1880–98), San Francisco; *Telegrapher's Advocate* (1883–85), New York; *Electric Age* (1883–1910), New York, called *Electrical Age* after 1899, which had a varied and sometimes brilliant career, particularly as an international journal under Louis Cassier, 1904–07; *Telegraph Age* (1883–current), New York, called *Telegraph and Telephone Age* since 1909.

were the *Electrical World*[75] and *Electrical Engineer*,[76] of New York; and the *Electrical Review*,[77] of Chicago.

RAILROADS AND THEIR TROUBLES

The driving of the last spike on the Union Pacific Railroad at Promontory Point, Utah, May 10, 1869, produced a spontaneous ebullition of enthusiasm all over the country. It was greeted as the beginning of a new era of American history. In celebration of the event, the *Nation* tells us, Chicago had a seven-mile procession; New York hung out bunting, fired one hundred guns, and held services in Trinity Church; and Philadelphia rang the Liberty Bell.[78] But soon the shrewd weekly just quoted was warning its readers against too much confidence in railroad investments:

The cotton and grain speculation, the real estate speculation, the gold and stock speculation, have all had their share of comment, favorable and otherwise; but the railroad-building speculation, which in magnitude far surpasses all the others, seems to have almost entirely escaped scrutiny.[79]

[75] Founded by W. J. Johnston, January 6, 1883, as a weekly. It was not a separate paper, however, until April 24 of that year. Johnston had been publishing the *Operator* and at the beginning of 1883 gave it the name *Operator and Electrical World;* then he separated the two in April, but the *Electrical World* retained numbering from the first of the year, its first separate issue being Vol. I, Number 17. The *World* eventually absorbed the *Operator*, in 1885, as well as half a dozen other periodicals in its field from time to time. T. C. Martin was editor, 1889–1909, following Johnston; and W. D. Weaver, 1899–1912. It has added various names to its title from time to time on account of consolidations. It has been well illustrated, and its patent record has been a prominent feature. It affords a remarkable history of electrical development since 1883.

[76] Published January 1882–March 2, 1899. F. L. Pope was editor, 1884–90. It began as a monthly called *Electrician*, changed title to *Electrician and Electrical Engineer* in 1884, and finally dropped the first part of its title in 1888. It adopted weekly publication in April 1890. Its contributors were among the leading electrical engineers; it was quite the equal of the *Electrical World*, with which it was finally merged.

[77] Founded February 15, 1882, as *Review of the Telegraph and Telephone; Electrical Review*, 1883–1921; *Industrial Engineering*, 1922–31; *Maintenance Engineering* (New York), 1931–32; *Factory Management and Maintenance*, 1932–current. It absorbed several other journals in its field. Charles W. Price, a great figure in the industry, was editor and publisher, 1891–1921.

[78] *Nation*, II, 365 (May 13, 1866).

[79] *Ibid.*, VIII, 185 (March 11, 1869).

Harper's Weekly had, however, pointed out, nearly four years before, the peril of investment in railroad stocks because of the ease in the manipulation of them by the financiers in control.[80] This manipulation was an outstanding scandal in an era of scandals. "Railroads are managed," said a writer in the *Atlantic*, "according to a system which enables directors to make enormous fortunes at the expense of those whose interests they are bound in honor and equity to protect." [81] The *Nation* returned to the subject again and again. "Railroad securities now constitute probably the most popular form of investment of a personal nature now open to the people of the United States," it said in 1872. "A sort of mania as regards them may be said to exist." Then it recalled that railroad speculation brought on the panic of 1857, immediately disclaiming any intention of predicting a panic at that time.[82] This was a year and a month before the crash actually came.

In the meantime there were many complaints about the high-handed conduct of the railroads in their dealings with shippers, passengers, and employes. To be sure, travel, as a writer in *Appleton's Journal* pointed out, was much pleasanter than ever before. There were "larger, finer, more convenient, and more comfortable cars"; [83] and the invention of the Westinghouse air brake made for both speed and safety. But the arrogance of the roads, financially and politically, created ill feeling. "The railroads have got the upper hand, and they seem likely to keep it," commented the *Scientific American* in 1870.[84] The railroad articles of Charles Francis Adams, Jr., in the *North American Review* were exceptionally able. The *Atlantic Monthly* in 1872 printed the story of an aggrieved passenger who summed the matter up as follows: "The public has been so busy in this new country that it has permitted the railroad men to steal away its liberties." [85] Even the *American Railroad Journal*, theretofore a special pleader for the roads, changed its policy in 1875 and promised "free and impartial discussions of the questions at

[80] *Harper's Weekly*, IX, 722 (November 18, 1865).
[81] *Atlantic Monthly*, XXXII, 510 (October 1873).
[82] *Nation*, XV, 102 (August 15, 1872).
[83] *Appleton's Journal*, IV, 114 (July 23, 1870).
[84] *Scientific American*, XXII, 7 (January 1, 1870).
[85] *Atlantic Monthly*, XXX, 642 (December 1872).

issue between the railroads and the public"; it believed that the railroads' power "now threatens to become greater than the source from which it was derived." [86]

The great agrarian discontent of the period was, in one of its phases, a war with the railroads. Freights on agricultural products seemed exorbitant. W. M. Grosvenor, writing in the *Atlantic*, spoke with passion:

> The bandits of modern civilization, who enrich themselves by the plunder of others, come with chests full of charters; judges are their friends, if not their tools; and they wield no weapon more alarming than the little pencil with which they calculate differences in rates.

Yet he thinks that the farmers should abandon their ideas of state control of rates, should adhere to the natural alliance between farm and road, and should look to tariff reform for their salvation.[87]

But if the railroads were threatened with rate control on the one hand, they were not, on the other, earning profits on their capitalization.[88] By 1873 the construction of new roads had declined greatly — "an encouraging sign," said the *Nation*.[89]

Less encouraging were the disputes with workmen, and as the decade progressed the signs of a labor revolt became more ominous. The widespread and bloody general railroad strike of July 1877 came, nevertheless, as a shock to the country; and the burden of comment in the periodicals was in the nature of protest against the violence of the strikers — their "insanity of passion, played upon by designing and mischievous leaders," to use the words of the president of the Pennsylvania Railroad in an article in the *North American Review*.[90] The *Nation* defended the wage cut which provoked the revolt,[91] and declared that the strikers should have been "confronted by trained bodies of men sufficient to overawe or to crush them at the first onset." [92] In its argument for a larger standing army to prevent such "insurrections," the *Nation* was joined by such periodicals

[86] *American Railroad Journal*, September 20, 1879.
[87] *Atlantic Monthly*, XXXII, 591 (November 1873).
[88] *Nation*, VIII, 186 (March 11, 1869).
[89] *Ibid.*, XXI, 1 (July 1, 1875).
[90] *North American Review*, CXXV, 352 (September 1877).
[91] *Nation*, XXV, 99 (August 16, 1877).
[92] *Ibid.*, XXV, 85 (August 9, 1877).

as the *Galaxy*[93] and *Harper's Weekly.*[94] The new *Puck*, in a moment of seriousness, presented a double-page colored cartoon called "The Rioters' Railroad to Ruin," in which a skeleton destroyer rode a locomotive propelled by strikers through a shambles of wounded combatants and burning houses, and commented:

Some of the events of the past week read like a chapter of the French Revolution. . . . After all, it was but a nine days' terror, and the object for which the vandalism and murder took place was not achieved. . . . *Puck* is no friend to railway monopolists, and is of opinion that to some extent they are responsible for the unsettled state of the country by their gross mismanagement.[95]

Several railroad magazines survived from the preceding period;[96] it is significant that the more important newcomers of the seventies were nearly all published in Chicago. There the *Railroad Gazette* began a new series in 1870 and the *Railway Age* six years later; the two were merged in 1908.[97] Fowler and Brooks' weekly *Railway Review* was published in Chicago 1868–1926. There were special union journals for conductors, firemen, brakemen, and mechanics, as well as periodicals for manufacturers of locomotives, cars, and equipment.[98]

[93] *Galaxy*, XXIV, 433 (September 1877).
[94] *Harper's Weekly*, XXI, 618 (August 11, 1877).
[95] *Puck*, I, 2 (August 1, 1877).
[96] See vol. II, p. 81.
[97] The first, or monthly octavo, series of the *Gazette* began in 1857 (see vol. II, p. 81). But when the weekly quarto series was begun in April 1870, with A. N. Kellogg as proprietor, a new series numbering was used, and soon the "whole numbers" were abandoned and the initial series, rare anyway, was forgotten. *Railway Age* was begun as a weekly, June 17, 1876, by E. H. Talbott. The merger with the *Gazette* occurred June 5, 1908; W. H. Boardman, E. A. Simmons, and others formed the publishing company, later called the Simmons-Boardman Company. Boardman, who had long been editor and publisher of the *Gazette*, was editor of the new paper three or four years, and Samuel O. Dunn has been editor since. (For Dunn, see *Reading for Profit*, I, 20, October 1933.) The *Gazette* had moved to New York in 1882, and the *Railroad Age-Gazette*, as the merger was called, was located there; the name was changed to *Railway Age-Gazette* in 1909 and to *Railway Age* in 1918.
[98] The *Railroad Conductors' Brotherhood Monthly* was published in Chicago during the great strike, 1876–78; it was followed by the *Railway Conductor's Monthly* (1884–current), later the *Railway Conductor*, edited by officials of the Order of Railway Conductors first at Elmira, New York, and then at Cedar Rapids, Iowa. *Locomotive Firemen's Magazine* was founded in 1873 at Cin-

Other means of transportation were being exploited by special journals. The *Electrical World* in 1883 thought that electric railways were the next big goal in sight in its own field. "The skeptics may expect to see electricity take the place of steam on the elevated railways of our city within a very few years," it declared;[99] and it recorded the first successful demonstration of electric traction, by Leo Daft at Saratoga, in 1884.[100] The coming of the electric street car in the middle and later eighties may be traced in the *Street Railway Journal*, founded in New York in 1884.[101] Shipping by water was covered by the *Nautical Gazette* and the *Marine Journal*, begun in New York in 1871 and 1878, respectively, and still extant.

And finally, looking forward toward aviation, the interest in certain ballooning experiments may be mentioned. The fiasco of Professor Wise and his partner Donaldson in connection with their project, promoted by the *New York Graphic*, to cross the Atlantic by balloon in September 1873 was fully chronicled in the pictorials.[102]

---

cinnati; in 1901 it became *Brotherhood of Locomotive Firemen's Magazine* at Peoria, Illinois, and six years later *Brotherhood of Locomotive Firemen and Enginemen's Magazine*, now published at Cleveland. The *Western Railroader* began in 1883 at Peoria, becoming the *Railroad Brakemen's Journal* two years later and the *Railroad Trainmen's Journal* in 1890; it is now published at Cleveland as the *Railroad Trainman*. The *Railway Master Mechanic* (1878–1916), Chicago, was called *Railway Purchasing Agent*, 1878–85. The Hartford *Locomotive* (1867–current) is the house organ of a boiler insurance company and specializes in steam power. The *National Car Builder* (1870–95), New York, became *National Car and Locomotive Builder* in 1886. The *American Journal of Railway Appliances* (1881–1901), New York, dropped the first word of its title in 1896. Another New Yorker was the *Official Railway Equipment Register* (1884–1932). Joseph Creamer's *Railroad Record and Investment Guide* was published (1883–1901) in Philadelphia, and Carl I. Ingerson's *Railway Register* (1873–91) in St. Louis. There were also many monthly railroad guides, and many short-lived periodicals for railroaders.

[99] *Electrical World*, I, 438 (July 14, 1883).

[100] *Ibid.*, V, 13 (January 10, 1885).

[101] In effect an organ for the American Street Railway Association, founded in 1882. It was changed from monthly to weekly publication in 1900, and its title was changed in 1908 to *Electric Railway Journal* and again in 1932 to *Transit Journal*. James H. McGraw was editor and manager, 1889–1902, after which the McGraw Company was organized to take it over, becoming McGraw-Hill Publishing Company in 1917. See "Forty Years of the *Electric Railway Journal*," LXIV, 947 (December 6, 1924).

[102] See *Scientific American* in September and October 1873 (Vol. XXIX).

THE GREAT PENNSYLVANIA RAILROAD STRIKE OF 1877

A typical *Harper's Weekly* page of sketches. These are by John W. Alexander and Jacob Beeson and appeared in the issue for August 11, 1877, over the title: "The Great Strike — Pittsburgh in the Hands of the Mob."

LYCEUM TALENT OF THE 1873–74 SEASON

C. S. Reinhart's drawing in *Harper's Weekly* of November 15, 1873. These lecturers may be identified as follows: Top Row — William H. H. Murray, Charles Bradlaugh, James Parton, Bayard Taylor, James T. Fields, Henry Carey Baird, David R. Locke ("Petroleum V. Nasby"). Middle Row — Louis Agassiz, John B. Gough, Henry Ward Beecher, Theodore Tilton, Elizabeth Cady Stanton, Susan B. Anthony. Lower Row — John Hay (?), Thomas Nast, Samuel L. Clemens, Wilkie Collins, Henry W. Shaw ("Josh Billings"). Acknowledgments for most of the identifications to Nevins' *Emergence of Modern America* (New York, 1927).

MANUFACTURERS' JOURNALS

Closely related to the magazines devoted to inventions and engineering were certain journals in the field of manufacturing and industry. There were, for example, the *Manufacturer and Builder* (1869–97), edited by William H. Wahl in New York; the *Manufacturers' Gazette* (1881–98), of Boston, which later went over to the lumber trade and was published in other cities; and the *Manufacturers' Record* (1882–current), of Baltimore, a weekly industrial journal for the South, edited successively by Edward H. Sanborn and Richard H. Edmunds. Chicago had a number of such periodicals, the two most important being the *Industrial World* (1873–98), which was called the *Chicago Commercial Advertiser* for its first seven years but later specialized in the iron industry; and the *Western Manufacturer* (1874–88), a general mechanical and scientific monthly. St. Louis had its *Midland Industrial Gazette* from 1866 to 1886. Some colleges which stressed the industrial arts issued periodicals in this field.[103]

Certain special lines of manufacture had their own groups of periodicals — boots and shoes, textiles, glass and pottery, iron and steel, paper, flour. Some of these were designed as much or more for the retailer as for the manufacturer. In the first group the two most important spokesmen came from Boston: the *Boot and Shoe Recorder* and the *Leather Manufacturer*, founded in 1882 and 1883, respectively, and still published.[104] In the textile field there were the New York *Manufacturers' Review and Industrial Record* (1868–96), the Philadelphia *Textile Colorist* (1879–current), and *Textile Record of America* (1880–1903). Pittsburgh was the center for glassware papers, led by the *National Glass Budget* (1884–current) and the *Pottery and Glassware Reporter* (1879–93).

[103] Two of the earliest were Kansas State Agricultural College at Manhattan, and Hampton Institute in Virginia; the former began the *Kansas Industrialist* in 1875 and the latter the *Southern Workman* in 1872. (For historical sketch see *Southern Workman*, LXIII, 9, January 1934. The *Workman's* field also includes the general consideration of race problems; see LXIII, 302–308, October 1934.)

[104] There were also *Shoe and Leather Review* (1877–1902), Chicago; *Boots and Shoes* (1882–1901), called *Boots and Shoes Weekly* after 1889, New York; *Leather Gazette* (1884–1913), called *Shoe and Leather Gazette* beginning in 1888, St. Louis.

The *Crockery and Glass Journal* (1874–current) was a New York trade paper.

Several important iron and steel journals continued from preceding periods, among which *Iron Age* was especially important;[105] and a dozen or more new ones were started. Among the new ventures perhaps the most important was the *Iron Trade Review* (1867–current), of Cleveland, which became *Steel* in 1930. The monthly *Bulletin of the American Iron and Steel Association* was published in Philadelphia from 1866 to 1912, and the *American Metal Market* in New York since 1882. The *Roller Mill* (1882–1912) was a Buffalo periodical.

A dozen grain-milling journals were scattered over the country.[106] Two of the best of them were launched in the panic year of 1873 — the *American Miller*,[107] Chicago, and the *Northwestern Miller*, Minneapolis, which still flourish, as do the *Southwestern Miller*, begun in 1879 at Kansas City; and the *Modern Miller*, begun at Moline in 1878 under the name of *Grain Cleaner* and moved about until it found its present home in Chicago; and the *Miller's Review* was established in Philadelphia in 1882.[108] The *Millers' Journal* (1863–86) was the leading New York periodical in this field.

The manufacture of paper was represented by Howard Lockwood's *Paper Trade Journal*, published since 1872 in New York; the *Paper Mill and Wood Pulp News*, founded by Lyman D. Post in Philadelphia in 1878 and published by him ever since, having been moved to New York in 1885; and the *Paper World* (1880–98), a lively and interesting Massachusetts journal founded at Holyoke but later moved to Springfield.

[105] See vol. II, p. 92. The *Iron Age* was a big paper, with large advertising patronage. It was published in the seventies by David Williams and edited by James C. Bayles. See George P. Rowell & Company, *Centennial Newspaper Exhibition* (New York, 1876), p. 225.

[106] Besides those named above, the following should be listed: *Millstone* (1875–92), Indianapolis; *United States Miller* (1876–94), Milwaukee; *Milling World and Chronicle of the Grain and Flour Trade* (1879–98), Buffalo.

[107] It was published at Ottawa, Illinois, for one year before it was moved to Chicago. Samuel S. Chisholm was the founder; he associated himself with Arthur J. and Harley B. Mitchell, who subsequently became owners and editors.

[108] Moved to Atlanta, Georgia, in December 1924, absorbing the *Dixie Miller* (1892–1924) and continuing as *Millers' Review and Dixie Miller*, a dollar monthly.

A number of labor journals were associated with the various manufacturing industries, sometimes combining the functions of a union organ with those of an exponent of the industry.[109]

CONSTRUCTION PERIODICALS

Journals related to building were also plentiful. Chief among those devoted to architecture was the weekly *American Architect*, founded by the famous Boston publishing firm of James R. Osgood & Company in 1876 under the editorship of William P. P. Longfellow.[110] In New York William T. Comstock's weekly *Building*, established in 1882, was the leader; it was devoted to such various themes as "art, architecture, archaeology, engineering, and decoration." [111] It was in New York also that David Williams founded *Carpentry and Building* (1879–1930) as a well-illustrated monthly of moderate price; it was called *Building Age* after 1910. The *Western Architect and Builder* was begun in Cincinnati in 1883, to become *Building Witness* thirty years later; and in Chicago the *Inland Architect and Builder* began in the same year as a dollar monthly, later to make itself famous in a more expensive edition for its large photogravure illustrations and special World's Fair numbers, and to be merged in 1908 with the *American Architect*. The *Northwestern Architect* (1882–94) was published in Minneapolis and the *California Architect* (1880–1900) in San Francisco; and both were devoted more to the building trade than to architecture as an art.

---

[109] Note, for example, *Carpenter* (1881–current), monthly organ of the United Brotherhood of Carpenters, published successively in Philadelphia, New York, and Indianapolis; and *American Glass Worker* (1882–current), Pittsburgh, which was called *Commoner*, 1887–1911, *Glassworker*, 1911–26, and *American Glass Review* thereafter.

[110] William Robert Ware was assistant editor at the beginning, and remained as editor until 1907, when he was succeeded by E. J. Rosecrans. The *Architect* was moved to New York in 1905; it was acquired by W. R. Hearst's International Publishing Company in 1929. Its original title (1876–1908) was *American Architect and Building News;* when it absorbed the *Architectural Review* in 1921 it added that name to its own. The various editions issued 1885–1908 are listed in *Periodicals*, I, 6 (October–December 1917).

[111] The title was changed in 1890 to *Architecture and Building*. In 1899 it absorbed the *Builders' Magazine* and changed title to *Architects' and Builders' Magazine*, but returned to *Architecture and Building* from 1911 to its end in 1932.

This was true of other journals which subordinated the professional aspects to the trade phases of building. The *American Journal of Art* (1868–95), begun in Chicago by Charles D. Lakey, became five years later the *American Builder* and, later, *Builder and Woodworker*. Also in Chicago *American Contractor*, now *General Building Contractor*, began in 1879; and in Cincinnati the *American Building Association News* was begun a year later, while the *Building Trades Journal*, of St. Louis, was published from 1883 to 1903. The local real estate journals were related to this class, and so were the special periodicals of the plumbers.[112]

Apparently the first periodicals devoted to lumbering were the *Lumberman's Gazette* (1871–98), of Chicago, and the *Mississippi Valley Lumberman* (1876–current), of Minneapolis. In the early eighties three strong lumber journals were established: the *Lumber World* (1881–98), Buffalo; the *Southern Lumberman* (1881–current), Nashville; and the *Lumber Trade Journal*, a semimonthly established in 1882 at Chicago, but continued 1896–1931 in New Orleans. San Francisco *Wood and Iron* was published 1884–1920. Closely related to these were several woodworkers' journals.[113]

The brick and tile trade had the *Brick, Tile and Metal Review* (1881–90), of Pittsburgh, called *Manufacturers' Chronicle* from 1887; and the *Clay Worker* (1884–1933), of Indianapolis, founded by Theodore A. Randall.

FLUSH TIMES IN THE OIL FIELDS

The exploitation of the Pennsylvania oil fields at the beginning of our period furnished one of the sensations of the times. The word "petroleum" came to stand for sudden wealth in the slang of the day. Periodicals soon sprang up to represent the new industry. At Oil City, the boom city of the field, were pub-

[112] *Metal Worker, Plumber and Steam Fitter* (1874–1931), which became *Sanitary and Heating Engineering* in 1921 and *Sanitary and Heating Age* in 1929; *Sanitary Plumber* (1882–1900); *Plumbers' Trade Journal* (1881–current) — all of New York.

[113] *Carpenter* (see note 109 above); *Wood Worker* (1882–current), Indianapolis; *American Woodworker and Mechanical Journal* (1882–1922), Cincinnati; *Furniture Workers' Journal* (1884–91), continued as *General Woodworkers' Journal* (1891–96), Baltimore.

lished the *Petroleum Monthly* (1870–72), which was succeeded by the *Monthly Petroleum Trade Report* (1873–82), and the *Oil City Derrick* (1871–current), said to have been subsidized by the Standard Oil Company,[114] now a local daily. The *Petroleum Age* (1881–88), first of its name, was issued from Bradford, Pennsylvania.

Many of the general periodicals commented upon the phenomena of the oil regions of western Pennsylvania, eastern Ohio, and West Virginia. Oil Creek, in Pennsylvania, was "the richest oil producing region on earth," according to the report of John S. Schooley in *Harper's*.[115] The *Journal of Science* reported C. A. Ashburner's calculation that 133,-262,639 barrels of crude oil had been taken from the Pennsylvania fields by the end of 1879, at a value of about $2.62 a barrel.[116] Picturesque accounts of life in the oil fields, which had "all the aspects of California mining towns in flush times" appeared in *Every Saturday*[117] and in other illustrated periodicals.

In this connection the leading artificial gas organ should be mentioned. It began in New York as the *Water-Gas Journal* in 1883, but in the next year adopted the title *Progressive Age*, which it bore for nearly forty years, during which time it represented gas, electricity, and water utilities.[118]

JOURNALS FOR PRINTING AND OTHER CRAFTS

There were many typographical journals begun in the years following the Civil War. One of the best of them was R. S. Menamin's modest *Printers' Circular* (1866–90), of Philadelphia. In the same year came the Cleveland *Printing Gazette* (1866–75). The *Pacific Printer* was published in San Francisco from 1877 to 1891, and the International Typographical Union's *American Model Printer* in New York from 1879 to 1884. The *Printing Trade News* (1882–1915) was another New York

---

[114] *McClure's Magazine*, XXVI, 451 (February 1906).

[115] *Harper's Monthly*, XXX, 562 (April 1865).

[116] *American Journal of Science*, CXIX, 168 (February 1880).

[117] *Every Saturday*, II, 299 (April 1, 1871).

[118] In 1912 it became *Gas Age*, and on absorption of the Chicago *Gas Record* (1912–21), *Gas Age-Record*.

journal. The *Inland Printer*,[119] of Chicago, began a distinguished career in 1883. Several printers' periodicals were mainly advertising sheets.[120]

The military profession was represented before 1879 chiefly by one periodical, which had been founded during the war — the *United States Army and Navy Journal*.[121] After that date *United Service*,[122] a well edited monthly, and the *Army and Navy Register* (1879–current), of Washington, a good weekly, shared this field. The Grand Army of the Republic had several journals, notably the *Grand Army Gazette* (1873–1900), New York. The Boston *Bivouac* (1883–85) and Washington *Vedette* (1879–83) were monthly veterans' journals independent of the G. A. R.

Barbers had the *American Hairdresser and Perfumer* (1879–current) in New York, and the *Barbers' National Journal* (1879–86) in Philadelphia. Launderers had the *National Laundry Journal* (1878–current) in Chicago, and the *American Laundry Journal* (1882–1902) in Troy, New York.

Incongruously enough, the leading undertakers' journal was begun as a little miscellany of jokes and anecdotes. It was called *Sunnyside* and was founded in 1871 by H. E. Taylor, a manufacturer of caskets, in New York; it was a four-page house journal distributed free. After a few years it was taken over by Frank H. Chase, a newspaper man, who made it a trade journal. In 1876 Albert H. Nirdlinger founded the *Casket* in Rochester; after his death his widow and later his stepson Simeon Wile continued the periodical, which was moved to New York in 1914 and placed under the same editorship as *Sunny-*

[119] It began as a dollar monthly of 24 quarto pages. Editors: H. H. Hill, 1883–84; Andrew C. Cameron (former editor of the *Workingman's Advocate*), 1884–92; Albert H. McQuilkin, 1893–1917; Harry Hillman, 1917–28; J. L. Frazier, 1928–current. From the first it was notable for excellence of typography and presswork and skillful editing. It emphasized the education of apprentices and practical hints for printers. Job and ad specimens became a specialty, with pictures in colors. It gave much attention to the history and biography of the printing art; its range has been encyclopedic.

[120] For example: The *Chicago Specimen* (1867–80), New York *Proof Sheet* (1870–91), Chicago quarterly *Electrotyper* (1871–90), San Francisco *Printers' Guide* (1871–90). For printers' journals persisting from the preceding period, see vol. II, p. 93.

[121] Treated more fully in vol. II, sketch 39.

[122] Treated more fully in sketch 31.

side. The two were not consolidated, however, until 1925, when they were made a single semimonthly under the title of the *Casket and Sunnyside*. Besides these, there were the *Western Undertaker,* founded at Grand Rapids in 1879 and called *American Funeral Director* since 1920; and other briefer ventures in this field, such as the Chicago magazine with the forbidding name of *Shroud* (1881–86).

The compiler of these lists presents his compliments to the bootblacks, nursemaids, and janitors, and regrets that they did not have their distinctive journals in this period. Nearly all other vocations were represented; practically every department of human endeavor had its periodical organs by 1885.

TRADE JOURNALS

The drug, dry goods, and grocery trade fields were plentifully supplied with representative organs, located for the most part in New York, Philadelphia, Chicago, and St. Louis. Many of these lasted for a decade or more, and several in each field have lived to celebrate semicentennials.

The druggists' papers are closely allied with the more scientific journals of pharmacy. Among them, the *American Journal of Pharmacy* and the *Druggists' Circular* were the veterans.[123] *New Remedies* was founded as a dollar monthly in folio form by William Wood & Company, of New York, in 1871; twelve years later its name was changed to *American Druggist*.[124] In the same city William O. Allison founded the *Oil, Paint and Drug Reporter* (1871–current) and the *Painters' Magazine* (1874–1933). Another less important New Yorker was *Drug Topics* (1883–current), an advertising paper. Chicago had its *Western Druggist* (1879–1933), whose name was changed to *Drug Bulletin* in 1904, and the *Paint, Oil and Chemical Review* (1883–current). The *St. Louis Drug Market,* begun in 1880, became *Meyer Brothers' Druggist* nine years later and then

---

[123] See vol. II, p. 92.

[124] In 1892 Ashbel R. Elliott bought it, making Caswell O. Mayo editor; and the next year he purchased the *Pharmaceutical Record and Market Review* (1881–93), a New York weekly, and consolidated the two under the name *American Druggist and Pharmaceutical Record*. The name was again shortened to *American Druggist* when Hearst's International Publishing Company purchased the property in 1927.

Meyer Druggist, ending in 1933; while the *National Druggist* was begun in 1882 by Frank L. James as the *St. Louis Druggist*, ending in 1935. And there were many others with shorter careers.

The dry goods trade had the old *United States Economist and Dry Goods Reporter*;[125] as well as several other journals of the textile trade in New York,[126] including the *American Silk Journal* (1882–current). The Chicago *Dry Goods Reporter* (1871–1929) was the most important of several papers of the kind in that city. The *Millinery Trade Review* has been published since 1876 in New York.

New York was also the home of the more important journals of the clothing and tailoring trade, one of which furnishes an interesting example of the progress of specialization in the trade journal field: the *Clothier and Hatter* (1872–79) was in 1880 divided into two papers — the *Clothier and Furnisher* [127] and the *Hatter and Furrier* — and the latter was divided in 1892 into the *American Hatter* (ended 1935) and the *Furrier* (now *Fur Trade Review*). The *American Fashion Review*, founded in 1874, has been called the *Sartorial Art Journal* since 1887. The *Furnishing Gazette* was founded in 1881 and was called the *Haberdasher* 1887–1931. These are only a few of many.[128]

Grocers were well represented by the *American Grocer* (1869–current) and the *Retail Grocers' Advocate* (1877–1934), both of New York; the *New England Grocery and Market* (1877–current), of Boston; the *San Francisco Grocer* (1874–1936); the Baltimore *Canning Trade* (1878–current), which has borne various names, such as *Trade*, and *Grocer and Canner*; the New York *Spice Mill* (1878–current); and many

[125] See vol. II, p. 93.

[126] Including the *American Journal of Fabrics and Dry Goods Bulletin* (1871–88), called *Merchant World* in its last two years; *Fabrics, Fancy Goods and Notions* (1875–1920), with variations of title; and *Fancy Goods Graphic* (1880–97) — all of New York. For textile manufacturing journals see p. 127.

[127] Merged in 1927 into the *Haberdasher* under the name *Haberdasher and the Clothier and Furnisher*.

[128] Others of importance were: *Tailors' Review* (1866–1903), owned by the Butterick Company in the nineties; *American Tailor and Cutter* (1880–1916); *Clothing Gazette* (1881–1903), begun as *Gibson's Monthly Review*. All the foregoing were published in New York. The *Glovers' Journal* was issued (1881–1909) from Gloversville, New York.

other periodicals in Philadelphia, Chicago, and other cities.[129]

Other important journals of the provision trades were the *Butchers' Advocate and Market Journal* (1879–current) and the *Fishing Gazette* (1884–current), both of New York; the *Milk Reporter* (1884–1930), of Sussex, New Jersey; the *Ice Trade Journal* (1877–1904), of Philadelphia; and the *Coal Trade Journal* (1869–current), of New York. The *American Elevator and Grain Trade* (1882–1930) and the *Grain and Provision Review* (1875–87) were published in Chicago. The *Confectioners' Journal* has been published in Philadelphia since 1874; the *Confectioners' Gazette*, founded in New York in 1881, had its name changed to *Candy* in 1929; the Chicago *Confectioner and Baker* (1875–1913) was published as a house organ under the title *Western Confectioner and Baker* for its first few years.

The *Tobacco Leaf* [130] was practically alone in its trade field until 1874, when the *Western Tobacco Journal*, of Cincinnati, and the *United States Tobacco Journal*, of New York, appeared. The Philadelphia *Tobacco World* entered the field in 1881. All these journals are still current.

The brewers and liquor sellers had the *American Brewer* (1868–current), the *American Brewers' Gazette* (1871–86), and *Bonfort's Wine and Spirit Circular* (1871–1919) in New York. The Chicago *Wine and Spirit Review* (1862–86) was at first called the *American Spirit and Wine Trade Review* and later the *Western Spirit*. The *Western Brewer* (1876–current) was founded in Chicago by J. M. Wing and H. S. Rich; its name was *Beverage Journal* from 1920 to 1932.

The *American Stationer* was published in Brooklyn from 1873 to 1928, and the *Western Stationer* in Chicago from 1880 to 1900; *Geyer's Stationer*, founded in 1877, is current in New York. The New York *Paper Trade Journal* and the Chicago *Paper Trade* (founded *Western Paper Trade*) were begun in in 1872 and 1875 respectively. Some booksellers' journals [131] also served the stationery trade.

[129] Among them were: New York *Grocers' Journal* (1879–1905); three Philadelphia papers — *Grocers' Price Current* (1873–86), *Cash Grocer* (1874–94), *Grocer* (1875–90); Cincinnati *Grocer* (1872–93); *Chicago Grocer* (1874–1903); *Grocer's Criterion* (1873–1912), Chicago; *St. Louis Grocer* (1878–1904).

[130] See vol. II, p. 213. [131] See pp. 235–36.

The *American Artisan* (1880–current), of Chicago, was formerly devoted chiefly to hardware but latterly to hot-air heating. *Stoves and Hardware Reporter* (1878–1913) was a St. Louis paper. *Tradesman*, begun in Atlanta in 1879, became the *Southern Hardware and Implement Journal* in 1919.

Three periodicals of the jewelry trade begun in the early eighties enjoyed long lives: the *American Jeweler* (1882–1929), Chicago; *Keystone* (1883–1934), Philadelphia; the *Manufacturing Jeweler* (1884–current), Providence.

The earliest of the important journals in the furniture and carpet trade were two New Yorkers begun in 1870 and still published: the *American Cabinet Maker and Upholsterer*, which became the *Furniture Buyer and Decorator* in 1919; and the *Carpet Trade Review*, now *Carpet and Upholstery Trade Review*. The *Furniture Trade Review* (1880–1932) was a subsidiary of the latter paper; and there were several others of importance in the same field.[132] The *Picture and Art Trade*, later *Picture and Gift Journal*, began in Chicago in 1880.

The hotel business had seven dailies in as many cities at the end of our period, but there were also several more widely circulated weeklies in the field. The *Western Hotel Reporter* (1873), of San Francisco; the *Hotel World* (1875), of Chicago; and the *Hotel Gazette* (1876), of New York, are all current. The *Hotel Mail* (1877–97) and the *Hotel Register* (1884–1912) were both New York periodicals. Most of the early hotel journals were little more than gazettes chronicling the arrival of buyers and merchants.

[132] Among them were: *Trade Bureau* (1874–93) and *Decorator and Furnisher* (1882–98), New York; *Carpet Trade* (1875–90) and *Carpets, Wall Paper and Curtains* (1879–89), Philadelphia; *American Furniture Gazette* (1880–1902), Chicago.

CHAPTER VI

MEDICINE, LAW, FINANCE, AND AGRICULTURE

PROFESSIONAL journals, besides those belonging to technology and trade, showed marked extensions during the years following the Civil War. These increases were owing in part to the multiplication of local journals and to the inauguration, especially in the field of medicine, of periodicals devoted to highly specialized departments.

POPULAR INTEREST IN MEDICAL MATTERS

Cholera, yellow fever, and smallpox epidemics were subjects of the gravest public concern in the seventies. Some six hundred persons died of cholera in New Orleans in the spring of 1873.[1] But the worst visitations of plague in the whole period were the yellow fever epidemics in Shreveport, Louisiana, and Memphis, Tennessee. This scourge was believed to have come to Shreveport from Havana; of the 4,500 persons who did not flee the devoted city, 3,000 were attacked by the fever, and, according to the report of the *American Journal of Medical Sciences*, 759 died of it in eight weeks.[2] That was in September and October 1873; in the following year it broke out at Memphis, which had already been chastened by smallpox and cholera. By October the Chicago *Advance* reported that the yellow fever had "spread so fast in Memphis that an exodus of the people is going on." [3] Some 2,000 died of the disease in that city, in spite of the firing of cannon and the use of coal gas and other more or less empirical remedies.[4] Smallpox was epidemic in many cities; and various "conceited ignoramuses" were calling in question "the beneficence of vaccination" for that disease, according to Dr. Austin Flint in the *North American Review*.[5]

Consumption was being studied more carefully than before

[1] *American Journal of the Medical Sciences*, LXVII, 480 (April 1870).
[2] *Ibid.*
[3] *Advance*, October 9, 1873, p. 5.
[4] *American Journal of the Medical Sciences*, LXVII, 348 (April 1874).
[5] *North American Review*, CXXXII, 588 (June 1881).

by medical men, as the pages of their journals attest. It was
"never more rife," declared the *Atlantic Monthly* in 1869, in a
series of articles on the subject; New England was declared to
be "its favorite seat." [6] Anaesthesia was another medical topic
that interested the public. The use of ether on the battlefields
of the recent war by Dr. Morton, the discoverer of its anaes-
thetic value, appealed to the popular imagination.[7]

Abuses in medical education were under fire. The sale of
medical diplomas, centering in Pennsylvania even after the legislature of that state revoked the charters of certain institutions, attracted much comment.[8] A writer in a leading medical
journal stated that in 1877 there were sixty-five medical schools
in the United States, exclusive of those of the homoeopathic,
eclectic, and botanic systems; and that only five of them had
three-year courses, and not more than twenty were doing even
"fairly good work." [9] Related to the problem of proper medical
education was "the continually renewed discussion" of the question which furnished a title to one of the *North American Review's* symposia in 1882: "Shall Women Practice Medicine?" [10]

The surgical treatment accorded President Garfield after he
received his mortal wound from Guiteau's pistol [11] and the
homoeopathic treatment of Disraeli in his last illness [12] were
also subjects of popular interest.

HEALTH MAGAZINES

Physical culture was attracting public attention.[13] Dr. Henry
Hartshorne, writing in *Lippincott's*, pointed out that this cult
"thrives now somewhat among us." Hercules, he says, is no
longer the gnarled and knotty figure of classical art. "We have
changed all that; the Hercules of today — the Windship or Dio
Lewis — is a person of good figure with the appearance of a

[6] *Atlantic Monthly*, XXIII, 51 (January 1869).

[7] *Harper's Monthly*, XXXI, 459 (September 1865).

[8] *Galaxy*, XXIV, 126 (July 1877). Mention of the matetr was frequent in
the medical journals.

[9] *American Journal of the Medical Sciences*, LXXVI, 185 (July 1878).

[10] *North American Review*, CXXXIV, 52 (January 1882).

[11] *Ibid.*, CXXXIII, 518 (December 1881).

[12] *Ibid.*, CXXXIV, 293 (March 1882) and CXXXVI, 77 (January 1883).

[13] For college athletics, tennis, bicycling, etc., see pp. 221–22.

gentleman and the language of a scholar." [14] He was doubtless also a reader of the *Herald of Health*, born *Water-Cure Journal*, and *Hall's Journal of Health*, both of them older New York magazines continued from preceding periods.[15] Begun after the war were *Good Health* (1866–current), of Battle Creek, Michigan; Dr. W. H. Hale's *Health and Home* (1871–91), begun in Port Chester, New York, but reaching a large circulation only when it was moved to Chicago from Washington at the very end of our period; *Dr. Foote's Health Monthly* (1876–95), a cheap New York paper; the *Sanitarian* (1873–1904), also a New York monthly, and devoted throughout much of its life to physical culture and allied matters; the *Annals of Hygiene* (1884–97), Philadelphia, a scientific journal; and *Laws of Health* (1878–87), called *Health* (1881–86), of Reading and other Pennsylvania cities. Health articles in the general magazines were not uncommon, especially in magazines for the home and in such miscellanies as *Harper's Weekly* and *Appleton's Journal*.

MEDICAL JOURNALS

There were forty medical journals listed in the first number of Rowell's *American Newspaper Directory*, published in 1869; by the end of our period, Ayer listed 150 such periodicals. Doubtless between 300 and 400 of them were published for longer or shorter periods between 1865 and 1885.

A number of these were holdovers from preceding periods,[16] the oldest among them being the *American Journal of the Medical Sciences*,[17] still under the editorship, throughout most of the postbellum period, of Dr. Isaac Hays; and the *Boston Medical and Surgical Journal*,[18] in whose editorial chair George B. Shattuck succeeded J. Collins Warren in 1881. The new medical journals tended more and more to fall into one or the other of two classes: either they were local organs of city or state medical societies, hospitals, or medical schools; or they were journals for workers in special fields of medical study and practice.

[14] *Lippincott's Magazine*, I, 646 (June 1868).
[15] See vol. II, p. 87.
[16] See vol. II, pp. 84–88.
[17] See Mott, *A History of American Magazines, 1741–1850*, p. 566.
[18] See vol. II, p. 84.

Some of the local periodicals, however, achieved circulations beyond their own regions, broadening their editorial policies accordingly. This was true of the *New York Medical Journal*,[19] founded in 1865, which gained the largest circulation among American medical magazines in the seventies, and which, under the able editorship of Dr. Frank P. Foster in 1880–1911, came to occupy a high position. Before the end of our period, however, the *Journal* was overtaken and passed in the circulation race by the New York *Medical Record*, founded in 1866 and under the editorship of Dr. George F. Shrady. Many years later, in 1923, these two magazines were to be merged first under a combined name, and then as the *Medical Record*. But the medical magazine which outstripped all in the eighties was the St. Louis *Medical Brief* (1873–1929), a dollar-a-year monthly founded by Dr. J. J. Lawrence and conducted by him for more than thirty years. Dr. C. F. Taylor's Philadelphia *Medical World* (1883–current) was another periodical which reached the higher circulation figures. These four were the only professional medical journals to circulate over 10,000 copies before 1885; a few others had over 5,000, but the great majority of them existed upon circulations ranging from a few hundred to 2,000. Of these, thirty or more enjoyed more than a quarter-century of life.[20]

[19] Monthly, 1865–82; weekly, 1883–1920; semimonthly, 1921–current. D. Appleton & Company were publishers 1868–95. Prominent editors besides Foster have been E. S. Dunster, James B. Hunter, Charles E. de M. Sajous, and Smith Ely Jelliffe.

[20] The following list contains the local, collegiate, and regional journals which were published for twenty-five years or more. A few of them enjoyed national circulations during parts of their lives. In the East were the *Albany Medical Annals* (1880–1922), issued by the Albany Medical College; the *Medical Bulletin of the Jefferson Medical Association* (1879–1908), Philadelphia; *Dunglison's College and Clinical Record* (1880–99), of the Jefferson Medical College, Philadelphia; *Philadelphia Medical Times* (1870–1903), called the *Times and Register* after its absorption of the *Medical Register* (1887–89); the *Medical Summary* (1879–1928), begun at Lansdale, Pennsylvania, but moved to Philadelphia in 1885; and the *New England Medical Monthly* (1870–1912), published in various Connecticut cities but chiefly in Danbury, and edited for many years by Dr. William C. Wile. In the South were the *Maryland Medical Record* (1877–1918), Baltimore, and the *Virginia Medical Monthly* (1874–current), both organs of state associations; two other Richmond journals — the *Southern Clinic* (1878–1919), edited and published by Dr. C. A. Bryce; and the *Richmond Medical Journal* (1866–1911), founded and edited by Dr. Edwin S. Gaillard, who moved

The *Journal of the American Medical Association*[21] began in 1883 as a thirty-page monthly devoted to the reporting of the official proceedings and papers of the Association.

First in point of time among the specialized journals was the *American Journal of Obstetrics and Diseases of Women and Children* (1868–1919), a quarterly which became a monthly in 1883. It was founded by Emil Noeggerath and B. F. Dawson; Paul F. Mundé was editor 1875–92. William Wood published this magazine as well as the *Archives of Ophthalmology and Otology*, founded in New York in 1869. The *Archives* had both American and German editions, Herman Knapp being editor in

---

it in its third year to Louisville, Kentucky, and published it as the *Richmond and Louisville Medical Journal*. Dr. Gaillard also founded in Louisville the *American Medical Weekly* (1874–83). In 1879 he took his monthly to New York, where it was published by his son, M. E. Gaillard, as *Gaillard's Medical Journal* until it was merged in 1904 in *Southern Medicine*, of Savannah, Georgia, to be published 1906–11 under the name *Gaillard's Southern Medicine*. Another Louisville journal was *Medical Progress* (1884–1928). The *Southern Medical Record* (1871–99), of Atlanta, was called throughout its first two years the *Georgia Medical Companion*. In Tennessee there were the *Southern Practitioner* (1879–1918), of Nashville; and the *Memphis Medical Monthly* (1881–1922), called 1881–88 the *Mississippi Valley Medical Monthly*. The *Texas Medical and Surgical Record* (1881–83), of Fort Worth, was continued by the *Texas Courier-Record of Medicine* (1883–1917). In Ohio were the *American Medical Compend* (1884–1913), begun at Attica but moved in 1890 to Toledo; *Cincinnati Medical News* (1868–91), called *Cincinnati Medical Repertory* for its first four years; and the *Columbus Medical Journal* (1882–1916). Indiana had the *Fort Wayne Journal of the Medical Sciences* (1881–1907), which became the *Journal of the National Association of Railway Surgeons* in 1888; the *Indiana Medical Journal* (1882–1908), Indianapolis; and the *New Albany Medical Herald* (1879–1931). The *Physician and Surgeon* (1879–1915) was published at Ann Arbor, Michigan, by Dr. John W. Keating; and the *Therapeutic Gazette* (1877–1927), which began as *New Preparations*, at Detroit. The *Chicago Medical Times* (1869–1910) and the *Chicago Medical Review* (1880–1915) represented the great midwestern metropolis, but the latter was soon transferred to St. Louis and assumed the name of that city. St. Louis also had the *Courier of Medicine* (1879–1907), and other Missourians were the *Kansas City Medical Record* (1884–1911) and the *St. Joseph Medical Herald* (1883–1933), later the *Medical Herald and Physio-Therapist*. The *Kansas Medical Index* (1880–1910) was published at Fort Scott until 1885, when it became the *Kansas City* [Missouri] *Medical Index*, adding *Lancet* to its title when it absorbed the *Kansas City Lancet* (1896–99). The *Northwestern Lancet* (1881–current), of Minneapolis, prefaced its title with *Journal of the Minnesota Medical Association* (1905–11) and since the latter year has been called the *Journal-Lancet*. The *Denver Medical Times* (1882–1933) was called *Western Medical Times* after 1915. The *California Medical Journal* (1880–1908) was published first in Oakland but was moved to San Francisco in 1890 and there adopted by the California Medical College.

New York; in 1879 it was divided into the *Archives of Oph-thalmology* and the *Archives of Otology.*[22] Both were then edited by Knapp and published by G. P. Putnam's Sons. The *American Journal of Ophthalmology* (1884–current) was a St. Louis monthly founded by Adolph Alt.[23] Monthly also was the *Chicago Journal of Nervous and Mental Diseases* (1874–current), which moved to New York in 1881 and became the official organ of the American Neurological Association. The monthly *Archives of Pediatrics* (1884–current) was begun in Philadelphia with William Perry Watson as editor, but was moved to New York in 1892. The *Medico-Legal Journal* (1883–1933) was edited successively by Clark Bell and A. W. Herzog and published by the Medico-Legal Society of New York. Other special journals had briefer lives.[24]

The *Bistoury* (1865–85) was a quarterly by T. S. Up de Graff, of Elmira, New York, "devoted to the exposition of charlatinism in medicine" and to medical news.

The homoeopathic school was represented by several periodicals which continued from the preceding period,[25] as well as by thirty or more which were founded between 1865 and 1885.[26] Most of these were organs of city or state associations, or represented colleges, hospitals, or pharmaceutical houses; several were vehicles for more popular propaganda addressed to the laity. Among the most important were the *Hahnemannian*

[21] To be treated more fully in a separate sketch in the succeeding volume of this work.

[22] The *Archives of Otology* ended in 1908. Arnold Knapp became editor of the *Archives of Ophthalmology* in 1918, and it was moved to Chicago in 1929. The first four volumes were published irregularly in nine numbers, after which the periodical was a quarterly until 1896, when both journals became bimonthlies.

[23] J. H. Chambers & Company were the original publishers, and Alt did not gain control until 1896. In 1918 it absorbed three other ophthalmological journals and began a third series in Chicago, with Edward Jackson as editor.

[24] The following may be listed: *American Journal of Syphilography and Dermatology* (1870–74), New York, which was followed by *Archives of Dermatology* (1874–82) and later by *Journal of Cutaneous Diseases Including Syphilis* (1882–1919), Chicago, organs of the American Dermatological Association; *American Journal of Otology* (1879–82), Boston; *Archives of Laryngology* (1880–83), New York.

[25] See vol. II, pp. 84–85.

[26] See W. A. Dewey's "History of the Periodical Literature of the Homoeopathic School" in William Harvey King, *History of Homoeopathy and Its Institutions in America* (New York, 1905), II, 13–34.

Monthly (1865–current), of the Homoeopathic Medical Society of Pennsylvania; the *New England Medical Gazette* (1866–1918), of the Boston University School of Medicine; the *Medical Advance* (1873–1915), founded in Cincinnati, but later published in Ann Arbor, Chicago, and Batavia, Illinois; the *American Homoeopathist* (1877–1908), founded in Chicago but moved to New York in its third year, there to become the *American Physician* in 1902; and the *Chironian* (1884–1918), of the New York Homoeopathic Medical College. A quarterly *Homoeopathic Journal of Obstetrics* (1879–1910), New York, became the *Journal of Surgery, Gynecology and Obstetrics* in 1905.

Eclectic medicine was represented by half a dozen new journals, most prominent among them being the *New York* (originally *New Jersey*) *Eclectic Medical and Surgical Journal* (1874–95) and the *American Medical Journal* (1873–1916) of St. Louis.

Chief among the dental journals which continued from the preceding period [27] was the *Dental Cosmos*. The Philadelphia *Dental Office and Laboratory* (1868–1908) continued the *Dental Quarterly*; and a score of publications representing local and state societies and dental supply houses [28] furnished periodical literature for dentists.

The veterinarians had the *American Veterinary Review* (1877–current), New York, called the *Journal of the American Veterinary Medical Association* since it was moved to Ithaca in 1916.

[27] See vol. II, p. 91. It was discontinued in 1936.

[28] Most of them were begun in the years 1879–83. Notable were the quarterly *Dental Advertiser* (1869–98), Buffalo, called *Dental Practitioner and Advertiser* after 1891; the Wilmington Dental Manufacturing Company's *Items of Interest* (1879–current), of Philadelphia, T. B. Welch editor, sold to the Consolidated Dental Manufacturing Company of New York in 1896 and Rodrigues Ottolengui made editor, called *Dental Items of Interest* since 1916; the quarterly *Dental Luminary* (1879–93), Macon, Georgia; *Odontographic Journal* (1880–99), a quarterly by the Rochester Dental Manufacturing Company; the quarterly *Dental Headlight* (1880–1910), Nashville, Tennessee; *Independent Practitioner* (1880–1905), Buffalo, which was moved to Philadelphia in 1889 to become the *International Dental Journal*; *Ohio State Journal of Dental Science* (1881–1925), Toledo, which, after other changes of name, became *Dental Summary* in 1901; *Southern Dental Journal* (1882–1900), Atlanta, which absorbed the *Luminary* (*supra*) and added its name to the title in 1893; *Texas Dental Journal* (1883–current), Dallas.

LEGAL PERIODICALS

Over a hundred legal journals were published during the postbellum period — some for less than a year, and some for the whole of the two decades. *Jones's Index* was covering 43 such journals by 1885. Many of these periodicals were merely weekly law reporters for city or state. Most of the larger cities had their daily court newspapers. There were legal journals, however, of a more general sort which contained articles and comment as well as case reports and details of court actions.

The majority of the legal periodicals counted less than 1,000 circulation, and only a few passed the 5,000 mark. Four of the older periodicals [29] were among those which enjoyed the larger circulations — the *Legal Intelligencer* and the *American Law Register and Review*, both of Philadelphia; the *Legal Journal*, of Pittsburgh; and the *Legal Adviser*, of Chicago. The most brilliant legal periodical of the times was the *American Law Review*, begun in Boston in 1866, and edited by such men as Arthur G. Sedgwick, Oliver Wendell Holmes, Jr., Moorfield Storey, Samuel Hoar, and Charles E. Grinnell. In 1883 it was moved to St. Louis, where it was published for nearly half a century.[30] St. Louis was also the home of the successful *Central Law Journal* (1874–1927), a weekly *Legal News* (1868–1925) and a monthly *Law Journal* (1880–1907). The *Albany Law Journal* (1870–1908) was one of the most widely circulated of the legal periodicals of the seventies; and the *Maryland Law Record* (1878–89), of Baltimore, claimed a considerable following by the end of our period. Other legal journals were widely scattered, especially through the East and Middle West.[31]

[29] See vol. II, p. 93.

[30] Quarterly, 1866–79; monthly, 1880–82; bimonthly, 1883–current. Little, Brown & Company were the *Review's* publishers while it was in Boston. Later editors have been S. D. Thompson, Lucien Eaton, Charles E. Grinnell, Leonard A. Jones, Hannis Taylor, John D. Lawson, and E. H. Robinson. It became the *United States Law Review* in 1929, and was moved to New York. For historical sketch see LXIII, 321 (July 1929).

[31] The *Washington Law Reporter*, begun in 1874, and the *Lancaster Law Review*, 1883, have lived to celebrate semicentennials; the latter has been edited and published by G. R. Eshleman since 1888. The *Kentucky Law Reporter* was published at Frankfort 1880–1908. *Legal Bibliography* (1881–1913), of Boston, first issued twelve numbers irregularly (1881–90) as *Soule and Bugbee's Legal Bibliography*, but began a new series in 1893 as a quarterly by the Boston Book

INSURANCE JOURNALS

The insurance journals were almost as numerous as those devoted to legal matters; and they were, on the whole, more prosperous and longer-lived.[32] And this in spite of the disasters suffered in the failure of prominent life and fire insurance companies in the early seventies. Writing after the collapse of two important New York life insurance companies, the editor of the *Nation* said, "The question of the morality and public policy of the system . . . has been revived by recent events." He pointed out that the total capital of New York life insurance companies was only about $10,000,000, while their annual income was four times that amount, and their risks exceeded $1,600,000,000.[33] In the realm of fire insurance, it was the great Chicago conflagration of 1871 that proved at once disastrous and beneficent to the system. It was disastrous in that it wrecked fifty-seven companies — a third of New York's fire insurance companies and three-fourths of those of Illinois — the total losses in American companies ($85,000,000) being in excess of the aggregate capitalization of all of them. It was beneficent, as the *Spectator*, a leading insurance journal, pointed out, because it caused the companies to raise rates and at the same time brought in a flood of new business.[34]

A number of important insurance periodicals founded in the preceding period continued to flourish, one of them — the *New York Underwriter* — leading the field in circulation. Those begun after 1865 which reached 5,000 circulation by 1885 were the New York *Insurance Critic* (1874–1926), the New York (later Philadelphia) *Spectator: an American Review of Life Insurance*

Company. The *Ohio Law Bulletin* was begun in 1876 under the title *Cincinnati Weekly Law Bulletin;* but in 1884 it absorbed the *Ohio Law Journal* and used both titles until 1913, when it adopted the simpler name. Then it was absorbed by the *Ohio Law Reporter* (1903–current) under the title *Ohio Law Bulletin and Reporter* in 1921. Another Cincinnati journal was the *American Law Record* (1872–87). *Western Jurist* (1867–73) was published at Des Moines, Iowa, and *Virginia Law Journal* (1877–93) at Richmond. Two specialists were *Journal of Banking Law* (1882–88), New York, and *Criminal Law Magazine and Reporter* (1880–96), Jersey City.

[32] For a good list of them see Marion V. Patch, "American Insurance Journals before 1900" (Columbia University thesis, 1930).

[33] *Nation*, XII, 54 (January 26, 1871).

[34] Quoted in *Bankers' Magazine*, XXVI, 458 (December 1871).

(1868–current), the *Philadelphia Underwriter* (1869–1906), J. C. Bergstresser's Pittsburgh *Insurance World* (1874–1924), and J. S. Bloomingston's Chicago *Investigator* (1874–1908). Some of these had editions for other cities. Circulations of insurance journals declined noticeably between 1880 and 1885, but no less than twenty of those that were founded in the postbellum period continued for half a century,[35] and nine are still published. Some insurance companies had their own house organs, as the *Aetna* (1868–1908), and the *Traveler's Record* (1865–1906), both of Hartford; and the *Equitable Record* (1871–1905), New York.

BANKERS AND MERCHANTS

In this period of financial excitement, bankers and brokers depended upon such veterans as Homan's *Bankers' Magazine* and *Thompson's Bank-Note and Commercial Reporter*,[36] and upon a dozen or more newcomers in the field of finance. Of these latter the most important were the *Commercial and Financial Chronicle*,[37] with its many supplementary numbers dealing

[35] *Baltimore Underwriter and National Agent* (1865–1931); *Western Insurance Review* (1867–current), St. Louis; *Northwestern Review* (1868–current), Chicago, which became *United States Review* upon its removal to Philadelphia in 1875, and upon successive absorptions added to its title the names of *Insurance World* (*supra*), and *Insurance News* (1883–1926), Philadelphia; *Insurance Times* (1868–1936), New York, which moved to Richmond, Virginia, in 1924; *Insurance Index* (1870–1935), New York; *Coast Review* (1871–1924), San Francisco; *Insurance Law Journal* (1871–current), founded in St. Louis but bought by C. C. Hine in 1873 and moved to New York; *Southern Underwriter* (1871–1929), Atlanta, called *Herald* (1871–76), *Argus* (1877–1913), *Insurance Herald-Argus* (1913–16); *Standard* (1872–current), Boston, called *Index* (1872–82); *Insurance Age* (1873–1936), Boston, called *Insurance Age-Journal* after absorption of *Insurance Journal* (1873–1924), Hartford; *Expositor* (1874–1922), New York, Philadelphia, Newark; *Rough Notes* (1878–current), Indianapolis; *Insurance Salesman* (1879–current), Indianapolis: *Mutual Underwriter* (1881–current), Rochester, published in Green Springs, Ohio, 1881–89; *Indicator* (1882–1936), Detroit; *Insurance* (1883–current), Newark, a continuation of *United States Insurance Gazette and Magazine* (1855–82), New York, called *Insurance and the Insurance Critic* since absorption of *Insurance Critic* (*supra*); *Vindicator* (1883–current), New Orleans, called *American Insurer* since 1916.

[36] See vol. II, pp. 94–95.

[37] Founded in 1865 by William B. Dana. It absorbed several other periodicals and added their titles to its own from time to time. It has always published a tremendous amount of statistics of trade and finance in quarto form, for a long time charging $10 a year for its thirty-two weekly pages. Its bimonthly investors' supplement began in 1875; in the nineties it added a monthly quotation

with varied fields of finance; *Bradstreet's*,[38] a high-class "journal of trade, finance, and public economy"; and [Bradford] *Rhodes' Journal of Banking* (1873–95), a monthly — both New York publications. Late in the period *Rand, McNally & Co.'s Bankers' Monthly* (1884–current) was begun in Chicago.[39] Others were more or less local or specialized.[40]

Hunt's Merchants' Magazine [41] gave way before the spirit of specialization in 1870, while *De Bow's Review* [42] hung on until 1880. John J. W. O'Donoghue's *Banking and Insurance Chronicle*, founded in New York in 1866, turned more and more to trade and after several changes of name became *Economic World* for a decade before its end in 1926. The *American Exporter* (1877–current), Charles K. Hammit's *American Merchant* (1881–87), and William E. Wilkins' *Merchants' Review* (1879–1908) were all New York monthlies. Most cities had their *Prices Current* or *Journals of Commerce*, some of them daily in issue, which specialized in commercial news; of these the *Boston Journal of Commerce*, a weekly periodical, filled seventy-two semiannual volumes from 1872 to 1908 and was merged with *Cotton* at the end.

Many cities had real estate journals, and there were also a

---

supplement, a quarterly street railway supplement, a semiannual state and city supplement, etc. (See *Union List of Serials*.) In 1928 it separated these supplements off as distinct periodicals at $5.00 a year each as follows: *Bank and Quotation Record, Railway Earnings Record, Railway and Industrial Compendium, State and Municipal Compendium* — all monthly except the last two, which were semiannual. The *Chronicle* has been notable for its commercial summaries, its editorials, and its weekly analysis called "The Financial Situation."

[38] Began as a semiweekly continuation in 1879 of an earlier bulletin, and changed to weekly publication the next year. It was combined with *Dun's Review* (1893–current), called *Dun and Bradstreet's Review* 1933–36.

[39] See the number for February 1934 for a historical sketch. The title now appears *Bankers' Monthly*.

[40] In New York were *Counting-House Monitor* (1869–current), which became *Bullinger's Monitor Guide* in 1880; *Underwood's United States Counterfeit Reporter* (1878–1931); *Bullion* (1879–85); and *Book Keeper* (1880–84), which became *American Counting Room* for its last year or two. The *Boston Economist* (1879–88) was moved to New York in 1884, but the *Banker and Tradesman* has occupied the Boston field since 1872. Others were the New Haven *Commercial Record* (1882–current), the *Dubuque* [Iowa] *Trade Journal* (1881–1906), and the San Francisco *Finance and Trade* (1884–1931). The last named was called *Western Finance and Trade* after 1928.

[41] See Mott, *op. cit.*, p. 696.

[42] Treated more fully in vol. II, sketch 10.

number of "booster" magazines devoted to the exploitation of favorite regions. The *Virginias* was published at Staunton, Virginia (1880–85), the *Northwest Magazine* at St. Paul (1883–1903), and the *West Shore* at Portland and Spokane (1875–91). The *National Real Estate Index* (1881–90), of Kansas City, had a considerable circulation.

THE "FARMERS' MOVEMENT"

The development of the farm journals in this period cannot be understood without some insight into the growth of agrarian discontent — what was often called the "farmers' movement" — and into the geographical, industrial, and mechanical changes in agriculture.

The shift of agrarian resources to the Middle West was generally recognized: "The centre of the grain-growing region, which has, within a few years, been transferred from Ohio to Indiana, and again to Illinois, is now west of the Mississippi," said an *Atlantic* observer in 1872.[43] Thus the political and industrial contests in which agriculture had become embroiled took on a sectional appearance, and the West seemed to array itself against the East. Eastern periodicals were apt to be contemptuous or indignant about the "farmers' movement." The *Atlantic Monthly* editorially condemned the leaders of the revolt for their "profound contempt for law, justice, and honesty" in their crusade against the railroads.[44] The *Nation* declared, in the year in which the granges were first organized:

> That it is from a general want of wisdom, information and enterprise, and a general prevalence of stupid self-conceit and shortsighted economy among our farmers, that the average crops and the profits of agriculture are so small as they are, there is abundant evidence.[45]

The Patrons of Husbandry were first organized in 1867, thus beginning what came to be called the "grange movement"; and in the autumn of 1873 an observer for the *Scientific American* reported 5,000 granges, with a membership of 300,000 and an

[43] *Atlantic Monthly*, XXX, 347 (September 1872).
[44] *Ibid.*, XXXII, 511 (October 1873).
[45] *Nation*, IV, 147 (February 21, 1867).

expectation of 50 per cent increase by the end of that year.[46] As a matter of history, grange membership more than tripled during the winter of 1873–74.[47] "It is in a great degree an educational institution," explained one of the grange's supporters, the *Prairie Farmer*, though

to ensure success it has been considered essential to provide an initiative ceremony of a secret nature. . . . This order gives the farmers the strength of a united interest, and at the same time promotes education and a love for rural life.[48]

It was in 1873, year of the panic and of extraordinary growth of granges, that Illinois leaders of the movement established the *Industrial Age* [49] in Chicago and that the *Prairie Farmer* began a department devoted to the grange. Within twelve months scores of grange papers sprang up all over the West and South;[50] soon state granges were founding or naming "official organs," and in 1877 the National Grange began the publication of its official *Grange Record* at Louisville, Kentucky, — but the movement was already declining by that date. About a hundred periodicals were either organs or allies of the Patrons of Husbandry.[51]

Another organized movement of agriculture was the Farmers' Alliance, which was first given effectiveness through the work of Milton George, of the *Western Rural*.[52] George had taken over this paper in 1877, making it a strong antirailroad organ; and

---

[46] *Scientific American*, XXIX, 128 (August 30, 1873).

[47] See Solon J. Buck, *The Granger Movement* (Harvard Historical Series, Cambridge, 1913) for an excellent treatment of this movement.

[48] *Prairie Farmer*, XXI, 288 (May 2, 1868).

[49] Ended 1877. J. A. Noonan, C. C. Buell, and others were editors.

[50] See Buck, *op. cit.*, pp. 288–290, 321–329. Among the more important of the grange papers were the *California Patron* (1875–89), San Francisco; *Southern Planter and Grange* (1873–80), Atlanta; *Western Granger and Home Journal* (1871–79), Lafayette, Indiana; *Farmers' Union* (1867–1924), Minneapolis, called the *Farmers' Tribune* after 1883; *Patron of Husbandry* (1873–83), Columbus, Mississippi; *Husbandman* (1874–93), Elmira, New York; *Dirigo Rural* (1874–87), Bangor, Maine; *Farmer's Friend and Grange Advocate* (1874–1902), Mechanicsburg, Pennsylvania; *Cincinnati Grange Bulletin* (1876–1906), called the *American Grange Bulletin* after it became in 1883 the organ of the National Grange, and succeeded by the present *National Grange Monthly*, of Springfield, Massachusetts.

[51] Buck lists ninety-nine for the seventies, *op. cit.*, pp. 321–329.

[52] See vol. II, p. 90.

in 1880 he promoted the first Cook County clubs of the Farmers' Alliance. But the great swarm of periodicals devoted to this cause came in a later period.[53]

Farmer's grievances were voiced at length in the agricultural press. Perhaps it was true, as the eastern *Hearth and Home* declared, that the granges did not quite know what they were after;[54] but they did know that the farmer was in trouble. "Good wheat will bring only forty cents in Iowa, and a slow sale at that,"[55] reported the *Prairie Farmer*; and the *Iowa Homestead* reported "Corn flat and dull at 23–28" in January 1871.[56] Those were the days when Iowa farmers burned corn for fuel.[57] The feeling against the railroads was intense. The *Michigan Farmer* asserted:

A bushel of wheat that ought to be conveyed to New York from Michigan for ten cents and then pay a reasonable profit on the actual capital invested in the road, now has to pay twenty-five cents. . . . This species of legalized robbery is fully as atrocious as that of the robber barons of the Rhine in the Middle Ages.[58]

"So silently have these iron coils encircled the country," said the *Prairie Farmer*, "so fascinated have these people been by the fiery eye of the engine, that not until they feel the grinding, crushing contraction do they become conscious of their condition and their doom."[59] In Illinois, state regulation of freight rates was attempted.[60] Another remedy which was widely tried was coöperative buying. The granges made a convenient nucleus for this movement; it began by merely clubbing together to buy tools and clothes,[61] but it later extended to actual manufacture and to mail-order buying on a large scale. Montgomery, Ward & Company was originally organized as a part of this movement.

Farming shared in the changes brought about in these years

[53] To be treated in the succeeding volume of this work.
[54] *Hearth and Home*, V, 614 (September 27, 1873).
[55] *Prairie Farmer*, XLI, 89 (March 26, 1870).
[56] *Iowa Homestead*, January 6, 1871, p. 8.
[57] *Annals of Iowa*, IV, 544 (October 1900).
[58] *Michigan Farmer*, January 15, 1871.
[59] *Prairie Farmer*, XLI, 112 (April 16, 1870).
[60] See *Prairie Farmer* through the early seventies.
[61] *Iowa Homestead*, March 10, 1871, p. 5.

by mechanical invention. The Oliver chilled plow with self-scouring moldboard, the cheap windmill, improved grain drills, and — most wonderful of all —

the self-binder, that perfection of farm machinery, that ghostly marvel of a thing, with the single sinister arm, tossing the finished sheaves from it in such a nervous, spiteful, feminine style [62]

— these revolutionized farm work. Agricultural machinery soon had its own journal — the *Farm Implement News* (1882–current), a Chicago monthly.

IMPROVEMENT AND INCREASE IN FARM JOURNALS

The rapid increase of agricultural journals is an indication of the interest of the farmers in improved methods, for these papers were not only exponents, in advertisement and editorial, of better machinery, but they were practical and scientific teachers of better farming. The *American Agriculturist* declared in 1869 that "the agricultural press was never half so well conducted or so influential as today." [63] It further pointed out that the general magazines were printing many articles on country life and farming, citing Donald G. Mitchell's work in the *Atlantic* and that of Charles Wyllys Elliott in the *Galaxy*. The farming articles by Solon Robinson and others in the weekly *New York Tribune* were famous; and indeed most newspapers, even in the larger cities, gave attention to agricultural matters, especially in weekly editions designed chiefly for farmer readers.

The census figures indicate about ninety agricultural periodicals for 1870, and nearly double that for 1880; and the directories show the addition of over a hundred more to the total by the end of our period in 1885. These journals will best be considered regionally, since few of them, because of climatic and topographical differences the country over, had more than a regional circulation.

EASTERN FARM PAPERS

The *American Cultivator* [64] at Boston was the leading New England farm journal at the end of the Civil War, and it main-

---

[62] H. H. Boyesen in *Scribner's Monthly*, XIX, 134 (November 1879).

[63] *American Agriculturist*, XXVIII, 325 (September 1869).

[64] Published 1839–1915; originally called *Boston Cultivator*.

tained a considerable circulation for many years thereafter. A third *New England Farmer* [65] was begun in 1865, to continue for half a century. Two years later the *New England Homestead* was founded at Springfield by Henry M. Burt; it flourished in weekly and monthly editions, and shortly after the close of our period it undertook a big experiment in agricultural journalism by a consolidation of important regional papers.[66] In 1880 the *Homestead's* monthly edition gave way to *Farm and Home* (1880–1925), a national journal which obtained a very large circulation at a low price. *Farm and Home* was following the example, in this kind of exploitation, of certain western journals [67] and of Augusta, Maine, mail-order papers. Of the Augusta farm papers, the Vickery company's *Farm and Hearth* (1878–87) was the largest. *Our Country Home*,[68] of Greenfield, Massachusetts, was another booming paper. A more modest and enduring New England venture was the *Connecticut Farmer* (1875–1927) at New Haven, called *New England Farms* after 1915.

The oldest of the farm journals published in New York City was the *American Agriculturist*,[69] generally considered in these years the foremost periodical of its class. During the first half of our period, it led all its fellows in circulation as well as in prestige. In 1868 D. D. T. Moore brought his *Rural New Yorker* [70] from Rochester to New York, where he soon went bankrupt; his creditors continued the paper, however, and it lived to find success again. *Hearth and Home* [71] had strong agricultural interests, though chiefly a literary miscellany. A new paper was formed in 1875 by the union of the *Working Farmer*, which had been published in New York since 1849, and the *National Agriculturist*, begun in Cleveland in 1860; the new

[65] The weekly edition was regarded as a continuation of Fessenden's *New England Farmer* (1822–46), and the monthly edition, begun in 1867, as a continuation of the second *New England Farmer* (1848–64). The monthly edition ended in 1871. Both were published by R. P. Eaton & Company.

[66] See the sketch of the *American Agriculturist* in Mott, *op. cit.*, p. 731.

[67] *Home and Farm*, Louisville, and *Farm and Fireside*, Springfield, Ohio. See p. 156.

[68] It began in 1884, a sister publication of the similarly exploited *Good Cheer* (1882–88), a home monthly; but it was moved to Boston in 1887, where it was published until 1894 under the name *Our Grange Homes*.

[69] See Mott, *op. cit.*, p. 728.   [70] See vol. II, p. 89.   [71] See p. 99.

name was the *National Agriculturist and Working Farmer*, but the paper perished in 1881 without ever having attained more than 6,000 circulation.

There were papers in Rochester to succeed *Moore's Rural New Yorker* when it was taken away to New York — among them the *American Rural Home* (1871–91), a dollar weekly which attained a large circulation, and the *Empire State Agriculturist* (1880–97), a fifty-cent monthly called *Farm Life* in its last decade. At Albany, Luther Tucker merged his weekly *Country Gentleman* [72] and monthly *Cultivator* [73] in 1866 under the name of the *Cultivator and Country Gentleman* — the title it retained until 1898. The *Orange County Farmer* (1881–1917) was a prosperous journal at Port Jervis, New York, called the *New York Farmer* during its last twenty years; and the *Chautauqua Farmer* (1869–98) was a smaller paper at Dunkirk.

In Philadelphia the *Practical Farmer* continued to lead the field until the distinctive little *Farm Journal*,[74] founded in 1877, forged far ahead of it. The *Farm Journal* was a small eight-page monthly sold at the low subscription price of twenty-five cents a year. Wilmer Atkinson, its founder and its editor for forty years, and such contributors as "Judge Jacob Biggle," with his Elmwood Farm letters, gave it a certain quality in spite of its cheapness. There was variety, and the antidote for "Peter Tumbledown" was found in the Experimental Farm articles. The homeliness of the *Journal*, its dry wit, its mass of practical hints, and its price brought it a large and constantly growing circulation. Albert J. Merrill's *Market Basket* (1880–1913) was a dollar weekly, and later, with a change of name to *Rural Farmer* in 1900, a fifty-cent weekly. *Farm and Garden* (1881–88) was a fifty-cent monthly with a considerable circulation.

[72] Treated more fully in vol. II, sketch 22.

[73] See Mott, *op. cit.*, p. 443.

[74] See "From Acorn to Oak," a historical pamphlet issued by the *Farm Journal;* the *Journal's* Fiftieth Anniversary number for March 1927; Sixtieth Anniversary number for March 1937; and *Wilmer Atkinson: An Autobiography* (Philadelphia, 1920). Atkinson's nephew, Charles F. Jenkins, became a partner in 1893; Graham Patterson has been publisher since July 1935. Current events became an important feature in 1936, Walter B. Pitkin being enlisted as "editorial director." Under its new ownership it took a strong political position against the Roosevelt "New Deal."

These were the chief Philadelphia farm journals of the period. The quarterly *Sugar Beet* (1880–1911) was a specialist in that city; and the *Pennsylvania Farmer* (1880–current) was founded at Mercer, Pennsylvania, as a dollar weekly and was moved successively to Meadville, Philadelphia, and Pittsburgh, cutting its price to fifty cents.

SOUTHERN FARM JOURNALS

In February 1866 the *American Agriculturist* remarked: "As an indication of returning prosperity at the South, we are glad to note the appearance of southern agricultural papers," and it pointed out that the *Southern Cultivator*, then published by William N. White at Athens, Georgia, was the only southern publication of its class which had survived the war.[75] White died in 1867, and a few years afterward the *Cultivator* was moved to Atlanta; in 1882 it absorbed the *Dixie Farmer* (1868–82), which had recently moved to Atlanta from Knoxville, Tennessee.[76] Another Atlanta paper was the *Plantation* (1870–73), founded by T. C. Howard and R. A. Alston as an agricultural and life insurance periodical, taken over by Ben C. Yancey and others in 1871, and made a monthly in the following year.

Baltimore was another center of southern agricultural journalism. The patriarchal *American Farmer*,[77] which had been suspended during the war, resumed publication there in 1866. The *Maryland Farmer* (1864–1902) was a war-born monthly which changed its name in 1877 to the *Farmers' and Planters' Guide*. Both Baltimore and Atlanta had their grange organs.[78]

Chief of the Virginia farm papers were the *Southern Planter*, of Richmond, which resumed publication in 1867 after a wartime suspension, and the *Rural Messenger* (1871–82), of Petersburg. At Raleigh the *North Carolina Farmer* (1876–93), called *Southern Farmer* in its last few years, was the leader, while the

[75] *American Agriculturist*, XXV, 49 (February 1866).
[76] It then changed its name to *Southern Cultivator and Dixie Farmer*, which it retained until it absorbed another Knoxville paper, *Farming* (1902–26), when it became *Southern Cultivator and Farming*.
[77] See Mott, *op. cit.*, p. 153.
[78] See p. 149, footnote.

Farmer and Mechanic (1877–1908), under newspaper ownership, was a home and farm miscellany. The *Rural Carolinian* (1869–76) was an earlier and briefer venture at Charleston. The *Cotton Plant* (1883–1904) began at Marion, South Carolina, soon moving to Columbia. The *Florida Dispatch* (1869–1910) was a Jacksonville advertising sheet which developed into a farm journal of standing and fair circulation, and the *Florida Agriculturist* (1879–1911) was E. O. Painter's paper at De Land.

The *Southern Agriculturist* (1869–current) was founded at Corinth, Mississippi, by Thomas J. Key as *Model Farmer*, but soon changed its name to *Agriculturist and Legal Tender*, and, with various changes of name and many changes of home office throughout the South, found a permanent home in the nineties at Nashville. Major Key was its editor for forty years. The *Sugar Bowl and Farm Journal* (1870–1910) began at New Iberia, Louisiana, moved to New Orleans in 1884, and changed title ten years later to *Sugar Planter*. E. F. Russell's *Rural Southland* was issued from New Orleans from 1869 to 1873, when it was consolidated with James H. Hummel's *Our Home Journal* (1871–75), of the same city. The *Arkansas Farmer* (1875–95) was a cheap paper published by the Arkansas Real Estate and Livestock Association at Little Rock throughout much of its life, and the *Rural and Workman* (1883–91) was another Little Rock paper, finally devoured by the *Farmer*, which did not long survive the meal. Texas had, besides livestock journals which will be considered later, two farm papers still current: the *Texas Farmer*, begun in 1880 as a grange organ at Belton, but made the Texas edition of the *Progressive Farmer* in 1913, with its home at Dallas; and the Dallas *Farm and Ranch*, largest of southwestern farm papers, founded by F. P. Holland in 1883.

WESTERN FARM JOURNALS

Louisville, second only to Cincinnati among the cities of the Ohio Valley, was both southern and western, and therefore happily situated to command circulations for its farm papers. The *Farmer's Home Journal* (1867–1932) was founded in Lexington by J. J. Miller, but was moved to Louisville in 1875 under the care of John Duncan; and Louisville had other shorter-lived farm and stock papers. But that city's outstanding success came with the founding of *Home and Farm* (1876–1918) by B. F. Avery and Sons. A semimonthly, sold at fifty cents a year, this paper soon reached a circulation of 100,000. The next year after it began its phenomenal career, P. P. Mast & Company, located at Springfield, Ohio, some 150 miles away, began their *Farm and Fireside* (1877–current) along the same lines and with the same success. In 1881 the Masts carried the war into their rivals' territory by issuing a "Southern Edition" from Louisville, and by the late eighties they had shot far ahead of the Avery paper.[79]

Two other low-priced Ohio farm papers won considerable circulations before the end of our period: the *Farmer's Home* (1880–1902), of Dayton, and *City and Country* (1882–99), of Columbus. But among papers of more nearly standard price and quality, the *Ohio Farmer*,[80] at Cleveland, maintained its leadership.

Thus also the Chicago *Prairie Farmer*.[81] The primacy of the latter in Chicago, however, was challenged by a strong field of competitors. Chief of these were General Charles H. Howard's *Farm, Field and Fireside* (1877–1925),[82] and Hannibal H. Chandler's *Farmers' Review* (1877–1918). The *Western Rural*[83] continued in spite of financial reverses. Chicago was also notable for its livestock papers and for other forms of journalistic specialization in the agricultural field. At Quincy, Illinois, was published the *Farmers' Call* (1881–1924), called the *Illinois Farmer and Farmers' Call* after 1909; and at Moline, Illinois, there was the *Western Plowman* (1882–1900), which

---

[79] Changes in the publishing organization eventually transformed Mast & Company into the Crowell Publishing Company. Herbert Quick, who was editor 1909–16, exercised considerable influence by his editorials on farm economics. His fiction serial, "The Brown Mouse," dealt with the problem of rural education. The title was changed to *Country Home* in 1930.

[80] See vol. II, p. 89. M. E. Williams was the most important of its editors during this period.

[81] See Mott, *op. cit.*, p. 444, footnote.

[82] Called *Farm, Field and Stockman*, 1885–93. It then returned to its former name, but in 1906 became *National Monthly Farm Press*, and in 1913 *Better Farming*. See F. W. Scott, *Newspapers and Periodicals of Illinois, 1814–79* (Springfield, 1910), p. 140.   [83] See vol. II, 90.

absorbed *South and West* (1880–86), of St. Louis, adding that name to its own title, and then moved to Chicago for its last few years.

At St. Louis the old *Valley Farmer* [84] changed its name at the beginning of our period to *Colman's Rural World*, but fell behind the *Midland Farmer* (1872–86) in the race for circulation. *Home, Farm and Factory* (1883–95) was a fifty-cent monthly.

The second *Western Farmer* (1882–1929) to be established at Madison, Wisconsin, became the second *Wisconsin Farmer* in 1891. The *Racine Agriculturist* (1877–current) became, after various minor changes of title, the *Wisconsin Agriculturist* in 1893.

At Minneapolis there were the *Minnesota Farmer and Stockman* (1877–87), H. E. Newton editor, and *Farm, Stock and Home* (1884–1929), long edited by S. M. Owen. The latter was transferred to St. Paul in 1929.

At Des Moines there were the veteran *Iowa Homestead*,[85] and the *Western Farm Journal* (1870–97); the latter, which was for a time consolidated with the *Homestead*, absorbed at least six other Iowa farm journals in the seventies and changed its name in 1887 to *Live Stock and Western Farm Journal* upon taking over the *Farm Journal and Live Stock Review* (1879–86) of Cedar Rapids, Iowa. A more famous Cedar Rapids paper was the *Iowa Farmer* (1878–92), which was edited for some years by James Wilson, later the first Secretary of Agriculture; apparently this was the forerunner of *Wallace's Farmer*, which furnished two more Secretaries of Agriculture.[86] The *Iowa Tribune* was founded in 1878 as an organ of the Greenback party and edited for a decade or more by General J. B. Weaver, that party's nominee for president in 1880, together with Congressman E. H. Gillette. It became increasingly a farm paper toward the nineties until its name was changed to the *Iowa Farmer's Tribune* in 1892; it was given to E. T. Mer-

---

[84] See vol. II, p. 88, footnote.   [85] See vol. II, p. 89.

[86] N. B. Ashby disposed of the paper in 1892 to Henry C. Wallace, of Ames, and the name underwent changes in which *Farm and Dairy* was prominent. It was moved to Des Moines in 1896. See Gerald Seaman, "Some Early Iowa Farm Journals" (Iowa State College thesis, 1936).

edith, later Secretary of Agriculture under Wilson, as a wedding present in 1895.[87]

The *Nebraska Cultivator and Housekeeper* (1869–89) was an Omaha paper; and the *Nebraska Farmer* (1877–current) lived at Omaha through a part of the nineties, though it had been published at Lincoln throughout most of its life. The *Missouri and Kansas Farmer* (1884–1920) was a Kansas City monthly which built up a considerable circulation at twenty-five cents a year. At Topeka the *Kansas Farmer* continued, Senator W. A. Peffer being its editor in the eighties.

The *Dakota Farmer* (1881–current) was founded at Huron, but moved to Aberdeen in the nineties. The *Northwestern Farmer* (1882–current) began in Fargo, Dakota Territory, as the *Sugar Beet News*; after changing its name it was moved in 1890 to St. Paul, there to become a second *St. Paul Farmer* in 1899.[88]

The *Rocky Mountain Husbandman* (1875–current) was published in the village of White Springs, Montana Territory, for many years by R. N. Sutherlin; it was moved by him to Great Falls in 1907. The *North Pacific Rural Spirit* (1879–current) was a Portland, Oregon, paper which became the *Western Breeders' Journal* in 1919. The *Willamette Farmer* (1869–87) began at Salem as the *Oregon Agriculturist*, and later moved to Portland. The *Northwestern Farmer* (1881–1928), of Portland, became the *Pacific Farmer* in 1887, and later the *Northwest-Pacific Farmer*.

In San Francisco the *California Farmer* continued until its merger in 1884 in the *Pacific Rural Press* (1871–current). The *Rural Californian* (1877–1914), of Los Angeles, was called *Semi-Tropic California* until 1882. At San José the *Santa Clara*

---

[87] See *Edwin T. Meredith 1876–1928, A Memorial Volume* (Des Moines, 1931), pp. 8–9. The paper had been bought by Thomas Meredith, grandfather of the young publisher, in 1893. It was sold in 1904 to a stock company which moved it to Sioux City. It was purchased by H. C. McMillan in 1905 and consolidated two years later with the *Farmer and Breeder* (which had been begun at Sheldon, Iowa, in 1895 and later was moved to Sioux City and published by John C. Kelly) but the title *Farmer and Breeder* was not adopted by the consolidated paper until 1911. It was moved to Sioux Falls, South Dakota, in 1921 and eight years later merged in the St. Paul *Farmer*.

[88] It absorbed *Farm, Stock and Home* (*supra*) in 1929, and became *Farmer and Farm, Stock and Home*.

TYPICAL FRONT PAGE OF SENSATIONAL BOYS' PAPER

How the word *sleuth* was popularized as a synonym for *detective*.

A SCENE FROM "THE BLACK CROOK"

A *Police Gazette* representation of the "desperate encounter" between Stalacta and the Black Crook in the mother of all burlesque shows.

Valley was begun in 1884, continuing through the nineties as *Pacific Tree and Vine,* and ending in 1913 at San Francisco as the *California Country Journal.*

LIVESTOCK JOURNALS

The general farm journal commonly treated livestock breeding, dairying, poultry raising, and horticulture, as well as the agronomical topics which formed its chief interest. There were, however, certain special journals, increasing in number, which were devoted to farm matters other than agronomy; and of these the livestock journals formed the most important group.

Chicago was the great livestock center. There the *National Live Stock Journal* (1870–91) was founded by George W. Rust, publisher, and John P. Reynolds, editor. James H. Sanders, who had published the pioneer *Western Stock Journal*[89] at Sigourney, Iowa, came to the *National Live Stock Journal* in 1874 as managing editor.[90] He left it, however, in 1881 to found the *Breeder's Gazette,*[91] taking with him many contributors and his son, Alvin H. Sanders. The latter soon took over the active management of the new journal, aided by such brilliant writers as William H. Goodwin and Joseph E. Wing. A third great livestock paper in Chicago was the *Drovers' Journal* (1873–current), founded by Harvey L. Goodall. It soon became a daily, but continued its weekly edition (changing the name in 1900 to *Goodall's Farmer*) until 1910.

At Lexington the *Kentucky Livestock Record* (1875–current) became in 1896 the *Thoroughbred Record* and eventually absorbed the *Kentucky Stock Farm* (1883–1912), also of that city. The *Live-Stock Indicator* (1873–1922), of Kansas City, began as *Price Current and Live Stock Record* and ended as the *Farmer and Stockman.*

In Texas, the *Live-Stock Journal* (1880–1913), of Fort

---

[89] A little monthly published in 1869–70, and then merged with the *National Live Stock Journal.* It was apparently the second of the livestock journals, the *American Stock Journal* (1866–72), Parkesburg, Pennsylvania, probably being the first.

[90] See W. E. Ogilvie, *Pioneer Agricultural Journalists* (Chicago, 1917), p. 70.

[91] *Ibid.,* pp. 72, 78; *Breeder's Gazette,* LXX, 1176 (December 21, 1916); Alvin H. Sanders, *At the Sign of the Stockyard Inn* (Chicago, 1915).

Worth, became "the first periodical in the world devoted to range stock." In the nineties it was moved to Dallas and called the *Texas Stock and Farm Journal*, and later, in Fort Worth, it appeared as the *National Co-Operator and Farm Journal*. Meantime the *Texas Stockman* (1881–1916) was being published in San Antonio, its title changed to *Texas Stockman and Farmer* after 1887.

In the East the *American Stockman* began in Pittsburgh in 1877 and gained a considerable circulation by the end of our period as the *National Stockman and Farmer*. It ended in 1921. The *Thoroughbred Stock Journal* (1881–89) was a fifty-cent monthly in Philadelphia.

Horse breeding will perhaps be better considered in connection with turf journals,[92] but two or three dairy papers may be mentioned here: the *American Dairyman* (1876–1907), of New York; and the *Jersey Bulletin* (1883–current), which was called the *Jersey Bulletin and Dairy World* after it absorbed C. S. Burch's *Dairy World* (1884–1905), of Chicago.

The *Swine Breeders' Journal* (1882–1928), of Indianapolis, went over to the Durocs in its fortieth year, prefacing its title with the word *Duroc*. The *American Berkshire Record* (1876–1923), of Springfield, Illinois, a mere chronicle of pedigrees issued by the American Berkshire Association, is supposed to have been the first periodical entirely devoted to hogs.

Probably the first American sheep journal was F. D. and A. H. Craig's *American Merino* [93] (1882–84), at Mazomanie and East Troy, Wisconsin. But the great periodical in this field was the *American Sheep Breeder and Wool Grower*, founded in Chicago in 1884 by C. S. Burch, a pioneer photoengraver and later a bishop of the Episcopal church, and conducted by the Burch family for many years.[94] It was a spokesman for the National Wool Growers' Association until 1911 and fought through many a campaign for the tariff on wool.

[92] See p. 215.

[93] See *American Sheep Breeder*, L, 5 (January 1930), which says the *American Merino* began in 1880. But there appear to be no files before 1882, and the volume for that year is Vol. I.

[94] See W. W. Burch's "Back of These Pages Is a Story," *American Sheep Breeder*, XL, 39 (January 1920).

POULTRY AND BEES

A flock of poultry journals began in the seventies. Three or four of the most important of them were published at Hartford, Connecticut, including the *Poultry World* (1872–96). The *American Poultry Journal* (1874–current), was founded in Cedar Rapids, Iowa, by C. J. Ward, but moved to Chicago in 1876. Then there were the Albany *Poultry Monthly* (1878–1902), the Chicago *Poultry Keeper* (1884–current), now published at Quincy, Illinois, and so on.[95]

Apiarists had the old *American Bee Journal*,[96] together with a number of new arrivals, such as the *Bee Keepers' Magazine* (1872–89), Chicago; the *Bee Keepers' Guide* (1877–93), Kendallville, Indiana; and the *American Apiculturist* (1883–95), Wenham, Massachusetts. Next to the *Journal, Gleanings in Bee Culture* (1873–current), of Medina, Ohio, is the oldest apiarists' periodical.

GARDEN AND ORCHARD JOURNALS

At the close of the Civil War, the Philadelphia *Gardener's Monthly*[97] was the leading horticultural and floral journal; it absorbed the New York *Horticulturist* in 1875. But in 1872 a rival had begun as the *Flower Garden*, a modest Brooklyn quarterly at twenty-five cents a year. When it was a year old it was acquired by a firm of seed and bulb dealers, Beach, Son & Company, with Mrs. C. Y. Beach as editor, and renamed the *American Garden*. But it was not until R. K. Bliss & Sons, of New York, made it a monthly in 1882, with F. M. Hexamer as editor, that it became important. It soon absorbed the *Ladies' Floral Cabinet* (1872–87), New York, which had been founded and named by a man who thought flowers woman's special perquisite, Henry T. Williams; and in 1888 it absorbed the *Gardener's Monthly and Horticulturist*. It became *American Gardening* in 1892, ending twelve years later.[98]

---

[95] Two or three others should be named: *Ohio Poultry Journal* (1880–1908), Springfield, toward the end of its life called briefly and successively *American Poultryman* and *Farm Stock Success; Fanciers' Gazette* (1883–1906), Indianapolis; *Poultry Raiser* (1884–1911), Chicago, which in 1888 became *American Farmer, Livestock and Poultry Raiser*. [96] See vol. II, p. 91. [97] See vol. II, p. 90.

[98] See "Fifty Years of Horticultural Journalism," *American Gardening*, XVII, 1 (January 4, 1896).

Vick's Illustrated Monthly Magazine (1878–1909), of Rochester, New York, was another floral journal published by a seed house. The *California Horticulturist* (1870–80) was a San Francisco periodical; *Bowditch's American Florist and Farmer* (1881–89) was issued from Boston; and *Orchard and Garden* (1878–92) was J. T. Lovett's fifty-cent monthly at Little Silver, New Jersey.

CHAPTER VII

EDUCATION AND ART

THE American people are "the most generally educated in the world," wrote Daniel Coit Gilman, lately become the first president of Johns Hopkins University, in a centennial article prepared for the *North American Review*. In connection with this declaration, he noted especially the spread of the public school system to all the states and territories.[1] And whether the general success or the numerous failures of education in America gave rise to the more lively discussions of educational topics, certainly the magazines and reviews of the postbellum period used their pages freely for debate upon the problems of the schools.

KINDERGARTEN AND PUBLIC SCHOOLS

These discussions ran the gamut from kindergarten to university. Froebel's kindergarten theories and methods received attention in both general and professional magazines. Elizabeth Peabody's *Kindergarten Messenger*, of Cambridge, was the organ of Bronson Alcott's school. It began in 1873, but three years later it became a small department in the *New England Journal of Education;* in 1878 it was merged with W. N. Hailmann's *New Education* (1877–82), of Milwaukee, which thereupon became the *Kindergarten Messenger and New Education*. The Boston *Primary Teacher* began in 1877, to continue with a considerable circulation under variations of name until 1916; and the *American Kindergarten Magazine* (1878–87), of New York, also underwent sundry alterations in title before its eventual merger with the *Phrenological Journal*.

Despite President Gilman's eulogy of the common school, that American institution was occasionally subjected to severe criticism. Abuses of the system were often complained of in the *North American Review* and other magazines of the eighties. "A great deal has been said of late, in newspapers and elsewhere, about overwork by the pupils of the public schools," [2] observed

---

[1] *North American Review*, CXXII, 191 (January 1876).
[2] *Ibid.*, CXXXVI, 295 (March 1883).

the *North American* in 1883; and two years later the *Andover Review*, noting that criticism of the common schools was "never so serious as at the present time," [3] devoted a series of editorials to comment on the health, morals, curricula, and methods prevailing in them.

THE COLLEGE CURRICULUM

But the big debate of the period in the educational field was that of the sciences versus the classics in college curricula.

Charles W. Eliot, who became president of Harvard in 1869, published in that year an important paper in the *Atlantic* on "The New Education." He advocated a system of electives based largely upon pure and applied science, living European languages, and mathematics, rather than upon the older fixed curriculum of Greek, Latin, and mathematics.[4] The controversy raised by the proposals in this article spread into many of the magazines. President Noah Porter, of Yale, in his treatise *The American College and the American Public*, published serially in the *New Englander* through 1869,[5] and in other papers took the negative, with its championship of classical education. Charles Astor Bristed, who had distinguished himself in an English university, wrote a two-part article for *Lippincott's* called "The Dispute about Liberal Education," in which he took the side of the classics.[6] President Andrew D. White, of Cornell, supported President Eliot in various articles. Nearly all the magazines were interested in the debate; the *Princeton Review* and *Popular Science Monthly* took prominent parts. But one outcome was possible, however, and President Eliot was able to write in *Our Continent* in 1882: "The adoption of what is called the elective or optional system of studies in the leading American colleges and universities, instead of a fixed and uniform curriculum, makes an epoch in the history of superior education." [7]

[3] *Andover Review*, III, 268 (March 1885). Article entitled "The Crusade against the Public Schools."

[4] *Atlantic Monthly*, XXIII, 203, 358 (February, March 1869). A forerunner of these articles is the alumni address of F. H. Hedge, published in *ibid.*, XVIII, 304 (September 1866).

[5] *New Englander*, XXVIII, 69 ff. (January 1869).

[6] *Lippincott's Magazine*, II, 295, 389 (September, October 1868).

[7] *Our Continent*, I, 24 (February 22, 1882).

In connection with this debate, it was pointed out by Professor Thomas R. Lounsbury, writing in the *New Englander:*

In many of our colleges a man might go through a four-year course and never once hear from the lips of any of his teachers the names of Shakespeare and Milton. . . . The student either picks up at haphazard any knowledge he may acquire of the structure of our own tongue, or does not acquire it at all.[8]

At about the same time the *Yale Literary Magazine* complained that "comparatively little interest is felt in college, in literary composition." [9]

Nevertheless, the college literary magazines multiplied, until by 1885 they had increased to well over a hundred.[10] The *Yale Lit* itself was one of the most flourishing of them: true, it had been referred to sarcastically by *Life* as "a powerful organ, devoted to foot-ball, amateur poetry, and other colossal interests," [11] but then *Life* was conducted by young men fresh from Harvard, and what could one expect from rivals? The *Brunonian* had been revived in 1868 by Brown University students, but had not yet bethought itself to flaunt a date which would make it older than the *Yale Lit.*[12] The *Nassau Literary Magazine*, another veteran,[13] was conducted by editor after editor at Princeton. The *Harvard Advocate* began its long career as a literary periodical in 1866, issued fortnightly at the beginning. The *Harvard Crimson* was originally a literary magazine.[14] At Columbia, *Cap and Gown* was published (1868–73) under the editorship of Seth Low and others; it was followed by the more

---

[8] *New Englander*, XXIX, 571 (October 1870).

[9] *Yale Literary Magazine*, XXXVII, 440 (July 1872).

[10] See Ayer and Rowell directories. Their lists include the student newspapers, but the great majority of periodicals listed are more or less literary. In 1882 a Collegiate Press Association was organized, John Kendrick Bangs, of Columbia, being its first president.

[11] *Life*, III, 58 (January 31, 1884).

[12] The *Yale Lit* was begun in 1836. (See Mott, *A History of American Magazines, 1741–1850*, p. 488; and vol. II, p. 99.) The *Brunonian* published twelve numbers (1829–31) and was then suspended until 1868. It was merged in 1898 with the *Brown Magazine*.

[13] See Mott, *op. cit.*, p. 489.

[14] Founded in 1873, it was called the *Magenta* for two years. In 1883 it was united with the *Herald* and became a newspaper. See *The Harvard Crimson Fiftieth Anniversary* (Cambridge, 1923).

illustrious *Acta Columbiana* [15] (1873–85). The *Acta* should have a niche of its own in the hall of fame for collegiate journalism. Under Harry Thurston Peck in 1879–80, under Nicholas Murray Butler (known as the *"Acta* Fiend") in 1880–81, and especially under John Kendrick Bangs in 1882–83, it was a gem of purest ray serene. Here Bangs won his first reputation as a humorous author, and under the names of Shakespeare Jones and T. Carlyle Smith ("the Great Collegiate Vituperator") he wrote pieces which not only gave flavor and charm to one of the best of college magazines, but were widely quoted in the general press.

The *Cornell Review* (1874–86) was a student monthly of literary proclivities. Further west the *Oberlin Review* began in 1873, the *Notre Dame Scholastic* in 1872, the monthly *Illini* at the University of Illinois in 1871, the monthly *Simpsonian* at Simpson College in 1870, and so on. These four were all mainly literary in intention when they were begun; but today they are newspapers, the *Illini* being a daily. Though these and others have continued without change of name, there was generally a lack of continuity in college periodicals because of changing student personnel.

Certain of the general magazines also had university affiliations. The *Atlantic Monthly*, for instance, had a peculiar interest in Harvard,[16] as did the *North American Review* before its removal to New York. The *New Englander* was a true son of Old Eli; at the very end of our period it acknowledged its parent by adding *and Yale Review* to its title. The *Princeton Review*, which became a general magazine in 1878, though transplanted to New York and lost to the "Princeton theology," had many ties binding it to the University. Of course, scholarly publications were generally published under university auspices or editorship; Johns Hopkins early made Baltimore a center for the publication of such journals.

[15] See *Columbia University Quarterly*, II, 350–353 (September 1900) and III, 135 (March 1901), for these magazines.
[16] The *Atlantic's* first editor, Lowell, was a Harvard professor throughout his editorship. Under Howells the magazine was less Harvardian.

EDUCATIONAL JOURNALS

Appleton's Journal, in a paragraph undoubtedly written by E. L. Youmans, asked in 1869:

Why is it that our educational journals drag out their existence at such a poor dying rate, that the presumptions are constantly against their continuance, while many of them can only maintain the breath of life by voluntary subsidies or State aid? It is not because the subject is uninteresting, for there is today, to the very borders of civilization, a deeper concern in educational questions than the world has ever before witnessed. . . . The reason is that educational journals are professional, and therefore appeal to a narrow constituency.[17]

Those observations are full of truth; yet when Professor Youmans objected to the trend toward specialization in magazine content he was kicking against the pricks. The general magazines might discuss some of the larger questions of educational policy, but the teachers were sure to have their own special journals which would interest the general public but little.

Ayer's directory of periodicals was publishing the names of over a hundred educational weeklies and monthlies by the end of our period, and it is safe to say that at least twice that many were issued for shorter or longer terms between 1865 and 1885.[18] Most of these were state publications, supported either by state aid or by teachers' associations.

Perhaps the most famous of the pedagogical journals of the time was Barnard's *American Journal of Education*,[19] which gained prestige when its editor was appointed United States Commissioner of Education in 1867. The *American Educational Monthly*,[20] a New York journal founded shortly before the end of the preceding period, had a much larger circulation in the late sixties than any other journal of its class. Most prosperous of the state-supported periodicals was the *Pennsylvania School*

[17] *Appleton's Journal,* I, 122 (April 24, 1869).
[18] The Ayer lists are much more inclusive than that of S. E. Davis, *Educational Periodicals during the Nineteenth Century* (Washington, 1919), a valuable authority. The 1880 census gave eighty-eight as the number of educational periodicals.
[19] Treated more fully in vol. II, sketch 24.
[20] See vol. II, p. 99, footnote.

Journal,[21] though California and some other states continued a degree of state support for their school periodicals throughout many years. Many other educational journals prominent after the war survived from earlier periods.[22]

In New England, all the important periodicals devoted to education were merged in 1875 in a weekly *New England Journal of Education*,[23] edited by T. W. Bicknell. It later dropped its place designation and continued as the *Journal of Education* at Boston. Bicknell was also editor of *Education*, founded by him in 1880 as an international technical and philosophical journal.[24] In New York the E. L. Kellogg Company was active in the publication of new teachers' magazines: its two most successful ventures were the *School Journal* (1871–1916) and the *Teachers' Institute* (1878–1906). The latter monthly achieved the circulation leadership among journals of its class by 1880; it absorbed the Chicago *Practical Teacher* (1877–85), adding that name to its title in 1885. C. W. Bardeen's *School Bulletin and New York State Educational Journal* (1874–1920) was published at Syracuse.

In the South the *Educational Journal of Virginia* (1869–91) was an association organ at Richmond; the *West Virginia School Journal* (1881–current) was originally published by school officials at Wheeling and later by state superintendents in other cities; Eugene Harrell's *North Carolina Teacher* (1883–95) was published at Raleigh, and J. L. Lampson's *Southwestern Journal of Education* (1883–95) at Nashville, Tennessee. The *Texas School Journal* (1883–1932) was conducted by state superintendents of education at Houston and other cities.

Westward, the *American Journal of Education* (1868–1920),

[21] See vol. II, p. 99, footnote.

[22] See vol. II, pp. 96–99.

[23] Parties to the merger were *Maine Journal of Education* (1866–74), founded by George M. Gage as *Maine Normal* at Farmington, but later made an association organ and moved to Portland; *Massachusetts Teacher* (see vol. II, p. 99); *Rhode Island Schoolmaster* (1855–74), Providence, Bicknell's magazine; *Connecticut School Journal* (1871–74), New Haven, a continuation of the old *Connecticut Common School Journal* (see Mott, *op. cit.*, p. 694); and the *College Courant* (1867–74), a Yale magazine.

[24] It began as a bimonthly, but became a monthly (except July–August) in 1886. In that year William A. Mowry became editor. Editorial terms have since run as follows: Frank H. Kasson, 1891–1901; Frank Herbert Palmer, 1892–current; R. G. Boone, 1901–07.

founded in St. Louis by J. B. Merwin, who edited it there for twenty-five years, maintained a circulation leadership threatened only by two or three cheaper midwestern monthlies. One of these was D. H. Gable's *Home and School Visitor* (1881–1927), of Greenfield, Indiana, which was sold for seventy-five cents a year. Two Ohio teachers' journals were begun in 1880: the *School Visitor*, of Ansonia, and the *Guernsey County Teacher*, of Cambridge. The former continued through 1914 under the editorship of John S. Royer; the latter, founded by John McBurney, ran till 1935 as *Ohio Teacher* at Columbus. The *Michigan School Moderator* (1880–1921), of Lansing, was called *Moderator-Topics* through the last half of its life. Two Illinois educational journals were founded in 1881: E. O. Vaile's *Schoolmaster*, of Oak Park, which was called *Intelligence* from 1884 until its end in 1905; and the more important *Illinois School Journal*,[25] founded by E. J. James and Charles De Garmo. The *Minnesota Journal of Education* was begun in St. Paul in 1881; after more than half a dozen changes of name [26] and nearly that many changes of residence, it survives as the *School Executives' Magazine* at Lincoln, Nebraska. Two Iowa teachers' journals were founded in 1877: the official *Iowa Normal Monthly*, published at Dubuque, and continued to 1912; and W. J. Medes' *Central School Journal* (1877–95) at Keokuk. The *Missouri School Journal* (1883–current) began as the unofficial organ of the State Department of Education, Jefferson City.

Besides the many general school journals, there were some specialists, such as the kindergarten magazines already mentioned,[27] and certain journals more appropriately discussed in the sections relating to music and art, the Chautauqua, and juvenile periodicals. A whole flock of shorthand journals took flight in the seventies and eighties: perhaps the best known of them was

[25] During its first six years it was published at Normal, Illinois, and then moved to Bloomington. In 1889 it became *Public-School Journal*, and in 1898 *School and Home Education*. It was followed by the *American Review* (1923–26). George P. Brown (with others) was editor 1886–1900.

[26] Other titles were *Journal of School Education, School Education, National School Digest, Educational Digest, American Educational Digest*. It was published in St. Paul, Rochester, Minneapolis, and Crawfordsville (Indiana) before moving to Lincoln.

[27] See p. 163.

Browne's Phonographic Monthly (1875–99), of New York, which became a *Weekly* in 1889 and was called the *Shorthand Educator* after 1893. Three journals devoted to penmanship were the *Penman's Gazette and Business Educator* (1876–86) and the *Penman's Art Journal* (1877–1916), of New York, both claiming 10,000 circulation by 1885; and A. N. Palmer's *Western Penman*, begun in Cedar Rapids, Iowa, in 1885, but now published in New York as the *American Penman*. A speech magazine, Edgar S. Werner's *Voice* (1879–1902), was said to be "devoted to the human voice in all its phases: music, drama, oratory, elocution, expression, delsarte sytem, vocal defects, articulation-teaching, vocal physiology and hygiene, visible speech." Begun at Albany, it was moved to New York in 1887, and its name changed two years later to *Werner's Voice Magazine;* later, as *Werner's Magazine*, it was merely a repository for readings.

LIBRARIES

Libraries also had their importance as educational institutions, and they flourished like the green bay tree. "Persons who have no means of information on such a subject would be astonished at the number of public libraries of all kinds recently established throughout the West," remarked a Chicago observer.[28] The statistics of American libraries found in the successive reports of the Commissioner of Education were frequently commented upon in the periodicals — particularly the *Special Report on Libraries* of the centennial year of 1876, which enumerated 3,682 public libraries, containing 12,276,964 volumes.[29] "The year 1876 markt a distinct library era," wrote one of the leaders of the movement many years later. (The commentator, it must be explained in order to account for the spelling in the quotation, was Melville Dewey, who, as an apostle of spelling reform, was wont to spell his name Melvil Dui.) He continued his remark about the epochal year 1876 by saying that

It saw the birth of A L A, *Library Journal*, Library Bureau and Decimal Classification; but chiefly of that new missionary spirit that

[28] *Dial*, I, 16 (May 1880).
[29] *Harper's Monthly*, LIV, 722 (April 1877); *Galaxy*, XXIII, 639 (May 1877)

has stampt American library work as something quite different from anything the world had seen before.[30]

Dewey himself was the first editor of the *Library Journal*,[31] which grew out of a department in the *Publishers' Weekly;* it soon became a coöperative project which engaged the services of a large board of librarians. Another periodical that gave much attention to libraries was the Chicago *Dial*, which ran a library department in 1880–81.

LYCEUM AND CHAUTAUQUA

The lyceum may also be considered as an educational agency. It underwent marked changes after the war; its old machinery of local organizations devoted to study and lecture courses was, for the most part, abandoned, and control passed to newly organized central lecture and entertainment bureaus which dealt with Y. M. C. A.'s and local lecture or library associations. Under the new system, commercialism displaced the traditional idealistic and reform elements; notoriety was exploited; and mere entertainment, by singers, bellringers, humorists, and "elocutionists," was paramount. "A showman gets his first invitation for the same reason that an author does," wrote Dr. Holland in an excellent article on the subject in the *Atlantic Monthly*, "because he is notorious." [32] "John B. Gough is the most popular lecturer and Anna E. Dickinson the most popular lecturess in the country," said the *Literary World* in 1870. "Both make over twenty thousand dollars a year." [33] Beecher is said to have received the first $1,000 fee, and Gough to have made more than $30,000 annually in his best years;[34] while Henry M. Stanley, fresh from darkest Africa, got $100,000 for a hundred lectures in 1872, according to Major Pond, his manager.[35]

---

[30] *Libraries*, XXXI, 270 (June 1926).

[31] Treated more fully in sketch 29.

[32] *Atlantic Monthly*, XV, 364 (March 1865).

[33] *Literary World*, I, 77 (October 1870).

[34] See "A Brief History of the Lyceum," by Anna L. Curtis, in C. Augustus Wright's *Who's Who in the American Lyceum* (Philadelphia, 1906). Gough received an average of slightly less than $175 for each lecture delivered in 1867. See his *Autobiography* (Springfield, Massachusetts, 1870), pp. 247–248.

[35] J. B. Pond, *Eccentricities of Genius* (New York, 1900), p. 540.

The *Nation* put its finger on the weakness of the lyceum system when it condemned the rhetorician on the platform, "ever ready to treat any theme at a hundred dollars an hour"; [36] and the *Round Table*, with its eye for abuses, spoke of the "flimsy foundations of the sham reputations which popular lecturers have." [37] But they were not all flimsy: there were real reputations behind Henry Ward Beecher, E. H. Chapin, George William Curtis, and even John B. Gough — four of the leading lecturers of the time. Many of the veterans of the lyceum fell out soon after the end of the war — Emerson, Sumner, and Greeley, for example — but Holmes, Higginson, Holland, Phillips, DuChaillu, Youmans, Whipple, and Douglass all did more or less lecturing during the seventies. [38] Two of the big hits of the decade were made by humorists — Mark Twain and Artemus Ward. Then there was a considerable group of "lecturesses" — Miss Dickinson, Mrs. Howe, Mrs. Stanton, Miss Anthony, Mrs. Livermore, Victoria Woodhull, Olive Logan, Kate Field, and others. The best defense of the popular lecture is that given by Holland early in our period:

There certainly has never been a time in the history of America when there was such a generous and general toleration of all men and opinions as now; and as the popular lecture has been universal, with a determined aim and a manifest influence towards this end, it is but fair to claim for it a prominent agency in the result. [39]

But by 1875, signs of the new order were plentiful. *Appleton's Journal* was deprecating the dry-as-dust lecturer on the one hand and the king's jesters on the other. [40] Most of the great platform men were, for one reason or another, retiring. English speakers, like Froude and Tyndall, were being imported to save the situation. [41] Great "star courses" were organized in the cities, featuring spectacular personalities and entertainment. Dr. Holland complained in *Scribner's* that the star courses were

---

[36] *Nation*, VIII, 271 (April 8, 1869).
[37] *Round Table*, I, 100 (January 30, 1864).
[38] See *ibid.*, VIII, 285 (October 31, 1868) and other periodicals for advertisements of the bureaus.
[39] *Atlantic Monthly*, XV, 369 (March 1865).
[40] *Appleton's Journal*, X, 281 (August 30, 1873).
[41] See pp. 249–51.

killing the lyceum.[42] Certainly the old, historic lyceum was passing.

To supplement and succeed it, however, a new movement appeared in the latter seventies. The Chautauqua began as a Sunday school assembly at Lake Chautauqua, New York, under John H. Vincent, later a bishop of the Methodist church, and Lewis Miller. From this beginning grew two more or less distinct movements — summer courses of lectures and entertainments, usually under tents or in rude "assembly halls," which spread mightily in later years;[43] and the Chautauqua Literary and Scientific Circle, an organization which provided systematic reading in history, literature, science, and art. This C. L. & S. C. was launched in the fall of 1878; in three months 8,000 students were registered for the four-year course proposed, and by 1885 about 20,000 men and women were beginning the course each year.[44] Shortly after the reading courses began, D. H. Post wrote in *Harper's* that many thousands of persons, "scattered all over the country, are pursuing a course of study which will give them the college student's outlook upon the world of men and matter." [45] Leading educators were equally enthusiastic.[46]

A monthly *Chautauqua Herald* was published 1878–80; out of it grew the *Chautauquan*,[47] organ of the C. L. & S. C., which eventually became a general magazine of wide circulation.

[42] *Scribner's Monthly*, VIII, 110 (May 1874).

[43] In 1876 three assemblies followed the lead of the one at Chautauqua Lake: the Sunday School Parliament on Wellesley Island, in the St. Lawrence River; the Bay View Assembly at Petoskey, Michigan; and the Sunday School Assembly at Clear Lake, Iowa. Assemblies founded later all over the country came to be called Chautauquas after the parent institution, and thus the name came to be attached to the itinerant courses under tents of later years. See Jesse Lyman Hurlbut, *The Story of Chautauqua* (New York, 1921), Chapter XXIV; John H. Vincent, *The Chautauqua Movement* (Boston, 1886), pp. 289–301; H. A. Orchard, *Fifty Years of Chautauqua* (Cedar Rapids), Chapters III–IV.

[44] *Chautauquan*, VI, 367 (March 1886).

[45] *Harper's Monthly*, LIX, 350 (August 1879).

[46] See Hurlbut, *op. cit.*, preface; and H. B. Adams' "Chautauqua: A Social and Educational Study," in *Report of United States Commissioner of Education for 1894–95*, I, 977.

[47] Treated more fully in sketch 34.

JUVENILE PERIODICALS

"A distinctive feature of American journalism, and one which has been carried further in this country than in any other, is the periodical adapted to juvenile reading," wrote S. N. D. North in his monograph on the periodical press of the United States which formed a part of the 1880 census report.[48]

American juveniles had been consistently wooden and unnatural before the Civil War; in the postbellum period more and more of them came to aim at children's actual interests. Indeed, a group of them, chiefly in the hands of dime-novel publishers, catered to youthful desires for the excitement and sensation of extravagant adventure. About half of the juveniles were secular, and the other half were Sunday school papers; but the secular papers exceeded the others in circulation, in spite of the fact that most of the Sunday school papers enjoyed the benefit of free distribution to scholars. Sixty or more juveniles were listed each year in the directories, with newcomers always on hand to fill vacancies left by suspensions.

A large part of the aggregate circulation of the secular papers for children was accounted for by the *Youth's Companion*,[49] the one important legacy to the girls and boys of this period from antebellum days. The subscription list of the *Companion* increased greatly in the seventies, under the stimulus of the premium system and through the holding power of such writers of serials as the inimitable C. A. Stephens. *Merry's Museum* was another oldtimer; it finished its course in 1872, the year which also saw the end of Oliver Optic's *Student and Schoolmate*.[50] The American Tract Society continued its juveniles,[51] adding the little *Apples of Gold* (1871–current), arranged for use in the primary departments of Sunday schools. Frank Leslie discontinued his *Boys of America* during his financial difficulties in the late seventies,[52] but kept the more widely popular *Frank Leslie's Boys' and Girls' Weekly* (1867–83) until near the end of our period; and he began the monthly *Frank Leslie's Chat-*

[48] S. N. D. North, *The Newspaper and Periodical Press* (Report of Tenth Census, Vol. VIII), p. 121.

[49] Treated more fully in vol. II, sketch 2.

[50] See vol. II, p. 100.

[51] See vol. II, p. 75.

[52] See p. 461.

terbox (1879–87) only the year before his death.[53] The *School-day Magazine* [54] was merged in *St. Nicholas* in 1875 and the *Little Pilgrim* [55] in *Wide Awake* in the same year.

In the opening year of our period two important juveniles were founded. One was *Our Young Folks*,[56] published by Ticknor & Fields in Boston, and edited by J. T. Trowbridge, Lucy Larcom, and "Gail Hamilton." This was a bright, amusing, literary magazine, with an excellent list of contributors, and had every claim on success; but its publishers decided to turn over its list to *St. Nicholas* when that periodical began its illustrious career. The other 1865 venture was the *Little Corporal*,[57] of Chicago, much loved by many readers. Emily Huntington Miller and Alfred L. Sewell were chief editors. In 1875 it was also merged in *St. Nick*.

Demorest's Young America (1866–75) began as a ten-cent monthly with little pages and colored pictures, promoted by the premium system. Later it was enlarged to octavo, but it never

[53] It was continued until 1892 as *Frank Leslie's Christmas Book*, sold chiefly as an annual. Bound yearly volumes of the *Chatterbox* had also been in favor as annual gift-books. An annual *American Chatterbox*, imitating the English favorite, had been published through the early eighties without serial numbers.

[54] See vol. II, p. 101.

[55] See vol. II, p. 100.

[56] Published January 1865–October 1873. "Gail Hamilton" dropped out of the editorial triumvirate in 1868. The illustrations in *Our Young Folks* were of a high grade, consisting of a frontispiece and several smaller woodcuts. There were music, charades, enigmas, and a "letter box," besides the articles and stories. Mayne Reid, Oliver Optic, Trowbridge, and Alger were among the authors of serials; and Mrs. Stowe, Whittier, Longfellow, Lowell, Higginson, Eggleston, and Miss Alcott were a few of the many distinguished writers of shorter material represented. Thomas Bailey Aldrich's *Story of a Bad Boy* was originally printed in *Our Young Folks*, but the most popular offering was the series of adventures of "Jack Hazard," as related by Trowbridge.

[57] Published July 1865–October 1875. Sewell was the founder, and for the first year, or until June 1866, he was sole editor and publisher. Edward Eggleston joined him then for nine months, and a few months after he had withdrawn Mrs. Miller took a share in the editorship. Her husband, John E. Miller, became a partner of Sewell in the publishing in 1870; and after Sewell withdrew in 1871, the magazine was published by Miller and edited by his wife until the end. *Little Corporal* began as an octavo with rather fine print, a few woodcuts, music, travel, verse, and tales. In 1869 it became typographically more attractive as a quarto. Correspondence with child readers was a feature. Mrs. Miller wrote most of the serials. The magazine had few well-known writers; but among contributors were "Olive Thorne" (the editor's pen name), Susan Coolidge, Josephine Pollard, Mary A. Denison, Harry Castlemon, and Mary E. C. Wyeth.

won a popular success. W. Jennings Demorest, of New York, was editor and publisher. Its life span almost paralleled that of *Oliver Optic's Magazine*,[58] published by Lee & Shepard in Boston. *Oliver Optic's* featured the exciting serials of its editor, William T. Adams; it was a weekly during its first three years, and then a monthly. Hurd & Houghton's *Riverside Magazine for Young People* (1867–70) was edited by Horace E. Scudder; it was a brilliant but unsuccessful illustrated monthly, merged after four years in *Scribner's Monthly*. For somewhat younger children was T. S. Arthur's *Children's Hour* (1866–72), of Philadelphia, issued in the older format of the juveniles — a square duodecimo. It was finally merged in that voracious devourer of smaller fish, *St. Nicholas*. *Burke's Weekly for Boys and Girls* (1867–71), of Macon, Georgia, was published by J. W. Burke and edited by T. A. Burke; it became a monthly during its last year, substituting *Magazine* for *Weekly* in its title. A sixth juvenile founded in 1867 was designed for the smallest readers — the *Nursery* (1867–80), published by John L. Shorey, of Boston, and edited by Fanny P. Seavers. This monthly was merged in 1880 into a periodical which had been started that year and which was subsequently called *Our Little Ones and the Nursery* (1880–99); it was edited for more than a dozen years by William T. Adams, far better known as "Oliver Optic."

Thus 1867, which saw the founding of these and several other juvenile periodicals, was the boom year in that field. But the story continued, with the *Young People's Magazine* (1868–87) by P. W. Ziegler in Philadelphia and (S. S.) *Packard's Monthly* (1868–70), "the young man's magazine," in New York. Mayne Reid's *Onward* (1869–70), in New York, was abandoned after fourteen monthly issues because of the ill-health of the editor. *Little Folks* (1869–77) was a Chicago imitator of *Little Corporal;* the *Young Folks' Monthly* (1870–83), another Chicagoan, was conducted by the editors and publishers of the *Prairie Farmer*.

St. Nicholas,[59] which began in 1873, shared with the perennial

---

[58] January 5, 1867–December 1875. Before 1874 the half title was *Our Boys and Girls*, and both this and *Oliver Optic's Magazine* were on the cover and title page.　　　[59] Treated more fully in sketch 25.

Youth's Companion the most distinguished success of these years. For its first thirty years it was under the wise editorship of Mary Mapes Dodge.

In 1874 Daniel Lothrop, of Boston, began his series of juvenile periodicals with the *Pansy* (1874–96), named after the pseudonym of the editor, Isabella (Mrs. G. R.) Alden. Mrs. Alden had already begun that shelf-full of "Pansy" books for Sunday school libraries which were avidly read by young moralists from one end of the country to the other. The magazine was issued in weekly parts as a Sunday school paper, and then in monthly numbers to mail subscribers at fifty cents a year. But the great Lothrop success was *Wide Awake*,[60] begun the year after the *Pansy* under the editorship of Ella Farman and Charles S. Pratt. The *pièce de résistance* of its menu was the series of serials by Margaret Sidney about the "Five Little Peppers" and how they grew and what they did. *Babyland* (1876–98), "the baby's own magazine," was conducted by the editors and publisher of *Wide Awake*.[61] Another Lothrop juvenile, designed for the ages between those served by *Babyland* and *Wide Awake*, and conducted by the same busy editors, was *Our Little Men and Women* (1880–1894), called for its first three years the *Little Folks' Reader*.[62] The Lothrop periodicals were more or less identified with the Chautauqua movement, and a *Chautauqua Young Folks' Journal* (1884–89) was the organ of its own "Reading Union."

Several more or less important juveniles sprang up in various cities in the late seventies. *Treasure Trove* (1877–93) was issued by the New York publisher of educational journals, E. L. Kellogg, and edited by his wife, Alice M. Kellogg. *Good Times* (1877–85) was a Boston monthly and the *Acanthus* (1877–84) an Atlanta monthly. The *Pictorial Gallery for Young Folks* (1878–93) was published by a Chicago engraving firm. But

[60] Treated more fully in sketch 27.

[61] After the death of Lothrop in 1892, it was conducted by E. Addie Heath, editor of *Litle Men and Women*; three years later it was bought by the Alpha Publishing Company and edited by Mr. and Mrs. Pratt. It was finally merged in *Little Men and Women*.

[62] Mrs. Frances A. Humphrey was editor in 1883. On Lothrop's death in 1892, E. Addie Heath became editor; but soon thereafter the Alpha Publishing Company, Mr. and Mrs. Pratt editors, took it over. The *Our* of the title was dropped in 1893. Mrs. Pratt was the former Miss Ella Farman.

far the most important of the group was the weekly *Harper's Young People*,[63] begun late in 1879. Copiously illustrated, and appealing to actual intellectual and emotional hungers of older children, it attained a fair circulation almost immediately.

In 1882 an ambitious youngster named Frank A. Munsey came to New York with a gripful of manuscripts, a mind buzzing with publishing plans, and forty dollars in his pocket. He started the weekly *Golden Argosy*, "freighted with treasures for boys and girls," in December of that year. First of these "treasures" was an Alger serial, "Do and Dare." Munsey had his troubles, but the *Argosy* [64] was the flagship for the successful fleet which came later. Munsey employed as a kind of contributing editor the famous dime-novel author, Edward S. Ellis, who had been, for the preceding two or three years, editor of James Elverson's *Golden Days for Boys and Girls* (1880–1907), of Philadelphia. Elverson was the publisher of the popular *Saturday Night*, and he found such authors for his juvenile as Alger and Ellis, Harry Castlemon, and Oliver Optic. *Golden Days* later lost this bright galaxy, and its luster was sadly tarnished.

Argosy and *Golden Days* will perhaps serve to bridge the gap between the "respectable" juveniles and the blood-and-thunder, bang-bang-bang type of cheap weekly for boys. These weeklies sprang up in the wake of the dime novel, and they were usually related to a series or "library" of sensational novelettes. The *Boys of New York* (1875–94) was begun by Norman L. Munro, who was later to reap golden harvests from the "Old Cap Collier" stories. *Boys of New York* was an eight-page folio in fine print, full of stories of bootblacks who stopped runaways and thereby saved the lives of little daughters of grateful millionaires, and others *mutatis mutandis*. The paper's unattractive

---

[63] Published November 4, 1879–October 1899. It changed its name to *Harper's Round Table*, April 30, 1895, and became a monthly in November 1897. Kirk Munroe was the first editor; he was followed by a Miss Van Duyne in the early eighties, and she by A. B. Starey in 1885. J. T. Trowbridge, Sophie Swett, and Captain Charles King wrote serials for it; Dan Beard did pictures and articles on building things; Benson J. Lossing and C. C. Coffin wrote historical sketches. The Order of the Round Table was founded by the magazine in 1891, and it was from this organization that the magazine took its second name.

[64] To be treated more fully in a separate sketch in the succeeding volume of this work.

typography and presswork were enlivened by exciting woodcuts; and when Frank Tousey, lately graduated from the wholesale distribution end of publishing to management of his own periodicals, took over *Boys of New York* in 1878, he put a slashing big action picture on the front page — a brave fire-laddie carrying a fainting damsel down a ladder placed against a flaming building, or a tremendous locomotive bearing down upon a poor gentleman lying on the track bound hand and foot [65] — and thus he set the type for the cheap boy's paper for two or three decades. Tousey's *New York Boys' Weekly* (1877–78) was merged with *Boys of New York* when he bought the latter, and his *Our Boys* (1876–78) was merged with a fourth Tousey juvenile, *Young Men of America* (1877–88). These were all as alike as so many peas in a pod. In the eighties there were many exciting serials involving mechanical invention. Frank Reade, Percy B. St. John, and Police Captain Howard were among the most popular of the boys'-paper authors. Beadle's *Belles and Beaux* (1874) and *Girls of Today* (1875–76), latterly called the *New York Mirror*, were cheap but well printed weeklies for girls, both unsuccessful ventures.

To what extent the dime-novel series were written and published for youth, it is difficult to determine. They seem to have been increasingly associated with clandestine reading of boys in haymows and attics, or inside "joggerphies" at school. Obviously Beadle's *Boys' Library of Sport, Story and Adventure* (quarto series, 1881–84; octavo series, 1884–90), with stories by Mayne Reid, T. C. Harbaugh, and Charles D. Clark, was a series for youth; [66] but the tales themselves are much like those of the standard "Dime Library." Tousey's *Wide Awake Library* (1878–91) was probably a boys' series.

There were some juveniles intended for farmers' children, such as *Young Folks' Rural* (1870–81), of Chicago, edited and published throughout most of its life by H. N. F. Lewis, of the *Prairie Farmer;* and *Our Little Granger* (1880–90), of Cin-

---

[65] In *Little Women*, Jo is moved to try her hand at fiction when she hears of the large sums received for such work by "Mrs. S.L.A.N.G. Northbury" — thin disguise for Mrs. E.D.E.N. Southworth. But Jo is clearly contemptuous of the papers with the exciting pictures.

[66] For this "Library," see *Collector's Journal*, IV, 493 (June 1934). For other dated series of dime novels in this period, see p. 43, *supra*.

cinnati, issued by the *American Grange Bulletin* organization.

Religious juveniles were usually published by the printing houses of the various denominations.[67] Practically all sects were provided with such papers, and many had a variety suited to various ages of childhood and youth. One of the best known of the interdenominational juveniles was the *Golden Rule* (1875–current), of Boston, organ of the Society of Christian Endeavor, and edited by its founder, Francis E. Clark; it became the *Christian Endeavor World* in 1897. Among the Sunday school papers, the Methodist *Sunday School Advocate* (1841–1921) reached what was probably the longest life under one name of the whole group. The Methodist *Classmate* (1879–current), for somewhat older children, has had distinguished editorship, especially since its new series began in 1895: Jesse L. Hurlbut, Thomas B. Neely, J. T. McFarland, and others. The Presbyterian *Forward* (1882–current) and the Baptist *Young People* (1881–current) have been high-grade papers of their class. The *Juvenile Instructor* (1866–current) was founded as the Mormon children's paper by Elder George Q. Cannon and edited by him for thirty-five years.

Still another type of juvenile was the paper edited by boys (and sometimes girls) for others of the same age. These amateur papers were almost always very short-lived, but in the later seventies hundreds of them were issued all over the country. They were small and chiefly devoted to editorial essays; and they made much of their "exchanges" with each other. Amateur press associations were active all through the seventies, and in the latter part of that decade attendance at the national conventions of such associations was considerable.[68]

POPULAR INTEREST IN ART

"As a means of culture, art is overrated," [69] observed *Appleton's Journal* in 1875. Although this dictum must not be taken as expressing the unanimous opinion of the American magazine

[67] A few of them are mentioned in the sections given to the periodicals of the various religious sects in Chapter III of this volume.

[68] See Thomas G. Harrison, *The Career and Reminiscences of an Amateur Journalist and a History of Amateur Journalism* (Indianapolis, 1883).

[69] *Appleton's Journal*, XIII, 148 (January 30, 1875).

public at the time it was uttered, still there can be little doubt that the attitude which it represents had been far from uncommon.[70] There had been, and was, much mistrust of art as something impractical, foreign, immoral. Yet by 1880 the *American Art Review* could print the following words in its salutatory:

> Within the last ten years a great change has taken place in public sentiment. The arts are no longer regarded as comparatively unimportant to our national growth and dignity, and an ever increasing enthusiasm has replaced languid interest or indifference. Our great cities have their museums, their art schools and their lectures; our colleges their art professors and their collections of casts and pictures; and our libraries their multiplicity of books upon art subjects whose circulation equals if it does not surpass books on other topics.[71]

What were the causes of this change? Doubtless one of them was the Centennial Exposition at Philadelphia in 1876. Thousands of people came to the great show from considerable distances, and then talked about "the Centennial" all the remainder of their lives. Dr. Holland noted in *Scribner's Monthly* during the Exposition

> the universal devotion to the art galleries. Every day testifies of it, and every writer speaks of it. Whatever portion of the superb show may be neglected, or only thinly attended, the art galleries are always full. However rapidly other departments may be skimmed over, here the crowd lingers.[72]

And the *Aldine* testified some years later:

> One of the most encouraging signs of the times, from the aesthetic point of view, is the growing interest manifested by large classes of the American people in every branch of the fine arts. The impulse received from the great art exhibit made at the Centennial Exhibition has been felt in every corner of the land; and the fervor, born at that time perhaps of sudden enthusiasm, has not diminished by the lapse of years.[73]

---

[70] A statement in such terms would scarcely have been made if there had not been conspicuous enthusiasms for art study. The *Literary World* had on September 1, 1870 (IV, 49) asserted that "today the public is greedy of art knowledge." There are many signs that the popular interest in art increased steadily after the Civil War.

[71] *American Art Review*, I, 1 (January 1880).

[72] *Scribner's Monthly*, XII, 126 (November 1876).

[73] *Aldine*, preface to Vol. IX (1878–79), p. 5.

Further, it cannot be doubted that the magazine reproductions on copper, steel, and wood, and the chromolithographs used so widely as premiums had something to do with the development of an art taste among the people. Of course some of this work was bad enough. *Appleton's* complained that chromolithographs were too often "showy and vulgar," [74] and "chromo" came at length to be a term of derision. Yet the part which this art played, in the hands of men like Louis Prang and Currier & Ives, is not to be treated lightly. Chromolithography, said that excellent magazine, the *Aldine*, in 1873,

is at its best in America. They admit in Europe that we have carried it to a higher degree of perfection than they have, and they declare that Mr. Prang is the man who has done it.[75]

This pride in American artistic achievement probably played a part in the fostering of popular interest in the arts themselves. The magazines, consciously or unconsciously, contributed to build up an art appreciation by such a psychology. George E. Pond, writing in the *Galaxy* in 1877, said:

Art has made greater strides in the United States within the past twenty years than in the century preceding. Twenty years ago there was comparatively no art public at all. There were not a quarter part as many foreign pictures here as today; there were not a fourth part as many artists. The department of American water colors has been substantially created within ten years. The facilities for art education have been quadrupled within the same period, and the wealthy who form galleries have been multiplied in like proportion. American progress in science and mechanism, though great, falls short of American progress in taste and American productivity in the fine arts.[76]

Ward, Saint-Gaudens, Powers, and Harriet Hosmer in sculpture belong to our period; in painting there were Church, Innes, Vedder, Hunt, Homer, LaFarge, and Durand; and in architecture, Richardson and Renwick. While critics found much mat-

[74] *Appleton's Journal*, I, 27 (April 3, 1869).

[75] *Aldine*, VI, 27 (January 1873).

[76] *Galaxy*, XXIII, 268 (February 1877). There was interesting comment on impressionism following the Ruskin-Whistler controversy; see *Our Continent*, II, 12 (July 12, 1882). The question of realism came up late in the period; see Cranch in the *Critic*, VI, 7 (January 3, 1885).

ter for debate in the work of the painters, the general tone was one of high praise; upon American sculpture, on the other hand, there was a divided verdict, and American architecture came in for much severe criticism.

ART CRITICISM IN THE MAGAZINES

For example, a writer in the *Atlantic* declared sculpture in America "an anachronism" in 1868;[77] but that magazine's art critic quarreled with the *Nation* in 1872 over Ward's work, which he defended vigorously and voluminously. *Appleton's* critic believed that though American genius was deficient in literature and in painting, in sculpture "it holds a prominent place."[78] But the *Critic*, somewhat surer of its standards, believed in the early eighties that "in painting and perhaps in sculpture also" American work was gradually improving, though it was astonished at the backwardness of architecture. American buildings, it asserted, "are the work of masters of mechanical and technical art as opposed to the fine arts"; and our architecture "represents the mere brute force of money more than anything else." But the *Critic* praised the Capitol at Albany;[79] certainly Richardson's work, spread though it was over so short a time, was outstanding in this period. Trinity Church, Boston, established his fame: it was finished in 1877, and its author was dead in 1886. "Certainly no architectural career so brief has been so epoch-making," wrote Montgomery Schuyler in the first number of the *Architectural Record*.[80]

Artists were inclined to complain that art criticism was ill-informed. "It is useless to ignore the fact that most of the art-criticism of the day, in this country, falls far below the standard of criticism on literature," wrote Christopher P. Cranch, poet and landscape artist, in 1867.[81] "What we need," declared *Harper's Weekly* about that time, "is a little more of honest frankness."[82]

---

[77] *Atlantic Monthly*, XXII, 564 (November 1868).

[78] *Appleton's Journal*, IV, 317 (September 10, 1870).

[79] *Critic*, II, 191 (July 15, 1882), for the former quotation; *ibid.*, I, 222 (August 13, 1881), for the Albany Capitol.

[80] *Architectural Record*, I, 15 (July 1891).

[81] *Galaxy*, IV, 77 (May 1867).

[82] *Harper's Weekly*, IX, 226 (April 15, 1865).

Some of the leading art critics of the day were Russell Sturgis, of the *Atlantic*; Eugene Benson, of the *Galaxy*; W. C. Brownell, of *Scribner's Monthly*; and S. S. Conant, of *Harper's*. The *Galaxy* had an art department in 1868, and the *Atlantic* in 1872. Neither department lasted very long; but both these magazines, as well as *Lippincott's*, *Putnam's*, *Harper's*, *Scribner's*, the *International Review*, and the *Penn Monthly*, gave much attention to the graphic arts during our period. *Harper's* and *Scribner's* were able, by means of their profuse illustration, to make their essays on art extremely effective. Various *Scribner* series are notable — D. O'C. Townley on living American artists in 1871, Clarence Cook on interior decoration in 1876–77, W. C. Brownell on art schools and painters at various times.

The important art exhibits were often reviewed in such weeklies as the *Nation*, the *Critic*, *Appleton's*, the *Round Table*, and the *Arcadian*. Certain western magazines evidenced the spread of the cultural attitude. The *Ladies' Repository*, of Cincinnati, famous for its steel engravings, added an art department in 1873. Chicago, whose Fine Arts Institute and Academy of Design were both established in 1872,[83] had F. F. Browne's art notes in the *Lakeside Monthly*. Benjamin P. Avery contributed a two-part article to the first numbers of the *Overland* on "Art Beginnings on the Pacific." Much space was given to art in the *Western*, of St. Louis, especially to William M. Bryant's criticisms of loan collections. But in noting the close of the St. Louis School of Design in 1879, the *Western* said, "There are many necessities which must be satisfied before our citizens can afford to give support to art." [84]

ART JOURNALS

But in the East there were publishers optimistic enough to expect support for a dozen or more art magazines. In New York the *Aldine* [85] began as a "typographical art journal" circulated by a printing company in 1868; but it turned its attention more and more to the graphic arts, to pictures, literature, and criticism. D. Appleton & Company issued an American edi-

[83] *New England Magazine*, N.S., VI, 411 (June 1892).
[84] *Western*, N.S., V, 411 (August 1879).
[85] Treated more fully in sketch 13.

tion of the London *Art Journal* (1875–87), with the addition of very creditable material from the United States, under the title of the *American Art Journal*; and the English Cassell & Company published (1878–1904) a New York edition of the *Magazine of Art* just a month behind their London edition. The *Art Interchange* (1878–1904) began as a fortnightly quarto published at five cents to foster home decoration — one of the many evidences of general interest in this department following the Centennial Exposition. It had Russell Sturgis, General di Cesnola, and William C. Prime as leading contributors. Later it became a monthly, raised its price, gave more attention to painting and sculpture, and used more elaborate illustration. Another New York periodical devoted largely to art in the home was the *Art Amateur* [86] (1879–1903), by Montague Marks. Marks was an Englishman who began his American career as a cowboy on the Plains and then entered upon newspaper work in New York. At first he wrote most of his monthly himself, but it was always well illustrated, instructive, and surprisingly wide in scope. It had a London edition and English correspondence. Of shorter life was the *Art Age* (1883–89), a beautifully printed monthly quarto distinguished by exquisite illustration. Arthur B. Turnure was its editor. Charles M. Kurtz tried to revive the old art union scheme [87] at the end of our period, issuing his *Art Union: A Monthly Art Magazine* (1884–85) as its organ.

The Boston *Art Student* was published briefly from 1882 to 1884; and there the much more distinguished but also short-lived *American Art Review* (1879–81) had its home. The latter was a sumptuous quarto published by Estes & Lauriat and edited chiefly by S. R. Koehler. It was beautifully printed and richly illustrated. Its specialty was etching; and Koehler's series, "The Works of the American Etchers," illustrated by impressions from original plates, was an important influence in the development of this art. W. J. Linton's valuable *History*

---

[86] Among contributors were J. Wells Champney, Ernest Knaufft, W. A. Rogers, R. Davis Benn, and William Patten. Stephen Fiske wrote on art in the theaters. Marks wrote the London letter for many years. In 1897 Marks sold to John W. Van Oost, who continued as publisher until the end. Van Oost was a practical woodcarver, metal worker, and designer. Roger Riordan and Margaret Humble assisted him in the editorial work, Marks continuing his London letter. Chromolithography and pyrography were specialties.   [87] See vol. II, pp. 190–91.

of Wood Engraving in America was published serially in the
Review; and such critics as John Sartain, C. E. Norton, S. G. W.
Benjamin, and G. P. Lathrop were contributors.

The *Art Folio* (1883–84), a popular monthly illustrated by
large woodcuts, was published at Providence. In Chicago there
were two early ventures in the field of the art periodical: J. F.
Aitken's *Art Journal* (1867–71), a sixteen-page monthly; and
E. H. Trafton's *Art Review* (1870–72), a monthly with excellent illustrations.

Chromolithography was represented by [Louis] *Prang's
Chromo* (1868–69), of Boston, a quarterly of which only five
numbers were issued; Charles Hart's New York *Lithograph*
(1874); and the *Chromatic Art Magazine* (1879–83), of New
York, also a quarterly.

Some of the photographic journals of the war period continued into postbellum years, chief among them the *Philadelphia
Photographer*.[88] The *American Journal of Photography* (1879–
1900) was another Philadelphian. In New York there were
Anthony's Photographic Bulletin (1870–1902) and the *Photographic Times* (1871–1915). The West produced several magazines devoted to the growing art of photography, chief among
them the *St. Louis Practical Photographer* (1877–1910), called
after 1887 the *St. Louis and Canadian Photographer*.

MAGAZINE ILLUSTRATION: APPLETON'S

The practical contribution of the magazines themselves to
the graphic arts deserves a more extended examination, chiefly
because of certain developments in wood engraving.

By 1865 there was a tendency to abandon the steel plates
which had been the usual means of "embellishment" before
1850, and to use wood engravings. Some of the older magazines
which had made their success by means of steel or copper plates
still retained them, sometimes supplementing them with woodcuts: in this class belong *Godey's*, *Peterson's*, the *Ladies' Repository*, and other women's periodicals, as well as the *Eclectic*,
with its portraits. Electrotyping, which came in shortly after
the opening of our period, took away the superiority of steel
over copper as a medium by making possible any number of

[88] See vol. II, p. 194, footnote.

impressions no matter what the original engraving had been made upon. Woodcuts, too, were electrotyped for long runs.

Appleton's Journal, founded in 1869, interestingly exemplifies, by its use of various types of illustration, the changes that were taking place. It published excellent steel plates by S. V. Hunt, R. Hinshelwood and W. Wellstood, after landscapes and seascapes by A. F. Bellows, W. S. Haseltine, J. F. Kensett, and others — views containing the figures, spires, fences, bridges, and boats usual in the landscape painting of the time. There were also some engravings from F. O. C. Darley's lively but not always realistic western pictures. Besides these, *Appleton's* frequently published large folding pictures from engravings on wood, printed on heavier calendered paper. The artists who drew not only these pictures but the drawings for many other woodcuts were Darley, Winslow Homer, Gaston Fay, Edwin Forbes, Thomas Hogan, A. R. Waud, and Harry Fenn. Perhaps Fenn was *Appleton's* chief artist. This reminds us that the publishers of the *Journal* were also the publishers of *Picturesque America*, a very important work in the history of American wood engraving, which was issued in monthly parts from 1872 to 1874, and for which Harry Fenn was largely responsible. The engravers for *Picturesque America* were the engravers for *Appleton's Journal*, and there was a certain amount of duplication. F. W. Quartley was prominent and admirable in the magazine, as were John Filmer, J. A. Bogert, and J. Harley. The Lintons — W. J. and Henry — were also represented there. But *Appleton's* illustrations dealt with many subjects besides natural scenery. They were particularly strong in the representation of typical scenes from the life of various American cities and in the portrayal of social life and types. After 1870, no steel engravings appeared in *Appleton's* and less care was taken in the printing of the woodcuts, though many of the good scenic blocks continued to appear.

THE NEW SCHOOL OF WOOD ENGRAVING

Scribner's Monthly was begun with Alexander W. Drake as art editor. It was fully illustrated by means of wood engraving and became at once a rival of *Harper's* in the field of the popular illustrated literary magazine. It showed great enterprise in wood engraving, developing especially the art of cutting from photographs made directly upon the wood.

When *Scribner's Monthly* was established [wrote Dr. Holland, its editor, in 1879], the men who could draw well upon the block . . . could almost be counted upon the fingers of the two hands. . . . Drawing upon the block has always been regarded by the artists as a cramped business; the freest handling is not obtainable in that way. But from the moment *Scribner's* began to avail itself of the art of photographing pictures upon the wood a great development took place, because that presented at once to the public the work of the best artists. The men who had hitherto been shut away from us could draw and paint their pictures, which could then be photographed upon the block.[89]

With these photographs on the block to work from, engravers soon learned to reproduce textures and even brush strokes with remarkable verisimilitude, and to achieve the effects of charcoal, pencil, clay, wash, or oils, which, as Holland remarked, could never have been secured with the "legitimate line" for which adherents of the older school contended. It was the complete discarding of this "legitimate line" of the graver that marked the emergence about 1877 of what came to be called the "new school of wood engraving." Sweeping lines gave place to very short lines so arranged as to reproduce most exactly a given detail. "At last it had become apparent," said Timothy Cole many years later, "that the old conventions were inadequate and that they had to go by the board. The line *had* to be tampered with in order faithfully to render the qualities characteristic of the artist's painting."[90]   Cole, Frederick Juengling, and Gustav Kruell were the leading exponents of this new method, but J. G. Smithwick, Henry Marsh, F. S. King, Robert Hoskin, J. H. Whitney, and Henry Wolf were also prominent. All of these except Cole worked for *Harper's Monthly* and *Weekly* as well as for *Scribner's Monthly* (later the *Century*) and *St. Nicholas*. Some of the most striking engravings of Juengling and Smithwick appeared in *Harper's Weekly*, which, in these days, was reproducing the fine work of artists like Edwin Abbey, F. S.

[89] *Scribner's Monthly*, XVIII, 458 (July 1879).
[90] Frank Weitenkampf, *American Graphic Art* (revised edition, New York. 1924), p. 128.

Church, and C. S. Reinhart. But *Scribner's Monthly* had a great asset in Theodore L. DeVinne, its printer. In October 1870 the *Literary World* observed that

the main difficulty with which American publishers have had to contend in the production of fine illustrations has been in the printing from the blocks. . . . Until recently our printers have been unable to command the requisite skill of manipulation and delicacy of machinery to secure a perfect impression.[91]

But DeVinne, although "warned by experts that it was ridiculous," used a cylinder press, with dry paper and a very hard impression, and achieved remarkable results on long press runs.[92] Clarence Cook pointed out in the *Princeton Review* in 1883 that *Harper's* always lagged behind *Scribner's* in the printing of its engravers' work.[93] In 1879 and 1881 *Scribner's* published portfolios of prints from some of their best blocks and thus provided a durable monument to the "new school." It was in 1881, too, that *Scribner's* instituted prizes for beginners in the art of wood engraving, in connection with which the magazine commented on the "freshness, variety and vigor" of the "new school," and named the following "commanding characteristics of wood engraving in the United States at the present time: (1) originality of style; (2) individuality, and (as a corollary) variety of style; (3) and chiefly, faithfulness in the reproduction of a wide range of subjects by diverse methods."

These new departures did not, of course, pass unchallenged. As early as 1874, *Every Saturday*, contending that wood engraving had declined in the preceding ten years, observed that "personal, spiritual quality, and not a chemical, mechanical one" was the desideratum in engraving. But it was W. J. Linton, the English-American engraver, who had come to this country in 1867, who made the strongest attack upon the "new school." His first onslaught was an article published in the *Atlantic Monthly* in 1879, in which he complained of photography on wood, of the use of the multiple graver, and of the

---

[91] *Literary World*, I, 72 (October 1, 1870).

[92] *Scribner's Monthly*, XX, 39 (May 18, 1880). In 1879 DeVinne wrote "Woodcuts: Concerning the Taking of Proofs and Prints" for the London *Printing Times*, and it was reprinted serially in the *Publishers' Weekly*.

[93] *Princeton Review*, 4th ser., XI, 319 (May 1883).

"fogginess," the lack of definition of line, and the use of the same "mess of meaningless dots and lines" for background, clothes and features, as practiced by Timothy Cole and other "followers after Baal." [94] Replies were immediately forthcoming in *Scribner's Monthly*, the *Nation*, the *New York Sun*, the *New York Times*, and other periodicals; Linton's rejoinder was a little book called *Some Practical Hints on Wood-Engraving for the Instruction of Reviewers and the Public*. Here Linton elaborated his case with some historical background and ill-temper. A better-considered work, and a very valuable one, followed three years later — *The History of Wood-Engraving in America*. Linton's position may be summed up thus: the engraver becomes a mere machine and betrays his art for hackwork when he is concerned altogether with reproducing with perfect exactitude his original, even to brush strokes, and if he is to keep an artistic integrity of his own he must adhere to the graver-line. There is not a little to be said on both sides. Perhaps the best defense of the "new school" is the argument of results: "the fact remains," says Weitenkampf, "that the new school did its work and did it well." [95] It was largely through their illustrations that *Harper's* and *Scribner's* were able to win an international reputation as the best general magazines in the world.[96]

DEVELOPMENT IN MAGAZINE ILLUSTRATION

If any general criticism is to be levied against the art work in these magazines it would be that there was too much of it. Charles T. Congdon, writing in the *North American Review*, in 1884, said of the *Century's* pictures that

there are so many of them that they become wearisome; but it is encouraging to think that we have at least reached the extreme point, beyond which we can no further go unless we give up letter-press altogether.[97]

[94] *Atlantic Monthly*, XLIII, 705 (June 1879).
[95] Weitenkampf, *op. cit.*, p. 131.
[96] E. E. Ellsworth, in his *Golden Age of Authors* (Boston, 1919), p. 70, quotes both the *Saturday Review*, of London, and the *London Graphic* as saying in 1880 that the best woodcuts were produced in America.
[97] *North American Review*, CXXXIX, 489 (November 1884).

This was an exaggeration, of course; and the general magazine was destined to go much further in volume of illustration before reaching a point of satiation. The *Century* and *Harper's* in 1884 commonly used about 15 per cent of their space for illustrations.

Among the well-illustrated periodicals the *Aldine* stands high. It published some of Linton's best work, as well as a number of blocks by Cole, Juengling, and others. The Appletons, in issuing their American edition of the London *Art Journal*, added excellent wood engravings by such men as Linton, Filmer, Karst, and Harley. The *American Art Review* was justly famous for its many fine etchings. The *Art Amateur* specialized in chromolithographs of famous paintings; but in spite of the *Amateur's* advocacy and the popularity of the genre in the premium field, the color lithograph had few adherents among the magazines. *Frank Leslie's Popular Monthly* was the chief user of them before *Puck*. In *Puck* three lithographed cartoons were presented in each number from the first, though they were not highly colored for the first year or two. Joseph Keppler was the genius of this weekly during our period, and its pictures made a brave show. Timothy Cole contributed some of his earliest blocks to the *Illustrated Christian Weekly. Our Young Folks* was well illustrated by woodcuts, and the art work for the *Riverside Magazine* and *Harper's Young People* was almost as good. The development of illustration in *St. Nicholas* was on the same high plane as that for its older sister, *Scribner's-Century*.

"Process" engraving was in the offing. It was used in the seventies by the New York *Graphic*, and it was a staple of the *Manhattan* when that magazine was begun by a group of young artists in 1883. In that year the *Critic* prophesied that the future of magazine illustration lay in the direction of "pictures without the intervention of an engraver's draughtsman." [98]

[98] *Critic*, III, 135 (March 24, 1883).

CHAPTER VIII

MUSIC, THE THEATER, AND SPORTS

G ROWING American interest in music was reflected in the magazines. This was true not only of the large group of national and local musical journals, but also of special articles and departments in the general magazines.

MUSIC AND THE GENERAL MAGAZINES

In the same year that Howells gave the *Atlantic* an art department, he added also a musical section edited by William F. Apthorp; moreover, following a custom common in earlier periods and still observed by such periodicals as the *Christian Union* and the *Independent*, he occasionally published a piece of music. *Scribner's* and *Putnam's* also had departments devoted to music. The progress of the New York Philharmonic Society, the organization of the New York and Boston symphony orchestras, the "series of unquestionable triumphs" [1] of Christine Nilsson on her visit to these shores in 1870–71, and the less successful appearances of Adelina Patti ten years later, the *succès du scandale* of Offenbach's *opéra bouffe*, the "Pinafore" mania, and the production of Wagnerian opera in New York and other cities were among the chief musical topics widely discussed in the magazines.

Of these, the last named was the most exciting. A good example of the attack to which Wagner was subject in those days is the large cartoon in the first number of *Puck* called "Wagner's Method Exposed," showing tin pans, anvils, cannon, cats, dogs, and pigs all in action as noise-makers. The irrepressible *Puck* returned to the attack many times in later months and years. [2] The *Galaxy*, in an article by Richard Grant White anent the production of "Lohengrin" in New York in the spring of 1874, cried Wagner down as dull, unoriginal, and uninspired. [3] But

---

[1] *Aldine*, IV, 35 (February 1871).
[2] See *Puck*, April 11, 1871, and March 17, 1878.
[3] *Galaxy*, XVII, 779 (June 1874).

the *Aldine*, which had a good musical department, had observed
the year before:

> Laugh and shudder and yawn as some of us may over the vagaries
> of some of this modern music, we cannot afford to ignore it; what all
> the world listens to we must grant a hearing; and even the most
> prejudiced must see that Wagnerism is making its way.[4]

It was. The *Atlantic's* music editor showed a discriminating
sympathy with it,[5] and its enthusiastic following is attested by
the following from the record of the *Critic*:

> A few years ago quite a commotion was excited among the musical
> people of the United States by a proposition to induce Richard
> Wagner to remove hither by an offer of a bonus of a million dollars.
> The scheme was the wildest folly. . . . It had the encouragement of
> some intelligent musicians.[6]

After his death in 1883, Wagner was the subject of much discussion in the magazines, with reviews of the memorial concert
given under the direction of Theodore Thomas, a devoted Wagnerian.

The visits of various European operatic stars, chiefly under
the Strakosch management — Christine Nilsson, Pauline Lucca,
Italo Campanini, the Pattis, Giuseppe Mario — were leading
events of the period, as were those of Anton Rubinstein and
Henri Wieniawski. The season of 1872–73, just before the
panic, was especially brilliant, most of the artists just named
being in the United States.[7] The Peace Jubilees at Boston in
1869 and 1872 were great popular musical events. In New York
during the season, opera was usually available, though not firmly
established until the opening of the Metropolitan Opera House
in 1883 under Abbey's management gave Mapleson's Academy
of Music a rival. New Orleans had its opera during the early
seventies, and operatic touring companies visited other large
cities.

The religious taboo which banned theater-going was extended
also to opera by stricter moralists, but there was a tendency

[4] *Aldine*, VI, 47 (February 1873).
[5] For example, in XXIX, 248 (February 1872).
[6] *Critic*, IV, 205 (May 3, 1884).
[7] See *Appleton's Journal*, VIII, 501 (November 2, 1872).

among the churchly to salve their consciences by calling the opera a concert: the Chicago *Advance* would "leave the settlement of this apparent inconsistency to Him who reads the heart." [8] Chicago music, incidentally, was well reviewed after 1880 in the *Dial*, which claimed that "outside of New York City there is no city where music is better patronized and pays better than in Chicago." [9] Chicago's great musical event was its May Festival, which in 1882 featured Theodore Thomas, later to represent the city's proudest bid for musical standing.

But if opera was allowed only a half-hearted success, such *opéras bouffes* as Offenbach's *La Belle Hélène*, with Mlle. Tostée, scored repeated triumphs. Moralists might damn the cancan, but even in Boston everybody flocked to see if it was as bad as others had said it was. Howells wrote in the *Atlantic* of the Italian, French, German, and English grand opera Boston had heard in the winter of 1868–69; and added:

> But best of all, and far more to our minds than her serious sisters, was the *opéra bouffe*, of which we had nearly a month, with Tostée, Irma, and Aujac. We greeted these artists with overflowing theatres. . . . It was not for Tostée's singing, which was but a little thing in itself; it was not for her beauty, for that is now scarcely more than a reminiscence, if it was not always an illusion; was it because she rendered the spirit of M. Offenbach's operas so perfectly that we liked her so much? "Ah, that movement!" cried an enthusiast, "that swing, that — that — wriggle!" She is undoubtedly a great actress. . . .[10]

In spite of a thread of irony in all this, there is some real enthusiasm, as though the chaste Mr. Howells and sedate Back Bay itself were going a bit "on the loose." Yes, as some of the periodicals had said, puritanic sanctions were weakening.[11]

Even more striking was the immense success of "Pinafore" in America. For four or five years from its pirated production at the Boston Museum on November 25, 1878, it was "all the

---

[8] *Advance*, October 7, 1869, p. 4.

[9] *Dial*, IV, 194 (December 1883).

[10] *Atlantic Monthly*, XXIII, 636 (May 1869). Apthorp, in a later number, calls Tostée "audacious and obscene." See XXIX, 509 (April 1872).

[11] See pp. 86–88.

rage." The visit of Gilbert and Sullivan to America and their premier production of "The Pirates of Penzance" in New York December 31, 1879, stimulated the vogue of light opera. The *Clipper* remarked in 1882 that "the astonishing demand for light comic opera, inaugurated by the unprecedented hit of 'Pinafore,' " set all the managers to producing all the available shows of that kind the stage would hold. "It seemed," says our commentator, writing after the craze had somewhat subsided, "that we were likely to remain on that diet for the rest of our lives." [12]

Popular appreciation of music was, according to Dwight, "making headway." [13] Parton reported that 25,000 pianos were sold in 1866, at an average of $600 each.[14] There were plenty of silly popular songs, those of the "nigger minstrels" being, it would seem, inexhaustible. *Punchinello* called "Shoo Fly, Don't Bodder Me" the "lay of the last minstrel";[15] but unhappily it was not, for even after what *Stage* called "that funny fly, that everybody is requesting not to be boddered with" [16] ceased from buzzing, the minstrel show kept on drawing crowds. Meanwhile, Thomas Wentworth Higginson's *Atlantic* article on Negro spirituals in June 1867, the first important critical appraisement of that important type,[17] had drawn attention to a more genuine Negro music. There was also a plethora of sentimental parlor ballads,[18] including Dexter Smith's, "Come, Put Me in My Little Bed," beginning

> Come, sister come,
> Kiss me goodnight,
> For I my evening prayers have said.

MUSICAL JOURNALS

Of the hundred or so musical journals of the period, only a few had much artistic importance. Most of them were advertis-

[12] *New York Clipper*, XXX, 546 (November 11, 1882).
[13] *Atlantic Monthly*, XXVI, 325 (September 1870).
[14] *Ibid.*, XX, 82 (July 1867).
[15] *Punchinello*, I, 30 (April 9, 1870).
[16] *Stage*, November 26, 1869, p. 2 (Vol. VII).
[17] Vernon Loggins, *The Negro Author* (New York, 1931), p. 358.
[18] *Atlantic Monthly*, XXXIII, 382 (March 1874).

ing sheets issued by dealers in musical instruments, sheet music, and choir and singing society books. A few, however, require special mention.

Dwight's Journal of Music, begun some ten years before the war and still enjoying the respect due the name of its editor, declined from about 2,500 circulation in 1865 to half that when it was discontinued in 1881. Lowell Mason's *Musical Review and Gazette* passed after the war under the control of Theodore Hagen and was published as the *New York Weekly Review* until 1873; while Mason Brothers proceeded to publish the *New York Musical Gazette* (1866–74). Henry C. Watson, a collaborator with Briggs and Poe on the old *Broadway Journal,*[19] the founder of two or three earlier and briefer musical journals, and himself a composer and singer and the music critic of the *New York Tribune,* began in 1864 the publication of *Watson's Art Journal,* a weekly devoted chiefly to musical criticism and trade news. Watson died in 1875, when his *Journal* came into the hands of his pupil, William M. Thoms, who improved it and finally merged it with the *American Musician* (1884–91).[20]

Boston was the home of more than a dozen musical journals during the seventies, most of them advertising sheets; and New York and Chicago did more than their share. But it was not until about 1880 that the larger crop of such periodicals appeared. The *Music Trade Journal* was founded in New York in 1879; it ran through half a dozen titles in its early years, but finally fixed upon *Music Trade Review.* The *Musical and Sewing Machine Gazette* began the next year in the same city, changing its name from *Gazette* to *Courier* after the third number, and eventually to *Musical Courier.* Under the enterprising and clever management of Marc A. Blumenberg and Otto Floerscheim it eventually built up a big success. Eben Tourgee, founder of the New England Conservatory of Music, began the

[19] See Mott, *op. cit.*, p. 757.
[20] This was in 1906, after the *American Musician* had been suspended fifteen years and the *American Art Journal* two months. The new periodical was called *American Musician and Art Journal* (1906–15) and was owned by the *Musical Courier's* publisher, purchaser of both of these competitors. The *American Musician* had been founded by John C. Freund and J. Travis Quigg as a weekly trade journal with good national and international music news.

Boston Musical Herald as its organ in 1880.[21] John C. Freund founded his *Music and Drama* (1882–92) for his son Harry E. Freund, who was not then of age. It began in the folio form, under the name of *Freund's Weekly*. Its criticism was full and fearless, and in some degree it took the place as a critical journal of Dwight's lately deceased monthly. Harry Freund's mother, writing as "Amelia Lewis," was a music critic of some ability. Before its end, however, *Music and Drama* went over largely to the trade field. Frederick Archer's *Keynote* (1883–97) was much like Freund's paper at its best, but had no dramatic criticism in its earlier years. Finally, the *Étude*, an eight-page monthly "publication for pianists and teachers of music," was begun by Theodore Presser at Lynchburg, Virginia, in 1883, and the next year moved to Philadelphia. It soon enlarged its size, adding many pages of compositions for the piano, as well as series of articles on musical history and biography, departments of teachers' helps, sketches of virtuosi, and news of concerts. It became the preëminent journal of the independent music teacher.[22] Such are the more important of the many musical journals of the two decades after the war.[23]

[21] It was purchased in November 1891 by George H. Wilson, and its name changed to *Musical Herald of the United States*. Articles on new works and their performance all over the world were featured; Krehbiel, Finck, and Henderson were leading contributors. But this continued for only two years, the paper ending in 1893.

[22] Its emphasis was not less on the needs of the young piano student. It added a voice department in 1897. Its prize essays were a feature, and it had an elaborate offering of premiums. James Francis Cooke became editor and publisher in 1910. Among associate editors, Henry T. Finck, Thomas Tapper, James Huneker, N. J. Corey, and Robert Braine have been listed. John S. VanCleve, C. B. Cady, and C. W. Landon were chief contributors in earlier years.

[23] Somewhat less important, perhaps, were: *Orpheus* (1865–80), *Folio* (1869–95), *Dexter Smith's Musical, Literary, Dramatic and Art Paper* (1872–78), *Organists' Quarterly Journal and Review* (1874–77), *Leader* (1875–1904), *Score* (1877–82), *Musical Record and Review* (1878–1903), and *Musician* (1879–94), all published in Boston; *Thomas' Musical Journal* (1880–94), Albany; *Loomis' Musical and Masonic Journal* (1867–1900); *Southern Musical Journal* (1871–82), Savannah, Georgia; [W. J.] *Warrington's Musical Review* (1877–86), New Orleans; the *Cincinnati College of Music's Courier* (1882–93), *Musical People* (1880–84), and *Church's Musical Visitor* (1871–97), all of Cincinnati; *Musical Harp* (1880–97), Berea, Ohio; *Whitney's Musical Guest* (1867–81), Toledo; *Brainard's Musical World* (1864–88), Cleveland; *Western Musical Review* (1866–80), begun in Indianapolis, changing title there to *Benham's Musical Review* in 1870, moved to Cincinnati as *Baldwin's Musical Re-*

At the very end of the period came E. Woodworth Masters'
Galop (1884–1900), a Boston monthly devoted to dancing,
music, and etiquette.

MAGAZINES OF THE THEATER

In 1879 the *New York Mirror* made a true summary of the
history of theatrical journalism in America, when it said: "The
dramatic profession of this country was for many years degraded by having its affairs treated in the professedly theatrical
papers side by side with prize fights, cocking matches, baseball,
and other sports." [24] The *New York Clipper*, devoted primarily
to sports, began to give increased attention to the theater soon
after the war and may be said to be the only theatrical paper of
the decade from 1865 to 1875. The *National Police Gazette*
gave no little attention in the later seventies to the rowdier kind
of theaters and to the new "burlesque," as did some of its imitators; and the *New York Illustrated Times* (1876–84) called
itself "the best theatrical and sporting journal in America."
There was a *Sporting and Theatrical Journal* in Chicago through
the eighties, and various other periodicals combined the amusements of sports with those of the theater.

But in 1875 C. A. Byrne started the *New York Dramatic
News*, an all-theatrical eight-page paper; and though after a
little over a year it adopted society news as an auxiliary and
added *and Society Journal* to its title, it remained primarily a
dramatic paper — and often "blackguardly to the point of
libel." [25] Then in 1879 Ernest Harvier founded the *New York
Mirror* [26] — and was almost immediately sued for libel by

view; Amphion (1874–85), Detroit; *Echo* (1883–1901), begun at Lafayette,
Indiana, and moved to Chicago; *Vox Humana* (1872–99), *Music Trade Indicator*
(1878–1930), *Musical Bulletin* (1879–83), *Song Friend* (1879–94), *Musical Times*
(1881–1926) merged in *Presto* (1884–current), all published in Chicago;
Kunkel's Musical Review (1878–1909), St. Louis; *Music and Drama* (1882–1901),
San Francisco.

[24] *New York Mirror*, I, 4 (January 11, 1879).

[25] See J. L. Ford, *Forty-Odd Years in the Literary Shop* (New York, 1921),
pp. 229, 233. It dropped its subtitle in 1883. In the nineties it absorbed *Dramatic
Times* and added its title to its own for a time. Edward S. Bettleheim has been
its editor and publisher ever since this consolidation.

[26] It changed title in 1889 to *New York Dramatic Mirror*, dropping the *New
York* in 1917. It ended in April 1922, having just changed to a monthly. Harrison Grey Fiske was editor and publisher for many years up to 1911; afterward

Byrne, whom he had accused of being a blackmailer. Byrne was forced out of the *Dramatic News* and founded the *Dramatic Times* (1881–96), which he continued to edit for five years. Meantime Harvier gave place on the *Mirror* to G. W. Hamersly, publisher, and Harrison Grey Fiske, editor. Thus by 1885 there were three flourishing dramatic papers in New York.

There were also Sydney Rosenfeld's New York *Rambler and Dramatic Weekly*, of 1879, which did not last the year out; and the more longevous but less distinguished Chicago *Play* (1877–83). *Freund's Music and Drama* had good notes on the theaters, as did J. F. Thrum's San Francisco *Music and Drama*. There were occasional publications of the playbill type, like the weekly *Stage* (1865–80) in New York, edited and published by D. H. Hopkinson. The front page was given over to the current playbill of the theater in which it was distributed, and the remainder was devoted to theatrical miscellany and advertising: the *Stage* was a four-page small folio distributed in a dozen or more New York theaters.

The theater was very popular in the years following the war, and the leading magazines gave it more or less constant attention. Among the monthlies, it was the *Galaxy* that followed the drama most closely: though it made no effort to review productions season by season, its articles by Lawrence Barrett, Henry James, Brander Matthews, and others on matters pertaining to the theater at home and abroad were of a high class. Among the weeklies, *Appleton's Journal*, the *Nation, Puck, Life*, the Boston *Saturday Evening Gazette*, the *Critic*, and the *Round Table* contained more or less distinguished dramatic criticism. The *Aldine* had a drama department in its later years. *Judge's* early volumes featured severe theatrical notices.

Frederick F. Shrader and Lyman O. Fiske had control, the former as editor. The *Mirror* was a matchless chronicler of the New York stage, and it also carried news letters from London, Chicago, and other cities. Winter's "Dramatic Diary," Nym Crinkle's "Feuilleton," and later Frank E. Woods's "Spectator" of the movie field were features. Burns Mantle was a notable contributor in the last few years. Mary H. Fiske had a well-known department called "The Giddy Gusher," and Charles Carroll was in charge of the music section. There was a legal department; the *Mirror* essayed to help members of the profession in their struggles against managers. Fiske was instrumental in the erection of the "Actors' Fund" in 1882. The Christmas numbers were a feature in the eighties.

Criticism of the theater was not usually very competent; newspapers believed too generally that the only background necessary to the critic was association with actors. Such work, said the *Round Table*, was chiefly in the hands of so-called bohemians — "long-haired and dirty-nailed men and unhooped and uncombed women . . . a Bacchanalian Mutual Admiration Society," not above petty bribery.[27] There were, however, such competent and brilliant critics as William Winter, Andrew C. Wheeler ("Nym Crinkle"), H. A. Clapp, Brander Matthews, and Laurence Hutton.[28]

ACTORS, PLAYS, AND CRITICS

Throughout the period, the theater was generally prosperous. There was a kind of theatrical boom after the close of the war; the hard times that followed seemed to interfere but little with the theaters, which continued to prosper amid the wrecks of other business enterprises;[29] and by 1883 Winter could write: "The stage continued to grow in wealth, power, and public consideration." [30]

But observers differed widely about artistic achievement in these years. The reader could run the whole gamut in the magazines. Kate Field declared in the *Atlantic Monthly* in 1868:

We have better theatres, better scenery, better costumes, more respectful and numerous audiences, better tendencies in our school of acting, and a better appreciation of one of the noblest of professions." [31]

And A. M. Palmer, one of the most intelligent of theater managers, wrote in the *North American Review* fifteen years later: "The present condition of the drama is, except in the quality of its literature, healthier, higher, nobler than it has ever been before." [32] But the *Critic* declared in the same year that Palmer made his gratulatory observation that "theatrical taste

[27] *Round Table*, I, 43 (January 2, 1864).

[28] Examples of dramatic criticism from the period are to be found in M. J. Moses and J. M. Brown, *The American Theatre As Seen by Its Critics, 1752–1934* (New York, 1934).

[29] *Galaxy*, XXI, 432 (March 1876).

[30] *North American Review*, CXXXVI, 598 (June 1883).

[31] *Atlantic Monthly*, XXI, 276 (March 1868).

[32] *North American Review*, CXXXVI, 591 (June 1883).

has reached its lowest point. Cheap melodrama reigns undisturbed."[33] And the actor John Gilbert wrote in the *North American*:

I believe the present condition of the drama, both from a moral and an artistic point of view, to be a subject for regret. A large number of our theatres are managed by speculators who have no love for true art . . . it is sufficient if a play is sensational and full of startling situations. Many of the plays that have been adapted from the French are open to the very severest criticism on the ground of immorality. . . . One great fault of the modern drama is over-decoration.[34]

The apparent confusion in such statements comes from the ease of generalization. When the attentive reader breaks such summary statements down into specific allegations, he finds little dispute over the main features of the situation: the theaters were prosperous, audiences were large and far better behaved than formerly,[35] there were some great actors on the boards, there was an overemphasis on settings, the dearth of good American dramatic writing was a national disgrace, a wave of cheap melodrama struck the theater in the early eighties, and certain new features of the stage were shocking to the moral sensibilities of many.

Criticism of the growing emphasis on settings ran from one end of the period to the other. In 1869 the dramatic critic of *Appleton's Journal* complained:

The pictorial art of the stage now more than rivals the actor. It has thrust itself into a first place in theatrical affairs, and not Shakespeare himself is now acceptable unless set forth with a wealth of scenic display.[36]

Charles Astor Bristed tells in the *Galaxy* of going to see the play "Acquitted," which was advertised as "One Unbroken Coruscation of Magnificent Effects, Startling Situations, and *Thrilling Battle Effects*, sustained by 160 Artists and Auxiliaries," and

[33] *Critic*, III, 49 (February 3, 1883).

[34] *North American Review*, CXXXVI, 586 (June 1883).

[35] An English observer in 1884 found the audiences in New York cold. See *Theatre*, Vol. II for 1884, p. 28. For boisterous behavior in earlier American theaters, see Mott, *op. cit.*, p. 431.

[36] *Appleton's Journal*, I, 25 (April 3, 1869); I, 154 (May 1, 1869).

being stunned by the noise and choked by the gunpowder; while a revival of "Niagara Falls" the same season employed "an entire stud of trained horses." [37]

The complaint about the lack of an American drama was not new; [38] it persisted through the seventies in spite of rather lonely efforts of Bronson Howard and James A. Herne. Laurence Hutton wrote in *Lippincott's* in 1886: "The American play is yet to be written. Such is the unanimous verdict of the guild of dramatic critics of America." [39] Two months later, probably in reply to Hutton's article, Manager Augustine Daly challenged this "verdict" in the *North American Review*, and contended that American playwrights had been doing some good work — not blatantly native, perhaps, and not based on American history, but, on the other hand, not written or adapted merely as starring vehicles. Daly named, among others, Howard's "Saratoga" and "The Young Mrs. Winthrop," Mrs. Burnett's "Esmeralda" (printed in the *Century* for February 1882), Henry Guy Carleton's "Victor Durand," Bartley Campbell's "My Partner," and Benjamin Woolf's "The Mighty Dollar." [40] The Madison Square Theater was dubbed "the Home of American Drama" at about this time by the *Critic*: [41] there such outstanding successes as "Esmeralda," "The Young Mrs. Winthrop," and MacKaye's "Hazel Kirke," were successively produced in the years 1880–82. [42]

Adaptations of foreign plays were, according to the critics, the bane of our dramatic literature. Many commentators of the seventies bore hard on Boucicault. *Puck* invented the verb *to boucicault* as a synonym for *to plagiarize*; and apropos of "Marriage," shown at Wallack's, it observed that "Five acts of epigram do not make a play. . . . Five acts of farcical incident do not constitute a drama." [43] The *Round Table* was characteristically violent in its attacks on "that managerial vampyre, Dion Boucicault." [44] But *Appleton's*, which had not

---

[37] *Galaxy*, XV, 410 (March 1873).
[38] See vol. II, p. 198.
[39] *Lippincott's Magazine*, XXXVII, 289 (March 1886).
[40] *North American Review*, CXLII, 485 (May 1886).
[41] *Critic*, III, 201 (April 28, 1883).
[42] *New York Clipper*, XXX, 490 (October 14, 1882).
[43] *Puck*, October 10, 1877.   [44] *Round Table*, I, 29 (December 26, 1863).

hesitated to call many a Boucicault production "trash," lauded the work of the actor-playwright when he and his wife appeared at Booth's in "Arrah-na-Pogue." "Their success has been very great," said this critic, "but no greater than they deserve. Without decided dramatic genius, they are almost perfect as artists." [45] Other reviewers generally agreed.[46]

As Daly intimated in his *North American* article, it was the necessity of fitting plays to the great actors and actresses that militated against the production of a drama by more literary American writers. "A little curious, isn't it," remarked a gossiper in the *New York Clipper*, "that people who can do purely literary work of the highest order are very apt to fail when they try to write a play?" [47] But it was not so "curious": Harte, Howells, and the others did not know the stage, and they did not write stars into their scripts. It was easier for theater hacks to revamp borrowed favorites, and far safer from a managerial standpoint. "The star," said an English critic in the London *Theater* in 1884, "seems to have been the sole attraction of the American theatre." [48] It was true, and the play was little more than the wagon hitched to the star.

To list the stars of the seventies and eighties would be no small task. The theatrical heavens were full of them, and some were of the first magnitude. Certainly one of the foremost was Edwin Booth. The brilliant history of his theater while he managed it, his unexampled record of one hundred nights in succession as Hamlet, and his triumphal 1876 tour of the country gave ample opportunity for comment — the more so because "Mr. Booth's rank as an actor has always been a disputed point."[49] As to Joseph Jefferson there was no such dispute: praise was universal. "By this time everybody has seen 'Rip Van Winkle,' " said *Punchinello* in 1870, "and everybody has expressed the same unbounded admiration for Mr. Jefferson's matchless genius." [50] Lawrence Barrett was also a major figure, manager

[45] *Appleton's Journal*, VIII, 501 (November 2, 1872).
[46] See, for example, *Critic*, II, 78 (March 11, 1882).
[47] *New York Clipper*, XXIX, 521 (October 29, 1881).
[48] Austin Brereton in *Theatre*, Vol. II for 1884, p. 29.
[49] *Appleton's Journal*, I, 185 (May 8, 1869).
[50] *Punchinello*, II, 183 (January 2, 1870). See also *Atlantic Monthly*, XIX, 750 (June 1876), and *Lippincott's Magazine*, IV, 167 (August 1869).

of theaters in New Orleans, San Francisco, and New York, Shakespearean star, producer of Boker's "Francesca di Rimini." John T. Raymond's Colonel Sellers was one of the big hits of the times, and he continued to appear in what the *Critic* called "Sellers characters." "May he long remain the central figure in a cyclus of Sellers plays!" was the *Critic's* devout prayer.[51] The same reviewer, whose comments are always both pointed and reliable, recorded the success of Lester Wallack in his own theater in Robertson's "Ours," with "applause so frantic that he may fairly claim, while still alive to have tasted of immortality." [52] Edwin Forrest declined to his death in 1872, and his disciple John E. McCullough fared but indifferently at the hands of the critics. Indeed, "Many have striven to possess themselves of the cast-off robes of the dead king," wrote Barrett in the *Galaxy*.[53] Charlotte Cushman died in 1876, after having taken, according to the *Clipper*, thirty-seven farewells of the stage,[54] "but none of us can regret her myriad reappearances after final retirements," wrote another magazine admirer.[55] John Gilbert won wide recognition, especially in the roles of old English gentlemen in comedies. The Drews and Barrymores, Laura Keene until her death in 1873, Clara Morris with her great successes in "Divorce" and "Article 47," "Our Mary" Anderson, and many other American actors and actresses made stage history in these years, and the periodicals witnessed to their talents and successes.

But the American stage was not monopolized by American players. From England, from France, from Italy, from Poland, from Germany flocked tragic and comic artists.

> There's more of them coming this way —
> Great Caesar, they're coming to stay!
> For the salaries meek Britain pays in a week
> They can collar out here in a day!

So the doggerelist of the *New York Clipper* heralded in 1883 the coming of a new regiment of foreign invaders.[56] Among

[51] *Critic*, III, 26 (January 20, 1883).   [52] *Ibid.*, III, 12 (January 13, 1883).
[53] *Galaxy*, XXIV, 534 (October 1877).
[54] *New York Clipper*, XXIX, 514 (October 29, 1881).
[55] *Galaxy*, XXIV, 292 (August 1877).
[56] *New York Clipper*, XXXI, 210 (June 16, 1883); also *ibid.*, XXX, 330 (August 12, 1882).

the foreigners on the American stage in 1882–83 were Tommasso Salvini, Mme. Modjeska, Mlle. Rhea, Mme. Seebach, Ludwig Barnay, Henry Irving, Ellen Terry, and Mrs. Lily Langtry. Salvini received superlative praises; according to the *Critic*, he could "carry his audience ravished into the clouds." [57] Irving and Terry also made a big success, though the former was severely criticized for his mannerisms. "No actor has ever made warmer friends or more bitter foes," said *Life*.[58] Barnay was a comparative failure. Mme. Seebach was hailed by *Punchinello* in 1870 as "the greatest actress of the century." [59] Mrs. Langtry, described by the *Continent* as "the world-renowned professional beauty," [60] met with much ridicule and only indifferent success on her first visit in 1882, but she was back next year with her own company. "The divine Sarah" Bernhardt, who had been heralded by Henry James in the *Galaxy* as the most "brilliant embodiment of feminine success" imaginable,[61] came over to "conquer her kingdom" here in 1880.[62] Adelaide Ristori and Ernesto Rossi were Italian visitors; the former became especially well known in America through a series of visits which began in 1866 and ended in 1885. Modjeska and Rhea were popular through many American seasons. In an article on Modjeska in the *Century*, J. Ranken Towse said that she was one of four foreign actors who had acquired "a permanent reputation in America," the others being Salvini, Ristori, and Bernhardt.[63]

The foreign invasion was frequently resented by some of the periodicals. *Puck* liked to refer to Bernhardt, for example, as "the great French dier," [64] in reference to her Camille; and the *Clipper* spoke of "the horde of professionals from abroad, all more or less British, and all more or less actors." [65]

[57] *Critic*, III, 123 (March 17, 1883).
[58] *Life*, II, 280 (November 29, 1883).
[59] *Punchinello*, II, 54 (October 22, 1870).
[60] *Continent*, II, 383 (September 27, 1882).
[61] *Galaxy*, XXIII, 449 (April 1877).
[62] *Lippincott's Magazine*, XXVII, 180 (February 1881).
[63] *Century*, XXVII, 24 (November 1883).
[64] *Puck*, December 15, 1880.
[65] *New York Clipper*, XXX, 536 (November 4, 1882).

MORALS AND THE THEATER

Another chapter was written during this period in the contest between the pulpit and the stage. One of its most colorful incidents was the controversy over the Reverend Mr. Sabine, who refused to bury the actor George Holland from his church, but remarked that there was "a little church around the corner" where an actor's funeral might be held: thus has the Church of the Transfiguration come to be called by a name given it in derogation. Among those who attacked Sabine most bitterly was Mark Twain, then editing a department in the *Galaxy*. Mark's comment was in part an earnest defense of the theater and in part a severe indictment of sanctimonious pretense: it ended by calling the reverend gentleman in question a "crawling, slimy, sanctimonious, self-righteous reptile!" [66] Some ten years later a Chicago preacher engaged in a widely advertised controversy with James H. McVicker over the morality of the stage.[67] This may have suggested a notable *North American Review* symposium on the subject in 1883.[68] Later in the same year Theodore L. Cuyler declared that "no good woman wants her sons and daughters" at the theater — a remark which the *Nation* thought perhaps excited more indignation than it called for." [69]

Certainly the "burlesques" which arrived in the later sixties on the heels of Offenbach and la Tostée were thoroughly shocking to many observers. Among these offerings were "The Black Crook," "The Devil's Auction," "The Forty Thieves," and "Sinbad." "Of the seven theatres now open in New York," said *Appleton's* in July 1869, "six are devoted to burlesque or pantomime." Pantomimes might be legitimate,

but the burlesque is a different thing. It sets out with respecting nothing — neither taste, propriety, virtue, nor manners. Its design is to be uproariously funny and glaringly indecent. It seeks to unite the coarsest fun with the most intoxicating forms of beauty. It presents women garbed, or semi-garbed, in the most luxurious and seductive dresses possible, and makes them play the fool to the topmost bent of the spectator. One is dazzled with light and color, with gay songs,

---

[66] *Galaxy*, XI, 320 (February 1871).
[67] *New York Clipper*, XXX, 54 (April 15, 1882).
[68] *North American Review*, CXXXVI, 581 (June 1883).
[69] *Nation*, XXXVII, 388 (November 8, 1883).

with beautiful faces and graceful limbs, and startled at the coarse songs, the vile jargon, the low wit, and the abandoned manners of the characters.[70]

And the scandal-loving *Police Gazette* observed, apropos of a revival of "The Black Crook" at Niblo's in 1879: "There can be no excuse for young men spending their time in low bar-rooms, in billiard saloons," and such, "since the grand, gorgeous, resplendent, bang-up, utterly incomprehensible Black Crook" is in town again.[71]

Some other critics were less severe. William Dean Howells, who must, to satisfy his shade, be here referred to as "a scandalous writer of the period," wrote in the *Atlantic* of the new burlesque troupe from London:

Of their beauty and their *abandon*, the historical gossiper, whom I descry far down the future, waiting to refer to me as "A scandalous writer of the period," shall learn very little to his purpose of warming his sketch with color from mine. But I hope I may describe these ladies as very pretty, very blonde, and very unscrupulously clever, and still disappoint the historical gossiper.

But the gossiper is heartened to find a little further along that

the burlesque chiefly betrayed its descent from the spectacular ballet in its undressing . . . in the burlesque there seemed nothing of innocent intent. No matter what the plot, it always led to a final great scene of breakdown, — which was doubtless most impressive in that particular burlesque where the scene represented the infernal world, and the ladies gave the dances of the country with a happy conception of the deportment of lost souls.[72]

Richard Grant White went to the burlesque, too, and while he found it "monstrous," he was rather fascinated with the greatest of the burlesque queens — Miss Lydia Thompson. Indeed he was unkind enough to suggest that

Some of the outcry that we hear against the costume which the burlesque actresses wear, in the way of their profession, has in it such a tone of personal injury, that it might come from mammas and papas

[70] *Appleton's Journal*, I, 440 (July 3, 1869).
[71] *National Police Gazette*, March 15, 1879, p. 16.
[72] *Atlantic Monthly*, XXIII, 640 (May 1869).

who, having a very poor article of young woman lying heavy on their hands, are indignant that there should be so good and so easy an opportunity of trying it by a very high standard.[73]

Punchinello was less refined than these gentlemen: "Lydia Thompson," observed that young rascal, nightly "offers up her fatted calves at the shrine of a prodigal New York audience." [74] In short, this discovery of calves was really epochal in the changing morality of America; for though, of course, only a comparatively small proportion of the population saw "The Black Crook," nearly everybody read about it and discussed it and, willy-nilly, accepted it as a part of contemporary life. In a way "The Black Crook" is as important in our period as the resumption of specie payments. Perhaps it is not pushing the matter too far to say that Miss Thompson's line in her character as "A Girl of the Period" in "Sinbad" may be taken as an epitaph of Puritanism: "We are aware of our own awarishness!"

VARIETIES AND TOURING TROUPES

In the latter years of our period nearly everything went on tour. By the beginning of 1885, the *Clipper* was listing 182 dramatic companies on tour, 28 musical troupes, 21 "variety combinations," and 9 minstrel shows.[75] No star was so effulgent as to be fixed in a single theater for long; they all had their orbits, the wider the better. Chicago, New Orleans, San Francisco, and St. Louis were especially good "show towns"; but many cities much smaller were visited by the great attractions. Popular plays like "Hazel Kirke," "Esmeralda," "Uncle Tom's Cabin," and "East Lynne" each had several companies on the road at once.

Negro minstrelsy declined toward the eighties in the number of companies, at the same time that it enlarged the individual troupes. A minstrel company became a kind of three-ring circus, with scores of members performing various specialties. The names of these companies exhausted the vocabulary of largeness: Duprez & Benedict's Gigantic Minstrels, Barlow & Wil-

[73] *Galaxy*, VIII, 260 (August 1869).
[74] *Punchinello*, I, 116 (May 21, 1870).
[75] *New York Clipper*, XXXII, 646 (December 27, 1884).

son's Mammoth Minstrels, the Female Mastodon Minstrels, Gardner's Behemoth Minstrels, and so on.

In the summers ten or a dozen big circuses were on the road, all in bitter rivalries which may be followed best in the *Clipper*. Forepaugh, Barnum & Bailey, Van Amburgh, Sells Brothers, John Robinson, Cole, Orrin Brothers — these are all names dear to the hearts of the youth of the period and not unknown to more self-conscious adult patrons. The Buffalo Bill shows came in during the early eighties, and the Jesse James spectacles with their horses and shooting invaded regular theaters.

SPORTS AND THE OUTDOOR LIFE

American interest in sports rose steadily throughout the post-bellum period. Recreations such as bicycling, hunting and fishing, and amateur baseball increased in importance; but even more striking was the exhibition of interest in sports as popular spectacles, such as racing, professional baseball, prize fighting, and pedestrian contests. Participating in games and watching others play them tended to become more and more separated as the various sports were organized nationally, until recreation for the individual came to bear little relationship to spectacles for the masses except in the one game common to both functions — baseball. The increase of leisure allowed time for both these interests in sport: a writer in the *Journal of Social Science* pointed out in 1880 that the annual vacation, then become almost universal, not only allowed but demanded more or less systematic programs of recreation.[76]

Among the general sports periodicals, such veterans as the *Spirit of the Times*, the *National Police Gazette*, and the *New York Clipper* were still active,[77] the first specializing in racing, the second featuring prize fighting, and the third sharing various sports with the theater. Some of the old Sunday papers, notably William Cauldwell's *New York Mercury*, gave much attention to popular sports. Boston's weekly *Sporting Times* of 1867–72 had a recrudescence in 1884–86, with half its former sixteen folio pages; and *Sports and Pastimes* was published there as a weekly folio of eight pages in 1883–86. In Boston also Adams

---

[76] *Journal of Social Science*, XII, 137 (December 1880).
[77] See vol. II, 203–04 and sketch 9.

& Company issued a little quarterly called *Sports and Games* (1870–74) at twenty-five cents a year. The *Young New Yorker* (1878–79) was a brief weekly "journal of recreation and the world of sports" published by the Adams & Company who were associates of Beadle & Adams. It also published fiction by "Jack Harkaway" and "Oliver Optic," but it was unsuccessful and was soon consolidated with Beadle's *Star Journal*. In Chicago, F. B. ("Yank") Adams conducted the *Sporting and Theatrical Journal* (1880–93), latterly called *Sporting Review*; and *Pacific Life* flourished as a sixteen-page folio in San Francisco (1876–85).

Hunting and fishing, part of the business of making a living in the frontier, tended more and more to become avocations of the sportsman. "America's play-house is all-out-of-doors," declared the *Chicago Field*, "and out-door sports are growing more popular." [78] It was to such sports that the *Field* (1874–current) catered.[79] *Forest and Stream* (1873–1930), a New York weekly of high class founded by Charles Hallock and edited by him until 1885, was active in founding the Audubon Society and wielded an important influence in game conservation reforms. A later New York journal was the *American Angler* (1881–1900), a monthly edited by William C. Harris. *Outing* [80] was founded by W. B. Howland at Albany in 1882 and soon became one of the best outdoor periodicals. These were the leaders of a score of hunting and fishing periodicals.[81]

A valuable outdoor journal of a somewhat different class was *Appalachia* (1876–1922), organ of the Appalachian Mountain Club, of Boston. It was issued irregularly and contained articles

[78] *Chicago Field*, X, 232 (November 23, 1878).

[79] It gave attention also to racing, baseball, checkers, and so on; and was especially concerned with the kennel, game laws, and guns. It was founded as *Field and Stream*, changing in 1875 to *Field* and in 1877 to *Chicago Field*. When it moved to New York in 1881 it changed to *American Field*, its present title. George W. Strell was its managing editor for many years.

[80] To be treated more fully in a separate sketch in a succeeding volume of this work.

[81] Others were *Fur, Fin and Feather* (1868–91), New York; *American Sportsman* (1872–77), West Meriden, Connecticut, called *Rod and Gun and American Sportsman* in its last two years; *Field and River* (1877–82), New Brighton, Pennsylvania; *Game Fanciers' Journal* (1879–1910), Battle Creek, Michigan; *Forest, Forge, and Farm* (1880–86), Ilion and Albany, New York; *American Sportsman* (1884–90), New York.

of a scientific nature, with maps and illustrations. Some of the natural history periodicals, oölogists' journals, and other collectors' magazines, discussed in an earlier chapter,[82] are closely related to the sportsmen's publications.

Brentano's *Aquatic Monthly and Sporting Gazetteer* was begun in New York in 1872, to be devoted chiefly to yachting, rowing, and swimming. Suspended through 1876–78, it became more general after its revival, signalizing its broader policy by changing its name 1880–91 to *Brentano's Monthly*. The Brentanos also founded the *American Canoeist* (1882–91), called *Sail and Paddle* in its last three years. Canoeing was a popular sport by the late seventies, and an American Canoe Association was formed in 1880.[83] Its activities were recorded in *Outing*, the *Clipper*, and other journals. The six unsuccessful attempts by British yachts to "lift" the *America's* cup during this period excited wide attention, as did the transatlantic race of 1866.

THE BICYCLE CRAZE

In 1868 began the first American bicycle craze, though the word bicycle had not yet supplanted *velocipede*. Winslow Homer in *Harper's Weekly* pictured the year 1869 coming in on a two-wheeled velocipede.[84] Henry Ward Beecher declared that the "coming man" was coming on a velocipede, and it was reported that thousands of attendants at Plymouth Church came on wheels. Charles A. Dana was an enthusiast in the new exercise. Charles G. Leland wrote a Breitmann ballad on learning to ride. Even a periodical devoted to the craze was begun, to flourish briefly in 1869 — the *Velocipedist*, a New York monthly. The best place to follow the developments of the popular enthusiasm is the "Velocipede Notes" in the *Scientific American*. In its issue for January 9, 1869, that journal said:

> The *furore* created by the introduction of the velocipede in Paris has extended to this country, and in our principal cities the demand for this elegant and graceful vehicle is so great that quite a number of extensive establishments are being devoted to its production, yet the demand cannot be supplied.[85]

[82] See p. 111.   [83] See *Outing*, V, 415 (December 1884).
[84] *Harper's Weekly*, XX, 67 (January 30, 1869).
[85] *Scientific American*, XX, 20 (January 9, 1869).

A few weeks later the same paper observed that its "exchanges teem with items of all sorts regarding the velocipede." [86] The "girl of the period" took up the sport in a costume of divided skirts "not unlike the trowsers of a Zouave." [87] These early machines were true bicycles, but they had no rubber tires; the wheels were of wood with iron rims. Solid rubber tires came in, however, in the early seventies. Schools for teaching the art of "velocipeding" became very popular in the cities, and elevated ways over the streets were proposed for cyclists.

The velocipede craze subsided nearly as suddenly as it had risen; but in the late seventies it came in again, mounted this time on a wheel some five feet high with a second smaller wheel following after. The first of these machines came from England in the fall of 1877,[88] but the next year saw Colonel Albert A. Pope manufacturing American bicycles in Boston.[89] *Outing* declared that Boston was "certainly entitled to be called the Hub of the Bicycle, as it is the centre of the sport in this country.[90] In 1882 the *Wheelman* estimated that there were 20,000 bicycles in use in the United States. "Never was known so rapid a spread of an invention," it said, "except, it may be, in the case of the sewing machine." [91] Tricycles, "particularly adapted for the other sex," were also popular.[92]

Riding a "bi," as the machine came to be nicknamed, was an exhilarating adventure. The rider, said the editor of the *Wheelman* in its first number,

feels, when perched high in air, that he is making a considerable spectacle of himself and needlessly eliciting public remark; both of which sensations are not agreeable to men of tender sensibilities. But these feelings soon wear off.[93]

The rider also risked bruises unwelcome to men of tender skins; but when he had once conquered the wheel, he developed an

---

[86] *Scientific American*, XX, 67 (January 30, 1869).
[87] *Ibid.*, XX, 228 (April 10, 1869).
[88] *Wheelman*, I, 401 (March 1883).
[89] *Ibid.*, I, 70 (October 1882).
[90] *Outing*, II, 23 (May 1883).
[91] *Wheelman*, I, 23 (October 1882).
[92] *Ibid.*, I, 71 (October 1882).
[93] *Ibid.*, I, 47 (October 1882).

excessive enthusiasm for it. One of the best of *Puck's* many puns ran:

> Oh, don't tell me of your sleighing — don't! Just
> please to go away!
> Better bicycle ten minutes than a cycle in a sleigh! [94]

The first bicycle club was organized in Boston in February 1878;[95] and in 1880 the League of American Wheelmen was formed and attained a membership of 1,500 within a year.[96] In 1883 it paraded in New York with 875 mounted cyclists in line.[97] There were feuds between horsemen and wheelmen, and Central Park was closed to bicycles until 1883.[98] Horse-and-bicycle races, fifty-mile bicycle races, and six-day races were common in the early eighties; and at the very end of our period the "safety" bicycle, with wheels of equal size, made its appearance.

The second bicycle periodical appears to have been Cunningham, Heath & Company's trade organ, the *American Bicycling Journal*, begun in December 1877 in Boston and published irregularly for nearly two years. It was then succeeded by the first magazine of importance in the field, Charles E. Pratt's *Bicycling World*.[99] E. C. Hodges & Company soon got control of it; and it had many editors, including Abbot Basset, head of the L. A. W., of which the *World* became the official organ. It printed the records of club tours and ultimately became a leading good roads advocate. Its chief New York competitor was the *Wheel* (1880–1900), a twelve-page weekly in quarto which sold for a dollar a year. The *Wheelman's Gazette* (1883–1908) was begun in Springfield, Massachusetts, but moved to Indianapolis in 1886 and there was conducted by L. B. Darrow. There were a few shorter-lived bicycle papers.[100]

[94] *Puck*, VII, 19 (March 17, 1880).   [95] *Wheelman*, I, 401 (March 1883).
[96] *Harper's Monthly*, LXIII, 285 (July 1881).
[97] *Outing*, II, 47 (June 1883).
[98] *Ibid.*, XVIII, 345 (July 1891).
[99] Published November 1879–February 1915. It was a biweekly during its first year, and then a weekly. It was called the *Bicycling World and the Archery Field* in 1880–81. In 1898 it absorbed *American Cyclist*, adding that name to its title; it absorbed *Wheel and Cycle Trade Review* in 1900, becoming *Bicycling World and Motorcycle Review*. In 1904 it absorbed *Motor-Cycle Magazine*, and was itself finally merged into *Motorcycle Illustrated*.
[100] The Boston *Wheelman* was published by Albert A. Pope, the bicycle manu-

RACING AND DRIVING

Under the patronage of men of standing and respectability like August Belmont, W. H. Vanderbilt, and General Grant, horse racing achieved a position shortly after the war beyond anything known before or since. The season of 1867 was extraordinary. Dexter trotted a mile in 2:17¼ on August 14 of that year, and was then purchased by Robert Bonner for $33,-000 and retired from the turf.[101] Goldsmith Maid was the heroine of the early seventies, and Rarus and St. Julien divided honors in the latter half of that decade. Then Maud S. came in with a burst of speed that won the plaudits of the world and lowered the mark for the mile in 1880, and again in 1884, and finally set a record in 1885 which was to stand for five years — 2:08¾.[102] *Wallace's Monthly*, when it began in 1875, declared:

> The national sport of horse-trotting, American in its origin and development, has grown to mammoth proportions in the United States, and absorbs a far greater share of public attention than any other of the public pastimes which contribute to the enjoyment of the people. . . . The names of the leading performers of the trotting turf are as familiar as household words among every class of society.[103]

An excellent review of American trotting which appeared in *Harper's Monthly* in 1873 pointed out, however, some of the evils which had grown up about the sport and a partial remedy:

> Prior to 1870 there was little or no system in the management of the trotting turf, and consequently it was difficult to put a stop to rascality. . . . A driver might be ruled off one course, but he cared little for this, since the punishment did not extend to other courses. In February, 1870, the different associations throughout the coun-

---

facturer, and edited by S. S. McClure, later founder of *McClure's Magazine*, October 1882 through December 1883. Pope then purchased *Outing, q.v.,* and merged the two. See S. S. McClure, *My Autobiography* (New York, 1914), Chapter V. The subtitle describes the magazine succinctly: "An Illustrated Magazine of Cycling Literature and News." The *Western Cyclist* (1883–86) was conducted by the Bicycle Club of Ovid, Michigan.

[101] *Atlantic Monthly*, XXI, 529 (May 1868).

[102] See *Munsey's Magazine*, VI, 247 (November 1891), and *Harper's Monthly*, XLVII, 611 (September 1873).

[103] *Wallace's Monthly*, I, 1 (October 1875).

try . . . organized the National Association for the Promotion of the Interests of the American Trotting Turf.[104]

This organization had its troubles, but it greatly improved racing conditions. Ladies were now seen at the tracks, and the great meets became society events.[105]

Wilkes' Spirit of the Times, which dropped the name of its proprietor from its title in 1868 and a few years later passed to other management, shared leadership among turf weeklies during the postbellum period with the New York *Turf, Field and Farm* (1865–1903). This latter paper was founded by S. D. and B. G. Bruce, who had bought the plant of the older, defunct *Spirit of the Times*. Colonel F. G. Skinner, son of the founder of the *American Farmer* and of the *Turf Register*, and a man with wide experience in European field sports, became field editor of the new paper in its second year and exercised a potent influence through it. Farming, stock raising, and gardening were within its sphere of interest, as well as cricket, baseball, whist, chess, and so on.[106] *Wallace's Monthly* (1875–94) was an illustrated octavo edited and published by John H. Wallace in New York; it, too, gave attention to general stock raising, but the horse was its "leading feature." [107] The Chicago *Horseman* (1881–1915),[108] the San Francisco *Breeder and Sportsman* (1882–1920), and the *American Horse Breeder* (1883–1913), of Boston, were famous horse periodicals; and there were several others of some importance.[109]

[104] *Harper's Monthly*, XLVII, 611 (September 1873).

[105] *Ibid.*, p. 613.

[106] For *Spirit of the Times*, see vol. II, pp. 203–04. B. G. Bruce, whose home was at Lexington, Kentucky, soon gave place on the editorial staff of *Turf, Field and Farm* to H. Millard. Hamilton Busbey was an editor from the beginning, and L. C. Bruce joined the staff in the seventies. Busbey was still editor when the paper was merged into *Sports of the Times*.

[107] Benjamin Singerly was publisher for the first year or two. It was bought by the American Trotting Register Company in 1891 and moved to Chicago.

[108] It absorbed the *Spirit of the Times* in 1903 and added that name to its own for title. Its illustrations were excellent, and it was famous for its Christmas numbers.

[109] Including Charles J. Foster's *New York Sportsman* (1875–92); *Dunton's Spirit of the Turf* (1876–81), Chicago; *Turf, Farm and Home* (1878–1911), Waterville, Maine; *Western Sportsman and Live Stock News* (1878–current), Indianapolis, called *Western Horseman* 1892–1920, and since then *Horseman and Fair World*; *Maine Horse Breeders' Monthly* (1879–92), Canton, Maine.

These journals did not neglect the draft horse for the farm, or the carriage horse for the parks and roads. This latter animal, though not quite so spectacular as his relative of the turf, played a considerable part in popular recreation. Coaching attained some popularity in the later seventies; coaching clubs were organized and long drives made to points of scenic beauty.[110] The cities all had their riding clubs, too, in the early eighties, and polo came in during the seventies.[111] City parks [112] were largely for driving: in 1869 *Appleton's Journal* printed the following paragraph:

Nothing can be more striking, more brilliant, or more vivid, than the appearance of the grand drive at the Central Park, on a fair day, in the fashionable season. . . . Probably nothing more fully exhibits the wealth, luxury, and taste of New York City than its fancy "turnouts" and private carriages. . . . At least fifty new carriages a day are produced by New York manufacturers. The fashionable styles are: the Clarence (large family or state carriage); landau (opening on the top); landaulet (opening on the top, with appliances to remove the front section if desired); coupé (for fair weather or fresh air); ponyphaeton (riding *al fresco*); and a four-in-hand drag, which, within a few years, has become one of the most conspicuous features of the Central Park drives.[113]

The carriage industry had its journals: not only the older *Hub* and *Harness and Carriage Journal*,[114] but such newer organs as the *Carriage Monthly* (1865–1930), of Philadelphia;[115] the *Carriage Journal* (1879–93) and the *National Harness Review* (1879–1920), of Chicago; the *Harness Gazette* (1882–1926), of Rome, New York; and the *Horse Shoers' Journal* (1875–1930), long of Detroit but latterly of Chicago and Indianapolis.

THE GROWTH OF BASEBALL

But we must return to the spectacular sports and consider the growth of baseball, second only to trotting in mass interest.

[110] *Harper's Monthly*, XC, 28 (December 1894).

[111] *Outing*, XVIII, 331 (July 1891).

[112] *Appleton's Journal* (I, 250, May 22, 1869) noted that "most of the leading towns in the United States are planning or executing" designs for parks.

[113] *Appleton's Journal*, I, 25 (April 3, 1869).   [114] See vol. II, p. 92.

[115] Called *Coach-Makers' International Journal* 1865–73, *Carriage Monthly* 1873–1915, *Vehicle Monthly* 1916–21, and *Motor Vehicle Monthly* 1922–30.

It increased tremendously in popularity immediately after the war. *Harper's Weekly*, announcing the coming of the Athletics of Philadelphia to New York for a series in 1865, commented:

The games of these athletes are most attractive. They are sometimes witnessed by not less than ten thousand persons, including ladies. There is no manlier game than base-ball, and the more it is cultivated, the better for the country.[116]

Three years later the *Galaxy* wrote editorially of baseball:

It is a mania. Hundreds of clubs do nothing but play, all summer and autumn. What pleasant days are not devoted to matches are spent in practice. When the "nines" are not contending with visitors, they themselves are traveling over the country, from Bangor to St. Louis. They make batting a business, and depend for money on the receipts from spectators. . . . Since the war, it has run like wildfire. Young soldiers, full of vigor, and longing for comradeship and manly exercise, found them in this game. . . .[117]

And by 1872 *Sports and Games* could declare, "Base Ball has become the national game of the United States." [118]

These were the days of amateur baseball. The Cincinnati Redstockings of 1868 were said to have been the first team to draw regular salaries,[119] but by the middle seventies professional baseball had spread to all the important cities. The National League was formed in 1876, succeeding the professional division of the old National Association; and five years later [120] a rival was erected in the American Association. The first championship series was held in New York in 1884 between the Providence Club, representing the National League, and the New York Metropolitans of the American Association; the weather was bad, and the crowds were so small that the teams wanted to call the games off.[121] But the next year attendance at the series between the Chicago and New York pennant winners in Chicago averaged 10,000 a game.

Henry Chadwick's weekly *Ball Players' Chronicle* (1867),

---

[116] *Harper's Weekly*, IX, 371 (June 17, 1865).

[117] *Galaxy*, VI, 563 (October 1868).

[118] *Sports and Games*, III, 112 (No. 3, 1872).

[119] *Outing*, XII, 117 (May 1888).

[120] It was organized in Cincinnati in November 1881 but not put in operation until the next year. See *New York Clipper*, XXIX, 556 (November 12, 1881).

[121] *Ibid.*, XXXII, 523 (November 1, 1884).

of New York, appears to have been the first journal devoted to baseball. More successful, however, was the weekly Philadelphia *Sporting Life* (1883–1926), which gained a large circulation, capitalizing on the bicycle craze as well as upon the general interest in baseball.[122] Papers like the *Clipper, Frank Leslie's Illustrated Weekly*, the *Spirit of the Times*, the *Young New Yorker*, the Boston *Sporting Times*, and many of the Sunday weeklies gave full and regular reports of the baseball games.

PRIZE FIGHTING AND PEDESTRIANISM

Another of the great American spectacular sports — prize fighting — fell upon evil days after the war. The trouble was that the ring lacked a hero. Between John C. Heenan of the sixties and John L. Sullivan of the eighties there was a succession of third-rate pugilists, duly chronicled in the *Clipper*, the *Police Gazette, Day's Doings*, and such loyal adherents of the manly art, to be sure; but not until the "Strong Boy of Boston" knocked out Paddy Ryan in nine rounds of savage slugging on the afternoon of February 7, 1882, was there a popular champion.[123] This great event took place in an improvised ring in a Mississippi town to which a special train was run from New Orleans for the occasion. The *Police Gazette* commemorated the occasion in a special supplement. Five months later, at Madison Square Garden a record-breaking crowd of 12,000 fight-fans saw Sullivan fail to knock out Tug Wilson of England in four rounds;[124] this match was important not for its effect on the championship but for its initiation of the tradition of great fight crowds in New York. Richard K. Fox, owner of the *Police Gazette*, was the great patron of prize fighting in these years.[125]

Much tamer surely, but extraordinarily exciting to the public in these years, were the great walking matches. Famous pedestrians like Weston had caught the popular imagination in the sixties, but it was not until the six-day international walking matches of the late seventies that great interest was aroused and great crowds attracted by what *Puck* called "this walking mad-

[122] It was suspended 1917–22, but resumed as a monthly devoted to general sports. The title was changed to *Sport Life* in 1924.
[123] *New York Clipper*, XXIX, 772 (February 11, 1882).
[124] *Ibid.*, XXX, 286 (July 22, 1882).   [125] See vol. II, pp. 328 ff.

ness." [126] *Harper's Weekly* testified in 1879 that "No sporting event has caused so much excitement in New York for many years as the great walking match at Gilmore's Garden between four redoubtable contestants, one of whom held the belt as champion of the world." [127] The contest was won by the English Howell.

THE MINOR SPORTS

One of the prominent sports of the period — a game which enjoyed a popularity at one time which made it a major diversion of the American people — was croquet. The *Nation*, promulgating in 1866 a set of rules just formulated by "a croquet parliament" in England, remarked that "of all the epidemics that have swept over our land, the swiftest and most infectious is croquet." [128] The June 1869 number of *Onward*, Mayne Reid's short-lived magazine for young men, was devoted wholly to croquet; and another observer claimed that this recreation was, in that year, "a strong rival of our national game." [129] It survived, however, not as a rival of anything in particular, but as a pleasant social diversion — one of the few games in which women could participate equally with men.

The girls played lawn tennis, too, but they were not permitted to enter the open tournaments because of the fears of the managers that their precious feminine modesty would suffer.[130] Certainly they could not have played on even terms with the men if they had worn the long beruffled skirts in which the tight-laced racquet girl of the eighties was pictured by such interpreters of the game as the *Wheelman*. "Although the youngest of outdoor pastimes, lawn-tennis has already won for itself a foremost place among polite sports," said a writer in that magazine in 1883.[131] At that time 40 clubs with a membership of 4,000 players belonged to the national association, organized in 1881; and there were, besides, many private and institutional clubs.

Proper young ladies played at archery, too. Like all the minor

[126] *Puck*, V, 485 (October 8, 1879).
[127] *Harper's Weekly*, XXIII, 247 (March 29, 1879).
[128] *Nation*, III, 113 (August 9, 1836).
[129] *Printers' Circular*, IV, 139 (June 1869).
[130] *Wheelman*, II, 467 (September 1883).   [131] *Ibid.*, p. 463.

sports, archery had its national association (organized in 1879);
but it remained a rather aristocratic society game. The
Archery and Tennis News (1882–86), of New York, underwent two or three changes of title; it was concerned with the
more polite sports. The *Bicycling World* also paid much attention to archery and tennis.

Roller skating was often very popular at the beginning of
the eighties. It was also a social diversion, and the rinks in the
smaller towns furnished needed recreation centers. But in the
cities the sport itself was ruined by the variety shows which
were brought nightly to the rink floors in the course of competition for crowds.[132]

Cricket, which had long been played in America, had something like a revival in the eastern states during the early eighties.
At least its matches attracted considerable crowds, especially in
Philadelphia. *Sporting Life, Turf, Field and Farm*, the *Clipper*,
and the *Spirit of the Times* reported cricket games with care;
and the *American Cricketer* (1877–1933), of Philadelphia, was
the devoted organ of the sport.

"The bowling alley," said a writer in *Harper's*, "is, as a rule,
the adjunct of what is known as a beer garden." [133] Billiards
were in somewhat better standing. They had the aid of Michael
Phelan's *Billiard Cue* [134] until 1874; and the *New York Clipper*,
with its consistent and long-continued sponsorship, exercised a
beneficial influence upon the game. Chess and checker matches
were reported in many periodicals, and several short-lived journals were devoted to the playing of each of these games. Perhaps the *Brooklyn Chess Chronicle* (1882–87) was the most
important of these papers.

ATHLETIC CLUBS, COUNTRY CLUBS, AND COLLEGE SPORTS

"New York is in a fair way to become the athletic capital of
the world," believed a writer for *Harper's Monthly* who was
profoundly impressed with the number of athletic organizations
functioning in that city in 1884.[135] By that time there were

---

[132] *Wheelman*, II, 300 (January 1885); *Outing*, VII, 340 (December 1885),
and VIII, 99 (April 1886). Also note announcements of rink shows *passim* in the
Clipper, Mirror, and *Dramatic News*.

[133] *Harper's Monthly*, LXVIII, 299 (January 1884).

[134] See vol. II, p. 203. [135] *Harper's Monthly*, LXVIII, 297 (January 1884).

seven general athletic clubs in New York, and "of clubs that make a specialty of one form of exercise there is no end." Nor was this popular athletic preoccupation limited to New York; athletic clubs specializing in racing, jumping, and other field sports were to be found in all the larger cities by 1885. Catering to these physical culturists were *Dio Lewis's Monthly* (1883–84), of New York, edited by that "energetic and eccentric" hygienist and educator,[136] as well as a considerable group of health magazines.[137]

The German *Turnvereins*, nationally organized under the name of the North American Turner Bund, which had been interrupted by the war, reformed at the end of 1864 and soon became a greater power than ever in New York, Cincinnati, Milwaukee, and all the cities with considerable German populations.[138] Their periodical *turnfeste* were reported in many of the English-language sporting journals.

Although some of the hunting clubs had lodges here and there, the first country club with proper home and grounds is said to have been the Brookline Country Club on the south shore of Massachusetts Bay.[139] Connected with this form of organized sports and social divertisement is much coaching history, as well as the story of the development of fox hunting and such elegant social pleasures. Golf was practically unknown in America until the later eighties.

Colleges became more and more athletically minded. "The gymnasium is today an essential part of a thoroughly equipped college," wrote Andrew M. Davis, a Harvard graduate, in the *Atlantic* of 1883;[140] but a contributor to the *North American* in the same year complained that athletes' competition crowded out the proper physical training of the average student.[141] "The most popular game," continued Davis, "not only with students

[136] The epithets are those of *Appleton's Journal*, who thought Lewis something of a charlatan (X, 730, December 6, 1873). The *Monthly* failed because of the dishonesty of the publisher, according to Lewis' statement in the last number. It was devoted to personal hygiene, diet, and physical culture; and it campaigned against the corset, the tyranny of the male, the mismanagement of insane asylums, etc. It had some excellent contributors.

[137] See pp. 138–39. [138] *Harper's Weekly*, XXXIV, 734 (September 20, 1890).
[139] *Harper's Monthly*, XC, 20 (December 1894).
[140] *Atlantic Monthly*, LI, 677 (May 1883).
[141] *North American Review*, CXXXVI, 166 (February 1883).

but also with the public is base-ball," and in second place was football. In the early seventies college baseball teams defeated the regular professional clubs.[142] Football, object of faculty suppression in many colleges in the sixties and early seventies, and after the adoption of the Etonian system in 1880 requiring only eleven men on a side, made long strides as a popular game. The Yale-Princeton Thanksgiving game of 1884 attracted a crowd of 10,000 watchers.[143] Lacrosse was also occasionally played by the colleges, as well as by independent clubs. It "has had in New York a sort of spasmodic career, living, dying, being resuscitated over and over, for the last fifteen years," wrote a *Harper* commentator in 1884.[144] Rowing was a major sport in several eastern universities, and after the formation of the National Association of Amateur Oarsmen in 1874 it had a wide following outside of the colleges.

CRITICISMS OF SPORTS

The rapid growth of sports brought out many criticisms. College observers thought "athletics, gymnastics, and aquatics" were the "chief subjects of college instruction."[145] Gambling, an integral part of such sports as prize fighting and horse racing, and prominent in baseball and football, brought such contests under the ban of moralists. "Gamblers spread their nets over all public sports," complained the *Galaxy*,[146] and *Harper's Weekly* added its testimony: "So common has betting become at baseball matches that the most respectable clubs indulge in it to a highly culpable degree."[147] This was in 1867; after the organization of the leagues, betting by clubs and consequent "throwing" of games tended to disappear.

Harper's Weekly was also inclined to scoff at the continually increasing attention given to championships — in games, in bicycle riding, in walking, in rowing, in nearly everything. "Have we not of late had something too much of all these 'championship' follies?" it asked reasonably.[148]

---

[142] *New York Clipper*, XXX, 860 (March 18, 1882).

[143] *Ibid.*, XXXII, 602 (December 6, 1884).

[144] *Harper's Monthly*, LXVIII, 304 (January 1884).

[145] *North American Review*, CXXXVI, 166 (February 1883).

[146] *Galaxy*, VI, 563 (October 1868).

[147] *Harper's Weekly*, XI, 685 (October 26, 1867).   [148] *Ibid.*

THE VELOCIPEDE MANIA

Thomas Worth's drawing showing what the craze for velocipedes might lead to, namely, supplanting all horse-drawn vehicles by the new-fangled two-, three-, and four-wheelers. Note that one velocipede draws a trailer. From *Harper's Weekly*, May 1, 1869.

A NAST CARTOON AGAINST ANDREW JOHNSON

From *Harper's Weekly*, November 3, 1866. "King Andy," with Seward as Prime Minister and Stanton as guardian of the throne, commands the beheading of a long file of his enemies — Sumner, Stevens, Morton, Greeley, and others.

CHAPTER IX

LITERARY PHASES OF POSTBELLUM MAGAZINES

A N ANALYSIS of the literary contents of the magazines of a given period does not necessarily indicate with any exactitude the more significant trends of literature for the years studied. What it does indicate is the trend of popular reading. But when we add to such an analysis an examination of the literary criticism contained in the magazines, we may arrive at some understanding of how literature was functioning on its various levels at the time.

SERIAL FICTION

"Fiction, to a very large extent, constitutes the reading of the masses," remarked the *Literary World* in 1872, "and in whatever education they receive from books (outside of school books, of course) it is the instrument." [1] The immense popularity of Dickens, Collins, George Eliot, Hugo, and other foreign novelists; the interest in Howells and James, and the less instructed but more general favor shown E. P. Roe and Mary Jane Holmes; the wide distribution of the dime novels of the Beadle, Street & Smith, and Munro houses; and the growing appreciation of the short story — all these contributed to place fiction higher than any other literary genre in the esteem of readers of periodicals.

Yet this class of reading did not occupy the overwhelming share of the magazine pages that fell to it later. True, it was dominant in most of the "family" weeklies and monthlies, but the more important general magazines were more conservative. One serial novel at a time was enough for most of the first-class magazines, though *Harper's* commonly drove a tandem, and it is possible to find issues of the *Atlantic* which contain installments of three serials. Two- and three-part stories were not uncommon, and two short stories in a number furnished the usual quota. But fiction filled more pages than any other type of writing; a study of the *Galaxy's* contents shows 37 per cent of

[1] *Literary World*, III, 56 (September 1, 1872).

its entire file given over to fiction, and it is safe to say that one-third was about the usual proportion.

England furnished most of the serials. This is not strange when one considers, first, the state of the copyright laws, and second, the prosperity of the English novel of the time. These are the English novelists whose work *Harper's* published serially before 1885: Dickens, Thackeray, Bulwer, George Eliot, Trollope, Collins, Lever, Reade, Miss Mulock, Black, Hardy, McCarthy, Anne Thackeray, and Blackmore. It is an array against which it would be hard to compete. American authors of serial fiction in *Harper's* were Henry James, Miss Woolson, E. P. Roe, and Julian Hawthorne. At the same time the *Atlantic* was publishing Nathaniel Hawthorne's posthumous *Septimius Felton* and novels by Holmes, Mrs. Stowe, Howells, James, Donald G. Mitchell, W. H. Bishop, Rebecca Harding Davis, William M. Baker, H. H. Boyesen, and Caroline Chesebrough. American novelists prominent in other magazines were J. G. Holland, J. W. DeForest, Bret Harte, Edward Everett Hale, Frances Hodgson Burnett, George W. Cable, and Marion Harland. Not one of these, unless we except Holland, with his *Sevenoaks*, and possibly Mrs. Burnett, enlisted the public interest very strongly. Eggleston's *Hoosier Schoolmaster* was printed serially in *Hearth and Home*, but attained its larger circulation in book form. Mark Twain did not publish his earlier novels in magazines. Roe's *Barriers Burned Away* was published more or less obscurely in the New York *Evangelist*, and others of his novels in the *Christian Union*, the *Christian Advocate*, and *Hearth and Home*. Many other American novelists with large and constant followings were not printed in the better magazines. Mrs. Mary Jane Holmes was found chiefly in the *New York Weekly*. Sylvanus Cobb wrote voluminously for the *Ledger* and a score of other low-priced weeklies, and Mrs. E.D.E.N. Southworth stuck rather closely to the *Ledger*. Mrs. Ann S. Stephens wrote serial after serial for *Peterson's*, and T. S. Arthur and Virginia F. Townsend did likewise for *Arthur's Home Magazine*. Mrs. E. F. Ellett, Marion Harland, and Mrs. Metta V. Victor wrote chiefly for *Godey's* and *Peterson's*. Hundreds of other industrious fictionists did serials for the cheap weeklies.

But compare the American showing of serialists with that of England, and the contrast is evident. The editors frequently complained of the dearth of high-class narrative talent in America. Let us allow the *Galaxy* editor to state the case:

Our historians stand in the front rank; we have scholars and critics whose writings command the attention of Europe; essayists and humorists of equal reputation we do not lack. American sculptors have placed the genius of their country in the plastic arts upon a pedestal before the world, and in poetry our achievements have been at least respectable; but our novelists are few comparatively, and only two or three are well known beyond our own shores. . . . It is for this reason, far more than because of any considerations connected with the absence of an inter-national copyright law, that we read novels chiefly written by British authors. American publishers are ready enough to publish good novels by American writers. Editors of American magazines are anxious to publish them; they are particularly anxious to publish short tales and sketches by native authors. . . . The narrative faculty is notably lacking among us. Our public has no notion whatever of the poor quality of almost all the writing in this department submitted to American publishers and editors. The defect generally is not in style . . . but simply in that power of interesting the reader which is the all-important desideratum.[2]

SHORT STORIES

It will be noted that our critic speaks especially of the lack of good short stories. It was a shortcoming which was noted also by *Appleton's Journal* in a paragraph that constitutes what was probably the ablest statement of the short story art between Poe's review of *Twice-Told Tales* in 1842 and Brander Matthews' "Philosophy of the Short-Story" of 1885. This succinct little article is the more remarkable because most critics did not think of the short story as an art form at all, but merely as a narrative too slight or unimportant to be worked out in a novel.

No doubt one of the most agreeable things in literature is a thoroughly good short story. At the same time it is one of the most difficult to obtain. We have few or no trained workers in this branch of composition. Our professional novelists rarely attempt the short story, and, when they do, are far from increasing their reputation

[2] *Galaxy*, XIX, 288 (February 1875).

thereby. Since the time of Poe there has been no one eminently successful in this branch — no one whose invention or art has been sufficient for great success. A good short story should have one fresh, central incident, two or three well conceived and sharply drawn characters, a certain symmetrical unity in construction, a deep significance in the catastrophe or climax — not necessarily a moral, as ordinarily understood, but as nothing should be purposeless, the short story should illustrate some defect or virtue in human character, or portray some special experience whereby the imagination of the reader may be gratified, his sympathies awakened, or his knowledge of the world increased. It is not easy to fix the limitations to the short story. Its construction is an art, far more so than is generally believed; it has its laws, and bears very nearly the same relation to the novel that the song does to poetry, which always properly possesses one definite idea thrown into a compact, symmetrical form. Writers of short stories cannot hope to attain success unless they make this form of composition a profound study; they must have brevity of expression, conception of character, keen feeling for unity and symmetry in art, and very dramatic perceptions. All these qualifications are necessary, but many of them can be acquired by study.[3]

Matthews' article in *Lippincott's*, called "The Philosophy of the Short-Story,"[4] insisted that "a Short-story deals with a single character, a single event, a single emotion, or the series of emotions called forth by a single situation," and by thus defining it he made a distinction between the "Short-story" and "the story which is merely short." This point of view was to affect the short story profoundly for two or three decades. Matthews recognized the "very great importance to the American magazine" of this literary type and believed that American practitioners of it had been supreme for half a century.

The great fault of the short fiction of this period, as with the longer romances of Mrs. Southworth, Miss Holmes, and Company, was its sentimentality. It was false and unreal to an incredible degree. This had been common in American magazines ever since the closing decade of the eighteenth century, when such periodicals as the *American Moral and Sentimental Mag-*

---

[3] *Appleton's Journal*, I, 282 (May 29, 1869).

[4] *Lippincott's Magazine*, XXXVI, 366 (October 1885). This is an elaboration of an article by Matthews called "The Short Story," published the year before in the London *Saturday Review*.

azine flourished;[5] and in the lady's books and annuals sentimentality had found congenial habitat. In the period after the war, the sentimental short story was largely the product of women writing for women. It flourished in *Harper's*, but it emitted its cheap perfume everywhere. There was less of it in the *Atlantic* than anywhere else, perhaps. The stories of James and Cable, and of the Misses Terry and Woolson, published chiefly in the *Atlantic*, the *Galaxy*, and *Scribner's*, were the healthiest and soundest short fiction of the day; but their work was slight in extent beside that of the sentimentalists. "Our band of heart-wrenching female dealers in false fiction was never, we think, so numerous as now," said the *Nation* in 1866.[6] An example of this kind of writing will be more effective than attempts at characterizing it. Here is the opening paragraph of a typical specimen:

In looking over some old papers the other day, I found, unexpectedly, this pile of yellow, worn sheets which now lies before me. The sight of them thrilled me with a strange, sharp pain, as if a lover, after a long succession of years had ebbed and flowed, should come all unawares upon the handful of dust that had once stood to him for all the world's beauty and sweetness; as he would turn, hastily, from marred cheek and faded curl, so I eagerly thrust these memorials of the past back into the dark where they had slept so long, and turned the lock. But not so easily could I turn the key upon memory; not so easily remand that forlorn ghost to the chambers of silence.[7]

And so she is moved to tell the story, which is a sad, sad one. This example is taken from the *Galaxy* (which printed much fiction of a better class), but it is of the type that the *Nation* said "the Messrs. Harper might almost take out a patent for." Dennett, in the *Nation*, never tired of poking fun at the magazine stories which "have the general truth of sentiment of a romance by the leading graduate of a young ladies' seminary." [8] But there can be no doubt of the wide popularity of this "chocolate fudge fiction." Bret Harte was able to win such a quick response not because of his local color alone, but also because of

[5] Mott, *A History of American Magazines, 1741–1850*, p. 43.
[6] *Nation*, III, 347 (November 1, 1866).
[7] *Galaxy*, VIII, 328 (September 1869).
[8] *Nation*, III, 347 (November 1, 1866).

a sentimentalism which was in tune with the times. When the quartet of more sincere writers named above ventured on a realistic strain, they were severely criticized. "The rather clever 'Story of a Masterpiece,' which Mr. Henry James, Jr., is publishing in the *Galaxy*," said the *Round Table*,

is likely to be ruined for most readers by the author's unaccountable insanity in making his heroine a round-shouldered fat girl with red hair . . . the round shoulders and the red hair we might forgive . . . but the fatness! Who can take any genuine interest in the fortunes of a fat girl? [9]

The *Atlantic Monthly* did much to encourage more honest short stories.[10] In 1869 such a good critic as the magazine reviewer of the *Printers' Circular* thought that "short stories are assuming a much higher tone than the namby-pamby style once considered appropriate." [11] Perhaps the work of Aldrich, Cable, James, and Harte helped him to that opinion. The short stories which made the great hits of the period were Mark Twain's "Jumping Frog," published in the *Saturday Press*, November 18, 1865; Harte's "Luck of Roaring Camp" and "Outcasts of Poker Flat," in the *Overland Monthly* for August 1868, and January 1869; Aldrich's "Marjorie Daw," *Atlantic Monthly*, April 1873; and Frank R. Stockton's "The Lady or the Tiger?" in the *Century* for November 1882. Anent the extraordinary sensation created by "Marjorie Daw" and "Mlle. Olympe Zabriski," the *Atlantic Monthly*, which had originally published both stories, remarked, in the course of a review of a volume containing them, that Aldrich had in them "almost created a new species in fiction," namely, the surprise-ending short story.[12]

An important incident of the magazine history of the late seventies and early eighties was the incursion of southern short stories.[13] George Egbert Craddock in the *Atlantic*, and Cable, Thomas Nelson Page, and Joel Chandler Harris in the *Century* were the outstanding writers of the movement.

[9] *Round Table*, VII, 54 (January 25, 1868).
[10] See vol. II, p. 501.
[11] *Printers' Circular*, IV, 297 (October 1869).
[12] *Atlantic Monthly*, XXXII, 625 (November 1873). See also, in regard to this story, vol. II, pp. 507–08.
[13] See pp. 48–49.

MAGAZINE POETRY

When Justin McCarthy came from England to America in 1868, he decided that the new land was much more sentimental than the older one. As an illustration, he says, "I have often been struck by the fact that so much of its poetry of the late Civil War was so purely sentimental in character."[14] And this character extended to the poems of the postbellum period as well. Verses and sketches signed by "Sophie May," "Jennie June," "May Mather," "Minnie Myrtle," "Fannie Fern," and such pretty names were common, and were appropriate to the writing. Mrs. Elizabeth Oakes Smith, in her reminiscences, says that N. P. Willis invented this trick of the alliterative name for the feminine writer in suggesting the name "Fanny Forrester" to Emily Chubbuck. "Who will read a poem signed Chubbuck?" he had asked.[15] In Fitz-James O'Brien's amusing satire "Sister Anne,"[16] the heroine is advised to call her sketches " 'Dried Leaves,' or some other vegetable title, and they will be sure to succeed." She calls them "Lichens," and signs herself "Matilda Moss," and does succeed — in marrying her adviser.

It was not an important period in American poetry, though the mere quantity of production was remarkable. The *North American Review* declared that "there is no more striking mental phenomenon than the interest felt by the American people in poetry."[17] The *Atlantic* was able to publish some notable poems from the decaying New England school, as well as the work of the Carys and Piatts, Stedman, Aldrich, Hayne, William Winter, Theodore Tilton, "H. H.," Nora Perry, Lucy Larcom, Celia Thaxter, Bret Harte, and Joaquin Miller. All these except the older New Englanders wrote for various other magazines, and most of them rather copiously. What an army of forgotten poets! "Howard Glyndon," and T. W. Parsons the dentist-poet, and Edgar Fawcett, and Mrs. Akers, and Anne M. Crane, and many, many others. Ella Wheeler, who made a sen-

[14] *Galaxy*, IX, 764 (June 1870).
[15] Mary L. Wyman, *Selections from the Autobiography of Elizabeth Oakes Smith* (Lewiston, Maine, 1924), p. 103. Miss Chubbuck later became the wife of Adoniram Judson, the missionary.
[16] *Harper's Monthly*, XII, 91 (December 1855).
[17] *North American Review*, CII, 1 (January 1866).

sation with her *Poems of Passion* in 1883 and added Wilcox to her name the next year, wrote and sold to periodicals from two to eight poems a day from the age of nineteen on.[18] "There never could have been a time when minor poetry was more plentiful," exclaimed the editor of the *Galaxy* in 1870;[19] but a few years later he complained of the low grade of verse he received, though the quantity remained great.[20]   Charles Astor Bristed wrote to him shortly after the *Galaxy* began: "If I were you I wouldn't make a point of verse.   Most of that which is current nowadays is really worse than nothing.   What rubbish is in the *Atlantic*, for instance!"[21]   And somewhat later the *Literary World* was mourning:

How little good poetry is given to America in proportion to the number of purveyors of that art!   Take the monthly magazines for a whole year, and you will hardly find two pieces that seem to call for a place in your scrapbook. . . . Why editors of magazines admit to their columns verses so thin and evanescent is a question that has no doubt perplexed many.   We can account for this laxity in censorship only on the supposition that they accept poor ones because they cannot get good ones.[22]

The poet Irwin Russell makes the same complaint in *Scribner's*.   "A poem of the period," he says, "or a periodical poem, is the thing that is altogether emotional, and is not intended to convey any idea in particular."[23]   But the best contemporary magazine pronouncement upon the poetry of the day is an article by that acute critic and brilliant essayist David A. Wasson, called "Modern Poetry" and published in the *Galaxy* in 1867.   "The characteristic fault of modern poetry," he says, is "its general want of significance. . . . It is a blowing of soap-bubbles.   Doubtless Keats did much to bring into vogue this description of poetry."[24]   And Whitman made essentially the same comment when he wrote in the *North American Review*

[18] *Lippincott's Magazine*, XXXVI, 539 (May 1886).

[19] *Galaxy*, IX, 869 (June 1870).

[20] *Ibid.*, XXI, 435 (March 1876).

[21] Letter in the possession of Mr. Willard Church, Montclair, New Jersey, date February 18 [1867].

[22] *Literary World*, VI, 144 (March 1876).

[23] *Scribner's Monthly*, XVI, 759 (September 1878).

[24] *Galaxy*, III, 786 (April 1, 1867).

in 1881 that he found "nowhere a scope profound enough, and radical and objective enough." [25]

Of the more significant poets, Lowell was printed chiefly in the *Atlantic*, Whitman in the *Critic* and the *Galaxy*, and Lanier in the *Independent*, *Lippincott's*, and the *Galaxy*. The magazine that dared print Whitman had to be prepared to weather a gale of criticism. Several of the weeklies published much poetry, but few published more of it or better than the *Independent*. That journal, and most of the others at rare intervals, published the work of English as well as American poets. *Harper's* and *Scribner's* were particularly partial to rather long narrative and sentimental poems by authors like Mrs. Akers, of Maine, Benjamin F. Taylor, of Chicago, and later Will Carleton, of Michigan. The first number of *Scribner's* started off with an eighteen-page poem, unsigned, but written by Dr. Holland, the editor. Usually these pieces were copiously illustrated.

MAGAZINE ESSAYS

The familar, or discursive, essay, belonging to the periodical by right of tradition from *Spectator* and *Tatler* days, was cultivated in the magazines of the postbellum period more than it was later.

A noteworthy fact in recent literature [observed a *Galaxy* writer in 1866] is the revival of the Essay. . . . *Fraser*, *Blackwood*, and the London weeklies set the example of concise, agreeable, colloquial papers on themes and traits of the day; and the *Atlantic Monthly* diversifies its pages with at least one thoughtful and suggestive article in each number on a topic of life, morals, or manners.[26]

The "Contributors' Club" of the *Atlantic* was not inaugurated until 1877, but there had been no lack of essays by Higginson, Burroughs, Howells, Holmes, Hale, and others. George William Curtis in *Harper's* "Easy Chair," Dr. Holland in *Scribner's* "Topics of the Times," Grant White in the "Nebulae" and Charles Astor Bristed in the "Casual Cogitations" of the *Galaxy*, an unknown essayist in the "Monthly Gossip" of *Lippincott's*, "Harry Franco" in *Putnam's* "Table Talk," Oliver Bunce in the "Editor's Table" of *Appleton's Journal*, and Edward Everett

[25] *North American Review*, CXXXII, 196 (February 1881).
[26] *Galaxy*, I, 577 (August 1, 1866).

Hale in the "Examiner" of *Old and New* were genial writers in magazine departments where informal chat and brief social and literary essays found themselves at home.

LITERARY CRITICISM

Criticism of literature was a staple commodity in the higher-class magazines. To estimate the value of the contemporary criticism of a day long past is not a simple task. It is easy to pick out judgments which have been overruled in the court of time, without realizing that criticism was often competent.

Book reviewing was seriously and creditably done in several magazines, and the period was notable for the critical work of Lowell, Norton, James, Howells, Stedman, Garrison, Whipple, and Stoddard. The *Critic*, defending American literary commentators of 1881, declared that

Mr. Stedman, in his criticisms of English and American poets, Mr. Henry James, Jr., in his volume on the French poets and novelists, and, in their more elaborate and critical articles, Mr. Stoddard and Mr. Howells, compare favorably with the leading English critics.[27]

Perhaps there was a more consistent excellence in the book reviews of the *Nation*, the *Critic*, the *Dial*, and the *Atlantic* than in those of other periodicals. Lord Bryce, speaking of Wendell P. Garrison, who had charge of the book reviewing for the *Nation*, said, "His standard of excellence was as high as that of the best literary journals of Europe." [28] And Henry Holt declared, many years after the event, that "the early *Nation* unquestionably did more than all other influences to raise the standard of our literary criticism." [29]

The *Nation* itself thus diagnosed the defects of American criticism in its first number:

We are not well out of the childish age of promiscuous and often silly admiration. . . . The great mischief has always been that whenever our reviewers deviate from the usual and popular course of panegyric, they start from and end in personality, so that the public mind is almost sure to connect unfavorable criticism with personal animosity. Any review thus inspired is worth exactly its weight in Confederate paper.[30]

[27] *Critic*, I, 164 (June 18, 1881).
[28] *Nation*, CI, 41 (July 8, 1915).
[29] *Ibid.*, CI, 46 (July 8, 1915).
[30] *Ibid.*, I, 11 (July 6, 1865).

The *Round Table* also had its say about "laudatory twaddle." "The American critic," it observed, "is deficient in a just and discriminating severity." [31] The *R. T.* itself was not afraid to be severe, however just and discriminating it may have been. Editor Theodore Tilton, of the *Independent*, thought criticism the worst department of American writing, with the single exception of fiction.[32] Editor Holland, of *Scribner's Monthly*, joined the chorus of complaint with the query, "How many competent critics have we in America?" and the laconic reply, "Not many." "It is probable," he adds, "that incompetence, flippancy, arrogance, partisanship, ill-nature, and the pertinacious desire to attract attention will go on with their indecent work." [33] In connection with these comments it may be noted that both Tilton and Holland were smarting authors. In short, it is quite evident, first, that literary criticism was then as now no better than it should be, and, second, that the postbellum period afforded no truce in the eternal war between author and critic.

CRITICISM, THE BOOK TRADE, AND PHILOLOGY

The only important journal between 1865 and 1880 which was devoted mainly to literary criticism was S. R. Crocker's *Literary World*,[34] of Boston. After Crocker's mental collapse in 1877, the editorship was taken over by Edward Abbott. Louis Engel's New York *Arcadian* (1872–78) was a weekly review of literature, art, drama, and music; John Fraser was an editor, and H. C. Bunner became a leading contributor. In its later years especially the *Arcadian* was an unusually severe critic. Henry L. Hinton's *Library Table* (1875–79) was a weekly New Yorker devoted to news and reviews. In Chicago the *Owl* (1874–76) was a monthly devoted to literary criticism and comment and edited by the librarian and bibliographer, Dr. W. F. Poole; and the *Literary Review* [35] (1879–80) was a journal devoted to the activities of the city's many literary clubs.

[31] *Round Table*, II, 8 (June 18, 1864).
[32] *Independent*, Vol. XVIII, April 26, 1866.
[33] *Scribner's Monthly*, IX, 626 (March 1875).
[34] Treated more fully in sketch 20.
[35] It was called the *Literary and Musical Review* in 1880, and a music critic was added to its staff.

In 1880 two important critical journals were founded — one in Chicago and the other in New York. The Chicago *Dial* [36] was under the scholarly care of F. F. Browne, formerly editor of the *Lakeside Monthly;* and the New York *Critic* [37] was founded by Jeanette Gilder and her brother Joseph; their brother was Richard Watson Gilder, of the *Century.* Of the two journals, the *Critic* was the livelier; but both won high standing and lived to a fair age as such things go in magazinedom.

Sidney S. Rider's *Book Notes for the Week* [38] (1883–1916), of Providence, had an interesting individuality. Its subtitle lists its principal contents: "literary gossip, criticisms of books, and local history matters connected with Rhode Island." But its editor was a freethinker and an independent judge of books, and he liked occasionally to flail away at the tariff or some other *bête noire.* A. P. T. Elder's *Literary Life* (1884–1903) was begun in Cleveland, but was moved to Chicago before its first year was out and edited for a time by Will M. Clemens. For a few months in 1886 Rose Elizabeth Cleveland, sister of the President, was editor at long range; but she disagreed with the owner,[39] and the monthly was suspended soon after. Its obituary was written by young Eugene Field in this wise:

For the information of our public we will say that the *Atlantic Monthly* is a magazine published in Boston, being to that intelligent and refined community what the *Literary Life* was to Chicago before a Fourth Ward constable achieved its downfall with a writ of replevin.[40]

But it fell to rise again in 1899 for a few more years of publication.[41]

---

[36] Treated more fully in sketch 33.   [37] Treated more fully in sketch 35.

[38] In spite of its name, this was a fortnightly. It was a four-page octavo at fifty cents a year. It was distinctly regional, and interested in local history, anti-Catholic, and opinionated.

[39] See Herbert E. Fleming, *Magazines of a Market-Metropolis* (Chicago, 1906), p. 523.

[40] *Ibid.,* p. 524, quoted.

[41] It was revived in New York as a weekly by the Montgomery Publishing Company, September 2, 1899. A year later it was taken over by the Abbey Press and made a monthly, becoming a good, lively, tart little magazine. A good feature was "The Worst Book of the Month." Will M. Clemens was a constant contributor. *Literary Life* always made a specialty of short stories and of paragraphing.

There were several important booksellers' journals in the period. Frederick Leypoldt, a New York publisher turned bibliographer, founded the monthly *Literary Bulletin* in December 1868; this was the parent stem of two periodicals — the *Publishers' Weekly*,[42] which became the country's leading book trade journal; and *Literary News* (1875–1904), which was an attractive monthly, chiefly eclectic, designed for the general reader rather than for the trade.[43] The American News Company's organ, the *American Booksellers' Guide* (1869–75) was distributed free to the book and periodical trade; it was succeeded by the *American Bookseller* (1876–93), which the company sold at a dollar a year. The *Western Bookseller* (1868–70), of Chicago, was the Western News Company's organ; it was revived (1679–88) by J. Fred Waggoner, publisher of the *Western Stationer*.[44] Joseph Sabin, bookseller and well-known bibliographer, edited the *American Bibliopolist* (1869–77) for his book trade; it attained distinction by its reprints from old books, its articles on various American libraries, and its news of auctions and lists of publications.[45] John Wanamaker's book department published the excellent *Book News Monthly* (1882–1918) in Philadelphia.[46] The *Bookmart* [47] (1883–90) was a

[42] Treated more fully in sketch 23.

[43] For relationship to other Leypoldt periodicals, see p. 492. A New Series was begun with a number for January–February 1880, and most files begin with it. *Literary News* was sent to subscribers to the *Literary Journal* as a supplement to it for several years. It was a fragmentary little eclectic for book-buyers, crammed full of items. After 1887 it was copiously illustrated with pictures from current books.   [44] See p. 135.

[45] It was a monthly, 1869–72, and a bimonthly thereafter. It published a good question-and-answer department.

[46] Talcott Williams had charge of the review department 1889–1908, but the magazine was chiefly eclectic until 1904. It began with the title of *Book News: A Monthly Survey;* it became *Book News Monthly* in 1906. It gradually built up in illustration, literary correspondence from Boston, New York, and Chicago, and in sketches of contemporary authors, all through the nineties. In 1906 it began home reading course outlines, colored reproductions of paintings, and numbers honoring individual authors. These latter, dealing with contemporary writers, were richly illustrated and valuable. Norma Bright Carson was editor for the last decade. A. H. Quinn, M. J. Moses, and Albert S. Henry were among the contributors.

[47] It was mainly eclectic, with news notes and gossip of American and foreign writers; but its main business was its lists of old books for sale by various dealers. Albert R. Frey had a Shakespeare department in 1887, and Julian Hawthorne a book review department the following year.

pleasant monthly issued in Pittsburgh to carry the advertising of dealers in old and rare books.

Some established publishing firms had distinctive house organs. Scribner's *Book Buyer* (1867–1918) grew to be much more than a periodical advertising its publishers' books. Its subtitle was "A Summary of American and Foreign Literature," and its foreign correspondence was always a feature.[48] D. Lothrop & Company, Boston, published a *Book Bulletin* 1877–90, and *Appleton's Literary Bulletin* (1881–90) was an eight-page offering, containing news notes and clipped reviews, and furnished free to libraries.

The distinguished *American Journal of Philology*,[49] which was edited at Johns Hopkins for forty years by Professor Basil L. Gildersleeve, was of an entirely different class from the foregoing periodicals. The *Publications of the Modern Language Association of America* (1884–current) did not become a regular quarterly until 1888.[50] William Rainey Harper's *Hebraica* [51]

---

[48] Originally it was only a house organ, quoting a price of twenty-five cents a year but mainly distributed free. A New Series at fifty cents was begun in 1884, and the scope enlarged and the price soon raised again, this time to a dollar a year. In 1903 the name was changed to the *Lamp*. But in 1905 the periodical returned to its first name and to its original policy as a monthly announcement for Scribner's publications.

[49] Treated more fully in sketch 32.

[50] Vol. I, called *Transactions of the Modern Language Association of America*, covered the years 1884–85; Vols. II–III, called *Transactions and Proceedings . . .* , covered 1886 and 1887; Vol. IV, called *Publications . . .* , was divided into four numbers for 1888–89; thereafter the serial was a regular quarterly under the title *Publications of the Modern Language Association of America*, with a cover-title *PMLA* in recent years. It has had distinguished editorship: A. Marshall Elliott, founder of the M.L.A. and its first secretary, 1884–92; James W. Bright, 1893–1901; Charles H. Grandgent, 1902–11; William Guild Howard, 1912–19; Carleton Brown, 1920–32; Percy Waldron Long, 1932–current. It has been published by the Association, and has grown from fifty or sixty pages a number to three hundred pages or more. In the first three volumes there were some articles on pedagogy; since then it has been devoted to scholarship in the modern languages and literatures. An American bibliography in these fields has been published in each March number since 1921. *PMLA* has had many famous contributors: among the earlier names are those of Lowell, Kittredge, Gummere, Lounsbury, and Bright.

[51] Its first three numbers were issued monthly; then it was changed to a quarterly and those numbers (March, April, and May 1884) were counted as Vol. I, No. 1, of the quarterly. In the last three volumes, numbers were doubled, making it really a semiannual. Except for Vols. III–VII, it was published in Chicago. Vols. III–IV were issued from New Haven, V from New York, and VI–VII from Hartford; the last four volumes were issued by the University of

(1884–95) was published "in the interests of Semitic study." Appleton Morgan's *Shakespeariana* [52] (1883–93) was sponsored by the New York Shakespeare Society.

OPINIONS OF AMERICAN AUTHORS

Whatever may be said of the actual accomplishment of the group of leading New England writers in the two decades immediately following the Civil War, the position of these men in the public esteem was ineluctably fixed. A *Nation* reviewer might refer to New England transcendentalism as a "not very important affair";[53] a leading writer for the *North American Review* might declare that the New England movement in thought, religion, and literature was "at the point of pause";[54] the book critics might want enthusiasm in their comment on Longfellow's translations or the leftovers from Emerson's table: but that select group which had won recognition in the forties, and which was the nucleus of the *Atlantic's* early staff of contributors, made up (at least in the years immediately following the war) an academy of immortals to which only New England-bred Bryant was admitted from among those who acknowledged other capitals than Boston. "Without doubt," wrote Garrison, of the *Nation*, in 1866,

the four living American poets who fill the highest places are Emerson, Bryant, Longfellow, and Lowell. Dr. Holmes, of course, has to be mentioned when talk is made of American poetic literature, and so have Mr. Bayard Taylor, Mr. Stoddard, Mr. Read, Mr. Stedman, and Mr. Aldrich. Whittier is in a class above these; [H. H.] Brownell is to be ranked above most of them; and there are [Forceythe] Willson and Howells, whose names, to be sure, are yet to be made, but who must not be omitted.[55]

Chicago Press. It was continued by this Press as the *American Journal of Semitic Languages and Literatures* with continuous numbering. Robert Francis Harper became editor in 1907 and J. M. P. Smith in 1915.

[52] It contained much of the Bacon controversy in 1886–87, reports from Shakespeare clubs in Cambridge, Philadelphia, Omaha, Atlanta, Topeka, etc. F. G. Fleay, J. Parker Norris, W. J. Rolfe, and others contributed series and notes on editors of Shakespeare, portraits of him, and so on.

[53] *Nation*, XXIII, 107 (August 17, 1876).

[54] *North American Review*, CXXXIII, 276 (September 1881).

[55] *Nation*, III, 386 (November 15, 1866).

Willson died the next year, and Brownell a few years later, and Howells turned definitely to the novel; but otherwise this is clearly the canon — with New Englanders in the front rank, a few New Yorkers in a second grade, and Whitman and Southerners like Lanier and Hayne quite out of the picture.

But by the end of our period, in 1885, Emerson, Bryant, Longfellow, Taylor, Read, Simms, and Lanier were all gone; and the New York *Critic* had just conducted a plebiscite among its readers to find who were esteemed the greatest living American authors. The following were the fifteen ranked highest in order of the *Critic* readers' vote: Holmes, Lowell, Whittier, Bancroft, Howells, Curtis, Aldrich, Harte, Stedman, White, Hale, Cable, James, Clemens, Warner. Whitman was in twentieth place.[56]

Popular esteem for Emerson reached its highest point shortly after the war; it is attested in many magazines.[57] His physical and mental decline from about 1872 until his death ten years later, made it possible for his publishers to issue only collectanea from his pen, and these brought a crop of reviews which were kind rather than enthusiastic. *Harper's Weekly* stated the case well in 1880 when it said on the occasion of his seventy-seventh birthday that Emerson possessed "an affection and respect which few men have ever enjoyed. It is a feeling which has grown constantly for more than forty years, and it is deeper, stronger, and more universal than ever." [58] After his death there was much of eulogy.

Dennett's characterization of Bryant's poetry in the *Nation* as "a chill wind which blows softly — not out of graveyards; it possesses hardly so much of human interest as that" [59] aroused a small storm of disapproval, for Bryant, too, sat in the seats of the mighty. Most of the articles about him were distinctly laudatory, though a writer in the *International Review* in 1874

---

[56] *Critic*, IV, 169 (April 12, 1884).

[57] See Nevius Ove Halvorson, "The Growth of Emerson's American Reputation" (University of Iowa thesis, 1925), Chapter XVII; and also Edward Everett Hale, *James Russell Lowell and His Friends* (Boston, 1898), p. 203.

[58] *Harper's Weekly*, XXIV, 370 (June 12, 1880).

[59] *Nation*, V, 459 (December 5, 1867).

lamented that he was too much forgotten.[60] Stedman appraised him in the *Atlantic* after his death in 1878.[61]

Criticism of Longfellow came more and more to be premised by two considerations: his high position and the admission of a certain sentimentality both in the according of that position and in the poet's work. Howells reviewed some new tales of the Wayside Inn for the *Atlantic*: "Many and many maturer readers," he said, "will be most tenderly entreated by them because they are so like Longfellow." [62] But Longfellow's death, like that of Bryant several years earlier and Emerson's in the following month, brought out little but praise. "He was easily the first of American poets," said Tourgée in *Our Continent*.[63]

Lowell's reputation grew steadily during the first decade after the war. His poems connected with the war, his editorship of the *North American*, and the publication of his critical essays combined to increase the estimate which was popularly made of his abilities. Garrison, commonly a stern critic, was an enthusiastic admirer of Lowell, whom he called at various times, in the *Nation*, "perhaps the best of living English critics," [64] "all things considered, the first" of American poets,[65] and "one of the wittiest of men." [66] Professor William C. Wilkinson,

[64] *Nation*, X, 258 (April 21, 1870).
[65] *Ibid.*, III, 387 (November 15, 1866).

writing in *Scribner's Monthly* about American literary reputations in 1872, declared:

Could a poll of the best instructed and most controlling editorial suffrages of the country be taken on the question, the well-nigh unanimous sentence would pronounce Mr. James Russell Lowell upon the whole, beyond controversy, if not the first, then certainly the second among living literary men.[67]

[60] *International Review*, I, 433 (July 1874), by Ray Palmer, D.D. See also *Appleton's Journal*, VI, 477 (October 28, 1871), by R. H. Stoddard; *Scribner's Monthly*, XVI, 479 (August 1878); *New Englander*, XXXIX, 614 (September 1880); *Dial*, I, 186 (January 1881).
[61] *Atlantic Monthly*, XLII, 747 (December 1878).
[62] *Ibid.*, XXX, 112 (July 1872).
[63] *Our Continent*, I, 179 (May 3, 1882). Whipple spoke of him as "probably the most popular of American poets" in *Harper's Monthly*, LII, 514 (March
[66] *Ibid.*, XII, 129 (February 23, 1871).
[67] *Scribner's Monthly*, VIII, 76 (May 1872).

Lowell's absence from the country on diplomatic missions during the second half of our period, and his consequent abandonment of literary production in those years, removed him somewhat from the American literary consciousness; but the welcome accorded him on his return in 1885, signalized by a special Lowell number of the *Literary World* on June 27, made him again one of two or three leading literary figures in the country.

Holmes, like the other major New Englanders, had an assured standing; but his work after the war was not popular, and except for the reviews of his books of this period the magazines printed comparatively little about him. His friend Underwood pointed out in 1879 that "the *Poet* [*at the Breakfast-Table*] is still further removed than the *Professor* from the sympathy and appreciation of the general public." [68] Holmes was wounded by what he justly considered the "stinging phrases" of the reviewer of his *The Guardian Angel* in the *Nation*.[69]

Whittier was a poet beloved of many. The *Atlantic* greeted his *Snow-Bound* in 1866 with the prophetic words: "What Goldsmith's 'Deserted Village' has long been to Old England, Whittier's 'Snow-Bound' will always be to New England." [70] Stoddard wrote articles about him for *Appleton's* and *Scribner's*; and the reviewer of *The King's Missive* in the *Dial* ranks its author with "the most venerated poets of the age." [71]

It was in the *Atlantic* that the poet John J. Piatt wrote in 1878: "Of the younger American poets . . . Mr. Stedman may fairly be held to rank among the very few foremost." [72] Stedman's critical writing, much of it published in *Scribner's Monthly*, came to attract rather more attention than his poetry. Although Aldrich had written some very popular poems in the fifties, and though he had published ten volumes of verse by 1881, it was as a short-story writer and essayist that he was chiefly known at the end of our period. Bayard Taylor's selection as the Centennial poet caused some comment upon his

[68] *Scribner's Monthly*, XVIII, 127 (May 1879).
[69] See John T. Morse, Jr., *Life and Letters of Oliver Wendell Holmes* (Boston, 1898), II, 223; *Nation*, V, 390 (November 14, 1867).
[70] *Atlantic Monthly*, XVII, 383 (March 1866).
[71] *Appleton's Journal*, V, 431 (April 15, 1871); *Scribner's Monthly*, XVIII, 569 (August 1879); *Dial*, I, 236 (March 1881).
[72] *Atlantic Monthly*, XLI, 313 (March 1878).

work; it was unfortunate that it became generally known that the choice was made only after Longfellow, Lowell, Bryant, and Whittier had declined the honor. Taylor's death in 1878 called forth interesting memorial essays by Stedman, Stoddard, and Boyesen.[73]

Whitman won some friends among the critics in the seventies, though attacks upon his work overshadowed the occasional friendliness.[74] *Punchinello* asserted that "Walt Whitman writes most of his poetry in the dissecting room of the Medical College, where he has a desk fitted up in close proximity to the operating table." [75] The *Northern Monthly* declared:

Mentally, he is of the brute brutish. He affects originality and despises grammar; he talks nonsense, and, strange to say, finds fools enough to declare it wisdom. His last published what-d'you-call-it he calls "A Carol for Harvest for 1867," and we strongly suspect it was originally intended for an agricultural catalogue.[76]

But the "Carol for Harvest" had received the distinction of publication in the *Galaxy*, and by 1877 the poet was rather elaborately defended in the *Atlantic Monthly*.[77] Nora Perry, herself a poet of a very different kind, had written an understanding article about him in *Appleton's* the year before. Even Dennett, who found him indecent, lacking "a pinch of so of brains," and "generally non-existent" with respect to art, had a word of praise for him as "a preacher of democracy." [78] The *Critic* was consistently kind to him in the eighties.[79]

The magazines published little about Lanier before his death, and general notice of his work seems to have waited upon the publication of his collected poems in 1884. The outstanding article is the one by William Hayes Ward in the *Century* which

[73] *Scribner's Monthly*, XIX, 81, 266 (November, December 1879); *Atlantic Monthly*, XLIII, 242 (February 1879); *Lippincott's Magazine*, XXIV, 209 (August 1879).
[74] Marian Reta Speaks, "Contemporary Criticism of Walt Whitman" (University of Iowa thesis, 1926), Chapter III.
[75] *Punchinello*, I, 22 (April 9, 1870).
[76] *Northern Monthly*, I, 598 (October 1867).
[77] *Atlantic Monthly*, XLVI, 749 (December 1877).
[78] *Nation*, VI, 8 (January 2, 1868).
[79] See Portia Baker's "Walt Whitman's Relations with Some New York Magazines," *American Literature*, VII, 274 (November 1935).

was used in amended form as an introduction to the volume. This was criticized as too laudatory in the *New Englander*.[80]

Parkman generally fared well with reviewers. Howells expressed his delight in *The Conspiracy of Pontiac* in the *Atlantic*; Julius H. Ward, writing in the *International Review*, said that Parkman's histories were "as nearly perfect as it is possible for such work to be"; Lowell praised him discriminatingly in the *North American*; and Edward G. Mason argued in the *Dial* that Parkman was "the first of American historians." [81]

F. Marion Crawford was much discussed in the early eighties and was generally praised for a certain freshness in his work. It was common to compare him with Thomas Hardy, the new English novelist of those years.[82]

The irruption of the wild and woolly West into the gentle Longfellowship of the East created a painful situation,[83] and many were the expressions of indignation which issued from retreats of men of letters. The Boston *Literary World* referred to "the coarse ribaldry of the dialect school." [84] The *Nation* suggested that it might "soon be necessary for the reputable members of society to hire somebody to write poetry on their behalf, so that we need not give all our admiration to gamblers, prostitutes, profane swearers, drunkards, murderers, and suicides." [85] The profusion of such picturesquely wicked characters in the work of Bret Harte and John Hay, and the sudden and immense popularity of those writers,[86] serve to explain the *Nation's* distress. In the year of the publication of Hay's *Pike County Ballads*, an anonymous critic in the Galaxy began an article on "The Pike Poetry" by saying:

It is a significant and not altogether satisfactory symptom of public taste that the two most marked poetical successes of the last year

[80] *Century*, XXVII, 816 (April 1884); *New Englander*, XLIV, 227 (March 1885); *Critic*, I, 289 (November 5, 1881); *Dial*, V, 244 (January 1885).

[81] *Atlantic Monthly*, XXXIV, 602 (November 1874); *International Review*, III, 509 (July 1876); *Dial*, I, 149 (December 1880); *North American Review*, CI, 625 (October 1865).

[82] *Catholic World*, XXXVIII, 781 (March 1884); *Literary World*, XIV, 6 (January 13, 1883) and XIV, 187 (June 16, 1883); *Critic*, III, 521 (December 22, 1883); *Atlantic Monthly*, LIII, 277 (February 1884).

[83] See pp. 59–60.   [84] *Literary World*, II, 56 (September 1871).

[85] *Nation*, XII, 43 (January 19, 1871).

[86] *Appleton's Journal* says that the poetry of Harte and Hay was "popular to an extent almost without example" (V, 294, March 11, 1871).

have been achieved by writers who are not poets, and the recognition of them has been forced upon the public by a class of people who do not read poetry. We allude to Mr. Bret Harte and Mr. John Hay.[87]

"The Heathen Chinee" and "Little Breeches" had, according to this commentator "probably been printed a million times." Of the former *jeu d'esprit*, Emily S. Forman wrote in *Old and New*:

> This is the piece that has run through the papers like the cry of "fire" in a country village; it has furnished more neat phrases and apt quotations than any other poem of the century; almost every line of it has passed into the current coin of everyday talk.[88]

Harte's stories were scarcely less popular, and they were more generally approved by the critics. Even the *Nation* commended Harte's work with dialect in fiction, though regretting "the extravagant praise of him now current." [89] Perhaps Parke Godwin's comment in *Putnam's* was in the mind of the *Nation's* writer:

> It is not enough to say of them [Harte's stories]: This is good work. Something fervid and emphatic is called for. We must say: This is the work of a man of genius. . . . We cannot understand how a man can read these stories and not believe in immortality and God.[90]

This is quite enough. We need only add that nearly everybody had something to say of Harte: "Few writers of modern times have been more discussed," said Noah Brooks in *Scribner's*.[91]

And Mark Twain's star was rising. William Dean Howells, later a close friend of the humorist, but then not even properly acquainted with his name, which he gave as "Samuel S. Clements," wrote, in a review of *Innocents Abroad*:

> This book ought to secure him something better than the uncertain standing of a popular favorite. It is no business of ours to fix his rank among the humorists California has given us; but we think he is, in an entirely different way from the others, quite worthy of the company of the best.[92]

[87] *Galaxy*, XII, 635 (November 1871).
[88] *Old and New*, VI, 714 (December 1871).
[89] *Nation*, XII, 43 (January 19, 1871).
[90] *Putnam's Magazine*, N.S., VI, 109 (July 1870).
[91] *Scribner's Monthly*, VI, 161 (June 1873). ·
[92] *Atlantic Monthly*, XXIV, 766 (December 1869).

After the publication of the *Innocents* — "a book which made a very remarkable sensation" — Mark Twain rose "on a flood-tide of popularity," said *Appleton's*;[93] and by 1876 E. P. Whipple named him in *Harper's* "the most widely popular" of the better class of humorists.[94] Yet he had not, by the end of our period, gained anything like the wide acceptance that was to be his later.[95]

As to Joaquin Miller, the general American verdict upon his work may be left to a writer (probably Stoddard) in the *Aldine*: "Byron was a great poet, but Byron is dead. Mr. Miller is not a great poet, and his spurious Byronism will not live. We shall all see the end of Millerism."[96]

"Gradually, but pretty surely, the whole varied field of American life is coming into view in American fiction," wrote Howells, with apparent satisfaction, in 1872.[97] He himself reviewed not only the works of the Far-Westerners, but those of DeForest, whom he believed in 1874 "really the only American novelist,"[98] and of Eggleston, of whom he said in the same year, "No American story-teller has of late years had greater success, of a good kind."[99] The *Manhattan* declared somewhat later that Edgar Fawcett was "beyond all doubt the foremost writer of the American society novel";[100] this seems a fairly general opinion, though the repetitious Fawcett themes are said to have made R. H. Stoddard resort to the pun of exasperation: "Won't somebody please turn this Fawcett off?"

Of Howells himself, his fellow novelist Henry James said in the *North American*, "His art ripens and sweetens in the sun of success," and called *A Chance Acquaintance* "a popular success."[101] This was doubtless a friendly exaggeration; the *Nation* was nearer the truth when it said in 1880: "He has always had too few admirers."[102] Howells returned the compliment in

[93] *Appleton's Journal*, XII, 17 (July 4, 1874).

[94] *Harper's Monthly*, LII, 526 (March 1876).

[95] See Maude Humphrey Palmer, "History of the Literary Reputation of Mark Twain in America" (University of Iowa thesis, 1925), pp. 7–21.

[96] *Aldine*, VI, 10 (January 1872).

[97] *Atlantic Monthly*, XXX, 487 (October 1872).

[98] *Ibid.*, XXXIV, 229 (August 1874). [99] *Ibid.*, XXXIII, 745 (June 1874).

[100] *Manhattan*, III, 287 (March 1884).

[101] *North American Review*, CXX, 208, 214 (January 1875).

[102] *Nation*, XXXI, 49 (July 15, 1880).

a pleasantly laudatory essay on James in the *Century* a few years later, but he did make the illuminating statement that editors had more or less forced James upon their readers and compelled them to like him.[103] It was in this article that Howells made a remark that brought many English brickbats whizzing about his ears: he called fiction "a finer art today than it was with Dickens and Thackeray." [104] But there was something to be said for that thesis. Howells and James stood for new ideals and practices in fiction. Said Julian Hawthorne in the *Princeton Review* in 1884: "Mr. James and Mr. Howells have done more than all the rest of us to make our literature respectable during the last ten years." [105] James, though Fawcett thought him "the first of English-writing novelists," [106] was unpopular. His fellow novelists praised him, but the Great American Reader paid scant attention to him. The criticisms of James often concerned matters of national pride, as when a *Galaxy* reviewer insisted that though "Mr. Christopher Newman is certainly a fair representative of a certain sort," he ought not to be set up "before the world as '*The* American;' " [107] and *Life* suggested that James was "the original of Hale's Man Without a Country." [108] But *Life*, and some other critics as well, occasionally attacked James on the score of dullness and unintelligibility:

The mystic and imaginative James gives us the subjective impression which the impulse of a hypothetical being to inchoate action might or would contingently have produced upon its own and the popular mind; he tells us how people struck each other (that is, mentally, not literally), but he never tells us anything that people did.[109]

But *Life* lived to see James go much further in hypothetical inchoation than he had gone in 1883.

Finally, a few words may be spared the phenomenon of the cheaper literature. *Appleton's Journal* pointed out in 1870 what an "immense hold" certain writers ignored by the critics

---

[103] *Century*, III, 25 (November 1882).

[104] It was an early skirmish in the war over realism. A collection of comments brought out may be found in the *Literary News*, n.s., IV, 137 (April 1883).

[105] *Princeton Review*, 4th ser., XIII, 13 (January 1884).

[106] *Ibid.*, 4th ser., XIV, 86 (July 1884).

[107] *Galaxy*, XXIV, 137 (July 1877).

[108] *Life*, V, 32 (January 15, 1885).   [109] *Ibid.*, I, 16 (January 10, 1883).

have upon a vast multitude of readers. . . . There are American writers, such as Mr. Cobb, Mrs. Southworth, Mrs. Stephens, Miss Holmes, Miss Evans, who, if the statistics were given, would be found, we think, to have an immense constituency, outlying in all the small towns and rural districts, such as no English writer possesses here.[110]

Scott's Monthly in 1867 invoked the "verdict of posterity" to place Augusta Jane Evans "at the head of American female novelists." [111] It may be assumed that no representative of posterity was present to dispute that "verdict." As a matter of fact, all the "American female novelists" of the period are practically forgotten except Mrs. Stowe, and she was scarcely to be considered by so ardent a champion of the South as *Scott's*. Of course, Miss Evans's work was by no means to be thought of as cheap in the sense of having a low aim. Of the more vicious class of novels *Scott's* also has something to say:

We are sadly in need of an *Index Expurgatorious* in this country at the present time. Well nigh every bookstall and news depot in the land is crowded with . . . Satanic literature. These volumes find a ready sale in all quarters, greatly to the detriment of private and public morals.[112]

The *Aldine* also speaks of "the flood of sensual and trashy literature." [113]

BEST SELLERS

The study of best sellers is not necessarily related closely to a survey of literary criticism, and yet best sellers occasionally find places of importance in the history of literature. No periodical, however, gave adequate and consistent reports of the largest book sales until twenty-five years after the close of the war. The *Literary World* and the *Dial* were not interested in such phenomena, nor, in its earlier years, was the *Critic*. Even

[110] *Appleton's Journal*, IV, 22 (July 2, 1870).

[111] *Scott's Monthly*, III, 244 (March 1867). Adverse criticism of Miss Evans is, however, found in another southern magazine — *De Bow's*. There the reviewer speaks of her work as a "huge mass of erudition" and "a farrago of false sentiment and conceit." (After-the-War Series, III, 268–273, March 1867.) But Miss Evans had imitators: see *Appleton's Journal*, I, 474 (July 10, 1869).

[112] *Scott's Monthly*, III, 231 (March 1867).

[113] *Aldine*, preface to Vol. IX, 1879.

the *Publishers' Weekly* of those years affords but a poor guide to the investigator anxious to compile a list of best sellers. But there are here and there enlightening notes about sales and the popularity of certain books; and from 1880 on, the monthly readers' contests of the *Literary News* afford at least some insight into what more discriminating readers thought were the most important books currently published.

Holland's *Kathrina* (1867) was a poetical best seller, 100,000 copies of it having been demanded.[114] All of Holland's works, poetry and fiction, were popular, though the *Publishers' Weekly's* assertion that "there is probably no other living author whose works show so large an average circulation and sale" may be questioned.[115]

Gates Ajar (1868), by Elizabeth Stuart Phelps, was widely read, though the author confessed some years later that it never quite reached, in America, a sale of 100,000. It had the symptoms of popularity, however: many household articles were named after it, and there were "Gates Ajar" cigars, patent medicines, collars, and tippets. Its author was the victim of the over-zealous orthodox. "Heresy was her crime, and atrocity her name. She had outraged the church; she had blasphemed its sanctities." [116]

In the same year came a book by another gentle New England spinster — *Little Women*, by Louisa M. Alcott. As best sellers go, this got only a fair start, but it continued without abatement for a long time, stimulated by the appearance of *Little Men*, which was even more popular, in 1871.[117]

Innocents Abroad (1869) sold a quarter of a million copies in five years,[118] a record probably exceeded then only by *Uncle Tom's Cabin*.[119] *Tom Sawyer* (1876) and *Huckleberry Finn* (1884) were also in the best-seller class, with another boys' classic of the seventies, Eggleston's *The Hoosier Schoolmaster* (1871). Two best selling juveniles came a little later — Anna

[114] See sketch of Holland in *Appleton's Cyclopaedia of American Biography*.
[115] *Publishers' Weekly*, V, 234 (February 28, 1874). For the "immense popularity" of *Sevenoaks*, see *Annual American Cyclopaedia* for 1876, p. 429.
[116] *McClure's Magazine*, VI, 515 (May 1896).
[117] See Ednah D. Cheney, *Louisa May Alcott, Her Life, Letters and Journals* (Boston, 1890), pp. 200, 261.
[118] *Appleton's Journal*, XII, 17 (July 4, 1874).   [119] See vol. II, pp. 142–44.

Sewell's *Black Beauty* (1877) and Margaret Sidney's *Five Little Peppers and How They Grew* (1881). *Josh Billings' Allminax* sold about a hundred thousand in 1870–71.[120]

E. P. Roe's *Barriers Burned Away* (1872) had a phenomenal sale, and thereafter successive novels from the Reverend Mr. Roe's pen could be depended upon to be booksellers' leaders. Albion W. Tourgée's *A Fool's Errand* (1879) ran through edition after edition as fast as the presses could put them out,[121] and *Bricks without Straw* the next year was "a second success only less remarkable" than the first.[122]

John Habberton's *Helen's Babies* shared leadership with *Tom Sawyer* in 1876 and "took immensely with the public." [123]

Ben Hur was published in 1880, but it was not until two years later that it began to show signs of growing popularity.[124] Thereafter it went on and on to new heights until more than a decade later it set about establishing one of the great all-time records for book sales. It was the religious demand that made *Ben Hur* so popular. It may be pointed out in this connection that the new Revised Version of the Bible (1881–1885) was also a best seller. The *Nation* spoke of the "enormous sale of it — something wonderful even in this age of enormous sales." [125]

Mary A. Sprague's *An Earnest Trifler* was a best seller of 1879,[126] Emily Pratt McLean's *Cape Cod Folks* of 1881,[127] F. Marion Crawford's *Dr. Claudius* [128] and John Hay's *Bread-Winners* [129] of 1883, and Henry F. Keenan's *The Money-Makers* of 1885.[130]

ATTITUDES TOWARD ENGLISH WRITERS

It must be remembered, however, that there were English and French best sellers in America which frequently outdis-

[120] John S. Hart, *A Manual of American Literature* (Philadelphia, 1872), p. 446.

[121] Advertisement, *Dial*, I, 63 (July 1880).

[122] *Critic*, I, 51 (February 26, 1881).

[123] *Annual American Cyclopaedia* for 1877, p. 454; *ibid.*, for 1878, p. 440.

[124] See *Lew Wallace, An Autobiography* (New York, 1906), II, 942.

[125] *Nation*, XXXII, 401 (June 9, 1881).

[126] *Literary News*, n.s., I, 7 (January–February 1880).

[127] *Literary World*, XII, 496 (December 31, 1881).

[128] *Ibid.*, XIV, 464 (December 29, 1883).

[129] *Annual American Cyclopaedia* for 1883, p. 450.

[130] *Ibid.*, for 1885, p. 530.

tanced the native product. Nationalists might rant and professedly American periodicals might bar foreign genius; but
the people of the United States loved their Dickens, Collins,
Hugo, and Dumas, their Tennyson and Browning. *Putnam's*
said in disgust in 1870 (the writer was probably Parke Godwin)
that

all the foreign quarterlies are regularly reproduced . . . four of the
principal monthly magazines resort to noted English authors for
their main attractions; four of our foremost illustrated weeklies are
little more than copies, as to their pictures, of the foreign illustrated
weeklies; and two if not three of our daily journals are chiefly edited
by men from abroad.[131]

In the same year Thomas Wentworth Higginson wrote in the
Atlantic: "The highest aim of most of our literary journalism
has thus far been to appear English, except where some diverg-
ing experimentalist has said, 'Let us be German,' or 'Let us be
French.' " [132]

Indignation doubtless magnified the evil, if it was an evil; but
it is true that Americans looked much abroad for their literature.
Or rather, many writers and their work were brought to Americans from abroad; for not only were the Harper publications,
the *Galaxy*, the eclectics, and many other magazines faithful
purveyors of English and French literature, but the authors
themselves crossed the Atlantic to visit the Americans, lecture
to them, and share their financial prosperity.

W. C. Brownell, writing on "English Lecturers in America"
in 1875, was able to name the following for the decade just ending: Charles Dickens, Edmund Yates, George Macdonald,
James Anthony Froude, Charles Kingsley, Edward Jenkins
(author of *Jinx's Baby*, an international best seller), Gerald
Massey, Wilkie Collins, Charles Bradlaugh, Dr. Porteous, John
Tyndall, and Richard A. Proctor.[133] He might have added Justin McCarthy, who remained in this country three years and
was an editorial contributor to the *Galaxy;* Goldwin Smith,
who was a professor at Cornell 1868–71; Thomas Hughes, who
came back ten years after his lecture tour to found a colony in

[131] *Putnam's Monthly*, N.S., V, 609 (May 1870).
[132] *Atlantic Monthly*, XXV, 57 (January 1870).
[133] *Galaxy*, XX, 62–72 (July 1875).

Tennessee; and James Bryce, who received but scant attention.[134] Nor does the Brownell list include English actors in American theaters.[135] In the later seventies came more author-lecturers: Monckton Milnes, Thomas Huxley, William Black, Arthur Penrhyn Stanley, Robert Louis Stevenson. The early eighties saw some of the most heralded visits: those of Edward A. Freeman, George Augustus Sala, Archibald Forbes, Herbert Spencer, Oscar Wilde, and Matthew Arnold. The *Current*, a chronic Anglophobe, cried: "It is time to stop the opening of our purses, our houses, and our hearts to distinguished English tramps who come over here to rob us!"[136]

Of these the visits most discussed were those of Dickens, Tyndall, Spencer, Arnold, and Wilde. Though some could not forget the irritation produced by Dickens' first American tour, and insisted that he was "a vulgar snob,"[137] others were more generous. The *Galaxy* insisted that this visit fixed an era. "We shall date from the time he came here to read, and he from the time he made pots of money in America," it said.[138] Tyndall's scientific lectures in New York were extraordinarily popular;[139] and Spencer's visit, sponsored largely by Youmans' *Popular Science Monthly*, was a great national event. Matthew Arnold's criticisms of American life and culture while a visitor here offended many; *Life* said he had "incurred the displeasure of all Boston by his criticism of Mr. Emerson."[140] His visit was in general a great success, however.

But it took the seriocomic tour of Oscar Wilde in 1881–82 to elicit a record-breaking mass of comment. Wearing knickerbockers, holding a lily in his hand, he lectured on aesthetics; and his appearances were, as the *Chautauquan* observed, "productive of much discussion concerning aesthetic principles." The *Chautauquan's* own contribution to the discussion was that Wilde was "utterly wanting in the essentials of aesthetic culture."[141] The *Critic* noticed that people went to see Wilde "as

---

[134] See *Century*, XXIII, 780 (March 1882), where the editor contrasts the neglect of Bryce with the excitement over Wilde.

[135] See pp. 204–05.　　　　　　　　[136] *Current*, I, 260 (April 12, 1884).

[137] *Northern Monthly*, II, 251 (January 1868).

[138] *Galaxy*, V, 255 (February 1868).　　　　　[139] See p. 107.

[140] *Life*, III, 30 (January 17, 1884).

[141] *Chautauquan*, II, 373 (March 1882).

they would go to a circus or a fair." [142] The periodicals were
full of jokes about him; many of them did not know that the
whole visit was a publicity stunt.[143]

But Wilde's visit was only a comic interlude; for many Eng-
lish writers the American critics had the highest esteem. When
Dickens died in 1870, grief was the keynote of the articles.
Donald G. Mitchell wrote in *Hearth and Home*:

> If half the monarchs of Europe had been smitten down, there
> would not have been so great grief in the hearts of so many. He was
> so old a friend! He was so dear a friend! There is no living man
> who in the last thirty years has given such cheer and joy to so many
> millions as this great master, whose living touch in any future story
> we shall wait for and welcome no more.[144]

"After Dickens there is no living novelist who enjoys a popularity which even approaches that of Wilkie Collins," asserted
the *Round Table* in 1869.[145] Certainly Collins, Reade, and Trollope were eagerly reprinted by competing periodicals. Reade's
Griffith Gaunt and *A Terrible Temptation* were severely criticized on the score of immorality: *Judge* condemned the author
as "prurient and incorrigible," [146] but the editor of the *Galaxy*
thought him, with all his faults, "one of the most gifted and
charming" of novelists.[147] The prolific Trollope, reprinted on
this side in some of the best magazines, was the subject of en-
comiastic comment after his death in 1882: "the name of no
English writer is so honored by American readers," said *Harper's Weekly*;[148] and the *Princeton Review* praised him because
"he could be a realist without ceasing to be pure." [149] Bulwer's
star had declined,[150] but that of George Eliot shone high in the
galaxy of new writers. "We lovers of matchless *Middlemarch*
are not going to tamely surrender its supremacy of fame to the

---

[142] *Critic*, II, 13 (January 14, 1882).
[143] See "Think of Faint Lilies" by Hubert H. Hoeltje, in the *Palimpsest*,
XVIII, 177 (June 1937) for the origins of the tour.
[144] *Hearth and Home*, II, 424 (June 25, 1870).
[145] *Citizen and Round Table*, VI, 357 (November 13, 1869).
[146] *Judge*, October 21, 1882, p. 3.
[147] *Galaxy*, I, 559 (July 15, 1866).
[148] *Harper's Weekly*, XXVI, 805 (December 16, 1882).
[149] *Princeton Review*, 4th ser., XII, 28 (July 1883).
[150] See *Atlantic Monthly*, XXXIII, 616 (May 1874).

pretensions of any *Deronda*," said one good critic, "though, to say sooth, we must rally apace if we would make head against the reviewers."[151]   Each successive novel added to George Eliot's reputation. Disraeli's return to fiction with *Lothair* made a real sensation in 1870. "Scarcely any work of fiction has received such wide-spread notice and such general commendation," said *Appleton's*. "The articles written upon it in England and this country would already fill many volumes."[152]   Stevenson won his first considerable hearing in America with *Treasure Island*, which the *Literary World* called "the most realistic English fiction of the year."[153]   The *Moths* of Ouida, who "spies about genteel society in search of vice," was said in 1883 to be the "chief rival" of Zola's *Nana* in the bookstalls;[154] and a contest among the readers of the *Literary News* in 1882 resulted in the naming of Ouida and Zola at the top of the list of "authors having the worst influence."[155]

Among the English poets, Tennyson was laureate in America as in his native Albion; but controversy raged about Browning. In the early seventies, Stoddard, on the one hand, named Browning as the greatest dramatic poet since Shakespeare;[156] on the other, Howells, in the *Atlantic*, insisted that to characterize *The Red Cotton Night-Cap Country* "the manure heap affords the proper imagery of 'dung' and 'devil's dung.' . . . The poem, if it is a poem, is as unhandsome as it is unwholesome; it is both bad art and bad taste."[157]   But by 1883 the *Manhattan* was observing that "there is no doubt that Browning has a considerable following of disciples, especially in our country,"[158] and indicated that the Browning club movement had begun. Swinburne was more roundly abused than Browning; there were many pages of attacks on his "immoral" verses. *Punchi-*

[151] *Galaxy*, XXII, 698 (November 1876). Charles Astor Bristed was the critic.

[152] *Appleton's Journal*, IV, 22 (July 22, 1870).

[153] *Literary World*, XV, 465 (December 27, 1884). The word *realistic* had not yet been corrupted by the controversialists. Here it means real-seeming, or vivid, as in Brownell's comment on the realism of romance in the *Nation*, XXXI, 49 (July 15, 1860).

[154] *North American Review*, CXXXI, 83 (July 1880).

[155] *Literary News*, N.S., III, 16 (January 1882).

[156] *Appleton's Journal*, VI, 535 (November 11, 1871).

[157] *Atlantic Monthly*, XXXII, 115 (July 1873).

[158] *Manhattan*, I, 504 (June 1883).

nello — even he — pretended to decline a contribution from Swinburne because "the morals of our paper must be preserved." [159] Rossetti had many ardent admirers. Father Walsh, of the *Catholic World*, placed him "on a higher pedestal than Tennyson," and his death in 1882 stirred his followers to renewed comment. Father Walsh thought that "next after Rossetti, if at all after, comes Morris." [160] And one of the remarkable phases of the criticism of the times is the incense so copiously burnt at Jean Ingelow's altar. "In thousands of American homes her gracious presence is recognized as that of a fondly cherished friend," wrote a critic in the *Aldine*.[161]

Carlyle's attitude toward the Civil War in America, and his scornful parable, "Shooting Niagara," infuriated many of his former friends. Walt Whitman, writing in the *Galaxy*, referred to "the comic-painful hullabaloo and vituperative cat-squalling" over Carlyle's criticisms of America.[162] The *Nation* spoke of the Niagara article as "pure rigamarole, the nonsense of a foolish and conceited old man." [163] But Carlyle still had friends in America who resented attacks upon him.[164] John Stuart Mill, Herbert Spencer, and John Tyndall received much attention in American journals, *Appleton's Journal* and the *Popular Science Monthly* being the chief interpreters of their work. Arnold's visit increased an interest in his writings which was already considerable.

CONTINENTAL WRITERS

"There seems to be an increasing demand for translations of foreign books," noted *Appleton's*, that busy observer, in 1869; [165] and the *Galaxy* a few years later spoke of the popularity of "the novelists of France, Germany, and even Russia." [166] Magazines generally reflected this interest by their reviews of European books and by the publication of translations. The *International*

---

[159] *Punchinello*, I, 203 (June 25, 1870).
[160] *Catholic World*, XXIII, 219–220 (May 1876).
[161] *Aldine*, IV, 67 (April 1871). See also *Galaxy*, IV, 573 (September 1867).
[162] *Galaxy*, IV, 926 (December 1867).
[163] *Nation*, V, 194 (August 29, 1867).
[164] See F. L. Mott, "Carlyle's American Reputation," *Philological Quarterly*, IV, 261 (July 1925).
[165] *Appleton's Journal*, I, 155 (May 1, 1869).
[166] *Galaxy*, XXIV, 564 (October 1877).

Review and the *Literary World* had French and German correspondents, and the *Dial* and *Critic* followed Continental literature with some care. The *Galaxy* and the *Atlantic* had departments devoted to French and German literature in the early seventies.

The work of "all the chief French novelists appears in translation within a few weeks after their publication in Paris," wrote Brander Matthews in 1883.[167] The general interest in Hugo, George Sand, Dumas, and Jules Verne, and the advent of Zola were the outstanding features of American interest in French literature in the period. "The popularity of Mme. Dudevant's writing is now at its zenith," observed one critic in 1870,[168] and her death in 1876 was the occasion for several evaluations. Hugo was now lauded, now excoriated; his references to American affairs in *L'Année terrible* caused some recriminations.[169] There was a persistence of the belief in many quarters that French life and letters were corrupt.[170] *Appleton's Journal* ascribes France's defeat by Prussia to moral degeneracy induced in part by a "flashy" literature. "The ablest, most fertile, and most noxious of this class," it declared, "is Alexandre Dumas, *fils.*"[171] But French literature continued to gain in America: the *Dial* commented in 1880 upon "the rapidly increasing popularity which contemporary French fiction is gaining in this country."[172] Zola was in part responsible. He soon became a storm center: he was called "the genius of the muckrake" in the *North American Review*,[173] and the *Critic* declared after *Pot-Bouille* that he should be "henceforth a literary outlaw."[174] Even such a confirmed Gallican as Matthews rejected him.[175]

What the *Penn Monthly* called "the growing interest in the

---

[167] *Princeton Review*, 4th ser., XII, 188 (September 1883).
[168] *Punchinello*, I, 254 (July 16, 1870).
[169] *Atlantic Monthly*, XXX, 370 (September 1872).
[170] See vol. II, p. 164.
[171] *Appleton's Journal*, VI, 162 (August 5, 1871).
[172] *Dial*, I, 75 (August 1880).
[173] *North American Review*, CXXXI, 79 (July 1880).
[174] *Critic*, II, 141 (May 20, 1882).
[175] *Princeton Review*, 4th ser., XII, 197 (September 1883). See also Herbert Edwards, "Zola and the American Critics," *American Literature*, IV, 114 (June 1932).

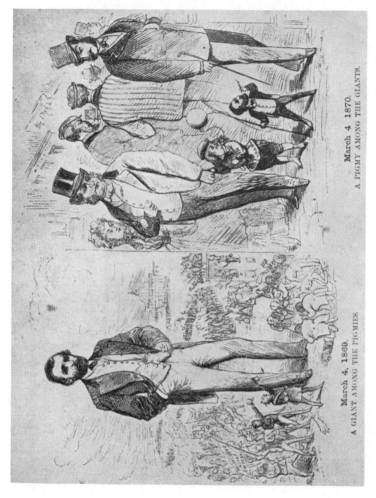

March 4, 1869.
A GIANT AMONG THE PIGMIES

March 4 1870.
A PIGMY AMONG THE GIANTS.

GRANT'S DECLINE

This cartoon by Henry L. Stephens appeared in *Punchinello*, April 2, 1870.

MARK TWAIN AND THE "INFERNAL *GALAXY* PORTRAITS"

Mark satirizes the portraits of the magazine for which he was writing a department by drawing a picture of King William which "*can not* be improved on, by making it either better or worse."

German language and literature" [176] was frequently commented upon.

> A good sign in our lighter literature [said the *Galaxy* in 1869] is the large number of translations from the German that have been made and published in this country of late. . . . These novels are a vast improvement on the French novels which have for a long time been thrown from our press. . . . We suppose the immense infusion of the German element into our population of late years has been the chief cause.[177]

Bayard Taylor's translation of *Faust*, published in 1871, stimulated that interest in Goethe which is most notable in the *Nation*, the *Critic*, and the *Atlantic Monthly*.[178] Auerbach and Ludwig were the German novelists most frequently discussed. An important two-part article by E. V. Blake in the *National Quarterly* dealt with Spielhagen, Auerbach, and others.[179]

Scandinavian literature also received some attention. The *Literary World*, citing the interest in Björnson, Hans Christian Andersen, and H. H. Boyesen, as well as that displayed in the work of the Russian Turgeniev, observes that "a favorable sign of the times in this country is the rapid extension of our acquaintance with the literatures of those nations of Europe of which we have hitherto had but small knowledge." [180] The coming of Boyesen to the United States in 1869 and his contributions to the magazines doubtless did something to stimulate interest in Scandinavian life and letters.

The praise of Turgeniev's work by James, Howells, and others brought him to American attention. He was constantly cited by the realists; and Lathrop, writing in the *Atlantic*, thought his example "likely to have the most general and far-reaching influence,"[181] while Julian Hawthorne called his work

[176] *Penn Monthly*, II, 17 (January 1871). See, for detailed treatment of this subject, Martin Henry Haertel, *German Literature in American Magazines, 1846 to 1880* (Bulletin of the University of Wisconsin, No. 263, 1908).

[177] *Galaxy*, VII, 773 (June 1869).

[178] See J. P. von Grueningen, "Goethe in American Periodicals, 1860–1900," *Publications of the Modern Language Association*, L, 1155 (December 1935).

[179] *National Quarterly Review*, XXXV, 83, 284 (June, September 1877).

[180] *Literary World*, III, 120 (January 1, 1873).

[181] *Atlantic Monthly*, XXXIV, 323 (September 1874).

"altogether the most important fact in the fiction of the last twelve years." [182]

THE ECLECTICS

The eclectic magazines, spreading their tables weekly or monthly with their poachers' game, did their share in fostering a taste for foreign literature. The old stand-bys, the *Eclectic Magazine* and the *Living Age*, were flourishing.[183] The *Albion* succumbed in 1875, after over half a century of "God Save the King." [184] The two most important new eclectics of the period were *Every Saturday* [185] in Boston and the *New Eclectic*, later the *Southern Magazine*,[186] in Baltimore. The *Library Magazine* was begun in 1879, to last until 1888.[187] There were several other journals of this type which continued from one to three years. The *Week* was an experiment in 1868, in New York, which was renewed in 1871–73. H. P. Chandler's *Every Other Saturday* (1884–85) was a Boston quarto. *Once a Month* was a venture by T. S. Arthur, of Philadelphia, in 1869. One of the cheap serials was the *Seaside Library*, which kept many typesetters busy through the late seventies in the daily publication of all the works its editor, George Munro, could pirate from abroad, ranging from Jane Austen's *Pride and Prejudice* to Anon.'s *The Arab Wife*. Many other periodicals were partially eclectic.

---

[182] *Princeton Review*, 4th ser., XIII, 7 (January 1884).

[183] See Mott, *op. cit.*, pp. 306, 747.

[184] See vol. II, p. 128; also Mott, *op. cit.*, p. 132.

[185] Treated more fully in sketch 5.

[186] See p. 46.

[187] It was a monthly duodecimo at first; but in July 1880 it began the policy of issuing bound volumes only, in bimonthly numbers. Then after a suspension through 1882, it began in February 1883 as a monthly quarto. At the beginning it was called *Library Magazine of Select Foreign Literature*, but upon the decision to include American selections in December 1880 it became *Library Magazine of American and Foreign Thought*. With the beginning of the quarto series, it became *Choice Literature*, but reverted in 1885 to the name *Library Magazine*. It was published in New York by the American Book Exchange, dealers in secondhand books, and succeeded their *Book Exchange Monthly* (1875–78). John Balden took it over in 1883. It carried no fiction, and was more serious than *Littell's Living Age* or the *Eclectic Magazine*. It returned to its policy of using chiefly English writings in 1883.

INNOCENTS ABROAD

Closely connected with American interest in foreign literature was the enthusiasm for European travel. How much of this was mere restlessness and how much ardor for European culture is difficult to say. Professor William Wells wrote in *Hours at Home* of the "necessity for men of culture and refinement to possess some knowledge of the polished nations of Europe." [188] And a similar attitude is represented by a *Galaxy* writer who thinks "there can be no better recreation for an American than to break away from his own restless, overworked country, and expand his mind by the calm contemplating of the historic monuments of Europe." [189]

After the war there was a great increase of foreign travel. *Appleton's Journal* in 1873 quotes a Swiss economist to the effect that

twenty-five thousand Americans visit Europe annually. There are comparatively large permanent colonies of Americans in Paris, Berlin, Dresden, Vienna, Hamburg, Frankfort, Geneva, Basle, Marseilles, Copenhagen, St. Petersburg, and in all the chief cities of Italy and England.[190]

Six years later *Scribner's* was approving "this continued interest in Europe, which seems really more fresh and strong with every passing year." [191]

A flood of travel books by Americans and Englishmen was published in the United States. We need mention only a few of the most prominent writers of this kind of literature in the post-war period: Bayard Taylor, Charles Dudley Warner, Henry James, John Hay, Thomas Bailey Aldrich, William Dean Howells, Helen Hunt, C. W. Stoddard, H. T. Tuckerman, Charles Godfrey Leland, Titus Munson Coan, and Mark Twain.

But a reaction had set in against the standard travelers' gush, and that even before the publication of *Innocents Abroad*. In the first number of the *Overland Monthly* Bret Harte noted:

The days of sentimental journeyings are over. The dear old book of travel . . . is a thing of the past. Sentimental musings on foreign

[188] *Hours at Home*, II, 256 (February 1866).
[189] *Galaxy*, XX, 42 (July 1875).
[190] *Appleton's Journal*, IX, 473 (April 5, 1873).
[191] *Scribner's Monthly*, XVIII, 782 (September 1879).

scenes are just now restricted to the private diaries of young and impressionable ladies, and clergymen with affections of the bronchial tubes. . . . A race of good-humored, engaging iconoclasts seem to have precipitated themselves upon the old altars of mankind. . . . Mr. Howells has slashed one or two sacred pictorial canvases with his polished rapier; . . . Mr. Mark Twain has used brickbats on stained-glass windows with damaging effect.[192]

"All Americans are by nature 'Passionate Pilgrims,' " declared J. G. Holland in *Scribner's Monthly.* "The Old World is a lodestone that is always drawing them to it. . . . An American magazine . . . must, if it wishes to keep its hold on the public attention at home, satisfy the appetite of its readers for knowledge of the past and present of the Old World." [193] Accordingly, magazines throughout the nineteenth century gave travel an attention second only to that devoted to fiction.

The illustrated magazines had a great advantage in their presentation of life and scenery in foreign lands. Stanley's finding of Livingstone in Africa stimulated interest in the dark continent, and there was continuing attention to the Orient.[194] Many of the serial stories published in the magazines combined the attractions of travel and fiction by emphasizing foreign settings.

HISTORY AND BIOGRAPHY

Two causes especially contributed to the popularity of history in our period: the nation's centennial anniversary had turned the thoughts of the people to their past, and the state and regional historical societies were active in organization and publication. But it must be admitted that local and family pride, rather than an interest in pure history, played a large part in keeping the historical periodicals alive; and genealogical records were a staple type of contents, especially in the East. There was some indication of the new critical spirit, as in the *North American,* but it may be said in general that the magazine history was nearer to John S. C. Abbott than to Justin Winsor.

---

[192] *Overland Monthly,* I, 101 (July 1868). The reference to Mark Twain was printed before the issue of *Innocence Abroad,* and was probably inspired by an article by Mark in the *Overland's* own first number.
[193] *Scribner's Monthly,* XXII, 146 (May 1881).
[194] See vol. II, p. 125.

Of the older historical journals,[195] the *New England Historical and Genealogical Register* continued, during this period chiefly under the editorship of Albert H. Hoyt; H. B. Dawson's *Historical Magazine* was discontinued on the eve of the Centennial because of postal difficulties; and the first series of the *Annals of Iowa* ended in 1874, not to be succeeded by the second series until the eighties.

Many new historical journals were begun, especially in the latter half of the period, and most of them, of course, in the East. Maine had three quarterlies: the *Maine Genealogist and Biographer* (1875–78), edited by Dr. William Berry Lapham (at the same time editor of the *Maine Farmer*) and published in Augusta by the Maine Genealogical and Biographical Society; *Old Times* (1877–84), devoted to the history of the village of North Yarmouth; and the *Maine Historical and Genealogical Recorder* (1884–98), published, with several intermissions, by Stephen Marion Watson, Portland librarian.[196] S. C. Gould's *Notes and Queries* (1882–1909), of Manchester, New Hampshire, was mainly devoted to historical miscellany.[197] New Hampshire's *Granite Monthly* [198] was also largely historical. In Boston, *Notices of Recent Publications* was begun in 1876 as a reprint of the literary notes from the *New England Historical and Genealogical Register*; it was continued as the *New England Bibliopolist* (1880–1901), which was devoted to reviews of books of history and biography. The Essex Institute, of Salem, added a monthly *Bulletin* to its quarterly *Collections* in 1869; but the *Bulletin* also became a quarterly in 1877. The *Antiquarian Papers* (1879–1885), of Ipswich, Massachusetts, were published irregularly on the basis of monthly installments. The *Newport Historical Magazine* (1880–87), called in its last three years the *Rhode Island Historical Magazine*, was a quarterly by Henry E. Turner and R. H. Tilley; it was largely devoted

---

[195] See vol. II, pp. 175–76.

[196] It was suspended 1890–92, 1894, and 1896–97. It was a quarterly except for the last year, when it was issued monthly.

[197] It was suspended 1903–04. Its first title was *Miscellaneous Notes and Queries with Answers;* in 1898 this was changed on covers and half titles to *Notes and Queries and Historic Magazine,* and in 1902 to *Historic Magazine and Notes and Queries.* The title page for 1898 bore the words *The Grand Man, Notes and Queries;* thereafter, *Notes and Queries.*

[198] See p. 36.

to publishing vital records. So was James N. Arnold's *Narragansett Historical Register* (1882–91), of Hamilton, Rhode Island.[199]

In New York the Genealogical and Biographical Society began to publish its quarterly *Record*,[200] still current, in 1870. An interesting journal was the *New Amsterdam Gazette* (1883–95), issued monthly by Morris Coster and containing "historical sketches and reminiscences of the Dutch Regime of New Amsterdam and the New Netherlands," with much genealogical data. The *Magazine of American History* [201] (1877–1917) became in 1883, with the accession of Mrs. Martha J. Lamb to the position of editor and owner, an unusually varied and elaborate historical journal.

The *American Historical Record* (1872–82), of Philadelphia, changed title in January 1875 to *Potter's American Monthly*. Under its earlier name it was devoted solely to history and biography, and Benson J. Lossing was its able editor; Lossing continued to contribute after John E. Potter had taken the magazine over and made it more general in character. It was well illustrated, and had such contributors as James Grant Wilson

[199] A quarterly "devoted to the antiquities, genealogy and historical matter illustrating the history of the Narragansett country, or southern Rhode Island." There was much documentary material; and some notable reprints, such as Captain John Mason's *History of the Pequot War*, were published.

[200] The *New York Genealogical and Biographical Record* began as an eight-page octavo, succeeding the *Bulletin* of the society, of which but one number was issued, December 1869; and it was gradually enlarged to forty-eight pages, small quarto. It has always been quarterly, and well printed. Though containing much of a general magazine nature, it has featured extended biographies of literary, political and military figures, genealogical records, church and probate data, and portraits. Chief editors in recent years have been H. S. Mott and J. R. Totten. Among the more famous early contributors were James Grant Wilson, Charles B. Moore, and Rufus King.

[201] A. S. Barnes & Company, New York, were publishers until 1883, with John A. Stevens editor 1877–81 and B. F. De Costa 1882–83; then Mrs. Lamb bought it, and is said to have made it a paying venture for the ensuing ten years. After her death on January 2, 1893, it was carried on by various hands through September 1893 and then suspended. Many well-known contributors appeared two or three times in its table of contents, and during the Lamb regime it was fully illustrated. It published documents, historical and biographical articles, news of the historical societies, the proceedings of the New York Historical Society, book reviews, and notes and queries. In December 1901 the name and numbering were resumed for a new dollar monthly published by Alvah P. French at Mount Vernon, New York; it ended in 1917, a war casualty, at Port Chester, New York.

and Elizabeth Oakes Smith.[202] The *Pennsylvania Magazine of History and Biography* (1877–current), though published by the state's historical society, was not, in earlier years, very strictly limited to historical matters. Mark Twain, Constance Fenimore Woolson, Thomas Wentworth Higginson, and Benjamin Silliman were found among its contributors. But in the main it was a handsomely produced quarterly of Pennsylvania history.[203] Philadelphia was also a center for Catholic historical publications — a distinction due to the activity of Martin I. J. Griffin and the American Catholic Historical Society of Philadelphia. *Griffin's Journal* (1873–1900) was finally merged in the quarterly *American Catholic Historical Researches* (1884–1912).[204]

There were several southern historical journals, all mainly devoted to presenting the southern view of the Civil War. *Our Living and Our Dead* (1873–76) was Colonel S. D. Pool's paper and an official organ of the North Carolina branch of the Southern Historical Society; it was given over chiefly to records of the battles of the war, but contained some educational articles and addresses.[205] The prospectus of the *Southern Historical Society Papers*, begun at Richmond as a monthly in 1876, stated: "The main object of our publication is to collect and

---

[202] *The American Historical Record, and Repertory of Notes and Queries. Concerning the History and Antiquities of America and Biography of Americans.* Such was the full title of this monthly during its first three years. Lossing was famous as a historical artist, and his magazine was brilliantly illustrated. It contained short historical articles, reviews of historical works, obituaries, reports of meetings of historical societies, etc. Chase & Town were publishers. Potter made it "an illustrated magazine of history, literature, science and art," with R. Grant Barnwell (later A. G. Feather) as editor. It dropped history and emphasized travel a year or two before its demise, and its contents deteriorated.

[203] It was the beneficiary of a privately subscribed publication fund for magazines and books in the hands of the historical society. Officers of the society were editors. See historical sketch in the Sixtieth Anniversary Number, LX, 305 (October, 1936).

[204] *Griffin's Journal* was a monthly except for 1883–94, when it was published fortnightly. It was under the aegis of the Irish Catholic Benevolent Union. The *Researches* began at Pittsburgh under the care of A. A. Lambing, but came under Griffin's direction in the second year and was moved to Philadelphia. The *Records of the American Catholic Historical Society of Philadelphia* (1884–current) was not a periodical until 1893 (Vol. IV), when it became a quarterly.

[205] It was published irregularly at Newbern, North Carolina, July 2, 1873–August 5, 1874, and then moved to Raleigh and published with new numbering, September 1874–March 1876. January–February 1876 was omitted.

preserve for the future historian material for a true history of the causes, progress and results of the great War for Southern Independence." After four years, J. William Jones, the secretary-editor, began issuing occasional quarterly numbers; and the *Papers* became annual in 1885. The *Alabama Historical Reporter* (1879–85) was issued by the state Historical Society at Tuscaloosa.

In Ohio there were two historical journals of some importance, the *Cincinnati Pioneer* (1873–85) and the *Magazine of Western History* (1884–93), of Cleveland. The latter journal had such contributors as James Ford Rhodes and Reuben G. Thwaites, as well as others less eminent and less reliable; it ended by going off to New York and falling into evil ways.[206]

Genealogy was carried far enough by the seventies to demand magazines devoted to special families, such as the *Paine Family Records* (1878–83), of New York; but these were usually brief and unpretentious. And there were also a number of obscure genealogical and historical journals of wider scope.[207]

[206] William W. Williams was the founder and editor until 1887. It published histories of western states, proceedings of historical societies, lives of pioneers, etc., including a good deal of Ohio material. Henry James Seymour's history of Pittsburgh appeared serially in 1885, C. W. Butterfield's histories of Ohio and Wisconsin in 1886–87, W. H. Venable's "Early Periodical Literature of the Ohio Valley" in 1888, and a railroad series in 1889. In October 1886 it became "the exponent of the Wisconsin Historical Society," edited at Madison and Cleveland, and "largely made up of matter relating to the Northwest." James Harrison Kennedy became editor in 1887, however, and moved it the next year to New York. It abandoned the West as a specialty, and in November 1891 became the *National Magazine*, "a journal devoted to American history," ending April 1893. But unscrupulous publishers later used the name for issues of a pretended magazine with contents taken from books and advertising improvised in order to get would-be notables to pay for steel portraits which were inserted in "ghost magazines" never sold or distributed. Some such issues of the *National Magazine* were printed as late as 1897. (See *Bulletin of Bibliography*, IV, 74, October 1905.)

[207] Among them were *Heraldic Journal* (1865–68), a Boston monthly, made a quarterly in 1866; *Chronotype* (1873–74) published in eight numbers by the American College of Heraldry and Genealogical Register at New York; *Southern Historical Monthly* (January, February 1876), Raleigh, North Carolina, of the same format as *Our Living and Our Dead*, and filling out the omitted numbers in that file, but a separate publication; *Our Country* (1876–78), New York; *Spirit of '76* (1875–77), in twelve numbers, New Haven; *Historical Register* (1883–84), Harrisburg, devoted to the history of the interior of Pennsylvania; *Confederate Annals* (June, August 1883), organ of the Southern Historical and Benevolent Association, St. Louis. Providence *Book Notes* (see p. 234) had a

Most of the standard magazines and reviews published more or less history. The *North American Review*, edited from 1869 to 1876 by Henry Adams, then assistant professor of history at Harvard, published a notable centennial number and did excellent work in reviewing current historical writing. It was at the very end of our period that the *Century* began its famous Civil War series.[208]

Biography was prominent in postbellum literature. Eugene L. Didier wrote in the *North American* in 1880: "One of the most striking features of the last decade has been the number of interesting biographies, memoirs, etc. . . . 'The cry is still they come.'"[209] Biography had long been prominent in American magazines. The indefatigable J. S. C. Abbott, who had contributed so much to the popularity of *Harper's* by his biographical serials, continued to fill many pages of that magazine, and contributed to others as well. The *Atlantic* published some notable autobiographies, such as that of Robert Dale Owen. There was a short-lived and unimportant *Biographical Magazine*, with woodcuts, in New York (1883–85).

THE COMICS

"America has of late years bristled with humorous writers as doth the porcupine with quills. . . . What persistent jokers!" exclaimed *Appleton's Journal* in 1874.[210] A year or two earlier the London *Examiner* had pointed out that in the literature of humor

America at the present moment and for some years past has fairly outstripped England. The vast majority of contemporary humorous books in circulation in this country are written by Americans and deal with American subjects. . . . The steady and abundant supply of humor, in verse and prose, that America yields, is now the principal source from which all English-speaking people derive their intellectual amusement.

---

special interest in Rhode Island history. See A. H. Shearer's list of historical periodicals, *Annual Report of American Historical Association, 1916* (Washington, 1919), I, 477.

[208] See pp. 468–70.

[209] *North American Review*, CXXX, 300 (March 1880).

[210] *Appleton's Journal*, XII, 16 (July 4, 1874).

In connection with these statements the *Examiner* named Lowell, Holmes, Saxe, Leland, Harte, Hay, Eggleston, Mark Twain, Josh Billings, and Artemus Ward. Our critic complains, however, that there is "no adequate artistic expression" for this school of humor.[211]

The attitude of American critics toward this humor that the English found so entertaining was frequently supercilious. "The very thought of American humor is becoming terrible," wrote an *Atlantic* reviewer of Eli Perkins;[212] and the *New Eclectic* said of the comics of 1869: "Their prevailing vulgarity saves us from the gloomy task of perusing the American journals that profess to be funny."[213] The Chicago *Advance* lamented the coarseness of Mark Twain and Josh Billings and wondered if mankind could not be taught to laugh "in a Christian way."[214] And the editor of the *Galaxy* was inclined to concur in such criticisms, especially so far as newspaper "funny columns" were concerned.[215]

It was another English observer who pointed out that

the Americans have not a single comic periodical like our *Punch*. . . . In the course of a dozen years many attempts have been made to establish such a print, but without success. *Vanity Fair* was the best of its class. . . . All the comic papers that flourished for a few years were only remarkable for the immense amount of bad wit they contained, for a wilderness of worthlessness, for an endless process of tickling and laughter. . . . There is hardly anything the Americans need more than a good comic paper.

This critic thought the lack arose from a dearth of good illustrators and enterprising publishers of the right sort.[216] But a better time was coming.

Several comic periodicals of the cheaper class — and most of them were cheap — had been founded in the preceding period.[217] To obtain files of all the funny papers begun between 1865 and 1885 is probably impossible: evidently not even the most aban-

[211] Quoted in *Every Saturday*, N.S., II, 458 (October 26, 1872).
[212] *Atlantic Monthly*, XLV, 666 (November 1880).
[213] *New Eclectic*, IV, 636 (May 1869).
[214] *Advance*, VIII, 682 (June 3, 1875).
[215] *Galaxy*, XXI, 579 (April 1876).
[216] *British Quarterly Review*, LIII, 5 (January 1871).
[217] See vol. II, pp. 178–85.

doned lover of puns in the land, nor the veriest devotee of the Pat-and-Mike anecdote, thought it worth while to save and bind such of these papers as were filled with coarse woodcuts and coarser wit. But fragments of files of many comics are to be found here and there,[218] and of the best of them there are sufficient materials for study.

Mrs. Grundy, one of the best of the lot, had a short life and a merry one in 1865. Dr. Alfred L. Carroll, an artist, was its editor; and Henry L. Stephens drew the full-page unbacked cartoon (usually on a political subject) which was its chief pictorial feature.[219] The monthly *Phunniest of Phun* also began in 1865 in New York. It was much cheaper and lasted until 1867; it was edited by the artist Frank Bellew and published by W. Jennings Demorest, and strongly satirized those who contended that the Civil War was not fought for the Negro but merely for the preservation of the Constitution. Out in San Francisco *Puck: the Pacific Pictorial* (1865–66) was published by Loomis and Swift. It began as a four-page weekly quarto, but after three weeks it became a monthly. Pascal Loomis, one of the proprietors, did many of the pictures; but Charles Nahl was perhaps the leading artist for this paper. There were some fine lithographed cartoons, many of them local satires.[220]

The best joke which George W. Carleton's *Kaleidoscope* cracked was in its subtitle: it called itself "An Intermittent Periodical," but it did not live even long enough to intermit, being compelled to demit after emitting its first number in June 1869. *Wild Oats* (1870–81), edited by "Bricktop," called

---

[218] Probably the best collection of them is that of Franklin J. Meine, of Chicago, to whom the author of these pages is much indebted.

[219] It ran July 8 through September 23, weekly. Its cover, drawn by Thomas Nast to win a $100 prize, showed Mrs. Grundy herself on the stage of a theater, with her back to the reader but facing an audience in which the artist depicted the features of some seventy-five famous men and women of the time. It was perhaps an ill omen that the audience was all very sober-faced. Other artists were Augustus Hoppin and E. F. Mullen. C. D. Shanly took Carroll's place as editor during an illness of the latter; and other editorial assistants were Howard Irving, Ashley W. Cole, and George Phoebus. *Mrs. Grundy* was intended as "*Vanity Fair* revived." It cost $600 a week, and its editor later testified that writers, artists, and readers in adequate number and quality were difficult to obtain. (See Carroll's "Can a Humorous Periodical Succeed in America?" in the *Round Table,* N.S., II, 97, October 21, 1865.)

[220] See *Collector's Journal,* IV, 438 (October–December 1933).

itself "an illustrated journal of fun, satire, burlesque, and hits at persons and events of the day." Some of its hits were too "very palpable," and Mayor A. Oakey Hall seized one of its early numbers for a cartoon called "Too Thick." [221] *Wild Oats* was usually anything but subtle; it was copiously illustrated by fairly good woodcuts. *Keepapitchinin* (1870–71) was "devoted to cents, scents, sense, and nonsense" — and also to puns.

Punchinello,[222] published for nine months in 1870, shares with *Mrs. Grundy* the honors of the early part of our period. It was backed by the Tammany organization and edited by Charles Dawson Shanly; it featured the pictures of Henry L. Stephens and Frank Bellew. *New Varieties* (1871–75) was an illustrated weekly quarto devoted to a cheaper type of wit and humor; it was published in New York by the Independent News Company and in Boston by John Stetson. Stetson tried *Cocktails* as a monthly in 1872, but shook up only four of them.

From Cincinnati came the *Fat Contributor's Saturday Night* (1872–75). A. Miner Griswold had made a reputation as the "Fat Contributor" to the *Cleveland Plain Dealer*; and he was able to capitalize it in a comic of his own, which he moved to New York in its second year. About the same time, C. H. Harris, who wrote in a German-American lingo under the name of "Carl Pretzel," began in Chicago a monthly publication called *Carl Pretzel's Pook* (1872–74); this he followed with his *Carl Pretzel's National Weekly* (1874–93), which came to have political and secret society alliances. In Boston, James R. Osgood & Company made a big hit with their daily *Jubilee Days*, an amusing journal issued during the World Peace Jubilee of 1872. Augustus Hoppin was the chief artist throughout the sixteen numbers, and William Dean Howells was editor.

Thistleton's Jolly Giant (1873–83) was a San Francisco monstrosity. It began as an attack upon a certain "lecturess" and reformer and continued as a bitter satirist of Catholicism and the Chinese. Its publication was occasionally interrupted

---

[221] See Brander Matthews' article originally published in the New York *Evening Post* and reprinted in the *American Bibliopolist*, VII, 199 (August 1875). This is the best summing up of the comics theretofore published in America. Winchell & Small were publishers of *Wild Oats*, which was at various times a monthly, a fortnightly, and a weekly.

[222] Treated more fully in sketch 18.

by the beating up or jailing of the editor. It was more scurrilous than "jolly," but it did have an individuality.[223] *Ye Giglampz* was Lafcadio Hearn's brief Cincinnati *jeu d'esprit* in 1874. Beginning June 21, it issued only nine weekly numbers; but they all had wit and a macabre distinction. "Published daily except week days," it was "devoted to art, literature and satire." [224] A second *Comic World* (1876–79), New York, was a merger of *Yankee Notions, Nick Nax,* and *Merryman's.*

Up to 1877 there had been no really successful humorous magazine in the United States. "The history of comic journalism in America," wrote Brander Matthews in 1875, "is merely a list of tombstones." [225] True, some of them, like *Yankee Notions* and *Frank Leslie's Budget of Fun,* had lasted out some two decades; but these were subliterary and inartistic — misbegotten children of Momus. The fatality which dogged the steps of the comics, said Matthews, "has not resulted in a survival of the fittest. The dead are honored; the living are despised." But in 1877 two men who had made a success with a German comic founded *Puck;*[226] and with Joseph Keppler as cartoonist and H. C. Bunner as editor, this witty weekly soon gained the high position which it held for many years in the field of satire. *Puck on Wheels* (1880–86) was an annual, as was, in our period, *Pickings from Puck* (1883–1923).[227]

The *American Punch* (1879–81) was a monthly published by a Boston engraving company. It borrowed much of its art and its jokes from its English model, though it printed some American cartoons.[228] An ambitious New York weekly was *Chic* (1880–81), which carried four pages of colored lithographs, mostly political cartoons, from the crayon of Charles Kendrick. Its theatrical department and its "Wall Street Ballads" were

[223] It began as a monthly, then became a semimonthly, and by 1874 was a weekly. George Thistleton was its perpetrator, and it was printed on cheap paper and illustrated by poor woodcuts.

[224] See George M. Gould, *Concerning Lafcadio Hearn* (Philadelphia, 1908), pp. 35 ff.

[225] *American Bibliopolist*, VII, 199 (August 1875).

[226] Treated more fully in sketch 30.

[227] The latter became a quarterly in 1897.

[228] Its monthly numbers sold for five cents except for about a year, 1879–80. William Henry Allen, William H. Mumler, and Earl Marble were successive editors; the last named was art and drama critic of the *Boston Budget.*

notable. In New Orleans the *Mascot* (1881–1900) continued through its two decades as an illustrated weekly of fair quality, with many changes of management.

In 1881 J. A. Wales, a cartoonist on the staff of *Puck*, quarreled with the owners of that magazine and enlisted two or three other artists with him under the banner of a new comic to be called *Judge*.[229] The venture appeared to flourish at first, but later met with such trials and tribulations that it was hard to keep laughing. *Judge* continued, however, as a high-grade periodical. In 1883 *Life* [230] was begun by a group of young men from Harvard. It was inclined to be more refined and subtle than *Puck*: then pen-and-inks of men like Kemble, Kendrick, and Attwood were far less boisterous and blatant than Keppler's two-page chromolithographic spreads. At any rate *Life* went on and eventually waxed and flourished. It was not a comic paper, but a gently satirical observer.

At the end of our period *Tid-Bits* (1884–90) put in an appearance as a cheap miscellany with many jokes accompanied by woodcuts; it was destined to great improvement after a year or two as a political and humorous paper.[231] In Chicago, Reginald DeKoven and Harry B. Smith turned aside from theatrical affairs to form the *Rambler* on the model of *Life*. The next year Elliott C. Flower took it over, making it more completely a humorous paper; but it perished in 1886.[232]

There were many other comics besides those that have just been reviewed, some lasting for only one number, and some for two or three years.[233] The college comic made its appearance in

---

[229] Treated more fully in sketch 36.

[230] To be treated more fully in a separate sketch in the succeeding volume of this work.

[231] The original publishers were the John W. Lovell Company. Wolcott Balestier became editor in 1886, making it wholly a satirical sheet, with theatrical and literary notes. Its name was changed to *Time* on June 23, 1888; it was enlarged to a quarto, and its illustration improved greatly. It was an ardent defender of Blaine in the campaign of 1884, being pitted against *Puck* in that torrid contest. Munsey bought it in 1890 and merged it with his *Weekly*.

[232] See Fleming, *op. cit.*, p. 528.

[233] Among them were *Phunniest of Awl* (1865), New York; *Little Joker* (1865–66), New York, edited by "Cousin Lizzie"; *Merry and Wise* (1867), New York; *Jolly Hoosier* (1867), Indianapolis, a four-page monthly; *Wag* (1868), cheap South Boston monthly; *Boneville Trumpet* (1868–69), Bridgeport, Connecticut, edited by "Alderman M"; *Comic News* (1869–72), New York monthly;

the seventies, the most prominent periodical of its class being the *Harvard Lampoon* (1876–current). College literary magazines commonly contained no little humorous writing: the *Acta Columbiana* [234] was an example.

Certain newspapers, begun as local weeklies, attained more than local reputations through the writing of humorist-editors. Mark M. ("Brick") Pomeroy edited the La Crosse, Wisconsin, *Democrat* (1860–70?) and there gained a national reputation for a kind of hard-hitting, witty political journalism. After the war he came to New York and founded *Pomeroy's Democrat* (1869–87), which gained a circulation of over a hundred thousand.[235] It was in Pomeroy's office at La Crosse that George W. Peck began his career in comic journalism, and *Peck's Sun* (1874–94) was founded at La Crosse. The paper was moved to Milwaukee, however, in 1878, and that city has the dubious honor of being the home of *Peck's Bad Boy* — the series that made the *Sun* famous.

Out in Laramie, Wyoming, Bill Nye founded the *Boomerang*,[236] named after the humorist's pet mule, in 1881. Like Pomeroy's paper, the *Boomerang* had a daily edition; but it was the weekly which, with a larger proportion of its columns given over to humorous writing, gained the wider hearing. Nye left the *Boomerang* in 1883, taking its reputation with him. Another westerner was *Texas Siftings* (1881–97), founded in Austin by

---

Chip Basket (1869–71), New York, a cheap monthly by John Silver; *New York Humorist* (1869); *Champagne* (1871), New York, Isaac G. Reed, Jr., editor, and Frank Leslie, publisher; *Thistle* (1872), New York, edited and written by Francis S. Saltus and published by S. M. Howard; *Brickbat* (1872), New York, edited by "Bricktop" and published by Frank Leslie and containing Matt Morgan's political cartoons from the *Illustrated Newspaper; Rutland* [Vermont] *Times* (weekly, listed as comic in E. Steiger, *The Periodical Literature of the United States*, New York, 1873); *Comic Weekly* (Steiger) Richmond, Virginia; *Comic Ventilator* (Steiger), Boston monthly; *Humorist* (1874), New York, a democratic paper edited by J. H. Rochacker; *Merry Masker* (1876), New York; *Uncle Sam* (1879), New York, A. Litchfield editor and Palmer Cox chief artist; *Wit and Wisdom* (1881), New York; *Punch and Judy* (1882), Boston; *Gilhooley's Etchings* (1883), Pittsburgh weekly; *Breeze* (1883), Chicago weekly; *Whip* (1885–86), St. Louis weekly.

[234] See p. 166.

[235] Pomeroy began the *New York Daily Democrat* in 1868. The weekly was merged in 1887 into *Pomeroy's Advance Thought*, a monthly 1887–96.

[236] See Frank Wilson Nye, *Bill Nye, His Own Life Story* (New York, 1926), Chapter VIII.

Alex E. Sweet and J. Armory Knox. It was from the beginning primarily a humorous sheet, but it contained some local and state news and had the appearance of a country newspaper. It moved to New York in 1885. Its specialties were witty paragraphs and the travel letters of its editors. Alas, how blunted the point of its wit now, even for the most indulgent reader! Its devotion to the pun for the pun's sake was pathetic.[237]

Somewhat similar in origin and history was Opie Read's *Arkansas Traveler* (1882–1916). It was founded at Little Rock and made a great hit with its sketches of back-country scenes and characters, reaching a circulation of 85,000 by its third year.[238] But these sketches were relished better by those who thought themselves more civilized than by the up-creek subjects of them; and when a man was elected to the legislature for having said he would like to tie a rope around the editor's neck and lead a mule from under him, Read decided to make the *Traveler* justify its title and moved to Chicago. This was in 1888, and thenceforward the paper dropped its news features entirely.[239]

Out on the coast, "Bill" Marshall earned some fame for his *California Maverick* (1883–86). And various newspapers gained wide reputations for their humor columns without losing their characters as newspapers.[240]

The general magazines published some humor. The most famous department devoted to it was the "Editor's Drawer" in

[237] When it was reduced in size to a quarto in 1886 it became a better paper, with art work by Thomas Worth and T. Ramsden. A. Miner Griswold, the "Fat Contributor," was added to the staff in 1887; he and Sweet became editors and Knox manager. Sweet was left in sole charge in 1891, and in December 1895 the paper came into the hands of Robert E. Morgan, who reduced the price but failed to save the paper's life. Probably Sweet's "Through Texas on a Mexican Mustang" in 1882 did as much as anything to make the paper famous. Opie Read wrote for it, and Howard Seeley was book reviewer and dramatic editor in 1890. A volume of *Sketches from "Texas Siftings"* was published in New York in 1882.

[238] See Opie Read, *I Remember* (New York, 1930), p. 182.

[239] Read's brother-in-law, P. D. Benham, was business manager. Read was forced out in 1892, and the paper deteriorated. Harry Stephen Keeler was editor in its last phase, and A. J. Gontier, later publisher of *Ten-Story*, was owner. Gontier bought it from Thomas Devereaux.

[240] For example: *Pittsburgh Chronicle-Telegraph*, William Henry Siviter; *Norristown* (Pennsylvania) *Herald*, J. H. Williams; *Chicago Herald*, Walter Wellman's "Train Talk"; *Chicago Daily News*, Eugene Field's "Sharps and Flats"; *Boston Courier*, George R. Jackson's "Pencillings"; *Toledo Blade*,

Harper's Monthly, edited during most of our period by the Reverend Irenaeus Prime. It was sometimes melancholy reading, as the *Nation* said; but at any rate it was chaste, and the illustrations added much to the text. *Scribner's* had its "Etchings," later "Bric-a-Brac," and "In a Lighter Vein." Neither was nearly as good as Mark Twain's "Memoranda" in the *Galaxy*; but Mark's successors in that magazine — Donn Piatt and then Kate Field — could not keep up his standard.

MAGAZINES AND NEWSPAPERS

It was not alone in the field of the comic periodical that the magazine and the newspaper approached each other so closely that distinctions become difficult. The Sunday newspaper, with its emphasis on magazine features, gradually gained popularity throughout the period.[241] On the other hand, magazines were closer to current news; the journalistic attitude adopted by the *North American Review* when Rice took it over in 1878 was a significant symptom.

The changing character of newspapers in the postwar period resulted in a decidedly critical interest in journalism on the part of the magazines. "In eight years the entire range and method of the newspaper business has undergone a revolution," observed a trade journal in 1869.[242] It was five years later that Frank B. Sanborn, writing on "Journalism and Journalists" in the *Atlantic Monthly*, said:

Since the death of Horace Greeley and the events which preceded and followed it, there is no difficulty in perceiving that we stand at the close of a long era of American journalism and are entering rapidly upon a new dispensation. The presidential campaign of 1872, and the death of Mr. Greeley, mark the end of partisan journalism in its old form.[243]

Chief subjects of magazine comment were the rapid increase in the number of papers, the growing emphasis on news instead

---

Petroleum V. Nasby; *Detroit Free Press,* M. Quad; *Danbury* (Connecticut) *News,* J. M. Bailey; *Burlington* (Iowa) *Hawkeye,* Robert J. Burdette.

[241] See vol. II, p. 34, for the beginnings of Sunday editions of newspapers. A typical attack on the early postbellum Sunday newspaper was that on Forney's *Philadelphia Press* in the *Round Table,* II, 256 (December 23, 1865).

[242] *Printers' Circular,* IV, 84 (May 1869).

[243] *Atlantic Monthly,* XXXIV, 65 (July 1874).

of political controversy, the growth of advertising, and the rise of the interview. The *Round Table*, which severely criticized newspapers from time to time for news sensationalism, editorial weakness, and disreputable advertising, was startled at their multiplication: it notes 300 new papers in the year following the war.[244] "What will journalism come to at the present rate of newspaper spawning?" asked the *Galaxy* three years later. "North, south, east and west, newspapers shoot up." [245]

The journalist E. V. Smalley, writing in the *Manhattan* at the close of our period, remarked upon the growing importance in the news of divorce suits, elopements, church scandals, bigamies, and murders, and the tendency to flippancy in the treatment of such matters.[246] An accompaniment of the change to news as the point of emphasis was the invention of the interview as a reporting device. The interview was strongly attacked by such magazines as the *Galaxy*, the *Nation*, and *Puck* because of its invasion of privacy. "Hardly a day passes without new offences by that abomination of our journalism, the interviewer," said *Every Saturday* in 1871;[247] and the *Nation* exclaimed:

> There are limits to people's endurance of printed impudence. . . . The "interview" as at present managed is generally the joint production of some humbug of a hack politician and another humbug of a newspaper reporter.[248]

Puck, in a page of pictures, shows an interviewer forcing doors, rummaging in bureaus and wine cabinets, and going down chimneys and manholes after his victims.[249] Richard Grant White, in a jeremiad against interviewing, wrote in the *Galaxy*: "It is the most perfect contrivance yet devised to make journalism an offence, a thing of ill savor in all decent nostrils." [250] A lawyer writing on newspaper libel in the *North American* in 1880 tells of the misdemeanors and crimes of the press: "On all sides we hear complaints of this license and abuse, and the courts are more and more resorted to for redress." [251]

[244] *Round Table*, III, 89 (February 10, 1866).
[245] *Galaxy*, VIII, 710 (November 1869).
[246] *Manhattan*, III, 361 (April 1884).
[247] *Every Saturday*, N.S., II, 66 (January 21, 1871).
[248] *Nation*, VIII, 66 (January 28, 1869).   [249] *Puck*, March 1877, p. 7.
[250] *Galaxy*, XVIII, 827 (December 1874).
[251] *North American Review*, CXXXI, 109 (July 1880).

The growth of advertising was thought by the critics to be full of peril to honest journalism. Smalley believed that the papers' increasing reliance on revenue from this source would bring them "under the thumb of the capitalist." [252] Charles T. Congdon, also a newspaper man, commented upon the corporate control of the press — especially Jay Gould's evil influence on certain western newspapers.[253] White thought the corruption of the press by advertising "very great." [254] *Puck*, on a somewhat different tack, was fond of lambasting the *New York Herald* for immoral advertising.[255]

But nowhere was the low esteem in which journalism was frequently held better illustrated than in the opinion that schools and departments of journalism were beneath the dignity of the college curriculum. A writer in *Hearth and Home* in 1872 said:

> Some time ago Washington College in Virginia invited the smiles of the incredulous by the announcement of a Department of Journalism. . . . [The course] drew more scoffs than scholars. But lately Cornell University has published a similar manifesto, and now the queer Virginia notion receives the lofty approval of no less venerable an imitator than Yale College. . . .[256]

Periodicals for journalists were intimately related to those for printers [257] and for the advertising business. *George P. Rowell & Company's American Newspaper Reporter and Advertiser's Gazette* (1868–84) was founded mainly as a house organ for a great advertising agency. In 1877 it was sold to W. H. Woodcock, dealer in printers' supplies, who changed its character somewhat.[258] A. N. Kellogg, publisher of syndicated "ready-prints" for country weeklies, began the *Publishers' Auxiliary* as a monthly in Chicago in 1869, combining the functions of trade journal and house organ.[259] The *American Journalist* (1872–77) was "a monthly review of American journalism" issued by

---

[252] *Manhattan*, III, 365 (April 1884).

[253] *North American Review*, CXXXVI, 88–99 (January 1883).

[254] *Galaxy*, VIII, 847 (December 1869).

[255] *Puck*, April 10, 1878.

[256] *Hearth and Home*, IV, 2 (January 6, 1872).

[257] See pp. 131–32 for journals of the printing trade.

[258] He also changed its name to *American Newspaper Reporter and Printers' Gazette*, and two years later to *Woodcock's Printers' and Lithographers' Weekly Gazette and Newspaper Reporter*.

[259] The Western Newspaper Union took it over when it bought out the Kellogg

the advertising agents Coe, Weatherill & Company, of Philadelphia; it added *and Advertiser's Index* to its title in 1876. There was another *American Journalist*, a more professional paper, edited by R. P. Yorkston at St. Louis 1883–85. The *American Press* (1882–current) was originally chiefly a house organ to advertise "boiler plate"; it carried news and hints for country weeklies. The Indianapolis *Printer and Publisher* (1882–current) was later to become the *National Printer-Journalist*.[260]

---

company in 1906. It had then been a weekly for many years. (Information from Elmo Scott Watson, present editor, and Wright A. Patterson, of the W. N. U., who was a Kellogg editor in 1890.)

[260] In 1888 it was consolidated with the *National Journalist*, founded in 1884 by B. B. Herbert, and changed its title to *National Editorial Journalist: Printer and Publisher*; and two years later it became *National Journalist for Editors*. It adopted the title *National Printer-Journalist* in 1893.

CHAPTER X

POLITICS AND ECONOMICS

SOMETHING has already been said of American relations with Europe in the postbellum period as they were formed by literature and travel,[1] but other and more political phases of international affairs much discussed in the magazines remain to be mentioned. "Every day brings us nearer," wrote Lowell in the *Atlantic* in 1867, "and enables us to see the Old World more clearly."[2] That there was an increasing interest in European affairs cannot be doubted. Americans took a deep interest in Prussia's conquest of Austria, in the Franco-Prussian War, and in the Congress of Berlin; while other matters more nearly affecting American affairs were closely watched. A writer in the *International Review* of 1882 named three foreign problems which were then interfering with American politics — Chinese immigration, Irish insurrections, and the importing of Mormon converts.[3]

IMMIGRATION

Immigration problems were closely linked with American interest in foreign affairs. Perhaps the great increase in America's German population by immigration had something — though certainly not everything — to do with the general interest in the rise of Prussia. "There are as many Germans in our large western cities as there are Americans," wrote J. J. Lalor in the *Atlantic* of 1873; "in some of them there are more. They are found scattered over the East; in the West they are thick as autumn leaves; they cover the country and swarm in the city."[4] The great wave of immigration, which reached nearly half a million in the single year of 1873, and after some recession in the middle and later seventies again passed beyond previous records in the eighties, produced social and economic effects which were frequently analyzed in the magazines.[5]

[1] See pp. 248–58. [2] *Atlantic Monthly*, XX, 619 (November 1867).
[3] *International Review*, XIII, 182 (August 1882).
[4] *Atlantic Monthly*, XXXII, 461 (October 1873).
[5] See, for example, *North American Review*, CXXXIV, 347 (April 1882), and CXXXVIII, 78 (January 1884); and *Century*, XXVIII, 761 (September 1884).

The Irish and Chinese were disturbing elements in this immigration. A *Puck* cartoon of 1878 shows a procession of Irishmen entering with banners carrying such legends as "Situation Wanted as Congressmen," "Liquor Store Wanted"; and another of Chinese, whose signs read, "Wantee Washee-Washee for Melican Man" and "Wantee Plentee Money to Takee Homee." [6] The Fenian troubles in Ireland had their reflexes in Boston and New York, which may be followed best in *Frank Leslie's Illustrated* and *Harper's Weekly*. The Chinese invasion of California aroused deep resentment. "Chinese immigration should be stopped with all the power of the government" was the text of a long and careful article in the *National Quarterly Review*.[7] Bret Harte's "Heathen Chinee" poem, more properly called "Plain Language from Truthful James," which was reprinted everywhere after its appearance in the *Overland*, expressed one phase of this "Chinese Question" in its famous lines:

> Which is why I remark,
>   And my language is plain,
> That for ways that are dark,
>   And for tricks that are vain,
> The heathen Chinee is peculiar, —
>   Which the same I am free to maintain.[8]

Which the same was not all comedy, but does indeed set forth one of the popular objections to the Chinese in California.[9] But the chief argument was economic and was voiced in many places — typically and humorously in a pretended symposium in *Scribner's*, where a German, an Irishman, a "Pike," and a Frenchman claim America for their own, and John Chinaman himself replies;[10] and more violently in *Thistleton's Jolly Giant*, of San Francisco, where "the filthy, dirty, abominable Chinaman" is said to be "not equal to any living human being." [11] The "Chinese Question" got into the national campaign of 1880 and

---

[6] *Puck*, March 17, 1880, center spread.

[7] *National Quarterly Review*, XLI, 302 (October 1880).

[8] *Overland Monthly*, V, 287 (September 1870).

[9] Ironically enough, Harte was not himself anti-Chinese. See George R. Stewart, Jr., *Bret Harte, Argonaut and Exile* (Boston, 1931), p. 178.

[10] *Scribner's Monthly*, XVII, 491 (February 1879).

[11] *Thistleton's Jolly Giant*, May 30, 1874, p. 2.

caused Garfield to lose California and Nevada.[12] After the Chinese Exclusion Act of 1882, the tension was relaxed somewhat.

Shortly after the close of the Civil War, the South was inviting immigration, seconded by such northern journals as *Harper's Weekly*, but with little success. At the same time ardent Southerners were advocating emigration to Brazil: "Let the proposed reconstruction measures be perfected," threatened *De Bow's*, "and emigration will proceed with the hurry and precipitancy of a *sauve qui peut*." [13]

ATTITUDES TOWARD VARIOUS NATIONS

England's treatment of Ireland aroused some feeling, especially among Irish-American citizens, and the Irish troubles were much discussed in the periodicals; perhaps the most notable articles were those by Parnell and Froude in the *North American Review* in 1880. It was in this magazine, too, that a writer discussed the annexation of Canada as "one of those important dormant issues never wholly out of sight." [14]

The general American attitude toward England after the Civil War is well summed up in Lowell's famous *Atlantic* essay, "On a Certain Condescension in Foreigners." The feeling toward the mother country, wrote the man who was to be minister to England a decade later,

is far from cordial. . . . Justly or not, we have a feeling that we have been wronged, not merely insulted. The only sure way of bringing about a healthy relation between the two countries is for England to clear their minds of the notion that we are always to be treated as a kind of inferior and deported Englishmen.[15]

A few years before this, W. M. Rossetti, in an illuminating article in the same magazine on "English Opinion on the American War," explained the English attitude on the ground that "the English as a nation dislike the Americans as a nation." [16] E. Dicey, writing to the *Nation* from London, thought the ill-

---

[12] *Penn Monthly*, XI, 909 (December 1880).
[13] *De Bow's Review*, After-the-War Series, III, 352 (April–May 1867).
[14] *North American Review*, CXXXVI, 326 (April 1883).
[15] *Atlantic Monthly*, XXIII, 94 (January 1869).
[16] *Ibid.*, XVII, 129 (February 1866).

feeling was mutual.[17] Whitman's noble "Democracy" essay in the *Galaxy* was a contribution to the controversy.[18]

And yet, in spite of these animosities and rivalries, English visitors were welcomed by curious and often enthusiastic crowds,[19] English fiction and poetry were reprinted everywhere,[20] English criticism was commonly quoted with a peculiar respect, English science was discussed on every hand, English internal politics were carefully watched and widely commented upon, and English persons and places were made the subjects of a very large number of magazine articles. Justin McCarthy, one of the visitors, expressed in the *Galaxy* his disappointment when he first reached New York upon hearing the bands play London tunes, noting placards that announced London actresses, and seeing bookshop windows full of London novels.[21]

The leading English reviews and magazines were regularly reprinted in New York as they had been for many years, but now they appeared through arrangement with the original publishers or from English-owned offices in New York. In 1865 Alexander Strahan, of London and Edinburgh, established a house in New York, from which he issued his *Contemporary Review, Good Words*, and *Sunday Magazine. Cassell's Monthly* set up a New York office in 1867. On the other hand, some American reviews had English editions; and in 1873 *Scribner's Monthly* led an invasion of England by the American illustrated magazine, soon to be joined by *Harper's.* By 1881, *Scribner's* was explaining:

> The success of American periodicals in a foreign market . . . is generally attributed almost wholly to the superiority of American engraving and the prodigality of illustration. . . . There are other causes at work; one of these is the interest taken by the people of Great Britain in American affairs.[22]

The success of the American magazines in England doubtless caused some imitation of their characteristics by English competitors, thus turning the tables at last. And yet, as we glance

---

[17] *Nation*, I, 336 (September 14, 1865).
[18] *Galaxy*, IV, 919 (December 1867).
[19] See pp. 249–51.
[20] See pp. 248–49.
[21] *Galaxy*, IX, 758 (June 1870).
[22] *Scribner's Monthly*, XXII, 145 (May 1881).

through a longer period, it is clear that there was more aping of English successes by American publishers in the fifties and sixties than there was of English imitation later. The *Atlantic's* cover plainly came from *Blackwood's*, and *Putnam's* also owed something to that magazine. The London *Spectator* was the model for the *Nation*, and the *Cornhill Magazine* for the *Galaxy*. *Harper's Weekly* was founded on the model of the *Illustrated London News*, as *Every Saturday* was on that of the London *Graphic* and Bonner's *New York Ledger* on the *London Journal*.

Lack of international copyright furnished a question which was chiefly Anglo-American. Though the bulk of the matter published on the problem favored the reform, a stubborn opposition advocated "free trade in brains"; and pirating of literature went on but slightly abated by "gentlemen's agreements." [23]

There was far more interest in things French than there had been for many years in America. Certain brilliant young magazine writers, such as Henry James and Eugene Benson, doubtless had much to do with spreading this enthusiasm for the Gallic. *Appleton's* published a rather controversial series on "French Morals and Manners" in 1869. Pierre Blot, the famous Parisian chef, came to New York in the sixties and wrote many articles for the *Galaxy* on French cookery and table manners. The Chicago correspondent of *Punchinello* remarked in 1870 that the French fever had spread among all classes in that burgeoning metropolis. "French teachers swarm like bees here. . . . We have had French parties, French plays, French lectures. We read French, speak French, sing French, and look French." [24]

Popular interest in the Franco-Prussian War did much to stimulate this "fever," and yet American sympathy was rather with Germany in that contest.[25] The size and influence of our German-American population was, of course, one reason for this sympathy; but it is true also that the Catholic question was involved and that Bismarck appealed to the American imagination. The Iron Chancellor's name became a conjuring word

[23] See p. 256. For earlier phases of the movement, see vol. II, pp. 128–30.
[24] *Punchinello*, I, 123 (May 2, 1870).
[25] *Appleton's Journal*, IV, 382 (September 24, 1870).

in the magazines: "his most inveterate enemy must confess that he has set his mark upon the age," said one writer.[26]

An international problem nearer home was that involved in the Cuban question, which continued to occupy many pages in American periodicals.[27] The *Nation*, which, upon the capture of some filibusters in 1869, had interpreted the popular feeling in the United States as mere indifference toward Cuban independence,[28] took quite another position after the Spanish atrocities of 1871. "The news from Cuba," it then said, "is of a kind to make foreign intervention in some form desirable and even probable." [29] It was two years after that, upon the slaughter of one hundred Cubans by the Spanish, that Julia Ward Howe wrote in her *Woman's Journal*: " 'The seals that hold the pestilence of war' are well nigh broken before us. . . . 'War, war!' is the general cry of those who passionately feel the outrage." [30] The Virginius affair of 1873 caused the war cry to be raised in many quarters; and it was not until the peace of 1878, which seemed liberal to many American observers, that attention in that direction relaxed.

American interest in the Orient had shifted from Japan to China, chiefly for two reasons: the Burlingame Treaty, which virtually admitted China to the family of nations; and the anti-Chinese sentiment in California. Nast's cartoon showing China, "the oldest member of the family, who desires our better acquaintance," presented to the other nations by America [31] expressed an idea that had caught the national fancy.

POLITICS IN THE MAGAZINES

After the war, politics were no longer taboo in the general magazines, as they had often been formerly. Magazines came to reflect more directly than ever before the current thought of the country not only in literature and the arts but in politics, economics, and sociology.

Even in *Harper's Monthly, Lippincott's, Old and New*, and the *Overland* there were occasional political notes, chiefly in the

---

[26] *Appleton's Journal*, IV, 700 (December 10, 1870).
[27] See vol. II, pp. 122, 139, for the Cuban question in the preceding period.
[28] *Nation*, IX, 24 (July 8, 1869).   [29] *Ibid.*, XIII, 362 (December 7, 1871).
[30] *Woman's Journal*, IV, 372 (November 22, 1873).
[31] *Harper's Weekly*, XII, 460 (July 18, 1868).

essay departments. Holland sometimes commented on political matters in his "Topics of the Time" in *Scribner's*. Arthur G. Sedgwick had a political department in the *Atlantic* for a few years, and political articles were not uncommon in that magazine. George E. Pond wrote politics for the *Galaxy*, which carried many political comments outside his department as well. Parke Godwin did politics for *Putnam's*. Robert Ellis Thompson gave the *Penn Monthly* a Republican bias. The *North American*, which published many political articles while it was a quarterly, redoubled its attention to that field when it became a monthly. The *National Quarterly Review* under Sears fought Grant and was otherwise politically active. *De Bow's*, while it lasted, attempted rather pitifully a leadership of the wasted South. Certain of the better religious quarterlies, like the *Princeton Review* and the *New Englander*, did not neglect politics. Among the weeklies, the independent *Nation* under Godkin exerted considerable influence upon the thoughtful, while the Republican *Harper's Weekly*, with Curtis and Nast, was a great force for Grant, against Tammany, later for Garfield, and still later against Blaine. The *Independent* belied its name in its devotion to Republicanism until Blaine's nomination. The *Round Table*, of shorter life, was nonpartisan but aggressive. The *Christian Union* paid some attention to politics in its department called "The Outlook." *Forney's Progress* was a strongly Republican weekly, but the course of Tourgée's *Continent* was rather indecisive. The comics frequently indulged in political comment; especially notable was *Puck's* campaign against Blaine.

None of the above periodicals was wholly or predominantly political in character, save possibly *Forney's Progress*. The *Republic* (1873–78), of Washington, was "a monthly magazine devoted to dissemination of political information" designed to aid the Republican party. It seems primarily an attempt to defend the party's reputation against the Crédit Mobilier and other scandals; but its partisanship was on a comparatively high plane, and the documents it published were doubtless valuable. The *Old Guard*,[32] Chauncey Burr's wild-eyed unreconstructed magazine, perished in 1870, the same year that saw the

[32] Treated more fully in vol. II, sketch 38.

very brief life of *Rutter's Political Quarterly*, of Memphis, "devoted to unearthing the sanctimonious political rats of the South, exposing radical scalawags and carpet-baggers." Political scurrility could no farther go.

One of the interesting phases of political development was a certain trend in the direction of independence from partisan bonds. This was reflected in the decline of the so-called "party press." Most of the prominent magazines just named as more or less political had no party allegiance, and even the Republican *Harper's Weekly* could support Cleveland in 1884, while the *Independent* refused to accept Blaine. In that year partisan independence attained proportions unknown before. "Party ties have become weak, and with multitudes have ceased to control," declared the *North American Review*. The people "demand a real issue, which the Republican and the Democratic parties no longer offer." [33] The *North American* itself was much given to symposia presenting two or more sides to a question; and its example was followed by other reviews, until in 1878 the *American Annual Cyclopaedia* declared that "a review among us [as contrasted with British reviews] now publishes the views of every party in town, or simultaneously, upon a given topic. . . . The word symposium . . . has become a frequent feature of the review 'of the period.' " [34] It was Henry Adams' move to loose party ties which had caused the internal revolution in the *North American's* affairs in 1876. The *Nation* was notoriously independent: "Treachery to party," wrote Godkin in the first Grant campaign, "is the very life and soul of political improvement." [35] W. C. Brownell, looking back on the *Nation's* history in later years, said that by 1876 "in circles of any political detachment, it was quite true, as I remember Mr. Sedgwick saying, that 'to call oneself either a Republican or a Democrat' was 'slightly ridiculous.' " [36] And a contemporary commentator on tendencies in journalism wrote in 1882: "In the spirit of no blind optimism, we may forecast the day in which there shall be full deliverance from all partisan political bondage." [37]

---

[33] *North American Review*, CXXXIX, 301 (October 1884).
[34] *American Annual Cyclopaedia* for 1878, p. 484.
[35] *Nation*, IX, 205 (September 9, 1869).   [36] *Ibid.*, CI, 42 (July 8, 1915).
[37] *North American Review*, CXXXV, 483 (November 1882).

RECONSTRUCTION

Periodicals like the *Nation*, the *Independent*, and *Harper's Weekly* followed the steps of governmental policy at the South week by week, while the reviews came on at their slower pace. *De Bow's* "After-the-War Series" reflected the point of view of the forward-looking South:

We call upon the people of the South to be manly, enterprising, hopeful. Their fortitude in adversity is even more admirable than their gallantry in the field. They are capable of great things and may achieve a high destiny. Let them turn away from the dead past, and look at the living future.[38]

The *Nation's* observer in the South, J. R. Dennett, found the people of New Orleans anxious for a return to normal business conditions: "The war is over, slavery is gone. They have no wish to see it restored; they want to see business reviving. . . . As for northern capital, they welcome it." [39] Dennett found the Freedmen's Bureau mistrusted; but *Harper's Weekly*, which for a long time carried a regular department reporting the Bureau's activities, declared: "The Freedmen's Bureau has always been an object of Democratic hatred; but no institution was ever more imperatively necessary, and none has been more useful." [40] A number of freedmen's journals were published for a few years after the war by private societies more or less allied with the Bureau. Among these were the *Freedman's Friend* (1864–83), Philadelphia; the *Freedmen's Record* (1865–73), Boston; and the *American Freedman* (1866–69), New York. Frederick Douglass' *New National Era* [41] was published for the freedmen themselves in Washington through 1869–75.

If the "carpetbaggers" were hated in the South, they were by no means admired in the North. The southern *Rutter's Political Quarterly* called them

the *Saintly Apostles of Reconstruction* turned loose upon the South, who have covered the land like locusts, and, like them, have eaten the

---

[38] *De Bow's Review*, After-the-War Series, I, 75 (January 1866).
[39] *Nation*, II, 269 (March 1, 1866).
[40] *Harper's Weekly*, XII, 467 (July 25, 1868).
[41] Douglass turned it over to his sons, who were printers, in 1872. It lost

heart and pith out of all manly advance toward social, political, or material prosperity,[42]

while the *Nation* described the carpetbagger more concretely as

a man who has not succeeded in any of the ordinary walks of industry, and who, while traveling in quest of better luck, has got employment from the southern negroes in managing the machine which the war threw into their hands, and with the nature of which they are not themselves familiar; and he does this with the firm determination of making all he can out of the job.[43]

The *Nation* often showed a sympathy with southern white viewpoints. It declared that "there is no more use in getting in a rage with Ku-Kluxery, and of sending cavalry and artillery after it, than of legislating against pestilence, as long as nothing is done to remove the causes." [44] But Tourgée, who had suffered at the hands of the K. K. K., lambasted it repeatedly in his *Continent*.

Other conditions at the South, such as the famine of 1867,[45] the craze of the Negroes for traveling,[46] and the mortality of the colored population,[47] were discussed in various periodicals. The *Atlantic* contained in 1877 a good exposition of the "Mississippi Plan" for white domination, which was said to have succeeded in South Carolina.[48] *Putnam's* had a striking article by J. W. De Forest about the conditions of the poor whites.[49]

Northern visitors were almost always kindly treated in the South. An observer for *Appleton's* reported, "It is universally the habit to disclaim in the most earnest way a supposed enmity toward the North." [50] Yet the old animosities died hard. It was after Lee's surrender that *Harper's Weekly* printed its horrible and incredible pictures of outrages on Federal soldiers in south-

---

about $9,000. See Douglass, *Life and Times* (Hartford, 1882), p. 408, and F. M. Holland, *Frederick Douglass* (New York, 1891), p. 324.

[42] *Rutter's Political Quarterly*, July 1870, p. 5.

[43] *Nation*, XIII, 364 (December 7, 1871).

[44] *Ibid.*

[45] *Harper's Weekly*, XI, 179 (March 23, 1867).

[46] *Atlantic Monthly*, XXXIX, 682 (June 1877).

[47] *Nation*, XV, 105 (August 15, 1872).

[48] *Atlantic Monthly*, XXXIX, 183 (February 1877).

[49] *Putnam's Magazine*, N.S., I, 704 (June 1868).

[50] *Appleton's Journal*, X, 299 (September 6, 1873).

ern prisons.[51] And it was actually after 1880 that a versifier in the *Southern Bivouac*, a repository of Confederate memories, wrote these lines:

> Nay, ask me not to love my foe;
> 'Tis Christian-like and right, I know,
>   And 'tis divinely great.
> Yet there's enough who will forgive;
> Then grant to me while yet I live
>   The luxury to hate.[52]

A SUCCESSION OF PRESIDENTS

The troubles of President Andrew Johnson received their share of notice in the periodicals. One quotation from the *Atlantic Monthly* will suffice to represent a common view:

The President of the United States has so singular a combination of defects for the office of a constitutional magistrate that he could have obtained the opportunity to misrule a nation only by a visitation of Providence. Insincere as well as stubborn, cunning as well as unreasonable, vain as well as ill-tempered, greedy of popularity as well as arbitrary in disposition, veering in his mind as well as fixed in his will, he unites in his character the seemingly opposite qualities of demagogue and autocrat.[53]

The attempt to impeach Johnson was closely followed by the hebdomadals, and the pictures in *Harper's Weekly* furnish a graphic history of the great trial.

Shortly after Grant was inaugurated in 1869, the *Atlantic Monthly* published an anonymous article on "The Intellectual Character of President Grant." Few carefully reasoned judgments of public characters have proved so mistaken: our analyst lauded the President's clear appraisal of men, his prompt intelligence, his broad views, and "his ability to control numerous and vast and complicated interests." [54] By the time Grant had been six months in office, the *Nation* was saying that he had been guilty of some of the worst appointments "ever made by a civilized Christian government." [55] The next year *Punchinello*

[51] *Harper's Weekly*, IX, 380 (June 17, 1865).
[52] *Bivouac*, II, 11 (September 1883).
[53] *Atlantic Monthly*, XVIII, 374 (September 1866).
[54] *Ibid.*, XXIII, 635 (May 1869).
[55] *Nation*, IX, 224 (September 16, 1869).

called upon the President, in verse as villainous as a presidential mistake, to

> rise up, to our joy,
> An' make a clean sweep of the crowd
> Of tinkerin' tools and blunderin' fools
> That put your wits under a cloud.[56]

A character in one of the editorial dialogues printed in the vituperative *Old Guard* doubtless expressed that magazine's opinion of Grant when he said: "If he were not President, and if I did not have a high respect for great officials, I should call him a nincompoop."[57] Indeed, the *Nation's* estimate of the retiring President in 1877 was not far different: it ascribed to him "entire ignorance of the intellectual and political life of modern society."[58] *Leslie's Illustrated*, with Keppler's cartoons, was Grant's consistent enemy; but the President had a champion in *Harper's Weekly*, where Nast drew him as the strong, silent hero.

The campaign of 1872 called forth some unusually bitter journalism, especially in the papers just mentioned. In *Leslie's*, Matt Morgan, fresh from his *Tomahawk* success in England, cartooned Grant as a drunkard, an embezzler, and a tyrant; while in *Harper's Weekly*, Nast's satires upon Greeley were unnecessarily cruel. *Appleton's* commented after the campaign was over: "On all sides the clamor was stunning and the fierceness amazing, in view of the few issues at stake."[59]

In retrospect, the campaign of 1876, hotly contested though it was, is overshadowed by the contest before the Electoral Commission which followed it. The article in the *North American Review* for July 1877, by Jeremiah S. Black, one of Tilden's counsel in the contest, presented one side with vigor and ability; the other view was expressed in the following issue by E. W. Stoughton, one of Hayes's counsel. Black declared that since the formation of the American government "no event not connected with violence or war has excited a feeling so intense as the act of 'counting in Hayes,'" and that the Electoral Com-

[56] *Punchinello*, I, 23 (April 9, 1870).
[57] *Old Guard*, VIII, 151 (February 1870).
[58] *Nation*, XXIV, 128 (March 1, 1877).
[59] *Appleton's Journal*, VIII, 706 (December 21, 1872).

mission had "betrayed the nation" by seating "a pseudo-president." [60]

The preconvention campaign of 1880 was unusually exciting because of the advocacy of a third term for Grant. "General Grant," said Black in the *North American*, "would make a tolerable king"; but after canvassing the matter, he decided that America did not wish a monarchy.[61] Even *Harper's Weekly* deserted the Grant standard, favoring the nomination of Senator Edmunds.[62] The convention finally rejected both the leaders — Grant and Blaine — and nominated Garfield. This suited *Harper's Weekly* well enough [63] and met with the fairly general acceptance of the party; it delighted the *Penn Monthly*, which had been one of Garfield's first proponents.[64] The rout of the Democratic party in this election was so decisive that there was no little talk (helped along by enthusiastic Republicans) of disbanding the party. "We do not know exactly how a party 'disbands,' " wrote Godkin, whose *Nation* had been independent in the campaign, "but it is plain that the hour for disbanding has arrived for our Democratic brethren. Neither man nor party ought to live after the brains are gone." [65]

The assassination of Garfield, so deeply mourned by the people and by the periodical press, and the accession of the little-known Arthur, handicapped the new administration; and when the next campaign unfurled its banners and lighted its torches, it was a Democracy heartened by the acquirement of a sturdy new candidate which faced a G. O. P. headed by a "plumed knight" unacceptable to certain eastern factions of the party. "The Republican opposition to Mr. Blaine in all of the states," said *Harper's Weekly*, which was supporting Cleveland, "is founded mainly upon the official record of his misuse of official position for his private advantage." [66] By the end of August,

[60] *North American Review*, CXXV, 1–34 (July 1877).

[61] *Ibid.*, CXXX, 222 (March 1880). This is from a symposium on the third-term question.

[62] *Harper's Weekly*, XXIV, 322 (May 22, 1880).

[63] *Ibid.*, XXIV, 402 (June 26, 1880), 338 (May 29, 1880).

[64] *Penn Monthly*, XI, 630 (August 1880).

[65] *Nation*, XXXI, 333 (November 11, 1880). See also Senator Edmunds' suggestion to the same effect in the *North American Review*, CXXXII, 19 (January 1881).

[66] *Harper's Weekly*, XXVIII, 592 (September 13, 1884).

Godkin noted that "the array of evidence against Mr. Blaine's political morality . . . is producing a profound effect." [67] After Blaine's defeat, the *Nation* referred to him as "this remarkable demagogue." [68] Throughout the whole campaign, *Puck* cartooned the Republican candidate as "the tattooed man," showing him repeatedly as marked all over by such legends as "Little Rock Railroad Bonds," "Monopoly," and "Mulligan Letters." Bernard Gillam's cartoon just before the Chicago convention was a characteristic *Puck* production: it was a travesty on the famous Gérôme picture and showed Blaine as Phryne, making classic exhibition of her charms before "the Chicago tribunal." Phryne hides her face coyly, but exhibits a body tattooed all over with the signs already familiar to *Puck's* readers. The expressions on the faces of the tribunal range from horror through shamefaced grins to Rabelaisian mirth.[69] After the election, a *Puck* cartoon showed Blaine diving into Salt River; only his tattooed legs were visible.[70] But Cleveland, too, suffered from personal attacks; and when revelations of a sexual irregularity came to light, many of the religious periodicals deserted his banner. The *Independent*, which had temporarily renounced its Republicanism after Blaine's nomination, ended by calling upon both candidates to withdraw.

RASCALS AND BOODLERS

So thought I, as with vague, mechanic eyes
I scanned the festering news we half despise
    Yet scramble for no less,
And read of public scandal, private fraud,
Crime flaunting scot-free while the mob applaud,
    Office made vile to bribe unworthiness,
    And all the unwholesome mess
The Land of Broken Promise serves of late
To teach the Old World how to wait. . . .[71]

Thus wrote Lowell in his ode to the memory of Agassiz published in the *Atlantic* in 1877; and though his lines aroused

---

[67] *Nation*, XXXIX, 166 (August 28, 1884).
[68] *Ibid.*, XXXIX, 447 (November 27, 1884).
[69] *Puck*, June 4, 1884, center spread.
[70] *Ibid.*, November 19, 1884.
[71] *Atlantic Monthly*, XXX, 586 (May 1874).

severe criticism, there were many to agree. A year or two before, the editor of the *Galaxy*, summing up the state of the country at the Centennial, had written:

That public life is shockingly corrupt; that public spirit has almost if not entirely died out; that the minority have no voice in affairs even as a minority; that all decent men revolt from politics; and that the greater number of those who control our political affairs at the present day may be justly characterized as corrupt, or unscrupulous, or ignorant, or as marked by all these traits of character, we fear must be admitted.

Three reasons are given for this condition of affairs: the mass of unassimilated immigrants, the sudden wealth of the country in its multiple expansion, and the American failure to plan for the future.[72]

Such scandals as those connected with the Crédit Mobilier, the Erie War, the Whisky Ring, and the Star Route Trials were recognized as national disgraces: the Federal responsibility was emphasized when H. V. Boynton showed in the *North American* that Secretary Bristow was compelled to fight a corrupt administration machine in order to dislodge the Whisky Ring conspirators.[73] Another effective *North American* article was Charles Francis Adams' "A Chapter of Erie" (July 1869), with its sequel "An Erie Raid" (April 1871). But it can scarcely be doubted that there was another American point of view which refused to think of boodling as a very serious crime. "The investigation," wrote a *Wild Oats* humorist of the inquiry into the Crédit Mobilier operations among members of Congress, "has revealed the fact that Senators are mortal, and Representatives are only the synonyms of frailty." [74]

Bribery was rampant in the state legislatures. "There is hardly a legislature in the country which is not suspected of corruption," declared the *Nation* in 1868.[75] Commenting upon the conviction of a member of the New Jersey legislature for bribery, the *Galaxy* said, "Legislative bribery, and its satellite, lobbying, have become the most grievous political evil of the

[72] *Galaxy*, XX, 432–433 (September 1875).
[73] *North American Review*, CXXIII, 280–327 (October 1876).
[74] *Wild Oats*, February 13, 1873, p. 4.
[75] *Nation*, VI, 386 (May 14, 1868).

country. They are destroying public virtue and sapping public honor." [76] *Punchinello* noted in 1870 that it had been proposed to "purify" the Pennsylvania legislature, but it believed such a project Utopian. "If Niagara were squirted through its halls," declared this critic, "the water would be dirtied, but the halls would not be cleansed." [77] In 1884 Wayne McVeagh assailed Pennsylvania boodlers quite as severely in the *Century*.[78] And Charles Francis Adams described a New York legislature in the *North American* as "a mart in which the price of votes was higgled over, and laws, made to order, were bought and sold." [79]

But we must turn from state to city government to reach the climax of crime in office for this period. That climax, at least so far as the size of the spoils was concerned, was reached by the Tammany boodlers of about 1870. An important exposé of the corruption in New York City politics appeared in the *North American Review* as early as October 1866. It was an able and fearless article by James Parton, and its revelations are not less than shocking. It was followed the next July by an equally frank article on "The New York City Judiciary." All this was from Boston and did not worry Tammany. But *Harper's Weekly* also said some sharp and bitter things: in 1870 it declared that "there are certain judges [in New York City] before whom no self-respecting advocate or honest man wishes to plead." [80] *Appleton's Journal*, too, spoke repeatedly of municipal misgovernment — but always rather plaintively, as if Tammany's malfeasance were something like original sin, a heritage of the human race; in 1869 it presented a picture of cannibal society in South Africa under the heading "Consolations for Misgoverned New Yorkers" in order to demonstrate that there were conditions in the world worse than those in its own city.[81] When at last the *New York Times* began its epochal fight against the Ring in 1871, *Harper's Weekly* was the only periodical which supported it very actively.[82] The *Nation* de-

[76] *Galaxy*, III, 687 (March 15, 1867).
[77] *Punchinello*, I, 84 (May 7, 1870).
[78] *Century*, XXVII, 672 (March 1884).
[79] *North American Review*, CIX, 103 (July 1869).
[80] *Harper's Weekly*, XIV, 114 (February 19, 1870).
[81] *Appleton's Journal*, I, 249 (May 22, 1869).
[82] See vol. II, pp. 478–80.

fended the *Times*, but acted, in the main, as an onlooker in the fight.[83] The New York *Evangelist* disgraced itself by a spirited defense of Judge Hilton, one of the corrupt judges. After it was all over, and the rascals had been brought to justice, the *North American* detailed the whole history of the ring in a fine series called "An Episode in Municipal Government," by Charles F. Wingate.[84]

Yet one lingers over the odorous personalities of some of the thugs who looted New York with a kind of sadistic affection. They were such consummate rascals! Take Fisk, for example, whom Wingate calls "a coarse, jovial, noisy thief and black-guard — a thorough debauchee, without the conception of a moral idea . . . the characteristic product of one of the most singular periods in history." [85] In 1872 the fellow was murdered spectacularly on the great stairway of the Grand Central Hotel by a jealous rival for the favors of one of his paramours: nothing in Fisk's life became him like the leaving of it! And so *Appleton's Journal* printed a delightful obituary of him, containing these words, which go far toward showing why this age loved its villains and made the going hard for its reformers:

> Even the story of Aladdin ceases to seem impossible when we think of this illiterate Vermonter stepping almost without an interval from his peddler's cart to take the reins of a great corporation, to purchase today a fleet and tomorrow a theatre, to make today a panic and tomorrow a statute, to buy legislatures and prima donnas, to dazzle Wall Street with the brilliancy of his thefts and Central Park with the splendor of his equipages, to complement Sardanapalus with Robert Macaire.[86]

New York furnished the great show, but other cities were probably about as bad. Indeed, *Life* thought Chicago much worse; it said in 1883:

> Carter H. Harrison was re-elected Mayor of Chicago a fortnight ago, by the criminal classes of that city, against the earnest protest

---

[83] *Nation*, XIII, 18, 300 (July 13, November 9, 1871).
[84] See numbers for October 1874, January and July 1875, and October 1876.
[85] *North American Review*, CXXIII, 394 (October 1876).
[86] *Appleton's Journal*, VII, 134 (February 3, 1872).

of every decent journal, corporation and firm in Cook County. . . .
New York has woes and shames, but at their worst they are glories
by the side of the degradation of Chicago.[87]

POLITICAL AND ECONOMIC ISSUES

The tariff was a moot question throughout the period. The
tariff changes of 1870 and 1873 and the general revision ten
years later kept the debate alive. The *Princeton Review* carried
a notable series of articles by David A. Wells through the early
eighties. The *North American* had a distinguished symposium
on the subject in September and October 1884. The *American
Free Trader* (1882–84) was the monthly organ of the American
Free Trade League, of New York; Worthington C. Ford was
its editor, and such economists as Wells and W. G. Sumner were
contributors.

It was the *North American,* too, that invaluable reflector
during the latter half of our period of the political, economic,
and social trends, which gave repeated attention to the growing
antimonopoly movement. "Monopoly and anti-monopoly represent the two great tendencies of the time," said one writer in
1884.[88] The Western Union Company was the object of various
attacks,[89] and space was given to a joint debate on government
ownership of telegraph lines shortly after the operators' strike
of 1883.[90] There was another debate over the Standard Oil
Company's activities, in which the total capitalization of that
organization's various departments was given as over a hundred million dollars.[91] *Puck* satirized Jay Gould's monopolistic
tendencies by picturing Hades two years after Gould's arrival:
by that time Satan was doing the janitorial work and Gould had
the trident and a majority of the stock.[92] That was good fun,
but there was serious feeling behind it; observers generally felt
some alarm in the early eighties over that concentration of
wealth through monopolistic enterprises. Even in unexcitable

---

[87] *Life,* I, 195 (April 26, 1883).
[88] *North American Review,* CXXXVIII, 552 (June 1884).
[89] *Ibid.,* CXXXII, 369 (April 1881).
[90] *Ibid.,* CXXXIX, 66 (July 1884).
[91] *Ibid.,* CXXXVI, 200 (February 1883).
[92] *Puck,* September 19, 1883. Cartoon by Opper.

Lippincott's Edward C. Bruce answered the question "Is the Monopolist Among Us?" with a fairly definite "yes." [93]

Bruce was, moreover, rather alarmed at the increase of corporate wealth in few hands: it had "reared its mass before our eyes like one of those eruptive islands which shoot up from the surface of a landless sea." Howard Crosby, alluding in the *North American* to the contemporary discussions of the "dangerous classes" in the slums,[94] asserted emphatically: "The 'dangerous classes' among us are those who are engaged in amassing colossal fortunes." [95] And the *Century*, discussing editorially the abuses of "watered stock," consolidations, and "corners," observed at about the same time:

Of the gigantic fortunes now held in this country, not a few have been gotten by legal robbery. Twenty years ago our millionaires could have been counted on the fingers of four hands. Today their enumeration would carry us into the thousands. Since the system of robbery has been perfected about twenty men have amassed fortunes which, taken together, exceed the debt of the nation.[96]

Undoubtedly there were, even in conservative quarters, signs of what one writer called "a destructive hostility toward moneyed corporations." [97] The *Nation* satirized the "Silverman" who never spoke of "the Money Power" without "that wild look in his eye"; [98] and another observer, writing in the *New Englander*, found the word *monopoly* "of late used in various vague senses" referring to all concentrations of wealth.[99]

In 1879 Henry George published his *Progress and Poverty*, which the *Critic*, half converted, called a "deeply interesting, exceedingly able and glowing book," [100] and which marked, according to Richard T. Ely's judgment expressed some years later in the *Christian Union*, "a noteworthy epoch in the history of economic thought both in England and America." [101] A writer

[93] *Lippincott's*, XXXV, 443 (May 1885).   [94] See pp. 27–28.
[95] *North American Review*, CXXXVI, 350 (April 1883).
[96] *Century Magazine*, XXV, 615 (February 1883).
[97] *North American Review*, CXXXVI, 457 (May 1883).
[98] *Nation*, XXVI, 91 (February 7, 1878).
[99] *New Englander*, XLV, 493 (June 1886).
[100] *Critic*, I, 90 (April 9, 1881).
[101] *Johns Hopkins Studies in Historical and Political Science*, III, 246 (April 1885). The article had been published the year before in the *Christian Union*.

in the *Princeton Review* called George "comparatively obscure though very able" early in 1882; [102] but the next year Francis A. Walker, turning all his batteries on "Henry George's Social Fallacies" in the *North American Review*, said that the single-tax advocate was "greeted in crowded public meetings as the apostle of great sociological and economic reforms," but there was "no reason to suppose that his doctrines have yet deeply infected the public mind." [103] Walker's fire had been drawn by a series of articles by George in *Leslie's Illustrated Newspaper*, later gathered together in a book called *Social Problems*. In 1885 the *North American* featured a "conversation" between George and David Dudley Field; by that time the single-tax theory was a more or less familiar magazine topic. The *Free-Soiler* (1883–84) was the official organ of a single-tax association called the American Free-Soil Society.

The "silver question" was actively discussed throughout most of the postbellum period. The demonetization of 1873, the Bland-Allison Act of five years later, and the agitation for the repeal of the latter legislation which came to a head immediately after Cleveland's election were the high points in a long controversy. A writer in the *Bankers' Magazine* in 1882 found it necessary to apologize for discussing "The Silver Question" because "so much has been written upon this subject." [104] The *Bankers' Magazine* itself, seeing "the world's dislike to silver" growing apace, opposed bimetallism.[105] The *Nation*, too, ranged itself among "the friends of honest money," and argued for the repeal of the Bland Act.[106] J. Laurence Laughlin wrote of "The Silver Danger" in the *Atlantic Monthly*: he expected coinage of "Bland dollars" to bring about depreciation.[107] On the other hand, Senator N. P. Hill, of Colorado, mine operator and leader of the coinage group in Congress, wrote in the *North American* that "the majority of the people of this country desire that silver as well as gold should be coined, at least to the limited extent provided for by the Act of 1878," as a measure to prevent

---

[102] *Princeton Review*, 4th ser., IX, 142 (March 1882).
[103] *North American Review*, CXXXVII, 147 (August 1883).
[104] *Bankers' Magazine*, XXXVI, 913 (June 1882).
[105] *Ibid.*, XXXVII, 653 (March 1883).
[106] *Nation*, XL, 172 (February 26, 1885).
[107] *Atlantic Monthly*, LIII, 677 (May 1884).

the aggrandizement of wealth and the impoverishment of the masses.[108] The *North American* carried two symposia on the silver question in 1885. An article in the *International Review* by J. W. Soderholm, of London, advocated a bimetallic union.[109]

Civil service reform was another political question which received much attention in the periodicals. George William Curtis, editor of *Harper's Weekly*, was the leading figure in the movement, and the first president of the National Civil Service Reform League. The *Nation* was one of the earliest and most persistent fighters for the reform. The *Century Magazine* seldom let a month go by without an editorial on the subject in its "Topics of the Time" department. The *North American* published many discussions of the reform. The *Independent* and the *Christian Union* were behind the movement, while *Lippincott's* opposed it. The cause was difficult to promote, however, partly because there was nothing about it that enlisted popular enthusiasm. It did not have "even the recognition, much less the comprehension, of the mass of the people," said *Lippincott's* in 1880: it was "a question of the closet." [110] But the death of Garfield, himself a civil service reformer, at the hands of a disappointed office seeker served to bring the matter into the public consciousness. "It is to be hoped that none of his successors will surrender what he won at the cost of his life," said the *Century*.[111] A new régime came with the passage of the Pendleton Act in 1883 and the adoption of the merit system for New York in the same year. The Boston Civil Service Reform Association published the *Civil Service Record* 1881–92, issuing it first as a propaganda clip sheet for newspapers, but gradually making it into a more pretentious monthly organ of the movement.[112]

---

[108] *North American Review*, CXXXVII, 307 (October 1883).

[109] *International Review*, XIII, 154 (August 1882).

[110] *Lippincott's Magazine*, XXXII, 690 (December 1880).

[111] *Century Magazine*, XXIII, 467 (January 1882).

[112] It began in May 1881 as a single folio sheet printed on one side only; in December it became an eight-page quarto at twenty-five cents a year. Editors: Arthur Hobart, 1881–82; Bancroft C. Davis, 1882–83; William V. Kellen, 1883–86; Robert P. Clapp, 1886–89; Richard Henry Dana, 1889–92. In July 1892 it was merged with the Baltimore *Civil Service Reformer* (1885–92) to form *Good Government*, which continued the *Record's* numbering. After July 1897 it was published very irregularly, with long suspensions, simultaneously in Washington

THE GREAT PANIC

"A strange craziness is abroad in the land," noted the *Round Table* in 1866. "Some mysterious spirit of evil has led our people into the blindest, wildest infatuation . . . wild and foolish speculation. . . . At least half the people are living beyond their means." [113] The *Round Table* was not the only periodical that noted the extravagance, the madness for speculation, and the lack of foresight among the people; warnings abounded. "There are ominous signs in the financial sky," observed *Harper's Weekly*, also in 1866; "they mean that about these days it may be well to beware of stocks." [114] The *Nation's* repeated warnings about railroad investments have already been referred to.[115] Many of the periodicals harped on the necessity for the contraction of the currency and the resumption of specie payments. "With a return to specie payments," wrote E. H. Derby in the *Atlantic*, "our current expenses must fall from thirty to forty per cent, and we can well afford to resign any premium on gold we now enjoy." [116] But there was opposition to such a policy in the West. "The great cry in the Northwest is 'more currency,'" reported the *Iowa Homestead* in 1870, "and the currency tinkers at Washington are striving to satisfy the demand." [117]

Came Black Friday, September 24, 1869, when Gould and Fisk, "the most unscrupulous gamblers of Wall Street," attempted to "corner" the American gold supply. Though they were defeated by the government's sale of four million dollars' worth of gold in Wall Street, the purchase of legislation at

---

and New York. It was moved to New York in 1900, and in July 1901 resumed regular monthly publication. As the organ of the National Civil Service Reform League it had considerable importance. There is much by Carl Schurz, Theodore Roosevelt, and Charles J. Bonaparte. Editors: Francis E. Leupp, 1892–94; George McAneny, 1895–1901; Henry Grafton Chapman, 1902–06; Albert de Roode, 1907–11; Robert W. Belcher, 1911–13; George T. Keyes, 1914–16; William A. Bird IV, 1917–19; Harry W. Marsh, 1920–27; H. Eliot Kaplan, 1928–current.

[113] *Round Table*, III, 344 (June 2, 1866).
[114] *Harper's Weekly*, X, 34 (January 20, 1866).
[115] See pp. 122–23.
[116] *Atlantic Monthly*, XVII, 624 (May 1866).
[117] *Iowa Homestead*, February 25, 1870, p. 4.

Albany for their protection and their immunity in venal courts demonstrated the alliance between political corruptionists and the financial powers and emphasized the economic peril in which the whole country stood.[118]

Jay Cooke & Company closed their doors September 18, 1873, and thereafter the panic which had been so long threatening swept over the whole country, leaving its wreckage of bankruptcies, unemployment, strikes, and suffering behind it. The Chicago *Advance* thought the hard times a judgment on the country: the people were being punished for their "perfect intoxication" with luxury. "Simplicity has departed, principle has been undermined, and the very churches have lost the savor of godliness," it said; and it rejoiced that at least "the system of building railroads with borrowed money has come to a dead stop." [119] The *Advance* was not the only periodical that saw some connection between the sufferings of the country and its sins. The *American Journalist* remarked in 1875:

There never has been in this country such a universal and utter prostration of business as the past two years have witnessed. . . . And there never have been before in this country such malfeasance in office, such awful rottenness in politics, such abominable corruption. . . .[120]

Horace White, editor of the *Chicago Tribune*, wrote some five years later, just as the depression was about to loose its hold, an able article for the *Journal of Social Science* in which he reviewed the course of the panic and pointed out that during these years the country had accumulated "such a plethora and surplus of unused capital as was never before dreamed of on this virgin continent." [121] But this did not prevent great suffering among the unemployed. "Few phenomena of the age are more remarkable than the increase of tramps," remarked one of the leading fraternal organs of the country; "they throng our highways, steal rides upon the trains, burn their tobacco in our haystacks and barns, beg our victuals. . . . In this I include female tramps." [122] The *Nation* told of the tramp evil

[118] See *Harper's Weekly*, XIII, 659 (October 16, 1869).
[119] *Advance*, October 2, 1873, p. 9.
[120] *American Journalist*, IV, 665 (July 1875).
[121] *Journal of Social Science*, No. 9, pp. 117–131 (January 1878).
[122] *Masonic Review*, L, 364 (September 1877).

in Massachusetts, where there were "gangs of vagabonds following theft and beggary as a profession, camping together by scores in the woods, begging, stealing, drinking and fighting." [123]

A symposium on the resumption of specie payments in the *North American* for November 1877 was perhaps influential in that matter. Resumption came gradually.

> The event of the past month [said the *Galaxy* in June 1876] has been the return to specie payments as far as the fractional parts of a dollar are concerned. . . . It is real money, which we have not seen in our daily transactions for fifteen years; and its appearance has made a sensation. And that sensation has caused a sort of hoarding of the pretty, fresh, white silver circles.[124]

Nor did normalcy return with a bound; but, as the *Commercial and Financial Chronicle* observed in 1879, "with resumption the country entered on the broad road to prosperity." [125]

LABOR UNIONS

The organization of workers into unions made tremendous gains during the postwar period. "This is preëminently an age of labor agitation," observed *Appleton's Journal*.[126] The journalist Richard J. Hinton contributed a history of labor organization to the *Atlantic Monthly* in 1871 and in connection with it gave some contemporary statistics. "At the present time," he wrote, "there are in the United States thirteen national and international trades unions, having 992 branches, and a membership of about 300,000 persons." Of these, the Knights of Crispin, the shoe trades' union, was the strongest, followed by the iron molders' union, the typographical union, and the bricklayers' and coal miners' unions.[127] At the end of our period it was said in the *Century* that "nearly every trade now has its union — some local, some national. . . . A coalition has been formed, not yet fully perfected, for the union of them all." [128] This was to come the next year, as the American Federation of Labor. Meantime the Knights of Labor spread widely, especially

---

[123] *Nation*, XXVI, 50 (January 24, 1878).
[124] *Galaxy*, XXI, 864 (June 1876).
[125] *Commercial and Financial Chronicle*, XXIX, 53 (July 19, 1879).
[126] *Appleton's Journal*, VII, 610 (June 1, 1872).
[127] *Atlantic Monthly*, XXVII, 558 (May 1871).
[128] *Century*, XXXI, 53 (November 1885).

during the decade following the great strike of 1877; but as T. V. Powderly, master workman of the order, explained in the *North American Review*, the K. of L. was not a labor union.[129]

The general public was far from accepting the labor union, and there was much debate over its utility and necessity. "Labor unions are the greatest foe to the elevation of the laborer himself," wrote Simon Newcomb in the *Princeton Review*.[130] Periodicals were rather generally unsympathetic with the organization of labor.

On the other hand, there were some four hundred labor papers by 1885, and even an Associated Labor Press.[131] Many were organs of the national unions of the various trades; [132] some represented the Knights of Labor and other orders; some were papers specializing in news of the unions and labor activities in general. Many labor papers were local in scope, and many were short-lived. The *Workingmen's Advocate* (1864–79), of Chicago, was the official organ of the National Labor Union, the first federation of wide scope among American unions; Andrew C. Cameron was its editor and publisher during its last ten years and made it the foremost labor voice of the country. Charles McKnight's *People's Monthly* (1871–75) was a Pittsburgh family paper featuring labor matters. A more important Pittsburgh paper was the *National Labor Tribune* (1873–current), edited successively by John M. Davis and Thomas A. Armstrong.[133] It was the organ of the Amalgamated Iron and Steel Workers, and a K. of L. paper in the eighties. Boston *Equity* (1874–75) was "a journal of Christian labor reform"; it was succeeded by the *Labor Balance* (1877–79). These two journals were edited by the Reverend Jesse H. Jones; Judge T. Wharton Collens, of New Orleans, and Edward H. Rogers, of Chelsea, Massachusetts, were leading contributors.[134] The *Sovereigns of Industry Bulletin* (1784–80) was founded

[129] *North American Review*, CXXXV, 124 (August 1882).

[130] *Princeton Review*, 4th ser., VI, 245 (September 1880).

[131] See *Johns Hopkins Studies in Historical and Political Science*, III, 285 (April 1885). These papers on "Recent American Socialism" were originally published in the *Christian Union* in 1884.

[132] See footnotes on pp. 125–26 and 129.

[133] Later editors were Thomas Telford and J. H. Vitchesbain.

[134] Letters from Rogers in the possession of the Boston Public Library.

in Worcester, Massachusetts, by R. H. Thomas and John Orvis, who soon moved it to Mechanicsburg, Pennsylvania. The *Journal of United Labor* (1880–1918) was begun as a monthly by the Knights of Labor at Marblehead, Massachusetts, but it soon moved to Philadelphia and became a bimonthly. It was edited by the Grand Secretary of the order, but Powderly was a regular contributor and the force behind it.[135] The Denver *Labor Enquirer* (1882–89), Joseph Buchanan editor, was first affiliated with the Knights of Labor, and later with the American Federation of Labor. Two influential printers' labor journals were the *Union Printer* (1882–93), of New York, and the Washington *Craftsman* (1883–91); the latter was the official organ of the International Typographical Union. *John Swinton's Paper* (1883–87) was the weekly organ of the social and economic views of an able journalist of the period; Swinton advocated the cause of labor, and its organization and federation, in forcibly written editorials.[136]

Closely related were the papers affiliated with movements for socialism, communism, and anarchy. The Oneida *Circular*,[137] chief communistic organ, was succeeded by the *American Socialist* (1876–79), also published by the Oneida group. Alcander Longley's *Communist* (1868–1917), of St. Louis, was published 1872–77 at Friendship Community, near Buffalo, Missouri. It was taken over by the Altruist Community of St. Louis in 1885 and became the *Altruist*. An adherent of the Social-Labor party, Longley engaged in a number of Utopian projects. The *Socialist* was begun in New York in 1876 by Hugh McGregor, as an organ of the Social-Democratic Working-Men's party. After four or five months it changed its name to the *Labor Standard*, deserting socialism in 1877 for federation

---

[135] It became a weekly in 1887, and in the following year the title became *Journal of the Knights of Labor*. It was changed to a monthly again in 1898, having been moved to Washington. It was a football of K. of L. politics for many years. After James R. Sovereign had displaced Powderly as General Master Workman, it attacked the latter, then a gold advocate. It advocated at various periods the eight-hour day, the single tax, and free silver. It supported Bryan for president in 1896. At one time it made Eugene V. Debs a hero, but later repudiated him. John W. Hayes was its editor in its later years.

[136] See Samuel Gompers, *Seventy Years of Life and Labor* (New York, 1925), I, 321.

[137] See vol. II, p. 207.

movements among labor unions, with J. P. McDonnell as editor; it was later moved to Paterson, New Jersey, where it was the "mainstay" of the International Labor Union movement.[138] It survived until 1900.

A number of Socialist-Labor papers were begun in 1876 and 1877, but none of them lasted more than a year or two.[139] The party founded the *National Socialist* (1878–79) at New York with John McIntosh as editor, but the paper's espousal of the Greenback movement caused it to be transferred to Frank Hirth in Chicago before a year was up.

Among the editors who adopted the doctrines of anarchy in these years was Benjamin R. Tucker. Tucker edited the *Word* in 1877, while its proprietor was in prison. The *Word* (1872–93), of Princeton, Massachusetts, was the libertarian organ of the American Labor Reform League; Ezra H. Heywood was its owner and the president of the League. Having acquired a taste for editorship, Tucker immediately established the *Radical Review* at New Bedford and published four quarterly numbers of it from May 1877 through February 1878. It was an excellent journal while it lasted, numbering D. A. Wasson, John Weiss, Sidney H. Morse, and John Fiske among its contributors. The philosophy of Proudhon was its ruling force, and "Down with authority!" its war cry. Then in 1881 Tucker established his *Liberty* (1881–1908), which for a quarter of a century advocated anarchy, free love, and other radical doctrines. *Liberty* was a fortnightly of four pages quarto which sold for fifty cents a year.

A similar paper came from Valley Falls, Kansas. It was called *Lucifer, the Light-Bearer,* and was produced weekly from 1880 to 1907 by Moses Harmon and E. C. Walker. Like *Liberty*, it advocated both anarchy and free love; and its editors apparently practiced the latter doctrine, though Mrs. Harmon eventually married Walker legally.[140]

---

[138] See Gompers, *op. cit.*, I, 128, 212.

[139] See Morris Hillquit, *History of Socialism in the United States* (New York, 1910, revised edition), pp. 204, 206.

[140] Harmon moved the paper to Topeka in 1890. January 6, 1897, he began a third series in Chicago, changing it from folio to quarto and devoting it chiefly to "sexology" — by which he meant sex freedom. Harmon was convicted of obscenity in the federal courts in 1904, and *Lucifer* was repeatedly held by postal

Truth (1882–84), a San Francisco "journal for the poor," was a weekly anarchistic propagandist of violence edited by Burnette G. Haskell. Finally, the Chicago *Alarm*, whose history belongs chiefly to the following period, was begun late in 1884 by A. R. Parsons.

PROPAGANDA, STRIKES, DYNAMITE

These and other radical and libertarian journals [141] purveyed the doctrines being currently bruited about the world — doctrines emanating from such sources as Proudhon, Bakunin, Marx, and Engels. Socialistic movements of the seventies were largely within the large German immigrant section of the population, and understanding of the whole complex labor movement as a world phenomenon made its way but slowly into the American consciousness. D. A. Wasson, one of the ablest essayists of the decade, wrote a rather unsympathetic history of the First International for the *Journal of Social Science* in 1873.[142] E. L. Godkin recorded the fact in the *North American Review* for July 1867, that "during the last year the industry of the four great manufacturing countries of the world — the United States, England, France and Belgium — has been in a state bordering on disorganization owing to incessant strikes." [143]

Strikes more or less violent occurred in many American industries from one end of the period to the other. Powderly, in the fourth number of the *Journal of United Labor*, tells of forty strikes during the first six months of 1880 and advocates the purchase of guns with which to fight the troops sent to quell strikers.[144] And this in spite of the fact that Powderly and the great order which he headed were not committed to the strike as a fundamental or permanent remedy for labor evils: "I fail

---

authorities. During part of 1905–06 it was marked "Censored by Postal Authorities before Delivery." The paper was dated (as was *Liberty*) by a chronology beginning with the burning of Bruno in 1600; thus 1897 was 297 E. M. (Era of Man). It was followed by the *American Journal of Eugenics.*

[141] See pp. 88–89 for liberal journals of religion. One libertarian paper, *Woodhull & Claflin's Weekly*, proved a divisive element in the International in America. See p. 446.

[142] *Journal of Social Science*, No. 5, pp. 109–121 (1873).

[143] *North American Review*, CV, 177 (July 1867).

[144] *Journal of United Labor*, I, 37 (August 15, 1880).

to see any lasting good in a strike," wrote Powderly in the *North American*.[145] This was not, however, a popular doctrine among labor leaders, and it eventually caused the decline of the Knights of Labor. The annoyance caused the public by multiple strikes had much to do with the general animosity to the union movement reflected in a majority of the periodicals. *Harper's Weekly* and the *Nation,* to take but two convenient examples, called loudly for federal intervention in the coal miners' strike in Pennsylvania in 1869 and the general strike in 1877.

One of the phases of the labor movement which aroused popular indignation was the violence of the "Molly Maguires" in the Pennsylvania coal fields. John T. Morse, Jr., writing in the *American Law Review* of conditions in five eastern Pennsylvania anthracite mining counties, said:

From their dark and mysterious recesses there came forth to the outside world an appalling series of tales of murder, of arson, and violent crime of every description. It seemed that no respectable man could be safe there, for it was from the respectable classes that the victims were by preference selected; nor could anyone tell from day to day whether he might not be marked for sure and sudden destruction. Only the members of one calling could feel any certainty as to their fate. These were the superintendents and bosses in the collieries; they could all rest assured that their days would not be long in the land. Everywhere and at all times attacked, beaten, and shot down, on the public highways and in their own homes, in solitary places and in the neighborhood of crowds, these doomed men continued to fall in frightful succession beneath the hands of assassins.[146]

It was the Pinkerton Detective Agency that finally accumulated evidence on which the "Molly Maguires" were brought to trial in 1875, convicted, and executed.[147]

A climax in strikes came with the great revolt of railroad employes in 1877, and the sympathetic strikes which accompanied it; this outbreak has been discussed in connection with railroad affairs.[148] But at the end of our period, it was evident

---

[145] *North American Review,* CXXXV, 124 (August 1882).

[146] *American Law Review,* XI, 233 (January 1877).

[147] *McClure's Magazine,* IV, 91 (December 1894) — "Stories from the Archives of the Pinkerton Detective Agency."

[148] See pp. 124–25.

to many observers that war clouds were gathering for another general conflict. Lyman Abbott, who followed such matters weekly in the *Christian Union*, wrote for the *Century* in 1885 an article showing both sides of the labor quarrel arming for conflict.[149] The *Alarm* was ringing violently: "Workingmen of America, learn the manufacture and use of dynamite — a weapon of the weak against the strong, the poor against the rich. Then use it unstintedly, unsparingly!" [150] And from the Pacific Coast: "*Truth* is five cents a copy and dynamite forty cents a pound. . . . Arm! I say, to the teeth! for the Revolution is upon you!" [151] And again: "Killing, burning — all means are justified." [152] The denouement waited upon the first years of a new period.

[149] *Century*, XXXI, 53 (November 1885).
[150] *Alarm*, November 8, 1884, p. 2.
[151] *Truth*, November 17, 1883, p. 2.
[152] *Ibid.*, November 3, 1883, p. 2.

CHAPTER XI

A POSTSCRIPT ON SOME FEATURES
OF THE PERIOD

THE preoccupation of the postbellum period with matters of manners and morals has been evident on many of the preceding pages of this volume. It has been noted in fiction, in poetry, in essays. Sketches of travel become studies in comparative manners, with interpolated bits of scenery. Politics center largely upon the moralties, or the want of them. Criticism is warped by ethics. All this, while it is true more or less in any period, was stressed in the one which followed the Civil War because a perceptible shift in manners and morals was then taking place.

"Puritanism" was being attacked even in its strongholds. It was possible for a woman to write in the *Atlantic Monthly* in 1868: "Puritanism has so long held us in rigid subjection, depriving us of even innocent amusements, that human nature is sure to be revenged. The pendulum will swing as far to one extreme as it has swung to the other."[1] She was talking of the cancan and of naughty plays — not approving them, indeed, but accepting them without too much fuss as a part of contemporary life. In 1882 Walt Whitman defended the frank acknowledgments of sex in literature and art, and the defence was published in the *North American Review*.[2] It is true that the Chicago *Current* asserted, in condemning Swinburne's verse at the end of our period: " 'Puritan' is an epithet of honor in this day and generation";[3] but the significant thing about this assertion is that the time had come when it was necessary to make it.

That the incursion of modern scientific ideas had something to do with the breakdown of the older religious taboos is indubitable, but there was little of the scientific spirit really per-

---

[1] *Atlantic Monthly*, XXI, 274 (March 1868).
[2] *North American Review*, CXXXIV, 546 (June 1882).
[3] *Current*, II, 77 (August 2, 1884).

ceptible in the popular thinking. In the special journals, yes; but not in the great mass of general and popular periodical literature. The editor of *Appleton's* was beyond question correct when he said that "the state of mind in this country . . . favors the multiplication of all kinds of mental extravagance." [4] This has been noted in the field of religious periodicals, where spiritualistic and millennial faiths were active; in that of medicine, where quackeries flourished intermittently; as well as in that of political and social reform, some of whose mutations and sports have just been noted.

Science played its part in the weakening of the power of religious sanctions, but other factors were active in bringing about that freedom of manners which gave alarm to the censorious in these years. The reaction from the tension of the war, the psychology of any postbellum era, was doubtless one influence on these modern *Relaxati*. There was also a late phase of frontier crudeness coming in contact with imported sophistication, the fusion taking place under the heat of sudden riches. Probably all these elements functioned in the process, and more. At any rate, the critics and carpers generally agreed that manners and morals were in a bad way. As the editor of the *Galaxy* put it, mildly enough: "Our manners and the tone of our society have suffered a great and widespread deterioration." [5]

MANNERS

There was, for instance, the "Girl of the Period." The phrase came from some bitterly satiric sketches in the *Saturday Review*, of London; but the skits were appropriate enough to American society, and the term, introduced by stage and press, quickly caught on. The *Round Table*, in the same year in which these sketches appeared, published a series of its own on types of American girls — "nice," "gushing," "fast," and so on. The "Girl of the Period" was, according to these satirists, scheming, cold-hearted, frivolous, sophisticated. The brilliant Eugene Benson wrote in *Appleton's* that modern society girls "do not afford us much sympathy and intelligent pleasure" [6] — *us* be-

[4] *Appleton's Journal*, I, 57 (April 10, 1869).
[5] *Galaxy*, V, 255 (February 1868).
[6] *Appleton's Journal*, III, 51 (January 8, 1870).

ing the lords of creation. Of course it was all part of the ancient war of the sexes, at this time somewhat emphasized by the woman's rights movement, and doubtless most of these critics were base traducers; but that the sentimental, shrinking-violet, duty-bound type of female, always ready to faint in a crisis, always painfully modest, was giving way to a more frankly self-reliant, athletic, and selfish girl was indicated on every hand. The *Galaxy* thought "the 'Girl of the Period' is apt to be what the Boy of the Period makes her." [7] There was truth in that, but it would have been better to say that she was what the changing times made her.

American behavior, public and private, in society, office, and home, was a topic of never-ceasing interest. Much of the magazine comment on this subject took English and French criticism as its text. In 1872 *Frank Leslie's Lady's Magazine* published a series of pictures illustrating "American Manners and Customs as Depicted by the European Press." The pictures are good fun. They deal with such supposed Americanisms as the prominence of the "spittoon" as a parlor ornament, universal smoking, chewing and drinking by both sexes, and the common use of the Bloomer costume.[8] But although the magazines might be by turns amused or angry over foreign comment on American idiosyncrasies, they were all more or less anxious to reform the bad manners of their countrymen. A schoolmasterish attitude was often adopted by the *Galaxy*, the *Round Table*, the *Nation*, and *Appleton's*, and to a less degree by *Scribner's*, the *Atlantic*, *Lippincott's*, and *Putnam's*. Charles Astor Bristed, discussing "what Sir Walter Scott called 'the manners or want of manners peculiar to Americans' " takes occasion to say:

> But after all, the reader may ask, "What's the use of discussing this matter? What have we to do with manners anyway? Are they not an institution belonging to 'the effete cockroaches of Europe,' as Mrs. Stowe felicitously puts it?" Reader, at the risk of boring you further, I must say that you are greatly mistaken if you think the subject of no consequence.[9]

[7] *Galaxy*, VI, 578 (October 1868).
[8] *Frank Leslie's Lady's Magazine*, XVI, 72 .(January 1865).
[9] *Galaxy*, XV, 181 (February 1873).

This was the creed of the magazines, and they preached it in and out of season and in many ways. Ignorance of etiquette, "tall talk," faults of taste, crudities developed by a highly individualistic pioneer society, were firmly and sometimes severely condemned. *Appleton's Journal* advocated teaching manners in the school.[10] The *Galaxy* published a number of articles on "The Art of Dining," most of them by Pierre Blot, a famous French chef of the time. One finds comment on such diverse subjects as shaving by barbers, railway-train manners, serenades, extravagant fashions, chaperones, and smoking, drinking, and swearing. Mrs. Stowe's "Chimney Corner" papers in the *Atlantic* dealt largely with such topics, as did her essays in the *Christian Union*. The urbane papers by George William Curtis in *Harper's Bazar* called "Manners Upon the Road" debated similar matters.

The discussions of burlesque shows which we have mentioned [11] had more to do with manners and morals than with art, and many of the articles on the "Woman Question" dealt primarily with manners. The Beecher-Tilton scandal of 1874–76, by all odds the greatest marital scandal of American history, furnished the text for much national analysis of social customs. Anthony Comstock's Society for the Suppression of Vice had been founded in 1873 and within a decade had destroyed the plates of 163 "obscene books" and "more than twenty-five tons of contraband matter." [12] Comstock played an important part in the suppression of *Woodhull & Claflin's Weekly*. His name had already become a symbol by the end of our period: *Judge* was calling him "a cheap and dirty tyrant, a sneak and a hypocrite." [13] In short, those twins that we call manners and morals were cutting up all kinds of didoes and shocking now the "high-toned" and now the "unco' guid."

POLITE SPEECH

Proper speech as a phase of good manners received a surprising amount of attention in the period. The editors and their public were interested less in the strictly philological aspects of

[10] *Appleton's Journal*, V, 685 (June 10, 1871).   [11] See pp. 206–08.
[12] *North American Review*, CXXXV, 489 (November 1882).
[13] *Judge*, April 1, 1882, p. 2.

the subject than in speech usages as a means of correct social intercourse. The *Galaxy* published over 450 pages of discussion of words and usages in less than twelve years of life, most of it by Richard Grant White. The *Nation* published Fitzedward Hall's replies, and the sanguinary war that ensued sometimes left something to be desired on the score of manners. The *Round Table* published a long series by G. Washington Moon, of the *Dean's English* fame. A series of "Hints on Language" appeared in *Godey's* in 1871–72. Indeed most general magazines gave attention to both popular and literary speech.

Many were the discussions of particular words. *Scientist* is under White's ban,[14] and *humanitarian* is questioned.[15] *Female*, after a long campaign by Mrs. Hale, of *Godey's*, is no longer *au fait* for *woman*. But *high-toned* is in excellent standing. "Anything that is admirable is nowadays said in slang phrase to be *dusty*," wrote George Wakeman in *Appleton's*, and he found classical lineage for such other slang words as *deadbeat*, *absquatulate* ("in the sense of leave"), and *skedaddle*.[16] But the periodicals which yield the richest treasure to the seeker after the slang of the day, especially of the urban sort, are the *National Police Gazette*, *Day's Doings*, and their kind. There one finds that *dizzy blonde* and *racket* (a swindling scheme) go back to the eighties; *the fancy* were followers of the ring; *fly* and *flash* were adjectives applied to "fast" gentry.

TEMPERANCE AND PROHIBITION

One of the most important of the reform movements of the period, enlisting far more adherents than the woman's rights crusade,[17] was the campaign for the prohibition of the liquor traffic. The number of temperance periodicals increased rapidly in the early eighties. Ayer's *Directory* for 1886 listed 134; 28 new ones had begun in 1885 and about as many the year before. Of these perhaps a fourth were "third-party prohibition" newspapers. Evidently the *Chautauquan* was right in speaking of the "rapidly gathering strength" of that cause in 1882.[18]

[14] *Galaxy*, XVII, 92 (January 1874).
[15] *Ibid.*, XVII, 181 (February 1874).
[16] *Appleton's Journal*, III, 133 (January 29, 1870).   [17] See pp. 90–96.
[18] *Chautauquan*, III, 56 (October 1882).

The leading temperance journals were the Philadelphia *Templar's Magazine;* [19] the *National Temperance Advocate* (1866–current), of New York; the Chicago *Lever* (1878–98), which was published during its first three years in Grand Rapids, Michigan, and was finally merged with the *Voice*; the Chicago *Union Signal* (1874–current); and the New York *Voice* (1884–1906). The *Union Signal* began as the *Woman's Temperance Union*, Jennie F. Willing, editor. Its name was later shortened to *Our Union*, and it was merged in 1883 with Mary B. Willard's *Signal* (founded in 1880 by Mrs. Matilda B. Carse), taking over the latter's editor and numbering. Mrs. Willard was a sister-in-law of the famous president of the W. C. T. U., and that organization purchased the *Union Signal* in 1910. The *Voice* began as a campaign daily, but continued in 1885 as a strong weekly. It was Funk & Wagnall's first periodical and gained a considerable circulation largely by generous free distribution financed by enemies of the "rummies." [20] The *National Anti-Slavery Standard* [21] became a temperance journal in its latter years, as the *National Standard*. Others were mainly local and state organs.[22]

The religious journals lent tremendous strength to the prohibition movement, though some of them were indifferent or opposed to it. The *New Englander* had an article headed "Prohibition Not Desirable" in 1885, in which the experiences of prohibition states were shown in unfavorable light.[23] The *Catholic World* said that its church "does not accept prohibition as a panacea for intemperance." [24] There were, however, a few Catholic temperance papers, chiefly organs of the Catholic

[19] See vol. II, p. 210.

[20] It published some miscellany not connected with the temperance cause, such as the "Samanthy Allen" sketches. It became *New York Voice* in 1896, *New York Voice and Chicago Lever* in 1899, and *New Voice* (Chicago) in 1902. In 1906 it was merged with the New York *Defender*.

[21] See vol. II, pp. 140–41.

[22] Some of the longest-lived were: *New Jersey Temperance Gazette* (1869–1911), Tom's River, Camden; *Living Issue* (1873–86), Utica, New York City; *Temperance Benefit* (1875–87), Easton, Pennsylvania; *Minneapolis Review* (1875–90), called *Northwestern Prohibitionist* 1888–90; *Washingtonian* (1876–93), Chicago; *Temperance Cause* (1878–1930), Boston.

[23] *New Englander*, XLIV, 706 (September 1885).

[24] *Catholic World*, XXXVII, 852 (September 1883).

Total Abstinence Union.[25] Among general magazines there was a tendency to keep hands off, though most of them were rather clearly against the proposed prohibitory amendment and usually against teetotalism. Articles of the antiprohibitory sort appeared in *Harper's Monthly*, the *Atlantic*, the *Galaxy*, and *Putnam's*. *Arthur's Home Magazine* was strongly against "the curse of the liquor trade" and carried a department called "The Reformer" which was largely devoted to the prohibition cause. *Dio Lewis's Monthly*,[26] like most of the physical culture and health magazines, advocated temperance without absolute prohibition.

There were some antiprohibition periodicals, such as the Chicago *Champion of Freedom and Right* (1878–1929), latterly called the *Champion of Fair Play*, edited for many years by R. J. Halle; and the Detroit *Public Leader* (1874–95). The brewers' journals [27] gave more or less space to fighting the reformers.

OTHER REFORM MOVEMENTS

A second series of the *Anti-Tobacco Journal* was published at Fitchburg, Massachusetts, in 1872–73.[28] James Parton, answering negatively his question "Does It Pay to Smoke?" in the *Atlantic Monthly*, acknowledged that the use of tobacco had "made bold and rapid encroachments of late years"; he was sure, however, that the "Coming Man" (almost as much a catchword in those days as the "Girl of the Period") would not smoke, simply because it was bad for him physically and the best men of the past had not been smokers. Parton boasted of having cured himself of smoking by the curious device of taking whisky whenever he was tempted to try a puff of the noxious weed.[29]

Henry Bergh's crusade against cruelty to animals in New York and the nation attracted attention largely because of Bergh's aggressive methods. The *Galaxy* poked fun at him, but

[25] See Apollinaris W. Baumgartner, *Catholic Journalism in the United States* (New York, 1931), p. 30.

[26] See *Dio Lewis' Monthly*, II, 46 (January 1884).

[27] See p. 135.

[28] The first series consisted of two volumes 1859–64.

[29] *Atlantic Monthly*, XXI, 129–145 (February 1868). *Lippincott's Magazine* published an answer to Parton, II, 147 (August 1868).

Harper's Weekly pointed out that "cock and dog fights take place almost every night in New York" and that "car and stage horses" were treated cruelly.[30] The Society for the Prevention of Cruelty to Animals was founded in 1866 with Bergh as president. *Our Dumb Animals* was begun in Boston in 1868 by George T. Angell and is still issued; the *National Humane Journal* (1872–1917) was founded in Chicago a few years later by Albert W. Landon; and the *Ark* was published briefly in Boston in 1875 for the same cause.

The *Advocate of Peace* [31] continued on its way, joined by the *Messenger of Peace* (1870–1931), begun at Richmond, Indiana, but more recently published at St. Joseph, Missouri. The Philadelphia *Peacemaker* (1883–1914) was long edited by Alfred H. Love.

Spelling reform made some converts. A freakish little magazine by T. R. Vickroy, of St. Louis, called the *Fonetic Techer* was published briefly in 1879. It proposed not only spelling reform but a "speshl fonetic alfabet."

A much more important crusade was that which was led against easy divorce. The subject was especially lively in the last three or four years of our period. Articles in the *Princeton Review*, the *New Englander*, the *Century*, and other stalwart journals deplored the increases in the divorce ratio; but Edward Quincy put himself on record as favoring easier divorce laws in the *International Review*,[32] and Elizabeth Cady Stanton wrote on "The Need for Liberal Divorce Laws" in the *North American*.[33] Howells' *A Modern Instance* was printed serially in the *Century* in 1882, and the editor saw fit to reprint in his own department, and heartily to commend, a speech of one of the characters which states the novel's thesis against divorce.[34] *Puck* was worried about what a much-divorced lady would do when she went to heaven, if she did: it pictured the divorcee's dilemma as half a dozen angel-husbands fly toward her with outstretched wings when she enters the golden portal.[35]

[30] *Harper's Weekly*, XI, 121 (February 23, 1867).
[31] See vol. II, p. 211.
[32] *International Review*, XIV, 128 (February–March 1883).
[33] *North American Review*, CXXXIX, 234 (September 1884).
[34] *Century*, XXIV, 941 (October 1882).
[35] *Puck*, January 22, 1879.

Many pages were printed in the magazines exposing and attacking the practice of polygamy in Utah; the passage of the Edmunds Act of 1882 was doubtless both cause and result of this phase of periodical literature. The Mormon immigration of the seventies — evidence that Mormonism was "a living, growing faith," [36] to be taken seriously — amazed and alarmed many observers. The *Anti-Polygamy Standard* (1880–83), of Salt Lake City, was an eight-page folio of no very great importance.

Though the great city as a problem — "the curse and the puzzle of our civilization" [37] — would seem to have fully emerged in this period, the fight against improper living conditions in populous centers was not yet prominent in the magazines. Much was printed of picturesque and mildly sensational aspects of the slums, of "the dangerous classes," and of "night life in New York"; [38] but the general magazines closed their eyes and their pages, as a rule, to the more sordid parts of the story. Such things did not make proper reading. "There is no paper — even the so-called police and sensational journals — that would dare print the facts, as reporters know them, of tenement life in this city"; thus spoke *Puck* in 1879, in one of its serious moments.[39] Prostitution was a problem scarcely mentionable. O. B. Frothingham pointed out in the *Nation* that it could not be discussed in the pulpit.[40] *Woodhull & Claflin's Weekly* talked about it frankly and frequently, as did some other women's reform journals. Perhaps the best discussion of it in the magazines of the period was Helen Campbell's "Studies in the Slums" in *Lippincott's* of 1883. The American Association for the Promotion of Social Science was organized immediately after the war and began to issue its proceedings in the *Journal of Social Science* (1869–1909) a few years later.[41] The National Conference of Charities and Correction was organized in 1874,

---

[36] *Appleton's Journal*, VIII, 470 (October 26, 1872).
[37] Charles Nordhoff in *North American Review*, CXIII, 321 (October 1871).
[38] See pp. 27–28.
[39] *Puck*, March 5, 1879, p. 3.   [40] *Nation*, IV, 220 (March 14, 1867).
[41] Issued irregularly, less frequently than quarterly, in forty-six volumes, in New York. Frank B. Sanborn, secretary, was editor, 1874–97. It had many distinguished contributors. A single-tax debate (October 1890) and another on free silver (November 1895) are notable.

and various state boards of public charities were formed in the seventies; their proceedings were usually published in annual numbers. There were several periodicals issued by city missions, such as the *Voice from the Old Brewery* (1861–current) of the Five-Points Mission in New York, called since 1898 by the less picturesque title of the *Monthly Echo*.

Prison reform was discussed in the proceedings of these charity boards, and in the Pennsylvania Prison Society's *Journal of Prison Discipline and Philanthropy*.[42] Charles Dudley Warner championed the new plan of the indeterminate sentence in the *North American* and *Harper's*.[43] Abolition of contract labor in the New York prisons furnished an issue discussed in the *Nation* and other journals. The state of common jails, "little in advance of those of fifty years ago" was deplored in the *Andover Review* and in the *Nation*.[44] One of the earliest of prisoners' periodicals was the *Summary*, published by the State Reformatory at Elmira, New York (1883–85).

Finally, reform in the treatment of the Indians, brought to popular notice by Helen Hunt Jackson's *A Century of Dishonor* and *Ramona*, was the subject of occasional articles. The Washington *Council Fire* (1878–89) was devoted to Indian rights.

SECRET SOCIETIES

In spite of attacks on them by Moody and other religionists, the secret societies flourished as never before. The Masons and the Odd Fellows were especially successful. Charles W. Moore's *Freemason's Monthly Magazine* pointed out that Masonry was "increasing in numbers with unprecedented rapidity" in 1867.[45] Of the many Masonic journals founded in our period,[46] the most important were the Philadelphia *Keystone* (1867–1905), a weekly folio; J. F. Brennan's Quarto Series of the *American Freemason* (1868–70), Cincinnati, successor of an *American*

[42] See vol. II, p. 212.
[43] *North American Review*, CXL, 291 (April 1885); *Harper's Magazine*, LXXII, 444 (February 1886).
[44] *Andover Review*, IV, 125 (August 1885).
[45] *Freemason's Monthly Magazine*, XXVII, 2 (November 1867).
[46] See vol. II, pp. 214–15, for Masonic journals founded in the preceding period and persisting to this time. See also the checklist of the Masonic Library of Cedar Rapids, Iowa, and Josiah H. Drummond, *Masonic Historical and Bibliographical Memoranda* (Brooksville, Kentucky, 1882, Second Edition).

Freemason published in New York by the same editor before the war; *Mackey's National Freemason* (1871–74), Washington, a monthly of high grade by Albert G. Mackey, one of the most famous of American Masons; and the *Liberal Freemason* (1877–91), Boston, by Alfred F. Chapman. The *Christian Cynosure* (1868–current) was and is an anti-Masonic journal published in Chicago.

Among the score or more of journals devoted to the I. O. O. F. may be mentioned the *Odd Fellows' Companion* (1865–82), of Columbus, edited by Henry Lendenberg; the *Odd Fellows' Talisman* (1868–1918), of Indianapolis, by John Reynolds; and the *New Age* (1865–95), of San Francisco, by Frank B. Austin and later W. F. Norcross.

The Ancient Order of United Workmen had a number of periodicals, most of them founded late in the seventies. Chief of them were the St. Louis *Overseer* (1879–1924); the *Pacific States Watchman* (1879–96), of San Francisco; the *Anchor and Shield* (1880–1918), of Paris, Illinois; and the *Empire State Workman* (1883–1910), of New York and later Buffalo. The Knights of Pythias had a score of periodical organs, of which the *Pythian Journal* (1874–1933) of Indianapolis, had the largest circulation. The Knights of Honor had several journals, led by the *Knights of Honor Reporter* (1875–1915), of Boston. Besides these, there were journals to serve the Ancient Order of Hibernians, the Chosen Friends, the Druids, the Foresters, the Knights of Maccabees, the Knights of the Golden Cross, the Knights of the Golden Eagle, the Knights of the Golden Rule, the Knights of St. George, the Legion of Honor, the Legion of the Red Cross, the Order of Harugari, the Red Men, the Royal Arcanum, the Sons of America, the Sons of Hermann, and the Sons of St. George.

SUPPLEMENT

SKETCHES OF CERTAIN IMPORTANT MAGAZINES
WHICH FLOURISHED 1865–1885

For an explanation of the ordering of the materials of this work into parts and supplements, the reader is referred to the Preface of Volume II.

The history of the *Saturday Evening Post* has been postponed to the final volume because it was incomparably more important after 1897 than before. Similarly, the following magazines which were founded in the early eighties had far less weight before 1885 than afterward and are therefore reserved for later discussion: *Andover Review, Argosy, Brooklyn Magazine, Forum, Journal of the American Medical Association, Ladies' Home Journal, Life, New England Magazine, Outing, Science, Woman's Home Companion.*

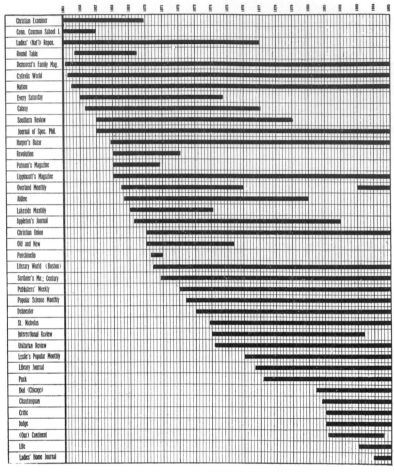

CHRONOLOGICAL CHART OF AMERICAN MAGAZINES 1865–1885
The following magazines were published during the whole of the period:

American Agriculturist
American Journal of Medical Sciences
American Journal of Science
American Railroad Journal
Bibliotheca Sacra
Church Review
Eclectic Magazine
Friend

Friends' Review
Godey's Lady's Book
Home Journal
Hunt's Merchants' Magazine
Independent
Journal of Franklin Institute
Littell's Living Age
Mercersburg Review
Methodist Quarterly Review

National Police Gazette
New Englander
New York Ledger
North American Review
Peterson's Ladies' Magazine
Princeton Review
Saturday Evening Post
Scientific American
Youth's Companion

THE ROUND TABLE [1]

IN DECEMBER 1863 Charles H. Sweetser, who had been graduated the preceding year from Amherst College, and his elder brother Henry E., who was night editor of the *New York World,* began a weekly journal of opinion in New York under the name of the *Round Table.* It was a large quarto of sixteen pages, priced at $6.00 a year. "Politics, the arts, literature, everything that can legitimately enter into the table-talk of a refined and intelligent circle" were declared to be the province of the new paper.[2]

A large part of it was written by the editors, and volunteer contributions were solicited. It was not long until the controversial spirit of the *Round Table* had developed a flourishing department of letters addressed to the paper. "Instead of organizing a regular corps of editors," it said at the end of its first brief series, "the columns of the paper were thrown open to all who chose to write for them." [3] One of the most important services performed by the *Round Table* was the gathering together of what was apparently a rather informal staff of cor-

[1] TITLE: *The Round Table.* Subtitles: (1) *A Weekly Record of the Notable, the Useful and the Tasteful,* 1863–64; (2) *A Saturday Review of Literature, Society and Art,* 1866–67; (3) *A Saturday Review of Politics, Literature, Society and Art,* 1867–68; (4) *A Saturday Review of Politics, Finance, Literature, Society and Art,* 1868–69.

FIRST ISSUE: December 19, 1863. LAST ISSUE: July 3, 1869.

PERIODICITY: Weekly. I, December 19, 1863–June 11, 1864; II, June 18–July 23, 1864, and September 9–December 30, 1865; III, January 6–July 28, 1866; IV, August 4–December 29, 1866; V–IX, regular semiannual volumes, January 5, 1867–June 26, 1869; X, July 3, 1869, only. Suspended July 30, 1864–September 2, 1865. Vol. II begins new paging and "New Series" with number for September 9, 1865.

PUBLISHERS: H. E. and C. H. Sweetser, New York, 1863–66; Round Table Association, New York, 1866–69.

EDITORS: Henry Edward Sweetser and Charles Humphreys Sweetser, 1863–66; C. H. Sweetser and Dorsey Gardner, 1866; C. H. Sweetser, Dorsey Gardner, and Henry Sedley, 1866; Henry Sedley and Dorsey Gardner, 1866–68; Henry Sedley, 1868–69.

[2] *Round Table,* I, 4 (December 19, 1863).

[3] *Ibid.,* I, 401 (June 11, 1864).

respondents in various cities. Periodicals in the sixties were commonly regional, but the *Round Table* had announced in its prospectus that it was to be "truly national in its character"; in its first number it had two columns on art in Chicago, and correspondents in Boston and Philadelphia were fairly regular. Alfred C. Lambdin sometimes wrote from Philadelphia and Justin Winsor from Boston.

Politics, though named first in the *Round Table's* list of its interests, were not first in its columns. Political comment — very outspoken, as was the brash young paper's habit — was, however, not neglected either in its local or national aspects. As the brilliant Charles Astor Bristed said, half jocularly, in its own columns after the war was over, the *Round Table* had not always been "thickly and thinly loyal" to the North, though "not as coppery as Bardolph's nose." [4] In other words, it was often severely critical of the conduct of the war. In New York politics, also, it spoke its mind: "New York politically is already the rottenest community on the face of the earth," it declared in its second month.[5]

In its comments on religious matters, too, it was ready with its criticisms. Particularly was the religious press the object of its attacks. Scurrilous use of personalities in debate and the printing of quack advertising were the chief faults for which it called such papers as the *Independent* and the *New York Observer* to task. Moreover, it was a censor of morals and manners, as well as of religious customs. It discussed smoking and drinking and eating, prostitution, "puffery," and the fads of dress and social behavior. It was always very sure of itself, always decided, and often severe. "It is nothing unless fault-finding; a vixen in its way," said the *Observer*.[6] It was, truth to tell, somewhat in danger of becoming a scold; but its freedom from conventional taboos, its honesty, its directness, and its general high-mindedness are so refreshing that one forgives its censoriousness.

But the *Round Table's* chief interest, perhaps, was in literary criticism. "We insist," it said, "that the great need of our

---

[4] *Round Table*, N.S., II, 76 (October 7, 1865).
[5] *Ibid.*, I, 133 (February 13, 1864).
[6] *New York Observer*, December 26, 1865.

national literature is criticism — criticism from an American standpoint. We have had too much of the mutual admiration style of reviewing. Let us have mutual detestation rather than that." [7] The *Round Table's* own pet detestations were sentimentality and prettiness. "What our literature wants," it said, "is power, vitality, distinctiveness, positiveness. We need a rougher, stronger race of literary athletes." [8] A comparison between Browning and Longfellow, it pointed out, showed "the difference between a great poet and a pretty one." [9] In its book reviewing the paper was sometimes acute and brilliant, but too much inclined to literalness and often lacking in scholarly background. Boston writers generally it found "crotchetty." [10] In art criticism it was noticeably less severe than in its comment on books.

In the number for July 23, 1864, it was announced that publication of the *Round Table* would be suspended, perhaps to be resumed in happier times. Begun in the midst of the war, it had confronted from the first the problem of rapidly rising costs of production. Thus, though it claimed in the last number before its suspension a circulation and an advertising patronage "greater than was anticipated," [11] its resources did not permit it to face the uncertainties of the situation. It was resumed a little over a year later, with a smaller quarto and a lower price — $4.00 — but the same set of principles and much the same group of contributors.

Articles in the *Round Table* were anonymous; but a list published at the end of the first volume [12] gives some help in identifying contributors, and hints are found in other places as well. Richard Henry Stoddard was an editorial assistant in at least the early months of the journal.[13] Thomas Bailey Aldrich's narrative poem "Judith" was published in two parts in April

[7] *Round Table*, II, 8 (June 18, 1864).
[8] *Ibid.*, II, 18 (June 25, 1864).
[9] *Ibid.*, I, 26 (December 26, 1863).
[10] *Ibid.*, I, 73 (January 16, 1864).
[11] *Ibid.*, II, 88 (July 23, 1864).
[12] *Ibid.*, I, 401 (June 11, 1864).
[13] See quotation from an autograph letter, "I was on the *Round Table* when the news of the death of W. M. T. was flashed under the sea," in catalogue of the Anderson Galleries, New York, for Sale No. 2298, p. 119. Thackeray died December 24, 1863.

1864; Sweetser is said to have remarked caustically to Aldrich that the praise given this poem by *Round Table* readers was as absurd as the poem itself.[14] Other members of the group of young literary New Yorkers who chiefly supported the *Round Table* were Edmund Clarence Stedman, William Winter, George Arnold, and Charles Dawson Shanly. The elder Sweetser's former associate on the *World*, David G. Croly, was a valuable aid. From Boston George S. Hillard and Robert C. Winthrop sometimes wrote, and from New Haven George P. Fisher, D. C. Gilman, and Noah Porter. J. J. Piatt and Kate Field wrote from Washington, and Moncure D. Conway from London. The editors complained, however, that they found it difficult to find bold and original writers; and though they had offered "extravagant sums," they had been unable to secure contributions from "the coterie of writers which revolves about Boston." [15]

The revived *Round Table* had the subtitle, "A Saturday Review of Literature, Society, and Art," and those were its three main interests. In criticism it was as outspoken as ever. "So long as there are bad books to be exposed, unprincipled publishers to be remonstrated with, corrupt society to be scathed, silly and extravagant fashions to be denounced," the *Round Table* pledged itself to man the breach, sit on the tripod, and wield the ferule.[16] In so doing, it made many enemies and lost some business. It once complained that while publishers and authors praised its intention to tell the truth and shame the devil, when the project was carried into effect publishers withdrew advertising and authors wrote indignant letters.[17] At least one author did more than that, for when the *Round Table* called Charles Reade's *Griffith Gaunt* "indecent" and "morally unfit for introduction into families," [18] Reade sued the editors of the paper for $25,000 damages. During the trial the novel was introduced as evidence, and half of it was read to the jury by George Vanderhof, "the well known elocutionist." [19] The jury found for the

---

[14] Ferris Greenslet, *The Life of Thomas Bailey Aldrich* (Boston, 1908), p. 70.
[15] *Round Table*, III, 440 (July 14, 1866).   [16] *Ibid.*, IV, 8 (August 4, 1866).
[17] *Ibid.*, II, 65 (July 16, 1864).   [18] *Ibid.*, III, 472 (July 28, 1866).
[19] For accounts of the trial see *New York Tribune*, February 27 (p. 7), March 2 (p. 5), March 3 (p. 8), 1869, and other New York papers. Suit had been brought in 1866 for publications in the *Round Table* for June 9, July 28, and October 13.

plaintiff and placed the damages at six cents; probably the plaintiff had actually benefited by the controversy. Reade's friends made counterattacks against the *Round Table,* accusing it of undue severity towards books not advertised in its columns; and we are told that Reade pasted such an article from the *American Gentlewoman's Newspaper* [20] into his scrapbook, heading it "The Brothers Sweetser . . . Blackguards." [21]

Art criticism occupied a considerable space in the *Round Table.* A series of sketches of publishers was a feature of 1866, followed by a series the next year on American journalism. G. Washington Moon, author of *The Dean's English,* published criticisms of philological works throughout these years. In 1867 the word *Politics* was introduced into the paper's title, and in the following year *Finance* was also added; but the *Round Table* never gained standing as either a political or a financial journal.

The circulation of the paper ranged between three and five thousand.[22] The price was raised to $5.00 in 1866; and the expense of publication, its readers were told in that year, was $800 a week.[23] With good advertising, such a business should find the balance on the right side; and accordingly the publishers stated at the end of 1866 that the paper "now pays a handsome profit." [24] Henry Sweetser had retired early in that year to reënter daily journalism; and Dorsey Gardner, who had been an assistant editor, was taken into partnership a few months later. Gardner had formerly been editor and publisher of the *Trenton Daily Monitor.* Henry Sedley, journalist and novelist, then made it a triumvirate for a short time; but in November 1866 Charles Sweetser withdrew to found the *New York Evening Mail,* leaving Sedley and Dorsey as editors and owners.

The new editors printed a statement at once in which they deplored "unwholesome bitterness" in journalism. "An idea has become somewhat widely prevalent," they said, "that this

---

[20] With date December 2, 1865.

[21] See E. G. Sutcliffe, "Charles Reade's Notebooks," *Studies in Philology,* XXVII, 70 (January 1930).

[22] Testimony in the Reade case was to the effect that the paper's circulation in 1866 was 3,700. See *New York Tribune,* March 3, 1869, p. 8.

[23] *Round Table,* III, 89 (February 10, 1866).

[24] *Ibid.,* IV, 357 (December 29, 1866).

paper lives but to destroy — that it has been a species of Ishmael among journals." This should be the case no longer.[25] Accordingly, the lion was taught to roar as gently as any sucking dove, and a year or two later we find the editor lamenting criticism that was "apt to make more foes than friends."[26] When it lost its belligerence, however, it lost much of its interest for readers; and besides, the *Nation*, founded in July 1865, had largely usurped the place which the *Round Table* had hoped to fill. In December 1868 Sedley became sole owner and told his readers of his resolution to make the paper "more racy, popular, and attractive."[27] Shortly thereafter he added a chess department. Art, which had been a prominent interest of the paper when the Sweetsers owned it, received more attention in 1869. But in the middle of that year Sedley gave up the struggle and merged his journal with the *New York Citizen*.

The *Citizen* had been founded in August 1864 as an independent political weekly, and two years later it had become the organ of the Citizen's Association, a reform society of which Robert B. Roosevelt was secretary. Charles G. Halpine ("Private Miles O'Reilly") and Roosevelt were editors and owners of the paper until the former's death in 1868. It was nearly a year after that event that Roosevelt bought the *Round Table* and merged it with his paper, changing the name to *New York Citizen and Round Table*. It was Democratic in politics, but occupied largely with its fight against Tammany. Roosevelt left it in 1871, after which it became more and more of a story-paper and reverted to the folio size as in the days before it was combined with the *Round Table*. It was being advertised as "the handsomest and best family and story weekly published" in 1873, but it seems to have drifted into limbo sometime late in that year.

[25] *Round Table*, IV, 283 (December 1, 1866).
[26] *Ibid.*, VIII, 3 (July 4, 1868).
[27] *Ibid.*, VIII, 383 (December 12, 1868).

DEMOREST'S MONTHLY MAGAZINE [1]

W. JENNINGS DEMOREST began his publishing career by founding the quarterly *Mirror of Fashions* in 1860, with "Mme. Demorest" as editor and "Jennie June" as assistant. The editor was Mrs. Ellen Louise Demorest, wife of the publisher; and "Jennie June" was Mrs. Jane C. Croly. In January 1864 Demorest bought the *New York Illustrated News*,[2] one of the first picture newspapers, but was forced to discontinue it in eight months.

Then at the beginning of the next year, he transformed his fashion quarterly into a magazine called *Demorest's Illustrated Monthly and Mme. Demorest's Mirror of Fashions*. It was a small quarto in size, priced at $3.00 a year, with a sentimental engraving for premium. It carried colored fashion plates (chromolithographs and hand-colored plates), woodcuts of fashions, music, serial fiction, poetry, sketches, and much miscellany. Virginia Townsend wrote the first serial, and the first issue contained a poem by Theodore Tilton and an essay by "Jennie June." George W. Bungay was the magazine's poet laureate during its early years.

But it was the tissue-paper dress pattern, stapled into the magazine as a kind of premium, that established *Demorest's*. This device was a great success and was continued for nearly twenty years.

[1] TITLES: (1) *Demorest's Illustrated Monthly and Mme. Demorest's Mirror of Fashions* (half title *Demorest's Monthly Magazine*), 1865; (2) *Demorest's Monthly Magazine and Mme. Demorest's Mirror of Fashions*, 1866–77; (3) *Demorest's Monthly Magazine*, 1878–89; (4) *Demorest's Family Magazine*, 1889–99.

FIRST ISSUE: January 1865. LAST ISSUE: December 1899.

PERIODICITY: Monthly. Regular annual volumes.

PUBLISHERS: W. Jennings Demorest, 1865–85; Henry C. and William C. Demorest, 1885–97; Arkell Publishing Company, 1898–99. All of New York.

EDITORS: William Jennings Demorest, Ellen Louise Demorest, Jane Cunningham Croly, 1865–85; Henry C. and William C. Demorest, 1885–97 (with Jane C. Croly, 1885–87).

[2] See vol. II, p. 45.

A SATIRE ON EARLY WOMEN'S CLUBS

From *Harper's Weekly*, May 15, 1869. The picture was drawn by Charles G. Bush and is entitled "Sorosis, 1869."

Mrs. Croly founded that most famous of early women's clubs, the Sorosis, in 1868, and was its president 1868–70 and 1876–86. In *Demorest's* she conducted for many years the "Ladies' Club" department, consisting chiefly of questions and answers. The magazine had many departments and was highly miscellaneous. By the late seventies Margaret Sangster was almost as much a stand-by as "Jennie June" herself. "The largest in size, the largest in circulation, and the only reliable fashions," boasted the publisher through the seventies. The size was 52 pages, small quarto; the circulation was about 50,000. In 1881, the price was reduced to $2.00 a year, without much resultant increase in circulation.

Demorest was one of the leaders of the prohibition party in the United States. He instituted a system of temperance recitation contests and donated before his death upward of 40,000 silver medals to the winners; hundreds of thousands of boys and girls committed temperance pieces to memory for these contests. He wrote strong editorials for his magazine advocating prohibition of the sale and manufacture of intoxicants.

In 1885 Demorest turned the magazine over to his sons Henry C. and William C., so that he could devote his time and his wealth to the prohibition cause. Mrs. Demorest had not been actively associated with the magazine for some few years, the subtitle *Mme. Demorest's Mirror of Fashions* having been dropped in 1878. Mrs. Croly continued with the new management for a year or two longer.

The young Demorests made several improvements in the magazine. A coupon exchangeable for a chosen dress pattern was substituted for the infolded tissue sheets which had distended the handsome form of the periodical. The illustration was improved under the art direction of Henry C. Demorest. A more distinguished group of contributors was introduced — Thomas Hardy, T. W. Higginson, Louisa M. Alcott, James Grant, and others. Julia Ward Howe contributed a serial in 1885, the year of the change. The colored fashions disappeared in the late eighties, and by 1890 less attention was paid to styles and more to the features of a general magazine. There was more of current events, of art, of travel. The name was changed to *Demorest's Family Magazine* in 1889.

Among the famous contributors of the nineties were Beatrice Harraden, Robert Louis Stevenson, and Amelia E. Barr. A remarkable feature was the printing of several pages of good half-tone portraits of the famous men and women of the past and the present in each issue; these pictures were unbacked, and subscribers were expected to cut them out and paste them into scrapbooks. There is no doubt that thousands of persons did this and were thereby edified.

The Arkell Publishing Company, owners of *Judge*, purchased the magazine in 1898, but continued it less than two years.

THE CATHOLIC WORLD [1]

FATHER ISAAC T. HECKER, founder of the Community of Paulist Fathers and of the Catholic Publication Society, began the *Catholic World* as a general magazine for Catholics in 1865. The first number consisted of 144 well-printed pages of selections from English and Italian periodicals (the latter translated by the editor), one original article, and brief departments devoted to science, art, and books. After the single original contribution of the first issue, however, came a rapid increase in such material; and soon the magazine became wholly original, and the word *Eclectic* was dropped from the subtitle.

Father Hecker set a high standard in literary tone and editorial enterprise. The *Nation*, which continually and severely criticized the controversial spirit of the magazine, admitted that it had "a more masculine tone than any of the other magazines" [2] — which was high praise from a journal that hated the namby-pamby sentimentalism current in periodicals generally. Hecker, who suffered from ill health, was an absentee editor during much of the later seventies and the eighties. The journalist J. R. G. Hassard was a member of the editorial staff. Father Hewit, assistant and successor, was the largest single contributor to the *World* during its first half century; and the leonine Orestes A. Brownson came next, with seventy articles. [3]

---

[1] TITLE: *The Catholic World: A Monthly Eclectic Magazine of General Literature and Science.* (The word *Eclectic* was removed from the subtitle October 1865.)

FIRST ISSUE: April 1865. Current.

PERIODICITY: Monthly. Semiannual volumes.

PUBLISHERS: Lawrence Kehoe, 1865–67; Catholic Publishing Society, 1867–88; Catholic World, 1888–current (since 1901 "under direction of the Paulist Fathers").

EDITORS: Isaac T. Hecker, 1865–88; A. F. Hewit, 1889–97; Alexander P. Doyle, 1897–1904; John J. Burke, 1904–22; James M. Gillis, 1923–current.

INDEXES: *Poole's* and *Readers' Guide.*

REFERENCE: John J. Burke's "The Catholic World," CI, 7 (April 1915).

[2] *Nation*, VI, 255 (March 26, 1868).

[3] *Catholic World*, CI, 10 (April 1915).

Church dignitaries have always been prominent in its pages. It published the first work of Agnes Repplier and Louise Imogen Guiney. Other distinguished writers familiar to its readers have been Alice Meynell, Katharine Tynan, John Gilmary Shea, Aubrey DeVere, Rose H. Lathrop, Joyce Kilmer, Hilaire Belloc, G. K. Chesterton, Padraic Colum, and Theodore Maynard.

The leading articles in each number have commonly dealt with distinctly Catholic questions; and discussions of educational, social, and literary matters have had a definitely Catholic angle. The *World* has not been primarily a theological journal, however; it has been a "popular" magazine, interesting to the general reader, but designed to support the doctrines of the church and to express Catholic views of literature, art, science, the drama, education, and society. It has not hesitated to reply to attacks on the church, or, for that matter, to attack on its own account the activities of Protestantism. Its too picturesque description of Luther as "the beery monk of Wittenberg" in 1873 gave the *Nation* much distress.[4]

Under the editorship of Father Burke, 1904–22, there was an effort to regain something of the literary quality the magazine enjoyed under the earlier administration of Hecker. In poetry the *World* has often been especially fortunate: the work of the Misses Meynell, Tynan, and Guiney, and of Kilmer, Colum, and Maynard has conferred distinction upon it. Elaborate Shakespeare (April 1916) and Dante (September 1921) numbers may be mentioned.

[4] *Nation*, XVI, 387 (June 5, 1873). The reference is to an expression in an article on Savonarola, *Catholic World*, XVII, 289 (June 1873).

THE NATION [1]

FREDERICK LAW OLMSTED was the prime mover in the project which culminated in the establishment of the *Nation* in 1865. Olmsted was the foremost American landscape architect of his time, the designer of Central Park in New York, and an active, practical thinker prolific in ideas and remarkably various in his interests. He felt the necessity for an American weekly paper which should enlist as contributors men of scholarship, brilliance, and independence. There were plenty of weekly story-papers, Sunday miscellanies, picture papers, religious weeklies, and specialized hebdomadals; but there was nothing to compare with the London *Spectator* or the *Saturday Review* in scholarship or in literary excellence. Olmsted was called west by a mining project before he had financed the new review, but not before he had interested Edwin Lawrence Godkin in it.

[1] TITLE: *The Nation.* Subtitles: *A Weekly Journal Devoted to Politics, Literature, Science and Art,* 1865–1908; *A Weekly Journal Devoted to Politics, Literature, Science, Drama, Music, Art, Finance,* 1909–current (*Finance* changed to *Industry* 1925).

FIRST ISSUE: July 6, 1865. Current.

PERIODICITY: Weekly, except for May–June 1866, when it was semiweekly. Regular semiannual volumes.

PUBLISHERS: Joseph H. Richards [for Nation Association], 1865–66; E. L. Godkin & Company, 1866–81; The Evening Post Publishing Company, 1881–99; New York Evening Post Company, 1900–14; The Nation Press Inc., 1915–20; The Nation Inc., 1920–current. All in New York.

EDITORS: Edwin Lawrence Godkin, 1865–81; Wendell Phillips Garrison, 1881–1906; Hammond Lamont, 1906–09; Paul Elmer More, 1909–14; Harold deWolf Fuller, 1914–18; Oswald Garrison Villard, 1918–32; Freda Kirchwey, 1933–current (with Henry Hazlitt, 1933; Ernest Gruening, 1933–34; Joseph Wood Krutch, 1933–37; Raymond Gram Swing, 1934–current; Charles Angoff, 1935; Max Lerner, 1936–current).

INDEXES: *Poole's, Poole's Abridged, Readers' Guide, Annual Library Index, Review of Reviews Index, Cumulative Index, Dramatic Index.*

REFERENCES: Semicentennial Number, *Nation,* July 8, 1915 (Vol. CI); Sixtieth Anniversary Number, *Nation,* July 1, 1925 (Vol. CXXI); Gustav Pollak, *Fifty Years of American Idealism* (Boston, 1915); Rollo Ogden, *Life and Letters of Edwin Lawrence Godkin* (New York, 1907), 2 vols.; [J. H. McDaniels, ed.], *Letters and Memorials of Wendell Phillips Garrison* (Boston, 1908); Carl Van Doren, *Three Worlds* (New York, 1936), chapter "Journalism."

Godkin, born in Ireland of English parents and educated in Ireland and England, was twenty-five years old when he came to America in 1856. He had been a newspaper correspondent since he had reached his majority, and his immediate purpose in crossing the Atlantic was to write articles for a London paper about conditions in the South. But he liked the new country and decided to remain. He was admitted to the bar in New York in 1858 and the next year married a granddaughter of Senator Foote, of Connecticut. Godkin was a born publicist, and Olmsted's plan for an intellectual weekly appealed to him strongly; but the plan to organize a stock company hung fire until the *Round Table*, begun at the end of 1863, appeared to have forestalled it.

But the *Round Table* suspended the next year; and when, in the spring of 1865, it was learned that a group of Philadelphia men led by James Miller McKim wished to put some money into a paper designed to aid the freedmen, a merger was effected between the Philadelphians, Godkin's backers in New York, and a group of Boston men headed by George L. Stearns and Charles Eliot Norton. In all, a company composed of forty stockholders put in $100,000 in cash, half of it coming from Boston and the balance being divided rather evenly between New York and Philadelphia.[2] Godkin was made editor,[3] with complete editorial freedom, "at a salary of $5,000 a year with twelve per cent of the profits after the payment of six per cent on the stock."[4] The first number of the new paper, which had been christened the *Nation*, was issued in New York on Thursday, July 6, 1865.

The publisher and the associate editor came from the staff of the *Independent*. The former was Joseph H. Richards, who remained with the *Nation* only a year; the latter was Wendell Phillips Garrison, third son of William Lloyd Garrison, the heroic editor of that old advocate of abolition, the *Liberator*,

[2] Ogden, *op. cit.*, I, 240.

[3] Whitelaw Reid said many years later that the editorship was offered to him and had prevoiusly been offered to George William Curtis, who had lately become editor of *Harper's Weekly* (Royal Cortissoz, *Life of Whitelaw Reid*, New York, 1921, I, 138). This is corroborated by Frank Preston Stearns, *The Life and Services of George Luther Stearns* (Philadelphia, 1907), p. 334.

[4] Ogden, *op. cit.*, I, 240.

now about to be laid to rest after its battles had been won. Young Garrison was a Harvard graduate and had been an editor of the *Independent* under Tilton for a year and a half; he was about to marry a daughter of McKim, one of whose reasons for wishing to found a paper was to create an editorial position for his new son-in-law.

The *Nation* was a small quarto of thirty-six pages. Paragraphs of comment on current affairs called "The Week" occupied the first three or four pages. These were followed by the leading editorials and correspondence from abroad, with some miscellany, a little poetry, and letters to the editor. Literary notes and reviews of new books occupied seven or eight pages. Discussion of art and music then filled two to four pages, followed by a brief scientific department and a financial review. The price was $3.00 a year.

In its prospectus the *Nation* had made a statement of purposes which may be summarized as follows: (1) To discuss current affairs, especially in their legal, economic, and constitutional phases, with more moderation than the party press; (2) to maintain true democratic principles; (3) to work for the equality of "the laboring class at the South"; (4) to enforce the doctrine that the whole country has the "strongest interest" in the elevation of the Negro; (5) to fix public attention on the importance of popular education; (6) to inform the country of conditions in the southern states; (7) to criticize books and works of art soundly and impartially.[5]

The emphasis upon reconstruction and freedmen's aid is apparent. A department headed "The Freedmen" was maintained through early issues, though the right of the new paper to speak for the Freedmen's Aid Association was challenged by Wendell Phillips and other members of the faction which, in opposition to William Lloyd Garrison, insisted on the perpetuation of the American Anti-slavery Society. Thus the *Nation* became heir to the last of the Garrisonian controversies: this fact, together with the new paper's championship of the freedman and the younger Garrison's connection with it, gives support to the later claim of its editors that the mantle of the old *Liberator* fell upon the new *Nation*. That sympathy for the freedman did much to

[5] Ogden, *op. cit.*, I, 1, 237.

shape the *Nation's* attitude toward reconstruction problems is obvious.

It is profitable to observe [wrote the editor in an early number] how the forces of conservatism, rallying after the signal failure of their efforts to defend and perpetuate the institution of slavery, are marshalling their strength to prevent the enlightenment, elevation, and enfranchisement of the Negro race.[6]

Trenchantly the *Nation* opposed this movement, at the same time that it did what it could to promote in the North a better understanding of the economic problems, the aspirations, and the possibilities of the South. One of its first enterprises was to send John Richard Dennett on a tour of the reconstructed states and to print his observations in an illuminating series entitled "The South As It Is." Upon his return, Dennett was made a member of the office editorial staff; and he remained an invaluable editor until his death in 1874.

But the *Nation* was far from being the organ of a single cause or group. Its interests were very wide from the first, and within less than a year it ceased what might be regarded as an over-emphasis on the freedmen's question. In the course of time its three great "causes" became civil service reform, tariff reform, and proportional representation. But its reformatory proclivities were not allowed to overshadow its week-by-week comment on affairs, always moderate, considered, forceful.

Quite as important as politics in the *Nation* was the criticism of books. "One principal object of the *Nation* is to promote and develop a higher standard of criticism," wrote the editor in his first number.[7] But it must be remembered that when we discuss book reviewing in the *Nation*, we are not dealing with a department or activity limited to belles-lettres, or functioning only as literary criticism proper, but with that broad survey of books as representative of the world's thought which has been characteristic of the great reviews. Book reviewing, to the *Nation*, meant criticism of the scholarship, the philosophy, the investigation, of the times. In order to present adequate criticism on so wide a front, Godkin and Garrison enlisted such an imposing

[6] *Nation*, I, 261 (August 31, 1865).
[7] *Ibid.*, I, 10 (July 6, 1865).

staff of reviewers as no American periodical had ever before assembled. Such were its resources that it actually "fitted" reviewers to books. Henry Holt, who began his publishing business in the same year that the *Nation* began, wrote later:

I still vividly remember my surprise and enlightenment when Dennett happened into my office just as the first volume of Taine's *Italy* came in from the binder, and I handed him a copy, and he said: "Let me see! To whom shall I send this for review? Who knows Italy?" And after a little reflection he decided to send it to Howells. Now, so far as I know, doing this as a matter of course was something new in American journalism.[8]

The list of the early contributors to the *Nation* enrolls most of the famous scholars and writers of the sixties and seventies.[9] Such a list should begin with the name of Charles Eliot Norton, to whom Godkin wrote: "Without your support and encouragement I do not think I should have been able to endure." [10] Norton contributed an appreciative review of Richard Grant White's first Shakespeare volume to Volume I, Number 1; and for the second number he wrote a memorably outrageous essay in which he called the United States "A Paradise of Mediocrities." This was the kind of facing of realities which was to become the mark of the *Nation's* high calling, though it did not "set well" with some of the brash young paper's readers in 1865. But Norton continued to write for the *Nation* on art and poetry and education with variety and acumen until his death in 1908. James Russell Lowell wrote some poetry (chiefly political) and a number of reviews for the paper in the mid-seventies, and was always its warm friend and eulogist. The Jameses — father and both sons — were contributors, both the elder and the younger Henry James being represented in the first number. William James's reviews of French and German philosophical works were notable. William Dean Howells wrote much for the *Nation* in its early years and for some months in 1865–66 was an assist-

---

[8] *Ibid.*, CI, 45 (July 8, 1915). Also in Holt's *Garrulities of an Octogenarian Editor* (Boston, 1923), p. 283.

[9] For such a roll, see Gustav Pollak's "The *Nation* and Its Contributors," *Nation*, CI, 57 (July 8, 1915), later expanded into an introduction to the same author's *Fifty Years of American Idealism*.

[10] Ogden, *op. cit.*, I, 250.

ant editor, just before he went to Boston to assist Fields in the editorship of the *Atlantic Monthly*. One of the *Nation's* most constant contributors over a long series of years was William Francis Allen, professor of history at the University of Wisconsin. His writing covered a very wide range of interests. Somewhat the same may be said of Michael Heilprin, whose command of history and of languages was phenomenal.

Professor E. W. Gurney's proficiency in the classics and in law and politics was evident in the *Nation* from the first number. Another *Nation* savant was George P. Marsh, long minister to Italy, who wrote on philology and science. Daniel C. Gilman foreshadowed his later activities in the founding of Johns Hopkins University when he discussed in the second number of the *Nation* the project for Cornell University; he was a lifelong contributor and cordial friend of the paper. Octavius B. Frothingham, historian of transcendentalism and liberal clergyman, and President Noah Porter, of Yale, also began long careers as *Nation* contributors with the second number.

Arthur G. Sedgwick, son of Theodore Sedgwick, of Boston, was not yet twenty-one when he made his first contribution to the third number of the *Nation*; for forty years he contributed largely to the paper on political subjects, always writing with the directness and clearness that characterized his mind. He left the *American Law Review*, which had been founded the year after the *Nation* and which he helped to edit, to become in 1872–84 an assistant editor of the latter periodical. His reminiscences of this period in the Semicentennial Number constitute his last contribution: he committed suicide in 1915. Another assistant editor of note was W. C. Brownell, critic of literature and essayist, who worked on the *Nation* 1879–81.

Three of the paper's chief writers on art in these years were Earl Shinn, who was studying in Paris, Professor Charles H. Moore, and Russell Sturgis. Henry T. Finck began his articles on music in the late seventies, sending his first contribution from Munich. The first London correspondent of the *Nation* was Edward Dicey, editor of the *Observer*; while Auguste Laugel wrote from Paris, Friedrich Kapp from Berlin, and Jessie White Mario from Venice. H. E. von Holst, the historian, was a German correspondent in the later seventies; and Willard Fiske,

Karl Hillebrand, and E. Gryzanowski wrote on Italian affairs. Alfred Webb admirably filled the difficult post of special writer from Dublin. Chief among English correspondents were Lord Bryce, Leslie Stephen, and Professor A. V. Dicey.

Among American scientists, two of the most faithful of the *Nation's* contributors were Simon Newcomb and Asa Gray. Of the historians, Francis Parkman, Henry C. Lea, and John Fiske may be named; the last wrote on philosophy and music as well as on history. General J. D. Cox, victim of the corruptionists of Grant's administration and lifelong friend of both Godkin and Garrison, wrote many articles for the *Nation*; he dealt most frequently, perhaps, with biographical material relating to the Civil War. Among active contributors in the field of economics were Charles Francis Adams, Jr., Horace White, and Professors W. G. Sumner and F. W. Taussig. Thomas Wentworth Higginson, John White Chadwick, and Goldwin Smith were publicists whose work was of great importance to the *Nation*. Judge C. C. Nott wrote extensively on legal questions. The list of university specialists who wrote frequently for the paper is very long, but the following must at least be mentioned: Fitzedward Hall, the philologer; George P. Fisher, the theologian and church historian; Elliott Coues, the ornithologist; Charles S. Peirce, the philosopher and mathematician; Charles W. Eliot, the educator; Basil L. Gildersleeve, the classicist; C. H. Toy, the Hebraist; and George L. Goodale, the botanist.

With so distinguished a faculty and with such varied resources, the *Nation* nevertheless managed a unity that gave it a distinct individuality. It was all, of course, anonymous. "Every Friday morning when the *Nation* comes," wrote Lowell to Godkin, "I fill my pipe and read it from beginning to end. Do you do it all yourself? Or are there really so many clever men in the country?" [11] This effect was produced partly by firm editing, especially by a severity of excision which one assistant called "ruthless" handling of authors, "though never interfering with their freedom of opinion in any task he had assigned them." [12] One service that the writing on the early

[11] Ogden, *op. cit.*, II, 74.
[12] *Nation*, CI, 44 (July 8, 1915).

Nation may be said to have performed for the whole body of American periodicals was to show that serious writing could be lively and readable. Godkin's own style had directness, zest, and wit; and he encouraged those qualities in his contributors wherever he found them.[13]

The new paper went to 5,000 circulation by its third number [14] and rapidly won the approval of the judicious. The die-hards of the old Anti-slavery Society at Boston attacked it bitterly, however; and Major Stearns, the largest *Nation* stockholder, soon became allied with them, though he based much of his opposition on another issue. These were years in which "nativism" still had demagogic potency, and it was possible to attack with some effectiveness an American editor for his display of bad judgment in being born in Ireland. Besides, the Irish question provoked strong emotional reactions, especially in Boston; and when Godkin inadvertently spoke of himself as English born, he was accused of bad faith, and both Irish and anti-Irish came down upon him. Dana, of the *Sun*, thought the *Nation* "too much like the *Spectator*," and "not an American journal." [15] Stearns sent out circulars against Godkin and the *Nation*; Phillips continued to assail everything and everyone connected with the project. But the paper went serenely on its way. It did not lack for friends and defenders as time went on. Emerson, who had been among the Boston disaffected at first, soon changed his opinion, and spoke to Norton "in warmest terms of its excellence, its superiority to any other journal we have or have had; its breadth, its variety, its self-sustainment, its admirable style of thought and expression." [16] Curtis wrote in *Harper's Weekly*, anent an attack on the *Nation* by its inveterate enemy, the *New York Tribune*, that Godkin's paper had

discussed every public question with a fullness and ripeness of thought, a candor, independence, conviction, and good temper which we and the *Tribune* and all our daily and weekly contemporaries may most profitably emulate. Its literary criticisms are not less commendable. A

[13] See p. 17.

[14] Ogden, *op. cit.*, I, 240.

[15] Charles F. Wingate, ed., *Views and Interviews* (New York, 1875), p. 63.

[16] *Ibid.*, I, 249. See also Stearns, *op. cit.*, p. 333, for Emerson's attitude to the early *Nation*. This volume presents (pp. 332–338) the grievances of Major Stearns against Godkin.

reader can actually judge by them whether a book is good or not, though "genial" criticism and indiscriminate praise must not be looked for in the *Nation*. Its science and other miscellany is accurate and to the date. Its brief comments upon the topics of the week are not only sparkling, but often witty.[17]

This statement from a rival weekly was not a "puff," reciprocal or otherwise: it was sincere appraisal. For good measure we may add Lowell's "deliberate" statement that the *Nation's* "discussions of politics had done more good and influenced public opinion more than any other agency, or all others combined, in the country." [18]

One might adduce many more such statements from high sources, but it is necessary to interrupt the flow of eulogy to make place for a single bald statistic: in its first half-century the *Nation's* circulation never got above 12,000. Indeed, it stuck at about half of that for its first few years. The number of pages was reduced after a few months; the subscription price was raised to $5.00 at the beginning of 1866, without greatly affecting the circulation; the experiment of semiweekly issue was tried in May and June 1866. By the end of the first year it was thought best to reorganize, eliminating the dissatisfied among the forty stockholders by purchase of their stock, and putting the paper on a somewhat more modest basis than that upon which it had been begun. For the next fifteen years, then, the business was conducted by E. L. Godkin & Company. Godkin's salary was only $2,000 a year in 1870,[19] with the circulation a little over 6,000. From there the list rose steadily to double that figure in the next five or six years.

Thus the power of the *Nation* came not from the number of its readers, but from their station and influence and from the frequency with which it was quoted. And a power it rapidly became, indubitably, in both politics and letters.

Godkin criticized President Johnson freely, but after the congressional election of 1865 the *Nation* was somewhat more indulgent toward the chief magistrate; he was "evidently not an unworthy successor of Mr. Lincoln." [20] But Johnson's intemperate speeches disgusted the *Nation*, which found his atti-

---

[17] *Harper's Weekly*, XII, 435 (July 11, 1868).   [18] Ogden, *op. cit.*, II, 78.
[19] *Ibid.*, II, 63.   [20] *Nation*, I, 742 (December 14, 1865).

tude of "sp'iling for a fight" vulgar and indecent; yet it still counseled moderation.[21] By February 1866 it observed that "those who have never admitted his wickedness are at present willing to have him impeached and deposed as an incorrigible dunce." It followed the impeachment trial judicially and found the "failure to convict regrettable," [22] while at the same time it rejoiced at the vindication of "the sacred rights of individual conscience" in the nonpartisan verdict. The reconstruction policy of Congress was pronounced in 1868 "as a whole unassailable." [23] The *Nation* "opposed all haste in bringing back the States to the Union," chiefly because "the weaker of the two races into which their population is unfortunately divided will go to the wall." [24]

The paper was for Grant in 1868, for three reasons: it expected him to be a strong force in reconstruction; he favored payment of the public debt; he was not "a regular politician." [25] But Godkin was disappointed in his hopes of Grant. He became alarmed at "the corruption which is at present so rife." [26] He championed the cause of Secretary Cox, who had defied the corruptionists. He pursued the bellicose Ben Butler through many years of his egregious career. In 1872 the *Nation* was a paper without a candidate. Said the republican *Penn Monthly*: "It almost despises one candidate, and hates the other most fervently." [27] Such was the case. On the one hand the *Nation* spoke of "the thoroughly corrupt and time-serving ring which has for some time past been managing the present administration . . . playing on General Grant's ignorance of affairs and desire for re-election"; and on the other it called Greeley "the final attempt of that large class of quacks, charlatans, ignoramuses, and sentimentalists who are engaged in every civilized country today in trying to substitute the heart for the head . . . to get control of the government." [28] In the Hayes-Tilden cam-

---

[21] *Nation*, II, 294 (March 8, 1866).
[22] *Ibid.*, VI, 164 (February 27, 1868); and VI, 404 (May 21, 1868).
[23] *Ibid.*, VI, 224 (March 19, 1868).
[24] *Ibid.*, VI, 264, 265 (April 2, 1868).
[25] *Ibid.*, VI, 345 (October 29, 1868).
[26] *Ibid.*, VIII, 469 (June 17, 1869).
[27] *Penn Monthly*, III, 519 (September 1872).
[28] *Nation*, XIV, 332–333 (May 23, 1872).

paign the *Nation* took much the same neutral position it had
occupied four years before; but whereas a defection in 1872,
with a divided party and a more or less perfunctory campaign,
might be forgiven, in 1876 the paper's criticism of both candidates was a heinous crime, and circulation dropped rapidly.
"Tell me," Godkin is reported to have said to his circulation
manager, "when only two subscribers are left; then I will consider what may be done." [29] After the voting, the *Nation* favored
inaugurating Hayes "in the interest of peace." [30] In the next
campaign the paper supported Garfield and Arthur, though it
made a wry face in swallowing the vice-presidential candidate;
Hancock it considered incompetent.

But the presidential campaigns were incidental in the course
of the *Nation's* political writing. Certain reforms were basic.
Judge Nott wrote in the Semicentennial Number:

> The *Nation* in those days was at war: war against slavery, war
> against the reconstruction iniquities, war against the Freedmen's Bank
> robbery, war for civil service reform, war against the District of
> Columbia ring, war against the republican bosses, war against the
> democratic party, war against the abuses in the departments. There
> were battles all the time, and the paper stood unsupported and almost
> alone, an authority among the intelligent few, and an influence among
> newspapers, but without a powerful circulation or a remunerative
> advertising patronage.[31]

This indicates rather more pugnacity than characterized the
Nation: it was intellectually critical, but not bellicose.

Its early battles for the freedmen soon became less important
than its campaign for civil service reform. "It advocated civil
service reform," claimed its editor in 1876, "before any other
paper in the country ever mentioned it, or mentioned it other
than jestingly." [32] It favored Grant for president in 1868 partly
because, not being "a regular politician," he would be "the first
president the country has had for many a long day on whom the
old party doctrines as to 'spoils' and 'claims' will have no influence." [33] But hopes of such a reform from Grant "did not sur-

[29] *World's Work*, IV, 2264 (June 1902).
[30] *Nation*, XXIII, 351 (December 14, 1876).
[31] *Ibid.*, CI, 48 (July 8, 1915).
[32] *Ibid.*, XXIII, 308 (November 23, 1876).
[33] *Ibid.*, VI, 345 (October 29, 1868).

vive his first year in office." [34] Nevertheless, the *Nation* strongly urged the Jenckes reform bill of 1868, and Secretary Cox was dear to its heart largely because he put his own department on a nonspoils basis. It heartily supported Hayes's efforts in that direction, and those of Schurz, new Secretary of the Interior.

The *Nation's* fight against Tammany began in its early numbers. By 1868 it was referring to "the notorious Supervisor Tweed" in connection with election frauds in New York City.[35] Two years later it was recording the fact that "Sweeny, Tweed & Co. are now masters of the situation," having organized the legislature and demonstrated their ability to bribe the minority.[36] But the *Nation* did not take an important part in the famous *Times-Harper's Weekly* fight on the Tweed ring; its leadership in the long war on Tammany was to come later.

In labor disputes the *Nation* was consistently on the side of capital. It opposed the eight-hour day, denied labor's right to dictate its own price, and opposed Chinese exclusion because the immigrants did "considerably more work at a lower rate of compensation" than American laborers.[37] It also showed anti-Catholic bias on many occasions. It was severe in its criticism of the railroads, it opposed high tariffs, it was strongly against currency inflation, and it favored minority representation as a basic principle. But whatever position the *Nation* took, whether readers agreed with it or disagreed, all had perforce to admit that it was always high-minded, dignified, candid. Not always did its critics use those terms, however; and to some its intellectual pride seemed priggish, or at least rather too aloof for human nature's daily food. Even Henry Adams spoke of "the elevated plateau of the New Jerusalem occupied by Godkin and the *Nation*." [38] Samuel Bowles wrote in the *Springfield Republican*:

> Often conceited and priggish, coldly critical to a degree sometimes amusing and often provoking, and singularly lacking not only in a generous enthusiasm of its own but in any sympathy with that generous American quality, . . . the paper yet shows such vigor and

[34] *Nation*, XIII, 172 (September 14, 1871).
[35] *Ibid.*, VII, 361 (November 5, 1868).
[36] *Ibid.*, X, 1 (January 6, 1870).   [37] *Ibid.*, VIII, 486 (June 24, 1869).
[38] *The Education of Henry Adams* (Boston, 1918), p. 244.

integrity of thought, such moral independence of party, such elevation of tone, and such wide culture, as to demand our respect and secure our hearty praise. . . . The *Nation* may not ever be popular in the common American sense, popular as the *New York Ledger*; as a sort of moral policeman of our politics, our society and our art, it can hardly expect to be; but it assuredly has been and will be most useful.[39]

In the *Nation's* literary criticism this unsympathetic attitude was complained of more frequently than in the other departments of its activity. Authors were accustomed to "genial" criticism. "Publishers," Henry Holt tells us, "had been used to having everything that was not glaringly ignorant or immoral gently treated, if not praised." [40] But the *Nation* refused to join in any such complaisant travesty; it reviewed books realistically; and as a result, a discriminating contemporary remarked on its twentieth birthday that literary criticism in American periodicals "has almost become a new art under its leadership." [41] The paper's comments on current literature were, on the whole, rigorous. Occasionally all the leading reviews would be condemnatory, and the praise seldom balanced the censure. Yet the *Nation* was not merely captious; it was usually acute, definite, and convincing. Moreover, its reviews were, more often than not, good reading. What may be called the casual brilliance and zest of the *Nation's* run-of-the-mill reviewing may be illustrated by the following paragraph on Miss Braddon's novels:

She knows much that ladies are not accustomed to know, but that they are apparently very glad to learn. The names of drinks, the technicalities of the faro-table, the lingo of the turf, the talk natural to a crowd of fast men at supper, when there are no ladies present but Miss Braddon — all these things — the exact local coloring of Bohemia — our sisters and daughters may learn from these works. . . . If one of her heroines elopes with the stableboy, she saves the proprieties by marrying him. This may be indecent, if you like, but it is not immoral.[42]

[39] George S. Merriam, *Life and Times of Samuel Bowles* (New York, 1885), II, 97. Quotation from the *Republican* of 1869. The *Nation* and the *Republican* were at the time allies in the attack on Benjamin F. Butler.
[40] *Nation*, CI, 46 (July 8, 1915) ; also Holt, *op. cit.*, p. 284.
[41] *Dial*, VI, 81 (July 1885).   [42] *Nation*, I, 593 (November 9, 1865).

Probably the *Nation's* reviewers made many mistakes in their evaluation of current belles-lettres: all reviewers are subject to such a charge. The early *Nation* was never quite friendly to fiction. It was contemptuous of Walt Whitman, saying that *Drum Taps* represented "the effort of an essentially prosaic mind to lift itself, by a prolonged muscular strain, into poetry."[43] On the other hand, it thought that H. H. Brownell's poems had "authentic power" and called them "magnificent." [44]

One department of the reviews deserves special mention — Dennett's monthly commentary on the current magazines. Lively, informative, specific, full of sound criticism — these notes still repay reading.

In June 1881 Godkin sold the *Nation* to the *New York Evening Post*, and for the next thirty-three years it was issued as the weekly edition of the *Post*. The price was reduced to $3.00 again. Henry Villard had bought a controlling interest in the *Post*; he was a brother-in-law of Garrison and was the primary mover in the merger. He made Carl Schurz editor of the *Post*, with Godkin and Horace White as associate editors. All three editors had stock in the paper. Villard, a financier and railroad promoter with a journalistic record behind him, agreed never to interfere with the editorial policy, and to confirm this agreement he made a trust comprising his entire holding which empowered the trustees to protect the editorial department against any interference from the ownership.[45]

As a part of the new arrangement, the *Post's* review department was greatly enlarged, and the *Nation* was filled each week with editorials and reviews which had already been printed in the daily. Garrison, who had been *de facto* managing editor from the beginning, succeeded to the general editorship without much change of duties; at the same time he became literary editor of the *Post*. Godkin remained as political and advisory editor, but he functioned less in the latter capacity after he was made editor-in-chief of the *Post* on Schurz's retirement in 1883.

But little difference was at first perceptible in the *Nation* after the change. It was in the same hands, followed the same

---

[43] *Nation*, I, 625 (November 16, 1865).
[44] *Ibid.*, I, 816 (December 28, 1865).
[45] *Memoirs of Henry Villard* (Boston, 1904), II, 339.

policies, and used the same format. But as time went by, a certain lack of freshness in the political department made itself apparent, and it became too easy to think of it as a mere *réchauffé* of the *Post*. The *Literary World* declared at the end of 1883 that "the *Nation* has lost its old position and power since it became a tender to the *New York Evening Post*." [46] It is doubtful if Godkin was as consistently pungent and vigorous on the daily paper as he had been on the weekly, and it is scarcely to be denied that he became at length too conservative for his generation — Brander Matthews thought him in his old age "impervious to every new idea." [47] This is, of course, often an infirmity of age, and Godkin's conservatism should not be overemphasized: his main significance continued to be his vigorous championship of the ideals of moderate and independent thinking in government. The chief loss of prestige to the *Nation* by the change of 1881 was owing to the fact that now nobody said, "This is what the *Nation* says"; it was rather, "Here is the *Evening Post's* view." Thus, in summarizing the *Nation's* political course, we but take a paragraph from the *Post's* history. [48]

Like most critics, the *Nation* was inclined to be lenient with Arthur's administration. When it came to the hotly contested election of 1884, Godkin was a leader in the attack on Blaine. The independent spirit of Cleveland, his practice with regard to the civil service, and his strong low-tariff views made the *Nation* his enthusiastic supporter in his three campaigns and throughout his two administrations — with one important exception. The exception was in respect to Cleveland's attitude (jingoistic, in Godkin's view) on the Venezuelan dispute with England. The *Post* and *Nation* were the President's first and severest critics on this policy.

It was in 1890 that Godkin struck his rudest blows against Tammany and its multiple corruptions. Bold, specific unmasking of the personalities of the ring's leaders was the Godkin technique. Several of the men attacked brought suits for libel,

[46] *Literary World*, XIV, 414 (December 1, 1883).

[47] Brander Matthews, *These Many Years* (New York, 1917), p. 52.

[48] See Allan Nevins, *The Evening Post: A Century of Journalism* (New York, 1922), Chapters XX–XXIV.

all of them promptly dismissed. A temporary triumph for reform came in 1894 with the election of William M. Strong as mayor.

In the national campaign of 1896, the *Nation*, with its "sound money" and antiprotectionist views, could muster little enthusiasm for either the high-tariff McKinley or the free-silver Bryan; but the danger it saw in the election of Bryan made it practically a McKinley paper. Godkin personally voted for Palmer, candidate of the gold Democrats.[49] The free-silver discussions in the *Nation* were written, for the most part, by Horace White, associate editor of the *Post*. The *Nation* watched the jingoism leading up to the Spanish War with foreboding and frequent censure; but when the country was at last at war, it did what it could to support American arms. On the issue of imperialism it trenchantly opposed the expansionist plans of the administration.

In 1899 Godkin retired from the editorship of the *Evening Post*, and he died three years later. Perhaps his work is best summed up by a sentence from A. G. Sedgwick's article in the *Atlantic Monthly* on his writings:

If Mr. Godkin's work be examined as a whole, it will be seen that there is not a distinctive principle underlying the independent movement of his period for which he has not found its best and most forcible expression, and not an impulse to action [in that movement] that has not received impetus, and in many cases life, from him.[50]

Associates of Godkin on the *Post* who became *ipso facto* writers for the *Nation* in the nineties were Horace White, Joseph Bucklin Bishop, Rollo Ogden, and Oswald Garrison Villard. The last named, a son of Henry Villard and a grandson of William Lloyd Garrison, joined the *Post* staff in 1897; he represented the majority holdings of the Villard family and eventually took over the financial control of the properties. He had, as Carl Van Doren has pointed out, a strong sense of family piety toward the *Nation*.[51]

The list of contributors in the eighties and nineties had a

[49] Ogden, *op. cit.*, II, 214.
[50] *Atlantic Monthly*, LXXIX, 122 (January 1897).
[51] Carl Van Doren, *Three Worlds*, p. 136.

remarkable continuity with that of the sixties and seventies: the *Nation* kept its contributors. Writers like Bryce and Dicey, Higginson and Norton continued to be outstanding. M. Laugel continued to write from France, and Signora Mario from Italy. Cox on history and biography, Sedgwick on politics, Finck on music, and Brownell on fiction were still stand-bys, with Michael Heilprin and W. F. Allen constantly useful. From the *Evening Post* came J. Ranken Towse, dramatic critic, and Alexander D. Noyes, financial writer. Such Harvard men as Channing, Hart, Royce, Kittredge, Shaler, and Winsor became *Nation* contributors; with Matthews and Woodberry, of Columbia, and Lounsbury, of Yale. Edward Eggleston, Gamaliel Bradford, and Joel Chandler Harris were occasional writers for the paper, as were William Roscoe Thayer, Fabian Franklin, and James Ford Rhodes.

In spite of an early distrust of realism, evidenced in the criticism of Howells, the *Nation* proved to be one of the most active channels of discussion of the new Russian novelists. Isabelle Hapgood, St. Petersburg correspondent, was high priestess of the movement in the *Nation*. The paper's literary correspondence from abroad was of great value. One of the earliest notices of European excitement over Ibsen, harbinger of a tide of popular American interest in the Norwegian dramatist, was in a *Nation* letter from Berlin, by C. H. Genung.[52]

Garrison's long editorship, which ended a few months before his death in February 1907, was characterized by remarkably consistent ideals of independence, competence, and good writing. Bryce doubted whether any European journal "maintained so uniformly high a level." [53] Garrison wrote comparatively little himself; but his unflagging industry, his careful planning, the relations of personal friendship maintained with his contributors, and his painstaking copy reading all marked him as one of the most competent of editors. "If anything goes wrong with you," Godkin wrote him in 1883, "I will retire into a monastery. You are the one steady and constant man I have ever had to do with." [54] Upon his completion of forty years of editorship, a large number of *Nation* contributors presented him

---

[52] *Nation*, XLIV, 116 (February 10, 1887).
[53] *Ibid.*, CI, 41 (July 8, 1915).   [54] McDaniels, *op. cit.*, p. 9.

with a commemorative vase, accompanied by the following note
of congratulation, prepared by Charles Eliot Norton, Goldwin
Smith, and James Ford Rhodes:

We wish to congratulate you on completing forty years as literary
editor and of late as director of the *Nation*. Your service, performed
quietly, but without rest or compromise, has been of great value. You
have made the *Nation* for more than a generation the chief literary
journal in America — the medium of the best criticism, and the mouth-
piece of high intellectual ideals. Long may you have the strength to
continue in this inestimable work. As we send you our greetings, we
cannot forget how easily and with what graciousness you transmute
your editorial relation into friendship.[55]

Garrison was an authority on punctuation and took infinite
pains in the small typographical matters that make the difference between slovenliness and the satisfying rightness of the
well-edited page. He also made the laborious and valuable
semiannual indexes. He doubtless lacked the originality and
personal force possessed by the greatest editors, but he was
both wise and thorough.

Garrison was succeeded in the editorship of the *Nation* by
Hammond Lamont, with Paul Elmer More as assistant. Both
came from the staff of the *Evening Post*, of which Lamont had
been managing editor after leaving a professorship of English
at Brown. But less than three years after assuming the editorship, Lamont died and was succeeded by More. More had
deserted a professorship of Sanskrit at Bryn Mawr for journalism when he accepted the literary editorship of the *Independent*
in 1901, joining the *Evening Post* two years later. He remained
as editor of the *Nation* for five years. Under his suzerainty a
divorcement between the literary department of the *Evening
Post* and the *Nation*, which had been begun under his predecessors, became much more marked; and it was practically complete under Harold deWolf Fuller, who came to the chair
when More withdrew to devote himself to more retired literary
work. Fuller had been assistant editor under More and an editorial writer on the *Post*; he continued the chain of Harvard
editors.

[55] McDaniels, *op. cit.*, p. 137.

Meanwhile, the political course of the *Nation* continued to parallel that of the *Evening Post*, and the articles on politics, though noticeably less important in the *Nation's* view, were chiefly by *Post* editors — Horace White, Rollo Ogden, O. G. Villard, Fabian Franklin. The paper supported Judge Parker rather than Roosevelt in 1904, largely because of disapproval of the latter's Panama activities. Its opposition to Roosevelt was, indeed, traditional — and mutual. "It fairly makes me writhe," wrote Roosevelt to Lodge in 1892, "to think of the incalculable harm to decency that scoundrelly paper [the *Nation*], edited by its scoundrelly chief, Godkin, has done." [56] In 1908 the *Nation* was behind Taft, though urging him to freedom from Rooseveltian domination; it could never stomach Bryan. In 1912 and again four years later it supported Wilson with some enthusiasm.

Shortly after Garrison's death there had been some change in layout in the *Nation*; the introduction of department headings broke a long adherence to a kind of typographical aridity that had been too characteristic of the paper. More prominence was given to current fiction. The department of letters to the editor continued to be one of the most interesting divisions of the periodical; in the long history of the *Nation* this department has been not only readable but often highly valuable. Among prominent contributors in these prewar years were Stuart P. Sherman, Irving Babbitt, J. E. Spingarn, Frank Jewett Mather, William Beebe, Norman Foerster, O. W. Firkins, H. W. Boynton, Morris Jastrow, W. P. Trent, F. J. E. Woodbridge, and Arthur S. Hardy. On the whole, in spite of its reliance on critics from the schools, the *Nation* by this time was not unfriendly to the newer and more experimental movements in letters. Dreiser's *Jennie Gerhardt* and *Sister Carrie* fared better than might have been expected; the experimental poets were somewhat less fortunate.

In March 1914, with the accession of Fuller to the editorship and some reorganization of management which accentuated the growing gap between the *Evening Post* and the *Nation*, the paper was made larger and fresher. It replaced the "Summary of the

[56] *Selections from the Correspondence of Theodore Roosevelt and Henry Cabot Lodge* (New York, 1925), I, 130.

News," which had once before occupied the place of honor, at the front of the journal; it added more foreign correspondence; it gave its readers some outdoor material, including even some staid sports; in general it became more human and less pedantic. Edmund Lester Pearson had a department of personalities, called "Books and Men." Dramatic criticism was enlarged, and William Archer wrote a monthly letter on London theaters. Such foreign correspondents as Louis Dyer in London, Stoddard Dewey in Paris, Arne Kildal in Bergen, A. Barnouw in The Hague, Mrs. A. von Ende in Berlin, and A. Alexander in Geneva continued their work for the *Nation*. In 1917 a new modernized "dress" emphasized the changing nature of the paper. By this time *Post* editorials were no longer used, and the *Nation* had its own Washington correspondent.

But it was in January 1918, when Oswald Garrison Villard became editor, with Henry Raymond Mussey, from the economics department of Columbia University, as assistant, that the great break occurred. Hundreds of thousands of the A. E. F. were in France by this time, and the *Nation* was valiantly supporting President Wilson, with criticisms now and then of such factors as the coal administration and the activities of Secretary Burleson. Once more the paper called its soul its own; once more it was endowed with vigor, independence, bold thinking. In July it announced its complete editorial separation from the *Evening Post*. But the paper was going ahead too fast to suit many of its old subscribers — too fast and in a direction far too much inclined to the left. A spokesman for them complained of the "excessive gall" in the *Nation's* comment on public affairs.[57] Circulation, which had stood at about ten thousand, declined rapidly.

But the tide turned in September, and the cause of its turning was the advertising given to the paper by the action of Secretary Burleson in holding up its issue of September 14. This issue contained more than one article which might have given offense to authority. The *Nation* itself preferred to think that one of its familiar satires on Samuel Gompers, in which he was called a "bagman of the war," was the bitter dose that made Burleson gag; but it is more likely that the general newspaper

[57] *Sewanee Review*, XXVII, 227 (April 1919).

opinion was correct and that the offending article was the one in which the drive on "slackers" and various acts of censorship were recorded, with the declaration that "personal liberty and freedom have disappeared in America." Whatever it was, the impolicy of suppressing the *Nation* was soon discovered; and the issue was handled by the postoffice department after a delay of five days. But from this time on, the *Nation* was more prosperous: H. L. Mencken claimed that it succeeded "because it began breaking heads." [58]

Circulation was further stimulated by the initiation, in October, of a biweekly "International Relations Section," in which foreign documents were published under the aegis of an "advisory council" consisting of such men as John Bassett Moore, Gilbert Murray, and James Harvey Robinson. Mussey wrote later:

We fed foreign news to a public hungry for facts, for years systematically starved of such facts by government censorship. Thenceforth even our enemies — and under our wholly independent auspices, with the flag of peace and reconciliation nailed to our masthead, they multiplied like flies in summer — even those who hated us worst had to come to us for facts at a time when facts were most unwelcome to those in authority. The circulation manager began to smile.[59]

Editor Villard himself covered the Versailles peace conference, sending his reports by cable, followed by stories of revolutionary Germany from his first-hand observation. The *Nation* became, in the ensuing months, an effective influence against American ratification of the Versailles treaty.

From the time of the deposition of Czar Nicholas in March 1917 the *Nation* watched Russia's struggle toward the light with interest and sympathy. Its editorial on the fall of Nicholas was almost a paean of triumph: "We are living in a Götterdämmerung of Kings and Viceregents of God!" it cried.[60] It protested against the sending of American troops into Russia in the next year, and it made a valiant attempt to interpret the Bolsheviki to the American people when the very name was being made a rallying cry of reactionary hatred. It was first

[58] H. L. Mencken, *Prejudices, First Series* (New York, 1919), p. 179.
[59] *Nation*, CXXI, 10 (July 1, 1925).
[60] *Ibid.*, CIV, 327 (March 22, 1917).

to print the new Russian soviet constitution in January 1919. Moreover, it championed the collective cause of the coal and steel strikers of 1919, the "Wobblies," and the political prisoners — all of whom suffered from the invocation of the "bolshevik scare." The *New York Times* said in 1920 that if the *Nation* was not "actually Bolshevist," it was "so near it that the distinction is not visible to the naked eye." [61] And the point is that this was the ultimate in condemnation.

The International Relations Section became a weekly department in 1920 and was eventually absorbed into the body of the magazine. The *Nation* continued a specialist in foreign affairs, however. It exposed in detail and at length "the foul record of our administration in Haiti," [62] beginning in the autumn of 1920. In a juncture of affairs which threatened a renewal of hostilities with Mexico, it sprang to the defense of President Obregón and his administration; and it continued for years an effort to interpret their southern neighbor to the people of the United States. Its interest in Russia was also maintained; Villard's own letters from that country in 1929 and the paper's advocacy of recognition until the triumph of 1933 were notable features. The Hitler régime in Germany has had no severer critic than the *Nation*; its editor was a German visitor just before the coup of March 1933.

Internationally minded though it was, beyond any weekly journal of opinion ever published in this country, it did not neglect American public affairs. In the quadrennial party nose counting, it generally checked in as a socialist paper. In 1920 it refused to support either Harding or Cox for president and advised its readers to vote for either Christensen, the Farmer-Labor candidate, or the Socialist Debs. In 1924 it supported LaFollette for president; but four years later it was not firmly behind any candidate, the staff being hopelessly divided between Alfred E. Smith, Democrat, and Norman Thomas, Socialist. In 1932 it urged its readers to help pile up an impressive vote for Thomas.

An important series of 1922–23 was "These United States," a sequence of surveys of the commonwealths by writers with

<hr>

[61] *Nation*, CXI, 467 (October 27, 1920). Quoted from *Times*.
[62] *Ibid.*

special information. Editor Villard kept his antimilitaristic views well to the fore in the *Nation's* pages. "The modern soldier is an utter anachronism," he remarked in an editorial entitled "The Military Menaces the World." [63] The threat of execution for Sacco and Vanzetti brought passionate protests from the *Nation*; and when the juggernaut rolled over them Villard wrote: "Massachusetts has triumphantly killed an Italian fishmonger and an Italian cobbler, but she has blackened the name of the United States across all the seas." [64] The individualistic philosophy of the Coolidge and Hoover administrations found little sympathy in the *Nation's* editorial room. "Mr. Hoover affects to contemplate America's false and dishonest individualism with pride and ecstatic veneration," said the paper in 1931.[65] It watched the "New Deal" go into effect with surprised approval. An editorial of 1934 said:

Although the *Nation* has questioned the probability that in the long run it would be possible to save an industrial system driven by the incentive of profits, it has regarded the Roosevelt program in general as the most intelligent means that could be taken toward that end.[66]

In criticism as in politics the *Nation* has been rather consistently pushed toward the left. The change in policy made in 1918 affected comment on letters as well as that on international and domestic affairs. Carl Van Doren, the paper's "Roving Critic" for several years, has pointed out that this shift represented a turning "from Sherman to Mencken." "The professors had been beaten by the journalists," he adds. [67] In another place Van Doren further explains the change:

With the break came a large increase in circulation, among readers, furthermore, who were notably concerned in the creative and speculative aspects of current literature, rather than with the erudite and technical. The literary department of the *Nation,* not so quick to respond to the change as its political columns, nevertheless did respond. It had the tact to see that its task was not to become less expert but to carry its old expertness into wider fields. For the past half dozen

[63] *Ibid.*, CXXIV, 306 (March 23, 1927).
[64] *Ibid.*, CXXV, 193 (August 31, 1927).
[65] *Ibid.*, CXXXIII, 330 (September 30, 1931).
[66] *Ibid.*, CXXXVIII, 346 (March 28, 1934).
[67] Van Doren, *op. cit.*, p. 149.

years [1918–24] it has gone on the assumption that, though it might not be called upon to examine every treatise or encyclopedia, it was called upon to examine every outstanding novel or play or book of poems or philosophy or political planning or economic reconstruction with the same precision which it would formerly have used with a treatise or encyclopedia.[68]

The drama and music have been given similar attention. Seasonal book, dramatic, and education supplements have appeared from time to time. Educational problems, prominently discussed in the paper from its first issue, have lost none of that emphasis in recent years. A later feature was the weekly cartoon, given a rather philosophical cast by the pencil of Hendrik Van Loon, or inspired with social passion by that of Art Young. Heywood Broun began a weekly page after his break with the *New York World* in September 1927; later, after he went back to daily journalism, he continued this contribution more or less regularly until, in 1937, he was irked by the *Nation's* giving space to the opposition to Roosevelt's court plan — a measure the editors approved.

There is a significance in what one commentator has called "the continual procession of bright young and able middle-aged men through the *Nation* office." [69] For some the *Nation* has been a trying ground, for others a convenient forum. Villard has had an affinity for likely young men of ambition and brilliance. Ernest H. Gruening, who wrote authoritatively on Haiti and Mexico, was managing editor 1920–22 and joint editor 1933–34. Carl Van Doren was literary editor 1920–22 and a contributing editor for some years afterward; his wife Irita was literary editor in 1924, and his brother Mark in 1925–28. Freda Kirchwey was managing editor in 1923, later literary editor, and then joint editor with Gruening, Krutch, and others, and finally owner. Joseph Wood Krutch was an associate editor for some years before he came to be called dramatic editor in 1928. John Macy was literary editor for a time in 1923, and Henry Hazlitt filled that position in 1930–32. Among the associate editors, Albert Jay Nock did notable essays for the *Nation* before his *Freeman* days; Lewis S. Gan-

[68] *Nation*, CXXI, 11 (July 1, 1925).
[69] *American Mercury*, XII, 456 (December 1927). By Edmund Wilson.

nett wrote brilliant literary criticism; Ludwig Lewisohn for some years followed the theaters and later wrote essays on varied subjects; Norman Thomas brought to the aid of his socialistic viewpoint a lucid and cogent reasoning power in his political articles. Other associate editors from 1918 to 1932 were William MacDonald, Lincoln Colcord, Arthur Warner, Arthur Gleason, Mabel H. B. Mussey, Dorothy Graffe Van Doren, Mauritz A. Hallgren, Devere Allen, and Margaret Marshall. For some years the paper carried a roll of "contributing editors," which included such names as the English John A. Hobson, the German Friedrich Wilhelm Foerster, the French Anatole France, and the American H. L. Mencken and Robert Herrick.

At the beginning of 1933 Villard retired from the chief editorship, making Gruening, Hazlitt, Krutch, and Miss Kirchwey joint editors; but Hazlitt soon resigned to edit the *American Mercury*, and a little later Gruening was lured away by the editorship of the *New York Evening Post*. R. G. Swing and Max Lerner then came in as co-editors. Villard remained, however, as contributing editor and until 1935 as owner. In spite of the many personalities which have been worked into the texture of the *Nation* since the World War, Villard managed to dominate it throughout the period — less, indeed, in the strictly literary columns than in the pages devoted to political and economic problems and to social reform in general. This domination was characterized by an incorrigibly optimistic idealism, surviving in spite of ever renewed indignations against oppression ever renewed.[70]

In 1935 Maurice Wertheim, banker, philanthropist, a founder of the Theatre Guild, and the director of the Civic Aid Foundation, bought the *Nation*, making his Foundation its publisher. The format was improved, David Low's cartoons were added, and the paper seemed to gain new vitality. Wertheim sedulously refrained from interference with the liberal and socialistic Kirchwey-Krutch-Lerner editorial management. But the *Nation's* endorsement of President Roosevelt's plan of Supreme Court reform was more than Wertheim could accept; he bought

[70] For Villard, *ibid.; World Tomorrow*, XIII, 440 (November 1930); *Outlook*, CLI, 384 (March 6, 1929).

space in the paper to record his disagreement, and in June 1937 he sold the property to Freda Kirchwey, who had been editorially connected with it for nineteen years. At that time it boasted a circulation of 43,000 — the largest in its history.

On the centenary of Edwin Lawrence Godkin's birth, Oswald Garrison Villard wrote a sentence which may serve to close this brief summary of seventy-odd years of the *Nation*: "As for the *Nation* of today, he would often find it crude, unpolished, and lacking the scholarship which under him made it unique; but he would perhaps recognize some of his own passion for social justice." [71] After all, that passion preserves the unity of the seventy years' history.

[71] *Nation*, CXXXIII, 354 (October 7, 1931)

EVERY SATURDAY [1]

TICKNOR & FIELDS, the leading Boston publishers, who were already proprietors of a general literary monthly, the *Atlantic*; a quarterly review, the *North American*; and a juvenile, *Our Young Folks*, began in 1866 the publication of an eclectic weekly under the editorship of Thomas Bailey Aldrich called *Every Saturday*. Aldrich, who was later to ascend the *Atlantic* throne, had published several volumes of verse, but had not yet achieved his wider reputation.

The selections in *Every Saturday* were chiefly from English periodicals, though there were a few from French and German magazines. Mrs. Aldrich tells in her autobiography of how she and her husband, having been charmed with Justin Winsor upon their first acquaintance with him, noted his shiny coat commiseratingly and conspired to give him work for *Every Saturday* translating articles from French and German, and of how they were comically surprised later, when he entertained them, to discover him anything but poverty-stricken.[2] But translating was more expensive than scissoring, and *Every Saturday* continued throughout to rely upon the English, though in 1873 a Turgeniev novel was printed serially. Serials were

[1] TITLE: *Every Saturday*. Subtitles: *A Journal of Choice Reading Selected from Foreign Current Literature*, 1866–69; *An Illustrated Weekly Journal*, 1870–71; *A Journal of Choice Reading*, 1872–74.

FIRST ISSUE: January 6, 1866. LAST ISSUE: October 31, 1874.

PERIODICITY: Weekly. Regular semiannual volumes, except for 1870, which has only one volume. [First Series], I–VIII, 1866–69; New [Second] Series, I (1870), II–III (1871); New [Third] Series, I–IV, 1872–73; New [Fourth] Series, I (January–June 1874), II (July–October 1874). Unpaged supplements weekly, April 9, 1870, through May 1870; also August–November 1870, except August 20 and October 1.

PUBLISHERS: Ticknor & Fields, 1867–68; Fields, Osgood & Company 1868–71; James R. Osgood & Company, 1871–73; H. O. Houghton & Company, 1874. All of Boston.

EDITOR: Thomas Bailey Aldrich.

INDEXED in *Poole's*.

REFERENCE: Ferris Greenslet, *The Life of Thomas Bailey Aldrich* (Boston, 1908).

[2] Mrs. T. B. Aldrich, *Crowding Memories* (Boston, 1920), pp. 91–93.

not begun until the second volume; but thereafter Edmund Yates, Charles Reade, Anthony Trollope, Charles Dickens, Anne Thackeray, and William Black furnished fiction — some of which was printed from advance sheets, but most from the English periodicals without a "by your leave." Indeed advance sheets were used little after the first volume. The serials were nearly all minor works for these novelists, though at the time our weekly ended it was printing Hardy's *Far from the Madding Crowd*. Original American productions appeared in the Second Series, and somewhat in the Fourth: in the latter, Mary Clemmer Ames's *His Two Wives* was serialized.

The most notable phase of *Every Saturday* was its Second Series, during which it was quarto in size and copiously illustrated with engravings on wood. "It is the intention of the publishers to make *Every Saturday* the handsomest illustrated journal in America," ran the announcement on January 1, 1870. The eclectic nature of the publication was gradually abandoned during 1870, and *Every Saturday* became a competitor of *Harper's Weekly* not only in illustration but also in comment upon politics, social life, and the arts. There was not much of original belles-lettres — a few poems by Hayne, Howells, and others; a series of reminiscences by Kate Field called *Leaves from a Lecturer's Notebook*; "Pike County" poems by John Hay and Bret Harte, which were taken from books about to be published by the magazine's proprietors. It was in 1871 that Bret Harte was paid $10,000 by Osgood for whatever he chose to write for the *Atlantic* and *Every Saturday* during the year, "not less than twelve pieces." [3] That the publisher thought this bargain was to entitle him to the author's exclusive production is shown by the announcement in *Every Saturday*: "Messrs. James R. Osgood & Company have made arrangements with Mr. Bret Harte by which he is to write exclusively for their publications, the *Atlantic Monthly* and *Every Saturday*." [4] There is plenty of evidence in other magazines, however, that Mr. Bret Harte did not so interpret his obligations.

[3] The *Atlantic* had declined Harte's early work because it "failed to interest," according to Jessie Benton Fremont, literary agent, writing in *Ladies' Home Journal*, IX, 18 (February 1892).

[4] *Every Saturday*, Second Series, II, 314 (April 8, 1871).

Two Harte bits fell to *Every Saturday's* share — a "condensed novel" and a poem on the Chicago fire.

Most of the pictures used in *Every Saturday* in 1870, and at least half of those used in 1871 were printed from electrotypes made from wood blocks which had been cut for the new London *Graphic*, one of the best of the popular illustrated journals of England. Since the *Graphic* paid much attention to the Franco-Prussian war, we find in *Every Saturday* a rather full pictorial history of that struggle. *Harper's Weekly* meantime copied many of the *Graphic's* pictures and thus robbed *Every Saturday* of most of what it had paid for. Much of the American engraving in the Boston paper, however, compared favorably with the English. W. J. Linton engraved a series of portraits for it in 1871. Its chief American artists were A. R. Waud, Winslow Homer, F. O. C. Darley, W. L. Sheppard, Sol Eytinge, and W. J. Hennessy. Eytinge did an admirable series of Dickens characters, and his double-page unbacked picture, "Mr. Pickwick's Reception," shows a vast crowd of people from the popular novelist's works.[5]

Greenslet, in his biography of Aldrich, has the following note on the art editor of *Every Saturday*:

Ralph Keeler, the vivacious author of papers in the *Atlantic* on "Three Years a Negro Minstrel," and "A Tour of Europe on $181," was appointed art editor of *Every Saturday* after its sea-change, and soon came to terms of comradeship with Mr. Aldrich. . . . In the course of a few years, however, the exciting progress of the Cuban insurrection became too strong for Keeler's spirit of adventure, and despite the remonstrances of his friends he set out for Cuba as a special correspondent of the *Tribune*. Before his departure Aldrich exacted from him the promise that when, with a halter about his neck, he should be carted out to the public square of Havana for execution, he would utter as his last words: "Ladies and gentlemen: If I had taken the advice of my friend Mr. T. B. Aldrich, author of *Marjorie Daw and Other People*, I should not now be in this place!" The pleasantry was turned to grisly earnest. Keeler was mysteriously lost at sea — probably murdered as the result of a political intrigue — before he reached the Cuban shore.[6]

---

[5] *Ibid.* (supplement for April 9, 1870).
[6] Greenslet, *op. cit.*, p. 100.

Keeler's most notable literary contribution to *Every Saturday* was a series of articles which he wrote and which A. R. Waud illustrated about the lower Mississippi and its cities from New Orleans to St. Louis.

Illustrations were abandoned at the end of 1871, and the magazine returned to its former size and policy. Edmund Clarence Stedman, who in 1868 had urged Osgood to bring the paper to New York, change its name to the *Atlantic Weekly*, and install him as editor, tells us that Osgood "afterwards had occasion to tell me that if he had followed my suggestion it would have saved him $125,000 — I think that was the loss." [7] Doubtless the flier in illustrated journalism did something to hasten the financial disasters that overtook Osgood in 1873 and made necessary the sale of *Every Saturday* to H. O. Houghton & Company at the end of that year. Houghton combined with it his monthly house organ, the *Riverside Bulletin*, in February 1874, making the *Bulletin* an editorial department of two pages in each issue. At the end of the year *Every Saturday* was disposed of to *Littell's Living Age*, which absorbed its list and thus became the only eclectic weekly in the country.

[7] Laura Stedman and George M. Gould, *Life and Letters of Edmund Clarence Stedman* (New York, 1910), I, 426.

THE GALAXY [1]

THE *Galaxy* was "born of a divine discontent with the *Atlantic Monthly*" and "the feeling that New York ought to have a monthly of its own." So the *Nation* thought,[2] and comments in contemporary periodicals and letters bear out that opinion. Perhaps the chief support, accordingly, came from New York, at least at the beginning of the project. There Edmund Clarence Stedman, for example, was urging his fellow literati to stand by the editors of the new magazine, who, he said, "are doing their bravest to establish a New York magazine and ought to be helped and encouraged by New York authors."[3] But encouragement came from other quarters too. From Philadelphia Rebecca Harding Davis wrote to the editors:

Both Mr. Davis and I have been interested in the *Galaxy* from the first issue, hoping to find in it that which will fill a vacuum in our literature more apparent every year — a national magazine in which the current of thought in every section could find expression as thoroughly as that of New England does in the *Atlantic*.[4]

And from the same city came the enthusiastic good wishes of George H. Boker, the poet and playwright. "I am glad to know

[1] TITLE: *The Galaxy: An Illustrated Magazine of Entertaining Reading.* (*Illustrated* dropped April 1872).

FIRST ISSUE: May 1, 1866. LAST ISSUE: January 1878.

PERIODICITY: Semimonthly, 1866–April 15, 1867; monthly, May 1867–1878. I, May–August 1866; II, September–December 1866; III, January–April 1867; IV, May–December 1867; V–XXIV, regular semiannual volumes, 1868–77; XXV, one number only, January 1878.

PUBLISHERS: W. C. & F. P. Church, New York, 1866–68; Sheldon & Company, New York, 1868–78.

EDITORS: William Conant Church and Francis Pharcellus Church.

[2] *Nation*, II, 534 (April 26, 1866).

[3] Laura Stedman and George M. Gould, *Life and Letters of Edmund Clarence Stedman* (New York, 1910), I, 380.

[4] Letter to F. P. Church, dated June 4, 1866, in the possession of Mr. Willard Church, of Montclair, New Jersey. Letters cited from Mr. Church's file of *Galaxy* correspondence will hereafter be referred to as from "Willard Church Collection."

that something without the imprint of Boston upon it is likely to establish itself with our people," he wrote.[5] From John Esten Cooke in Virginia came good wishes and promises of reinforcements: *Harper's* he believed to be "sectional and dull," and the *Atlantic* "a New England coterie affair altogether." [6]

The two editors whom Stedman was justified in thinking so brave were William Conant Church and Francis Pharcellus Church, known in New York literary journalistic circles as Colonel Church and his brother Frank, publishers of the *Army and Navy Journal*. At the end of the war, the *Journal* being an assured success, the two brothers had decided to capitalize the apparent sentiment in favor of a New York literary magazine by starting one of their own. The *Galaxy* was the result.

Oliver Wendell Holmes, who had named the *Atlantic Monthly*, may have named the new magazine. "Metropolitan" had been first proposed, but six weeks before the first number of the magazine appeared Howells wrote the editors, "The other night Dr. Holmes told me that he was engaged in the great work of trying to give a name to the new magazine. Is it christened yet?" [7] Soon thereafter the new name was announced. Odd though it seems for these anti-Bostonians to go to the Back Bay for a godfather, is it not true that "Galaxy" sounds very like a Holmes echo? One thinks of Holmes's own "Star-Drift" in *The Poet at the Breakfast-Table*, and of the doctor's love for correlating the phenomena of natural science with literature.

Stedman later told Lowell [8] that he had had the refusal of the editorship of the *Galaxy*, but when the magazine appeared the Church brothers were both publishers and editors. And editors they remained throughout the *Galaxy's* history,[9] though Sheldon & Company became publishers and joint proprietors at the end of the magazine's second year, with Colonel Alexander E. Sheldon active in the magazine's affairs. Associated

[5] Letter to W. C. Church, dated June 15, 1866 (Willard Church Collection).
[6] Letter dated March 26, 1866 (Willard Church Collection).
[7] Letter dated March 13, 1866 (Willard Church Collection).
[8] Stedman and Gould, *op. cit.*, I, 380.
[9] F. P. Church appears to have dropped out of the management, however, some months before the end.

with the Churches were Frederic Beecher Perkins as office editor and Richard Grant White as an editorial contributor. Perkins was a well-known librarian and an experienced editor, a cousin of Henry Ward Beecher. Theodore Tilton called him "a born magazine writer." [10] The length of Perkins' *Galaxy* service is not known, but White was a fairly regular writer of special articles and editorial notes throughout the magazine's career. As departments came to be added later, other writers were called upon. George E. Pond, who had been associate editor of the *Army and Navy Journal*, wrote an editorial department (chiefly political) called "Drift-Wood" under the name of "Philip Quilibet" during the last ten years of the *Galaxy*, being engaged meanwhile as editorial writer first on the *New York Times* and then the *Philadelphia Record*. S. S. Conant, who was editor of *Harper's Weekly* for fifteen years prior to his mysterious disappearance in 1885, did criticism for the *Galaxy's* fine arts department. James F. Meline, who contributed reviews of French and German books until his death in 1873, presented the paradox of an ardent Catholic writing for a magazine unfriendly to his faith. Professor E. L. Youmans, the famous popularizer of scientific knowledge, edited the "Scientific Miscellany" from 1871 to 1874. He was followed in the science department by John A. Church, a brother of the editors of the *Galaxy* who had been a professor of mineralogy in the Columbia School of Mines, and editor of the *Engineering and Mining Journal*.

One of the most interesting figures connected editorially with the *Galaxy* was that of the almost forgotten "Carl Benson." In private life he was Charles Astor Bristed, and so he was known in social centers of Europe and America. His father was an English emigrant who had been successively lawyer, editor, and clergyman, his mother a daughter of John Jacob Astor. "Carl Benson" was always a brilliant author — daring, cultivated, inclined to be cynical, decided. He was a tonic writer, and his "Casual Cogitations" and other contributions to the *Galaxy* were a decided asset to that magazine.

But the best-known *Galaxy* editor of them all was Mark Twain, who conducted a department called "Memoranda" from

[10] *Independent*, June 7, 1866.

May 1870 to April 1871.[11] Mark Twain had just acquired incontestable fame by his *Innocents Abroad*; he had married and settled down at Buffalo in a house which, as he boyishly wrote Colonel Church, " a generous father-in-law has built and furnished at the comely figure of $42,000"; and he had bought an interest in the *Buffalo Express*, which, he says, "pays me an ample livelihood, and does it without my having to go near it. I write sketches for it, and occasional squibs and editorials — that is all. I don't go to the office." [12] Thus he was in a position to demand liberal compensation for his magazine work. The *Galaxy* had already used one sketch of his and had rejected at least one, for there is a letter to "Friend Church — Confound it, when a man sends you an article and you don't want it, why in the mischief don't you return it at once and give him a chance to use it elsewhere? . . . This isn't right, you know." [13]   But this was before *Innocents Abroad*: now he writes:

> If I can have entire ownership and disposal of what I write for the *Galaxy*, after it has appeared in the magazine, I will edit your humorous department for two thousand ($2,000) a year [14] — and I give you my word that I can start out tomorrow or any day that I choose and make that money in two weeks, lecturing.

This amounted to some seventeen dollars a page, or nearly double the *Galaxy's* highest rate of payment to its other contributors of prose; but it was a good investment, for it brought the magazine the largest circulation it ever attained.

In his salutatory, Mark Twain outlined his program:

> . . . In this department of mine the public may always rely upon finding exhaustive statistical tables concerning the finances of the

[11] Inclusive; omitting, however, the installment for March 1871, and cutting the August 1870 installment to two pages.

[12] Letter to W. C. Church, dated February 9 [1870] (Willard Church Collection).

[13] Letter to W. C. Church, dated February 22, 1868 (Willard Church Collection).

[14] Mr. Albert Bigelow Paine, in his *Mark Twain: A Biography* (New York, 1912), II, 403, puts the contract figure at $2,400; but this letter dated March 11 [1870], together with a signed acknowledgment of "$334, full payment for July & Sept." dated September 5 [1870], shows that $2,000 was the amount. Letter and receipt are in the Willard Church Collection.

country, the ratio of births and deaths, the percentage of increase of population, etc., etc. — in a word, everything in the realm of statistics that can make existence bright and beautiful.

Also in my department may be found elaborate condensations of the Patent Office Reports. . . .

And finally, I call attention with pride to the fact that in my department of the magazine the farmer will always find full market reports, and also complete instructions about farming, even from the grafting of the seed to the harrowing of the matured crop. I shall throw a pathos into the subject of Agriculture that will surprise and delight the world.[15]

But however lightly the new editor might treat the subject of agriculture, he showed more than once in the "Memoranda" that vein of savage satire which is so important a phase of the true Mark Twain. In the very first installment he attacked the Reverend Mr. Talmadge for certain reported remarks tending to bar workingmen from his congregation because of their odor. His indignation was also aroused against the persecution of Chinese in America, and, on the other hand, against idealization of the Indian. His most bitter attack was upon a clergyman who had refused to bury an actor from his church.[16]

An interesting incident of his connection with the *Galaxy* was the one related to the *Saturday Review* hoax. Mark, having had his attention directed to a rather stupid review of *Innocents Abroad* in the *London Saturday Review*, conceived the idea of burlesquing it and passing off his production as the original. In the burlesque [17] the reviewer proceeds with ponderous and asinine gravity to rebuke the author for his exaggeration, for his levity, and for his ignorance.

He is vulgarly ignorant of all foreign languages [says the mock reviewer] but is frank enough to criticize the Italians' use of their own tongue. He says they spell the name of their great painter "Vinci, but pronounce it Vinchy" — and then adds with a naïveté possible only to helpless ignorance, *"foreigners always spell better than they pronounce."*

There was much more in the same manner. The burlesque was well done — too well, indeed. For some papers, while they

---

[15] *Galaxy*, IX, 717 (May 1870).
[16] *Ibid*., XI, 320 (February 1871). See p. 206.
[17] *Ibid*., X, 877 (December 1870).

were completely deceived about the authenticity of the piece, thought they perceived that the reviewer had actually seen all the humor of *Innocents Abroad* and was employing a humor of his own in "writing it up." A writer in the *Cincinnati Enquirer* was so delighted with this supposed discovery that he printed this paragraph:

Nothing is more uncertain than the value of a fine cigar. Nine smokers out of ten would prefer an ordinary domestic article, three for a quarter, to a fifty-cent Partaga, if kept in ignorance of the cost of the latter. The flavor of the Partaga is too delicate for palates that have been accustomed to Connecticut seed-leaf. The finer it is in quality, the more danger of its not being recognized at all. Even Mark Twain has been taken in by an English review of his *Innocents Abroad*. Mark is by no means a coarse humorist, but the Englishman's humor is so much finer than his that he takes it for solid earnest, and "larfs most consumedly." [18]

Of course Mark then confessed that "I wrote it myself — every line of it," and the joke should have been on the *Enquirer*; but the *Enquirer* fellow, valuing his dignity more than the joke, stubbornly maintained that the review actually did appear in the London paper and that he had a copy of it to prove his good faith. Things were now in a rather bad snarl; and Mark proceeded to post, through the *Galaxy*, a thousand-dollar reward, half payable to the *Enquirer* man or his agent if he produced the copy of the London paper containing the review as published in the *Galaxy*, and the other half payable to him if Mark failed to produce a copy of the *Saturday Review* containing an entirely different article on *Innocents Abroad*.[19] "If any man doubts my word now, I will kill him," exclaimed Mark. "No, I will not kill him; I will win his money." And he wrote to Colonel Church:

Oh, please don't fail to get this delicious thing in — now *don't*. Don't wait to ask the Sheldon's whether they'll back me for $1,000 — I hereby give them authority to secure themselves amply by means of my share of my pamphlet which they are about to publish. Or let them call for the *money* if it is won, and I'll furnish it instantly. I've got these *Enquirer* idiots just where I wanted *some*body — don't

[18] *Galaxy*, XI, 158 (January 1871).
[19] *Ibid.*, XI, 319 (February 1871).

you see why? Because half of the people don't know now whether to believe I wrote that thing or not, or whether it *was* from the *Review*, or whether it is all a sell, and no criticism ever *was* in the London paper. Now, over the shoulders of this Cincinnati fool, I'll make the whole thing straight.

Don't let that paragraph get lost for your life.

I've got the *original* London *Saturday Review of Oct. 8 with the silly original critique in it right under my nose at this moment* — and I'll lock it up till that idiot *dares* to call for it — which he never will! [20]

This example of the griefs of a hoaxer was overshadowed by greater private griefs, and the next month, instead of the "exposure" of the *Enquirer* which had been promised, there was this note:

The friends of Mr. Clemens (Mark Twain) will share our regret that the sudden and alarming illness of his wife deprives us this month of his usual contribution to the *Galaxy*. [21]

And the installment for the following month contained his "Valedictory":

I have now written for the *Galaxy* a year. For the last eight months, with hardly an interval, I have had for my fellows and comrades, night and day, doctors and watchers of the sick! During these eight months death has taken two members of my home circle and malignantly threatened two others. All this I have experienced, yet all the time been under contract to furnish "humorous" matter once a month for this magazine. . . . I think that some of the "humor" I have written during this period could have been injected into a funeral sermon without disturbing the solemnity of the occasion.[22]

But it should have been plain enough from the beginning that Clemens would do well to last the year out. Ten small-type, double-column pages a month required too much of a "grind." When the year was only half gone, he wrote Colonel Church: "Sometimes I get ready to give you notice that I'll quit at the end of my year because the *Galaxy* work crowds book work so much, but I am very fond of the Memoranda, and take a

---

[20] Letter to W. C. Church, dated December 23 [1870] (Willard Church Collection).

[21] *Galaxy*, XI, 478 (March 1871).

[22] *Ibid.*, XI, 615 (April 1871).

live interest in it always." [23] In the end, he was very glad to be free of it, and he wrote to his brother Orion that he had informed the *Galaxy* he would not furnish another installment for less than $500, and preferred not to do it at all.[24] This would have been three times what he had been getting, and prohibitive. He parted from the *Galaxy* on good terms with its editors, however.

For a few months after Mark Twain's departure, Donn Piatt edited the *Galaxy's* humorous department, now called "The Club Room," and then the editors themselves tried to run it. Indeed they did run it; but the effect, as the *Nation* observed, was rather "doleful" than merry. In July 1872 Kate Sanborn took charge of it and conducted it for a little more than a year, after which it was discontinued. Under Miss Sanborn it was an amusing, literary, scrapbookish essay of four pages in each number.

Passing from editors to contributors, we may note that of the four chief writers for the magazine's pages during its nearly twelve years of existence, two sustained some editorial connection with it. These four writers, outstanding because of the quantity as well as the importance of their contributions, were Richard Grant White, Justin McCarthy, Henry James, and Eugene Benson.

White probably wrote more of the "Nebulae" — the chief editorial department of the magazine — than any other writer, and was frequently referred to as the *Galaxy's* editor. He never was that, however; on the contrary, he occasionally found reason to complain of the way his copy was edited, and once went so far as to withdraw temporarily because of dissatisfaction with the way his work was handled. White's signed articles were related generally to what may be termed the state of civilization in America, and especially in New York. He "really writes as much on cultivation," said the *Nation*, "as though he were not in full possession of it." [25] His topics were Shakespeare, the stage, journalism, music, language, and manners; and the last-named topic managed to insinuate itself into most of the

[23] Letter to W. C. Church, dated October 18 [1870] (Willard Church Collection).

[24] Paine, *op. cit.*, II, 431.   [25] *Nation*, IV, 433 (May 30, 1867).

articles on the other six. Most notable was his series on "Words and Their Uses" and the controversy with Fitzedward Hall which grew out of it. Readers of the *Galaxy*, unless they also read Hall in the *Nation*, could scarcely know that Hall pretty thoroughly demolished White; White certainly pommeled Hall with vigor — "Punishing a Pundit," he called it. But Grant White was a valuable aid to the *Galaxy*, contributing to nearly half its numbers.

Justin McCarthy, Irish journalist and politician, was for a time minister unofficial and journalistic from England to America, and during a visit which stretched from a few months to three years became editorial contributor of informative articles and comment on the staffs of the *New York Times* and the *Independent*, as well as the *Galaxy*. Besides this, he contributed short stories and serial novels with miraculous fecundity to the *Galaxy*, *Harper's*, and other periodicals. His *Galaxy* articles dealt mainly with English political and literary figures with whom he was more or less acquainted personally, though he occasionally considered French or Italian politicians. The *Galaxy* published four fiction serials by this brilliant writer, of which *Lady Judith* was the best known. McCarthy was represented almost constantly in the *Galaxy's* pages from 1869 onward.

Henry James, Jr., as he then signed himself, had contributed two short stories to the *Atlantic* and many unsigned reviews to the *North American* before the *Galaxy* was begun. But the new magazine gave the young James an audience outside the Boston circle, though at first it printed an average of only about a story a year. In 1875 it began to print James's articles of travel and criticism; and for more than a year before its end, it had been printing a James article nearly every month. The *Europeans* was in the hands of the *Galaxy* for serial publication at the time of its merger with the *Atlantic* and was turned over to the surviving magazine.

Then there was Eugene Benson. Benson was a painter who was also a critic, and, as he would have said, a *frondeur*. He spent most of his life abroad, and his contributions to the *Galaxy* and the *Atlantic* were episodic in his career rather than integral, but (perhaps for that reason) they have a freshness, a vividness, a spirit of gallant tilting at conventions which did much to confirm the reputation of the *Galaxy* for liveliness. Benson was a leader of the revolt against American Puritanism. He was an admirer of French manners, he hated the "preachy-teachy-prosy motive" in American life, and he had a love for what was exquisite though fleshly. His first article in the *Galaxy*, "The Pagan Element in French Art," branded him as a pagan element in American letters. Even the *Galaxy* editors were rather frightened at their own temerity in printing his second article and openly criticized it in the next number for its "attack on reserve and decency." Yet they continued to publish Benson very frequently during their first three years. The "tomahawk man of the *Nation*" did not like Benson's ideas or his way of expressing them. An editorial in 1868 unites condemnation of the ambitions of Benson and Whitman for American literature in one anathema.[26] Benson's earnestness is shown by a letter to Church:

> . . . Thiers in the French Chamber once appealed with great effect to his countrymen by saying: let us be Frenchmen. My dear Church, I will say: Let us be young men together. You who come in contact with all sorts of people may know better than I why you should withhold yourself from any but the makers of academies, etc. — but I do not, and you will let me speak from my personal conviction.
>
> Why should not all of us young men, without formal organization, give ourselves to the ideas that hold the most liberty, the best future, the greatest veracity? Are there not enough of us in New York among painters, poets and journalists? You in your place (unless you have personal convictions against it) should certainly try and leaven the Sheldonites, and the Philistines, with as much of the *frondeur* literature as you can smuggle or boldly carry into your magazine. If not, the *Galaxy* gets soggy, flabby, and becomes a dead weight against our youth and our hope. . . .[27]

Benson's contributions helped give character to the *Galaxy* during its first four years, but nothing from his pen appeared in it after November 1869. He had by that time renounced literature and America and established a studio in Florence.

[26] *Nation*, VI, 7 (January 2, 1868).
[27] Letter dated July 30, 1866 (Willard Church Collection). "Sheldonites" refers to the publishers of the *Galaxy*.

The writer who outruns all other contributors except McCarthy and White in the number of pages printed in the *Galaxy* is Mrs. Annie Edwards. Six serial stories from her pen were printed in the magazine, and her contribution, averaged among the 153 numbers of the entire file, would make some ten pages for each issue. These serials were published contemporaneously in English magazines and printed in the *Galaxy* from advance sheets. Mrs. Edwards was a third-rate English novelist who sometimes rose to second-rate power in her handling of emotional interest. She was much praised for her ability in characterization, but her characters, though vivid and memorable, were too much in black and white; they must be either villains or heroes. She dealt with English and continental society; she was fond of an international group. A candid reviewer said in the *Galaxy*, in describing the heroine of one of Mrs. Edwards' twenty-one novels:

She does things, like most of Mrs. Edwards' heroines, which are upon the very verge of propriety, even of prudence, even of right; but she is always very right and pure at heart, and she is in person, in mind, and in manner a very alluring and captivating creature.[28]

Such were all Mrs. Edwards' *Galaxy* heroines. That our authoress was as frankly commercial as most English novelists of the day is evidenced by a letter to Colonel Church in which she says:

I am recommended by the London publishers to put more 'sensation' into my new story. Probably the advice is good. What do you say? What would be the opinion generally of American readers? [29]

The *Galaxy* was never without a serial story, and sometimes it had two or three going at full blast. About two-thirds of them were English serials, printed from advance sheets. Two reasons may be assigned for this use of English fiction: the editors thought the English novelists greatly superior to the American, and they knew that advance sheets of English novels were, sometimes at least, cheaper than original American manuscripts. Mrs. Edwards received less than $2.00 a page for the

[28] *Galaxy*, XIX, 277 (February 1875).
[29] Letter to W. C. Church (Willard Church Collection).

advance sheets of her stories,[30] and Trollope probably little more,[31] while for the American J. W. DeForest's *Overland* the *Galaxy* paid over $5.00 a page,[32] and no doubt quite as much for Rebecca Harding Davis' *Waiting for the Verdict*.[33]

Trollope's *The Claverings*, *The Eustace Diamonds*, and *An Editor's Tales*, William Black's *Madcap Violet*, Reade's *Put Yourself in His Place*, and the serials of McCarthy and Mrs. Edwards were the English contributions. Mrs. Davis' serial was the first American novel to appear, and it was followed by Marion Harland's *Beechdale* and Jane G. Austin's *Cipher*. Colonel DeForest's love and adventure story of the Far West, *Overland*, attracted wide attention by a refreshing tendency toward the realistic — a tendency also of Mrs. Davis' work. The *Galaxy* also printed *The Wetherell Affair* and continued to publish short stories by DeForest for several years. One other serial must be mentioned — H. H. Boyesen's delightful *A Norseman's Pilgrimage*, which supported pleasantly the *Galaxy's* ambition to print the fresh and different.

In the field of the short story the magazine seems to have had no very fixed policy. It found its short stories where and when it could, sometimes printing one in a number, sometimes three or four. Aside from James, McCarthy, and DeForest, its short story writers were chiefly women. Rose Terry Cooke made a real contribution to the realistic movement in short fiction in some of her *Galaxy* contributions, as, for example,

[30] Letters in Willard Church Collection, showing that Mrs. Edwards' price was £100 for each serial. They usually ran to 250 or 300 pages.

[31] See Trollope's *Autobiography* (London, 1923, Oxford Edition), p. 281, in which the novelist doubts whether his publishers, who had the disposal of his advance sheets, received for them 5 per cent of the price paid him for his novels. The highest price ever paid him for a noval was £2,800, of which 5 per cent would be £140. McCarthy, however, got a higher rate than this for his American serial rights. The *Galaxy* stated in March 1870 (IX, 416) that the "advanced sheets of the best foreign novels, as a rule, command a higher price from American publishers than the original manuscripts of American novelists." Nevertheless, the *Galaxy* paid less for an Edwards serial than for an American serial, in the average. But the statement quoted should be given due weight in considering the general question of English serials in American magazines.

[32] DeForest was paid $1,200 for *Overland*, which made about 225 pages. There were twelve installments, and letters acknowledging $100 per installment are in the Willard Church Collection.

[33] The *Galaxy* always paid Mrs. Davis $8.00 a page for short stories, and it is unlikely that she would be paid less than $5.00 a page for a serial.

in "Too Late," published in January 1875. Rebecca Harding Davis and Constance Fenimore Woolson were upon somewhat the same path, and a number of Turgeniev translations were published in the seventies. Caroline Chesebrough, whose short stories are now neglected by reader and critic alike, but who published largely in the very best American magazines for the twenty-five years before her death in 1873, is well represented in the *Galaxy*; as were the brilliant but less important writers, Louise Chandler Moulton and Harriet Prescott Spofford. Though realism had its innings in the *Galaxy*, sentimentality, with its handmaiden melodrama, scored the more heavily. Maria Louise Pool, Jane G. Austin, and a score or two of unknowns postured through many pages. Miss Pool began to write for the *Galaxy* when she was twenty and should have been in boarding school. What bucketfuls of tears somebody must have shed over the stories in these old magazines! It is impossible to give an idea of what they were like without quoting, and the keynote of the story's sentiment is usually to be found at the end; so we quote the closing paragraph from "A Summer at Newport," published anonymously by the *Galaxy* in September 1873:

Harry restrained himself until the man was gone, then he caught the cross from the table and pressed it wildly to his lips. [Here we must interrupt to say that the cross was the only memento of his dead sweetheart. We now have Harry's soliloquy:] "O love, love!" he moaned, "you stood there in the bleak autumn night, despairing, wretched, wild, deeming that you were forsaken and that I was faithless. O love! you did not know how I loved you. O my Florence, my dead darling, what must have been your anguish when death was your only refuge and your only hope! Do you know *now*, darling, why I failed to heed your sweet faithful summons? Behold, I have kept faith at last. I am here to bear you to your resting place, and instead of this cross, our last love-token, I bring you another gift; not the wedding-ring that I promised you, my love, my Florence, but a coffin and a tomb."

The *Galaxy*, though it may be searched in vain for masterpieces in poetry, and though it printed a great deal that might better have been left unprinted, published nevertheless much verse that is entirely worthy a first-class magazine. Four Whitman poems were printed (and Whitman's essay on "Democracy" appeared in December 1867). A few poems by Sidney Lanier were published in 1877, including the charming sonnet, "The Mocking Bird," and Paul Hamilton Hayne was represented frequently. Edmund Clarence Stedman and Bayard Taylor were occasional contributors of verse, especially in the early years of the magazine. Such composers of the popular and rather sentimental lyric of the day as the Cary sisters, "H. H.," William Winter, and the Piatts, were printed with more or less regularity. Certain writers remembered each by a single poem made less fortunate contributions to the *Galaxy*: Nora Perry, of "After the Ball"; Elizabeth Akers, of "Rock Me to Sleep, Mother"; Thomas Buchanan Read, of "Sheridan's Ride." Some forgotten poets of ability and a vanished popularity contributed often to the *Galaxy* — among them Edgar Fawcett, "Howard Glyndon" (Laura C. R. Searing), Robert Weeks, Julia C. R. Dorr, and Alfred B. Street. Edward Rowland Sill contributed a number of poems. Bret Harte and Joaquin Miller were slightly represented, and Emma Lazarus contributed three lyrics in 1877. The humor-poets, John G. Saxe and C. D. Shanly, appeared in the latter numbers. William Cullen Bryant was represented by a passage from his translation of the *Iliad*. The distinctively New England poets were conspicuous by their absence.

To analyze the special articles that appeared in the *Galaxy* from 1866 to 1878 would be to analyze the life and thought of its period. This magazine touched popular life at more points and more directly than most other important magazines have. "The *Galaxy* has swung quite clear of the old traditions of our literary pharisaism," remarked the *Independent*.[34] "Without any affectation of originality, it pays little attention to established methods; its topics are fresh, its illustrations salient, its discussions sometimes tinctured with the petulance of youth, but usually spiced with the aroma of vital juices." The sentence is unmistakably Theodore Tilton's. "The *Galaxy* is a monthly newspaper in the sense of always being of current interest," remarked the *Nation*.[35] Even more significant are

[34] *Independent*, January 2, 1868.
[35] *Nation*, X, 355 (June 2, 1870).

the words of the *New York Graphic*: "It is more in accordance
with the feelings of the reading public of America than any
other magazine that is published." [36] Contemporary judgment
was in general agreement that the *Galaxy* articles were, in the
first place, fresh, various, and original; and in the second
place, bold, vigorous, and direct. The second group of characteristics may require some qualifying. The *Independent*, in the
editorial quoted above, speaks of "the almost rustic simplicity
with which it expresses earnest convictions in bold words";
yet a study of the *Galaxy's* editorial policy as shown in the
magazine itself (especially in the "Nebulae"), and of the
correspondence between editors and contributors, indicates
a marked caution which always kept it from being really
extremist.

Next to fiction, criticism occupied the largest space in the
Galaxy.[37] Its literary criticism was, and still is, important.
Its department of "Current Literature" was hampered little,
if at all, by the incubus of publishers who were also in the
book business, for Sheldon & Company issued but few books,
and *Galaxy* reviewers were quite as frequently severe in dealing with Sheldon books as with any others. Reviews were intelligent and honest. The leading writers of literary criticism
in the magazine were Richard Grant White, Edmund Clarence
Stedman, Henry James, J. F. Meline, John Burroughs, and
W. C. Brownell. Of these, James and Meline wrote chiefly
of foreign literature; and for a time the magazine printed special departments devoted to German, French, and Italian
literature. James and White also wrote dramatic criticism; and
Brander Matthews contributed, during the latter half of the
magazine's life, some articles about the continental theater.
Olive Logan, too, had some very lively articles about the stage.

History and biography bulked very large in the *Galaxy*, as

[36] Quoted in an advertisement for the *Galaxy* in the *Christian Union*, XVI,
500 (December 13, 1876).

[37] Analysis of subject matter in the *Galaxy* file shows the average number of
pages per volume (6 issues) as follows: Serial fiction, 191; short stories, 131;
literary criticism, 75; history, 65; science, 62; travel, 35; biography, 33; sociology, 28; religion, 23; manners, 22; art, 22; poetry, 20; economics, 17; foreign
politics, 17; drama, 15; philology, 15; domestic politics, 14; feminism, 12; journalism, 6; unclassified, 57.

they have done in most American magazines. In the post-bellum period this phenomenon was the more marked from two causes — the popularity of Civil War narratives, and the occurrence of the national centennial. The recollections of Generals Custer and James Grant Wilson appeared in the *Galaxy*, and the excellent narratives of James Franklin Fitts were a good feature. Custer's *Life on the Plains* was cut short in its serial course through the magazine by the death of the author at Little Bighorn. Political reminiscences by Thurlow Weed, Jeremiah S. Black, and Gideon Welles gave rise to much controversy. J. S. C. Abbott, who was writing copiously for *Harper's* at the same time, contributed some of his popular European history to *Galaxy* pages.

Quite as striking as the amount of space given to history was the extent of the scientific articles. A scientific attitude appeared in various special articles written by physicians and professors and was especially notable in the writings of that group of professional magazinists which developed after the war.

Current politics, which the *Galaxy* began by avoiding, soon came to occupy a considerable place. Pond's more or less political department, "Drift-Wood," was concerned chiefly with the United States; but foreign politics bulk larger than the domestic variety.

Twenty-two pages per volume of the *Galaxy* file were devoted to topics related closely to manners; but that is not a fair indication of the interest shown by the magazine in this subject, for a large proportion of the articles, and even of the fiction, show constant occupation with this theme. Manners, social customs, etiquette, behavior were very important to many contributors. One of the *Galaxy's* most popular series was by Pierre Blot, a French chef residing in New York, on the art of dining. The foreign-educated Bristed, the imported McCarthy, and the reforming Benson thought largely in terms of manners. Richard Grant White set himself up as an *arbiter elegantiarum*. Journalism, literature, politics, sociology, feminism, all were viewed more or less from this angle of "the manners or want of manners peculiar to Americans."[38]   Eating,[39] smoking cigarettes,[40]

---

[38] The phrase is credited to Sir Walter Scott by Bristed in the *Galaxy*, XV, 181 (February 1873).

[39] *Galaxy*, XXII, 187 (August 1876).   [40] *Ibid.*, XXIII, 471 (April 1877).

chaperonage,[41] swearing,[42] women's drinking,[43] shaving by barbers,[44] and hundreds of other topics of the kind were treated at length. The "woman question" was a part of this general subject, and so also was the matter of language. An average of two or three pages to the volume on philological questions may surprise the reader of today until he learns of the importance ascribed, justly enough, to good language as a social convention.

The Messrs. Church belonged to the class of editors-tyrants. They were the absolute monarchs of their magazine, and they did not esteem the rights of contributors very highly. Consequently there are many authorial protests in the *Galaxy* correspondence files. If we take one example only, let it be from Rebecca Harding Davis, who had been forced to cut away large portions of her serial, "Waiting for the Verdict": "You are the first in the six years I have been writing for the press who have asked me to alter or abridge a line. I have been perhaps unusually favored by the old etiquette of the sanctum. . . ." She had. She had been a contributor to the *Atlantic*, but she had just missed the cutting and polishing editorship of Lowell and had doubtless found Fields an easier master. And she was wrong about her "old etiquette of the sanctum," for the iron editorial hand was a heritage from the older days of anonymity, when it was suffered more easily.

As to rates of payment for contributions, the *Galaxy* had no fixed scale. Payment for prose ranged from $10 for a 500-word page to $3.00 for a 750-word page, or from two cents to less than half a cent per word. McCarthy received the high figure, while Mrs. Davis got about a cent a word, as a rule, for short stories. The average was doubtless below rather than above $5.00 for the normal 750-word page. Benson and Abbott were paid $5.00. DeForest began at $3.00 and in a few years was receiving $8.00. We find two Boston writers, each represented in the *Galaxy* file by a single contribution — William Dean Howells and Edward Everett Hale — both asking rates somewhat in excess of the *Galaxy's* usual standard — a fact which may help to explain, or may not, the paucity of New England representation in the *Galaxy*. The *Atlantic* was paying about

[41] *Ibid.*, XXIV, 451 (October 1877).   [43] *Ibid.*, I, 752 (August 15, 1866).
[42] *Ibid.*, XXV, 60 (January 1878).   [44] *Ibid.*, XV, 627 (May 1873).

$10 a 750-word page at the time to its more favored writers.
For poetry the rate seems to have varied from $5.00 to $50 a
poem. "H. H." was dissatisfied with $5.00 for a sonnet; she said
that *Harper's* and the *Independent* paid her $10 apiece, which
seems indeed to have been a common *Galaxy* rate. Bayard
Taylor wrote, "The remuneration I now receive from other
magazines is fifty dollars on acceptance." [45] On the whole, the
Galaxy treated its authors as well as or better than they were
treated elsewhere.

In considering its rates to authors, we must remember that
the *Galaxy* was not making a financial success. It struggled
along with five or six thousand circulation for its first two years,
made an unusual gain at the end of 1868, and came steadily up
to 23,000, which it reached early in 1871, when Mark Twain's
"Memoranda," Justin McCarthy's *Lady Judith*, Col. DeForest's
Overland, and Thurlow Weed's *Autobiography* were running
simultaneously in the magazine. This was the high point in
Galaxy circulation, which thereafter declined steadily but surely
until it had reached 7,000 in 1878. The subscription rate was
$4.00 yearly, and the advertising rate published in Rowell's
Directory in 1872 was $100 a page. Advertising probably never
contributed very largely to the *Galaxy's* receipts, however.
Though it frequently carried as much as twenty-five pages of
advertisements during the years 1868 to 1871, they were largely
announcements of periodicals and books taken on an exchange
basis.

The magazine was octavo in size, usually of 144 pages. It
was a semimonthly for one year and thereafter appeared
monthly. Its first cover was a striking creation of gilt printing
on chocolate-brown stock in the ornamental style of the period;
this was superseded the next year by a red, green, and maroon
effect equally bizarre, which lasted out another year; after that
followed the design printed in black on a grey stock which came
to be familiar to readers. It was doubtless too architectural
and too symbolical, as well as astronomical, for the taste of the
present, but it was distinctive, and an improvement over the
earlier trials. The *Galaxy* was never as well printed as *Lippin-*

[45] Letter dated May 10, 1869, in Willard Church Collection, which also furnishes the data for most of the other statements in this paragraph.

cott's, the *Overland*, or the *Atlantic*;[46] but it was by no means distressing in its letterpress. The *Galaxy* illustrations, as a whole, were mediocre or worse. At the beginning, each issue had a wood engraving as frontispiece. These were very wooden indeed, having little of grace or truth, and much of styles in dress and beards. J. P. Davis-Speer engraved most of them from drawings by others. In 1868 there was an effort to illustrate more adequately, and W. J. Hennessy, Gaston Fay, Winslow Homer, and Sol Eytinge contributed with great inequality of production. In May of this year the *Galaxy* announced that the engraving had been put into W. J. Linton's hands, but very few Linton engravings ever found their way into the *Galaxy* pages. The author of an article about Fannie Kemble wrote the editors in November 1868: "The portrait of Mrs. Kemble is horrible indeed, calculated to inspire equal disgust and dismay in anyone familiar with her fair face." [47] This engraving was by Hennessy, concerning one of whose illustrations for her serial, "Waiting for the Verdict," Rebecca Harding Davis had written enthusiastically that it was "equal to the finest poem, I think." Both critics were perhaps right; some of the best and some of the worst engraving that appeared in the *Galaxy* was signed by Hennessy. Winslow Homer contributed some attractive pieces. But the portraits grow worse and worse, and their badness became more emphatic when the *Galaxy* discontinued other kinds of illustration altogether. In January 1871 Mark Twain gave more than two pages of his "Memoranda" to a satire on the *Galaxy* portraits. The article begins:

I never can look at those periodical portraits in the *Galaxy* without feeling a wild, tempestuous ambition to become an artist. I have seen thousands and thousands of pictures in my time — acres of them here and leagues in the galleries of Europe — but never any that moved me as the *Galaxy* pictures do.

There is the portrait of Monsignore Capel in the November *Galaxy*; now could anything be sweeter than that? And there was Bismarck's, in the October number; who can look at that without being purer and stronger and nobler for it? And Thurlow Weed's picture in the Sep-

---

[46] Volume VI was notably better printed than the others.
[47] Letter from Mrs. L. W. Thompson ("Maria Potter") dated November 24, 1868 (Willard Church Collection).

tember number; I would not have died without seeing that, no, not for anything this world can give. But look back still further and recall my own likeness printed in the August *Galaxy*; if I had been in my grave a thousand years when that appeared, I would have got up and visited the artist.

Mark tells then how these portraits have inspired him to study art himself, and how, through the gradations of fence painting, whitewashing, roofs, and signs he has come now within six months to portraits.

The humble offering which accompanies these remarks — the portrait of His Majesty William III., King of Prussia [William I of Germany] — is my fifth attempt at portraits, and my greatest success. It has received unbounded praise from all classes of the community, but that which gratifies me most is the frequent and cordial verdict that it resembles the *Galaxy* portraits.

Then, after presenting his burlesque portrait, he adds a series of "Commendations," such as:

There is nothing like it in the Vatican. — *Pius IX.*

There is a benignant simplicity about the execution of the work that warms the heart toward it as much, full as much, as it fascinates the eye. — *Landseer.*

Send me the entire edition — together with the plate and the original portrait — and name your own price. And — would you like to come over and stay awhile with Napoleon at Wilhelmshohe? It shall not cost you a cent. — *William III.*

Why did the *Galaxy* publish such a severe satire on its own "embellishments"? Well, Mark Twain was scarcely to be resisted. When he sent his copy it was accompanied by this note:

Friend Church. The matter referred to in the last paragraph of this "Memoranda" is a quiet satire on your infernal Galaxy portraits and is accompanied by a ghastly likeness to King William which I have worried over until it is bad enough to suit me. It must be engraved exactly as I have drawn it or it will suffer damage. It *can not* be improved upon, by making it either better or worse.

The whole thing is good, but if you do not want it, just drop off the paragraph which refers to it and I will understand, and will publish it as a lithograph, through Prang.[48]

[48] Letter dated October 18 [1870], in the possession of F. L. Mott.

The *Galaxy* portraits survived, however, for more than a year after the Mark Twain lampoon. The last one appeared in March 1872, and in the latter half of its life the magazine was without illustration.

The *Galaxy* list was sold to the *Atlantic Monthly* in 1878. When the *Atlantic* welcomed *Galaxy* subscribers in February of that year, it said:

> The *Galaxy* and the *Atlantic* more than any other two American magazines have appealed to kindred tastes. . . . Each had its advantages, and these advantages are now united. . . . The freshness, the brightness, the alertness that gave tone to the *Galaxy* will not cease, we hope, in the alliance which makes the *Galaxy* and the *Atlantic* one. . . . Retaining its chief writers, we shall aim to perpetuate the finest characteristics of a magazine which for eleven years has been a presence in our periodical literature so distinctly agreeable and useful that it could not wholly pass away without great public regret.

And so the *Galaxy* was submerged in the *Atlantic*, a phenomenon which suggested to the pun-loving mind of one *Galaxy* contributor the idea for a sonnet, ending:

> The stars go out, extinguished by the sea,
> Lost in the great Atlantic's rhythmic sweep.[49]

[49] Manuscript sonnet "Imperium in Imperio," by Mary B. Dodge (Willard Church Collection).

THE SOUTHERN REVIEW [1]

ALBERT TAYLOR BLEDSOE had one of those versatile and many-talented minds that lend themselves easily to work on periodicals. After a West Point education, he entered the practice of law at Springfield, Illinois, where he was a colleague of Lincoln; but he left the law for the Episcopal ministry. His views upon some theological questions caused him to withdraw from this work, though not from the denomination until later. He became professor of mathematics at the University of Virginia. At the beginning of the Civil War he was made a colonel in the Confederate army, but was soon relieved to work upon a constitutional defense of the southern position, to gather material for which he went to England. Returning, he found his old friend, Jefferson Davis, on trial for treason, and used the material he had been gathering as a defense for him.

Bledsoe then joined forces with William Hand Browne, the historian, to issue at Baltimore, in January 1867, the first number of the quarterly *Southern Review*, second of its name.[2] It was intended partly as a southern apologia and partly as a representative of the literary cultivation and scholarship of the South. Northern contributions were not unwelcome, and we find Bledsoe expressing gratitude for them,[3] but the *Southern*

[1] TITLE: *The Southern Review.*

FIRST ISSUE: January 1867. LAST ISSUE: October 1879.

PERIODICITY: Quarterly. I–VIII, semiannual volumes, 1867–70; IX, annual volume, 1871; X–XV, semiannual volumes, 1872–74; XVI, January 1875; XVII, April 1875; XVIII, July, October 1875; XIX–XXV, semiannual volumes, 1876–79.

PUBLISHERS: Bledsoe & Browne, Baltimore, 1867–68; A. T. Bledsoe, Baltimore, 1869; Henry Taylor & Company, Baltimore, 1870; Poisal & Raszell, Baltimore, 1871; Southwestern Book & Publishing Company, St. Louis, 1871–75; Bledsoe & Herrick, Baltimore, 1875–79.

EDITORS: Albert Taylor Bledsoe and William Hand Browne, 1867–68; A. T. Bledsoe, 1868–77; Sophia Bledsoe Herrick, 1878–79.

INDEXED in *Poole's* (except last volume).

[2] See Mott, *A History of American Magazines, 1741–1850*, p. 382, for the earlier *Southern Review.*

[3] The cover of the number for January 1868 says: "Northern friends by contribution of valuable articles have afforded valuable assistance."

Review was all that its name implied; it was southern through and through. Moreover, it might almost be called an official exponent of the lost cause. "Doctor," wrote Robert E. Lee to the editor, "you must take care of yourself; you have a great work to do; we all look to you for our vindication." [4] A notable series of articles in the first volume was one in which Bledsoe traced the causes of the war to the constitutional convention of 1787. Sectional feeling colors everything. One would be sadly lacking in the historical sense, however, who would find only condemnation for that steady flame of courageous self-assertion which burned in the *Southern Review* against its dark background of despair. "There can be no forgetfulness," quoted the reviewer of Simms's *War Poetry of the South*. As an interpretation of the postbellum mind of the intellectual South, the file of Bledsoe's *Southern Review* is almost incomparable.

It seems natural to speak of the *Review* as Bledsoe's; his was the commanding personality, though Browne was joint editor and publisher for the first year or two. Following Browne's retirement, Major Richard M. Venable was associate editor for a year.

Until 1871 the *Review* was not religious in aim; but in that year it was adopted by the Methodist Church South, whose former review had been suspended since 1861. Bledsoe had long had leanings toward Methodism and ultimately became a Methodist minister. The change in his journal enabled him to indulge his bent toward theology and to substitute religious for political controversies. Controversy of whatever kind was dear to his heart. The extent to which he employed personalities detracted perhaps from the dignity of the *Review;* his attacks upon D. D. Whedon, leading journalist of the Methodist Church North, were not very creditable. But Bledsoe felt that the castigation of his enemies was one of his editorial duties, and if he failed to discharge upon them a concentrated fire of hot shot in a given number, he apologized and promised to do better in the next. He comforts his readers in one issue by assuring them that "we have several rods in soak." [5]

[4] Edwin Mims in *The South in the Building of the Nation* (Richmond, 1909), VII, 464.
[5] *Southern Review*, XIX, 491 (April 1876).

Controversy was, of course, only one phase of the *Review*. For its type, it was uncommonly good in its literary phases. Paul Hamilton Hayne wrote literary criticism for it. The charming essays of the editor's daughter, Sophia Bledsoe Herrick, who was associate editor from 1875 until her father's death, were a pleasant feature; she wrote of literature, nature, and history. Bledsoe's theological works, of which the *Edwards on the Will* and *The Christian Cosmos* are the most notable, were printed in the *Review*. Bledsoe died December 8, 1877, and his daughter maintained the *Review* for two years thereafter, drawing chiefly on her father's work, but writing much herself. The resumption of the *Quarterly Review* of the M. E. Church South in 1879 caused Mrs. Herrick to give up her review at last. She was later a member of the *Century* staff.

A comparison of Bledsoe and Brownson [6] is almost inevitable. Of all American theological review editors, these two showed the strongest personalities in their journals. Both were masters of nervous, effective style, both were thoroughly earnest, both were lovers of controversy, and both felt the irresistible urge for self-expression. ("To abandon the *Southern Review* would be like the pang of death to me," wrote Bledsoe in 1870.) Bledsoe had a better appreciation of belles-lettres and wider interests, but less of dignity in controversy than his northern contemporary. Both were profoundly and personally affected by the Civil War. Bledsoe is less open to the charge of having overwritten himself, but his position as a theologian is doubtless lower than that of Brownson.

[6] See Mott, *op. cit.*, p. 685, for Brownson's reviews.

JOURNAL OF SPECULATIVE PHILOSOPHY [1]

I T WAS shortly before the Civil War that H. C. Brokmeyer, of St. Louis, a German-born lawyer who later became lieutenant governor of Missouri, undertook to teach Hegel's larger *Logic* to William T. Harris, then a young man of twenty-three fresh from Yale, and two other young St. Louisans. That was the beginning of "the St. Louis Movement in Philosophy." Shortly after the war was over, the St. Louis Philosophical Society was formed, and it fostered the organization of various other clubs and classes with the object of studying German idealistic philosophy. Brokmeyer, Harris, Denton J. Snider, and George H. Howison were among the founders of the Society.[2]

Out of the "St. Louis Movement" sprang the *Journal of Speculative Philosophy,* founded and edited for twenty years by William Torrey Harris. The first number, issued for January 1867, was a modest octavo of sixty-four pages, and four quarterly issues were sold for $3.00. "A journal devoted to the interests of speculative philosophy is a rare phenomenon in the English language," observed Harris in his salutatory.[3] It was, indeed. "Why, who cares for such things in America?" asked *Scribner's Monthly* in a commendatory notice of it. "What attraction could it possess for busy Americans?" [4] Yet it rather surprisingly continued quarter after quarter, and in its

[1] TITLE: *Journal of Speculative Philosophy.*

FIRST ISSUE: January 1867. LAST ISSUE: December 1893.

PERIODICITY: Quarterly. I–XXI, 1867–87, regular annual volumes; XXII, January–April (double number) 1888, September 1892, December 1893.

PUBLISHERS: W. T. Harris, St. Louis, 1867–77; G. A. Jones & Company, St. Louis, 1878–79; D. Appleton & Company, New York, 1880–93.

EDITOR: William Torrey Harris.

INDEXED in *Poole's.*

REFERENCES: Charles M. Perry, *The St. Louis Movement in Philosophy* (Norman, Oklahoma, 1930); Edward L. Schaub, "The Journal of Speculative Philosophy," *Monist,* XLVI, 80 (January 1936).

[2] Perry, *op. cit.*

[3] *Journal of Speculative Philosophy,* I, 1 (January 1867).

[4] *Scribner's Monthly,* I, 685 (April 1871).

third year doubled its number of pages. On its cover it carried a motto from Novalis: "Philosophy can bake no bread, but it can give us God, Freedom and Immortality."

The early volumes consisted largely of translations of Hegel, Schelling, Schopenhauer, Leibnitz, Fichte, and Rosenkranz, not before available in English. Many of the translations were made by Snider, A. E. Kroeger, Thomas Davidson, and others of the St. Louis group. Bronson Alcott and Frederick H. Hedge were published in the first volume, as were also Brokmeyer, D. G. Brinton, the poet Anna C. Brackett, and the editor himself. There was much of aesthetics, from Goethe, Winckelmann, Hegel, and others; there were Harris' own essays on art, some discussion of music by E. Sobolewski and others, and occasional poems.

When, at the end of the *Journal's* first year, Harris wrote a preface for Volume I, he noted that some had objected to it as being unoriginal; but he replied that American originality was not above instruction. He did not neglect American philosophy, however. Three articles from the pen of Charles S. Peirce appeared in the second volume, one from James and one from Royce in that for 1878, and one from Dewey in 1882. These were all among the very earliest writings of men destined to be leaders in American thought. William Ellery Channing, John Weiss, J. Elliot Cabot, G. Stanley Hall, Edwin D. Mead, and A. P. Peabody were among the more faithful American contributors. In the *Journal*, philosophy afforded strong support to religion, but there was much also of political and social aims and some discussion of science.

Harris went to Concord in 1880 to associate himself with Alcott in the leadership of the Concord School of Philosophy; but he continued the *Journal*, which now had slightly less of translation and also less of aesthetics, and was published by Appleton in New York. In spite of the fact that its annual deficit had to be paid out of his personal income,[5] Harris kept his magazine up to its same high level throughout two decades, winning for it golden opinions at home and abroad. When, however, he was appointed United States Commissioner of Education in 1889, his public duties forced him to neglect it; and after

[5] Perry, *op. cit.*, p. 66. Statement of Harris' son Theodore.

filling out the 1888 volume with single numbers in 1892 and 1893, he wrote finis to the journal's file.

The *Journal of Speculative Philosophy*, wrote a commentator in the *Educational Review* after Harris' death, was the most important work

in a philosophical sense yet undertaken in this country. . . . Each contribution is of a very superior order. . . . Its publication put Dr. Harris in close correspondence with many of the foremost thinkers of Great Britain, Germany, France and Canada.[6]

Its chief services seem to have been two. One of them is partially described by a recent biographer of Harris when he says that the *Journal's* "critical articles offered the first systematic study of German philosophy to appear in this country";[7] to this should be added acknowledgment of the value of the large number of translations from the German which the periodical published. The other service was rendered in presenting the earliest philosophical writings of some of this country's greatest modern thinkers.

[6] *Educational Review*, XXXIX, 132 (February 1910). Statement of James M. Greenwood.
[7] Ernest Sutherland Bates in *Dictionary of American Biography*, VIII, 329.

HARPER'S BAZAR [1]

ONE day shortly after the end of the Civil War, Fletcher Harper broached to his brothers, who were associated with him in one of the strongest publishing houses in the United States, the idea of a new periodical for women, to be called *Harper's Bazar*, after *Der Bazar*, of Berlin. But his partners were not favorable. The house already had two periodicals — the *Monthly* and the *Weekly* — both very successful; and they preferred to let well enough alone. Fletcher did not accept their refusal, however, and he finally said to them: "Well, I wish we could go into it as a firm, but if we cannot I will publish it myself." "No, you will not," contradicted brother John. "We'll defer to your judgment, and you shall have your *Bazar*." [2]

So on November 2, 1867, the new periodical appeared, with the subtitle, "A Repository of Fashion, Pleasure and Instruction." The editor was Mary L. Booth, historian of the city of New York, a translator of experience, and a woman of unusual abilities. The venture prospered from the first number, and within ten years had a circulation of 80,000 — "the most rapid success ever known in journalism," said its editor in an interview. [3]

The first *Harper's Bazar* consisted of sixteen pages in small folio, containing patterns, many large woodcuts of styles and

[1] TITLE: *Harper's Bazar* (spelled *Bazaar* since 1929).
FIRST ISSUE: November 2, 1867. Current.
PERIODICITY: Weekly, November 1867–April 1901; monthly, May 1901–current. I, 1867–68; thereafter regular yearly volumes. (Vol. LXVIII is properly called "69th Year" (1935), and this discrepancy continues.)
PUBLISHERS: Harper & Brothers, New York, 1867–1913; International Magazine Company, New York, 1913–28; Harper's Bazaar, Inc., 1929–36; Hearst Magazines, Inc., 1936–current.
EDITORS: Mary L. Booth, 1867–89; Margaret Sangster, 1889–99; Elizabeth Jordan, 1900–13; William Martin Johnson, 1913–14; Harford Powell, 1914–16; John Chapman Hilder, 1916–20; Henry Blackman Sell, 1920–26; Charles Hanson Towne, 1926–29; Arthur H. Samuels, 1929–34; Carmel Snow, 1934–current.
INDEXED in *Readers' Guide, Dramatic Index.*
[2] J. Henry Harper, *The House of Harper* (New York, 1902), p. 252.
[3] Charles F. Wingate, ed., *Views and Interviews on Journalism* (New York, 1875), p. 259.

other subjects, serial fiction, and miscellany, and was priced at
$4.00 a year. It was a ladies' *Harper's Weekly*, with the same
type of English serials, double-page pictures, miscellany, and
humor, and with fashions and patterns taking the place of politics and public affairs. The art work was excellent, with cartoons by Nast and engravings by the great *Weekly* group.

For many years the fashion plates came directly from Berlin
in the shape of duplicate electrotypes made by *Der Bazar*,
which, according to the first number of its American offspring,
"supplies the fashions to the newspapers of Paris." [4] With the
plates came advance proofs of the letterpress describing the
continental modes. The Harper staff added to this fashion
material its own descriptions of New York styles. For a time
"supplements" were issued occasionally to present the fashions
and the cumbersome German patterns; later, tracing patterns
were enclosed with each number, as came to be the custom
among American fashion papers in the late seventies. Fancywork and household problems occupied an important place in
the paper.

Among the novelists whose work appeared serially in the
early *Bazar* were Wilkie Collins, William Black, Miss Braddon,
and Justin McCarthy. There was a considerable amount of
verse from both English and American sources. "Gail Hamilton" lent her brilliance to the paper's pages. George William
Curtis for some years wrote, over the deceptive signature, "An
Old Bachelor," a charming and wise department called "Manners Upon the Road," in which he treated of familiar social
topics. This series was followed by a similar essay department
by Thomas Wentworth Higginson, begun in 1885 and called
"Women and Men."

There were many articles on domestic economy, the interior
arrangement of houses, and, by the nineties, house and garden planning. The paper improved consistently through the
eighties and early nineties, both in physical appearance and
in literary quality. William Dean Howells' *Heroines of Fiction*
was a pleasant feature in the nineties, and many of Mary E.
Wilkins' stories found their way into the *Bazar*.

In 1888 John Kendrick Bangs, who had just undertaken the

[4] *Harper's Bazar*, I, 2 (November 2, 1867).

editorship of the humorous department in the *Monthly*, was placed in charge of the "Facetiae" page of the *Bazar*, a department which had been a pleasant feature of the magazine from the beginning, but which Bangs made notable by his own contributions. In it he serialized his *Coffee and Repartee*, his *Celebrities at Home*, and *The Dreamers: A Club*. The Idiot papers found a place in the body of the magazine in 1895.

Margaret Sangster succeeded to the general editorship after Miss Booth's death in 1889, and retained it for a decade and until the failure of the Harper firm in 1899, after which Elizabeth Jordan came to the *Bazar* from the *New York World* staff. In 1901 weekly publication was abandoned, and the *Bazar* became a monthly of the square octavo shape.

It had been losing money for a good many years [5] when the International Magazine Company, William Randolph Hearst, president, purchased it in 1913. It immediately became more sophisticated, gay, and "smart." The fact is that, although the magazine had been designed for well-to-do homes, it had always inclined to hark back to the Methodistic Harper Brothers: it had been Harperish, but now it became Hearstian. A succession of short-term editors appeared and disappeared before Henry B. Sell, editor 1920–26, seemed to fix the type of the periodical rather definitely. Under Sell it contained many pages of the latest designs in styles, and on the literary side it printed Compton Mackenzie and Laurids Bruun serials, with John V. A. Weaver and Mildred Cram, and such English writers as Arnold Bennett, W. L. George, and Robert Hichens.

In 1926 Charles Hanson Towne succeeded Sell for a four-years editorship. The conventional spelling of the title name was substituted in 1929 for that which had been taken from the old Berlin *Bazar*. Arthur H. Samuels and Carmel Snow have been successive editors since 1929, and the *Bazaar* has been a well printed, sophisticated magazine devoted to fashions and literature. "The Ladies' Whiskey Primer" was the feature article in March 1935. Each number has a specialty — cosmetics, travel, fabrics, midsummer fiction, etc. Alexey Brodovitch has been art director since 1935.

[5] *Harper's Weekly*, LVII, 3 (May 31, 1913). The statement is that of George Harvey, then president of Harper & Brothers.

THE REVOLUTION [1]

I N JANUARY 1868 Theodore Tilton noted in the *Independent* that "the *Revolution* is the martial name of a bristling and defiant new weekly journal." He continued:

When we mention that it is edited by Mr. Parker Pillsbury and Mrs. Elizabeth Cady Stanton, all the world will immediately know what to expect from it. Those two writers can never be accused of having nothing to say, or of backwardness in saying it. Each has separately long maintained an individuality of tongue and pen. . . . The lady is a gay Greek, come forth from Athens; the gentleman is a sombre Hebrew, bound back to Jerusalem. We know of no two more striking, original, and piquant writers.[2]

As usual, Tilton rather overdid it; and the notice was more "piquant" than the paper it described. The *Revolution* turned out to be more energetic and belligerent than brilliant and original. It was a well-printed sixteen-page quarto at $2.00 a year, containing detailed reports of the various woman-suffrage gatherings, correspondence from home and abroad telling of the progress of the cause of women's rights, some literary miscellany (often including verse and sprightly character sketches) also dealing with the "cause," editorials, a financial department, and three pages of advertising. For the most part, it was lively and readable; it was less concerned with developing a connected and consistent philosophy of woman's place in the world than it was with presenting the news of an active reform movement and calling unsympathetic critics to account.

[1] TITLE: *The Revolution.*
FIRST ISSUE: January 8, 1868. LAST ISSUE: February 17, 1872.
PERIODICITY: Weekly; semiannual volumes.
PUBLISHERS: R. J. Johnston, New York (Susan B. Anthony, owner), 1868–70; Revolution Association, New York, 1870–71; J. N. Hallock, New York, 1871–72.
EDITORS: Elizabeth Cady Stanton and Parker Pillsbury, 1868–69; Elizabeth Cady Stanton, 1869–70; Laura Curtis Bullard, 1870–71; W. T. Clarke, 1871–72.
REFERENCE: Ida Husted Harper, *The Life and Work of Susan B. Anthony* (Indianapolis, 1898), Volume I, Chapters XVIII–XXI.
[2] Quoted in Harper, *op. cit.*, I, 296.

The proprietor, manager, and responsible financial head of the *Revolution* was Susan B. Anthony. Miss Anthony had gained a national reputation as a speaker and organizer for prohibition, emancipation, and woman suffrage. She and Mrs. Stanton had just completed a campaign for a suffrage amendment to the Kansas constitution, followed by a national lecture tour. In this they had been assisted financially as well as in the actual speaking by George Francis Train, the eccentric financier, traveler, author, and champion of causes; and it was before an audience at Junction City, Kansas, that Train announced, much to the surprise of Miss Anthony, who shared the platform with him, the name, motto, staff, and price of the new paper.[3] After the return to New York, Train enlisted in the enterprise David M. Melliss, financial editor of the *New York World*; and the two engaged to supply funds until the paper was on a paying basis, on condition that they were allowed space to express their opinions in the paper.[4] As a result of this arrangement, Train wrote correspondence for the paper on Fenianism and his other "isms," and Melliss maintained a financial department.

Train's connection with the paper offended many supporters of suffrage, and there is no doubt that he was a liability rather than an asset to the periodical. The first number of the paper was no sooner out than the restless adventurer announced that he was leaving immediately for Ireland. He handed Miss Anthony $600, assured her that he had arranged with Melliss to meet all obligations, took the next boat to Dublin, was arrested for complicity with the Fenians as soon as he made his first speech in Ireland, and was thrown into a Dublin jail, where he languished for a full year. He sent his letters to the *Revolution*, but no cash; and though Melliss did his best, the paper maintained its existence with difficulty.[5] It had 2,000 circulation at the beginning of 1869, and 3,000 by the next year.[6] After his return from Ireland, Train renewed his financial support, though he wrote less for the paper; after a few months both he and Melliss dissolved their connection with it, Train's valedictory appearing in the number for May 1,

[3] *Harper, op. cit.*, I, 290.
[4] *Ibid.*, I, 351.
[5] *Ibid.*, I, 299.
[6] *Ibid.*, I, 354.

1869. Two months later, Pillsbury's name was dropped as co-editor, though he remained as a contributing editor.

Meantime, there were difficulties regarding the support of the paper by the American Equal Rights Association, quarrels among the leaders in the reform movement, and finally the dissolution of the original society and the organization of the American Woman Suffrage Association. These developments were duly followed in the paper, as well as the organization of a workingwomen's association and Miss Anthony's activities in connection with the National Labor Union Congress in 1868. The woman suffragists were told by national leaders that they must await the full enfranchisement of the Negro before they pressed their case; and the Fifteenth Amendment was opposed by the *Revolution* because it extended the franchise only to Negro men, disregarding the women, and thus placed black men above white women.

The *Revolution's* original platform called for many reforms — among them "educated suffrage, irrespective of sex or color; the eight-hour day; abolition of standing armies; science, not superstition; personal purity; practical education; cold water *versus* alcohol and medicine; greenbacks, an American system of finance; organized labor," and so on.[7] The problems of working women were frequently discussed, with education for women and women's standing before the law. But despite the many causes it espoused at first, the *Revolution* became, after the first year at least, a paper devoted to what may be called inclusively "the woman question."

Many well-known writers and publicists were represented in the paper from time to time. Anna E. Dickinson was a faithful friend and contributor; Theodore and Elizabeth R. Tilton both wrote for it sometimes; Mary Clemmer Ames, Olive Logan, Louise Chandler Moulton, and Eugene Benson may be noted in its columns. The Cary sisters were contributors and close friends of Miss Anthony; and Alice wrote a serial story on the sufferings of a pioneer mother, called "The Born Thrall," for the *Revolution* — a story finally cut short by the death of the author. Harriet Beecher Stowe, her sister Isabella Beecher Hooker, and Paulina Wright Davis were contributing editors

[7] *Revolution*, I, 1 (January 8, 1868).

for a few months in 1870; and all three had written for the paper before that.

The *Woman's Journal* was founded under strong auspices at Boston at the beginning of 1870, and this made the *Revolution's* position all the more difficult. In May 1870 for one dollar in hand paid, Miss Anthony made over to Laura Curtis Bullard the title, list, and goodwill of the periodical, assuming herself the indebtedness then payable, amounting to about ten thousand dollars.[8]

Mrs. Bullard had been a foreign correspondent for the *Revolution*. In assuming the management of the paper, she was promised the aid of Theodore Tilton; [9] but it is uncertain how much help she received from him, for his hands were already pretty full. She enlisted Augusta Larned and Phoebe Cary, however, as assistant editors.[10] The paper immediately became less bellicose; from a paper fighting for equality, it changed to "a journal devoted to the welfare of women." True, it advocated suffrage, equality before the law, and better pay for women's labor; but it tried to do so without hurting anybody's feelings and with the mildness required of ladies. The price, which had been raised to $3.00 in 1869, was brought again to $2.00. It had been the boast of Mrs. Stanton and Miss Anthony that "no advertisements of quack remedies" appeared in their columns; [11] now pills, troches, sarsaparillas, and "Dr. Walker's California vinegar bitters — *not* a vile fancy drink" proclaimed their virtues in black type on the pages not devoted to women's welfare.

But neither pills nor bitters were of much help for what ailed the *Revolution*, and it was disposed of in October 1871 to J. N. Hallock, long publisher of the *Liberal Christian*, a Unitarian weekly. Hallock took the *Revolution* over at the suggestion of the Reverend W. T. Clarke, a former editor of the *Liberal Christian*, and now an associate editor of Tilton's *Golden Age*, who thought that he could make something out

[8] Harper, *op. cit.*, I, 362.
[9] *Ibid.*, I, 361.
[10] Elizabeth Cady Stanton, *History of Woman Suffrage* (Rochester, 1889), I, 46.
[11] See Theodore Stanton and Harriet Stanton Blatch, *Elizabeth Cady Stanton as Revealed in Her Letters, Diary, and Reminiscences* (New York, 1922), p. 215.

of it by turning it into a home journal. Thus Clarke became editor, while Miss Larned remained as associate editor. Women's "rights" were not forgotten, but now the paper was "devoted to women's rights and duties," with the emphasis on "duties." "Love," said the new editor, "is the inspiration of all true reform." [12] There was more miscellany, and the paper was more literary in a mediocre fashion; but in February 1872 it was merged in the *Liberal Christian*.

[12] *Revolution*, October 28, 1871, p. 2.

LIPPINCOTT'S MAGAZINE [1]

I N LIPPINCOTT'S MAGAZINE Philadelphia, long the
headquarters of worthless magazines, will have a very
respectable specimen of periodical literature," remarked
the *Nation* upon the appearance of *Lippincott's* first number.[2]
The *Nation's* critic guessed that George H. Boker was the
editor; but Boker, who in a few years was to go abroad as
minister to Turkey and then to Russia, was never more than
a faithful contributor. The editor for seventeen years was John
Foster Kirk, author of *Charles the Bold* and the industrious
bibliographer to whom we are indebted for the *Supplement*
to Allibone's *Dictionary of Authors*. Supported by the publishing house which issued the magazine, Kirk contributed his own
character for modest excellence to it. It was one of the best
printed of American magazines; its contents, though conservative, were usually of an admirable quality; and its departments
"Our Monthly Gossip" and "Literature of the Day," if not
brilliant, were often instructive and always pleasing. There
were no illustrations at first; but woodcuts began to appear
in the magazine's second year; and thereafter until 1885 there
were pictures, limited in number as compared with *Harper's*
and *Scribner's*, but good in quality.

[1] TITLES: (1) *Lippincott's Magazine of Literature, Science and Education,*
1868–71; (2) *Lippincott's Magazine of Popular Literature and Science,* 1871–85;
(3) *Lippincott's Magazine: A Popular Journal of General Literature, Science and
Politics,* 1886–1903; (4) *Lippincott's Monthly Magazine: A Popular Journal of
General Literature,* 1903–14; (5) *Lippincott's Magazine,* 1915; (6) *McBride's
Magazine,* 1915–16.
FIRST ISSUE: January 1868. LAST ISSUE: April 1916.
PERIODICITY: Monthly; semiannual volumes. XXVII–XXXVI also called
New Series, I–X.
PUBLISHERS: J. B. Lippincott & Company, Philadelphia, 1868–1914; McBride,
Nast & Company, New York, 1914–15.
EDITORS: John Foster Kirk, 1868–84; J. Bird, 1885; William Shepherd Walsh,
1885–89; Henry Stoddart, 1889–96; Frederic M. Bird, 1896–98; Harrison S.
Morris, 1899–1905; J. Berg Esenwein, 1905–14; Louise Bull, 1914; Edward
Frank Allen, 1914–16.
INDEXES: *Poole's, Poole's Abridged, Readers' Guide, Annual Library Index,
Cumulative, Jones' Index, Engineering Index, Review of Reviews Index.*
[2] *Nation,* V, 496 (December 19, 1867).

In its first number, issued for January 1868, the management declared that "it is no part of the publishers' plan to ask any-one to do something for nothing," and stated that it would pay contributors reasonably.[3] Its roll of authors was a notable one from the beginning, and a striking fact about the list is its national breadth. From Philadelphia there were Boker, L. Clarke Davis and his wife Rebecca Harding Davis, John S. Hart, Charles Godfrey Leland, Thomas Buchanan Read, S. Weir Mitchell, Frank R. Stockton, and others; from New England, George M. Towle, Harriet Prescott Spofford, and Rose Terry Cooke sent articles and short stories; from New York, Charles Astor Bristed, James Grant Wilson, Emma Lazarus, Brander Matthews, Henry James, the Stoddards, and the Carys sent their contributions; from the West came work by Charles Warren Stoddard, Maurice Thompson, Robert Dale Owen, and "Octave Thanet"; while southern writers for *Lippincott's* included William Gilmore Simms, Paul Hamilton Hayne, Sidney Lanier, John R. Thompson, George W. Bagby, John Esten Cooke, Margaret J. Preston, William M. Baker, Schele DeVere, and Edward A. Pollard. The South was, indeed, liberally represented; *Lippincott's* did more in the seventies to afford encouragement to southern writers than any other magazine in the country, and this despite the more spectacular work of its rival, *Scribner's Monthly*.

Lippincott's had at the first the ambition to print American serials only, like the *Atlantic*. It began with one by Rebecca Harding Davis called *Dallas Galbraith: an American Novel*, and followed with Robert Dale Owen's *Beyond the Breakers*, also subtitled *An American Novel*; but in its fourth volume it followed after foreign idols by running a Trollope novel, and it published thereafter English and American work indiscrimi-nately. In short fiction, *Lippincott's* kept company with the four or five leading magazines of the country, by means of stories by Henry James, Thomas A. Janvier, Mrs. Spofford, Mrs. Cooke, and Miss Woolson. "Ouida" was perhaps not quite at home in the *Lippincott's* of the seventies, but some of her best stories were published there, such as "A Leaf in the Storm" and "A Dog of Flanders." Much of Frank R.

[3] *Lippincott's*, I, 114 (January 1868).

Stockton's earliest work was printed in *Lippincott's* in the late sixties, and some of "Octave Thanet's" first tales ten years later. "Christian Reid" and Mrs. Lucy H. Hooper were other faithful contributors, the latter being associate editor during the magazine's first two or three years.

Special mention should be made of *Lippincott's* interest in travel. Illustrated articles by tourists in the southern and western United States and in foreign countries were prominent from the magazine's second year forward. George Kennan, Edward King, Henry James, and Edward Strahan were among the travel writers. Another distinctive department was that of literary criticism and book reviewing; the "Literature of the Day" section was of unusually high grade, ranking with similar work in the *Atlantic* and the *Nation*. There was an interest, too, in art; a series in 1872 on private art collections in Philadelphia may be mentioned.[4] *Lippincott's* was fortunately located for special attention to the great Centennial Exposition of 1876. Science was given constant if not very distinguished attention. Politics, too, were touched upon occasionally both in the "Monthly Gossip" and in unsigned articles probably by the editor; to take one example, the magazine opposed the civil service reform being urged upon the country in 1880. And manners, of course, furnished a subject always important in the seventies. "Articles descriptive of life and manners, graphically written and interspersed with anecdote and lively pictures of society at home and abroad" were promised readers of *Lippincott's* in the prospectus for 1873. Bristed, Lady Blanche Murphy, and Kate Field helped provide this menu. The offerings in verse were not, on the whole, very distinctive, nor indeed very extensive. Boker, Miss Lazarus, Edgar Fawcett, Bayard Taylor, the Stoddards and Carys, and the southern writers named above were the chief poets. Perhaps the most notable poetical contributions were by Sidney Lanier, whose "Corn," "Symphony," and "Psalm of the West" appeared in 1875–76.

In 1881 *Lippincott's* attempted an alteration in policy. It had certainly not been successful financially; it refused to

---

[4] These articles were signed "E. S.," initials which probably stood for Edward Strahan, who in the following years wrote much for the magazine on travel.

quote its circulation to the agencies, and it carried only ten or a dozen pages of advertising besides that of the Lippincott books and certain exchange announcements for other periodicals. Now it was to be "somewhat lighter." [5] Its price was reduced from four to three dollars, and a new series was begun. Little change in contents is to be noticed, however; perhaps the magazine became a little less academic, but somewhat more interested in social and political questions. It was unavoidably in competition with the two great New York magazines, *Harper's* and the *Century*, and it was unable to make headway against their abundant letterpress and copious illustration. A Boston observer remarked in 1883 that *Lippincott's* stood "only just behind its New York neighbors, with a quality of reading matter and illustration which would seem ample if it were not for the surpassing supply furnished by its two powerful rivals." [6] The fact is that it was more like two less prosperous contemporaries, the *Atlantic* and the *Galaxy*. In typographical excellence, in the quality of its book reviewing, and in dignity it resembled the former; while in breadth of interests, geographical and intellectual, it was more like the latter. It had, however, a distinct individuality of its own. The *Nation's* magazine reviewer, an exigent critic, wrote often of *Lippincott's* "distinctive flavor" [7] and "comparative freedom from staleness and familiar routine." [8]

In 1885 the magazine dropped illustration entirely; in 1886 it changed its familiar neat double-column page for a single-column spread; in 1887 it adopted the policy, later to dominate the magazine, of publishing an entire novel in each issue. Kirk had retired, and William S. Walsh, a grandson of one of Philadelphia's old-time editors, Robert Walsh of the *American Quarterly Review*, was at the helm.

There were still some short stories, some articles and poems, and the "Monthly Gossip" and review departments. Brander Matthews' "Philosophy of the Short Story," important for its effect on short story criticism for many years to come, appeared

[5] Prospectus for 1881.
[6] *Literary World*, XIV, 414 (December 1, 1883).
[7] *Nation*, XV, 221 (October 3, 1872); XVI, 31 (January 9, 1873); XVI, 240 (April 3, 1873).
[8] *Nation*, XIX, 157 (September 3, 1874).

in *Lippincott's* for November 1885. But the long fiction usurped the chief attention and claimed the lion's share of space. Some very notable novels were published, and many, of course, which had little or no value. Oscar Wilde's *The Picture of Dorian Grey* shocked many readers, and Amélie Rives's *The Quick and the Dead* made an even bigger sensation. The latter was, indeed, one of the "hits" of its decade. Conan Doyle's *The Sign of the Four* introduced Sherlock Holmes to an American audience, and Kipling's *The Light That Failed* nursed the growing reputation of another author. These were English writers; but American novelists were in the majority, with Charles King's historical novels, H. H. Boyesen's Norwegian stories, and work by Edgar Saltus, Julian Hawthorne, and John Habberton, and by women novelists like Julia Magruder, Louise Stockton, Grace King, Ruth McEnery Stuart, and Amelia E. Barr occupying places of prominence. In the nineties came new writers, including Gertrude Atherton, Gilbert Parker, Robert Barr, and Paul Leicester Ford.[9] James Lane Allen's *The Choir Invisible* was printed in 1897. One of *Lippincott's* chief poets in these years was Paul Laurence Dunbar; and among the best short stories were Lafcadio Hearn's "Karma," Anna Katharine Green's "A Mysterious Case," W. N. Harben's "The Sale of Uncle Rastus," Maurice Thompson's "A Friend to the Devil," Paul Laurence Dunbar's "The Strength of Gideon," and Owen Wister's "Philosophy 4." [10] Stephen Crane's European series was a prominent feature.

Walsh's editorship ended in 1889, but he was succeeded by Henry Stoddart, who had been his managing editor for several years. In 1899 Harrison Smith Morris, poet and art critic, came to the editorship; and in 1905 came J. Berg Esenwein, who was later to become a prominent teacher by correspondence of the writing of fiction. Esenwein accepted Mary Roberts

[9] Other contributors to *Lippincott's* in its second phase were Joseph A. Altsheler, Robert Montgomery Bird, Cyrus Townsend Brady, Alice Brown, Will Levington Comfort, Edgar Fawcett, Marion Harland, Bret Harte, Maurice Hewlett, Mary Jane Holmes, Richard Malcolm Johnston, John Luther Long, Francis Lynde, Alice Duer Miller, S. Weir Mitchell, Maria Louise Pool, Albert Bigelow Paine, Christian Reid, Charles G. D. Roberts, Marie Van Vorst, C. N. and A. M. Williamson, and Carolyn Wells.

[10] These stories appeared, in the order named, in the numbers for May 1890, March 1891, September 1894, August 1895, October 1899, and August 1901.

Rinehart's first novel, induced Carolyn Wells to enter the field of detective writing,[11] and did much to sustain the magazine's reputation for entertainment in fiction. Miss Louise Bull succeeded him briefly, giving place in 1914 to Edward Frank Allen, whose editorship of McBride's *Travel* was interrupted by his superintendence of the last two years of *Lippincott's*. McBride, Nast & Company had bought the magazine in December 1914, moving it to New York to be "in the center of American literary activities." [12] In September of that year the name was changed to *McBride's Magazine*; but after eight months' effort under the new title, the attempt at resuscitation was abandoned, and *McBride's* was merged in *Scribner's*.

The publication of a long story in each issue had its disadvantages as a magazine policy: the novels had to be short ("novelettes," they were called); it was difficult to keep to a uniform quality in such work; and the whole gave a certain fragmentariness to the complete file for the year and lost to the magazine that individual personality which had meant so much to it in its first phase. Moreover, it proved to be impossible to educate the public to a liking for novels in paper covers, chosen in advance by editors of a series. Though some of the *Lippincott* novels made popular successes, they made them chiefly after they were placed between boards.

Lippincott's, however, must be given a high rank among American magazines. In its career of almost half a century it printed much, particularly of fiction, poetry, and travel, which still seems important.

[11] Letter to the author from Mr. Esenwein dated September 21, 1926.
[12] *Lippincott's*, XC, 128 (December 1914).

THE OVERLAND MONTHLY [1]

T HE founder of the *Overland Monthly* was a San Francisco bookseller and publisher named Anton Roman. The weekly *Californian* [2] had just passed away, leaving a void in the literary empyrean of California which, thought Roman, should be filled with a good monthly having the double purpose of "boosting" California and offering a medium to a group of lively young San Francisco writers. The men he chose to edit the new magazine were Francis Bret Harte, secretary to the director of the mint at San Francisco and a writer for the *Californian* and *Golden Era*; Noah Brooks, editor of the *Alta California*, a daily newspaper; and W. C. Bartlett, editor of the

[1] TITLES: *The Overland Monthly*, 1868–1923; *The Overland Monthly and Out West Magazine*, 1923–35. Variable subtitles.

FIRST ISSUE: July 1868. LAST ISSUE: July 1935.

PERIODICITY: Monthly. [First Series], I–XV, semiannual volumes, July 1868–December 1875. Suspended, 1876–1882. Second Series, I–LXXIX, semiannual volumes, January 1883–June 1922; LXXX, July 1922–April 1923; LXXXI, May–December 1923; LXXXII–XCIII, annual volumes, 1924–35 (omitted February 1933; June, September, October 1934; January, February, May 1935).

PUBLISHERS: A. Roman & Company, San Francisco, 1868–69; John H. Carmany, 1869–75; California Publishing Company (Warren Cheney, manager), San Francisco, 1883; Samuel Carson & Company, San Francisco, 1883–85; Overland Monthly Publishing Company, San Francisco (Charles H. Shinn, manager, 1885–94), 1885–1900; Frederick Marriott, San Francisco, 1900–20; B. G. Barnett, San Francisco, 1920–21. Since 1921, editors have been publishers.

EDITORS: Francis Bret Harte, 1868–70; W. C. Bartlett, 1871; Benjamin P. Avery, 1872–73; Walt M. Fisher, 1874–75; Milicent W. Shinn, 1883–94; Rounsevelle Wildman, 1894–97; James Howard Bridge, 1897–1900; Frederick Marriott, 1900–03; Florence Jackman, 1903; P. N. Beringer, 1903–05; Thomas B. Wilson, 1905; P. N. Beringer, 1906–11; Frederick Marriott, 1911–20; Herbert Bashford, 1921; Almira Guild McKeon, 1921–22; D. R. Lloyd and Mabel Moffitt, 1923; Harry Noyes Pratt and Mabel Moffitt, 1924–25; V. V. Taylor and Hamilton Wayne, 1925; B. Virginia Lee and S. Bert Cooksley, 1925–26; R. D. Hart, 1926–28; Arthur H. Chamberlain, 1928–35.

INDEXED in *Poole's Index, Readers' Guide, Annual Library Index, Cumulative Index, Jones' Index, Review of Reviews Index, Engineering Index, Dramatic Index.*

REFERENCES: George R. Stewart, Jr., *Bret Harte, Argonaut and Exile* (Boston, 1931), Chapters XX–XXIII; James Howard Bridge, *Millionaires and Grub Street* (New York, 1931), pp. 191–217. *Overland Monthly*, anniversary number, July 1898 (Vol. XXXII, Second Series).

[2] See p. 118.

San Francisco *Bulletin*. But as in most editorial boards, one member soon emerged as the most active and reliable: Brooks and Bartlett were busy men, while Harte's job at the mint was a political sinecure, and all were soon agreed that Harte should be the chief editor.[3]

The first number, issued for July 1868, contained a sketch by Mark Twain, "By Rail Through France," Harte's poem "San Francisco from the Sea," a poem by Ina Coolbrith, a discussion of "Art Beginnings on the Pacific" by B. P. Avery, and articles on other western topics, with book reviews and a department of magazinish "table-talk" called "Etc." So far as "boosting" was concerned, there was very little of it, though its subtitle marked the magazine as "devoted to the development of the country." The new periodical was dignified, handsome, literary — a western *Atlantic Monthly*. Indeed, there were many who thought it imitated the *Atlantic* in format; but the practiced eye of an eastern printers' journal discovered that it was almost "a facsimile of *Lippincott's*." [4] The *Atlantic* or *Lippincott's*, it made no difference: it certainly belonged to the group of the best-printed magazines.

In the second number of the *Overland* appeared a story which made history. Roman was probably responsible for directing Harte's talent toward the materials of the mining camps; until this time the young author had scorned the coarse manners and loose morals of the forty-niners.[5] But now he wrote a tale called "The Luck of Roaring Camp," in which he showed that there were fine sentiments in hearts that beat beneath red flannel shirts and a basic human kindliness underlying bad grammar and "cuss words."

The "cuss words," by the way, almost made an end of this famous story before it was fairly born. A maidenly proofreader in the publishing office was deeply shocked by the introduction of a "dissolute, abandoned" woman in the second paragraph of the tale; she was indignant when she read that when "Cherokee Sal" was suffering the pains of childbirth the men stood about outside and made bets on whether "Sal would get through with

[3] Roman in *Overland*, Second Series, Vol. XXXII.
[4] *Printers' Circular*, III, 240 (October 1868).
[5] Stewart, pp. 162–166.

it"; and when the proofreader found the profane exclamation of "Kentuck" when the babe took hold of his finger, "He rastled with my finger, the d——d little cuss!" she grasped the proof sheets determinedly in one hand and, manipulating her long skirts with the other, swept into the publisher's office, red with outraged modesty. The dash between the *d's* did not placate her; pure though her mind was, she strongly suspected that here lay hidden a swear word, and she thought it her duty to communicate her suspicion to her employer. It took an editorial conference to determine the issue, but finally the story went in, *d*——*d* and all.[6]

"The Luck" made an immense success. The *Nation* was quick to declare that here was a story that belonged not to "mere magazine writing," but to "literature."[7] The *New Eclectic* had "an unpleasant sensation that our eastern civilization is stale and insipid by contrast" with Harte's West.[8] The *Atlantic's* publishers wrote to "The Author of 'The Luck of Roaring Camp'" — since everything in the *Overland* was unsigned — asking for contributions. The success of this first story was repeated by that of "The Outcasts of Poker Flat" in the number of the *Overland* for the next January, "Miggles" in the following June, and "Tennessee's Partner" in October. Then came a "hit" of another kind. It was in September 1870 that the magazine published some verses by its editor entitled "Plain Language from Truthful James." Harte had a low opinion of the poem and printed it only as a filler;[9] but it caught on and was reprinted in thousands of papers from Maine to California and Minnesota to Texas, usually under the title, "The Heathen Chinee."

But though its editor made all the "hits" of the early *Overland*, he was by no means the only contributor. Besides Brooks and Bartlett, Miss Ina Coolbrith, the poet, was an associate

---

[6] Some doubt has been cast upon the authenticity of this story, but it is too good not to be true. Both Harte and his assistant editor Noah Brooks related it; Brooks even gave, somewhat tentatively, the modest proofreader's name. See T. E. Pemberton, *The Life of Bret Harte* (London, 1903), p. 87; *Overland Monthly*, Second Series, LII, 10 (July 1908).

[13] See p. 14, footnote.

[8] *New Eclectic*, III, 379 (November 1868).

[15] See pp. 413–14.

in the editorship. Charles Warren Stoddard, a close friend of Harte, contributed some of his "South Sea Idylls," and Benjamin P. Avery his "Sierra Pictures." Clarence King wrote some mountaineering sketches; Josephine Clifford, Harte's office assistant,[10] did some short stories; J. Ross Browne contributed occasional humorous pieces; and John S. Hittell wrote articles on mining. Roman procured some two-thirds of the contributions; but Harte did his part with his short stories, poems, and the editorial "table-talk."

California business men had guaranteed the success of the *Overland* by contracting for $900 worth of advertising a month.[11] If the magazine had not made a circulation success, these guarantors, who expected a "booster" periodical, might have complained; but within six months the *Overland* went to 3,000 and a little later to 10,000, at $4.00 a year. Roman sold it, however, within its first year, because he was ill and unable to attend to it properly. The purchaser was John H. Carmany, and he paid $7,500 for the nine-months-old magazine.[12] Harte demanded from the new publisher $2,000 a year as salary, extra payment at regular rates [13] for any contributed matter outside of the regular editorial departments, and a private office.[14] The terms were reasonable enough; but if they had been unreasonable Carmany would have had to meet them, for Harte had become indispensable to the magazine.

It was a sad blow, then, when the indispensable editor resigned at the end of the next year. But Harte felt the call of the East inescapably. He was really an expatriate in California; he longed for a more "civilized" environment. Besides, he had an offer to edit a magazine in Chicago, which may have seemed more civilized to him — until he saw it.[15] Carmany made every effort to hold Harte, offering him $5,000 a year as salary, plus $100 apiece for contributions and a fourth-interest in the magazine; finally he offered to sell him the whole property for

---

[10] For reminiscences by Josephine Clifford McCracken, see *Overland*, LXVII, 1 (January 1916); *American Magazine*, LXXIX, 51 (June 1915).

[11] B. E. Lloyd, *Lights and Shades in San Francisco* (San Francisco, 1876).

[12] Roman in *Overland Monthly*, Second Series, XXXII, 74 (July 1898).

[13] See p. 14, footnote.

[14] Geoffrey Bret Harte, ed., *The Letters of Bret Harte* (Boston, 1926), p. 7.

[15] See pp. 413–14.

$13,000.[16] But Harte's mind was made up, and off he went in February 1871, speeded on his way by one of those convivial all-night fêtes with which the San Francisco bohemians sometimes complimented their favorites.

Carmany was left "holding the sack." In the next five years he lost $5,000 to $6,000 annually trying to make the *Overland* a success. He once remarked, with a bitterness that exaggerated the fact, that he spent $30,000 to make Bret Harte famous.[17]

Bartlett took over the editorial work for nearly a year after Harte's departure; then Benjamin P. Avery, a journalist and engraver, and an early contributor to the magazine, was editor until his appointment in 1874 as minister to China. After that, Walt M. Fisher occupied the editorial chair[18] until the magazine was suspended at the end of 1875. Miss Coolbrith, Miss Clifford, and Charles H. Phelps were assistants. The former contributors continued, with others, including Prentice Mulford, Ferdinand Ewer, and Joaquin Miller. Certain members of the University of California faculty wrote for the magazine — Edward Rowland Sill, Presidents Daniel Coit Gilman and John Le Conte, Professor Joseph Le Conte, and others. But Carmany gave up the struggle at the end of the fifteenth semiannual volume.

Five years later Roman again made an attempt to found a California magazine, this time in conjunction with Fred M. Somers, who had been associated with Ambrose Bierce on the *Argonaut*. The magazine was called the *Californian, a Western Monthly*,[19] and was begun in January 1880. As before, Roman withdrew after about a year, and Charles H. Phelps became editor and owner until he was succeeded by Warren Cheney in the fall of 1882. Carmany now made a gift to Cheney of the name of the *Overland Monthly*, and the latter rechristened his periodical the *Californian and Overland Monthly*. In January 1883 this name was shortened to the old *Overland Monthly*, of which Cheney began a "Second Series" with new number-

[16] Carmany in Supplement to *Overland Monthly* for February 1883.

[17] Ella Sterling Cummins [Mighels], *The Story of the Files* (San Francisco, 1893), p. 145.

[18] Quotation from *San Francisco Bulletin* in *Publishers' Weekly*, February 12, 1876.

[19] See p. 56.

ing. Bierce promptly christened the revived magazine the "Warmed-Overland"; and the unhappy designation stuck.[20]

Milicent W. Shinn, who had entered upon a journalistic career by the advice and aid of the poet Sill,[21] and who had served as managing editor of the *California and Overland*, was the editor for its first twelve years of the Second Series of the *Overland Monthly*. Miss Shinn had that faculty for pleasant acquaintance with writers which is so important for a magazine editor. Besides Sill, who contributed poetry and criticism under his own name and miscellaneous articles under various pseudonyms, there were several of the supporters of the First Series to be found in the magazine in the eighties — Stoddard, Miss Coolbrith, Brooks, and Joseph Le Conte. Dan De Quille and Charles Howard Shinn were frequent contributors, and two newcomers to the University of California — Josiah Royce and Albert S. Cook. Several academic contributors from the East were also prominent, such as Richard T. Ely and George Frederick Wright. General O. O. Howard wrote about Indian wars; John Vance Cheney and Clinton Scollard contributed verse; Maria Louise Pool and Sara D. Halsted wrote short stories. California, pioneer history, the Indians, mining, the Chinese, and South America were favorite topics. The *Overland* confessed itself "local in its subjects," and acknowledged its preference for California writers even when their work was less finished than that of transmontane authors.[22] Always closely related to the University of California, of which its editor was a graduate and many of its contributors professors, it published a notable series of articles on that institution in 1892. It was not wholly local, however; it kept abreast of current affairs, and it published departments of book reviews and general editorial comment. Some illustrations entered its pages in the late eighties.

The *Overland's* circulation, which had been quoted at 18,000 in 1888, showed tobogganing tendencies in the early nineties. Reducing the price to $3.00 in November 1891 helped but little. In 1894 Rounsevelle Wildman became editor and owner

[20] Bridge, *op. cit.*, p. 194.
[21] *Overland Monthly*, Second Series, XL, 265 (September 1902).
[22] *Ibid.*, X, 443 (October 1887).

for three years; when he left to become consul to Hong Kong, he sold the magazine to James Howard Bridge. The managing editor under both Wildman and Bridge, both of whom were often absentee editors, was Charles S. Greene, who had been on the editorial staff since 1887. A graduate of the University of California, a ready writer of both prose and verse, and an active manager, Greene did much to revive the declining magazine. The price was reduced to ten cents a copy to meet the competition of the eastern low-priced magazines. By the end of 1896, the editor could write:

> In three years the *Overland* has trebled its subscription list, wiped out nine-tenths of its debts, added three hundred per cent to its assets, doubled the number of its illustrations, doubled its advertising patronage, doubled its office expenses, and become a power for good among its great army of readers.[23]

The magazine was occasionally active in California politics. In the late nineties it had a special edition including an educational department edited by A. B. Coffee, which sold for $1.50 a year and was adopted as the official organ of the state's board of education. This placed 3,341 schools on the *Overland's* subscription list.

Among the contributors in these years were Willa Cather, Horace Annesley Vachel, James Hopper, Gertrude Atherton, Robert J. Burdette, Oliver Curwood, Edwin Markham, George Sterling, and John G. Neihardt. The magazine paid the unknown Jack London $5.00 for his "To the Man on Trail" in 1899; according to London's story, Editor Bridge said he could not pay more because he received only $30 a page for advertising.[24]

In 1900 Frederick Marriott, of the *San Francisco News Letter*, gained control of the *Overland*. The circulation at this time was 30,000; it continued to increase gradually until it reached 75,000 in 1912. In 1907 it was able to pay a very popular Jack London fifteen cents a word for his stories.[25]

[23] *Overland Monthly*, XXVIII, 599 (November 1896).
[24] Charmian London, *The Book of Jack London* (New York, 1921), I, 267. Bridge says, however, that he paid London $25 for it. See Bridge, *op. cit.*, p. 202. London's story is very convincing. Bridge makes an error in the title of the story.
[25] *Ibid.*, II, 150.

It was now a handsomely printed and illustrated magazine, much given to promotion, selling at fifteen cents. It carried a department by Pastor Russell from 1909 until his death in 1916. It published an excellent Japanese number in January 1910 and one devoted to Joaquin Miller in February 1920. A department of "Oriental Affairs" was a valuable feature of 1919–20. The price went to twenty-five cents after the war.

In 1923 the *Overland* absorbed *Out West Magazine*, a Los Angeles periodical. The *Overland Monthly and Out West Magazine* gave special attention to poetry and the arts, as well as to material which concerned California institutions and activities. Arthur H. Chamberlain, the last editor, moved it to Los Angeles in 1931. It was discontinued July 1935.

THE ALDINE [1]

SUTTON, BOWNE & COMPANY, a firm of New York printers, began in August 1868 to issue a house organ called the *Aldine Press*. It was a four-page folio printed on calendered paper with glossy ink, and was filled with selected miscellany and some advertising. It was distinguished by the reproduction of Gustav Doré's illustrations of scenes from Don Quixote and the Bible; the Doré pictures were made from imported French blocks by Pisan and others and were exceptionally well printed. The paper, which bore the subtitle, "A Typographical Art Journal," was circulated free among the patrons of its publishers.

In January of the following year the number of pages of the new journal was doubled, and an annual subscription price of one dollar was named, though some free circulation was still maintained. The contents continued to be chiefly "selected," but some original contributions found their way into the paper before the end of the year. W. H. Ingersoll became a contributor on art subjects. Special attention was given to insurance affairs; and the insurance companies, which were the leading patrons of Sutton, Bowne & Company's printing establishment, carried most of the advertising in the paper. Doré's pictures continued as a chief feature, accompanied by other borrowed woodcuts. In 1870 the number of pages was increased to twelve, more variety was introduced in the pictures, and departments for art, music, and books were established. The price rose to $2.00 a year.

[1] TITLES: (1) *The Aldine Press, a Typographic Art Journal*, 1868–70; (2) *The Aldine, a Typographic Art Journal*, 1871–73; (3) *The Aldine, the Art Journal of America*, 1874–79.

FIRST ISSUE: September 1868. LAST ISSUE: Part 12 [December], 1879.

PERIODICITY: Monthly, bimonthly. I, September–December 1868; II–VI, regular annual volumes, 1869–73; VII–VIII, biennial volumes of 24 undated "parts" each, 1874–77; IX, 12 undated "parts," 1878–79.

PUBLISHERS: Sutton, Bowne & Company, 1868–October 1870; James Sutton & Company, November 1870–1873; Aldine Company (James Sutton, president), 1874–79. All of New York.

EDITORS: Richard Henry Stoddard, 1871–75; James Sutton, Jr. (?), 1876–79.

In 1871 the *Aldine* outgrew its swaddling clothes. The word
Press was dropped from its title; the magazine was transformed into a quarto of twelve to sixteen pages. The alliance
with the insurance business was abandoned, and advertising
was dropped altogether. Original woodcuts were used, including some of W. J. Linton's best work; [2] and the printing and
typography were raised to an even higher level. Richard Henry
Stoddard, recently resigned from the literary editorship of the
New York World, was made editor and soon brought into the
handsome pages of the new magazine some of his many literary
friends. The price was increased to $2.50; and the next year it
was doubled, with a chromo to palliate the increase.

Besides Stoddard and his wife, such writers as John R.
Thompson, Junius Henri Browne, Harriet Prescott Spofford,
Caroline Chesebrough, Julian Hawthorne, Julia C. R. Dorr,
Margaret J. Preston, and C. D. Shanly were frequent contributors during the next few years. There were notes on the arts,
including music and the drama. But the emphasis in the *Aldine*
continued to be placed upon graphic art and especially upon its
engravings on wood. Full-page unbacked cuts with tint blocks
were features. Thomas Moran, John D. Woodward, John S.
Davis, and Eliza Greatorex were among the artists, with several French painters; and W. J. and Henry Linton, J. P. Davis,
J. A. Bogert, F. W. Quartley, Davis & Spier, and Kingdon &
Boyd were leading engravers. Some of the early work of
Timothy Cole and Frederick Juengling appeared in the *Aldine*.
Blocks by Maurand and Jonnard were imported from France,
and Germany and England were also represented.

In 1876 Stoddard apparently retired from his editorial
direction of the magazine, and the number of pictures was
increased; in 1878 general literature was abandoned, and the
only letterpress consisted of discussions of art and comment
on the illustrations, which became even more profuse. Elihu
Vedder, E. H. Blashfield, and Granville Perkins appeared.

If there is any idea in which the *Aldine* is more interested than
any other [wrote the editor (probably James Sutton, Jr.,) in 1878]
it is certainly that of art education. . . . We can see nothing better

[2] See W. J. Linton, *The History of Wood-Engraving in America* (Boston,
1882), p. 33.

at present than the constant reproduction for the public of first class engravings from the best pictures.[3]

The successive "parts" were, however, issued only bimonthly now; and at the end of 1879 the magazine was discontinued.

The *Aldine* was never important in literary publication, in spite of Stoddard's efforts; but in the printing of good engraving and in typography it was a distinguished effort. Charles Dudley Warner, praising its typography, wrote that it had been "one of the most powerful means in the revival of what is really one of the fine arts." [4]

[3] *Aldine*, IX, 169 (Part 5).
[4] *Ibid.*, VII, 6 (Prospectus).

THE LAKESIDE MONTHLY [1]

WHEN Bret Harte was at the height of his popularity as exponent of the picturesque life of the California mining camps, he decided to leave the scenes of his early exploits in literature and seek his fortune in the East. Searchers for crude gold might go west, but seekers after literary prosperity must journey eastward. When he came to Chicago, Harte stopped for a visit with relatives. But he had another reason for breaking his journey there: he had been receiving overtures from some Chicagoans who wished to start a magazine in that ambitious city and make him the editor of it. On the evening of Harte's visit he was invited to one of the most expensive banquets ever spread in that not too inexpensive metropolis; there were thirty guests, and the cost to each was a thousand dollars. The money, however, did not go for food or service. It was designed as working capital for the new magazine, and the prospective editor was to be surprised by seeing thirty thousand-dollar checks pressed upon him. But alas for the well-laid plans of mice and men! — Bret Harte did not attend that dinner. Whether he was indisposed, or whether Mrs. Harte was offended by some fancied discourtesy, or whether one glance at Chicago had been enough,

[1] TITLES: *The Western Monthly*, 1869–70; *The Lakeside Monthly*, 1871–February 1874.

FIRST ISSUE: January 1869. LAST ISSUE: February 1874.

PERIODICITY: Monthly. Regular semiannual volumes. Omissions: October 1870; November, December 1871.

PUBLISHERS: H. V. Reed and E. C. Tuttle, January–March 1869; Reed, Browne & Company, April–December 1869, May–October 1871; Western Monthly Company, 1870; Lakeside Publishing Company, January–April 1871; University Publishing Company, January–September 1872; J. J. Spalding & Company, October 1872–April 1873; F. F. Browne & Company, May 1873–February 1874.

EDITORS: H. V. Reed, January–April 1869; F. F. Browne, May 1869–February 1874.

INDEXED in *Poole's Index* and in *Jones' Index*.

REFERENCE: Herbert E. Fleming, "The Literary Interests of Chicago," *American Journal of Sociology*, XI, 398–404 (November 1905), published separately as *The Magazines of a Market-Metropolis*.

has never been satisfactorily explained.[2] We know Harte had other offers, and generous ones, from eastern publishers. At any rate he gave Chicago the cut direct, and the capitalists pocketed their checks, along with the snub.[3]

The magazine which it was planned that Harte should take in charge was the *Western Monthly*, lately rechristened the *Lakeside*. The *Western* had been founded by H. V. Reed in January 1869, but after a few issues Francis Fisher Browne had acquired an interest; and although Reed retained his connection with the publication for two or three years, Browne became its chief (and after the fire of 1871, its sole) conductor. He had been born a New Englander and trained a printer. He had excellent literary judgment and soon rescued the *Western* from those vices of local magazines — indiscriminate "boosting" and "selections."

It was, however, always a distinctly sectional periodical. "Our magazine," said the editor in the first number, "is intended to be purely an institution of the West." And then he added the complaint grown familiar in the East as against England, in the South as against the North, and in the West as against the East: "Our writers have learned to look upon those of the East with unbecoming awe, and fear to cope with them in the literary arena."[4] Another writer in the first issue boldly exclaims, "If we have earned the title of the Granary, let us strike for that of the Brainery of the nation."[5] Before many months the magazine was advocating the removal of the national capital to the Mississippi Valley.[6] When the *Independent* attacked the *Western* for "narrow-minded sectionalism," it answered vigorously:

The East — we say it more in sorrow than in anger — the East regards the West as the great consumer of her wares — mechanical

[2] It has been stated by a close friend of the Hartes that Mrs. Harte was offended because the cousins with whom they were staying in Chicago were not invited. See *Overland Monthly*, LXVII, 1 (January 1916).

[3] J. H. Carmany named the sum contributed as $500 a guest in his address at the *Overland* dinner of 1883. (*Overland*, February 1883, Supplement, p. 12.) But the sketch of Browne in the *Dial* for June 16, 1913 (LIV, 489) says $30,000 was raised by thirty guests.

[4] *Western Monthly*, I, 57 (January 1869). The same plaint is voiced at length by G. Nelson Smith in the March 1869 number (I, 159–162).

[5] *Ibid.*, I, 35 (January 1869). Nathan Sheppard is the writer.

[6] *Ibid.*, I, 390–399 (December 1869).

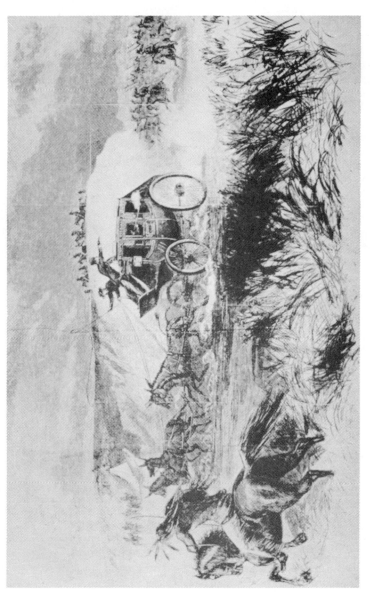

INDIAN ATTACK ON OVERLAND DISPATCH

Theodore R. Davis' sketch in *Harper's Weekly* of April 21, 1866. The coach bears the lettering "Butterfield's Overland Dispatch." As is shown by the defective joints, this cut was a composite of 18 blocks, separately engraved (see p. 454).

LASSOING A BEAR IN CALIFORNIA

One of F. O. C. Darley's spirited drawings of western life. There were critics who complained that Darley was more spirited than accurate in this series. Engraved by Francis Holl, this plate was used first for the book *Picturesque America*, and then for the March 5, 1870, number of *Appleton's Journal*.

and intellectual — while she declines everything looking toward reciprocity. Our efforts in science, literature, and the practical arts are ignored. . . . What western book has received a generous commendation in an eastern magazine? [7]

Yet sectional propaganda had no very strong appeal for Browne, and probably if it had not been for the recent striking success of the *Overland* in that kind he would have made a more national magazine.

As it was, Browne's change of the name in 1871 from the *Western* to the *Lakeside Monthly* made the title, if actually more local in signification, less blatantly sectional. The Lakeside Publishing Company was founded, with a capital of half a million, to publish not only the *Monthly* but many other periodicals [8] and do a general printing and publishing business. It was at this time that the Harte fiasco occurred. Then came the great conflagration of 1871. The *Lakeside* had already had its baptism of fire in the autumn of 1870, when its October number had been burned, and a fire in the stereotype foundry had delayed the issue of the following January; but those were light misfortunes compared to the disaster of a year later. The publishing company's great new building was destroyed, with all the magazine's plates, equipment, and material on hand. The November and December numbers were omitted; but in January 1872 the *Lakeside's* famous fire number (now a collector's item) was published, and the magazine continued. At the time of the fire the circulation was 9,000; by 1873 it had reached 14,000, which represented at least a self-supporting basis. Then came the panic of 1873, with its Black Friday of finance; and in the ensuing subscription season the Chicago magazine lost more than a third of its list. This was the final calamity. Some $50,000 had been invested already, without returns; [9] Browne's health was broken; and it was resolved to suspend publication. *Scribner's Monthly* offered to take over the list, but Browne decided to preserve the magazine's integrity by letting it die as it had lived, with Chicago's banner floating over it.

---

[7] *Western Monthly*, II, 434 (December 1869).

[8] In 1871 it was advertising three weeklies, eleven monthlies, two bimonthlies, and three quarterlies — religious, professional, philanthropic, and general.

[9] *Western Monthly*, IV, 335 (November 1870).

The *Lakeside Monthly* was, considering its difficulties, an admirable magazine. There are not many famous names connected with it, to be sure; but it boasted at the end of 1870 that it had "developed a corps of writers who, although without previous magazine experience, have shown versatility and a capacity for magazine writing." [10] The Reverend Robert Collyer contributed many articles and even a serial story which the suspension of the magazine left in midair. There was not a great deal of fiction, though short stories increased latterly. James Grant Wilson, Francis E. Willard, Eben E. Rexford, and Mrs. M. L. Rayne were prominent contributors. Poetry came to the *Lakeside* pages from Benjamin F. Taylor, Edgar Fawcett, "Howard Glyndon," Joaquin Miller, and others. William Matthews wrote philological and miscellaneous essays, and Moses Coit Tyler wrote literary criticism. Browne's own "Chit-Chat" was really bright and incisive; it did not appear after the fire. Some attention was given to art, music, and drama, especially early in 1873, after the visits of such artists as Rubinstein, Wieniawski, and Edwin Booth. Theodore Thomas was prominent. The contents had much that was indigenous to the region in which it was published, and much that was attractive, although the didactic note was doubtless too pronounced for a general literary magazine.

After the first few numbers, the magazine was uniformly well arranged and exceptionally well printed. Except for some portraits in 1869, there was no illustration.

A later commentator on the life and work of Browne said very justly of the *Lakeside*, by way of summary:

> For that helpful conservatism which spurns the taint of sensationalism, and for typographical taste, it probably deserves the palm amongst all; while in other respects suffering by comparison less in average quality than in the celebrity of some of the writers.[11]

It remains to this day the most important general literary magazine of a consistently high class ever published in Chicago.

[10] *Dial*, LIV, 490 (June 16, 1913).
[11] *Ibid.*, p. 489.

APPLETON'S JOURNAL [1]

FEW periodicals of the years following the Civil War furnished a better picture of the varied life of the times than the weekly *Appleton's Journal* did from 1869 to 1876. It had great variety; its articles were, as a rule, short and readable; not quite a newspaper, it was very close to current ideas and interests.

Omitting ordinary news and avoiding partisan advocacy, both political and sectarian, the *Journal* will be devoted to general literature, to science, art, and education, and to the diffusion of valuable information on subjects of public importance [ran the introductory announcement]. It is intended to make use of all resources, original and selected, domestic and foreign, which can give interest and variety to its pages.[2]

Edward L. Youmans, a member of the staff of the publishing house of D. Appleton & Company, was the first editor. His chief interest was the popularization of science, and he later became famous as a scientific lecturer and editor. He conceived of the new *Journal* as chiefly a reporter of contemporary scientific ideas. He had been sent abroad by the Appletons to procure material for book publication and for the projected journal, and in England he had established contacts with famous

[1] TITLES: (1) *Appleton's Journal of Literature, Science and Art*, 1869–June 1876; (2) *Appleton's Journal: A Monthly Miscellany of Popular Literature*, July 1876–1878; (3) *Appleton's Journal: A Magazine of General Literature*, 1879–81.

FIRST ISSUE: April 3, 1869. LAST ISSUE: December 1881.

PERIODICITY: Weekly, 1869–June 26, 1876; monthly, July 1876–1881. I, April 3–August 14, 1869: II, August 21–December 25, 1869; III–XV, 1870–June 26, 1876; New Series, I–XI [XVI–XXVI], July 1876–1881. Supplements with separate paging accompany Nos. 2, 4, 8, 11, 14, 17, and 18 in Vol. I; 22 and 32 in II; 43, 46, 50, 51, 54, 56, 57, 59, 61, 63, and 65 in III; 70, 74, 79, and 83 in IV.

PUBLISHERS: D. Appleton & Company, New York.

EDITORS: Edward Livingston Youmans, 1869–70; Robert Carter, 1870–72; Oliver Bell Bunce and Charles Henry Jones, 1872–81.

INDEXES: *Poole's, Jones'*, and *Subject-Contents Index*.

[2] *Appleton's Journal*, I, 22 (April 3, 1869).

scientists which were to prove more important to later ventures than to *Appleton's Journal*. For science, after all, became only one of several fields of knowledge exploited almost equally in the new periodical. After several numbers had been published, Youmans wrote to Herbert Spencer:

> The paper is having a curious experience. The bare announcement that it would give attention to science and valuable thought raised an almost universal condemnation of it in advance as a certain failure. And although we have had no science in it, and made it as vacant of ideas as possible, it is voted heavy.[3]

These are the exaggerations of disappointment; yet it is a fact that science was emphasized but little more in *Appleton's* than it had been in several contemporaries, and it is also true that such success as the new journal had at its beginning came from its serial publication of Victor Hugo's *The Man Who Laughs*.

It is safe to guess that a large proportion of the direction of *Appleton's* in these days, as well as later, fell to the lot of Oliver Bell Bunce, who had been trained as both a publisher and a popular writer, and who had the capacity for detail and the sympathy with popular taste which go to make an editor. A novel by Mrs. Oliphant was soon started to pursue its serial course alongside Hugo's; short articles on subjects connected with science, art, the drama, education, travel, biography, feminism, etc., appeared in great variety; there were some short stories and poems; and several departments made up of brief paragraphs occupied the last pages of the periodical. Eugene Benson, John Esten Cooke, Richard Henry Stoddard, Paul Hamilton Hayne, Schele DeVere, James Grant Wilson, and George M. Towle were prominent among the early contributors.

After about a year of discouraged editorship, Youmans retired, to found, a few years later, the *Popular Science Monthly* [4] under the aegis of the same publishers. He was supplanted by Robert Carter, who had had various experiences as an editor and publisher. He had, for example, been James Russell Lowell's partner in the production of that brief but excellent

[3] John Fiske, *Edward Livingston Youmans* (New York, 1894), p. 260.
[4] See p. 496.

magazine, the *Pioneer*,[5] and Lowell had once addressed him as his "dear, good, kindest, best friend"; [6] but when Carter now asked his former partner to contribute to *Appleton's*, Lowell was too busy and had refused too many offers that seemed more flattering.[7] Carter got along without Lowell's name and continued as editor for two years, yielding in 1872 to a team composed of Bunce, who had been his associate as well as Youmans', and Colonel Charles H. Jones, a journalist who was later to be editor of the *New York World*.[8]

Bunce had made his first literary success in the field of drama, and his play "Love in '76" holds a place in stage history as one of the most successful of dramas dealing with the American Revolution. Since that time he had been general publisher, novelist, and writer of popular history. He evidently was responsible for most or all of the "Table Talk" in *Appleton's Journal*, for he published the year after the magazine was discontinued a book of sayings and comments called *Bachelor Bluff*, much of which had appeared in slightly different guise in this department. These little essays made pleasant and sometimes incisive comments upon timely matters. In tone and scope they were strikingly like Richard Grant White's "Nebulae," which were appearing in the *Galaxy*: both Bunce and White had the aesthetic viewpoint, both were preoccupied with the subject of American manners (Bunce actually wrote a book on etiquette), both were conservatives in art, and both had a wide range of interests.

Probably the most distinguished editorial work of Bunce's life was done in connection with the most sumptuous of the period's illustrated works — *Picturesque America*, of which, though it bore William Cullen Bryant's name as editor, Bunce "had sole editorial charge." [9] This work originated in *Appleton's Journal*, which began to publish a series of pictures and sketches under the title later given to the separate work, in

---

[5] See Mott, *A History of American Magazines, 1741–1850*, p. 735.

[6] H. E. Scudder, *James Russell Lowell* (Boston, 1901), I, 111.

[7] *Ibid*. II, 144. He did, however, contribute one sonnet.

[8] See Don C. Seitz, *Joseph Pulitzer* (New York, 1924), *passim*.

[9] Appleton's *Annual Cyclopaedia*, XV, 638. In the completed work Bryant's name appears only in the second volume; that of Bunce appears only as author of several of the sketches.

1870, with Harry Fenn and A. R. Waud as artists and F. W. Quartley, J. A. Bogert, and others as engravers, while Bunce, T. B. Thorpe, John Esten Cooke, and various other writers did the descriptive sketches.

The original system of illustration for *Appleton's* called for either a large folding "cartoon" [10] on wood (usually a metropolitan scene) or a steel plate or a fully illustrated "art supplement" with each number, besides a number of woodcuts in connection with the letterpress.[11] Winslow Homer, Gaston Fay, F. O. C. Darley, and Edwin Forbes were among the artists. After 1870, however, this plan of illustration was abandoned; and though many illustrated articles appeared thereafter, including some numbers of the "Picturesque America" series, there were no more steel plates or folding "cartoons." It is evident enough that the magazine was not financially successful and that retrenchments had become necessary.

Appleton's was distinctively of New York, though there are not a few southern and western articles, chiefly by way of travel sketches. Such southern writers as Cooke, Thompson, and Hayne, and such westerners as Thorpe and Miss Woolson were represented. But New York scenes, theaters, art, and manners were predominant. Foreign influence was important throughout the file. Most of the serials were by English, French, and German novelists, the editor having a very low opinion of the American novel.[12] Foreign travel had an important place, especially after Bunce took full charge: Lucy H. Hooper had a French series, C. E. Pascoe an English series, and so on.

In 1876 the magazine abandoned weekly publication and became a monthly. Its character, however, changed little. It kept the same contributing personnel, in which Rossiter Johnson, Julian Hawthorne, Edgar Fawcett, Mrs. Sherwood (M. E. W. S.), Junius Henri Browne, and Constance Fenimore Woolson played important parts. Perhaps the most notable of the original pieces by Americans published in *Appleton's*, from a literary point of view, were a number of stories

---

[10] This term is used by *Appleton's* to designate a large picture printed from a woodcut, separately from the letterpress. See I, 409 (June 26, 1869).

[11] For further treatment of *Appleton's* illustration, see p. 187.

[12] See, for example, I, 474 (July 10, 1909).

by Miss Woolson, some poems by Hayne, a few essays by Burroughs, literary criticism by Stoddard, and certain southern sketches by Cooke and Thompson. Important occasional contributors were Bryant, Taylor, Fiske, "Carl Benson," and D. C. Shanly. Among later comers were Maurice Thompson, Rebecca Harding Davis, George Cary Eggleston (writing of Russia), Brander Matthews (writing of the stage, ever stressed in *Appleton's*), and Justin McCarthy.

After the first five volumes of the monthly — that is, after 1878 — the magazine became practically an eclectic. From the beginning there had been some use of English and French periodicals for material; now these and the German magazines furnished practically everything but the departments of criticism. Thus, before its discontinuance at the end of 1881, *Appleton's Journal* lost most of its original distinction.

16

THE OUTLOOK [1]

A BAPTIST paper called the *Church Union* was established in New York in 1867 by Henry E. Childs. At the end of its first year it claimed 16,000 circulation; but in the fall of 1869 its editor and owner of that year, the Reverend Crammond Kennedy, was trying to give the paper, with its debts and its 2,000 subscribers, to J. B. Ford & Company if they would carry it on. The Fords were publishers of Henry Ward Beecher's *Life of Christ* and of *Plymouth Pulpit*, the weekly periodical which printed Beecher's sermons; and they conceived the idea of putting their famous preacher into the editorship of the *Union* and exploiting it as the Beecher paper. Beecher had been a great success as editor of the *Inde-*

[1] TITLES: *The Christian Union*, 1870–93; *The Outlook*, 1893–1928; *The Outlook and Independent*, 1928–32; *The New Outlook*, 1932–35.

FIRST ISSUE: January 1, 1870. (Preliminary numbers under the title *The Christian Union* were issued October 9–December 25, 1869, but they are actually a part of the file of the *Church Union*, of 1867–69.) LAST ISSUE: June 1935.

PERIODICITY: Weekly, 1870–1932; monthly, 1932–1935. I–LIV, semiannual volumes, 1870–96; LV–CLIX, three volumes a year, 1897–1931; CLX, January 6–September 1932; CLXI, October 1932–June 1933; CLXII–CLXV, semiannual volumes, July 1933–35. Suspended May–August 1932.

PUBLISHERS: J. B. Ford & Company (John R. Howard, managing publisher), 1870–75; Christian Union Publishing Company, New York (H. M. Cleveland and Horatio C. King, managers), 1875–77; New York and Brooklyn Publishing Company, 1878–81; Christian Union Company, New York (Lawson Valentine, president, 1881–91; Lawrence F. Abbott, president, 1891–93), 1881–93; Outlook Company, New York (Lawrence F. Abbott, president, 1893–1923; Harold T. Pulsifer, president, 1923–27; Francis Rufus Bellamy, president, 1927–32; Frank A. Tichenor, president, 1932–35), 1893–1935.

EDITORS: Henry Ward Beecher (George S. Merriam, managing editor, 1870–75; Charles L. Norton and John Habberton, managing editors, 1875–76; Lyman Abbott, joint editor, 1876–81), 1870–81; Lyman Abbott (H. W. Mabie, associate editor, 1884–1916), 1881–1923; Ernest Hamlin Abbott (Harold Pulsifer, managing editor), 1923–28; Francis Rufus Bellamy, 1928–32; Alfred E. Smith, 1932–34; Francis Walton, 1934–35.

INDEXES: *Poole's, Poole's Abridged, Annual Library, Readers' Guide, Cumulative, A. L. A. Portrait.*

REFERENCES: Lyman Abbott, *Reminiscences* (Boston, 1915); Lyman Abbott, *Henry Ward Beecher* (Boston, 1903); John R. Howard, *Remembrance of Things Past* (New York, 1925); Edwin W. Morse, *Life and Letters of Hamilton Wright Mabie* (New York, 1920).

pendent some years before,[2] and the idea of renewing such a connection appealed to him. The Fords therefore took over the *Church Union* in September 1869, changing its name the following month, at Beecher's suggestion,[3] to the *Christian Union* in order to broaden its appeal. Kennedy was retained as managing editor, but the paper was gradually changed from a specialized religious journal into a general family periodical. Beecher had declared that he would not assume the editorship until a year or more later, but he was drawn into it by premature announcement;[4] and at the beginning of 1870 his name appeared as editor, and the paper entered upon a new career with new serial numbering.

It was a large quarto of sixteen pages — increased, as advertising grew, to twenty-four. It was not particularly well printed on paper not especially good; but what could one expect from a weekly at $3.00 a year? As to contents, the editor's "Lecture-Room Talks" were doubtless the chief attraction, for Beecher was immensely popular; and second only to these were the contributions of the editor's famous sister, Harriet Beecher Stowe, whose serial, "My Wife and I," in 1871 excited much attention, and who also wrote other serials as well as many little essays for the paper. Other constant contributors were the editor's wife, who conducted a domestic economy department in the late seventies; his brother Edward, who was an assistant editor; his half-brother Thomas K., who wrote moral essays; and his nephew, Frederic Beecher Perkins, a littérateur of some reputation already in the magazine world. How many more Beechers were masked under such pen names as "Aunt Fanny" and "Aunt Nelly" one can only guess.[5] But it would be quite wrong to assume that the *Christian Union* was merely a family affair: its list of contributors was long and distinguished. Louisa M. Alcott, George Macdonald, and Edward Eggleston shared with Mrs. Stowe the distinction of furnishing the paper's earliest fictional serials. Eggleston's *Circuit*

[2] See vol. II, pp. 371–72.
[3] Howard, *op. cit.*, pp. 243, 257.
[4] *Ibid.*, p. 259.
[5] "Aunt Patience" was the wife of a later editor, Lyman Abbott, several of whose relatives, including his father and uncle, were contributors.

Rider, illustrated by small woodcuts, was an attractive feature of 1873–74, and its author was a member of the *Union's* editorial staff in those years. Edward Everett Hale and George P. Fisher were among those who wrote the short moral essays which filled an important place in the *Christian Union's* bill of fare. Oliver Johnson, who had come to the new paper as office editor from the *Independent*, contributed his reminiscences of *Early Anti-Slavery Days* as a serial in 1874. E. L. Youmans wrote brief scientific sketches, John W. Chadwick wrote both verse and prose, George M. Towle did political and economic articles, and Charles L. Brace was the author of some sociological essays. Charles Dudley Warner, a neighbor of Mrs. Stowe's at Hartford, furnished pleasant sketches. There was some poetry, of course, though it was not very remarkable: Whittier, Hayne, "H. H." and Mary B. Dodge were among the *Union's* early poets. "Grace Greenwood" and "Olive Thorne" Miller wrote for the children. "Gail Hamilton" contributed many of her lively essays in 1874. Rose Terry Cooke and Louise Chandler Moulton were well known to the paper's readers. Young Moses Coit Tyler was literary editor in 1873–74.

Altogether, there was great variety: instruction in sermon, essay, and informational article; and entertainment in the fiction of a type not at all vain or amatory, but edifying; besides poetry, and even jokes and puzzles. The periodical type was that of the "family paper," highly departmentalized for old and young, male and female. By the middle seventies there were some eighteen departments: "The Outlook," a department of shorter, informative editorials; the serial; Beecher's "Lecture-Room Talk"; "Public Opinion," later called "Uppermost Topics," which contained scissored extracts from periodicals and books; "Books and Authors," a review department; the editorial page; "Inquiring Friends," a question-and-answer column, chiefly theological; the Sunday school lesson; "Selections," another eclectic department; "Truths and Trifles," paragraph miscellany; a section devoted to ecclesiastical news, called "The Church"; "The Week," a news department; "The Household," of the helpful essay type; "The Little Folks," juvenile miscellany; puzzles; "Farm and Garden"; the publisher's department, containing notices about the paper, premiums, etc.; and a financial section, chiefly advertising. There were eight pages of advertising by 1873.

The paper was a great success from the first number. "It was greeted with a chorus of protest and derision which was not always free from personalities," according to Lyman Abbott; [6] but much of this was sour-grapes criticism. J. B. Ford & Company was an enterprising firm, of which Edward Lloyd Ford and John R. Howard were active members; and it had ample financial resources, as well as the benefit of Beecher's shrewd advice.[7] The Reverend Mr. Kennedy soon found himself out of step with a pushing, popular paper; and in May 1870 he was replaced in the managing editorship by George S. Merriam, of Springfield, Massachusetts. Dorsey Gardner, a journalist who had held a similar position on the *Round Table*, was literary and news editor; while Charles L. Norton, James H. Dwight, Robert L. Raymond, and Charles W. Jenkins were staff writers.

Howard, stimulated by Beecher's suggestions, built up a good editorial staff; the editors produced a good paper; but it was the promotional genius of Captain Ford which crowned the whole effort with circulation success. Ford was the man who introduced the chromolithograph as a subscription premium, and who first sent canvassers from door to door to sell magazine and chromo, as the subscription book companies had taught him to do it. He began by using a steel engraving of Stuart's Washington as a premium in 1870, and sending out canvassers. This ran the list up to 35,000 by the fall of 1870. The next spring Captain Ford went to Paris and bought chromolithographic prints of two child's heads — "Fast Asleep" and "Wide Awake" — for his 1871 campaign. These doubled the circulation that year; and the following year new chromos almost doubled it again.[8] Thus in three years the *Christian Union* reached the largest circulation which had ever been attained by a religious periodical.

Then came troubles and reverses, not singly but in sickening succession. The panic of 1873 cut into both circulation and

[6] Abbott, *Reminiscences*, p. 330.

[7] Howard, *op. cit.*, Chapters XXX–XXXI.

[8] *Ibid.*, pp. 245–246. Howard's figures do not correspond exactly with those in Rowell, who gives 102,000 in 1871 and 132,000 in 1873.

advertising. Captain Ford's health broke down, and he had to leave New York. A disastrous fire destroyed a part of the company's plant. But worst of all, the Beecher-Tilton marital imbroglio destroyed for the time that phenomenal Beecher popularity which had been the very corner stone of the *Christian Union*. Beecher refused to defend himself in his paper, which lost three-fourths of its circulation within two years and by 1877 was quoted at only 10,000 circulation. J. B. Ford & Company, whose business had been founded on the paper and on Beecher's books, now unsalable, was forced into bankruptcy in 1875.

In the reorganization that followed, Beecher sold the controlling interest, which the Fords had presented to him at the start, for $10,000; [9] but he remained as titular editor. He had never, indeed, been actual manager. Merriam was succeeded as managing editor (after a brief interregnum by Charles L. Norton and John Habberton) by Lyman Abbott, a disciple of Beecher and a religious journalist of great abilities.

The changes in the paper effected by Abbott made the *Union* somewhat less a miscellany and somewhat more a journal of opinion. The editorials and critical departments were massed at the front of the journal. A larger type was mercifully adopted. The array of contributors was not quite so brilliant as in the palmy Ford days, but many of the older writers were retained, including Mrs. Stowe. Ford's *Plymouth Pulpit* had been discontinued, and its contents — Beecher's sermons and Star Papers — were transferred to a department in the *Union*. Judge Tourgée's *Mamelon* was serialized in 1876. Joseph Cook's popular "Boston Monday Lectures" were a feature of the late seventies. John Burroughs wrote some nature studies, Phillips Brooks religious essays, and E. P. Roe one of his characteristic serial stories for the paper. There was some political commentary, Republican in sympathy, yet denunciatory of official corruption.

In 1881 there was another reorganization, in which Lawson Valentine, friend and former parishioner of Abbott, who had bought stock in the *Christian Union* when Abbott became ed-

[9] *New York Sun*, February 16, 1876. See also the Ford statement about ownership in *Publishers' Weekly*, July 31, 1875.

itor, gained financial control of the magazine. Valentine was a man of property, and from 1881 until his death ten years later he was a shrewd and sympathetic manager.[10] At this juncture, too, James Stillman, a neighbor of Abbott, helped out in the reorganization by buying a small block of stock: in later years this "taint" of Standard Oil was made the basis of criticism of the *Outlook* by "muck rakers." [11] Beecher, who had long since ceased to give attention to the paper, withdrew upon the reorganization of 1881. Hamilton Wright Mabie, a young lawyer who cared far more for belles-lettres than briefs, had been recommended by Edward Eggleston in 1879 when the *Union* needed an editor for its church news department, and Abbott had hired him; [12] but Mabie soon demonstrated his ability in book reviewing and in literary essays, and within a few years he became Abbott's chief lieutenant. In 1884 Mabie's name was posted at the head of the editorial page as associate editor, and there it remained until his death in 1916. Another assistant editor in the early eighties was Eliot McCormick.

Circulation remained at about 20,000 throughout most of the eighties. The paper's biggest "hit" in that decade was probably the serialization of Helen Hunt Jackson's *Ramona* in 1884, which brought a circulation flurry.[13] Beecher's sermons were printed; and when Abbott succeeded to Plymouth pulpit upon the death of Beecher in 1887, his own sermons frequently appeared, varied occasionally by those of other famous preachers. Abbott's Sunday school lessons were another feature. Public affairs were discussed on the editorial pages; and though the *Union* always seemed to have a Republican bias, party politics were in the main avoided. In the campaign of 1884, for example, the editor, unable to accept either Blaine or Cleveland, pronounced a curse on both their houses and urged his readers to vote for St. John, the prohibition candidate.[14] Such writers as Joel Benton, Washington Gladden, Julia C. R. Dorr, and Thomas Wentworth Higginson became frequent contributors

[10] *Outlook*, XLVIII, 7 (July 1, 1893).
[11] See *Arena*, XLI, 106 (January 1909); *Outlook*, XC, 597 (November 21, 1908).
[12] *Ibid.*, CXV, 49 (January 10, 1917).
[13] See *Critic*, VI, 11 (January 3, 1885).
[14] *Christian Union*, XXX, 388 (October 23, 1884).

in these years. Mabie's light essays headed "In the Forest of Arden" began in 1888; his book reviews defended romance and sentiment against the ogre of realism. There was rather more of music and art than formerly; and correspondents in Washington, Boston, and Chicago extended the paper's news coverage. In the closing years of the decade the *Union* improved greatly in typography, printing, and paper stock.

In 1891 Valentine, the publisher, died and was succeeded by Lawrence F. Abbott, son of the editor. The *Christian Union* was in that year made a smaller quarto, with forty-eight pages and a cover — a "new dress" that gave it a handsomer appearance than it had ever worn before. Agnes Repplier and Austin Dobson were brought in as new contributors, with F. Hopkinson Smith, Thomas Nelson Page, H. C. Bunner, and Richard Watson Gilder. For the next few years there was much of the great Fair at Chicago.

Then in July 1893 the managers made a decisive change in the periodical: they discarded the old name and christened the paper the *Outlook*. This had been the title of a department of editorial comment ever since March 1873; and in raising it to the masthead, the paper was marking a change of emphasis from religious news and comment to the broader fields of public affairs and arts and letters. Not that it proceeded to abandon its attention to religion: it continued to emphasize its "Religious World" department, and for the next thirty years or more it preserved a distinctly religious tone and attitude. But the current specialization in periodicals as in nearly everything else demanded that the paper should become either an out-and-out religious periodical or a journal of opinion; it had already chosen the latter course, and its change of title merely recorded that choice. "The *Outlook*," said the editor in the first issue under the new name, "is a weekly family newspaper. It is a running history of the year in fifty-two chapters. Its editorials, contributed articles, and departments deal with the things of today in the broadest and most dispassionate spirit." [15]

Besides Abbott and Mabie, the staff now consisted of R. D. Townsend, who remained for many years as managing editor; Charles B. Spahr, writer on industrial and social subjects; Mrs.

[15] *Outlook*, XLVIII, 6 (July 1, 1893).

Lillian W. Betts, who continued the home department until 1900; Elbert Francis Baldwin, who was an *Outlook* editor for more than thirty years; Amory H. Bradford and James M. Whiton, both clergymen, scholars, and writers. These editors kept the *Outlook* abreast of the times and made it high-minded and rather serious, but readable. It steadily gained a little in circulation, in spite of the hard times of the middle nineties, passing the 30,000 mark in 1894.

At the beginning of 1897 it made another change — this time in format. It reduced its page size to octavo, making the first issue of each month (later changed to the fourth) an "illustrated magaine number" of about 120 pages, while the other three or four numbers of the month carried no illustration and consisted of 68 pages. At that time Abbott wrote a sentence which expresses so well a basic characteristic of the *Outlook* under his editorship that it must be quoted here. He expressed his belief and the belief of his magazine

in the immortality of the spirit and in change of forms, in the old religion and in a new theology, in the old patriotism and in new politics, in the old philanthropy and in new institutions, in the old brotherhood and in a new social order.[16]

Abbott began his *Theology of an Evolutionist* in the first "magazine number," to be followed the next year by his *Life and Letters of Paul*; Mabie began his series of "Literary Worthies"; and Justin McCarthy's life of Gladstone was started on its serial course. "Ian Maclaren," then at the height of his popularity, became a contributor. Daniel Gregory Mason wrote the first of his many *Outlook* articles on musical topics. James Grant Wilson and Clifton Johnson were frequent writers for the magazine. In 1898 Edward Everett Hale's *James Russell Lowell and His Friends* was published serially in the "magazine numbers," with copious illustration.

Somewhat more attention was given to politics as the *Outlook* approached the turn of the century. Theodore Roosevelt emerged as the great leader, and his praises echoed in the *Outlook's* pages. It was for the *Outlook* that Roosevelt wrote his eulogy of General Wood in January 1899. Four years later

[16] *Ibid.*, LV, 15 (January 2, 1897).

Jacob A. Riis published his *Theodore Roosevelt the Citizen* in the same paper — an effective contribution to the presidential campaign of 1904; and the authorized publication of T. R.'s "The Man with the Muck-Rake" took place in the *Outlook* for April 21, 1906. The paper maintained a good record of current events, with running commentary upon them. George Kennan was its Washington correspondent from 1902 until he was sent to the Far East to cover the Russo-Japanese War in 1905.

Three important autobiographies were published serially in the *Outlook* in 1900–02 — Booker T. Washington's *Up from Slavery*, Jacob A. Riis's *The Making of an American*, and Edward Everett Hale's *Memories of a Hundred Years*. The problems of immigration occupied the paper frequently, Riis, Spahr, and Edward A. Steiner being the chief writers in that field. Literary discussion was prominent: "the *Outlook* is a book-lovers' and a book-readers' paper," Abbott once wrote.[17] Mabie's most ambitious work in the direction of criticism was published serially in 1900 — his *William Shakespeare, Poet, Dramatist and Man*. The tone of the book reviewing continued to be conservative, but there was an especial friendliness to younger writers. There was a short story in every "magazine number," but the only serial story of these years was Stewart Edward White's *The Forest*. Mabie reprinted famous short stories of the past in 1907–08, in a series with critical introductions; these were followed by a similar series of great poems. Vachel Lindsay's "Adventures of a Literary Tramp" was a pleasant feature of 1909.[18] Art occupied a rather prominent place, with Paul Van Dyke a leading critic; gardens and trees were discussed by J. Horace McFarland; and travel, music criticism, and poetry were well represented.

In 1902 the *Outlook* reached 100,000 circulation, and it remained slightly above that figure for the next twenty years. These were great days for the paper — days of influence, of respect, of prosperity. When Roosevelt, on the eve of retiring from the presidency, looked about him to choose a periodical upon which he might employ his ready pen, he fixed upon the

[17] *Outlook*, XLVIII, 6 (July 1, 1893).
[18] Published in book form as *Adventures While Preaching the Gospel of Beauty*. White's *The Forest* had the book title, *The Magic Forest*.

Outlook. "The *Outlook* has stood for righteousness," he wrote in his first editorial, "but it has never been self-righteous. It stands for the things of the spirit, but it remembers the needs of the body." [19] The Abbotts had suggested a contributing editorship to Roosevelt while he was still President,[20] and the announcement of his acceptance was made in November 1908. He entered upon his duties immediately after he left Washington, in March 1909, attending the weekly editorial conferences and sharing staff discussions. His yearly salary was $12,000.[21]

According to our mutual agreement [wrote Lawrence Abbott later], he was to be free to express his own views over his own name, and the *Outlook* was equally at liberty to state its opinion even when it varied from his on public questions. We rarely differed, but when we did he accepted the difference of opinion with perfect loyalty to the understanding which was the basis of our joint work. He believed in what he called "team-work," and practiced his belief. He listened to the views of his colleagues, and often modified his own as a result of the interchange of opinion. He never wrote an article that he did not, before publication, submit to one of us, and he almost invariably accepted our suggestions.[22]

Soon after beginning this work, however, Roosevelt left for Africa to hunt big game; and while some of his editorials appeared in his absence, and Lawrence Abbott, who joined him after his emergence from the jungle, sent on some of his speeches and statements, he did not resume his active editorial work until the spring of 1910. It was then that he wrote the series of little essays on "Nationalism and Progress" later called *The New Nationalism.* A series on "The American Worker" followed the next year. In spite of the fact that a member of its staff was a candidate for president in 1912, the *Outlook* kept an even keel and presented both sides as it had been accustomed to do in former campaigns, though of course it strongly favored Roosevelt editorially. The Roosevelt *Autobiography* came in

[19] *Outlook,* XCI, 511 (March 6, 1909).
[20] Lawrence F. Abbott, *Impressions of Theodore Roosevelt* (Garden City, 1919), p. 13.
[21] Henry Cabot Lodge, *Selections from the Correspondence of Theodore Roosevelt and Henry Cabot Lodge* (New York, 1925), II, 311. See also Lawrence F. Abbott, *op. cit.,* p. 210.
[22] Lawrence F. Abbott, *op. cit.,* p. 14.

1913, and articles from South America the next year; but in July 1914 Roosevelt resigned from the *Outlook* in order to give more time to his work for the Progressive cause in the ensuing congressional campaign.

It is difficult to put into a paragraph the mood and tone of the *Outlook* in these years before the war. Through the magazine ran three main motives, interweaving the whole pattern: a liberal religion, without sensationalism or belligerence; social-mindedness, with political implications, expressed with decision but commonly with calmness; a love of letters and fine arts, not quite scholarly and by no means professional, but rather fine and appealing. Abbott stood for the first element, Roosevelt the second, and Mabie the third; but all three men represented in some degree all three elements. A paragraph from one of Mabie's letters in 1910 is illuminating:

We celebrated Christmas in good old *Outlook* fashion, and Dr. Abbott's seventy-fifth birthday at the same time on Monday evening. He is stepping lightly and radiantly along with a clear, strong mind, a beautiful spirit of peace and faith, and a gentleness and courtesy of manner which make him very dear to us. Mr. Roosevelt is great fun; a warm-hearted, affectionate, companionable giant, who makes everybody that knows him his friend — as unlike the newspaper pictures of him as I am unlike Tim Sullivan. No office could be more interesting than ours, and none filled with a finer atmosphere of mutual devotion to the higher things of life.[23]

Notable non-Rooseveltian features of the magazine in these years were the articles of Harold J. Howland from England, Mabie's papers from Japan, Frederic C. Howe's articles on governmental and economic questions, Frederick M. Davenport's political observations, Riis's "Life Stories of the Other Half," and Lyman Abbott's *Reminiscences*. Woman suffrage was discussed: Abbott was opposed to it, but he allowed others to present the case for the suffragists. There was an annual review of educational progress, usually written by President Butler. When the Mexican troubles came up, Gregory Mason was sent to the Border as a special correspondent. The custom of presenting occasionally a cross section of newspaper opinion

[23] Morse, *op. cit.*, p. 228.

or a particular subject under the heading "Poll of the Press" was adopted in these troublous times.

Pictures in the *Outlook* were increased when a section of "Illustrations of Current Events" was inserted in each issue; they had up to this time been limited to the monthly "magazine numbers." In 1917 the "magazine number" idea was abandoned, and the page size increased again to quarto.

Mabie died on the last day of 1916. Much of his writing in his latter years was on ethical subjects, of the *Life of the Spirit* type. His rank as a literary critic was not high: he was, as his chief said after his death, "rather an interpreter than a critic." [24] He is more fully expressed in *Books and Culture* than in his study of Shakespeare. To many he was a personal guide in problems of both literature and life.

The *Outlook* followed the World War with care in articles, pictures, and editorials; but it gave special attention to the home reactions. Arthur Bullard was the magazine's correspondent at the European battle front; Gregory Mason wrote from Russia; and Joseph H. Odell wrote from American cantonments, from Washington, and from France. Meanwhile, the other *Outlook* phases were maintained. Abbott's "Knoll Papers" continued to appear; commentary on government, social reform, economics, and education, now chiefly under the direction of the editor's second son, Ernest Hamlin Abbott, lost none of their authority; the literary features, supervised after Mabie's death by Harold T. Pulsifer, a grandson of Lawson Valentine, continued to be attractive. A sequel to Lyman Abbott's *Reminiscences* appeared serially in 1921 under the title, "Snapshots of my Contemporaries."

In 1923 the editor died, at the age of eighty-eight. He had directed the paper editorially for forty-seven years and been chief owner for thirty-two. He had seen the world's aspect change marvelously before his eyes, but he had as fresh and clear interest in it in 1923 as in 1876, when he had first come to the *Christian Union*. E. H. Abbott, who had been trained in the Congregational ministry, but who had been his father's active assistant on the *Outlook* for some twenty years, now

[24] *Outlook*, CXV, 49 (January 10, 1917).

became editor-in-chief; and Pulsifer became managing editor and president of the publishing company, succeeding L. F. Abbott, who retired to a contributing editorship. There was a special effort made to introduce the *Outlook* into schools as a chronicle of current events in these years, with some success; but the circulation slowly and steadily declined after the war.

In 1927 a controlling interest in the magazine was sold to Francis Rufus Bellamy, a journalist and author, who became its editor as well as publisher. A board of a dozen associate editors was listed, including E. H. Abbott and Pulsifer from the old staff. The next year Bellamy took over the *Independent*, whose development had for many years more or less paralleled that of the *Outlook*, and called the merged periodical the *Outlook and Independent*. The circulation decline was thus stayed for a time (85,000 was the figure in 1929), but soon it was once more on the toboggan. In March 1932 monthly publication was adopted.

The magazine under Bellamy was bright and interesting, but it lacked the old "feel" of strong personalities. Stéphane Lauzanne wrote well on international affairs, and Sir Oliver Lodge had some stimulating articles. Christian A. Herter and William O. Scroggs, associate editors, were familiar contributors; and Ernest Boyd had a book department for a time. T. Y. Ybarra, Allen W. Porterfield, and W. B. Pitkin were prominent in the magazine's pages. Motion pictures, theaters, music, books, and business were given special departments.

In September 1932, after a suspension of four months, the magazine was put up at auction; and Frank A. Tichenor, publisher of the *Spur*, the *Aero Digest*, and other periodicals, bought it, changed its name to the *New Outlook*, and installed Alfred E. Smith as editor. Smith had been defeated a few months before for the Democratic nomination for President, he had a large personal following, and he needed an organ for the expression of his ideas on public affairs. He was not, however, a literary man by nature, for whom such expression was a necessity; and in a year and a half he had tired of the task of writing his monthly article for the *New Outlook*. Francis Walton, who had been called managing editor while Smith's name appeared on the cover, succeeded to the editorship. The *New Outlook* specialized in incisive short articles on economic and social questions until its final suspension after the issue of June 1935.

Though assailed from time to time on both religious and political grounds,[25] the *Outlook*, on the whole, maintained a high position in the public estimation, and throughout its change of emphasis from the moral and religious to the sociological and political was continually of genuine service in the development of American thought and culture.

[25] See, for example, the *North American Review*, CC, 178 (August 1914); *Arena*, XLI, 106 (January 1909).

OLD AND NEW [1]

EDWARD EVERETT HALE, of Boston, Unitarian minister, short story writer of distinction, and trained journalist, wrote to his brother Charles from New York on October 6, 1869:

> I am here to confer about the establishment of a monthly Journal by the funds of the Unitarian body. It will absorb the *Christian Examiner* and the little *Monthly* [*Journal of the American Unitarian Association*], but will be very different from both; a *Blackwood* or an *Atlantic* whose pervading tone will be as pure religion as we know of, instead of Toryism as in *Blackwood* or literature as in the *Atlantic*.[2]

Things went very smoothly; the American Unitarian Association agreed to lend the new magazine $8,000 on very favorable terms—so favorable that it was never repaid [3]—and Hale, W. B. Weeden, W. Sawyer, and Adams Ayer each put in $1,000. A few weeks before they were ready to issue their first number, James T. Fields came to Hale trying to sell him the *North American Review* to "unite with the team," offering easy terms. "I confess that I am strongly tempted," wrote Hale; but before he had had time even to finish the letter in which he confessed his temptation, Houghton, his publisher, had come in and

---

[1] TITLE: *Old and New.*
FIRST ISSUE: January 1870. LAST ISSUE: May 1875.
PERIODICITY: Monthly; semiannual volumes. The last volume (XI) has only five numbers.
PUBLISHERS: H. O. Houghton & Company, Boston, January–June 1870; Roberts Brothers, Boston, July 1870–December 1874; Lee & Shepard, Boston, January–May 1875. (E. E. Hale and others, owners.)
EDITOR: Edward Everett Hale.
INDEXED in *Poole's Index* and *Jones' Index.*
REFERENCE: E. E. Hale, Jr., *Life and Letters of Edward Everett Hale* (Boston, 1917).
[2] Hale, Jr., *op. cit.*, II, 101.
[3] *Ibid.*, II, 106. It was to be repaid $1,000 a year when the circulation reached 13,000 a month for one year. "If it does not come to that in three years we are never to pay." It never came to that.

Old and New was never a great success. It seems never to
the idea," Hale wrote; and no more was heard of it.[4]
thrown cold water on the proposition. "Houghton pooh-poohs
have exceeded 9,000 circulation, in spite of the chromos and
croquet sets it gave away as club premiums. It also published
for use as a premium *The Christmas Locket,* which was called
"a holiday number of *Old and New,*" but which was not a part
of the file, as it was irregularly issued solely for use as a premium. It was written chiefly by *Old and New* contributors.

The magazine's difficulty seems to have been that it was trying to do two things, each of which hindered the other. Bellows
had tried to make the *Examiner* both a denominational review
and a forum of free discussion. Hale was trying an even bolder
experiment.

We took the ground [he wrote later] that literature and politics
and theology and religion might be discussed within the same covers
and read by the same readers. If you please to take the language of
the trade, we believed that the stories and the poems in our journal
would float the theology and the religion.[5]

But neither those who wanted a religious review nor those
who wanted a story magazine were satisfied. A letter from a
"well known and esteemed Unitarian clergyman" published
as an advertisement in the *Monthly Religious Magazine* for
February 1870 expressed the hope that that periodical would
become a Unitarian review, now that the *Examiner* was gone,
and *Old and New* was "outside of Unitarian christianity." Hale
later wrote that before the end of its span of less than five years

the Unitarian Association had long since tired of us, for it was impossible to make the directors of a denominational society understand that we were doing their work — as we were — better than
they could do it themselves.[6]

One reason that the stories and poems would not "float" the
theology was that the theological articles were rather heavy
for floating. "You have no idea how eager my friends are to

[4] Hale, Jr., *op. cit.,* II, 103.
[5] E. E. Hale, *A New England Boyhood and Other Bits of Autobiography*
(Boston, 1900), p. 333.
[6] *Ibid.,* p. 334.

choke and stifle the Journal by their stupidities," Hale wrote his brother.[7] But the editor worked nobly against this tendency to founder the craft by mere weight. The outstanding theological contribution to *Old and New* was the series by James Martineau, running through the latter half of the file, and later published as *The Transient and Permanent in Religion*.[8] James Freeman Clarke was a valuable contributor of theological papers also.

But the outstanding personality in *Old and New* was, of course, that of its editor. "Conducted by Edward E. Hale" was always prominently printed on the front cover. "It had a flavor all its own," said Dr. Holland when he welcomed the homeless readers of the *Old and New* to the shelter of *Scribner's* in 1875, "which was derived mainly from the personality of the editor." [9] The *Lakeside Monthly* had a clever way of commenting on Hale's pervasiveness in his magazine:

We have received and read *New and Old*, the latest born of the magazines. We salute it in the language of the response of the witches to the invocation of Macbeth:

> First Witch. — All Hale!
> Second Witch. — All Hale!
> Third Witch. — All Hale!

It will have to encounter the keen rivalry of the *Atlantic* and *Galaxy*, but we trust that it will prove

> Greater than both, by the All-Hale hereafter.[10]

One would expect Hale to make a good editor. Intelligent, informed, lively, witty, the elements were so mixed in him that he would surely have made a successful magazine of the kind he purposed, if only he had been able to find his public. There is much excellent material in the *Old and New* file. It must be admitted, however, that there seems to have been a lack of vigorous, driving motive. "It was as pure as snow," said Dr. Holland over its grave. Yes, and as tasteless; somehow its favorite premiums — chromos and croquet sets — seem to express it too completely.

[7] Hale, Jr., *op. cit.*, II, 111, February 13, 1870.
[8] One hundred dollars each was the price offered for the installments of about 7,500 words apiece. *Ibid.*, II, 112.
[9] *Scribner's Monthly*, X, 378 (July 1875).
[10] *Lakeside Monthly*, III, 80 (January 1870).

Perhaps the most important serials, aside from Hale's own of that kind, were Mrs. Stowe's *Pink and White Tyranny*, and novels by George Macdonald and Anthony Trollope. Just as Howells had hoped for Charles Reade to pull the *Atlantic's* circulation up a few years before and been "disappointed of it," [11] *Old and New* evidently banked on the diverse Englishmen, James Martineau and Anthony Trollope, to do the same for it; for, illustrating the magazine's double purpose, the theologian's series and the romancer's novel *"The Way We Live Now"* appeared together in the last volume of *Old and New*. But the serial stories were, in the main, mediocre or worse. It was "difficult," Hale complained, "to find brilliant and powerful writers." [12] Charles Dudley Warner's *Sorrento Days* in the third volume is one of the most attractive serials in the file, and Robert Dale Owen's war papers appeared in the second and third volumes. Poems by Christina Rossetti were features of distinction; and papers by Charles Francis Adams, Frank B. Sanborn, Andrew D. White, and Julia Ward Howe were worthy of any journal. Frederic B. Perkins, grandson of Lyman Beecher and a versatile magazinist of the time, was an assistant editor. Book reviewing was done with care: Hale made it a rule "to place a work for review in the hands of a friendly critic who was an expert on the subject of the volume." [13] Considerable attention was given to educational questions; and the July numbers of the magazine's last three years were college numbers, containing college directories.

By the middle of 1875 its editor had "tired of the strain," and *Old and New* was merged in *Scribner's Monthly*.

[11] See vol. II, p. 508.
[12] *Old and New*, VIII, 740 (December 1873).
[13] *Century Magazine*, XXIX, 340 (January 1885). Article on Hale by William Sloan Kennedy.

PUNCHINELLO [1]

A GROUP of the men who had worked on *Vanity Fair*,[2] convinced that the demise of that journal was owing chiefly to lack of financial backing, in 1870 induced four New York financiers to put $5,000 apiece into a new comic. As a result, the following prospectus was issued in March:

With a large and varied experience in the management and publication of a paper of the class projected, and with the still more positive advantage of an Ample Capital to justify the undertaking, the Punchinello Publishing Company, of the City of New York, presents to the public for approval the new illustrated humorous and satirical weekly paper, *Punchinello*, the first number of which will be issued under date of April 2, 1870, and thereafter weekly. Punchinello will be *National*, and not *local* . . . will be entirely original; humorous and witty, without vulgarity, and satirical without malice. . . . The Artistic department will be in charge of Henry L. Stephens, whose celebrated cartoons in *Vanity Fair* placed him in the front rank of humorous artists, assisted by leading artists in their respective specialties. The management of the paper will be in the hands of William A. Stephens, with whom is associated Charles Dawson Shanly, both of whom were identified with *Vanity Fair*.[3]

It was not announced, however, that the four financial "angels" of the venture were Jay Gould and Jim Fisk, heads of the Erie Railway; and William M. Tweed and Peter B. Sweeny, heads of Tammany.[4] Whether this "tainted money" was a handicap to *Punchinello* it is difficult to say. The paper cannot be classified as a Tammany organ, though it did lambast

[1] TITLE: *Punchinello*.
FIRST ISSUE: April 2, 1870. LAST ISSUE: December 24, 1870.
PERIODICITY: Weekly. I, April–September; II, October–December.
PUBLISHER: Punchinello Publishing Company, New York.
EDITORS: William A. Stephens and Charles Dawson Shanly.
[2] See vol. II, sketch 33.
[3] Printed in the advertising section of *Punchinello* for several weeks.
[4] Statement of Brander Matthews in *American Bibliopolist*, VII, 201 (August 1875), and also in *Outlook*, CXVII, 50 (September 12, 1917).

the "Young Democrats" in the fall campaign. It occasionally poked fun at its benefactors, especially at Fisk and Sweeny; and it occasionally indulged in mild criticism of paving abuses and of Mayor Hall. Its satires were never very biting; it seemed incapable of any high indignations.

Punchinello was a sixteen-page quarto selling for ten cents. It carried one full-page unbacked political cartoon drawn by H. L. Stephens and engraved on wood by Wevill [5] & Hammar: thus in format as in name, it was an imitator of the London *Punch*. Besides the big cartoon, there were six or eight smaller cuts in each number, illustrating social or political satires. These were drawn by Stephens, Frank Bellew, George B. Bowlend, F. T. Merrill, W. L. Sheppard, Augustus Hoppin, and others.

The paper had a regular theatrical department by "Matador," and correspondence, real or pretended, from Philadelphia, Boston, and Chicago. It devoted much attention to foreign affairs — to Louis Napoleon, Bismarck, and others. It ran a department purporting to condense the proceedings of Congress, and sometimes got off some good hits on national figures. It kept a rod in pickle for President Grant. Of course it satirized woman suffrage, the summer vacationists at watering places, and the New York horsecars. Dana, Greeley, Bennett, and the other New York editors came in for a good deal of criticism. There was a serial comic zoology, and another series on Mother Goose characters. Orpheus C. Kerr contributed "The Mystery of Mr. E. Drood" — a satire on public characters and types based on the Dickens story which was just then exciting popular interest. Kerr's travesty was called "a comic serial," but the comedy, if there ever was any, has evaporated with the years. Other regular writers for *Punchinello* signed themselves Sarsfield Young, Hiram Green, and so on. James E. Brown, writing under the name of "Mose Skinner," contributed a serial to the last few numbers. Some of the best writing in *Punchinello's* brief career was done by Charles A. Jones, who, as "Dick Tinto," had won some fame on the *Cincinnati Gazette* and later in the first series of *Putnam's*, and who wrote for the new comic some letters supposedly emanating from Paris.

[5] George Wevill was a brother-in-law of H. L. Stephens.

Punchinello offered a monthly edition composed of the weekly numbers bound for monthly issue. Prang's chromos were given as premiums, but they were not enough to save the paper from early death.

In spite of its efforts, or perhaps because of them, *Punchinello* was not very funny. At best it was mildly amusing. Perhaps its best joke was the one it played on its quartette of "angels." They were all rich rascals, and they were all headed straight for disaster in the year of 1870: *Punchinello* gained their attention for a moment, held them up, asked them to laugh at its clowning, ridiculed them a little, and dropped their money in a well.

WOODHULL & CLAFLIN'S WEEKLY [1]

THE history of *Woodhull & Claflin's Weekly* is a chapter in the career of one of the most remarkable of American women, Victoria Claflin Woodhull. The Claflins, back in Homer, Ohio, had been "trash." Buck Claflin was quarrelsome and violent and was suspected of counterfeiting and arson; his wife was "queer"; the children, who had been given curious names by their parents, were ill-cared-for young animals. The whole tribe seemed to have some strange qualities of personality which made their neighbors distrust them. Roxy, the mother, was a star performer at those annual winter orgies known in the villages as protracted meetings. She had visions, too; and her youngest daughter, Tennessee, got to having visions. Then the older daughter, Victoria, the beauty of the family, developed mesmeric powers. Those were the days of spiritualism and mesmerism and table tippings and rappings — a world of phenomena immediately familiar to the Claflins. So when Homer found them unbearable and drove them out, they became itinerant spiritualists and patent-medicine vendors. Little Tennessee was chiefly exploited, telling fortunes, diagnosing by magic, and prescribing her own "Elixir of Life." In Ottawa, Illinois, however, they became too ambitious and found themselves in serious trouble. There they had established an "infirmary" for the cure of cancer by some kind of clairvoyance, and after the death of one of their patients Tennessee was indicted for manslaughter. This necessitated a change of base.

In the course of her travels Victoria Claflin acquired a

[1] TITLE: *Woodhull & Claflin's Weekly.*

FIRST ISSUE: May 14, 1870. LAST ISSUE: June 10, 1876.

PERIODICITY: Weekly. Semiannual volumes; numbers paged separately. Suspended June 29–October 26, 1872, November 9–December 21, 1872; minor irregularities, especially in 1873.

PUBLISHERS AND EDITORS: Victoria Claflin Woodhull and Tennie C. Claflin [with James H. Blood].

REFERENCE: Emanie Sachs, *"The Terrible Siren,"* Victoria Woodhull, *1838–1927* (New York, 1928).

doctor-husband named Woodhull; somewhat later, in St. Louis, she picked up another husband, Colonel James H. Blood, who married her after he had secured a divorce from his wife. There is no need to try to untangle the skein of Victoria's divorces and marriages with these men; when the Claflins came to New York, the proper scene of their larger activities, both Woodhull and Blood were in their entourage.

Their first coup in New York came when Buck Claflin arranged an interview between Tennessee, now grown up, plump, attractive, flirtatious, with Commodore Vanderbilt. The Commodore was old and sick, and Tennessee's brand of magnetic healing seemed to be just what he needed. Eventually he asked her to marry him, but later withdrew his proposal and married another young lady more acceptable to his family and to society. But what he did do for the Claflins was to give Victoria and Tennessee (he was fond of both of them) a big check to set them up as "lady brokers" on Wall Street.

The lady brokers made a fine newspaper success and some money — though certain shady deals got them into court. Tennessee (she now wrote it Tennie C.) was the more frivolous of the two; but Victoria never failed to impress those whom she met by her beauty, her intelligence, and her very extraordinary personal magnetism. She had boundless ambition, no scruples, and unusual histrionic ability. Then she met Stephen Pearl Andrews, scholar and mystic. Andrews was a follower of Swedenborg and Fourier, master of half a dozen languages (he wrote textbooks in Chinese and French), one of the chief promoters of the use of shorthand in America, and an advocate of woman suffrage, spiritualism, and free love. He agreed with Colonel Blood, who was a bold promoter and an active partner in the Woodhull and Claflin firm, that Victoria was the ideal protagonist for a comprehensive and sensational drama of reform. Victoria, who knew by means of visions that she was destined for great things, agreed.

The prologue to the drama was the announcement in the *New York Herald* of April 2, 1870, of Victoria C. Woodhull's candidacy for the presidency of the United States. The pronunciamento was probably written by Andrews and Blood.[2]

[2] Sachs, *op. cit.*, p. 60.

The first act in the play centered about the founding on May 14 of *Woodhull & Claflin's Weekly*.

This famous, and ultimately sensational, paper began calmly. It was a well-printed small folio of sixteen pages of four columns each. Under the name plate was the motto "Onward and Upward," which soon gave place to "Progress! Free Thought! Untrammeled Lives! Breaking the Way for Future Generations." Victoria was supported for the presidency, suffrage was advocated, such sports as baseball and boating were given attention, and there were dramatic and financial departments.

Victoria, by a bold stroke, now put herself in the forefront of the suffrage reform. Through the intercession of her sponsors, now including Benjamin F. Butler, she got a memorial, signed by her and asking for the enactment of suffrage legislation, presented in both houses of the national Congress, and obtained a hearing before the judiciary committee of the House; and the date for this hearing was fixed on the day on which the national suffrage convention, whose leaders had snubbed her, opened in Washington. The Woodhull stole the show, the next day she was invited to sit on the platform with Mrs. Stanton and Miss Anthony at the convention, and for the next few years she was one of the recognized suffrage leaders. Her *Weekly* reported suffrage activities, and soon it was doing much more in that direction: it was extending the discussion of the "woman question" to the realms of prostitution, the marriage relation, and free love. There was much of this sort of writing:

> We hear of abandoned women, but not a word of abandoned men; and yet there are ten times the number of abandoned men than there are of women. Eight millions of dollars paid by men in the city of New York to support this infamous business by which they gratify their damnable lusts. . . . Men reeking with the foul abomination of fancy houses and street walkers, just from the moral degradation of promiscuous and polluted beds, bought with money and the price of souls, are countenanced and fellowshiped by virtuous men and chaste women.[3]

Of course the *Revolution*,[4] conducted by Miss Anthony and Mrs. Stanton, had protested against the double standard almost

[3] *Woodhull & Claflin's Weekly*, June 3, 1871, p. 11.
[4] See sketch 10.

as picturesquely. "I read your journal with great pleasure," wrote Mrs. Stanton to Mrs. Woodhull. "It is the ablest women's journal we have had yet." [5]

But the Woodhull soon became a clear liability to the suffrage cause. The Claflin family could not keep out of the courts. Living now in luxurious quarters, they remained as quarrelsome as in the old days in Homer, Ohio. In May 1871 Mother Roxy had a quarrel with Colonel Blood, which she took to court. She told the judge that there was "a gang of free-lovers" at their house — Woodhull and Blood and Andrews. This, of course, was a fine newspaper sensation. That Mrs. Woodhull handled the whole matter without gloves in the *Weekly* of June 3, by way of reply to an attack in the *Independent,* made little difference; few doubted that the household at 15 East Thirty-Eighth Street was founded on immoralities.

Andrews' high-sounding "Weekly Bulletins on the Pantarchy" helped the matter little. Most readers did not know what the Pantarchy was all about, but they soon discovered the Andrews advocacy of free love. It sounded much like the later "companionate marriage" formula as Andrews stated it in the *Weekly* during the summer of 1871.[6] Not until that winter did the Woodhull herself reach the advocacy of free love.

Meantime she had been nominated for the presidency of the Victoria League, an organization built up by the *Weekly.* She had lectured widely for suffrage. She had been elected president of the National Society of Spiritualists. She had gained control of Section Twelve of the workingmen's International. Then on the night of November 20, at Steinway Hall, she addressed a large audience on "The Principles of Social Freedom, Involving the Questions of Free Love, Marriage, Divorce, and Prostitution." In the course of that lecture she declared herself a free lover, "with an inalienable, constitutional, and natural right to love whom I may, to love as long or as short a period as I can, to change that love every day if I please!" [7] From that time forward the *Weekly* was more outspoken in its free-love propaganda.

[5] Sachs, *op. cit.,* p. 81.
[6] *Woodhull & Claflin's Weekly,* August 26, 1871, pp. 10–11.
[7] Sachs, *op. cit.,* p. 135.

VICTORIA WOODHULL AS MRS. SATAN

Thomas Nast's cartoon of Mrs. Woodhull in *Harper's Weekly*, February 17, 1872. The figure in the background is that of a wife bearing heavy burdens of legitimate marriage; she is saying, "I'd rather travel the hardest path of Matrimony than follow your footsteps."

A *PUCK* COVER SATIRIZING THE NEW BICYCLES

The picture, by Frederick B. Opper, appeared in lithographic colors.

It printed comment on many other matters. It discussed the strike in the anthracite coal region of Pennsylvania, defending the strikers. It exposed scandals in insurance companies and bond deals; it was a really valuable muckraker. It printed items about women in industry and business gleaned from here and there. Its articles often represented advanced thought which would have met the approval of liberals of a somewhat later day. But it published columns about the Pantarchy, and spiritualism, and mystic healing. *"Woodhull & Claflin's Weekly,"* said an enlightened contemporary observer, "has voices from the 'seventh heaven,' and gabblings from a frog-pond . . . yet the amazing journal is crowded with thought, and with needed information that can be got nowhere else." [8]

It carried four pages of advertising, chiefly of bankers and brokerage houses, during its first year or two. But in 1872 its advertising dropped off, in spite of its repeated threats to expose the status of certain of the banks. There can be no doubt that the *Weekly* blackmailed not only its advertisers, but many persons of social and political distinction. Again and again it published threats to reveal scandals at which it hinted more or less darkly. In one instance it threatened to use the contents of a ledger that had been kept for some years by the proprietress of a house of ill-fame, giving the names of visitors.[9] On another, a proof of an article attacking personally the women who led the suffrage movement was shown to them as a threat, but never printed.[10] The *Weekly* even went so far as to rationalize blackmailing. "If the laws will not protect women," it said, "they must protect themselves by the same crude justice that invented the blackmail system." [11]

But the most sensational episode of a saffron career consisted of the *Weekly's* part in the greatest of American domestic scandals — the Beecher-Tilton affair. Of course the Claflin crowd would be sure to hear the gossip about Beecher and Mrs.

---

[8] Edward H. G. Clark in his *Thunderbolt*, May 1873. Quoted in Sachs, *op. cit.*, p. 205, which contains a photographic reproduction of a part of the *Thunderbolt*, a "single-shot" periodical.

[9] *Woodhull & Claflin's Weekly*, December 16, 1871.

[10] Sachs, *op. cit.*, p. 164.

[11] *Woodhull & Claflin's Weekly*, April 6, 1872.

Tilton; Victoria heard a circumstantial story about their relations from no less a person than Elizabeth Cady Stanton. Once
in possession of a credible story of this kind, it was impossible
for blackmailers to make no use of it. What the Woodhull
wanted more than money was the support of both Beecher and
Tilton in her grandiose schemes for personal advancement.
She got Tilton's; he was infatuated with her, and she was his
mistress for six months.[12] In his new periodical, the *Golden
Age*, Tilton lauded the Woodhull along with Lucretia Mott,
Elizabeth Cady Stanton, Julia Ward Howe, Mary A. Livermore,
and two or three other suffragists, in an article entitled "A Leg-
end of Good Women." Of Victoria he wrote: "If the woman's
movement has a Joan of Arc, it is this gentle but fiery genius.
She is one of the most remarkable women of her time. . . . In
moral integrity, she rises to the full height of the highest."
In one part of his eulogy he compared her to St. Theresa.[13]
When Victoria returned the favor by a laudatory sketch of
Tilton in the *Weekly*, *Frank Leslie's Budget of Fun* proposed
"Theodore Woodhull for president and Victoria Tilton for
vice!" [14]

But the rapport between Theodore and Victoria could not
last. It was dissolved in June 1872, the same month that saw
the suspension of the *Weekly* because of the bankruptcy of its
owners and editors. The Claflin tribe was desperate in the
summer of that year. They had tried raising the price of the
Weekly from two to three dollars in April, they had resorted to
petty blackmailing, they had borrowed wherever they could.
But their advertising and circulation declined, they were sued
for debts, they were attacked on every side. Victoria was even
refused a hall for some of her lecture engagements —the ultimate indignity.

In November they made good their threats to lay the Beecher-
Tilton scandal wide open. The *Weekly* was revived to do it:
the issue of November 2, 1872, filled pages nine and ten with
the ungodly mess. It was an extraordinarily clever article.

[12] Sachs, *op. cit.*, pp. 106, 230, and *passim*.
[13] *Golden Age*, July 1, 1871, p. 6. A later and longer *Account of Mrs. Woodhull* by Tilton was published as a *Golden Age Tract* and used as a campaign
document.
[14] *Frank Leslie's Budget of Fun*, January 1872, p. 2.

I propose [wrote the Woodhull], as the commencement of a series of aggressive moral warfare on the social question, to begin in this article with ventilating one of the most stupendous scandals which has ever occurred in any community. I refer to that which has been whispered broadcast for the last two or three years through the cities of New York and Brooklyn touching the character and conduct of the Rev. Henry Ward Beecher in his relations with the family of Theodore Tilton. I intend that this article shall burst like a bombshell into the ranks of the moralistic social camp.

The story was specific and detailed, but its author used it as a text from which to preach her generalized doctrine of the folly of marriage as an institution, and her panacea of free love, which would make such scandals impossible. She said that Beecher had confessed to her personally his belief that "marriage is the grave of love." She said that the love between Mrs. Tilton and Beecher was "the most natural in the world and intrinsically the most innocent."

The exposé was indeed a bombshell. The *Weekly* sold as fast as it could be printed, and then faster: copies are said to have changed hands at ten dollars apiece. But in a few hours another element entered the game. In the same issue that exploded the bombshell had appeared a second exposure story in which one Luther C. Challis, a wealthy broker and a former intimate of Tennie's, was accused of having seduced two young girls; and such details of the seductions were given as convinced young Anthony Comstock, then just beginning his activities as secretary of the Society for the Suppression of Vice, that the publication was obscene. There was some confusion at first whether the arrest which Comstock caused, resulted from indignation at the attack on Beecher and Plymouth Church or to a real belief in the obscenity of the Challis article. Obscenity then, as now, was hard to define exactly. At any rate, Victoria and Tennie were arrested and thrown into the Ludlow Street jail. Bail was fixed at $8,ooo apiece, which George Francis Train, that eccentric friend of the woman's rights movement, offered to advance.[15] There is no need to go into the

[15] Train himself published in November two numbers of a paper called the *Train Ligue* in order to get himself arrested by Comstock and make a test case; the first contained statements from the *Weekly* of November 2, and the second

legal history of the various arraignments and trials of Victoria and Tennie, Blood and Andrews, which grew out of the famous second of November number of the *Weekly*. The women were in jail four weeks.

As soon as she got out, Victoria arranged for a lecture in Boston on her experiences; but the governor of the state interfered to prevent the delivery of the speech. The *Weekly*, which had not been published since the Beecher-Challis number, was again revived December 28 to present, in large type, "The Suppressed Boston Speech," which was called "Moral Cowardice and Modern Hypocrisy; or, Four Weeks in Ludlow Street Jail." A little later Comstock attempted to prevent a lecture on "The Naked Truth" at Cooper Union by a trick arrest; but Victoria, who was undoubtedly the most effective female orator of her time, foiled him and gave her lecture triumphantly amid the acclaim of a large audience.[16] She was arrested again, however.

By this time public sympathy began to turn toward the Woodhull; the repeated arrests looked like persecution, and was she not, possibly, telling the truth about Beecher? Mere volume of newspaper publicity builds up a kind of popularity, and certainly the arrests and the sensational lectures won plenty of newspaper publicity. *Day's Doings*, which should have been an authority on sensationalism, observed that what it liked to call "the Free-Love-Beecher-Challis-Woodhull-Claflin-Blood scandal" was "one sensation that had held its own," despite the demands on newspaper space of the disastrous Boston fire of November 9 and 10.[17] Resolutions against the "persecution" were passed by public meetings, letters of sympathy poured in upon the sisters, and the circulation of the *Weekly* leaped to a new high record of some 40,000 copies. When the American News Company refused to display the paper on its newsstands, friends sprang up to put it on sale in other places. The "Victoria

---

some passages from the Bible under sensational headlines. Comstock had him arrested, and he served five months in the Tombs before he was brought to trial. He was then acquitted on the grounds of insanity.

[16] For the incidents in which Comstock appears, see Heywood Broun and Margaret Leech, *Anthony Comstock, Roundsman of the Lord* (New York, 1927), Chapters VII and VIII.

[17] *Day's Doings*, X, 2 (November 30, 1872).

Leagues" renewed their activity; spiritualist societies pledged their faith in their leader. Then Victoria had a very serious illness, when it was generally reported that she was dying; and that helped to win sympathy for her. But the *Weekly*, despite its unwonted prosperity, was irregular in issue through the early months of 1873; repeated arrests, trials, lectures, and illnesses were not conducive to orderly publication.

Eventually the sisters were acquitted of publishing obscene matter, and Challis lost his suit against them for libel. The latter action did not come to trial until March 1874.

In the meantime the paper was filled with the echoes of the conflict. On May 17, 1873, the entire Beecher article was re-printed. Biographical articles lauded the Claflin attorneys. There was much of George Francis Train and his campaign for the free press. Victoria's lecture tours were featured; the *Weekly* was a promotion journal for the lectures, and in return it gained circulation by its sale to audiences.

Tennie retired from her share in the editorship of the *Weekly* in May 1873. She was advance agent for Victoria on her lecture tours, and Colonel Blood was platform manager. When they were all away, the *Weekly* was in charge of George Blood, the colonel's brother, and Robert W. Hume, an advocate of land reform.[18] The paper teemed with the Beecher-Tilton-Bowen trouble from this time forward until the trial of Tilton's suit against Beecher for the alienation of his wife's affections, which ran through the first six months of 1875. Andrews, who no longer wrote for the *Weekly*, was the only one of the Claflin group who testified in the famous trial, though Mrs. Woodhull's letters from Tilton were subpoenaed.

In the winter of 1875–76 many of Victoria's lectures were canceled because of illness. It may be that this was sometimes merely an excuse, objection being frequently raised to the granting of a hall for a free-love lecture. Then early in 1876 a change came over the whole of Victoria's "teaching." The emphasis was shifted from free love to biblical interpretation of sex, founded especially on Revelations. Her lectures became a strange mélange of eroticism and religionism. The *Weekly* printed a series of articles designed to show that the Garden

[18] Sachs, *op. cit.*, p. 237.

of Eden was in woman's body, and perfect sex the great object of existence. Purity of marriage was advocated, though the interferences of the law with such a state were somewhat vaguely referred to. In the last number of *Woodhull & Claflin's Weekly* — that for June 10, 1876 — Victoria wrote these words:

It is I who believe in the institution [of marriage] as a divine provision, but law alone cannot make it divine. There must be honesty, purity, intelligence, goodness. . . . Nor do I believe in the loose system of divorces now so much in vogue.

No reason was given for the abandonment of the *Weekly*, but one may conjecture that the falling away of those interested in its free-love propaganda had not been balanced by any acquisition of support from erotic mystics. The free-love support came largely from the spiritualists, and Victoria had seen fit to resign her presidency of their national society. And perhaps an even more potent reason was the loss of Colonel Blood and his brother George from the *Weekly's* staff. The St. Louis Mrs. Blood had turned up in Brooklyn, and the colonel had furnished her some money; when Victoria learned of this treachery, she acceded to Mother Roxy's often reiterated pleas and sent the Bloods packing. Hume had resigned when Victoria had begun to be apocalyptic instead of reformatory.

Later Victoria and Tennessee both went to England and married rich husbands. For many years they spent much energy and thousands of pounds in the rather unheroic business of laying the ghosts of old scandals. Victoria, now Mrs. Woodhull-Martin, published one number of a paper, *Woodhull & Claflin's Journal*, in London on January 29, 1881, for the purpose of traducing Blood and Andrews as the authors of calumnies against her and her sister; and still later she published the *Humanitarian*, a prosy periodical devoted to an unusually unscientific kind of eugenics.[19] She died at eighty-nine, a grand old lady in her fine old English manor house. Tennie survived her husband, Sir Francis Cook, by several years, but preceded her sister in death; Lady Cook's benefactions were bizarre, as all her life had been.

[19] Issued in London, July 1892–December 1901, as a monthly. It had an American edition during its later years. Victoria's daughter, Zulu Maud, was associate editor, and later American editor.

Victoria's able biographer sums her up very well in a paragraph:

When Theodore Tilton called Victoria Woodhull the Joan of Arc of the woman's movement, it was not such a wild exaggeration. Victoria fought the folkways that oppressed her sex as audaciously, as courageously as the Maid of Orleans fought the enemies of France. Like her, Victoria heard voices from the other-where, and had the strange power which often is their source, or their effect. She, too stirred the imaginations of men. She was an absurd extremist, but extremists are useful. No doubt she was unscrupulous under stress; she was a fraud and a pretense, and yet she might have been the historical symbol for man's release from fundamental fears and artificial shames. She might have dramatized the sex hygiene that Havelock Ellis founded on scientific realism, that Sigmund Freud popularized with scientific eroticism. She was on the way to sociological significance when she took the turning that led to fortune instead of fame — a turning that made her an interesting phenomenon instead of a heroine of history. And probably she took it because of sickness and poverty.[20]

As to the *Weekly*, which Victoria abandoned just before she took her fateful "turning," it was by turns the propagandist of grandiose schemes for human betterment, and an advocate of confused absurdities— a ringing voice in behalf of the downtrodden, and a shrill scream raised against the decencies — a banner lifted high for liberty and equality, and a blackmailing sheet.

[20] Sachs, *op. cit.*, p. 267.

THE LITERARY WORLD [1]

THE Boston *Literary World* was founded in 1870 as a monthly "help and monitor to book buyers and readers." S. R. Crocker, the editor and publisher, had been trained as a lawyer; but he was widely read and had a flair for literary criticism, a studious habit, and tremendous industry. The *World* was his personal organ, but such were his versatility, breadth of interests, and voracity that it became a fairly well-rounded literary paper.

A small quarto of sixteen pages, it sold at first for fifty cents annually; but after its second year it increased the subscription price to a dollar. It contained several pages of longer reviews of the more important books, a page or two of editorials on literary matters, a couple of pages of "Minor Notices," a department of notes and queries, a generous supply of literary and publishing news notes, and a list of forthcoming books. Advertising was very light in its early years, and was never heavy.

The *World* claimed to be an

absolutely independent journal. It is under no bonds, expressed or implied, to anybody. . . . It has no favor for writers of this school or that . . . none for North or East in preference for those of the West or the South.[2]

Crocker did accept, however, in 1872, a position with Little, Brown & Company, publishers; but if this resulted in any

[1] TITLE: *The Literary World: A Review of Current Literature.* (The word *Fortnightly* was inserted in the subtitle 1879–1900.)

FIRST ISSUE: June 1870. LAST ISSUE: December 1904.

PERIODICITY: Monthly, 1870–78, March 1900–1904; fortnightly, 1879–February 1900. I–VIII, annual volumes, June 1870–May 1878; IX, June–December 1878; X–XXXV, regular annual volumes, 1879–1904.

PUBLISHERS: S. R. Crocker, Boston, 1870–77; Edward H. Hames, Boston, 1877–1903; L. C. Page & Company, Boston, 1903–04.

EDITORS: S. R. Crocker, 1870–77; Edward Abbott. 1877–88, 1895–1903; N. P. Gilman, 1888–95; Bliss Carman, 1903–04.

INDEXES: *Poole's, Cumulative.*

[2] *Literary World*, IX, 10 (June 1878).

favoritism for Little, Brown books it was slight and difficult to discern.

Crocker was, on the whole, a rather indulgent critic. "May it not be," he asked, "that our canons of criticism are too strict, and that a more attainable standard of merit would more surely draw the public taste and intelligence up to its level?"[3] Toward the end of his career, the *New York Evening Post* summed up Crocker's critical position as follows:

. . . that criticism, to be of any worth either to literature or to the readers immediately addressed, must be in the main friendly . . . that our literature needs the encouragement of praise where praise is honestly due, even more than it needs censure for its faults.[4]

This sounds like namby-pamby criticism; but, as a matter of record, the fact is that Crocker did not hesitate on occasion to condemn unsound work and faults where he found them. His reviews, though "friendly" as a rule, were apparently honest and fairly discriminating. The *World* was informative, conservative, and inclined to dullness.

Crocker's health declined in 1876, and in the following year he became hopelessly insane; he died in a hospital in 1878. Edward H. Hames became publisher of the *Literary World* in 1877; and the Reverend Edward Abbott came to its editorship from the *Congregationalist*. The *World's* circulation had up to this time been small, and it was little known in the South or West.[5] An attempt was now made to broaden its scope, both in contents and in circulation. B. P. Bowne, Arthur Gilman, Henry Cabot Lodge, Robert Carter, Charles F. Thwing, Margaret J. Preston, and other littérateurs became contributors. Thomas Wentworth Higginson wrote a series of "Short Studies of American Authors"; Justin Winsor wrote on American libraries; W. J. Rolfe began a department of Shakespeareana which was to run for a decade or more; and a series of "*World* Biographies" of literary leaders was begun. There was a special Whittier Number in December 1877, and one devoted to Emerson on May 22, 1880. In 1879, having absorbed *Robinson's*

---

[3] *Ibid.*, V, 88 (November 1874).
[4] Quoted *ibid.*, VII, 120 (January 1877).
[5] Statement in *Western*, IV, 385 (May 1878).

Epitome of Literature,[6] the *World* became a fortnightly, at $2.00 a year. It was thereafter more varied and more interesting, but it never reached a circulation figure above 3,500.

In the eighties such men as Richard Grant White and N. S. Shaler were added to the list of contributors. Asa Gray reviewed some scientific works. Frederic B. Perkins edited the department of "Notes and Queries." Attention to foreign literature had heretofore been limited to translations; now there were, at various times, correspondents in England and Germany, as well as in New York. But Edward Rowland Sill wrote to his friend Aldrich that the *Literary World* was "sort o' philistine, heavy," [7] and he was unquestionably right.

N. P. Gilman, who had been assistant editor, relieved Abbott of the editorship through 1889–95, after which the latter came back again. There was a vast amount of conscientious reviewing of books in these years, but the *World* was clearly inferior to both the New York *Critic* and the Chicago *Dial*. In 1903 L. C. Page & Company took the paper over and placed the poet Bliss Carman in charge. The appearance of the journal was greatly improved, and it was given more liveliness and variety, but it persisted in its habit of losing money. At the end of 1904 it was absorbed by the *Critic*, which was thereupon called the *Critic and the Literary World* until it was itself merged with *Putnam's Monthly* less than two years later.

[6] Published May 1877 to August 1, 1879. It began as *Bentley's Book Buyer*, a monthly; it was fortnightly at the end.

[7] W. B. Parker, *Life of Edward Rowland Sill* (New York, 1915), 273. Letter dated December 27, 1885.

SCRIBNER'S MONTHLY — THE CENTURY MAGAZINE [1]

SCRIBNER'S MONTHLY was founded by three men — Dr. Josiah Gilbert Holland, who came to the editorship from lecturing and writing; Roswell Smith, who came to the business managership of the new periodical after training in both publishing and the law; and Charles Scribner, of the publishing firm of Charles Scribner & Company. A magazine publishing company was organized by these men under the name of Scribner & Company; and, as a basis for the new subscription list, it took over the literary and religious monthly which Charles Scribner & Company were already publishing, *Hours at Home*. With its second number (December 1870),

[1] TITLES: (1) *Scribner's Monthly, an Illustrated Magazine for the People,* 1870–81; (2) *The Century Illustrated Monthly Magazine,* 1881–1929; (3) *The Century Quarterly,* 1929–30.

FIRST ISSUE: November 1870. LAST ISSUE: Spring 1930.

PERIODICITY: Monthly, November 1870–August 1929; quarterly, Autumn 1929–Spring 1930. I–CXVII, semiannual volumes, November 1870–April 1929; CXVIII, May–August 1929; CXIX, Autumn 1929; CXX, Winter, Spring 1930. New Series, I–XCVI, same as whole numbers XXIII–CXVIII, November 1881–August 1929.

PUBLISHERS: Scribner & Company, New York, 1870–81; Century Company, New York, 1881–1930.

EDITORS: Josiah Gilbert Holland, 1870–81; Richard Watson Gilder, 1881–1909; Robert Underwood Johnson, 1909–13; Robert Sterling Yard, 1913–14; Douglas Zabriskie Doty, 1915–18; Thomas R. Smith, 1919; W. Morgan Shuster, 1920–21; Glenn Frank, 1921–25; Hewitt H. Howland, 1925–30. (Assistant editors: Gilder, Frank R. Stockton, Johnson, Clarence Clough Buel, L. Frank Tooker, William Carey, Sophie Bledsoe Herrick, Harriet Bliss, T. R. Smith, Carl Van Doren, Anna Lord Strauss, etc.)

INDEXES: *Index to Volumes I–X* (New York, 1876); *Index to Volumes I–XXX* (New York, 1886); also indexed in *Poole's Index, Poole's Abridged, Jones' Index, A. L. A. Portrait Index, Annual Library Index, Contents-Subject Index, Cumulative Index, Review of Reviews Index, Engineering Index.*

REFERENCES: William Webster Ellsworth, *A Golden Age of Authors* (Boston, 1919); Rosamund Gilder, ed., *Letters of Richard Watson Gilder* (Boston, 1916); Robert Underwood Johnson, *Remembered Yesterdays* (Boston, 1923); Algernon Tassin, *The Magazine in America* (New York, 1915), Chapter XI; L. Frank Tooker, *Joys and Tribulations of an Editor* (New York, 1924); "The *Century Magazine* 1870–1924," *Pan-American Magazine,* XXXVII, 341 (July 1924).

the new magazine absorbed *Putnam's* (second series) and a Boston juvenile, the *Riverside Magazine*.[2]

The project for *Scribner's Monthly* really grew out of the proffer by Scribner of the editorship of *Hours at Home*, then filled by Richard Watson Gilder, to Dr. Holland. Holland, having little confidence in the future of that magazine, refused; but he could not get the thought of what it would mean to him to be editor of a popular magazine out of his mind, and when he met Roswell Smith abroad he broached the matter to that ambitious young business man. It was on a certain bridge in Geneva that Holland and Smith planned their magazine; so they were fond of recounting.[3] As soon as they returned to America, they laid the matter before Scribner and easily persuaded him to take four-tenths of the stock, while they divided the balance equally between them.[4] Holland thought it seemed a little "selfish" to name the magazine after one of the three partners;[5] but the publishing houses of Harper, Putnam, Appleton, and Lippincott had done the like, and it was thought that the Scribner name might help to inspire confidence.

It would not have been inappropriate to name the new magazine after its editor. Holland was already famous in American literary circles. He had begun life under difficult circumstances, teaching penmanship and making daguerreotypes to pay his way through medical school; then, after failing as a physician, as the publisher of a family paper, and as a teacher, he had at last found his true place as a writer of moral essays in the *Springfield Republican*, of which he eventually became part owner with Samuel Bowles. His "Letters to Young People, Married or Single," signed with the Thackerayan pseudonym "Timothy Titcomb," attracted wide attention when printed in the *Republican* and were very successful when the Scribners issued them in book form. Holland's long poems *Bitter-Sweet* and *Kathrina* were even more popular, the sales of the latter exceeding that of any other American long poem except *Hiawatha*.[6] Holland was criticized, it is true, even in his own

---

[2] In July 1875 *Scribner's Monthly* absorbed Edward Everett Hale's *Old and New*.   [3] *Scribner's Monthly*, XXII, 302 (June 1881).
[4] Ellsworth, *op. cit.*, p. 9.
[5] *Scribner's Monthly*, XXII, 302 (June 1881).
[6] *Century*, XXIII, 165 (December 1881).

times, for triteness and banality, as well as for moral bigotry. Elizabeth Cady Stanton nicknamed him "the American Tupper": [7] but Edward Eggleston expressed the far more general opinion when he said, just after Holland's death:

> He was the most popular and effective preacher of social and domestic moralities of his age; the oracle of the active and ambitious young man and of the susceptible and enthusiastic young woman, the guide, philosopher and schoolmaster of humanity at large, touching all questions of life and character.[8]

At any rate, he was a man of wide intellectual curiosity and of decided opinions; a good friend and a good fighter; six feet tall, erect, with coal-black hair and an appearance suggesting an Indian chief. Such was the editor of *Scribner's Monthly*, who, whatever his faults, should be named in any list of the half-dozen greatest American magazine editors.

Holland's personality was strongly impressed upon the whole of the magazine from the first. It was expressed most directly in the editorial department "Topics of the Times," for which, "with a few exceptions, he wrote with his own hand every article" until his death in 1881.[9] These "articles" were tabloid essays on morals and manners, politics, religion, current events, and popular tendencies. They were the Timothy Titcomb papers of Holland's later years and were considered important enough to be reproduced between book covers; incidentally, they show a perceptible ripening and broadening of the editor's mind in their eleven years' course. Doubtless W. W. Ellsworth, long associated with the business management of the magazine, was right when he said that New York life was good for Holland, "opening up the Puritan prison-house he had built for his soul — at any rate putting a piazza on it." [10]

Another department was "The Old Cabinet," which was written by Richard Watson Gilder, associate editor and a poet of some distinction. This department, says L. Frank Tooker,

---

[7] *Revolution*, I, 10 (January 8, 1868). But newspaper critics also applied this insult to Holland; see Johnson, *op. cit.*, p. 85.

[8] *Century*, XXIII, 164 (December 1881). See also George S. Merriam's *Life and Times of Samuel Bowles* (New York, 1885), I, 201; *Century*, XXIII, 310–316 (January 1882); Johnson, *op. cit.*, pp. 85–88.

[9] *Century*, XXIII, 311 (December 1881).

[10] Ellsworth, *op. cit.*, p. 44.

a later assistant editor, was "a sort of tinkling harpsichord accompaniment to Dr. Holland's bass-viol solo." [11] It was distinctly reminiscent of Holmes's breakfast-table series. Begun in the second number, it was maintained until 1878, when Gilder's editorial work became heavier because of Holland's failing health. Gilder's chief enthusiasms were for literature and art, and he played an important part in the development of *Scribner's* distinction in illustration; but he also had a capacity for public affairs, largely undeveloped until he became editor on Holland's death.

A third department was at first called "Etchings," soon altered to "Bric-à-Brac." It was largely devoted to light verse and pictures, and Richard Henry Stoddard had charge of it for a time in the middle seventies.[12] As a humorous department it was not a distinguished success. Later, in the times of the *Century*, it became "In Lighter Vein," and survived until 1918. "Home and Society" was a department devoted to manners, rather homely social hints, moral advice, and something of fashions. "Culture and Progress" was given over to literature and the arts at home and abroad; in the *Century* it gave way to a "Literature" department. "Nature and Science" completes the roll of departments in *Scribner's Monthly*. This began in May 1872, under the editorship of Dr. John C. Draper, but was abandoned after three years with the explanation that it was impossible to make it either entirely scientific or entirely popular, when it should have been both; and a department of current events called "The World's Work," edited by Charles Barnard, took its place. When the series of Civil War articles came on in 1883, with its pressure for space, all departments were dropped except "Topics of the Times," "Bric-à-Brac," and a section devoted to "Open Letters." The "Topics" held a place, with changes of name, until 1916.

Holland was his own best contributor of serial fiction to the *Monthly*. He began, however, by using some foreign serials, as *Harper's* and the *Galaxy* were doing — one by George Macdonald, one by Mrs. Oliphant, and a third by Jules Verne — but the policy of American serials was soon adopted, and with

[11] Tooker, *op. cit.*, p. 33.
[12] *Publishers' Weekly*, April 11, 1874.

the third year Holland's own *Arthur Bonnicastle* was begun, to run through six volumes. It was followed by the editor's best work, the Dickensy *Sevenoaks*; and then came *Nicholas Minturn* to complete the trilogy of Holland's novels in the magazine. Alice Trafton, Rebecca Harding Davis, George E. Waring, Jr., and H. H. Boyesen were other earlier contributors of serial fiction. After his own magazine *Old and New* had been merged with *Scribner's*, Edward Everett Hale contributed his *Philip Nolan's Friends* to the survivor. Frances Hodgson Burnett wrote *That Lass o' Lowrie's*, a very successful serial, for *Scribner's* of 1876–77; and in the following year the magazine carried both Stockton's inimitable *Rudder Grange* and Eggleston's interesting *Roxy*. Among other continued stories were Henry James's *Confidence*, Bret Harte's *Gabriel Conroy*, and (more important and successful) George W. Cable's *The Grandissimes*.

Most of these writers contributed shorter fiction also. Stockton, Cable, Boyesen, Julian Hawthorne, Constance Fenimore Woolson, Harriet Prescott Spofford, Hans Christian Andersen, and Helen Hunt may be named among the leading writers of short stories for *Scribner's Monthly*.

The star performer in this field during the early years of the magazine was Miss Hunt (later Mrs. Jackson), with her series of rather stirring common-life tales written under the name of "Saxe Holm." She was by no means an artist in the short story; and though pleasantly poetical at times, she occasionally lapsed into morbid sentimentality. But whatever her faults, as now viewed in perspective, the readers of *Scribner's* liked her very much indeed. Her stories began in the magazine's first year and were kept going through almost a decade. Doubtless the mystery of their authorship added to the general interest in them. "Who is Saxe Holm?" became a common newspaper question; and when the game waxed too "warm," Miss Hunt was forced to perpetrate a literary lie by publicly denying authorship. There were plenty of claimants, however. Robert Underwood Johnson, then an editorial assistant in the *Scribner* office, told later of how a gentleman once called upon Gilder to reveal the secret and asked permission "to bring the lady who had written them and who had another story to offer" — unaware that Gilder was one of two friends of the author who were "in the know." When the claimant appeared, she explained how she came to part with the stories which *Scribner's* had already published, and which she assumed had come anonymously into the magazine's possession.

She was on her way to offer them to a magazine when she was accosted by a young man, pale and evidently ill, leaning against a wall, who begged for assistance. On impulse, she gave him the manuscripts, saying, "Silver and gold have I none, but such as I have give I unto thee." Mr. Gilder treated her with great politeness and received her new story for examination. As he had expected, it had no likeness to its predecessors and was on a far lower level of writing. He felt it his duty to inform the lady's sponsor that she was self-deceived, but this tolerant gentleman chose to regard the matter as a feminine foible and soon after made her his wife.[13]

Perhaps they had been trying to raise funds to set up housekeeping. At any rate, the lady's romantic prevarication was itself worthy of Saxe Holm.

Another popular fictionist for *Scribner's* in these years was Stockton. He had made his beginnings on newspapers, in the *Southern Literary Messenger*, and in *Beadle's* and the *Riverside*, and had joined *Scribner's* staff when it was founded; but when *St. Nicholas* was begun by the publishers of *Scribner's* in 1873, he became its associate editor,[14] resigning his place on the older magazine to the twenty-year-old Johnson. Stockton was greatly beloved of the whole Scribner personnel. Robert Louis Stevenson became acquainted with him at the *Century* office and wrote the rhyme —

> If I my Stockton should forget,
>   It would be sheer depravity,
> For I went down with the "Thomas Hyke"
>   And up with Negative Gravity.[15]

— which would be a good motto for all Stocktonites — now, alas, too few.

With three poets directing the course of *Scribner's* — Hol-

---

[13] Johnson, *op. cit.*, p. 119.
[14] See p. 500.
[15] Ellsworth, *op. cit.*, p. 29; Johnson, *op. cit.*, p. 106.

land, Gilder, and Johnson — unusual excellence in the department of verse might be anticipated. Such an expectation would, however, be disappointed. To name a few of the magazine's poets will be sufficient comment: Elizabeth Akers Allen, author of "Rock Me to Sleep, Mother"; Kate Putnam Osgood, author of "Driving Home the Cows"; Mrs. A. D. T. Whitney, author of *Faith Gartney's Girlhood*; as well as the better known Joaquin Miller, E. C. Stedman, R. H. Stoddard, Emma Lazarus, P. H. Hayne, and J. G. Saxe. An early Negro dialect poem, by Sidney and Clifford Lanier, gave a certain interest to the number for June 1875; and Irwin Russell's first magazine offering appeared in the "Bric-à-Brac," as well as his most famous poem, "Christmas Night in the Quarters."

The *Scribner* achievement in the essay was more striking than that in poetry. Charles Dudley Warner's *Back-Log Studies* ran through the second, third, and fourth volumes. John Burroughs, John Muir, and T. W. Higginson wrote with literary charm on nature subjects. Stedman did his series on Victorian poets for *Scribner's*; and W. C. Brownell, D. O'C. Townley, and Clarence Cook wrote on American art. E. S. Nadal had a pleasant group of articles on London social life. Politics occupied comparatively little space in these early volumes, though Holland in his "Topics" advocated prohibition, attacked woman suffrage, and pleaded for the reform of the civil service.

Oddly enough, *Scribner's Monthly* early found itself arrayed among the heretics on religious questions. Its heresy seems very mild now, but those who gave aid and comfort to the "higher critics" were listed among the hosts of darkness by most evangelicals of the seventies. The Reverend Samuel W. Duffield's "Freedom of the Pulpit," in three parts, started a small war, to be continued on *Scribner's* side by an article on "The Liberty of Protestantism," in July 1873, which alleged that there was none, and pleaded for tolerance; but it was a series of articles on "Modern Skepticism," beginning in the following number, which really spilled the theological beans. "The magazine has betrayed its trust," exclaimed the Boston *Watchman and Reflector*, the leading Baptist newspaper of the country, and continued, "One thing is clear to a vast number of those who subscribed to *Scribner's* at the beginning of 1873 or earlier under the impression that it was true to the faith of the evangelical churches — they have been disappointed, if not deceived." The difficulty the magazine faced rose from its inheritance of the subscription list and traditions of *Hours at Home,* which had been, especially in its earlier years, a religious magazine. Holland stuck to his guns, however, and the *Watchman and Reflector* later acknowledged *Scribner's* as "the purest, safest, and best of the monthly periodicals," and not to be judged as a theological review.[16]

The most spectacular series of articles published by *Scribner's* was *The Great South,* projected by Roswell Smith, written by Edward King, and copiously illustrated by J. Wells Champney. At the completion of the papers Dr. Holland wrote of them as follows:

It has been an enterprise involving an amount of labor and expense unprecedented in popular magazine literature. Neither pains nor money have been spared to make it all that we promised it should be. It has occupied, in all, about 450 pages of the magazine, and involved the production of more than 430 engravings. Mr. Edward King, who has written the papers, and Mr. Champney, the artist, who accompanied him and made the original sketches for the pictures, have traveled more than 25,000 miles in carriage, stagecoach, and saddle (in the latter 1,000 miles), in personal survey of the immense tract of country presented, and our readers have the result of what has cost the magazine more than $30,000. It is with no ordinary pride and satisfaction that we thus record the completion of a task undertaken with the desire to enlighten our country concerning itself, and to spread before the nation the wonderful natural resources, the social condition, and the political complications of a region which needs but just, wise, and generous legislation, with responding goodwill and industry, to make it a garden of happiness and prosperity. . . . The whole of the Southern papers will soon be republished in a beautiful volume.[17]

The *Nation,* which eight years before had published a more analytical and studied series,[18] made the obvious criticism of

[16] See quotations and controversy in *Scribner's Monthly,* VII, 237 (December 1873), *et seq.*

[17] *Scribner's Monthly,* IX, 248 (December 1874).

[18] See p. 334.

King when it called him "a fluent rather than a weighty reporter"; but it added that "he seems to have a clear notion of affairs and is often graphic and amusing." [19] *Scribner's* was able to give its series much greater circulation than the *Nation* had given Dennett's in 1865, and besides the time was now far more propitious for the cultivation of a friendly interest in the South on the part of Northerners. There can be no doubt that King's series was an effective factor in sectional reconciliation. A further service which King performed was more definitely literary. Mainly by accident he had become acquainted in New Orleans with a young warehouse clerk named George Washington Cable, who put into his hands a few stories which he had written to depict Creole life in that city. Cable's " 'Sieur George," published in October 1873, was the first of a long line of southern stories to appear in *Scribner-Century*, by Cable, Joel Chandler Harris, Thomas Nelson Page, James Lane Allen, Richard Malcolm Johnston, Harry Stillwell Edwards, Grace King, John Fox, Jr., and Ruth McEnery Stuart. Most of the *Nights with Uncle Remus* stories appeared in the *Century*, beginning in 1883; and Harris acknowledged Gilder's effective aid in working them out.[20]

After King's southern series, *Scribner's* printed many other series and separate articles on the American scene by King, John Muir, J. W. Powell, and others. It was also strong, especially at the close of the seventies, in the discussion of such themes as education, popular science, and farming. Sophie B. Herrick, daughter of A. T. Bledsoe, of the old *Southern Review*, who had become an assistant editor of *Scribner's*, wrote a series of illustrated articles on microscopy for Volumes XIII and XIV.[21]

Articles on science, travel, and art were especially suited for

[19] *Nation*, XVII, 427 (December 25, 1873).

[20] Julia C. Harris, *Life and Letters of Joel Chandler Harris* (Boston, 1918), pp. 201–234.

[21] Among contributors to *Scribner's Monthly* not otherwise mentioned may be listed: John Bigelow, Noah Brooks, Susan Coolidge, Schele DeVere, Thomas Dunn English, James T. Fields, Mary Hallock Foote, John Hay, George Parsons Lathrop, B. J. Lossing, James T. McKay, Brander Matthews, Donald G. Mitchell, Albert Rhodes, Eugene Schuyler, H. M. Stanley, C. A. Stephens, Benjamin F. Taylor, Celia Thaxter, Charles F. Thwing, James T. Trowbridge, Francis A. Walker, Williams Hayes Ward, William Wells, and W. C. Wilkinson.

illustration. And pictures printed from woodcuts formed one of the cornerstones of the *Scribner* edifice. "The feature of illustration has been adopted to meet a thoroughly pronounced popular demand," wrote Dr. Holland in the first number.[22] This demand had been shown by the popularity of *Harper's*. There can be no doubt that the success which came to *Scribner's* was due in large measure to the quality and quantity of its illustration. A sequel to Holland's statement of 1870 is found in a summary of accomplishment at the end of the *Monthly's* file and almost at the end of the editor's life:

> I suppose that if anyone were asked what, more than anything else, had contributed to the success of the magazine, he would answer: its superb engravings, and the era it introduced of improved illustrative art. This feature of our work is attributable to Mr. Richard Watson Gilder and Mr. Alexander W. Drake, the former the office editor and the latter the superintendent of the illustrative department.[23]

Drake was certainly one of the greatest art editors of American magazines. His promotion of the method of photography on wood as an aid to the engraver was perhaps his most striking single contribution to the art of illustration. For nearly half a century — from 1870 almost until his death in 1916 — Drake kept *Scribner-Century* art work on a high plane. William Lewis Fraser became his associate in the late eighties. The most famous of the magazine's engravers was Timothy Cole, who cut blocks for it during almost as long a period as was represented by Drake's service. He was a leader in the "new school" of wood engraving.[24] The spokesman for the older school, William J. Linton, also did some work for *Scribner's* in its earlier years; as did such engravers as Atwood, Juengling, Kruell, and Wolf.

The work of Theodore Low DeVinne, the magazine's printer from 1874 until 1914, was of inestimable value to the art department, for DeVinne learned to excel all other printers in handling wood engravings on the press.[25] In typography also

---

[22] *Scribner's Monthly*, I, 105 (November 1870).

[23] *Ibid.*, XXII, 303 (June 1881).

[24] For an explanation of the principles of the "new school" and the part of *Scribner's* in its development, see pp. 187–90.

[25] See p. 189.

his achievements were notable,[26] and the *Century* gained the reputation of being the best-printed magazine in the world. The cover, originally a kind of scroll-saw effect on greyish lavender stock, gave way in 1880 to a beautiful design by Stanford White and Augustus Saint-Gaudens printed in brown on a tan cover-paper.

In circulation promotion, inevitably the barometer of success, there had never been room for doubt from the first. "Of the first edition of the magazine," says Ellsworth, "40,000 copies were printed, and there were never any fewer." [27] The price was increased from $3.00 to $4.00 in the second year without noticeably affecting circulation. The panic of 1873 caused no tremors in the *Scribner* organization, and by 1880 the circulation had passed well beyond the 100,000 mark. An English edition was begun in November 1873, with 20,000 copies; it was successful until *Harper's* entered the English field in December 1880, just before *Scribner's* raised the price of its English edition.[28]

The year 1881 saw three marked changes in *Scribner's,* none of which appears to have affected its general policy: its management was divorced from the Scribner publishing house, its name was changed and a new series begun, and its editor died. The cause of the change of ownership was a difference of opinion between Charles Scribner's Sons, book publishers, and Scribner & Company, magazine publishers, as to whether the latter had the right to issue books.[29] The elder Charles Scribner had died in less than a year after the founding of the magazine named after him.

The present Mr. Charles Scribner and I [wrote Dr. Holland in June 1881] have now ceased to be proprietors, and Mr. Roswell Smith has acquired about nine-tenths of the stock. The remainder has been divided among the young men who have done so much and worked so faithfully to make the magazine what it has been and is.[30]

---

[26] See DeVinne's article on the printing of the magazine, *Century*, LXXXVIII, 151 (May 1914).
[27] Ellsworth, *op. cit.*, p. 42.
[28] Johnson, *op. cit.*, p. 98.
[29] *Ibid.*, pp. 82–83.
[30] *Scribner's Monthly*, XXII, 302 (June 1881).

In the transfer of stock the property was valued at half a million dollars.[31] Charles Scribner's Sons agreed not to start another magazine within five years; *Scribner's Magazine* was not founded, as a matter of fact, until six years later. On his part, Roswell Smith agreed to alter the title of his magazine; and it was named the *Century Illustrated Monthly Magazine*, from the Century Club of New York, at Gilder's suggestion.[32] The publishing company, now controlling the two magazines, the *Century* and *St. Nicholas*, and engaged in the book business, was called the Century Company. The death of Dr. Holland occurred on October 12, 1881; he contributed to but one number of the *Century*. Gilder, associate editor from the first, now became editor-in-chief.

The great enterprise of the early years of the *Century* was the famous Civil War papers. This extensive series had its rise in two articles on the John Brown raid written from opposing viewpoints. L. Frank Tooker tells how the idea grew:

In July Mr. Buel [Clarence C. Buel, assistant editor] had gone away on his vacation, and sitting one day under the chestnut trees that bordered a stream in Chautauqua county, and with the John Brown articles in mind, possibilities of a series of articles by the men who directed the battles of the Civil War suddenly came to him. He immediately outlined his suggestions in a letter to Mr. Robert Underwood Johnson, the associate editor. The letter was written July 17, and Mr. Johnson, on receiving it, had forwarded it to Mr. Gilder, who returned it with his approval, subsequently committing the matter to the charge of Mr. Johnson, with Mr. Buel as his assistant.

Mr. Buel's original suggestion had been for a series of eight or ten articles on the decisive battles of the war, to be written by the opposing generals in command. But elaboration of the plan, the task of securing contributors, and the editing of the series was shared by the two editors, Mr. Johnson directing the main part of the work during the organization, and Mr. Buel having entire charge of the editing for nearly the whole of the second year.

For beginning in November, 1884, the series did not really close until November, 1887. In the great success of the enterprise, the original plan was quickly swamped. In the second year, the monthly circulation had increased from 127,000 to 225,000, and there were

---

[31] Johnson, *op. cit.*, pp. 82–83.
[32] Ellsworth, *op. cit.*, p. 23.

times when the normally quiet editorial rooms were like the head-quarters of an army on the eve of a great battle, with generals and privates, confederates and federals, coming and going.[33]

Generals Grant, McClellan, Eads, Porter, Johnston, Hill, Longstreet, Beauregard, and many others contributed to the series. Even unmilitary Mark Twain told of his Civil War experience. Grant's contributions furnished the basis for his later *Memoirs*. It was necessary for Johnson to return Grant's first attempts in this direction and tactfully indicate the difference between a concise military report and a readable narrative.[34] But the Grant articles, when published, were greatly successful; and the *Century* paid their author $1,000 apiece for the four of them — double the amount at first agreed upon.[35]

A contemporary observer declares that the *Century* war papers "created in this country the greatest interest ever felt in any series of articles published in a magazine." [36] The newspapers all discussed them: never was there such a fighting over of old battles. Of course the satirists eventually had their comments to make. "We cannot but feel," wrote John Kendrick Bangs in *Life*, "that in showing us how much mightier our heroes are with the pen than with the sword, our esteemed contemporary has done us a great service." And he goes on to tell of the man who had sent a substitute to the war, and who now found that substitute's chapters so affecting that he died of wounds received on the twelve-thousandth page.[37] The series had its humors even in the *Century* office.

It was not long [wrote Johnson afterwards] before we found ourselves knee-deep in controversy. . . . It must be remembered that every battle produces usually at least four points of view: first, that of the one who gets credit for the victory; second, that of the one or more who think they should have had the credit; third, that of the

[33] Tooker, *op. cit.*, pp. 45–46. Cf. Johnson, *op. cit.*, pp. 189–224, and Ellsworth, *op. cit.*, pp. 232–234.

[34] Johnson, *op. cit.*, pp. 213–216.

[35] *Ibid.*, p. 213. But the Century Company did not get the publication of the *Memoirs*. See Johnson, *op. cit.*, pp. 216–219, and Ellsworth, *op. cit.*, pp. 234–242.

[36] *Current Literature*, II, 3 (January 1889).

[37] *Life*, VIII, 88 (August 12, 1886).

one who is blamed for the defeat, — the other commander; and fourth, that of the one who is blamed by him.[38]

One of the controversies led to a challenge to a duel received by Johnson from an ex-Confederate officer living in New York. "I laughed it off," writes the editor, "and he afterward apologized handsomely, attributing his combativeness to an excess of mid-day champagne at the Union Club." [39]

The series in the magazine and the book which it made in the end, called *Battles and Leaders of the Civil War*, earned more than a million dollars for the Century Company.[40] As a sequel to it, the *Century* published Nicolay and Hay's *Lincoln*, for which it paid $50,000,[41] and which, abridgment though it was, ran through the monthly issues from November 1887 to February 1890. An aftermath of articles springing from the war series and the Lincoln biography kept coming to the *Century's* pages for twenty years.

At the beginning of the *Century* departure, the editors confessed that "it was many years before *Scribner's Monthly* thoroughly grasped and adopted the scheme for presenting, as the best of all magazine material, the elaborate discussion of living, practical questions," and it then promised that "this kind of discussion will have special prominence in the new series." [42] In pursuance of this plan the *Century* showed, while not by any means a preponderating political interest, at least a serious and intelligent regard for public affairs and problems. The advocacy of civil service reform was carried over from *Scribner's*. The great Gilder campaign was against unsanitary tenement houses. Other *Century* causes then and later were forest conservation, international arbitration, international copyright, abolishment of the Louisiana lottery, antibossism, and the Australian ballot reform. Washington Gladden, Theodore Roosevelt, Francis A. Walker, and C. C. Buel were among the writers on these and other subjects of public interest: and the editorial department, "Topics of the Times," gave much

[38] Johnson, *op. cit.*, p. 193.
[39] *Ibid.*, p. 197.
[40] *Ibid.*, p. 190.
[41] *Ibid.*, p. 208.
[42] *Century Magazine*, XXIII, 144 (November 1881).

attention to such matters. When the muckraking era came in, however, the *Century* did not join in the almost universal pastime, but was satisfied to quote the aphorism of Woodrow Wilson, one of its contributors: "All life is not running to a fire." [43]

Three of Howells' best novels were published serially in the early numbers of the *Century*: *A Modern Instance, The Rise of Silas Lapham*, and *The Ministers' Charge*. Cable's *Dr. Sevier* and James's *The Bostonians* were others; but the great success was an anonymous serial attacking the rising power of the labor unions, *The Breadwinners*, written by John Hay. In spite of the fact that it became a best seller, its authorship was not revealed until the novel had been practically forgotten. Mrs. Catherwood's best novels were printed in the *Century* in the eighties and nineties, when Eggleston, Amelia E. Barr, Mrs. Burton Harrison, and F. Marion Crawford were also among the *Century's* writers of serial fiction. Mrs. Humphrey Ward and May Sinclair came later, as well as Jack London, with his *Sea Wolf*, which, Tooker tells us, was nautically incorrect when it came to the office of the *Century*.[44] The *Sea Wolf*, coming the next year after *The Call of the Wild*, was one of those "seconds" that failed to keep the promise of their highly successful predecessors: the *Century* had taken Mrs. Ward's *Sir George Tressady* hoping to duplicate the popularity of her *Robert Elsmere*, Mrs. Rice's *Sandy* after *Mrs. Wiggs of the Cabbage-Patch*, Bacheller's *D'ri and I* after *Eben Holden*, and so on.[45] But S. Weir Mitchell's *Hugh Wynne* was a genuine premiere "hit," though it was followed by less successful novels from the same pen. It was one of the several historical serials which the *Century*, falling in with the taste and mood of the end of the nineties, offered its readers. Crawford's *Via Crucis* was one of the best of the group.

The *Century* had unusual success in the short story field. The southern school was prominent in its earlier volumes, as has been noted. Page's "Marse Chan" and "Meh Lady" did much to invite that flood of dialect fiction which characterized

---

[43] *Ibid.,* LXXX, 955 (October 1910).
[44] Tooker, *op. cit.,* pp. 279–282.
[45] *Ibid.,* p. 269.

the decade centering on 1890. The former of these stories, long and almost entirely in dialect, was held for four years by fearful editors who were reassured only by the growing popularity of the apostrophe in literature. Tooker thought the greatest story the *Century* ever published was Kipling's "The Brushwood Boy," [46] which may very well be; but the biggest "hit" was made by Stockton's "The Lady or the Tiger?" of November 1882.

Almost as important as the serial fiction in the *Century* was the serial biography. Eugene Schuyler's *Peter the Great* had appeared late in the old series, and the great *Lincoln* came late in the eighties; immediately following this came Joseph Jefferson's *Autobiography*, and some three years later Professor W. M. Sloane's *Napoleon*, followed by General Horace Porter's *Grant*, Paul Leicester Ford's *Franklin*, John Morley's *Cromwell*, John Bach McMaster's *Webster*, A. C. McGiffert's *Luther*, and (as a theological antidote for the *Luther*) Maurice Francis Egan's *St. Francis*. It was a great procession of biography.

Another procession was that of the elaborately illustrated art series. Timothy Cole spent twenty-eight years in Europe engraving old masters for the *Century*, doing the work "directly before the original pictures." [47] He was in Italy ten years and afterward spent four or five years each in Holland, England, Spain, and France, returning then to engrave American masterpieces. Each series had letterpress by Cole himself or by some other critic-historian of painting. A series on cathedrals, with illustrations by Joseph Pennell (a leading *Century* artist) and articles by Mrs. Schuyler Van Renssalaer ran intermittently from 1886 to 1909. La Farge's *An Artist's Letters from Japan* were printed in 1890–91; and there were many other articles and series which, treating of art, were well adapted to illustration. The half tone vanquished the woodcut in the nineties, much to the regret of Gilder; [48] but the *Century* reverted to the older medium for occasional pictures for many years. Among the artists prominent in the magazine in the nineties were

[46] Tooker, *op. cit.*, p. 266.

[47] *Bookman*, VIII, 323 (December 1898). See also Alpheus P. and Margaret W. Cole, *Timothy Cole, Wood Engraver* (New York, 1935), for Cole's long relationship with the *Century*.

[48] *Outlook*, LXI, 320 (February 4, 1899).

E. W. Kemble, Frederic Remington, Howard Pyle, Charles Dana Gibson, André Castaigne, Maxfield Parrish, A. B. Frost, Albert Sterner, and Jay Hambidge.

One of the most important of the many series of articles undertaken by the *Century* during Gilder's long editorship was that of George Kennan on *Russia and the Exile System*. In the course of a perilous journey through Siberia, made on an assignment for the magazine, Kennan and his artist Frost collected material which made an international sensation and caused the *Century* to be banned by the Russian government. Starting out with opinions opposed to the exiled revolutionists, Kennan was converted by what he saw to a hatred of czarism. His book has been called by Robert Underwood Johnson "the *Uncle Tom's Cabin* of the Siberian exile." [49]

Still another series was that on the California gold hunters, published in 1890. The *Century* had several features dealing with the West. It was an ardent advocate of forest conservation and published many articles by John Muir preaching that doctrine.

Gilder was editor of the *Century* for twenty-eight years, and before that he had been Holland's assistant for eleven years. In a letter to John Burroughs he once wrote this phrase, after a mention of the *Century* " — the soul of which is, in a way, my own soul." [50] It is pleasant to dwell upon the character of Gilder, with its twin passions for art and citizenship; its native courtesy, so that Bill Nye said of him that "he could return rejected manuscripts in such a gentle and caressing way that the disappointed scribblers came to him from hundreds of miles away to thank him for his kindness and stay to dinner with him"; [51] and its not quite austere morality. This last characteristic was a *Century* tradition. Gilder, however, was more liberal than Dr. Holland, who had called Whitman an "old wretch," and had been with difficulty persuaded to print Stedman's moderately commendatory article on him, though it belonged to a series which the *Monthly* was publishing.[52]

[49] Johnson, *op. cit.*, p. 224.
[50] Gilder, *op. cit.*, p. 400.   [51] *Ibid.*, p. 387.
[52] Johnson, *op. cit.*, p. 337. Whitman told Traubel that Holland once rejected a poem "with a note of the most offensive character," Horace F. Traubel, *With Whitman in Camden* (New York, 1908), II, 184.

Gilder admired Whitman, but he could say of Mark Twain that "at times he is inartistically and indefensibly coarse" — and then send Mark a copy of the letter in which he had made the statement! [53] And he could boast of the "most decided difference" between the "Huckleberry Finn" of the *Century* and that of the unexpurgated book, though the editing of the chapters used in the magazine seems today almost inexplicable. All of which gives point to a practical joke played upon him by his office staff.

He had been invited by Smith College [writes one of the jokers] to prepare a poem for commencement exercises, and when the proof was ready, as a matter of courtesy, he sent it to the master of ceremonies. This fact was known to the other members of the staff, who much admired the lines. The next day one of our assistants, William Carey, who had a waggish Irish wit, entered into a conspiracy with Buel, the assistant editor, which took this course. By the aid of the operator at the nearest office of the Western Union, a telegram was drafted and sent in to Mr. Gilder with all the appearance of genuineness. It was dated "North Hampton," and signed by the professor to whom Mr. Gilder had sent proofs, and read: "Faculty doubt morality of fourth stanza. Can it be changed?"

Gilder, who "wrote no line that dying he would wish to blot," at once came out of his room to the adjoining one, where his assistants were installed, and asked Carey for a proof of the poem. After he had apparently made a study of the "objectionable" stanza, he appeared at the sliding door and asked for a book of telegraph blanks, and then closing the door was closeted with himself for fifteen minutes. Carey made an excuse of office business to interrupt him and discovered him much perturbed and evidently very indignant at the aspersion on his poem, a dozen discarded telegrams in the wastebasket giving evidence of the difficulty he had in expressing himself. Carey could hardly keep a straight face, but went out and closed the door gently after him. Soon Gilder came out again suddenly, and detected the two conspirators in a chuckle which revealed the plot.[54]

James L. Ford established his reputation as a humorous writer by a series of sketches in the satirical paper *Truth* in 1894, which were devoted chiefly to making fun of the *Century's* false delicacy. But Ford's butt was Johnson, whom he was pleased to call "unquestionably the one dominant figure in

[53] Gilder, *op. cit.*, p. 399.
[54] Johnson, *op. cit.*, p. 93.

American literature today." [55] Whatever may be said against puritanical attitudes of the editors of *Scribner-Century*, however, it is clear enough that the magazine's readers generally approved such editing.

Century circulation reached its highest point in the closing years of the eighties, when it ran well over 200,000. Roswell Smith died in 1892 and was succeeded by Frank H. Scott as president of the Century Company. By that time circulation was down somewhat, by the end of the nineties it had declined to 150,000, and in the next decade it was quoted at 125,000. Advertising, which had run as high as fifty pages in the old *Scribner's*, more than doubled in quantity in the nineties, at a greatly increased rate. The *Philistine* announced in 1895, with its customary sarcasm, that "The *Century*, it is said, will insert a page or two of reading matter between the Italian art and the ads." [56]

The increased prosperity which the Spanish War and its aftermath brought to the lower-priced magazines does not appear to have been shared by the *Century*. Not that that there was, as yet, any financial distress in the magazine's affairs. Contents shifted with the times. General Shafter, Admiral Sampson, and Lieutenant Hobson wrote on war matters; Cleveland contributed his reminiscences, particularly of the Venezuelan troubles; Secretary Taft had an article on the Panama Canal. The magazine favored the gold standard and international arbitration, and opposed violent strikes and boycotts. It was resplendent with color plates from about 1904 to 1909, and indeed color continued in the *Century* until the policy of full illustration was abandoned in 1921. Among the outstanding color pictures were Jules Guérin's French châteaux and other foreign subjects, Maxfield Parrish's villa and garden studies, decorative designs by Beatrice Stevens, and work by George DeForest Brush, Sigismond de Ivanowski, and N. C. Wyeth. There were color portraits of actresses from 1905 to 1908, followed by an American artists' series. [57] Frank Crowninshield was art editor 1910–13.

[55] James L. Ford, *The Literary Shop* (New York, 1895), p. 63.

[56] *Philistine*, I, 3 (June 1895).

[57] See *Printing Art*, X, 241 (December 1907) for a review of color printing in leading American magazines

An exciting incident of 1908 related to the *Century's* attempt to print William Bayard Hale's account of his interview with Kaiser Wilhelm of Germany. The Kaiser's remarks to Hale had been incredibly reckless: British statesmen were called "ninnies," and the dismemberment of the British Empire was predicted; the Japanese were called "devils," and the necessity of uniting against them was pointed out; a hatred of Catholicism was expressed, and the Pope was called a "zealot." Hale toned the interview down somewhat so that he hoped it might pass the scrutiny of the German Foreign Office; but when it reached the Kaiser's censors, the heart of it — the attack on Japan — was deleted, though some of the indiscreet flares of anger against England and the Catholic church were allowed to remain. The Kaiser had specified that the interview was to be printed in "the leading American magazine," and the emasculated copy was accepted by the *Century* and widely advertised for the December 1908 number. But by the first of November certain other mad utterances of the Kaiser which had been printed in an English paper had got him and his Foreign Office into hot water; and the cables began to hum with messages designed to suppress the Hale interview entirely. In the end the publishers of the *Century* had to yield, stop the presses which were even then printing the article, and box up and secrete every sheet of the printed interview and every scrap of copy and proof. When the news of the suppression got out, there was a sensation in the daily press. The *New York American* published a shrewd reconstruction of the interview, and the *World* a different one based on less accurate surmises. But Hale and the *Century* kept the secret faithfully, and the plates and the boxes containing the sheets were turned over to representatives of the German government. The plates were melted up, and some months later the cruiser *Bremen* took the boxes of sheets on board and steamed away to the Caribbean. Somewhere in the southern seas, the boxes were thrown overboard; looking back, the ship's officers saw with consternation that the boxes were not sinking — so hard it was to lose the ill-fated interview with his Imperial Highness! So the ship put about and sent out boats, and the sailors picked up the boxes, and they were again heaved back on deck. Then they were taken down to the engine room, the stokers were sent up on deck, and twelve German officers, stripped to the waist, spent hours feeding their emperor's hot words to the hotter flames. Thus perished William Bayard Hale's "An Evening with the German Emperor." The Foreign Office paid the *Century* publishers $2,000 to cover their losses, but Hale's humiliation and loss of time and effort were disregarded.[58]

Upon the death of Gilder in 1909, Johnson succeeded to the editorial chair, and Buel became associate editor. Like Gilder's, Johnson's service on *Scribner-Century* extended over about forty years; but he was editorial head for only three and a half years of this term. "I was the apostolic as well as the editorial successor of Gilder and Holland," he wrote;[59] and during his brief career as editor-in-chief there was no change in the magazine's policy. He had been ardent in the prosecution of the various reforms which his magazine had pressed, and Albert Shaw had given him a major share of credit for victory in the long fight for international copyright.[60] He was the chief mover in the establishment of Yosemite National Park, was active in the founding of the American Academy of Arts and Letters; and after his resignation from the *Century* in 1913, he was ambassador to Italy. Among the interesting features of the magazine under his editorship were the Luther and St. Francis biographies, Hichens' articles on the Holy Land, and an "After-the-War Series" to which Henry Watterson, George F. Edmunds, and others contributed articles on the Johnson impeachment, reconstruction, the Greeley campaign, and so on.

But efforts to stir fire from the old embers were vain. After the death of Frank Scott, president of the company, it was decided that a new policy was needed for the magazine — something more journalistic and less aloof.[61] This decision brought Johnson's resignation in 1913 and the appointment in his place of Robert Sterling Yard, a newspaper man. "It is time we looked this question of the present squarely in the eye," said

[58] For the interview itself, see *Atlantic Monthly*, CLIII, 513 (May 1934); for the circumstances of the incident, *ibid.*, CLIII, 696 (June 1934), and Johnson, *op. cit.*, pp. 229–237.

[59] Johnson, *op. cit.*, p. 140.

[60] *Review of Reviews*, III, 217 (April 1891).

[61] See *Writer*, XXV, 90 (June 1913); Tooker, *op. cit.*, p. 326.

Yard's salutatory, rather vaguely.[62] The matter became some-what less vague when the next number appeared, with Roosevelt's article on "The Progressive Party." Edward A. Ross's papers on immigration were a feature of the magazine in 1913–14, and H. G. Wells's "Prophetic Trilogy" appeared in 1914. Modernism in art — post-impressionism, cubism and the other "isms" — which had been under the ban before 1913, now had its innings. "Topics of the Times," sole departmental survivor from Holland's days, now gave place to "The Spirit of the Century," and that to "Current Comment," where public affairs were discussed with more or less freedom; and there was a new cover. In 1914 a sale of the magazine was arranged to a company of which Robert M. McBride was to be the president and Yard the vice-president; but the deal fell through after its announcement,[63] and shortly thereafter Yard was replaced by Douglas Z. Doty, secretary of the Century Company.

There was much of the European War by 1916. In June of that year the *Century* published Frank B. Vrooman's address advancing the theory that America should make the world safe for democracy — a philosophy soon to have more distinguished advocacy. George Creel was found much in the pages of the *Century* after the United States entered the war. Russia was discussed frequently, and the bolshevik movement condemned: Lothrop Stoddard, who wrote many articles for the magazine in these years, named as the two great modern heresies the German idea of the overman, and the bolshevik fallacy of the underman.[64] By 1919 the *Century* carried less illustration; the magazine was devoted mainly to public affairs and short stories.

In 1920 W. Morgan Shuster, president of the Century Company, became editor; and Glenn Frank undertook the editorial comment, which had lapsed a year or two before. Frank's department, called "The Tide of Affairs," was well displayed in the magazine and became a real success; and in the following year Frank succeeded Shuster as editor. Illustration by half

---

[62] *Century*, LXXXVI, 791 (September 1913).

[63] See announcement in *Bookseller, Newsdealer and Stationer*, XLI, 22 (July 1914). *Cf.* Tooker, *op. cit.*, p. 328.

[64] *Century*, XCVIII, 237 (June 1919).

tones was now abandoned, egg-shell-finished paper was introduced, and pictures were all by line cuts. Rockwell Kent's
Voyager's Log, with its woodcuts, was published in 1923.

The *Century* under Frank was filled with the color of the
modern scene, but at the same time it had a distinctively literary
tone. Its serials in 1921 were Donn Byrne's *Messer Marco Polo*,
Charles Hanson Towne's *Loafing Down Long Island*, and
chapters from Charmian London's *Book of Jack London*.
Carl Van Doren, the magazine's literary editor, contributed
an attractive series of criticisms of writers, chiefly contemporary, as well as other essays. In 1924 Konrad Bercovici's
Around the World in New York was serialized, and also chapters of Tooker's editorial reminiscences. Lothrop Stoddard
wrote a department of current comment in 1922 and later
contributed a series of articles on political and social subjects.
Among other prominent contributors were Henry Seidel Canby,
Bertrand Russell, Lincoln Steffens, Walter Tittle, Harry A.
Franck, Frederick O'Brien, and Herbert Adams Gibbons in
the department of feature articles; in that of fiction, James
Branch Cabell, Anzia Yezierska, Algernon Blackwood, and
Joseph Hergesheimer; in poetry, Amy Lowell, Robert Frost,
and George Santayana.

Another change took place when Frank left the *Century* in
1925 to become president of the University of Wisconsin, and
Hewitt H. Howland came to the editorial tripod. Illustration
was now entirely discarded, articles were all comparatively
short, fiction was less important. John Erskine's "The Cen-
turion" and Van Doren's "The Roving Critic" were features in
1925–26. Silas Bent and Lyle Saxon became prominent contributors, and Joseph Anthony began his "Reading Room" in
August 1926.

The expiring breath of the magazine — or rather, the three
last breaths — were the three quarterly numbers which closed
the file in 1929–30. Henry Hazlitt and Herbert Gorman had
departments in the *Century Quarterly*, which differed from its
monthly predecessor only in size and frequency. It was good,
if not very exciting, reading; but it had sunk below 20,000 in
circulation, and after the "Spring Number" for 1930 it was
merged in the *Forum*.

The *Scribner-Century Magazine* was of great importance in the development of American literature throughout a life of sixty years, and its pages are filled with materials of significance for the study of American life in that period. It was characterized by the highest aesthetic and moral ideals and was often an effective force in political and social reform.

THE DELINEATOR [1]

IN 1863 Ebenezer Butterick, a tailor of Fitchburg, Massachusetts, patented a special type of the tissue-paper dress pattern,[2] evolved from his long experience in making clothes for boys and men. In June of that year he put his first patterns on the market. They made an immediate success; the sewing machine for the home was just being popularized, and Butterick's patterns came in the nick of time to play a highly important part in the development of home dressmaking. In 1864 Butterick moved to New York, hired assistants, and published the first fashion plates designed to exploit his patterns. One of the men he hired was Jones Warren Wilder, who became his general agent for distribution; and another was Albert W. Pollard, Mrs. Butterick's brother, who became office secretary. In 1867 E. Butterick & Company was organized, Wilder and Pollard being taken into partnership; and the *Ladies' Quarterly Report of Broadway Fashions* was founded. The next year this paper was joined by the *Metropolitan*, a two-dollar fashion monthly also designed to promote the pattern business. The *Metropolitan* was later continued as an illustrated folio at three

[1] TITLE: *The Delineator.* Subtitles vary.
FIRST ISSUE: January 1873. LAST ISSUE: April 1937.
PERIODICITY: Monthly, with regular semiannual volumes. July 1920 was omitted, causing Volumes XCVII–CI to begin with August and February; Volume CI, however, contains but five numbers (August–December 1922), and CII begins the regular semiannual volumes again.
PUBLISHERS: E. Butterick & Company, New York, 1873–80; Butterick Publishing Company, New York, 1881–1937.
EDITORS: Robert S. O'Loughlin, 1873–84; H. F. Montgomery, 1885–94; Charles Dwyer, 1895–1906; Ralph Tilton, 1906; Theodore Dreiser, 1907–10; George Barr Baker, 1911–14; Mrs. Honoré Willsie Morrow, 1914–20; Mrs. William Brown (Marie Mattingley) Meloney, 1921–26; Loren Palmer, 1926; Oscar Graeve, 1927–37.
REFERENCES: John Adams Thayer, *Astir* (Boston, 1910), Chapters IX–XI; Charles Hanson Towne, *Adventures in Editing* (New York, 1926), pp. 121–160; Mabel Potter Daggett, "When the *Delineator* Was Young," *Delineator*, LXXVI, 365 (November 1910).
[2] *Frank Leslie's Ladies' Gazette of Fashion* had issued tracing patterns as early as 1855. See Vol. II, p. 437, of this work.

dollars a year, called *Metropolitan Fashions*.[3] In 1872 E. Butterick & Company, which was now doing a large and profitable business in patterns, determined to found in the following January a dollar magazine of fashions, which it named the *Delineator*.

The new periodical was subtitled "A Monthly Magazine Illustrating European and American Fashions," and it consisted of forty-eight pages in square octavo. There were various departments: "Seasonable Styles," "Styles for Misses and Girls," "Styles for Little Folks," "Hats and Bonnets," "Stylish Lingerie," and other sections for fancywork, hairdressing, fabrics, gardening, and correspondence. Woodcuts illustrated these departments adequately. Patterns were given as premiums with annual subscriptions.

Robert S. O'Loughlin was the first managing editor. By 1877 circulation had passed the 25,000 mark; and in 1880 it reached 85,000, according to publishers' claims. In the following year the company was reorganized under Wilder's presidency, with Pollard as treasurer; and the founder, who had already amassed a fortune, turned most of the work over to his younger associates. Butterick Publishing Company, Limited, was the style of the new firm. The circulation went to 100,000 within the year, and by 1888 to twice that. In 1885 H. F. Montgomery succeeded to the editorship, though O'Loughlin remained with the company, and Charles Dwyer became an associate editor. Other periodicals were undertaken, as the *Quarterly Plate*, the *Ladies' Review*, and the *Tailor's Review*.

In the late eighties the *Delineator* was expanded to eighty pages, and the plain cover was exchanged for one depicting a Grecian lady, seated, admiring herself in a small mirror propped up in her lap. New departments were introduced: one devoted to styles for men and boys, another called "Tea-Table Talks," and a third which commented on new books. Articles appeared on motherhood, the serving of meals, and so on. Several serials ran at length — one on interior decorating, another on etiquette, and still others on lace making and other home arts.

George Warren Wilder joined the Butterick organization in

---

[3] In the early nineties this became an advertising sheet, and then the semi-annual *Metropolitan Catalogue of Fashions* at fifty cents a number.

1891; his father, J. W. Wilder, died three years later. The younger Wilder was largely responsible for the growth of the *Delineator* during the next two decades. Thousands of agencies for the patterns and the *Delineator* were established throughout the country. Circulation for June 1892 was 500,000; and that figure stood for average monthly circulation in 1894. The number of pages in the magazine increased to between 150 and 200 in the latter year. Much the same editorial policy as that of the eighties was maintained, with rather more material on fancywork, and the addition of some travel articles and serials on evening amusements, the care of children, cosmetics, the new art of pyrography, and "The Delsarte System of Physical Culture." In 1893 a series by a staff writer, A. B. Longstreet, celebrated the Columbian Exposition; and Columbus before Queen Isabella supplanted the Grecian lady on the cover for several months. There were plenty of woodcuts, though the paper stock was inferior. In spite of the use of some more general articles, the *Delineator* was still predominantly a fashion magazine.

In 1894 Charles Dwyer took over the editorship, and a broader policy was noticeable. In that year and the next there were three notable series — "The Women's Colleges of the United States," by women well known in education; "Employments for Women"; and "The Social Code," by Mrs. Roger A. Pryor. There was some verse by Edith M. Thomas and others, and occasionally a piece of music. Illustration was more brilliant in 1896, with many half-tone engravings and a few colored lithograph and oleograph fashion plates. Department headings became decorative, and a section of the magazine was printed, text and all, in color. In this year also the *Delineator* published its first fiction — a story by Francis Lynde — and in 1897 it announced "a complete Story each month by a famous Novelist." Its fictioneers, however, were not of the loftiest fame; the best-known were Lynde, Molly Elliot Seawell, and Cornelia Atwood Pratt. The magazine was now printing authors' names rather generally, without producing an effect of galactic brilliance; Joel Benton, Octave Thanet, and Charles G. D. Roberts were occasional contributors. There were notes about women's club work, a new department on flowers conducted by E. C.

Vick, a series of "Talks on Health and Beauty" by Dr. Grace Peckham Murray, and various articles on child welfare by Mrs. Alice Meynell. The Grecian lady at last abdicated the *Delineator* cover in 1898, and her successors in the oval displayed modern modes. After 1900, covers varied monthly.

Butterick and Pollard withdrew entirely from the organization in 1899, selling their holdings to the sons of Jones W. Wilder and a few associates. Of the older Butterick men, O'Loughlin remained with the new company, serving as its president for the first three years. George W. Wilder was vice-president, and his brothers C. D. and B. F. were respectively treasurer and secretary. John Adams Thayer, one of the most brilliant advertising men in the country, was employed. Both circulation and advertising showed a sharp upturn, owing partly to newspaper advertising;[4] and in 1902 George W. Wilder financed another reorganization, with himself as president, capitalizing the Butterick Company (patterns) and the Butterick Publishing Company (periodicals) at $12,000,000. The *Delineator's* circulation now started for the million mark, and its annual advertising revenue for the million-dollar goal — both of which objectives were attained in 1912. Meantime the Butterick Publishing Company had become interested in *Everybody's Magazine*, finally taking over the ownership of the Ridgway Company, its publisher, in 1909 by the issuance of $3,000,000 more of stock. Butterick's was now one of the largest magazine companies, publishing thirty-two periodicals, including the editions of the *Delineator* in the United States, England, France, Germany, and Spain. The English edition had been in existence for many years, and by 1912 the Paris edition had a larger circulation than any other French fashion magazine.[5]

The *Delineator's* art work improved noticeably after the Wilder reorganization. Colored fashion plates increased in number, recipes were illustrated by half tone, and stories began to be accompanied by pictures. By 1902 the magazine had enlisted some of the best artists in America: Orson Lowell, Albert Levering, Henry Hutt, Howard Chandler Christy, Charles Grunwald, J. C. and F. X. Leyendecker, Jules Guérin. The

[4] Thayer, *op. cit.*, p. 215.
[5] *Everybody's Magazine*, XXVI, 56 (January 1912).

magazine's contents began with about a dozen full-page fashion plates, some in color, in 1902; but the next year fashions were pushed back in the book and replaced by a full-page illustration of fashionable society life, followed by a picture which accompanied the chief fictional offering of the number. Fashions, indeed, no longer dominated the magazine. They had formerly occupied about three-fourths of the *Delineator's* space; now they had somewhat less than half, having given way to home departments, society matter, general articles, and fiction.

Among the articles, public affairs had little place. The Spanish-American War and the problems it brought were outside the magazine's sphere. Interest in the Orient excited by the Boxer troubles is reflected, however, in several articles in 1900–01. The Pan-American Exposition at Buffalo was the subject of an illustrated series by N. Hudson Moore, who wrote much for the magazine in these years. Opera, life in royal palaces and in the White House, and athletics for women were among the newer topics to compete with the perennial themes of child welfare, clubs, art, women's occupations, and the kitchen and garden. In 1906 the magazine devoted a good many pages to a campaign against untrustworthy foods and fabrics — the first of its crusading efforts.

The *Delineator's* first serial story was Amelia E. Barr's *Thyra Parrick*, in 1902; this was followed the next year by Mary Hartwell Catherwood's *The Bois-Brûlés*. Other prominent writers of fiction in these years were Cyrus Townsend Brady, Will N. Harben, Carolyn Wells, Josephine Dodge Daskam, John Luther Long, F. Hopkinson Smith, Richard Le Gallienne, Alice Brown, Hamlin Garland, Anthony Hope, and Zona Gale. Among the poets were Edwin Markham, Theodosia Garrison, and Edmund Vance Cooke.

Theodore Dreiser became editor of the *Delineator* in 1907. He had already written *Sister Carrie* and seen it published, withdrawn, and republished, and during his editorship he was writing *Jennie Gerhardt;* but he had too keen an editorial sense to try to impart to the *Delineator's* pages anything of that freedom in regard to sex problems which distinguished those novels, or anything of the somewhat grosser sex interest which had characterized the *Broadway* or *Smith's* under his editorship. Indeed he was a definitely conservative editor.[6] In the Butterick magazines, illustrators were instructed never to picture a man smoking a cigarette, never to show a wine glass on a table.[7] Dreiser was general editor of these magazines, which included, besides the American and English *Delineators*, the *Designer* and the *New Idea* (later *Woman's Magazine*). Robert Mackay was managing editor of the *Delineator*, and Sarah Field Splint editor of the juvenile department; Charles Hanson Towne soon became fiction editor, and Arthur Sullivant Hoffman came to the staff as an associate editor. "We had a huge staff," writes Towne.

Every department of the organization was under the control of Mr. Dreiser. Not a detail escaped his vigilant eye. He O. K.'d every manuscript that we accepted — read them all, in fact, and continually gave out ideas to the entire staff, and saw that they bore fruit.[8]

Dreiser eventually parted company with some of the *Delineator's* editorial traditions. Current problems entered the magazine, which came to have a distinctly controversial and reformatory trend. "Matrimonial unrest," divorce, "race suicide," woman suffrage, the high cost of living, spiritism, failures of the public schools, the decline of the churches — these were all subjects for articles and symposia, usually by famous or authoritative writers. The fight against fraudulent merchandise was continued, and there was a more spectacular crusade to rescue children from orphan asylums and promote the welfare of underprivileged children.

Another innovation was the pursuit of big names: Kipling, Conan Doyle, Woodrow Wilson, William E. Borah, Julia Ward Howe, Jacob Riis, John Burroughs, Charles H. Parkhurst, Elbert Hubbard, and Oscar Hammerstein compose a list which may indicate the scope of the magazine's roll of authors. The chief serials were by Francis Marion Crawford, Mrs. Burton Harrison, and C. N. and A. M. Williamson. There were several contests, climaxed by a big short-story competition in 1911

[6] See Burton Rascoe, *A Bookman's Daybook* (New York, 1929), p. 59.
[7] Towne, *op. cit.*, p. 126.
[8] *Ibid.*, pp. 134, 135.

which was won by Zona Gale;[9] other writers of short fiction included David Graham Phillips, Honoré Willsie, Mary E. Wilkins Freeman, Dorothy Canfield, and James Oppenheim. A short short-story department was added, with a book-review section by Frederic Tabor Cooper, an architecture department for small homes, and a humorous "Man's Magazine Page" with contributions by Franklin P. Adams, Homer Croy, and H. L. Mencken. In 1909 the size was changed to a large quarto.

After Dreiser left at the end of 1910 to devote himself to writing fiction, his crusading policy seemed to continue for a time by its own impetus; but the fire was rather gone out of it. George Barr Baker, who had been associate editor of *Everybody's,* became managing editor under the supervision of Erman J. Ridgway, who had come in with *Everybody's* as general publisher. Ridgway had a rather crass editorial department called "Conversazione," at first in the middle of the book but later moved to the front. The chief crusade after Dreiser left was one for the legal rights of women and children, conducted in monthly articles by William Hard. The *Delineator* confessed in 1913 that it had as much interest in reform as in fashions; yet the latter continued to occupy nearly half the book. (One kind of "reform" the magazine became interested in, by the way, was weight reducing.) The juvenile department had been building up for a number of years, and child welfare and the schools received much attention. The serial fiction was by Richard Le Gallienne, Samuel Hopkins Adams, Mary Stewart Cutting, Robert Hichens, William J. Locke, and Mary Roberts Rinehart; and there was some serial autobiography by the Princess Eulalia, of Spain, and Mrs. William Howard Taft. Among the newer illustrators were Penrhyn Stanlaws, Oliver Herford, W. T. Benda, and N. C. Wyeth. The standard of the art work was high, and there were some excellent engravings on wood; but toward 1914 the appearance of the magazine was less attractive, and the number of pages was reduced to about sixty-four. Circulation declined slightly, perhaps because of the increase of the annual subscription price. The magazine had always sold for fifteen cents a number; but the annual rate was

[9] *Ibid.,* p. 127, for a full account of this contest.

$1.00 until November 1911, when it was set at the more reasonable figure of $1.50.

Honoré Willsie was the war editor of the magazine. Ridgway was talking preparedness two or three years before the United States entered the war; and once this country was in, the *Delineator* became thoroughly a war magazine. A "Women's Preparedness Bureau" was established to advise readers of methods of supporting the war, a series on thrift was published, and most of the articles and practically all of the editorials were martial. By 1918 the magazine was almost hysterically anti-Hun, with a series of morbid articles by Brand Whitlock on German atrocities. Dorothy Canfield Fisher had some excellent "Vignettes from Life at the Rear." The war was in everything, even the styles. An "Adopt a Town" campaign was carried on to aid war victims in France. The wife of General Funston was given space each month in which to "advise soldiers' mothers, daughters, wives, sisters, and sweethearts," and there was another department of "Special War Subjects." Less definitely connected with the war and its emotions was the magazine's crusade against infant mortality.

After the war the *Delineator* continued its aid in the rehabilitation of French towns ruined by the war, and also carried on a campaign to find homes for French orphans. There were still a few articles on the war and on returned heroes. Editorially the magazine supported the prohibition amendment, though in later years it reversed this policy. In 1920 there was much about "red" activities, postwar morals, the drug evil, and the movies. In that year, too, came the magazine's "Beautify Your Town" campaign. The proportion of fiction to fashions changed in these years, the former gaining, though never quite reaching a parity. Samuel Merwin's *Hills of Han* was a 1920 serial, and Arnold Bennett's *Mr. Prohack* appeared the next year. Edna Ferber, Joseph C. Lincoln, Fannie Kilbourne, Ethel M. Dell, and many others contributed shorter fiction.

During the war the price had been raised to twenty cents, and in 1920 it was jumped to twenty-five. Two years later it went back to twenty, but in 1926 it was twenty-five again. Circulation, too, fluctuated somewhat, but by the middle twenties it was climbing steadily above the million mark. In

1921 Mrs. Marie Mattingley Meloney, who had been editor of the *Woman's Magazine*, succeeded to the editorship of the *Delineator*. James Eaton Tower continued as managing editor, a position he had filled since 1919.

During Mrs. Meloney's suzerainty, which continued until 1926, there were serials by Zona Gale, Arnold Bennett, Dorothy Speare, A. S. M. Hutchinson, George Barr McCutcheon, and others; a series of dog stories by Albert Payson Terhune; and short fiction by a long list of good writers, including John Galsworthy, Hall Caine, Edgar Wallace, W. L. George, A. A. Milne, John Erskine, Arthur Train, and Owen Johnson. Autobiographical serials by women became a marked feature; and Mme. Curie, Ethel Barrymore, Mme. Louise Homer, and Kathleen Norris wrote of their own experiences for the magazine. The crusades of these years were for better homes and for the improvement of teaching. Calvin Coolidge and Herbert Hoover were *Delineator* contributors.

In 1926 the magazine began to change its character somewhat, and the alteration became more marked with the accession of Oscar Graeve to the editorship in the following year. The *Delineator* became "smart." An air of piquancy, of sophistication, of exclusiveness characterized it. Crusading lost favor; there were, instead, reviews and pictures from the theater, discussions of Hollywood and beauty methods and international marriage and women celebrities, as well as occasional articles on politics, world peace, and books. The art department went modernistic. Fashion sketches were elegant, some of them being printed on special rough paper. Such artists as Bernard De Monvel, Pierre Brissaud, Ricco Lebrun, Covarrubias, and R. F. Schabelitz gave an exotic note to *Delineator* illustration. Rockwell Kent also did work for the magazine, as did Leonard Dove, Ralph Barton, Everett Shinn, Rose O'Neill, and many others. Helen Dryden and, later, Dynevor Rhys drew excellent cover designs. Leading serials were Edith Wharton's *The Gods Arrive* and Grace Hegger Lewis' *Half a Loaf*. John Galsworthy, Sir Philip Gibbs, Hugh Walpole, and others from overseas continued to give a somewhat English look to the short fiction; but Peter B. Kyne, Elsie Singmaster, Ben Ames Williams, and Bess Streeter Aldrich helped restore the balance, while

Achmed Abdullah and Konrad Bercovici contributed exotic elements.

The magazine absorbed the *Designer*, long a sister Butterick periodical, in 1928 and lowered its price to ten cents. Circulation responded to these moves and to the new editorial and art policies, reaching 2,000,000 the year of the panic and later adding 450,000 more. In typography, presswork, and art it became swankier than ever.

It was a surprise move when the *Delineator*, now ranking fifth among the big-circulation women's magazines, was combined in May 1937 with the fourth on that list — *Pictorial Review*, a Hearst periodical.

The history thus abruptly ended is divided into two nearly equal periods. For its first thirty years the *Delineator* was one of the most popular of American fashion magazines, giving secondary attention to household helps and, after 1894, to fiction and books; during its latter thirty years it showed itself extraordinarily responsive to the popular moods and tastes of the American audience.

THE PUBLISHERS' WEEKLY [1]

I N THE late sixties the book publishing house of Leypoldt & Holt occasionally issued a little circular listing new foreign publications, which it supplied to the book trade with the imprints of the dealers. This circular was prepared by the senior member of the firm, Frederick Leypoldt; and it was the germ of the *Literary Bulletin*, a monthly imprint circular for booksellers modeled on Brockhaus' German bulletin and begun with a Christmas number for 1868. In September of the next year the *Monthly Book Trade Circular* was founded, utilizing the trade announcements and news of the *Literary Bulletin*, which it superseded. In 1871 Leypoldt, who was by nature and calling a bibliographer, withdrew from his partnership with Holt and from book publishing, because he realized the impropriety of conducting a periodical for the whole trade while still connected with a single house. In January of the next year he launched the *Publishers' and Stationers' Weekly Trade Circular*, which he distinguished as a new journal by beginning it with a Volume I, Number 1; and within the month he purchased "at a considerable cost" the *American Literary Gazette and Publishers' Circular*, of Philadelphia, and merged it with his *Weekly Trade Circular*.[2]

The Philadelphia paper was older than Leypoldt's earliest venture. It had been founded in May 1851 by Charles B.

[1] TITLES: (1) *The Publishers' and Stationers' Weekly Trade Circular*, 1872; (2) *The Publishers' Weekly*, 1873–current. Variant subtitles.

FIRST ISSUE: January 18, 1872. Current.

PERIODICITY: Weekly. Semiannual volumes.

PUBLISHERS: Frederick Leypoldt, New York, 1872–79, 1880–84; R. R. Bowker, New York, 1879–80, 1884–1933; Frederic G. Melcher (president R. R. Bowker Company, New York), 1933–current.

EDITORS: Frederick Leypoldt, 1872–79, 1880–84; Frederick Leypoldt and Richard Rogers Bowker, 1879–80; R. R. Bowker, 1884–1918; R. R. Bowker and Frederic G. Melcher, 1918–33; Frederic G. Melcher, Mildred C. Smith, Sanford Cobb, and Alice P. Hackett, 1933–36; F. G. Melcher, M. C. Smith, A. P. Hackett, Eugene Armfield, 1936–current.

[2] See *Publishers' Weekly*, IX, 10 (January 1, 1876), for Leypoldt's account of these origins.

Norton under the title, *Norton's Literary Advertiser;* but the title was changed at the beginning of the next year to *Norton's Literary Gazette and Publishers' Circular.* Its contents were adequately indicated by its subtitle: "A Monthly record of works published in America, England, Germany, and France; with a review of the current literature of the day; contents of leading American and English periodicals; advertisements of the trade, &c, &c." A quarto, usually of twelve pages, it was priced at a dollar a year. It had been first planned as an advertising sheet, but it soon acquired trade correspondence from Boston, New York, New Haven, Cincinnati, and other cities; it printed news of libraries, learned societies, historical associations, and so on, and offered itself to booksellers, publishers, libraries, and "reading men." Originally "sent gratis," it soon acquired a paid subscription list, took over *Wiley's Literary Telegraph,* and in 1854 started a semimonthly New Series at $2.00. In September 1855 George W. Childs, of the book publishing firm of Childs & Peterson, bought the periodical and superseded it by the *American Publishers' Circular and Literary Gazette,* octavo in size and designed primarily for the bookselling trade. The *Criterion* [3] was merged with it in 1856, and Charles R. Rode, the editor of that literary journal, came to the editorial chair of the *Circular.* In 1863 Childs retired from the book publishing business to become the conductor of the *Public Ledger;* and the *Circular* became more a journal of literary notes, with the title *American Literary Gazette and Publishers' Circular.* It was still a two-dollar semimonthly when Leypoldt bought it and absorbed it in his weekly.

One other bibliographical complication of this confused set of origins, so frequently misstated, remains to be mentioned. *Leypoldt's Monthly Book Trade Circular,* discarded when the *Weekly Trade Circular* was started in 1872, was revived in 1875 under the new title of *Literary News,* an eclectic monthly which thus claimed a beginning in 1869. It began a New Series in 1880 and lasted through 1904.

Leypoldt changed the name of his *Weekly Trade Circular* to the *Publishers' Weekly* in 1873. Its first subtitle shows the breadth of the fields it attempted to cover in its early years:

[3] See vol. II, p. 159.

"A journal devoted specially to the book and stationery trades," and, three years later, "The American book trade journal." Thus it gradually centered upon the book trade.

Publishers' announcements were of primary importance in the *Weekly*. Eventually this meant the listing of all books published in the United States; and these lists were cumulated, beginning in 1876, in the *American Catalogue*. Announcements were also made, with more freedom on the part of the publishers, in the advertising pages. Eight to ten pages of advertising were carried in each number, but the special Christmas issue usually contained seventy-five to a hundred pages of such matter. The advertising rate was low, however — $18 per octavo page in the seventies. Trade news, book trends, personal items about booksellers and book publishers, some gossip about authors, and much of booksellers' problems occupied the pages left from announcements and advertising. The *Weekly* fought the booksellers' battles and reported their convention proceedings. It was the organ of the Publishers' Board of Trade and of booksellers' organizations. In the middle seventies there were many articles about the Centennial Exposition, especially in its relations to publishing. An annual review of American publishing became an important feature of January numbers.

In 1879 Leypoldt, whose ambitions and industry in bibliography had outrun his pecuniary ability, was rescued financially [4] by R. R. Bowker, who had become asociated with him in connection with the editing of the *Library Journal*.[5] Bowker was publisher of the *Weekly* for about a year; after which he left for England as the representative of the House of Harper abroad, leasing the paper back to Leypoldt. But Leypoldt died in 1884, and Bowker returned to assume the management of the company's various publications — a task which he did not wholly relinquish until his death in 1933.

Bowker's editorship changed the *Weekly* only in certain phases related to England. There was always, after 1884, much of English attitudes toward American books, much of English books, and much of the copyright question. On this latter controversy Bowker became an authority, publishing in the *Weekly*

[4] *Publishers' Weekly*, XCCIV, 1764 (November 18, 1933).
[5] See p. 518.

most of the material that later went into his definitive history of international copyright. Adolphus Growoll, the bibliographer, was an assistant editor in the eighties.

It was not until about the time of Leypoldt's death that the *Weekly* passed the 2,000 mark in circulation; and it remained in that neighborhood for the next thirty years. In the nineties the number of pages was considerably increased, and advertising patronage grew to large proportions. The advertising sections of the *Publishers' Weekly* have always been interesting and instructive. The World's Fair at Chicago, the Du Maurier and Kipling crazes, the growth of historical fiction, and the popularity of the "kailyard school" of writers may be studied in the *Weekly* of the nineties.

In 1906 the price was advanced from $3.00 to $4.00 a year, and some fifteen years later to $5.00. About the beginning of the World War the *Weekly's* circulation began to mount, passing 7,000 in 1929. Frederic G. Melcher, a prominent bookseller, became joint editor with Bowker in 1918, and vice-president of the publishing company. Upon the death of Bowker in 1933, Melcher succeeded to the presidency and the chief editorship. The magazine has continued its now traditionally established policy, increasing the attractiveness of its format, and giving new emphasis to the art of book making, the merchandising and collection of old books, and kindred topics.

POPULAR SCIENCE MONTHLY [1]

PROFESSOR Edward L. Youmans edited in the latter sixties a succession of scientific works published under the general title, "International Scientific Series." For this series he persuaded Herbert Spencer to write a volume to be called *The Study of Sociology*, promising serial publication in English and American magazines before it was issued in book form. Youmans then arranged with the *Galaxy* to use it in the United States, the first installment to appear in May 1872. But whether the *Galaxy* editors repented of their bargain, or whether the arrival of the advance sheets only a few weeks before the time agreed upon for beginning the serial made it impossible for the *Galaxy* to coöperate in simultaneous publication in the two countries (as the editors said), the fact is that Youmans had the sheets in his hands in the middle of April, but had found no periodical to print them. It was then that he and his publishers, D. Appleton & Company, decided to found a magazine of their own and make the Spencer serial its leading feature. "In less than two weeks after the first conception of the project," wrote Youmans' sister after his death, "and two days before the *Galaxy* appeared which was to have contained the delayed article, the first number of the *Popular Science Monthly* appeared." [2]

[1] TITLES: (1) *The Popular Science Monthly*, 1872 94; 1900-current; (2) *Appleton's Popular Science Monthly*, 1895–1900.

FIRST ISSUE: May 1872. Current.

PERIODICITY: Monthly. I–LXVI, semiannual volumes beginning May and November 1872–1905; LXVII, May–December 1905; LXVIII–current, regular semiannual volumes.

PUBLISHERS: D. Appleton & Company, New York, 1872–1900; McClure, Phillips & Company, New York, 1900–01; Science Press, New York, 1901–15; Modern Publishing Company, New York, 1915–22; Popular Science Publishing Company, New York, 1922–current.

EDITORS: Edward Livingston Youmans, 1872–77; E. L. and William Jay Youmans, 1877–87; W. J. Youmans, 1887–1900; James McKeen Cattell, 1900–15; Waldemar Kaempffert, 1915–20; Kenneth W. Payne, 1920–22; Sumner Blossom, 1922–30; Raymond J. Brown, 1930–current.

INDEXES: *Poole's, Poole's Abridged, Readers' Guide* (before 1916), *Cumulative, Jones' Legal. General Index*, 1872–82 (New York, 1883).

[2] *Popular Science Monthly*, XXX, 688 (March 1887).

It was not founded quite so casually as this sounds, however. Youmans had long meditated the need for an American journal which should bring to thoughtful readers without scientific training some knowledge of scientific thought and progress in Europe. He had tried to turn *Appleton's Journal* science-ward in 1869, but its publishers had had other plans.[3] Youmans was an enthusiastic admirer of the work of Spencer, especially, and he was but little less interested in that of Darwin, Tyndall, and Huxley. Moreover, he had the instincts of a missionary; he felt a strong necessity urging him to do his utmost to disseminate the work of these men.

The first number of *Popular Science Monthly* was a well-printed octavo pamphlet of 128 pages. The two leading articles were the first installment of the Spencer serial, and the beginning of Quatrefages' *Natural History of Man*, translated from the French by the editor's sister, Eliza Ann Youmans. There were selections from other periodicals and books, chiefly European, as well as an "Editor's Table," a section of book reviews, and a department of shorter scientific miscellany.

"The stroke is unusually applauded," Youmans had written Spencer a few days after the first announcement of the magazine, "and the incoming support is more than we expected." [4] And on the second of June he wrote:

We printed 5,000 each of Numbers 1 and 2, have printed 2,000 of each since, and they are now both out of print. We shall print 7,000 of Number 3, and it would not surprise me if the first three numbers went up to 10,000.[5]

The general interest in science among the American people at this time was amazing,[6] and to this interest Youmans himself no doubt contributed much. A considerable amount of matter by and about Tyndall appeared in the first volume, in anticipation of his approaching visit to America; the *Popular Science Monthly* did its part to make his lectures the immense success they were.

[3] See pp. 417–18.
[4] John Fiske, *Edward Livingston Youmans, Interpreter of Science to the People* (New York, 1894), p. 302.
[5] *Ibid*. "Its success from the start has been exceptional," said the Chicago *Advance*, VI, 11 (January 2, 1873).
[6] See pp. 104–07.

But this blowing of horns for the evolutionists could not, of course, pass without criticism. Among the critics was Dr. Holland, in *Scribner's Monthly*, who was distressed to find the new journal upsetting established convictions. Youmans retorted with some contempt that Holland would do better to "stick to his fiction and verse-making." Evolution, he said,

is a great and established fact — a wide and valid induction from the observed order of Nature, the complete elucidation of which is the grand scientific task of the future. It is in this sense that we hold to the doctrine of Evolution.[7]

Holland returned to the attack in the next year, and the church papers occasionally trained their editorial batteries against the "evolutionist monthly." "The religious press is beginning to threaten us," wrote Youmans to Spencer early in the controversy;[8] but at the beginning of 1874 he was able to report: "We continue to print 12,000, though the magazine fluctuates around 11,000 and seems to be stationary the last few months."[9]

For an eclectic monthly, quite without entertaining features, and selling at $5.00 a year, this was an excellent circulation for the times. There were a few illustrations — the portrait of a famous scientist as a frontispiece to each number, and woodcuts for one or two articles. Some original papers appeared after the first few years, and an increasing number in the eighties and nineties. Likewise, American scientists were represented with greater frequency as the file lengthened; they were chiefly college and university professors. Addresses on important academic occasions or before learned societies were often printed. But Spencer continued a leading author for many years.

In his first number Youmans had expressed his aim "to meet the broadening conception of science as analysis of mind";[10] and the magazine became notable for its application of the scientific method to sociology, psychology, economics, and politics, as well as to natural science. Hartmann's *Philosophy of the Unconscious* was translated for the second volume. C. S. Peirce's "Illustrations of the Logic of Science" ran through several numbers in 1877–78. The leading articles in two successive

[7] *Popular Science Monthly*, II, 115 (November 1872).
[8] Fiske, *op. cit.*, p. 303. [9] *Ibid.*, p. 314.
[10] *Popular Science Monthly*, I, 113 (May 1872).

numbers in the fall of 1880 were a discussion of the "Kearney Agitation in California" by Henry George and a dissertation on "The Science of Comparative Jurisprudence" by William M. Ivins.

Professor Youmans was joined in the editorship of the *Monthly* in 1877 by his brother, Dr. William Jay Youmans. Dr. Youmans had studied in England under Huxley, and he brought much material by his former teacher into the pages of the magazine. The two editors now undertook a *Supplement to the Popular Monthly* which was virtually a new monthly magazine. It published the same kind of material used in the parent journal, but without illustration and with fewer pages, at $3.00 a year. The *Supplement* began in May 1877 and ran through the next year; it then ended with one number of a new series in February 1879, and the regular *Monthly* was now increased to 144 pages.

Through the eighties and nineties the magazine continued on much the same lines as those along which it was originally designed. The chief variation from the first numbers was in the use of more original material and more articles by American writers. The balance between natural science and the social sciences remained about the same. David A. Wells was a frequent contributor on economic subjects for many years; and such writers as David Starr Jordan, J. Laurence Laughlin, and the Duke of Argyll contributed original articles. Andrew D. White's *New Chapters in the Warfare of Science* was an important feature of 1894–95.

Professor Youmans died in 1887, and his brother edited the magazine alone until 1900, when the publishers disposed of the property to McClure, Phillips & Company. The new editor was Professor J. McKeen Cattell, of Columbia, who was already the successful editor of *Science;* in 1901 the Science Press took over the publication responsibilities. Cattell conducted the journal with much the same policies as those followed by the Youmans brothers. The price was now $3.00, and the circulation for a long time had been considerably under 10,000.

In 1915 the name, which seemed to the owners unsuited to their publication,[11] was sold to the Modern Publishing Com-

[11] *Popular Science Monthly*, LXXXVII, 309 (September 1915).

pany, proprietor of the *World's Advance*, a popular journal devoted chiefly to mechanical development and devices. This company took the name and numbering of *Popular Science Monthly*, but continued the policy and type of contents of the *World's Advance.* Meantime, Science Press, which had retained the subscription list of the older *Popular Science Monthly*, began a new periodical, edited by Cattell, on the lines of the former magazine but under the title *Scientific Monthly*.

The new *Popular Science Monthly* was a copiously illustrated magazine for readers who were interested in science or mechanics as a hobby, and was filled with scientific information presented in a definitely popular fashion. Waldemar Kaempffert, who had for some years been associated with the *Scientific American*, was editor for five years. He was succeeded in 1920 by Kenneth W. Payne; two years later there was a reorganization of the publishing company, and Sumner Blossom came to the editorial chair. When Blossom went to the *American Magazine* in 1930, he was succeeded by Raymond J. Brown. The new *Popular Science Monthly* passed its 300,000 mark in circulation in 1926. It still teaches science, as Youmans' magazine did, but with far less of philosophy and more of the definitely practicable and objective.

ST. NICHOLAS [1]

ROSWELL SMITH, who had been one of the founders of *Scribner's Monthly* in 1870, projected a magazine for children three years later to be named after the saint connected in many minds with the celebration of Christmas.[2] For editor he secured Mrs. Mary Mapes Dodge, author of a masterpiece for juvenile readers, *Hans Brinker and His Silver Skates,* and a journalist experienced in the conduct of monthly periodicals through her work on *Hearth and Home.* Frank R. Stockton, a popular contributor to *Scribner's,* much of whose earlier work had been done for juvenile readers, was associate editor; and a third member of the staff was William Fayal Clarke, a young man of twenty.[3] The publisher was the founder, Smith, who acted for the owners, Scribner & Company;

[1] TITLES: *St. Nicholas: Scribner's Illustrated Magazine for Girls and Boys,* 1873–80; *St. Nicholas: An Illustrated Magazine for Young Folks,* 1881–1930; *St. Nicholas for Boys and Girls* (called *St. Nicholas Magazine* on contents page), 1930–current.

FIRST ISSUE: November 1873. Current.

PERIODICITY: Monthly. Annual volumes November–October. Beginning with Vol. VI, each volume was divided into Parts I and II, with title page for each.

PUBLISHERS: Scribner & Company, New York, 1873–80; Century Company, New York, 1881–1930; American Education Press, Columbus, Ohio, 1930–34; Educational Publishing Corporation (Roy Walker), New York, 1935–current.

EDITORS: Mrs. Mary Mapes Dodge, 1873–1905; William Fayal Clarke, 1905–27; George F. Thompson, 1928–29; Albert Gallatin Lanier, 1930; Mrs. May Lamberton Becker, 1930–32; Eric J. Bender, 1932–34; Chesla Sherlock, 1935; Vertie A. Coyne, 1936–current.

INDEXES: Harriet Goss and Gertrude A. Baker, comps., *Index to St. Nicholas: A Complete, Comprehensive Index and Dictionary Catalogue to the First Twenty-Seven Volumes* (Cleveland, 1901); Anna Lorraine Guthrie, comp., *Index to St. Nicholas 1873–1918* (New York, 1919). Indexed also in *Annual Library Index, Readers' Guide, Cumulative Index, Review of Reviews Index.*

REFERENCES: W. F. Clarke, "Fifty Years of *St. Nicholas,*" *St. Nicholas,* LI, 16 (November 1923); William Webster Ellsworth, *A Golden Age of Authors* (Boston, 1919), Chapter VI; W. F. Clarke, "In Memory of Mary Mapes Dodge," *St. Nicholas,* XXXII, 1059 (October 1905); Sixtieth Anniversary Number, November 1932.

[2] There had been an earlier *St. Nicholas* published briefly in Oswego, New York, in 1853.

[3] *St. Nicholas,* LI, 21 (October 1923).

and that firm was a joint partnership of Smith, Editor Holland of *Scribner's,* and the book publishing house of Scribner, Armstrong & Company.

Mrs. Dodge had decided ideas about the children's magazine as a type. It must not, she said,

be a milk-and-water variety of the periodical for adults. In fact, it needs to be stronger, truer, bolder, more uncompromising than the other; its cheer must be the cheer of the bird-song; it must mean freshness and heartiness, life and joy. . . . Most children of the present day attend school. Their heads are strained and taxed with the day's lessons. They do not want to be bothered nor amused nor petted. They just want to have their own way over their own magazine. They want to enter one place where they can come and go as they please. . . . Of course, they expect to pick up odd bits and treasures. . . . A child's magazine is its playground.[4]

St. Nicholas was a handsome magazine from the first — a large square octavo of 48 pages, later increased to 64, 80 and 96. It sold for twenty-five cents; and in spite of the fact that it was started in the year of the panic, it seems to have gained a satisfactory circulation at once and to have kept in the neighborhood of 70,000 for many years. It was beautifully printed by the DeVinne press and copiously illustrated by the artists and wood engravers who were at the same time doing distinguished work on *Scribner's.*

In the first number there were articles, stories, and poems by "Olive Thorne" Miller, Noah Brooks, Rebecca Harding Davis, Lucretia P. Hale, Celia Thaxter, Lucy Larcom, and Donald G. Mitchell. Stockton began a serial. Mrs. Dodge wrote the "Jack-in-the-Pulpit," a department for younger children. Of course there were riddles, too, and a "Letter Box." As number succeeded number, all the leading writers for children came in. After a few months *Our Young Folks* was absorbed by *St. Nicholas* and brought with it its editor, John T. Trowbridge, as a leading contributor; his *The Young Surveyor* and his "Jack Hazard" serials, dear to the heart of boyhood, were published year after year. Louisa May Alcott's *Eight Cousins,* Noah Brooks's *Boy Emigrants,* and other serials by Stockton, Olive

[4] *Ibid.,* XXXII, 1063 (October 1905). The anonymous article on "Children's Magazines" in *Scribner's Monthly* for July 1873 was by Mrs. Dodge.

Thorne, Mrs. Oliphant, and Susan Coolidge appeared in the seventies.

These were the Stockton years. Stockton was never long absent from the pages of *St. Nicholas* in the seventies: his *Floating Prince, Castle of Bim, Jolly Fellowship, How the Aristocrats Sailed Away*, and so on, made a matchless series of tales. Many anecdotes are told of the relations of the whimsical associate editor to other members of the staffs of *St. Nicholas* and *Scribner's*. One day he startled them by announcing that a little Mary Mapes Dodge had come to live at his house. They knew he was something of a chicken fancier, but they did not suspect for some time that his announcement had meant only that they had named a chick after the editor of *St. Nicholas*. Later he told them regretfully that the chick had turned out to be Thomas Bailey Aldrich.[5] Stockton gave up his associate editorship in 1878, so that he might devote himself more fully to writing for adults; and his staff position was taken by Clarke.

In the general reorganization of 1881, the Scribner house withdrew from any ownership in either *St. Nicholas* or *Scribner's Monthly*, and the latter became *Century Magazine*. The relation between the two was of great value to the juvenile, for the printing and art facilities of the very prosperous *Century* were made available to it.

One of the most famous *St. Nicholas* serials of the eighties was Mrs. Burnett's *Little Lord Fauntleroy*, which not only gave juvenile literature a popular (if priggish) hero, but also, with its illustrations by R. B. Birch, set a fashion in boy's costume which pleased the mothers, however much unregenerate sons might resent it. Charles E. Carryl's *Davy and the Dragon* was a delightful masterpiece. Other serials of that decade which old men and women still recall with pleasure were Edward Eggleston's *Hoosier School Boy*, Harry M. Kieffer's *Recollections of a Drummer Boy*, E. S. Brooks's biographical and historical works, E. P. Roe's *Driven Back to Eden*, Thomas Nelson Page's *Two Little Confederates*, and others by Edward S. Ellis, Mayne Reid, Maurice Thompson, William M. Baker, H. H. Boyesen, and Horace E. Scudder. The Agassiz Associ-

[5] Robert Underwood Johnson, *Remembered Yesterdays* (New York, 1923), p. 104.

ation, with hundreds of chapters all over the country, was organized by the magazine; and brief reports of activities and offers, for exchange, of natural history specimens were printed in the "A. A." department. Tudor Jenks became an assistant editor in 1887, to serve for fifteen years; and S. A. Chapin was also on the staff in the late eighties.

Outstanding serials in the nineties were Mark Twain's *Tom Sawyer Abroad*, Theodore Roosevelt's *Hero Tales from American History*, and Howard Pyle's *Jack Ballister's Fortunes*. Kate Douglas Wiggin, who had contributed to *St. Nicholas* in the days when she was Katharine D. Smith, wrote for the magazine again — *Polly Oliver's Problem* and other stories. Laura E. Richards, for many years one of the most faithful contributors to *St. Nick*, contributed to it *Captain January* and the Hildegarde books. The *Lakerim Athletic Club* stories of Rupert Hughes were popular. Other serialists were R. M. Johnston, Brander Matthews, Robert Louis Stevenson, James Otis, Tudor Jenks, and G. A. Henty. But most captivating of all, for some readers at least, were the *Jungle Book* stories of Rudyard Kipling. As a boy, Kipling had "scrambled for" *St. Nicholas*;[6] and now he was happy to accept Mrs. Dodge's suggestion that he should do a series for his old favorite. Mowgli was the result, and such stories as "Rikki-Tikki-Tavie."

Walter Camp wrote articles on football and baseball for *St. Nicholas* in the early nineties, and William T. Hornaday on natural science. Articles, short stories, and poems came from Howells, Stedman, Cable, Harte, Burroughs, Warner, Hay, and others as well known. The "Letter Box," "Puzzle Box," "Jack-in-the-Pulpit," and Agassiz Association departments continued, and also a little section in large type "For the Very Little Folks." Illustrated jingles were a feature of each number, many of them written by Mrs. Dodge. Palmer Cox's immensely popular "Brownies" began in 1887 and continued to appear for thirty years; they might be out for some months, or even a year or two, only to be welcomed back again. Gelett Burgess' "Goops" were a feature in 1899. The illustration continued to be first-class: the *Quarterly Illustrator* observed in 1893 that "nearly every illustrator of talent and note has got his handi-

[6] *St. Nicholas*, XXXII, 1064 (October 1905).

work between the covers of *St. Nicholas*." [7] Among the more notable were Frank Beard, Sol Eytinge, C. S. Reinhart, Howard Pyle, E. W. Kemble, Oliver Herford, Mary Hallock Foote, Livingston Hopkins, and Frederick B. Opper.

As *St. Nick* entered the twentieth century, it showed, to a critical eye, a certain flagging in vitality, perhaps less regard for high literary standards, and a slow but alarmingly regular decline in circulation. The "St. Nicholas League" was organized to award prizes to readers for short original contributions of prose, verse, and pictures; among the juvenile contributors were E. Vincent Millay, Conrad William Faulkner, Ringold W. Lardner, and others who later became famous.[8] Hildegarde Hawthorne conducted a department of book reviews. The "Watch Tower, A Review of Current Events," was edited by Edward N. Teall. There was clearly more emphasis on departments and less on articles and stories. Ralph Henry Barbour became the leading writer of continued stories; others were Carolyn Wells, Amelia E. Barr, George Madden Martin, Alice Hegan Rice, John Bennett, and Frederick Orin Bartlett. Hezekiah Butterworth and C. A. Stephens, of the *Youth's Companion*, were contributors, as was John Kendrick Bangs.

Mrs. Dodge died in 1905, having edited *St. Nicholas* for nearly a third of a century. She was succeeded by Clarke, who had been virtually in control for several years. The articles continued to emphasize art and science; and Barbour's stories of athletics remained a feature. Alden Arthur Knipe and Samuel Scoville, Jr., wrote serials. Albert Bigelow Paine's *Boy's Life of Mark Twain* was published in 1916. Charles J. Finger's folk tales and A. A. Milne's poems delighted many readers in these years. Departments devoted to short plays, to science, and to philately were prominent.

The price was raised from $3.00 to $4.00 a year in the expensive days after the war, or two years for $6.50. In 1926 the size was increased to quarto, following a fashion which pleased advertisers because it mixed the text with their displays. In 1928 George F. Thompson became editor, Clarke retiring after fifty-five years of service on the staff of the magazine. Two

---

[7] *Quarterly Illustrator*, I, 293 (December 1893).
[8] See article in *Nation*, CXXXIX, 728 (December 26, 1934).

years later the Century Company went out of the magazine business, suspending the *Century Magazine* and selling *St. Nicholas* to the American Education Press, of Columbus, Ohio. Mrs. May Lamberton Becker became editor for two years; she was succeeded in 1932 by Eric J. Bender. At the end of 1934 the magazine was purchased by Roy Walker, who moved it back to New York and placed it under the editorship of Chesla Sherlock, who had a few years before served as editor of the *Ladies' Home Journal;* he was succeeded after about a year by Vertie A. Coyne.

St. Nicholas continues to be highly departmentalized, to encourage contributions from its readers, and to "supplement, to some extent, the work of the schools."

THE UNITARIAN REVIEW [1]

WHEN that masterpiece of Unitarian journalism, the *Christian Examiner*,[2] was transmogrified into *Old and New*,[3] the *Religious Magazine*,[4] which had for some time been publishing one theological review article in each number, added the word *Review* to its title and tried to take advantage of whatever demand there was after the disappearance of the *Examiner* for a theological review of the Unitarian faith. *Old and New* also did something of this kind, but soon discarded the more theological planks of its editorial platform. Thereupon, in March 1874, about a year before *Old and New* was merged in *Scribner's Monthly*, the *Religious Magazine* decided to become an out-and-out review and was issued, renamed and revamped, with new serial numbering, as the *Unitarian Review and Religious Magazine*.

The *Unitarian Review* is one of the periodicals that contain in their dusty files so much matter of interest and value that it seems strange they should be so little remembered. Its projectors stated in their prospectus that they aimed to make "a review that should represent the best theological culture and Christian activities of the Unitarian denomination. The original aim of the *Magazine* will not, however, be wholly lost sight of."

Some of the best *Examiner* contributors wrote for the new review, including such former editors as Frederick H. Hedge,

---

[1] TITLE: (1) *The Unitarian Review and Religious Magazine*, 1874–86; (2) *The Unitarian Review*, 1887–91.

FIRST ISSUE: March 1874. LAST ISSUE: December 1891.

PERIODICITY: Monthly. I, March–July 1874; II, August–December 1874; III–XXXVI, regular semiannual volumes, 1875–91.

PUBLISHERS: Leonard C. Bowles, Boston, 1874–76; Unitarian Review, Boston, 1876–91.

EDITORS: Charles Lowe, 1874; Henry Wilder Foote, 1874; John Hopkins Morison and Henry H. Barber, 1875–79; Henry H. Barber and James DeNormandie, 1880–84; Joseph Henry Allen, 1885–91.

INDEXED in *Poole's Index*, and *Jones' Index*.

[2] See Mott, *A History of American Magazines, 1741–1850*, p. 284.

[3] See sketch 17.

[4] See vol. II, 72, footnote.

George E. Ellis, Henry W. Bellows, and Joseph Henry Allen.
Three editorial contributors are named — Henry W. Foote, of
King's Chapel, Boston; Charles H. Brigham, of the Unitarian
society at Ann Arbor, Michigan; and Martha Ann Lowe, wife
of the first editor of the *Review*, and a poet of some reputation.
James Freeman Clarke and Andrew P. Peabody were faithful
contributors, with Thomas Hill, Rufus Ellis, and C. C. Smith.
Some foreign writers were also enlisted during the eighties. It
was in these later years that such well-known authors as Josiah
Royce, Moncure D. Conway, N. S. Shaler, C. P. Cranch, and
J. S. Dwight became contributors.

The *Review* began under the editorship of Charles Lowe,
secretary of the American Unitarian Association, who died after
editing only four numbers. Henry H. Barber held the editorial
desk for the longest term, sharing it first with John H. Morison,
the last *Religious Magazine* editor, and a former editor of the
Christian Register, and then with James DeNormandie, who
had some fame as a preacher and religious author. Joseph
Henry Allen, the classical scholar and an editor of the *Examiner*,
was the *Review's* last and ablest editor. John W. Chadwick,
himself a *Review* contributor, declared in the course of an
obituary article on Allen that American Unitarianism had seldom produced "writing that speaks so directly from man to
man as his editorial pages in the *Unitarian Review*." [5]

While theology was dominant in the magazine, literature was
the second interest; and art and music were occasionally discussed. There was some verse, especially in the earlier years.
Social and economic questions, as well as travel, received
attention. The *Review* once boasted "a hospitality to free
investigation, a carefulness of criticism, a rich scholarship, and
a religious life of which any denomination might well be
proud." [6] It was not too much to say. Always it maintained,
moreover, the high standard of book reviewing set by the
Examiner. But its circulation never exceeded 1,500 copies.

In 1891 it was decided that quarterly publication was better
suited to the theological review type of periodical, and accordingly at the end of that year the *Unitarian Review* was discontinued, to be succeeded by the *New World*.

[5] *New World*, VII, 307 (June 1898).
[6] *Unitarian Review*, XXIII, 66 (January 1885).

WIDE AWAKE [1]

DANIEL LOTHROP, of Boston, publisher of books for children, founded *Wide Awake* in 1875 as one of a group of juvenile periodicals.[2] Miss Ella Farman, of Battle Creek, Michigan, who had written several books for children which Lothrop had published, was chosen as editor; and Charles Stuart Pratt became associate editor.

Wide Awake was a small quarto of sixty to seventy-two pages, well illustrated by woodcuts and filled with original material of a high class. It appealed to the same public — children of about ten to eighteen — that *St. Nicholas* had been founded some two years before to reach; it had a larger page and larger type than *St. Nicholas*, but was not as fully illustrated and was somewhat more old-fashioned in its literary and educational policy. That is to say, it was more inclined to give the children what was thought by their elders to be good for them in the way of instruction and entertainment than to consult their own tastes and preferences.

Series of articles on such subjects as American poets and American artists were frequent in *Wide Awake;* but there were also puzzles, stories, articles on games, and so on. Among the well-known authors who wrote fiction, poetry, and articles for the magazine were Edgar Fawcett, Mrs. S. M. B. Piatt, Louise Chandler Moulton, Elizabeth Stuart Phelps, Mary H. Catherwood, Edward Everett Hale, Charles Egbert Craddock, Louise Imogen Guiney, Mrs. A. D. T. Whitney, Sarah Orne Jewett, and James Whitcomb Riley. Another list might be made to name leading *Wide Awake* writers who specialized in distinc-

---

[1] TITLE: *Wide Awake: An Illustrated Magazine for Boys and Girls.* (Subtitle varies slightly; title pages, 1875–81, bear title *Wide Awake Pleasure Book.*)

FIRST ISSUE: July 1875. LAST ISSUE: August 1893.

PERIODICITY: Monthly. Regular semiannual volumes. Title pages do not bear numbers, but letters A–Z, then AA–JJ [I–XXVI, XXVII–XXXVI].

PUBLISHER: D. Lothrop & Company, Boston.

EDITORS: Ella Farman Pratt, 1875–91; Ella F. Pratt and Charles Stuart Pratt, 1891–93.

[2] See p. 177.

tively juvenile literature; it would have to include Hezekiah Butterworth, Emily Huntington Miller, "Sophie May," John T. Trowbridge, Kirk Munroe, and Margaret Sidney.

Doubtless the most important of all these writers to *Wide Awake* readers was the one last named. Miss Sidney wrote a series of continued stories for the magazine, beginning in 1880 with *Five Little Peppers and How They Grew*, which achieved immediate popularity, and which enthralled several generations of small readers when published in book form.

The magazine organized the Chautauqua Young Folks' Reading Union in 1882, a kind of junior auxiliary of the Chautauqua Circle, and devoted a supplement to its activities during the years 1882–88. The books used for it were, of course, published by the Lothrop house.

Semiannual volumes of *Wide Awake* were bound up for use as birthday and holiday gifts, with the title *Wide Awake Pleasure Book*. With pictures by such preëminent artists as Howard Pyle, W. T. Smedley, and Sol Eytinge, they made attractive gift-books.

Editor and associate editor were married in 1877; in the last few volumes of the file their names appear as co-editors. Elbridge Streeter Brooks was office editor. Lothrop died in 1892, and in the next year *Wide Awake* was merged with *St. Nicholas*.

THE AMERICAN MAGAZINE [1]

FRANK LESLIE added a ninth to his family of periodicals when he issued the first number of *Frank Leslie's Popular Monthly* in January 1876 — a $2.50 magazine in competition with the standard $4.00 monthlies. It was the year of the nation's centennial, there were hopes of returning prosperity, and the Leslie periodicals were apparently flourishing. Certainly the new member of the group did well from the first; as a three-year-old, it boasted a circulation of 60,000. But it was in the *Monthly's* third year that its proprietor went into bankruptcy — not, if we may believe the scandal of the time, because his periodicals were not making good profits, but because he and his wife were reckless spenders.[2] Isaac W.

[1] TITLES: (1) *Frank Leslie's Popular Monthly*, January 1876–February 1904; (2) *Leslie's Monthly Magazine*, March 1904–August 1905; (3) *American Illustrated Magazine*, September 1905–May 1906; (4) *The American Magazine*, June 1906–current.

FIRST ISSUE: January 1876. Current.

PERIODICITY: Monthly. I–XLV (January 1876–June 1898), regular semiannual volumes: XLVI (July–October 1898); XLVII–LXIII (November 1898–April 1912), semiannual volumes; LXXIV (May–November 1912); LXXV (December 1912–June 1913); LXXVI–current (July 1913–current), regular semiannual volumes.

PUBLISHERS: Frank Leslie, 1876–July 1878; Frank Leslie Publishing House, August 1878–August 1905; Colver Publishing House, September 1905–September 1906; Phillips Publishing Company, October 1906–June 1916; Crowell Publishing Company, July 1916–current. All of New York except Crowell Publishing Company, Springfield, Ohio, and New York.

EDITORS: Frank Leslie, 1876–80; Mrs. Frank Leslie, 1880–99; Ellery Sedgwick, 1900–1906; John S. Phillips, 1906–15 (with Lincoln Steffens, 1906–08; Peter Finley Dunne, 1906–10; William Allen White, 1906–10; Ida M. Tarbell, 1906–15; Ray Stannard Baker, 1906–15); John M. Siddall, 1915–23; Merle Crowell, 1923–29; Sumner N. Blossom, 1929–current.

INDEXES: XXIX–LX in *Review of Reviews Index*, LX–current in *Readers' Guide*, LX–LXII in *Poole's Index*, LXVII–current in *Dramatic Index*.

REFERENCES: "Thirty Years Backward and One Forward," by Frederic L. Colver, in LIX, 358 (January 1905); Lincoln Steffens, *Autobiography* (New York, 1931), Chapters XXVI, XXXI.

[2] See Fulton Oursler's "Frank Leslie," *American Mercury*, XX, 101 (May 1930). Many of the statements in this sketch are to be taken guardedly, as rather too much reliance has been placed upon popular rumors and upon a scurrilous pamphlet — *Territorial Enterprise Extra* (Virginia City, Nevada, July 14, 1878).

England, of the *New York Sun*, became receiver for a few years, and the *Monthly* apparently continued its even and prosperous course. Nor did Leslie's death in 1880 affect the magazine noticeably; the widow, her own name legally changed to "Frank Leslie," carried on quite as efficiently as the indefatigable founder-editor had.

As a matter of fact, the virtual (though not the nominal) editor of *Frank Leslie's Popular Monthly* during its first ten or a dozen years appears to have been John Gilmary Shea, historian of the Catholic church in America and a mainstay of the Leslie house. The *Monthly* was a royal octavo of about 128 pages, copiously illustrated by wood engravings and chromolithographs. Its contents were very miscellaneous: it had the customary serial, short stories, and travel articles, with a little poetry and some essays in science, art, literature, and anthropology, with plenty of recipes, jokes, curiosities, and olla-podrida. Some material was taken from English magazines, without credit. The *Monthly's* first serial was Joaquin Miller's *The Pink Countess*. Other contributors of fiction were Amelia E. Barr, Jane G. Austin, Harriet Prescott Spofford, and Horatio Alger. Popular magazinists like A. H. Guernsey, Frank Lee Benedict, Richard B. Kimball, and George M. Towle are frequently met in its pages. Ella Wheeler, not yet Wilcox or famous, Eben E. Rexford, C. W. Stoddard, Lucy H. Hooper, and Madison Cawein contributed verse. Whittier, Harte, Andrew Lang appeared a time or two. Brander Matthews wrote of the drama, Lady Blanche Murphy of European society, and Evert A. Duyckinck and Sarah K. Bolton of contemporary literature.

Meanwhile circulation kept the upward curve, even when the price was raised to $3.00: by 1884 it had passed 100,000, and in 1887 it was quoted at 125,000. But the hard times of the early nineties brought it down to about half the latter figure, and the competition of the ten-cent magazines did not help the situation. In 1895 Mrs. Leslie, who had managed the *Monthly* with ability for fifteen years, leased it to a group headed by Frederic L. Colver. Colver had been with the magazine for six years and was secretary-treasurer of the publishing company which Mrs. Leslie headed. But after the Colver group had been in charge three years, Mrs. Leslie again took over the reins, decreased the page size to regular octavo, lowered the price to ten cents, and watched the circulation climb in a few years to 200,000. In 1900 she resigned the presidency of the company to Colver again, and turned the editorial work over to young Ellery Sedgwick, who had been assistant editor of the *Youth's Companion;* but she continued to hold an interest until 1903.

Under Sedgwick, *Leslie's Monthly,* as it came to be called in 1904, came closer to public events than it had before; but it did not participate in the muckraking diversions of the day. Burton J. Hendrick and Harvey J. O'Higgins interpreted public affairs; and certain well-known characters like Wu Ting Fang, Secretary Long, and Admiral Evans contributed articles. Stephen Crane, Frank R. Stockton, Samuel Merwin, Stewart Edward White, Emerson Hough, and others furnished the fiction. There was some emphasis on wit and humor; and Marietta Holley, Sewell Ford, and Ellis Parker Butler were drawn upon. Butler's "Pigs Is Pigs," the title of which was suggested by Sedgwick,[3] was a great "hit" of 1905. The name of the periodical was changed to the *American Illustrated Magazine* in the fall of 1905, the word *Illustrated* being dropped a few months later.

In 1906 a group of the leading contributors to *McClure's Magazine*, having had difficulties with S. S. McClure, resolved to secede and to buy a magazine which they could run to suit themselves. John S. Phillips, dissolving his partnership with McClure, organized the group and became its executive head. The magazine acquired was the *American*, and it was said that a debt of $400,000 was assumed by the purchasers.[4] The "leading contributors" referred to were five: Ida M. Tarbell, Lincoln Steffens, Ray Stannard Baker, Finley Peter Dunne, and William Allen White. With them in the secession from *McClure's*

---

[3] Proposed titles "Guinea Pigs in Pawn" and "The Dago Pig Episode" were discarded. See American Art Association-Anderson Galleries catalogue for Sale Number 4325 (New York, 1937), frontispiece and pp. 10–11, showing original MS.

[4] See Upton Sinclair, *The Brass Check* (Pasadena, California, n.d.), p. 81. Mr. Sinclair's data are, of course, sometimes untrustworthy. He thinks this debt made the *American* subservient to Wall Street, especially in the matter of the "Barbarous Mexico" articles.

came others, including Albert A. Boyden and John M. Siddall of the editorial staff.

It was a spectacular movement in the magazine world and attracted no little public attention, for the writers were among the best known in the country. The first three were preëminent in the great campaign of muckraking which was just passing its apogee, and it was felt that decks were being cleared for action. What actually happened has been described by Steffens:

We began the making of the *American*, and we met to assign one another subjects. I was to do William Randolph Hearst; Dunne was to write some "Dooley" articles, Phillips editorials, and so on. It was a feast of fun at first. . . . We all knew one another pretty well, excepting only Peter Dunne, who was new as an office companion. He provided most of the entertainment.[5]

Thus it started out a good deal like a picnic. But after the scheme had been well tried, Steffens decided:

The editing of the *American Magazine* by a group of fellow writers was a scattered control which was more cautious and interfering than S. S. McClure's dictatorship. . . . All the writers on the editorial board of our own magazine took an interest in what I was writing, and they had an appeal that *McClure's* lacked. I had — we all had — a financial interest in the *American* — stock. I was asked to "go easy" at first, because we were just starting and needed friends. This I defied. . . .[6]

But he found eventually that he *was* "going easy," and he resigned from the group after somewhat over two years of work with it. In two years more, White and Dunne were missed in the *American's* pages.

But before this happened, there had been much wielding of the muckrake. There had been exposés of graft and crime in high places presented in the careful, scholarly fashion which had distinguished the best work of that kind in *McClure's*.[7] Miss Tarbell wrote a history of the tariff in recent years and followed it by some articles showing the relation of the Standard Oil Company and other corporations with certain phases of

[5] Steffens, *op. cit.*, p. 536.
[6] *Ibid.*, p. 575.
[7] For this phase of the magazine's history, see C. C. Regier, *The Era of the Muckrakers* (Chapel Hill, 1932), *passim*, but especially p. 155.

government. Steffens wrote on the San Francisco graft prosecutions. Parts of Upton Sinclair's *The Metropolis* pilloried the idle rich. White's *The Old Order Changeth* was printed in 1909. Four installments of John Kenneth Turner's *Barbarous Mexico*, exposing the barbarities of the Diaz regime, were featured in all the panoply of blackface type in 1909–10; but disagreements between the author and the editor [8] caused Turner to take the remainder of his articles to the *Appeal to Reason*, leaving the *American* to complete its anti-Diaz campaign with pieces from various other hands. The palmy days of muckraking were over, anyway; fickle public taste had veered, and the novelty had worn off.

Other phases of the magazine were stressed more and more by Phillips and his associate editor Siddall. Baker had found relief from the strains of exposure-reporting in his idyllic "Adventures in Contentment," and they were followed by other "Adventures" stressing the simple joys of common things. The "Interesting People" department began in 1908. Little prize contests on such subjects as "My Biggest Piece of Luck," "The Bravest Thing I Ever Did," and "The Meanest Thing I Ever Did" emphasized the ordinary human qualities. The magazine seemed to drive a tandem: an interest in the simple and homely affairs of the average man and woman, and a high-minded interest in civic reform. The latter phase was represented in these later years by Jane Addams' "Twenty Years at Hull House," LaFollette's autobiography, and an ardent support of the insurgent movement in politics. Among fiction writers, Marion Crawford, O. Henry, John G. Neihardt, Edna Ferber (here making her first appearance), and Lincoln Colcord became prominent. Humorists were much in evidence: among them were Stephen Leacock, Walt Mason, George Fitch, Wallace Irwin, Oliver Herford, and Gelett Burgess.

It was the human interest side of the tandem that ran away with the magazine in the course of time. The change became complete when the Phillips Publishing Company sold the property in 1915 for $350,000 to the Crowell Company of Spring-

[8] Sinclair (*op. cit.*, p. 82) thinks that Editor Phillips was forced to "back down," but the continuance of the anti-Diaz series without Turner makes that contention untenable. See Regier, *op. cit.*, p. 188.

field, Ohio, publishers of *Farm and Fireside* and the *Woman's Home Companion*, and put John M. Siddall into the editorial chair. Siddall had the average American family in mind in his editing. "The *American Magazine*," said a prospectus which appeared shortly after he took the reins, "is made to appeal to certain strong interests that exist in all families." [9] Convincing stories of personal and domestic life, articles which showed industry rewarded by financial success, and sketches of men and women who had worked to their goals in spite of handicaps, came to be characteristic of the *American*. "Sid," in his little sermonettes, preached the optimism which his whole magazine breathed; but he did more than preach success — he dramatized it. The secret of the magazine's prosperity, wrote a staff member after the editor's death in 1923, "was that John Siddall loved people and knew what interested them." [10]

Siddall's formula was indeed successful. It increased the *American's* circulation from 400,000 to 1,720,000, quadrupling it in the eight years of the Siddall editorship.

Merle Crowell, trained under Siddall, succeeded his chief as editor. Naturally, he continued the successful policies; the magazine went on up to 2,300,000 circulation. S. S. Van Dine's detective serials excited wide attention, and Clarence Budington Kelland began his "Scattergood Baines" stories. In 1929 the *American* printed two articles in which Calvin Coolidge, who had just retired from the presidency, commented on the everyday duties of the chief executive: each of these articles was somewhat less than four thousand words long, and for each of them the magazine paid $15,000 [11] — about $3.80 a word. They were followed by five articles by Mrs. Coolidge on life in the White House, purchased for $10,000 apiece.

Crowell crystallized the magazine's creed thus:

A magazine must be, first of all, a friendly publication. Back of each page must be an honest interest in human beings — a sympathy with the decent ambitions of the average man and woman. . . . I believe in going straight to the individual and telling him only those

[9] *American Magazine*, LXXIX, 3 (June 1915).
[10] *Ibid.*, XCVI, 7 (October 1923).
[11] Letter from Mr. Crowell. The cost to the magazine was reduced somewhat by the sale of republication rights.

things that are in some way tied up with the universal problems and interests of human life. . . . By steering clear of the morbid and the "racy," the magazine records a conviction that there are other things in life more dramatic than gloom and more helpful than disillusionment. . . . I believe in a magazine that is not controversial — that deliberately wounds no one. . . . Its pages should be clean and wholesome. They should galvanize — but they ought never to shock the finer sensibilities. . . .[12]

But when, in 1929, Crowell gave way to Sumner Blossom,[13] the *American* within a few months took on a somewhat more sophisticated tone. Like another *Cosmopolitan,* its page layouts displayed movie stars, legs, and bathing beauties. Whether or not "the finer sensibilities" of readers were shocked by this sojourn among the fleshpots, the prodigal returned, after a year or two, to an editorial policy which seemed to represent some compromise with the traditional Siddall ideas. Clever page layout, much color, a long detective story in each issue, striking short stories, personality articles, and features on public affairs characterize the later *American Magazine.*

[12] Doris Ulmann, *A Portrait Gallery of American Editors* (New York, 1925), pp. 38, 41.
[13] Blossom had been editor of *Popular Science Monthly* before coming to the *American.*

THE LIBRARY JOURNAL [1]

I N ITS issue for January 15, 1876, Frederick Leypoldt's *Publishers' Weekly* [2] began a department devoted to libraries and librarians. This departure aroused so much interest among library workers that Leypoldt resolved to found a periodical to be devoted to the rapidly growing library interests of America. He called into counsel a contributor to the *Weekly*, Melvil Dewey, then acting librarian at Amherst College and an ambitious and enthusiastic young promoter of new movements. It was decided that the new journal should be widely representative, and twenty-one associate editors were enlisted from all parts of the country. This board included such

[1] TITLE: (1) *The American Library Journal*, 1876–77; (2) *The Library Journal*, 1877–current.

FIRST ISSUE: September 1876. Current.

PERIODICITY: Monthly, 1876–1919; semimonthly, 1920–current. I, September 1876, Nos. 2–3 November 1876, Nos. 4–5 January 1877, regular February–August 1877; II, September, October, November–December 1877, January–February 1878; III, regular March–December 1878; IV, 1879, July–August and September–October being combined numbers; V, 1880, September–October and November–December being combined numbers, and two July–August numbers (numbered 6–7 and 7–8); VI, 1881, September–October being combined; VII, 1882, July–August being combined; VIII, 1883, March–April and September–October being combined, supplements; IX, 1884, regular, supplements; X, 1885, September–October being combined, supplement February; XI, 1886, August–September being combined; XII, 1887, January–February and September–October being combined; XIII, 1888, March–April and September–October being combined; XIV, 1889, January–February and May–June being combined; XV–current, regular annual volumes.

PUBLISHERS: Frederick Leypoldt, New York, 1876–84; R. R. Bowker, New York, 1884–1922; R. R. Bowker Company, 1923–current.

EDITORS: Melvil Dewey and Richard Rogers Bowker, 1876–79; Frederick Leypoldt and Melvil Dewey, 1880; Charles Ammi Cutter and Frederick Leypoldt, 1881–84; C. A. Cutter, 1884–86; C. A. Cutter and R. R. Bowker, 1887–89; C. A. Cutter and Paul Leicester Ford, 1890–93; R. R. Bowker, 1893–1933; Bertine E. Weston and Frederic G. Melcher, 1933–36; Bertine E. Weston, 1936–current.

INDEXES: General Index to I–XXII (1876–97); also indexed in *Poole's Index, Cumulative, Annual Library, Jones' Index, Engineering, Review of Reviews, Contents-Subject, A. L. A. Portrait.*

REFERENCE: *Library Journal*, LVIII, 1001 ff. (December 1, 1933), Part II.

[2] See sketch 23.

men as Justin Winsor, Frederic B. Perkins, John Fiske, William F. Poole, W. T. Harris, J. L. Whitney, and Charles A. Cutter.

The first number of the *American Library Journal* was issued in September 1876. Its plan, its readers were told, was "to cover the entire field of library and bibliographical interests." [3] It contained articles on library economy, editorial notes, proceedings of library conferences, news of librarians, bibliographical matter, and notes and queries. The second issue did not appear until the end of November; it and the third issue (published January 31, 1877) were double numbers. In February 1877 the word *American* was removed from the title, and English names were added to the editorial board. In the fall of that year R. R. Bowker, a young New Yorker with various literary and publishing connections, who had been connected with the magazine from the start, became general editor. Dewey's editorial work was of the long-distance variety; he never removed from his Boston home, where he was engaged in many other activities. In 1880 Bowker went to London as the representative of Harper Brothers; and in the following year Charles A. Cutter, librarian of the Boston Athenaeum, who had done some bibliographical work for the *Journal* from the beginning, became joint editor with Leypoldt.

Proceedings of library conferences were featured in the *Journal* throughout these years. There was some English material, and something of library buildings as well as of library administration and economy. In the March–April number 1883 the *Journal* began to publish, in supplements, a "Co-Operative Index to Current Periodicals," edited by W. I. Fletcher. This was intended to supplement the Poole indexes by making references to periodicals available monthly, the same matter appearing later in the Poole volumes. The indexes continued to be issued with the *Journal* until and including February 1885, after which they were published separately.

The *Journal* experienced financial difficulties throughout its first decade, and there was grave danger of suspension, especially in the early eighties.[4] The price was originally $5.00 a year, but the number of pages was reduced and the price lowered

[3] *American Library Journal*, I, 12 (September 1876).
[4] *Bulletin of Bibliography*, VI, 3 (October 1909).

to $3.00 in 1881. When the index supplements were added in 1883 the subscription was set at $4.00. Leypoldt died in 1884, and Cutter continued in the editorship alone until 1887. By that time Bowker had returned from England and reorganized Leypoldt's publishing business; he became owner and, with Cutter, joint editor, increasing the number of pages and raising the price again to $5.00. At that price the quarterly index to periodicals and the *Literary News* were furnished in addition to the *Library Journal* — a successful combination.

Paul Leicester Ford, then known chiefly as a bibliographer, was joint editor with Cutter, 1890–93. From then on for forty years Bowker was editor-in-chief, with various managing editors, including Helen E. Haines, 1897–1908, and Fremont Rider, 1913–17.[5]

The magazine increased to sixty pages in 1902. Its circulation remained under 2,000 until about 1915, after which it mounted steadily to 4,500 in 1930. In 1920 it became a semimonthly, with two monthly numbers in the summer. From the first it has been especially strong in bibliography, in library administration, and in publishing records and proceedings of library conventions. The description of it which Miss Haines wrote in 1909 still holds: "the only current chronicle of the modern library movement, and the chief source from which its history must be compiled."[6] Following the death of Bowker in 1933, Miss Bertine E. Weston, who had been managing editor, has collaborated with Frederic G. Melcher in the general editorship.

[5] See statements, however, concerning Bowker's editorial control from the beginning, in *Library Journal*, LI, 735 (September 1, 1926), and LI, 880 (October 15, 1926).

[6] *Bulletin of Bibliography*, VI, 3 (October 1909).

PUCK [1]

O N HIS eighth birthday *Puck* indulged in a versified
retrospect, from the pen of its editor, H. C. Bunner.
The poet looked back to the year of the saucy periodical's nativity:

> Hayes and Tilden were counted in;
> The *Sun* was having a Vision of Sin;
> Corruption reveled in places high;
> War in Europe was drawing nigh;
> And such cheerful matters were taking place
> As make up the average year of grace —
> When,
> Just then
> Out of the turmoil and trouble and doubt,
> Fearless and fresh came springing out,
> Ready for good or evil luck —
> *Puck!*
>
> Nothing he had but his native worth
> And a swallow-tail,
> And a will to fight all the wrong on earth,
> And not to fail,
> And a merry smile and an opera-hat —

[1] TITLE: *Puck.*

FIRST ISSUE: March [14], 1877. (The first fifteen numbers did not bear the
full date, but only the month and year. Counting back, however, from the issue
dated June 27, 1877 (No. 16), we find that the first of the three March numbers
would regularly have been dated March 14. The second June issue (No. 14) is
erroneously labeled "May.") LAST ISSUE: September 1918.

PERIODICITY: Weekly, March [14], 1877–June 6, 1917; fortnightly, June 20,
1917–February 5, 1918; monthly, March–September 1918. I–LXXX, semiannual
volumes, 1877–1916; LXXXI, January 20–September 5, 1917; LXXXII, September 20, 1917–February 5, 1918; LXXXIII, March–September 1918.

PUBLISHERS: Keppler & Schwarzmann, New York, 1877–1913; Puck Pub-
lishing Company, New York (Nathan Straus, Jr., president, 1914–16; M.
DeWitt, president, 1917), 1914–17; International Magazine Company, New
York, 1917–18.

EDITORS: Sydney Rosenfeld, 1877–78; Henry Cuyler Bunner, 1878–96; Harry
Leon Wilson, 1896–1902; John Kendrick Bangs, 1904–05; Arthur Hamilton
Folwell, 1905–16; Karl Schmidt, 1916.

One of the species that shut up flat —
　But *that*
Puck was not, whatever his hat:
He was never shut up, and he never was flat.[2]

But *Puck* did not spring, full-panoplied in swallow-tail and opera hat, from the sea of 1877's troubles. He came, and stayed, only after certain predecessors had subsided ignominiously. Joseph Keppler, Viennese immigrant, actor, and artist, tried in St. Louis two comics in the German language in 1870 and 1871, the second of which was called *Puck*, but neither of which lived out a year. Then he came to New York, where he worked on *Leslie's Illustrated*. But he still thought he could make a success of a satirical weekly, and in 1876 he formed a partnership with A. Schwarzmann, a printer, to publish a German comic to be called *Puck* in New York. This began in September of that year — a twelve-page quarto, edited by Leopold Schenck and with political cartoons in lithograph by Keppler. Sydney Rosenfeld, the playwright, saw this journal and was delighted with it; he thought it was too good to be confined to readers of German and suggested an English edition which should utilize the stones already cut.[3] Schwarzmann and Keppler readily assented. Rosenfeld was made editor, and he employed Henry Cuyler Bunner, who had reached his majority in the month before the German *Puck* was started in New York, to be his assistant.

The first number of the English *Puck*, issued in March 1877, was a rather large quarto of sixteen pages, selling for ten cents, with one double-page and two full-page cartoons by Keppler, a poem by Bret Harte, a satire on purifying the stage by Rosenfeld, the first installment of "Fitznoodle" by B. B. Valentine, the first of a two-part story, some theatrical reviews, a good deal of brief satirical comment, and some advertising.

Most attempts to found American comics before this time had been based upon imitation of the London *Punch*, but here was a periodical that appeared to have original vitality of its own. It was this vitality that attracted readers in growing num-

---

[2] *Puck*, XVII, 2 (March 4, 1885).
[3] *Scribner's Magazine*, XX, 287 (September 1896).

bers, drew advertising patronage, pulled *Puck* through the uncertain first months, and built up a circulation within five years of some 80,000. The German edition was continued for about fifteen years, but it was soon eclipsed by its lusty offspring.

Three men were chiefly responsible for *Puck's* success — Schwarzmann, Keppler, and Bunner. Rosenfeld withdrew after about a year, leaving the literary editorship to Bunner. Of Schwarzmann, "a little, undergrown typesetter," [4] not much has been written; but the prosperity of the magazine's business affairs testifies to his competence. Keppler and Bunner, however, "the incomparable two," [5] have been praised by many and objurgated by not a few.

Keppler was a man of remarkable energy and fecundity of ideas; his mind, said one associate, "was in a constant state of eruption." [6] Every week for the first two or three years of *Puck* he drew three large, bold cartoons, as well as several smaller pictures for the text and even some for advertising. The cartoon on the front page and the double-spread in the middle were political in character, while the one on the back cover was more often a social satire of some kind. These cartoons — the outstanding feature of the magazine — were lithographs at first backed by a tint block; in the second year an effective variety was produced by two tint blocks; but by 1879 the resources of chromolithography produced the brilliant, overcolored, slashing pictures, clearly of the German school, which came to be characteristic of *Puck*. The writer of *Puck's* obituary note after his death in 1894 referred to Keppler as "the artist-founder" of the magazine, and paid tribute to his industry as well as to his ability as an artist: "The work he did in the first days of *Puck* was the work of three men." [7]

Bunner's was a talent of far more delicate and subtle cast. A writer in the *Critic* phrased the matter well: "To make the fine, violinlike tones of his 'comments' heard through all the trumpet-blast of Keppler's cartoons was no easy task, yet Bunner

[4] *Rambler and Dramatic Weekly*, June 4, 1879, p. 8. This is a severe attack, evidently by a man with a personal grievance.

[5] *Puck*, March 12, 1902. Harry Leon Wilson's twenty-fifth anniversary editorial.

[6] W. A. Rogers, *A World Worth While* (New York, 1922), p. 284.

[7] *Puck*, XXXV, 18 (February 28, 1894).

accomplished it." [8] His friend Brander Matthews has explained:

At first he did not care for politics. . . . But he soon saw how great an influence might be wielded by the editor of a comic paper who would accompany the political cartoon with persuasive comment; and with this perception came a sense of his own responsibility. He began at once to reason out for himself the principles of political action. He did his own thinking in politics as in literature.[9]

But he wrote much more than political comment for *Puck;* like Keppler, he was a hard worker, and Matthews tells us that in the magazine's early years

there were many weeks when nearly half of the whole number was written by Bunner. . . . Into the broad columns of *Puck* during the first ten years of its existence, Bunner poured an endless stream of humorous matter in prose and verse. Whatever might be wanted he stood ready to supply — rhymes of the times, humorous ballads, vers de société, verses to go with a cartoon, dialogues to go under a drawing, paragraphs pertinent and impertinent, satiric sketches of character, short stories, little comedies, nondescript comicalities of all kinds. . . . The average was surprisingly high, and the variety extraordinary.[10]

Bunner's literary reputation was founded upon his short stories chiefly — the *Short Sixes* and other compact, clever tales that appeared in *Puck*. But the contrast of his mannered *jeux d'esprit* with the strong warfare of Keppler sometimes led to unjust comparisons, as in Bierce's cruel lines, addressed to *Puck:*

> Giant with pencil, but with pen,
>   Pigmy! . . .
> Great Keppler, if I do you wrong
>   To couple with your name the sleek
>   Fat-witted fool whose words make weak
> The pictures that you made so strong. . . .
>
> I link your fame with his dispraise;
>   Forgive me. Lo, he eats your bread,
>   Owes you the fat that fills his head,
> And dares to glimmer in your blaze.[11]

[8] *Critic*, XXVIII, 362 (May 23, 1896).
[9] *Scribner's Magazine*, XX, 288 (September 1896).   [10] *Ibid.*, pp. 287, 289.
[11] Quoted in *Echo*, III, 161 (September 12, 1896).

But anybody who worked at the *Puck* anvil had to protect himself against flying sparks. *Puck* himself attacked individuals and institutions with almost unbelievable severity; his satire was at times Swiftian, *Tomahawk*-like, devastating, almost sadistic. On November 28 of his first year the Puckish gibe "What fools these mortals be!" appeared as the magazine's motto. As he saw the folly and injustice about him, *Puck* forgot sometimes to be funny; and the impish grin on his lips turned to a snarl of anger. On his fifth birthday he said of himself:

He has seen about him death and defeat, injustice and incompetence, all forms of wrong and tyranny; he has seen the wrong triumph over the good; he has seen hope grow weary and courage fail. The merry laugh which he brought to earth with him has been checked now and again while tears of sorrow or sympathy ran down his rosy cheeks.[12]

The chief political objects of *Puck's* attack in its first decade were Tammany and Blaine. In the warfare on Tammany, Keppler had to yield first place to Nast, of *Harper's Weekly*, who had a priority in that field;[13] but in the campaign of 1884 against Blaine, *Puck's* cartoons attracted for the first time a national attention, and they had a large share in Blaine's defeat. It was Bernard Gillam, however, and not Keppler, who pictured Blaine as the tattooed man and drew the masterpiece showing him as Phryne before the Chicago tribunal.[14] Grant was attacked, too, mainly on the score of his drinking; President Hayes was berated, on the other hand, for banishing wines from the White House table. Garfield suffered for his connection with the Credit Mobilier scandal: Keppler drew his famous "Forbidding the Banns" in 1880. In it Garfield, dressed in women's clothes and a coy expression, is about to be married to Uncle Sam. Schurz and Reid are bridesmaids, and the clergyman has a ballot box for a head. But W. H. Barnum, chairman of the Democratic national committee, is rushing in, vigorously

[12] *Puck*, X, 2 (March 8, 1882).

[13] See vol. II, pp. 478–80.

[14] See p. 288. The idea of the tattooed man is said to have come from Carl Hauser, then editor of the German *Puck*. James L. Ford, *Forty-Odd Years in the Literary Shop* (New York, 1921), p. 299.

protesting against proceeding with the ceremony, and bearing in his arms a babe labeled "$329 Credit Mobilier." "But," protests the demure bride, "it was such a little one!" [15] Keppler constantly attacked Ben Butler, whom he pictured as a snake, as well as Tilden and Jay Gould. He assailed monopolies, especially in oil and telegraph lines, and their handmaiden high tariff; but he also opposed free silver, showing Uncle Sam in 1886 riding a high bicycle, the wheels of which were silver dollars, "To National Bankruptcy."

But perhaps *Puck's* most constant protest was registered against political corruption — "the vast growth of shameless jobbery and conscienceless misuse of power . . . hideous forms of corruption." [16] This was a nonpartisan campaign: in 1882 appeared Graetz's double-page cartoon, "The Political Sodom and Gomorrah," showing the Republican party as one city and the Democratic party as the other, with fire and lightning playing upon them and an angel in the foreground leading out of the doomed cities the forces of political honesty and wisdom.[17] The paper's favorite reforms were the merit system in the civil service, lower tariffs, and correction of ballot abuses; and it considered Cleveland's election in 1892 a victory for all three.[18]

Puck came to be a political power through sheer force and reiteration in its cartoons. In 1883, which was not a "political year," 60 per cent of its colored cartoons dealt with domestic politics, and 12 per cent more with international politics — including seven lambasting Ireland. It was these cartoons, with their large strength, their sometimes lurid coloring, and occasionally their broad suggestiveness, that gave *Puck* its standing. "It is not refined humor that makes *Puck* a political power," observed the *Critic* in 1886: "it is the coarse strength of its cartoons, which thus far have been drawn almost uniformly in the interests of popular morality and political integrity." [19] J. A. Wales joined Keppler as cartoonist in 1879, Frederick Opper came in 1881, and F. Graetz and Bernard Gillam were recruited in 1882. Wales, however, left in 1881 to found *Judge*,

[15] *Puck*, August 25, 1880.
[16] *Ibid.*, XVI, 386 (February 18, 1885).
[17] *Ibid.*, May 10, 1882.
[18] *Ibid.*, XXXII, 186 (November 16, 1892).
[19] *Critic*, VIII, 24 (January 9, 1886).

and Gillam joined him on that paper four years later. When Keppler was in Europe in 1883, Graetz, Opper, and Gillam did all the cartoons for *Puck*. The custom at this time and afterward was for a weekly "conclave" to discuss the ideas and possibilities for the cartoons, and to decide upon and assign the work.[20]

Puck also took a great interest in religious matters: he was not especially religious himself, or at least not churchly; but he had a stern eye for the abuses of religionists. Beecher he despised; he believed all the scandal about the famous preacher and often pictured him as a Turk or a Mormon. Talmadge was an even more frequent butt, for *Puck* resented sensationalism in the pulpit — "a vice," he said, "that seems to be spreading among the American ministry,"[21] and which he called "Talmadge-ism." Talmadge was commonly pictured as all one huge mouth. In 1880 *Puck* was more than usually concerned with churchly abuses — high pew rents, sensationalism, fairs, and camp meetings. It ran a series of cartoons in this year on campmeeting evils. Later Keppler had a cartoon showing churchmen protecting themselves by the umbrella of bigotry from the "Light of Reason" projected from Darwin, Tyndall, Haeckel, Voltaire, Franklin, Paine, Kant, and others.[22] From the first volume there was a heavy attack on the Catholic church, much of it occasioned by the ascension of Leo XIII to the papacy. In reply to criticism of "ruthless caricatures" of Pius IX and his successor, the editor said that Keppler was a Roman Catholic, but that *Puck* himself was "neither Catholic, Protestant, Hebrew, nor Mohammedan."[23] He continued the attacks. Finally, *Puck* had a good time abusing the Mormons. The cartoon of 1877 which excited the most attention of all Keppler's efforts in that year was one imitated from a picture in Mark Twain's *Roughing It*. Printed soon after the death of the Mormon leader, it was entitled: "In Memoriam: Brigham Young. 'And the Place That Knew Him Once Shall Know Him No More!'" The picture showed twelve weeping women in a very wide bed, with a bow of crape in the center. This was con-

---

[20] Illustrated Supplement of *Puck*, March 2, 1887, p. 4.
[21] *Puck*, October 3, 1883.
[22] *Ibid.*, March 8, 1882.   [23] *Ibid.*, March 6, 1878.

sidered obscene by critics; but the edition of the number in which it appeared was soon exhausted, and it was later published as a broadside.[24]

Social topics were discussed as trenchantly as those related to politics and religion. *Puck* never tired of poking fun at the woman-suffragist.[25] Easy divorce it disapproved with equal vigor.[26] Masonry was "so much bigod nonsense."[27] Like all comics, it laughed at the fashions in dress and at such passing fads as pedestrianism, Barnum's baby show, Oscar Wilde's visit, and velociceding. Keppler's favorite butts are all portrayed in a double-page cartoon in 1881, in which the artist is shown asleep while his victims are all busy drawing themselves for once as they see themselves. Talmadge draws himself as a dignified divine, Ben Butler as a beauty, Grant as "Imperator," Beecher as the modest ascetic, Tammany Chief Kelly as "the stainless statesman," Bennett as Apollo Belvedere, Conkling as Jupiter Tonans, Tilden as a heavyweight, Peter Cooper as "ever youthful."[28] Jay Gould was also a frequent victim in the early eighties; he was shown variously as a whale swallowing railways, telegraphs, and newspapers (with *Puck* the harpooner), and as a bowler wearing diamond pants-buttons and rolling balls of trickery to overturn broker and banker ninepins.[29] New York newspaper editors "caught it" frequently — Bennett, Pulitzer, Dana, Godkin. It is interesting to note that Pulitzer had tried to buy into the *Puck* firm before he came to New York; he had known Keppler in St. Louis.[30]

There was, of course, much lighter wit and humor. Puns, chief diet of so many early comics, were scarcely to be neglected. When someone spoke of "the genesis of Mark Twain," it was objected that he was not a Genesis but a Levity-cuss. Which will be quite enough of *Puck's* puns. "Puck's History of the United States" ran through many numbers in 1877–78 and was

[24] See *Puck*, April 3, 1878, p. 15. The cartoon had appeared September 5, 1877. In the number for February 13, 1884, Keppler, Graetz, Opper, and Gillam each drew a cartoon against the Mormons.

[25] See pp. 91–92.

[26] See p. 312.

[27] *Puck*, August 20, 1879.

[28] *Ibid.*, August 10, 1881.

[29] *Ibid.*, January 26, 1881; March 29, 1882.

[30] See Don C. Seitz, *Joseph Pulitzer* (New York, 1924), p. 92.

followed by a "History of Oireland." Valentine's "Fitznoodle in America" continued for several years, but its author later quarreled with *Puck's* proprietors and sued them at law.[31] The theaters and musical performances were reviewed with some regularity, W. J. Henderson being the leading critic.

R. K. Munkittrick, who had been a *New York Ledger* contributor, wrote verse and sketches regularly for *Puck* after its first year. A. E. Watrous and Robert J. Burdette were also prominent early contributors; and in the middle eighties came F. Marshall White, Williston Fish, James L. Ford, Ed. Mott, and Manley H. Pike.

In 1881 fine, large, colored lithographs were issued as monthly supplements under the name of "Puckographs": they were *portraits chargés* by Keppler. A new series of them began in December 1885, with one of Mark Twain, "America's Best Humorist." Eugene Zimmerman drew much for *Puck* in the early eighties, and Frederick Opper became one of the paper's most popular artists by the middle of the decade. J. A. Mitchell, of *Life*, wrote of Opper in 1889: "The number of types he has produced, and even created, for our amusement would fill a volume. They all have character, and there is movement, and plenty of it." [32] Movement there was in most of the drawing for *Puck:* its pictures were usually full of action. Wales, Gillam, and Graetz had all left *Puck* by 1886; Charles Jay Taylor, Louis Dalrymple, and A. B. Shults were on the art staff. Among contributors in the late eighties were A. B. Frost, C. G. Bush, M. A. Woolf, E. N. Blue, and J. S. Godwin. The *Critic* once pointed out *Puck's* "lamentable weakness in the pictorial commentary on society" for which French and English comics were notable.[33] Taylor later supplied this lack somewhat, but *Puck* was always fondest of the middle and lower class types of men, such as those that Opper, Frost, and Zimmerman drew.

Puck claimed a circulation of nearly 90,000 as it entered the decade of the nineties; and *Puck's Library*, the paper's monthly sister, which had, since 1887, retailed *Puck's* witticisms at second-hand, claimed over 60,000. The *Library* was not the

[31] *Journalist*, VI, 4 (February 11, 1888).
[32] *Scribner's Magazine*, VI, 731 (December 1889).
[33] *Critic*, II, 50 (February 25, 1882).

only one of *Puck's* camp followers: *Pickings from Puck* was published irregularly from 1883 on, to become a quarterly in 1897; and *Puck on Wheels* was an annual devoted to the bicycling craze in 1880–86. *Puck's* circulation declined in the hard times of the middle nineties, to recover again for a while in the boom which followed the war with Spain.

For several years *Puck* was a good Cleveland paper. True, it was sometimes critical in his first administration; and the *New York World* charged that Keppler had tried to get an appointment for a relative and had failed — to which Keppler entered categorical denial, adding that he had never had private relations with Cleveland: "What we have to say we say in the paper; and if Mr. Cleveland cares to know what we think, he must buy his *Puck* like any other citizen." [34] But in the campaign of 1888 *Puck* supported Cleveland and Thurman valiantly, and four years later Cleveland and Stevenson. In the contest of 1892 it gave no quarter to such Republican "bosses" as Hill, Platt, and Quay: it wrote of Platt's "low cunning, trickery, sordid ambition, greed and duplicity"; [35] and it called Quay an "embezzler and defaulter." [36] Later it attacked the free silver panacea, and it warned the Democratic party in 1894 that "its days of supremacy are numbered" unless it "vindicates itself" by reforming the tariff. [37]

In its comment on labor troubles *Puck* was a conservative. Its antimonopolistic tendencies gave it a sympathy for labor, but it was quick to resent excesses and abuses by the unions. A strong Graetz cartoon appeared August 1, 1883, called "The Tournament of Today; A Set-to Between Labor and Monopoly"; it showed ill-nourished Labor mounted on a skinny horse, Poverty, while Monopoly is clad in full armor and rides on a gigantic steed which travels on the wheels of a locomotive. But three years later it was picturing the anarchist, the "walking delegate," and the boycotter as the three enemies of the workingman. February 23, 1887, Taylor had a cartoon showing a "walking delegate" lazily reclining in a chair which was carried

---

[34] *Puck*, XXI, 382 (August 10, 1887).
[35] *Ibid.*, XXXI, 406 (August 7, 1892).
[36] *Ibid.*, XXVII, 306 (July 9, 1890).
[37] *Ibid.*, XXXV, 194 (May 16, 1894).

on the back of a workingman up the steps of hardship, distress, poverty. The Chicago anarchists were called by the editor of *Puck* "simply cut-throats, murderers, rioters, and robbers." [38] "Coxeyism," said the same authority, "may be defined as the belief that happiness and prosperity are to be achieved by Acts of Congress"; [39] and in the same number a double-page cartoon by Taylor shows McKinley, Harrison, and Reed blowing bubbles for Coxey to chase.

But politics and economics yielded gradually to art and lighter satires in the nineties. Bunner's *Short Sixes*, *The Runaway Browns*, *Made in France*, and "The Suburban Sage" were prominent, with sketches by George H. Jessop, Charles F. Lummis, Charles Battell Loomis, Harry Leon Wilson, and many others. The paper had a building at the World's Fair in Chicago and published a World's Fair *Puck* there.

Keppler died in 1894 and Bunner two years later. Joseph Keppler, Jr., succeeded his father; he and Taylor, Dalrymple, and Ehrhart, did most of the cartoons which attacked Bryan in 1896. The younger Keppler commonly used fewer figures than his father, but was quite as successful with facial expression and sometimes with action. Other artists who became prominent in *Puck* in the late nineties were John Cassel, O'Neill Latham, and Frank A. Nankivell. The work of the last named was notable for its decorative poster effects.

Harry Leon Wilson succeeded Bunner as editor. Edwin L. Sabin, Carolyn Wells, Thomas L. Masson, Joseph C. Lincoln, Tom P. Morgan, and Katharine Perry were among the most frequent contributors at the turn of the century. The butts of *Puck's* satire in these years were Bryan (in the 1900 campaign), Tammany Chief Croker, the walking delegate, the prohibitionist, Kaiser Wilhelm of Germany, the Boxers in China, and the missionaries. The pieces were all short, and there was less of literary flavor to the paper than under Wilson's predecessor or under his successor.

John Kendrick Bangs became editor in 1904. He came to *Puck* from *Harper's Weekly*, of which he had been editor; he had a reputation as one of the country's chief humorists. In his

[38] *Puck*, XIX, 338 (July 28, 1886).
[39] *Ibid.*, XXV, 130 (April 18, 1894).

brief incumbency his "Alice in Stageland," a clever serial of dramatic criticism, was one of the paper's most popular features. He also collaborated with Bert Leston Taylor and his associate editor, Arthur Hamilton Folwell, in a historical novel which burlesqued the type then so popular. Grant Hamilton's cartoons attacking Theodore Roosevelt were another feature of that year. L. M. Glackens joined the force of cartoonists, to be an effective force on the paper for the next decade. Otto J. Schneider's delicate artistry was notable.

After Folwell became editor, Franklin P. Adams, Freeman Tilden, Arthur Guiterman, and Charles Hanson Towne appeared in the paper; and Albert Levering became a contributor of art, followed a little later by Arthur Young and Gordon Grant. *Puck* favored neither presidential candidate in the campaign of 1908, but laughed at Taft, Roosevelt, Parker, and all the chief figures of the show. Four years later it was for Wilson. Young "Kep," Glackens, and Will Crawford were the chief political cartoonists of these years; Keppler did some of his best work in 1908.

Puck's page grew smaller in the middle of 1915; its traditional chromolithographic spreads gave place to color printing from half tones; and soon after the war began, the paper shortage compelled the use of a cheap paper stock. By 1916 color was abandoned except for the cover. In short, *Puck* looked a bit strange and out-at-elbows even to his best friends, and this in spite of the fact that he had been adopted by the young millionaire, Nathan Straus, Jr., of Macy's Department Store, in 1914. Straus was publisher and a kind of superintending editor for three years.

But the contents of the magazine were lively enough after 1914. Ralph Barton was a Paris correspondent echoing the war, George Jean Nathan wrote about New York plays, Dana Burnet did the news in rhyme, and James Huneker conducted a brilliant department called "The Seven Arts." Henry Mayer's pictures were a prized feature, and Mayer was made "contributing editor" of the magazine. Other prominent artists were Tony Sarg, W. E. Hill, John Held, Jr., Raphael Kirchner, and W. J. Enright. Frederick Opper was still a contributor. *Puck* became very militant shortly before the war. It was strongly pro-Wilson in 1916 and published one cartoon showing how the name of Pennsylvania Avenue in Washington would be changed to Hindenbergstrasse in case of the election of Hughes.[40]

In 1917 *Puck* was sold down the river. Hearst's International Magazine Company was the new owner. It was now better printed, on fine paper, and it numbered Stephen Leacock, Bruno Lessing, "B. L. T." "K. C. B.," Carolyn Wells, George Jean Nathan, and Gustav Michelson among its contributors. Louis Raemaekers was the leading cartoonist, though such pictorial comment on public affairs as had once made *Puck* loved and hated was now subordinated in the magazine to theaters and lighter persiflage on society and fads. Alan Dale wrote on the theaters, and actresses indulged their artful exhibitionism on many pages. But circulation had been declining sadly for several years. The magazine became a fortnightly in 1917 and a monthly in March of the next year. It was discontinued in September 1918.

Puck of the eighties and nineties was an institution *sui generis*. American journalism never had anything else quite like it, and this in spite of imitations. Its boldness, its incisive cleverness, its robust comedy, its real literary and artistic values made it a factor in politics and in social life. "It was never shut up, and it never was flat."

[40] *Puck*, LXXX, 14 (September 23, 1916).

THE UNITED SERVICE [1]

LEWIS R. HAMERSLY founded *United Service* in Philadelphia in 1879 as "A Quarterly Review of Military and Naval Affairs," changing it to a monthly in the following year. He himself had charge of the naval department of the journal, and George A. Woodward of the military section. The new magazine was a handsomely printed large octavo of over 120 pages at $4.00 a year, containing articles of professional interest contributed by officers in the two services, translations from foreign military journals, reviews of military and naval literature, and some entertaining miscellany.

United Service represented "an honest effort to afford its readers both instruction and entertainment." [2] The instruction came from the professional articles, such as the series on artillery in foreign countries by Major J. P. Sanger, and the contributions by General J. Watts de Peyster, former editor of the *Eclaireur*. The entertainment came from the serial fiction by Captain Charles King and "Tom Bowline," "Whiffs from an Old Sailor's Pipe" by "E. Z.," and so on. There were articles of reminiscence, some historical essays by David Graham Adee and others, and occasional verse.

[1] TITLES: (1) *The United Service*, 1879–1906; (2) *Army and Navy Life and United Service*, 1906–08; (3) *Army and Navy Life*, 1908–09; (4) *Uncle Sam's Magazine*, 1909.

FIRST ISSUE: January 1879. LAST ISSUE: July 1909.

PERIODICITY: Quarterly, 1879; monthly, 1880–1909. [First Series], I, 1879; II–XIII, regular semiannual volumes, 1880–85; XIV, January–April 1886. Suspended May 1886–December 1888. New [Second] Series, I–XVI, regular semiannual volumes, 1889–96; XVII, January–April 1897. Suspended May 1897–December 1901. Third Series, I–VII, regular semiannual volumes, 1902–June 1905; VIII, July 1905–June 1906; IX–XIII, regular semiannual volumes, July 1906–December 1908; XIV, January–July 1909.

PUBLISHERS: Lewis R. Hamersly & Company, Philadelphia, 1879–84; T. H. S. Hamersly, New York, 1885–86; Lewis R. Hamersly & Company, Philadelphia, 1889–1901; Lewis R. Hamersly, New York, 1902–04; L. R. Hamersly, Jr., New York, 1904–05; Army and Navy Press, New York, 1906–09; *Uncle Sam's Magazine*, New York, 1909.

EDITORS: Lewis R. Hamersly and George A. Woodward, 1879–84; T. H. S. Hamersly, 1885–86; L. R. Hamersly, 1889–1904; Lewis R. Hamersly, Jr., 1904–05; W. D. Walker, 1906–08; T. N. Horn, 1908–09; W. D. Walker, 1909.

INDEXED in *Poole's Index* and *Review of Reviews Index*.

[2] *United Service*, I, 650 (October 1879).

In 1885 T. H. S. Hamersly, a son of the founder, took the magazine to New York and attempted to enlarge its scope to include the Civil Service; but the experiment was a failure, and publication was suspended after the issue for April 1886. In January 1889 Lewis R. Hamersly revived the magazine in Philadelphia, with portraits in half tone of prominent military and naval personages, a department devoted to the Military Order of the Loyal Legion, and a good humorous department called "Service Salad." But the New Series did not survive the hard times of the middle nineties and was forced to suspend in 1897. Thus an ironical fate cut it off just before it might have shared in the prosperity of military and naval affairs at the time of the war with Spain. Following that war, it was revived once more, however, in New York in January 1902 at $3.00 a year, soon reduced to $1.00.

Upon the death of the founder two years later, his son, Lewis R. Hamersly, Jr., became editor and publisher; but the magazine was sold at the end of 1905 to *Army and Navy Life*, which had just been founded in New York by W. D. Walker. Walker combined the titles of the two periodicals and continued the serial numbering of the older one. *Army and Navy Life and United Service* was a well-illustrated square octavo containing news of the services, fiction, poetry, articles dealing with sports and the theater, and much editorial advocacy of increased armaments. It was "conducted by officers of the American Army, Navy, and National Guard"; and the list of associate editors was headed by the names of Rear Admiral Robley D. Evans and Joseph B. Coghlan.

The journal's big-navy propaganda attracted no little attention from the newspapers, and the magazine was both praised and abused for it. The *Boston Transcript*, for example, thought it was trying to frighten the country into building battleships by "blood-curdling . . . bugaboos and bogies." [3] But the magazine stood by its guns.

In May 1908 Captain T. N. Horn took over the conduct of *Army and Navy Life;* but after ten months it was turned back to Walker, who changed its name to *Uncle Sam's Magazine* for five issues and then abandoned it. Its highest circulation appears to have been under 20,000 copies.

[3] Quoted in *Army and Navy Life*, XII, 512 (May 1908).

THE AMERICAN JOURNAL OF PHILOLOGY [1]

BASIL L. GILDERSLEEVE was president of the American Philological Association in 1878, and in the course of his presidential address he reproached the philologers of the country with their lack of a special journal. The issue in May 1879 of the prospectus of the *American Journal of Philology* was the result partly of this address and partly of the suggestion of President Gilman that it was Professor Gildersleeve's "manifest duty to follow the lead of the *American Journal of Mathematics* and the *American Journal of Chemistry*" — other Johns Hopkins periodicals.[2] The prospectus brought a "comparatively long list of subscribers";[3] the University agreed to become "a large subscriber";[4] and Gildersleeve issued the first number in February 1880 — a handsome octavo to be published quarterly.

The editor apologized in the first number for the preponderance of studies in Greek, but asserted that the *Journal* had been

[1] TITLE: *The American Journal of Philology.*

FIRST ISSUE: February 1880. Current.

PERIODICITY: Quarterly. Annual volumes. Parts are given numbers instead of month-dates.

PUBLISHERS: B. L. Gildersleeve, 1880–97, 1911–18; Johns Hopkins Press, 1898–1910, 1919–current.

EDITORS: Basil Lanneau Gildersleeve, 1880–1919 (with C. W. E. Miller, 1915–19); Charles William Emil Miller, 1920–34 (with Maurice Bloomfield, 1920–28; Hermann Collitz, 1920–34; Tenney Frank, 1920–34; Wilfred P. Mustard, 1920–32; D. M. Robinson, 1920–34; Roger M. Jones, 1932; Harold Cherniss, 1934, and B. D. Meritt, 1934); Benjamin Dean Meritt, 1934–35 (with Cherniss, Collitz, Frank, Robinson, and Kemp Malone); Tenney Frank, 1936–current (with Cherniss, Robinson, Meritt, and Malone).

INDEXES: Vols. I–X in Vol. X; contributor indexes for decades in Vols. XX, XXX and XL; "Index Scoliodromicus" (index to Brief Mention department), XLII, 370–382; "Indiculus Syntacticus" (index to materials on syntax), XXXVI, 481–487; I–XXVII in *Poole's Index;* XXVIII–current in *Readers' Guide*, Supplement.

REFERENCES: Introduction to C. W. E. Miller, *Selections from the Brief Mention of B. L. Gildersleeve* (Baltimore, 1930); "Retrospect," XXV, 486–490 (No. 4, 1904).

[2] *American Journal of Philology*, XXV, 487 (No. 4, 1904).

[3] *Ibid.*, I, 2 (No. 1, 1880).

[4] *Ibid.*, XXV, 487 (No. 4, 1904).

promised the coöperation of scholars in other fields. Of the nineteen leading articles in Volume I, however, twelve dealt with topics related to the classical languages. This proportion continued through the first four volumes, after which there was more of Sanskrit and Hebrew, as well as Anglo-Saxon, Norse, and Icelandic. A series on the American revision of the Bible by Charles Short, of Columbia, a member of the committee on revision, appeared in 1882–84; and a series on American dialects in the late eighties. There was much in Teutonic fields in the nineties; but Greek was always the *pièce de résistance*, and this emphasis became more and more marked after the turn of the century.

William D. Whitney, of Yale, who had been a fellow student with Gildersleeve at Berlin, was one of the editor's chief lieutenants in the establishment of the *Journal* and brought many Yale scholars into the pages of the magazine. C. H. Toy, of Harvard, was another helper. Gildersleeve visited England in 1880 (Charles D. Morris doing the editorial work on the *Journal* during his absence), and there he secured the coöperation of such scholars as Henry Nettleship and Robinson Ellis, of Oxford, and Lewis Campbell, of St. Andrews. Fitzedward Hall was also recruited; but Gildersleeve later wrote, "I am mortally afraid of my transplanted fellow-countryman, Dr. Fitzedward Hall." [5] Maurice Bloomfield and Professor Morris were especially active from Johns Hopkins, J. A. Harrison from Washington and Lee, Albert S. Cook from Yale, and G. L. Kittredge from Harvard.

The AJP was distinctly Gildersleeve's, however. He wrote a great deal for it himself — articles, thorough reviews of books and of scholarly journals, and his famous "Brief Mention." This last-named department was begun to furnish a place for that mass of short reviews which accumulates on the desk of the editor of a learned journal; but under Gildersleeve's management it soon took on the aspect of an editorial department in which a vital and pungent writer commented on men and things, books and ideas. It became the confirmed habit of all readers of the *Journal* to turn first to the "Brief Mention," there to find a rare combination of scholarship with ebullience, wit

[5] *American Journal of Philology*, XVIII, 124 (No. 1, 1897).

with authority. Paul Shorey has observed that, however trivial some of these comments ("native wood-notes," their author smilingly called them) may seem singly,

in the mass they were anything but insignificant. There were few topics of interest to classical scholars, few important books which he did not somewhere touch upon, and he touched nothing which he did not illuminate as well as adorn. . . . Anyone who goes to the stacks to look up some particular point in the back numbers of the journal will find himself reading on and on in the old "Brief Mentions" and discover that they are still excellent reading.[6]

In 1930 *Selections from the Brief Mention* brought together in a separate volume a considerable number of these short reviews and comments.

Morris died in 1886, and Whitney in 1894; new names appeared in the *Journal* — Francis B. Gummere, Paul Shorey, J. P. Postgate, Fred C. Conybeare, E. J. Goodspeed, Paul Haupt, and many others. In 1902 nineteen of the twenty-two leading articles dealt with Greek or Latin topics. Though contributors were more abundant than in the early years of the review, its editor still wrote much.

Essential scholar though Gildersleeve was, by training and inner necessity, he thought of himself as a journalist as well. He had had "considerable journalistic experience"[7] as an editorial writer in the *Richmond Examiner* during the war, and he undoubtedly had the journalistic gift. It is doubtful if the editor of any other American scholarly quarterly, among the multitude of them, has approached Gildersleeve in his exercise of the diverse qualities of editorship. "His journal," says Shorey, "was the one publication to which ambitious young scholars looked. . . . His applause was most prized, his censure most feared."[8]

In the early days of the AJP, finances seem to have given some trouble. Gildersleeve complained in 1882 that "the support accorded to the journal by the philological public of America is far from being adequate to the original plan."[9] But the cooperation of the Hopkins Press, of which Nicholas Murray was

[6] *New York Times Magazine*, January 27, 1924, p. 3.
[7] *American Journal of Philology*, XXV, 487 (No. 4, 1904).
[8] *New York Times Magazine*, January 27, 1924, p. 3.
[9] *American Journal of Philology*, III, 138 (No. 1, 1882).

superintendent, and the increasing support of scholars enabled the review to continue. In the nineties, what our philologist called "the fissiparous multiplication of philological publications" [10] tended to reduce the numbers of both subscribers and contributors.

Impaired health led Gildersleeve in 1915 to ask the editorial assistance of his colleague, C. W. E. Miller; and when his sight was affected a few years later, he resigned the work wholly. "The privilege of dying in harness has been denied me," he wrote, "and henceforth I must surrender to the too long neglected claims of the contemplative life. Rachel must have her rights." [11] On his ninetieth birthday Volume XLII (1921) was dedicated to the founder; it included an index to his "Brief Mention" called "Index Scoliodromicus," by Lawrence H. Baker.

Following the forty-years' editorship of Gildersleeve, the AJP has continued upon the high levels set by him, emphasizing classical philology, but including oriental, comparative, and modern fields. The amount of space given reviews has been reduced somewhat. The Johns Hopkins University Press, to which Gildersleeve transferred the *Journal* before his resignation, has since been the publisher. Professor Miller retired in 1934 and has been followed in the editorship first by Benjamin Dean Meritt and then by Tenney Frank.

[10] *American Journal of Philology*, XVII, 390 (No. 3, 1896).
[11] *Ibid.*, XL, 451 (No. 4, 1919).

THE DIAL [1]
(of Chicago and New York)

FRANCIS F. BROWNE, who had edited and published the *Lakeside Monthly* [2] in Chicago from 1869 to 1874 and had later conducted the literary department of the Chicago *Alliance*, began in 1880 a monthly journal of literary criticism. All sorts and conditions of periodicals were being founded in the exuberant metropolis by Lake Michigan in those years, and it is not a matter for wonder that a critical journal should be attempted; but the remarkable fact is that Browne's *Dial* should have lived and prospered in Chicago for more than a third of a century, gaining a high reputation for honest and conservative criticism.

Browne was fortunate in finding an established firm of wholesale book jobbers to act as his publishers. He himself had some money in the venture from the first,[3] but his friend A. C. McClurg furnished not only sympathetic coöperation but a business connection of the utmost value. Eastern publishers might have refused book advertising to Editor Browne, but they found it difficult to say no to Wholesale-Book-Jobber McClurg.

The *Dial* consisted of twenty-four pages, small quarto, with

[1] TITLE: *The Dial.* Subtitles: *A Monthly Review and Index of Current Literature*, 1880–92; *A Semi-Monthly Journal of Literary Criticism, Discussion and Information*, 1892–1917 (*Fortnightly* beginning March 1915); *A Fortnightly Journal of Criticism and Discussion of Literature and the Arts*, 1917–18.

FIRST ISSUE: May 1880. LAST ISSUE: July 1929.

PERIODICITY: Monthly, 1880–August 1892; semimonthly, September 1892–February 1915; fortnightly, March 1915–November 1919; monthly, 1920–29. I–XII, annual volumes, 1880–April 1892; XIII, May–December 1892; XIV–LXXXV, regular semiannual volumes, 1893–1928; LXXXVI, January–July 1929.

PUBLISHERS: Jansen, McClurg & Company, Chicago, 1880–86; A. C. McClurg & Company, Chicago, 1886–92; The Dial Company, Chicago, 1892–1914; Henry O. Shepard Company, Chicago, 1914–15; The Dial Publishing Company, New York, 1916–29.

EDITORS: Francis F. Browne, 1880–1913; Waldo R. Browne, 1913–16; Clinton Joseph Masseck, 1916; George Bernard Donlin, 1917–18; Robert Morss Lovett, 1919; Scofield Thayer, 1919–26; Marianne Moore, 1926–29.

INDEXES: *Poole's, Readers' Guide, Dramatic Index.*

[2] See sketch 14.　　　　　　　　　　　　　　[3] *Dial*, XIII, 85 (July 1892).

excellent typography, at $1.50 a year. It contained reviews of the leading books, brief notices of others, literary news notes, lists of new books, and publishers' announcements. The reviews were often a little heavy, as the typography was inclined to solidity; it was evident at a glance that the *Dial* was to be conservative and dignified. It was intelligent, however; and the editor was not afraid to publish a review with an edge to it. He himself wrote about half the paper at first,[4] but he soon gathered a group of contributors (most of them Midwesterners) who could be depended upon to discuss books in special fields with understanding and to share the editor's general viewpoint. Among these men were Joseph Kirkland, William F. Poole, Melville W. Fuller, Charles Mills Gayley, David Starr Jordan, William Morton Payne, O. F. Emerson, Paul Shorey, Richard Burton, and Joseph Jastrow.

In 1892 Browne resigned his position as editorial adviser for the publishing business which McClurg had built up, and became his own publisher. Relations with McClurg, who continued to write occasional reviews, remained friendly; but it was believed that a critical journal ought to have no business affiliation with a publisher of books. Browne at once made his journal a semimonthly at $2.00, running its circulation to 5,000 in 1893 — the highest point it reached while in Browne's hands. The scope of the journal was broadened a little in 1892; there was some material about the World's Fair, and a series on the teaching of English in various universities. Notice was taken of the Ibsen "craze"; the *Dial* was generally unfriendly to the Norwegian dramatist. Very little attention was given, however, to literature in foreign languages: the only reason Ibsen came into the *Dial's* ken was that he had become a factor in the English and American drama. Nor was the theater given attention; only the literary phases of plays were of interest. British literature was important, however, in the *Dial's* contents. In spite of the journal's location in Chicago and its editor's former feeling against the East,[5] there was little or no sectionalism. A New York letter by Arthur Stedman was carried for about two years, beginning late in 1893.

The *Dial* believed the New England group of writers "one of

---

[4] *Dial*, XXXVIII, 306 (May 1, 1905).   [5] See pp. 414–15.

the most remarkable in the history of literature." [6] It declared that "most unvitiated stomachs reject with involuntary but decided symptoms of disapproval the mixture of wine and bilgewater, nectar and guano" which Walt Whitman had compounded in *Leaves of Grass*.[7]

The *Dial* was a journal with Standards. Browne, Payne, Melville B. Anderson, William Henry Smith, Richard Henry Stoddard, and Hiram M. Stanley kept it so. But what shall we say of an editor who, summing up in 1894 the status of the American novel, says, "The place of honor among our living novelists should probably be given to Dr. Holmes. . . . What other living American has given us two novels (or even one) of such enduring interest" as *Elsie Venner* and *The Guardian Angel*? [8] A corollary is found in McClurg's comment on Crane's *The Red Badge of Courage*: "a book and an author utterly without merit." [9]

Browne died in 1913, and his son Waldo R. Browne became editor of the *Dial*, with Charles Leonard Moore as an associate; and the same policies which the paper had pursued for a generation were continued. But in 1916 there was a reorganization, Martyn Johnson becoming president of the Dial Publishing Company and C. J. Masseck, professor of English at Washington University, editor; then in the latter part of the same year the journal was moved to New York. George Bernard Donlin was now made editor, first with Travis Hoke as associate, and later with Harold E. Stearns. A long list of "contributing editors" was printed, including Conrad Aiken, Randolph Bourne, Van Wyck Brooks, Padraic Colum, and John Macy.

This was indeed a transformation. Browne's name was still carried as "founder," but Browne would not have been recognized now. "The good old *Dial* since it left Chicago has hardly been itself," sighed the *Bulletin of Bibliography*.[10] The fact is that it had suddenly emerged into the light of the modern day. The newer schools were welcomed; originality was praised. Foreign literature, the arts, and public affairs found their way into pages once sacred to the classics and their imitators. Early

[6] *Dial*, VII, 275 (April 1888). [8] *Dial*, XVI, 353 (June 16, 1894).
[7] *Dial*, II, 219 (January 1882). [9] *Dial*, XX, 227 (April 16, 1896).
[10] *Bulletin of Bibliography*, XI, 2 (January–April 1920).

in 1918 H. M. Kallen, a "contributing editor," wrote for the *Dial* a significant series on "The Structure of a Lasting Peace."

These were exciting times, and the young men who conducted the journal were gradually drawn off from literature to public affairs. A new staff committed to a mission of leadership in world reconstruction took charge of the *Dial* in October 1918, consisting of Donlin, Stearns, Clarence Britten, and Scofield Thayer, with three additional members "in charge of Reconstruction Program" — John Dewey, Thorstein Veblen, and Helen Marot. Of real distinction and significance were such series as that by Dewey on the League of Nations and Veblen's "The Modern Point of View and the New Order." Other important contributors were Harold J. Laski, Charles A. Beard, Norman Angell, Robert Morss Lovett, and Gilbert Seldes. The *Dial* became a journal of opinion, radical in the older sense of that word. It rapidly mounted to a circulation of 10,000. It would have been made a weekly (as it doubtless should have been) but for the scarcity of paper caused by the war. But there were staff difficulties, growing pains, financial crises; and in November 1919 Scofield Thayer, who had left the *Dial* ten months before, returned to become its editor and to change it into a very handsome octavo monthly of modern letters and arts. At that time Thayer and J. S. Watson, Jr., purchased the controlling interest from Martyn Johnson, retaining it to the end.[11]

And now it became the spokesman for all that was modern in these fields. The leaders of all the new movements were found in its pages; there were reproductions of modernistic drawings and paintings and sculpture by Cézanne, Matisse, Epstein, and many others; lively music, art, and book departments were important features. Letters were printed from various foreign centers of activity in the arts: Paul Morand wrote from Paris, James Stephens from Dublin, T. S. Eliot from London, Thomas Mann from Berlin, and so on. This correspondence and the many contributors from abroad gave the *Dial* an international aspect.

It was definitely critical in spirit, and it had something of the review about it; but it was primarily a literary magazine, containing fiction, poetry, drama, and essays. To name the authors who appeared in the *Dial* would be calling the roll of all the more

[11] Letter from Mr. Thayer.

important of the newer writers of that yeasty era, as well as many of the older and long established men of letters who were sympathetic with modern movements. Among prose writers were Sherwood Anderson, Waldo Frank, George Santayana, A. E. Coppard, D. H. Lawrence, George Moore, Anatole France, Gerhardt Hauptmann, Johan Bojer, and Manuel Komroff. Among the poets were William Butler Yeats, Edwin Arlington Robinson, Amy Lowell, and Edna St. Vincent Millay, as well as T. S. Eliot, Ezra Pound, E. E. Cummings, and Gertrude Stein. Perhaps the magazine's greatest sensation was scored by Anderson's serialized *Many Marriages* in 1922–23. Thomas Mann's *Death in Venice* appeared in 1924, as did Jules Romain's *Lucienne*. Rémy de Gourmont's epigrams, called "Dust for Sparrows" and translated by Ezra Pound, appeared serially in 1920–21. Parts of Oswald Spengler's *The Decline of the West* were printed in 1924–25. Bunin's "Gentleman from San Francisco" appeared in the number for January 1922.

For the last four years of the magazine, Marianne Moore was editor and Scofield Thayer "adviser." Gilbert Seldes was associate editor 1920–25. Kenneth Burke, Stewart Mitchell, and Alyse Gregory were also identified with the editorship at various times.

The *Dial* of 1920–29 was so fully representative of certain points of view that it seems a pity it could not have continued. Like so many other magazines that seemed to deserve long life, it died of inadequate circulation. It was always beautifully printed and sold for $5.00 a year.

Looking at the whole career of the *Dial*, we see that it was divided into three parts — its life as a conservative journal of literary criticism, 1880–1916; a brief period as a radical journal of opinion, 1916–19; and a ten years' picnic as a literary, artistic, and critical organ of modernism, 1920–29. Has any other American periodical so well represented the scholarly and conservative point of view in literary criticism as the *Dial* in its first phase? Or did any editorial staff present fundamental principles in a crisis more forcefully than the Dewey-Veblen-Bourne combination in its second phase? Or did any periodical so perfectly adumbrate the whole after-the-war state of the arts as the last *Dial*? In all three periods it was an unquestioned leader.

THE CHAUTAUQUAN [1]

B Y 1880 the Chautauqua Literary and Scientific Circle had enrolled in its reading groups many thousands of ambitious students.[2] For four years it had been served by the *Assembly Herald*, which was published as a daily for the three weeks of the August "Assembly" at Chautauqua, New York, in 1876 and 1877; then in the next two "Assemblies" it was a monthly with a daily edition. It was a folio of newspaper size and contained the addresses delivered by the notable speakers who appeared at the great gatherings on the shore of Chautauqua Lake. The editors and publishers of the paper were Theodore L. Flood, a former Methodist minister, and Milton Bailey.

But Flood conceived the idea of publishing a monthly magazine which should be tied in with the prescribed reading courses of the Chautauqua Literary and Scientific Circle, the yearly subscription price to be included in the student's fee. Accordingly,

---

[1] TITLE: *The Chautauquan*. Subtitles: (1) *A Monthly Magazine Devoted to the Promotion of True Culture, Organ of the Chautauquan Literary and Scientific Circle*, 1880–89; (2) *A Monthly Magazine*, 1889–99; (3) *A Magazine for Self-Education*, 1900–02; (4) *Issued Monthly with Illustrations*, 1903–13; (5) *A Weekly Newsmagazine*, 1913–14.

FIRST ISSUE: October 1880. (There was a preliminary number in September 1880). LAST ISSUE: May 23, 1914.

PERIODICITY: Monthly except August and September, 1880–89; monthly, 1890–May 1913; weekly, June 1913–May 23, 1914. I–IX, annual volumes (October–July), 1880–July 1889; X–XXIX (New Series, I–XX), semiannual volumes, October 1889–September 1899; XXX–XXXVI, semiannual volumes, October 1899–March 1903; XXXVII, April–August 1903; XXXVIII–XLIII, semiannual volumes, September 1903–August 1906; XLIV–LXX, quarterly volumes, September 1906–May 1913; LXXI, June 7–August 23, 1913; LXXII, September 6, 1913–May 23, 1914. The last two volumes were paged consecutively.

PUBLISHERS: Theodore L. Flood, Meadville, Pennsylvania, 1880–1899; Chautauqua Press, 1899–1914 (at Cleveland, 1899–1902; Springfield, Ohio, 1902–04; Chautauqua, New York, 1904–14).

EDITORS: Theodore L. Flood, 1880–99; Frank Chapin Bray, 1899–1914.

INDEXES: *Poole's, Poole's Abridged, Readers' Guide, Annual Library Index, Cumulative Index, Review of Reviews Index, Engineering Index, Dramatic Index*.

[2] See p. 173.

the new monthly appeared in octavo form in the fall of 1880. The first number was printed by Bailey at Jamestown, New York; but Flood, with the assistance of George E. Vincent, son of the founder of Chautauqua, financed the purchase of a printing plant at Meadville, Pennsylvania,[3] which soon became the *Chautauquan's* permanent home.

Volume One, Number One, opens with "Required Reading: History of the World," written by the Reverend Richard Wheatley, of New York. It begins with the sixth day of the Creation — the sixth because man was made on that day, and he immediately began to make history. Readers were assured on the first page that the fashioning of Eve out of Adam's rib was intended to show her natural subordination to him.[4] The first volume of the *Chautauquan* was much occupied with this history; but it also contained lectures delivered at Chautauqua, Sunday school helps, and readings in other courses — in science, theology, and standard authors. John H. Vincent conducted a department, and there was a section devoted to current events. By the end of the eighties, however, the magazine was printing such important writers as J. P. Mahaffy, H. B. Adams, John Burroughs, and H. H. Boyesen. Courses by W. T. Harris, Arthur Gilman, E. E. Hale, and others appeared serially. The *Chautauquan* had one great advantage over all other general magazines: it could use a strong and successful self-culture organization to draw into its net all — or nearly all — the big fish in the intellectual sea. Its table of contents soon became a distinguished roll call, and it paid the central association $1,400 a month for the articles it used for required reading. Its own subscription price was $1.50 a year.

But its great disadvantage was, of course, this very alliance, which might have made it a dry and dreary magazine indeed. But Flood realized the danger and proceeded to give more and more variety to the contents, with less space to the required readings. There was always a religious tinge and sometimes much more than a tinge — a dye. Homer's polytheism was apologized for in 1881; prohibition was stoutly supported; there was a good deal of Methodism, probably more or less un-

[3] *Review of Reviews*, IV, 87 (August 1891).
[4] *Chautauquan*, I, 1 (October 1880).

conscious. Clergymen and reformers were numerous in the magazine's pages.

In the fall of 1889 a radical change was made in the *Chautauquan*. It enlarged its page and raised its price to $2.00. It discontinued the long serials for required reading and introduced more articles of literary criticism, travel, politics, science, art, history, and biography. It even printed a little fiction. It began its "Woman's Council Table," containing short pieces relating to women's activities, frequently by famous women. Its department of "Current History and Opinion" gave excerpts from editorials of leading newspapers. But with all this miscellany, the *Chautauquan* still remained the official organ of the Chautauqua Literary and Scientific Circle. Its articles were required reading for students enrolled, and it printed questions on the courses, news of local circles and summer assemblies, and Bishop Vincent's selected Sunday readings.

The *Review of Reviews* called the new *Chautauquan* "one of the chief educational publications of the world . . . an organ without sacrifice of freedom." [5] Its range of topics was indeed remarkable, and its list of contributors impressive. In one number (January 1891) it printed two future presidents of the United States — Theodore Roosevelt and Woodrow Wilson — together with Edward A. Freeman, G. P. Fisher, J. C. Ridpath, Sarah Orne Jewett, Harriet Prescott Spofford, and so on. But it was still too didactic. It was printed for readers who were deadly serious in their passion for information; and while there was some graceful writing, the classes were in session from one end of the magazine to the other, and it was a long time until recess.

In 1899 Flood relinquished ownership and editorship together, saying, "My monument will be the *Chautauquan*: I ask no loftier fame." [6] The ownership passed to the central association, and the Chautauqua Press became the publisher. Frank Chapin Bray, a journalist trained from youth in Chautauqua ways,[7] was made editor. It was now less a general magazine and more an organ, though there were more illustrations, especially

[5] *Review of Reviews*, IV, 87 (August 1891).
[6] *Chautauquan*, XXIX, 326 (July 1899).
[7] Jesse L. Hurlbut, *The Story of Chautauqua* (New York, 1921), p. 274.

for art and travel articles. Social and civic reform, book reviews, news of assemblies, and current events were important.
Bray was a traveler and was interested especially in the East.
His Constantinople series was used for leading articles through
many issues — until one is tempted to complain that there is too
little yeast and too much East in the periodical.

The size was changed to duodecimo in 1906, and the contents
were limited chiefly to Chautauqua announcements and news.
The place of publication was changed to Chautauqua, New
York. The Chautauqua Literary and Scientific Circle gradually
declined in its countrywide enrollment until at length there
seemed to be little need for the magazine. June 7, 1913, it was
transformed into "a weekly newsmagazine," quarto, of current
events; but after a year of this experiment it was absorbed by
the *Independent*.

The old files of the *Chautauquan* contain some valuable material. It was a unique periodical, and it fulfilled its special
function well.

THE CRITIC [1]

JEAN and Joe start a paper here next Saturday," wrote Richard Watson Gilder, then editor of the *Century*, to a friend of the family, in January 1881. "It is to be called the *Critic*. It is a wild thing to do, but they have had . . . lots of encouragement." [2] To begin a periodical is doubtless always "a wild thing to do," and in this instance the more so because of slender resources. But Jeannette and Joseph Gilder had courage and industry; and Jeannette, who had been literary editor for the *New York Herald* and other papers, was experienced in the trade of reviewing.

Its departments of reviews, the drama, fine arts, and news notes were not all of the *Critic* in its early numbers, however. Walt Whitman soon became a leading contributor, his series "How I Get Around at Sixty, and Take Notes" beginning in the first volume. A few of Whitman's poems were published, but most of his contributions to the *Critic* were in prose and included notes on Emerson, Tennyson, Poe, Longfellow, Shakespeare, the Bible as poetry, "Walt Whitman in Camden" (signed "George Selwyn"),[3] and so on. An early discovery was Joel Chandler Harris, who contributed many "Nights with Uncle

---

[1] TITLES: (1) *The Critic*, 1881–83, July 1884–1904, 1906; (2) *The Critic and Good Literature*, January–June 1884; *The Critic and Literary World*, 1905.

FIRST ISSUE: January 15, 1881. LAST ISSUE: September 1906.

PERIODICITY: Biweekly, 1881–82; weekly, 1883–June 1898 (except combination issue, July–August 1898). [First Series], I–III, annual volumes, 1881–83; New Series, I–XXIX (IV–XXXII), semiannual volumes, 1884–June 1898; XXXIII–XLVIII, semiannual volumes, July 1898–June 1906; XLIX, July, August, September 1906.

PUBLISHERS: J. L. and J. B. Gilder, January–March 1881; The Critic Printing & Publishing Company, March 1881–January 1884; Good Literature Publishing Company, February–December 1884; The Critic Company, 1885–98; G. P. Putnam & Company, 1899–1906.

EDITOR: Jeannette L. Gilder, 1881–1906 (with Joseph B. Gilder, 1881–1901).

INDEXES: *Poole's, Poole's Abridged, Annual Library Index, Readers' Guide, Cumulative Index, Review of Reviews Index, Contents-Subject Index, A. L. A. Portrait Index.*

[2] Rosamund Gilder, *Letters of Richard Watson Gilder* (Boston, 1916), p. 106.

[3] See *Critic Pamphlet No. 2* for proof of Whitman's authorship of "Walt Whitman in Camden," as printed in the *Critic* February 28, 1885. "One of the

Remus" to the first volume — the first of these papers to be published outside of Atlanta.[4] Other writers represented were Stedman, Stoddard, "H. H.," Emma Lazarus, Julia Ward Howe, Edith M. Thomas, and James Lane Allen. These contributed chiefly poetry, except Allen, whose pleasant essays attracted considerable attention; and most of them continued to write for the *Critic* throughout its life.

But most important, of course, was the book reviewing. It was usually bright, incisive, and impartial, with a tendency to be conservative in judgments and not very profound. The two editors did much of it, but James Herbert Morse helped them from the first; and they gradually built up an able staff of reviewers which included such specialists and scholars as James A. Harrison, Tudor Jenks, G. Stanley Lee, W. J. Rolfe, N. S. Shaler, W. I. Fletcher, Charles DeKay, and J. Ranken Towse. Other less frequent contributors were Thomas Bailey Aldrich, Richard Watson Gilder, Edward Everett Hale, Noah Brooks, and Thomas R. Lounsbury.

Though it disclaimed any "national bias," there is discoverable in the *Critic's* pages a tendency to be unusually severe upon English authors; and it remarked casually in 1882: "We have poets whose fame does not yield to that of Tennyson and Morris; we have novelists whose merit is as great as that of Messrs. Hardy, Black, and Blackmore."[5] No specification is advanced. Moreover, the *Critic* was plainly not saddened as much as it should have been by the case of plagiarism which one of its contributors found against Hardy's *Trumpet Major*, especially in view of the fact that the borrowing was from an American book.[6] But in spite of the anti-British attitude, there was a considerable amount of English reprinted material in the *Critic* during the years 1884 and 1885, though the eclectic feature grew less thereafter. Little or no attention was given to continental literature.

---

things of which I am most proud," wrote Miss Gilder later, "is that the *Critic* was the first publication of its class to invite Walt Whitman to contribute to its pages." Charles N. Elliot, *Walt Whitman as Man, Poet, and Friend* (Boston, 1915), p. 97.

[4] Julia C. Harris, *Life and Letters of Joel Chandler Harris* (Boston, 1918), p. 167.

[5] *Critic*, II, 72 (March 11, 1882).

[6] *Ibid.*, II, 25, 55 (January 28, 1882). The alleged plagiarism was from Longstreet's *Georgia Scenes*.

Special numbers were sometimes printed — an admirable issue on the centenary of Irving's birth, one on Lowell's seventieth birthday, one on Tennyson's death, and so on. Drama, music, and the fine arts were well represented, except in the middle eighties, when the departments devoted to them either deteriorated or lapsed for a time. A Shakespeareana section was conducted by W. J. Rolfe in the nineties. Notes upon current magazines continued throughout. Special Boston correspondence, by William H. Rideing, Alexander Young, and Charles E. N. Wingate, successively, began in 1886; and about the same time a London letter written first by L. B. Walford and later by Arthur Waugh and Clement K. Shorter. When the Columbian Exposition in Chicago began, the *Critic* inaugurated a Chicago letter on art and literature by Lucy Monroe which continued for some time. A series of *American Authors at Home* was started in 1885 and ran through several volumes.

Popular fads in literature and society were freely commented upon in the *Critic*. The popularity of Amélie Rives's *The Quick and the Dead,* which the *Critic* was inclined to consider a *succès du scandale*; the bicycle craze, to which a special number was devoted; the popular esteem for E. P. Roe's innocuous novels; the Kipling madness, when it seemed that all writers wished "to kipple"; and the even more virulent *Trilby* rage, during which the *Critic* maintained a department of "Trilbyana" — all these phases of the passing show were chronicled in our journal.

It was the *Critic* which suggested, April 24, 1889, that the Washington Memorial Arch, which had been constructed in wood for the Centennial, be reproduced in marble. This, with no little help from the *Critic* in the campaign for funds, was done, and the arch finished in 1892. The *Critic* was also active in the campaign to free art products from tariff restrictions.

In 1898 the magazine was purchased by the Putnams, who retained the former editors but adopted monthly publication and reduced the page to the usual size for monthlies of the time — octavo. It was resolved to print "less matter for the sake of the record . . . a greater number and variety of essays and special articles." [7] In short, the *Critic* was to become more magazinish. A "Bookbuyers' Guide," which consisted of many very brief

[7] *Critic*, XXXIII, 3 (July 1898).

reviews left more room for the longer articles and poetry.
Rupert Hughes, Gelett Burgess, William Archer, Andrew Lang,
and others were added to the roll of contributors. Charles
Hemstreet's *Literary Landmarks of New York* and F. B. Sanborn's *A Concord Notebook* were among the later serials. Most
attractive of the changes of 1898 was the addition of illustrations. The *Critic* had begun by using a portrait on wood in each
issue, but the cuts were mediocre and were soon discontinued.
Now with the advent of halftones and the willingness of publishers to furnish plates freely for notices of their own books,
illustration had become much simpler.

Another promise made by the publishers in 1898 was to give
more space to "The Lounger." This was a department of book
chat written by Miss Gilder and displaying the charms of her
mind and manner at their best. It henceforth led off each issue.
During the last five years of the *Critic*, Miss Gilder was sole
editor; her brother, who had been gradually relinquishing his
part of the work for some time, retired at the end of 1901.

In October 1906 the *Critic* was merged with a revival of *Putnam's Monthly* under the name *Putnam's Monthly and The
Critic*. Miss Gilder was retained as editor, and her "Lounger"
was a department of the new magazine. Speaking of the *Critic*,
Putnam's took occasion to say: "The list of its contributors during the quarter century of its existence includes most of the best
known names of recent English literature"; and again, "The
Critic has always stood for good literature." [8] To which deserved encomia we may fittingly add that of Edmund Clarence
Stedman in a letter to the editors: "You maintain a high and
impartial standard of criticism, and have brought out the talent
of new and excellent writers." [9]

The *Critic* was never, however, a money-maker. Its circulation remained in the neighborhood of 5,000 during most of its
life. It absorbed *Good Literature* in 1884 and the *Literary
World* in 1905. Its subscription rate was only $3.00, and its
advertising was light. That it was maintained for so long a time
on a comparatively high plane was owing to the industry and
persistence of Jeannette Gilder.

[8] *Putnam's Monthly and The Critic*, I, 82 (October 1906).
[9] *Critic*, X, 278 (May 28, 1887).

JUDGE [1]

IN 1881 the comic weekly *Puck* had made a conspicuous success, under the management of Keppler and Schwarzmann; but certain quarrels and personal disagreements had broken out among the art staff. In the summer and fall of 1881 these troubles came to a head, and a group of artists headed by James Albert Wales seceded to found *Judge*, or, as it was first called, *The Judge*. Wales himself was an able caricaturist. He brought with him to the new paper Livingston Hopkins, who could write as well as draw; Thomas Worth, who had done the "Darktown" Negro travesties for Currier & Ives and was already a veteran of the comic press; Frank Beard, another writer-artist; E. W. Kemble, a second illustrator of Negro life, but more sympathetic than Worth; and "Chip," a son of Frank Bellew. Grant E. Hamilton, who was to be one of the *Judge's* greatest political cartoonists for many years, apparently deserted *Puck* for *Judge* some little time after the latter had made its beginning.

It was on October 29, 1881, that *The Judge* first donned wig and robes and surveyed the world from his lofty bench. A sixteen-page quarto with *Puck*-like chromolithographs for covers and for center spread, it sold for a dime a number. Frank Tousey, a successful publisher of cheap papers and a partner in the powerful American News Company, was associated with Wales in the ownership and business management of the Judge Company.

[1] TITLES: *The Judge*, 1881–85, 1938–current; *Judge*, 1886–1937.
FIRST ISSUE: October 29, 1881. Current.
PERIODICITY: Weekly, 1881–1931; monthly, 1932–current. Annual volumes.
PUBLISHERS: Judge Company, 1881–1909; Leslie-Judge Company, 1910–27; Judge Publishing Company, 1927–31; Judge Magazine, Inc., 1932–current. All in New York.
EDITORS: J. A. Wales, 1881–85; I. M. Gregory, 1886–1901; Henry Tyrrell, 1901–07; Burges Johnson, 1908; James Melvin Lee, 1909–12; Carleton G. Garretson, 1912–17; Dougles H. Cooke, 1922–27; Norman Anthony, 1927–28; Jack Shuttleworth, 1929–36, 1937–38; Monte Bourjaily, 1936–37; Robert T. Gebler, 1938–current.
REFERENCE: *American News Trade Journal*, June 1920, pp. 13 ff.

"I have started this paper for fun," declared the *Judge* in the opening editorial. "Money is no object. Let sordid souls seek that; I have got all I want." [2] It was a brave but reckless gesture, though typical enough of the early issues. And the paper flourished at first. It was a good deal like *Puck*, with the same bold, free satire, the same good drawing, and the same handsome format. But the trouble was that it was too much like *Puck* to win a place in competition with that irrepressible youngster, and after a year or two it fell off; money became a very needful and rare "object." His Honor was about to quit the bench, when Albert H. Smyth, Philadelphia author, traveler, and educator, and Harry Hart, a wealthy young Philadelphian, took it over. They did not move it from its native New York, and they put their Philadelphia money into it to no avail; lively though it was in its quips on the theater, politics, and the arts, from a circulation standpoint *Judge* languished.

In 1884 came the great Blaine-Cleveland contest in which *Puck* did spectacular work in its onslaughts upon Blaine. This phenomenon opened the eyes of Republican leaders to the effectiveness of a comic paper in a political campaign. And the next year appeared W. J. Arkell, "a young man of unusual force and enterprise," [3] to reorganize the Judge Company with substantial G. O. P. aid. He took as editor Isaac M. Gregory, who had been editor of the *Elmira Gazette and Free Press*, in New York state. He lured Bernard Gillam, chief cartoonist (after Keppler) for *Puck*, by a partnership in the company; and he hired Eugene Zimmerman, another *Puck* artist with a remarkable gift for grotesquerie. The leading cartoons were now political; Gillam, Hamilton, and Zimmerman got in many a telling blow against the Democratic administration in the smashing double-page colored spreads. Tammany was a special object of its attacks. Writing in *Judge* was anonymous. The theatrical reviews were generally severe; *Judge* was inclined to hit all heads in drama, literature, journalism, society. Anthony Comstock was a bête noire, Grover Cleveland a clown.

But circulation and advertising boomed; the advertising rev-

[2] *Judge*, October 29, 1881, p. 2.
[3] *American News Trade Journal*, June 1920, p. 13.

enue for the Christmas number in 1887 ran to $7,000,[4] and
the circulation gradually increased from a few thousand to
50,000 in the early nineties. The Harrison campaign in 1888,
though comparatively dull, was a circulation stimulant for
Judge. In 1887 the Judge Company began *Judge's Library:
A Monthly Magazine of Fun*,[5] and in 1890 *Judge's Quarterly*.[6]
Frank Leslie's Illustrated Newspaper was purchased by the
Judge Company in 1891.

In the campaign of 1892 Grant Hamilton and Bernard and
F. Victor Gillam drew most of the political cartoons; but it
was Hamilton who made the great hit of the McKinley-Bryan
campaign in 1896. He it was who set up the "full dinner pail"
as the Republican symbol at that time. We are told that

It was declared by William McKinley, as well as by his manager
Mark Hanna, that the series of *Judge* cartoons originated by Grant E.
Hamilton in that campaign, based on the idea of "the full dinner
pail," was the greatest single factor in McKinley's election.[7]

After this campaign the circulation of *Judge* went up to
85,000, where it remained until the financial disturbances of
1907. John A. Schleicher, who had for some years been editor
of *Leslie's Weekly*, became chief owner of the Judge Company
in 1898, supplanting Arkell.

Among the artists enlisted after the turn of the century were
Art Young, E. Flohri, Penrhyn Stanlaws, James Montgomery
Flagg, and R. F. Outcault. The magazine in these years was
mildly amusing, with a modicum of rather gentle social satire,
some good anecdotes, and pictures in many styles. Occasionally the light verse, by such writers as W. J. Lampton, W. D.
Nesbit, S. E. Kiser, and R. K. Munkittrick, was excellent. The
chromolithographic political cartoons continued as in the nineties; battle was waged against all "trust-busters" and against
the perennial ogre Bryan.

[4] *Journalist*, December 10, 1887, p. 3.

[5] Each number was devoted to a single topic, as the hired girl, married life,
"Uncle Josh," etc. It reached a circulation of 100,000 in 1898, but later de-
clined greatly. It was changed to the *Magazine of Fun* in 1913 and ended in
June 1915. The early numbers were without dates. It was continued by
Film Fun.

[6] Continued until 1913. Its price was twenty-five cents a number, and it
reached a circulation of 60,000 in 1899.

[7] *American News Trade Journal*, June 1920, p. 13.

In 1910 there was a reorganization of the publication company, now called the Leslie-Judge Company. The G. O. P. partnership was dissolved; politics no longer rested on the paper like an incubus. The page became somewhat smaller, the contents somewhat brighter. James Melvin Lee came to the editorship, but left it after two or three years to head the School of Journalism at New York University, giving place to Carleton Garretson. Carolyn Wells, Ellis Parker Butler, Homer Croy, and G. H. Jessop appeared in *Judge* pages. By 1912 the 100,000 mark was reached in circulation. Ever since the late nineties, *Judge* had been well ahead of *Life*; now it forged ahead of *Puck*, which gave up the struggle in 1918.

Another shake-up came in 1922, when Douglas H. Cooke became editor and publisher and Norman Anthony, a free-lance artist, became managing editor. *Leslie's Weekly* was merged with *Judge*, which was made more than a comic; it became a departmentalized magazine. William Allen White wrote its editorials until he tired of long-distance editing after a few months; Walter Prichard Eaton did book reviews; Heywood Broun edited a sports department; Ruth Hale handled movies; and George Jean Nathan wrote on the theater. Radios and automobiles also had their sections. The wit and humor and art were all far smarter than in the years before the Great War had changed the aspect of things. John Held, Jr., and W. E. Hill were among the more prominent comic artists. Ring Lardner was a star performer. The price was increased to fifteen cents a number, but the circulation rose to 250,000 in 1923.

Came the years of crossword puzzles and of the crusade against prohibition — two games in which *Judge* proceeded to join with zest. Some of the departments of 1922 were dropped, but Nathan was still "Judging the Shows," and William Norris Houghton was "Judging the Movies."

Comic pictures of the later models and light brevities by men like S. J. Perelman, Jefferson Machamer, William Gropper, Don Herold, and Milt Gross are characteristic of the more recent *Judge*. Cynical disillusion accepted with a smile was the mood for some years. Contract bridge was an important feature; Sidney S. Lenz was the expert until displaced by Philip Hal Sims and later by others.

It was not easy for *Judge* to be funny during the depression of the thirties. Its price was reduced to the older ten-cent rate; but circulation did not respond, and in 1932 it became a monthly at fifteen cents a number. Four years later it bought the subscription list and "the humorous tradition and features" of its old rival *Life* from Time, Inc., which kept merely the name for its own new picture magazine. At the same time Monte Bourjaily, a feature syndicate manager, purchased *Judge* from Kable Brothers, its printers, who had held financial control for some years. Bourjaily was publisher and editor for just a year, after which he was succeeded by Harry Newman, promoter and former publisher of the journalists' trade paper, the *Fourth Estate*.

THE CONTINENT [1]

ALBION W. TOURGÉE, author of a best-selling novel telling of his experiences as a carpetbagger in the South under the title *A Fool's Errand, by One of the Fools*, engaged in February 1882 in a venture which proved more disastrous to him than that "errand" of reconstruction days. In brief, he started a magazine. He and Robert S. Davis, a Philadelphian of means, organized a $150,000 corporation in which they were the chief stockholders to finance what they confidently expected to make one of the best and most profitable periodicals in America. Several public men, friends of Judge Tourgée, bought shares: among others, former President Grant put in $1,000. Associated with Tourgée and Davis in the management was Dr. Daniel G. Brinton, editor and owner of the Philadelphia *Medical and Surgical Reporter* and an ethnologist of some fame. C. L. Norton was managing editor.

The new journal was called *Our Continent*. It was a weekly of sixteen well-printed small folio pages, excellently illustrated by such distinguished artists as Will H. Low, W. T. Smedley, Joseph Pennell, Howard Pyle, Kenyon Cox, Frank Bellew, and A. B. Frost. And this roll of illustrators was equaled by a remarkable galaxy of writers of articles, fiction, and verse. Tourgée, who was a man of great projects, planned to make *Our Continent* at once the equal of the best monthly magazines in quality, and to win a greater popularity than any of them by weekly publication. An unusual staff was assembled — Donald G. Mitchell in charge of art, Kate Field in a dressmak-

[1] TITLES: (1) *Our Continent*, 1882; (2) *The Continent*, 1883–84.

FIRST ISSUE: February 15, 1882. LAST ISSUE: August 13, 1884.

PERIODICITY: Weekly. I, February 15–July 5, 1882; III–V, regular semi-annual volumes, July 12, 1882–June 25, 1884; VI, July 2–August 13, 1884.

PUBLISHERS: A. W. Tourgée, Daniel G. Brinton, and Robert S. Davis, Philadelphia, 1882; A. W. Tourgée, 1882–84 (Philadelphia, 1882–83; New York, 1883–84).

EDITOR: Albion Winegar Tourgée.

REFERENCE: Roy F. Dibble, *Albion W. Tourgée* (New York, 1921), Chapter IV.

ing department, Louise Chandler Moulton in a society section, Max Adeler for humor, and Helen Campbell editing household notes. All were stars; but with the exception of Adeler, they seem not to have been well cast in these rather humble parts. Leading contributors, besides the editors, were E. P. Roe, J. T. Trowbridge, William M. Baker, Noah Porter, and Joel Chandler Harris — all of whom were in the first number; and Julian Hawthorne, Harriet Beecher Stowe, Edward Everett Hale, George H. Boker, Rebecca Harding Davis, Sarah Orne Jewett, Charles W. Eliot, Richard T. Ely, and so on. It was a fine list, and the contents were varied and attractive. In three days after the first issue was out, 58,000 copies of it had been sold. Tourgée told his wife to write in her diary that he expected to have $100,000 in the bank in a year's time.

But it was soon evident that the expense of such a paper was tremendous, and that the $4.00 subscriptions were not going to pour in with the spontaneity and in the quantity that had been hoped for. Davis became frightened and sold out to Tourgée for $10,000 after only a few months, and with him went Brinton and some of the departmental editors. The format was changed to a thirty-two page quarto, the name simplified to the *Continent*, and Judge and Mrs. Tourgée worked harder than ever to build their great weekly magazine. Tourgée's own novel, *Hot Ploughshares*, a story of the antislavery crusade, was serialized; other serials were by Rhoda Broughton and Marion Harland. Felix Oswald had a series on the national parks, famous educators talked shop in another series, there were "Uncle Remus" and Orpheus C. Kerr sketches. In politics the journal had declared for an independent policy; but the editor could not restrain vigorous expression of his strong opinions in defense of the Negro, in support of Republican policies, in opposition to alcohol, and against the K. K. K.

In December 1883 the *Continent* moved to New York, but found there no more success than at Philadelphia. Circulation dropped to about 4,000 in 1884, and the paper was discontinued in August, in the midst of the Blaine-Cleveland campaign. Politically, Tourgée may have been glad to be out of it, for he did not like Blaine, and he disapproved of party irregularity, so that he seemed rather bewildered. But financially it was a bad blow. Grant lost his $1,000,[2] but Tourgée lost all of the $60,000 he had realized from his novels and had besides been forced to mortgage his home estate and the future sale of his published books.[3]

Tourgée's own explanation of the *débâcle* is found in one of his letters:

A very rich man induced me in 1881 to engage with him in publishing the *Continent* magazine. When his extravagance and pretence had swamped what ought to have been a success, he dug out and I very foolishly undertook to resuscitate the corpse. Had I been brave enough to cut expenses down to bed-rock, I should have succeeded. But I was not.[4]

[2] Dibble, *op. cit.*, p. 90.
[3] *Ibid.*
[4] *Ibid.*

CHRONOLOGICAL LIST

CHRONOLOGICAL LIST

THIS list of periodicals founded 1865-1884 gives only the more important changes in title and in place of publication. It includes only periodicals mentioned in the text. End-dates are given following places of publication. A part of the title carried through only part of the file is noted, when important, within parentheses.

1865

American Journal of Conchology. Philadelphia. 1872.
American Miscellany. Boston. 1874.
Ave Maria. Notre Dame (Indiana). Current.
Baltimore Underwriter and National Agent. 1930.
Bistoury. Elmira (New York). 1885.
Carriage Monthly, later *Motor Vehicle Monthly.* Philadelphia. 1930.
Catholic World. New York. Current.
Commercial and Financial Chronicle. Current.
Demorest's Monthly Magazine. New York. 1899.
Evangelist. Oskaloosa (Iowa), Chicago. 1882.
Frank Leslie's Chimney Corner. New York. 1885.
Freedmen's Record. Boston. 1873.
Gazlay's Pacific Monthly. New York. 1865(?).
Hahnemannian Monthly. Philadelphia. Current.
Heraldic Journal. Boston. 1868.
Hours at Home. New York. 1870.
Little Corporal. Chicago. 1875.
Little Joker. New York. 1866.
Mrs. Grundy. New York. 1865.
Nation. New York. Current.
National Baptist. Philadelphia. 1894.
New Age. San Francisco. 1895.
New England Farmer. Boston. 1915.
New York Medical Journal (and Record), later *Medical Record.* Current.
Odd Fellows' Companion. Columbus. 1882.
Orpheus. Boston. 1880.
Our Young Folks. Boston. 1873.
Petroleum Gazette and Scientific Journal. Cincinnati. 1865.
Phunniest of Awl. New York. 1865.
Phunniest of Phun. New York. 1867.
Puck: the Pacific Pictorial. San Francisco. 1866.
Radical. Boston. 1872.
(Religio-) Philosophical Journal. Chicago, San Francisco. 1905.
Saturday Night. Philadelphia. 1902.

Scott's Monthly. Atlanta. 1869.
Stage. New York. 1880.
Tobacco Leaf. New York. Current.
Traveler's Record. Hartford. 1906.
Turf, Field and Farm. New York. 1903.
Western Watchman. St. Louis. 1934.

1866

American Freedman. New York. 1869.
American Journal of Mining, later *Engineering and Mining Journal.* New
    York. Current.
American Journal of Numismatics. Boston. 1919.
American (later *United States*) *Law Review.* Boston, St. Louis, New York.
    Current.
American Stock Journal. Parkesburg (Pennsylvania). 1872.
Banking and Insurance Chronicle, later *Economic World.* 1926.
Baptist Record. St. Louis. 1868.
Baptist Visitor. Baltimore, etc. 1878.
Boston Journal of Chemistry, later *Popular Science.* 1902.
Bulletin of the American Iron and Steel Association. Philadelphia. 1912.
Catholic Standard (*and Times*). Philadelphia. Current.
(*Chicago*) *Mining Review* (*and Metallurgist*). 1907.
Children's Hour. Philadelphia. 1872.
Christian Witness. Columbus (Ohio). 1886.
Christian (*at*) *Work.* New York. 1926.
Crescent Monthly. New Orleans. 1867.
Demorest's Young America. New York. 1875.
Episcopal Methodist. Baltimore. 1894.
Esquimaux. San Francisco. 1867.
Every Saturday. Boston. 1874.
Fireside Companion. New York. 1907.
Frank Leslie's Pleasant Hours. New York. 1896.
Galaxy. New York. 1878.
Good Health. Battle Creek (Michigan). Current.
Gospel Advocate. Nashville. Current.
Harvard Advocate. Cambridge. Current.
Inventor's and Manufacturer's Gazette. Boston. 1886.
Journal of Applied Chemistry. New York, etc. 1875.
(*Juvenile*) *Instructor.* Salt Lake City. Current.
Land We Love. Baltimore. 1869.
Maine Normal, later *Maine Journal of Education.* Farmington, Portland.
    1874.
Medical Record. New York. 1923.
Messenger of the Sacred Heart. Woodstock (Maryland). 1909.
Midland Industrial Gazette. St. Louis. 1886.
Missouri Baptist, later *Central Baptist.* Palmyra (Missouri), Kansas City.
    1913.

National (Temperance) Advocate. New York. Current.
National Sunday School Teacher. Chicago. 1882.
New England Medical Gazette. Boston. 1918.
New York Musical Gazette. 1874.
Northwestern Chronicle. St. Paul, Minneapolis. 1936.
Pacific Churchman. San Francisco. Current.
Presbyterian. St. Louis. 1894.
Printers' Circular. Philadelphia. 1890.
Printing Gazette. Cleveland. 1875.
Richmond Eclectic, later *New Eclectic,* later *Southern Magazine.* Richmond, Baltimore. 1875.
Richmond (and Louisville) Medical Journal. 1911.
(Southwestern) Christian Advocate. New Orleans. Current.
Tailors' Review. New York. 1903.
Western Educational Review, later *Western.* St. Louis. 1881.
Western (later Benham's, Baldwin's) Musical Review. Indianapolis, Cincinnati. 1880.
Western Presbyterian. Danville (Kentucky). 1869.

1867

Advance. Chicago. 1917.
American Naturalist. Salem (Massachusetts), Philadelphia, Boston, New York. Current.
Apostolic Guide, later *Christian Guide.* Covington, Louisville. 1902.
Art Journal. Chicago. 1871.
Ball Players' Chronicle. New York. 1867.
Baptist Quarterly. Philadelphia. 1877.
Book Buyer, later *Lamp.* New York. 1918.
Burke's Weekly for Boys and Girls. Macon (Georgia). 1871.
Chicago Specimen. 1880.
Christian Index. Jackson (Tennessee). 1937.
Christian Standard and Home Journal. Cincinnati. 1906.
Church Union. Brooklyn. 1869.
College Courant. New Haven. 1874.
Ehrick's Fashion Quarterly. New York. 1887.
Farmers' Home Journal. Lexington (Kentucky), Louisville. 1932.
Farmers' Union, later *Farmers' Tribune.* Minneapolis. 1924.
Frank Leslie's Boys' and Girls' Weekly. New York. 1883.
Guardian Angel. New York. 1909.
Harper's Bazar. New York. Current.
Iron Trade Review, later *Steel.* Cleveland. Current.
Jolly Hoosier. Indianapolis. 1867.
Journal of Speculative Philosophy. St. Louis, New York. 1893.
Journal of the Telegraph. New York. 1914.
Keystone. Philadelphia. 1905.
Locomotive. Hartford. Current.
Ladies' Quarterly Report of Broadway Fashions. New York. ?

Loomis' Musical and Masonic Journal. New Haven. 1900.
Lyceum Banner. Chicago. 1872.
McGee's Illustrated Weekly. New York. 1882.
Mason's Coin and Stamp Collectors' Journal. Philadelphia. 1882.
Merry and Wise. New York. 1867.
New England Farmer (monthly). Boston. 1871.
New England Homestead. Springfield (Massachusetts). 1880.
Northern Magazine. Newark (New Jersey). 1868.
Oliver Optic's Magazine. Boston. 1875.
(Our Little Ones and) The Nursery. Boston. 1899.
Our Monthly. Clinton (South Carolina). Current.
People's Journal. Philadelphia. 1875.
Pittsburgh Quarterly Magazine. 1868.
Riverside Magazine for Young People. Boston. 1870.
Southern Review. Baltimore. 1879.
Southern Society. Baltimore. 1868.
Spiritual Republic. Chicago. 1870(?).
Sporting Times. Boston. 1886.
Standard. Chicago. 1920.
Star of Zion. Charlotte (North Carolina), etc. Current.
Twelve Times a Year. Louisville. 1871.
Utah Magazine. Salt Lake City. 1869.
Western Insurance Review. St. Louis. Current.
Western Jurist. Des Moines. 1873.
Western Soldiers' Friend, later *Gem of the West and Soldiers' Friend.*
　　Chicago. 1874.
Whitney's Musical Guest. Toledo. 1881.
Wood's Household Magazine. Newburgh (New York), New York. 1881.

1868

Aetna. Hartford. 1908.
Alaskan Herald. San Francisco. 1876.
Aldine (Press). New York. 1879.
American Brewer. New York. Current.
American Freemason. Cincinnati. 1870.
American Journal of Art, later *American Builder,* later *Builder and Wood-
　　worker.* Chicago. 1895.
American Journal of Education. St. Louis. 1920.
American Journal of Obstetrics. New York. 1919.
American Journal of Philately. New York. 1906.
Boneville Trumpet. Bridgeport (Connecticut). 1869.
Brunonian. Providence. 1898.
Cap and Gown. New York. 1873.
Chicagoan, later *Universe.* 1869.
Christian Cynosure. Chicago. Current.
Cincinnati Medical News. 1891.
Communist, later *Altruist.* Buffalo (Missouri), St. Louis. 1917.

Day's Doings. New York. 1876.
Dental Office and Laboratory. Philadelphia. 1908.
Dental Quarterly, later *Dental Office and Laboratory.* Philadelphia. 1908.
Dixie Farmer. Knoxville, Atlanta. 1882.
Free Methodist. Aurora (Illinois), Sycamore (Illinois), Chicago. 1935.
Fur, Fin and Feather. New York. 1891.
George P. Rowell and Company's Newspaper Reporter and Advertiser's Gazette, later *Woodcock's Printers' and Lithographers' Weekly Gazette and Newspaper Reporter.* New York. 1884.
Golden Censer. Albany. 1880.
Hearth and Home. New York. 1875.
Illustrated Chicago News. 1868.
Insurance Times. New York, Richmond. 1936.
Last Sensation. New York. 1868.
Legal News. St. Louis. 1925.
Leisure Hours. Pittsburgh. 1870.
Lippincott's (later *McBride's*) *Magazine.* Philadelphia, New York. 1916.
Manufacturers' Review and Industrial Record. New York. 1896.
Metropolitan (Fashions). New York. 1899(?).
News from the Spirit World. Chicago. 1870.
Northwestern (later *United States*) *Review.* Chicago, Philadelphia. Current.
Occident. San Francisco. 1900.
Odd Fellows' Talisman. Indianapolis. 1918.
Our Dumb Animals. Boston. Current.
Overland Monthly (and Out West Magazine). San Francisco. 1935.
Packard's Monthly. New York. 1870.
Plymouth Pulpit. New York. 1884.
Prang's Chromo. Boston. 1869.
Present Age. Chicago. 1872.
Putnam's Monthly Magazine. 1870.
Railway Review. Chicago. 1926.
Revolution. New York. 1872.
Sorosis. Chicago. 1869.
Southwestern Presbyterian. New Orleans. 1908.
Spectator. New York, Philadelphia. Current.
Stetson's Dime Illustrated. New York. 1868.
Sunday School Journal. Philadelphia. 1926.
Wag. Boston. 1868.
Week. New York. 1873.
Western Bookseller. Chicago. 1888.
Western Home. Chicago. 1871.
Young People's Magazine. Philadelphia. 1887.

1869

Agitator. Chicago. 1869.
American Bibliopolist. New York. 1877.

American Booksellers' Guide. New York. 1875.
American Grocer. New York. Current.
American Horological Journal. New York. 1873.
Appleton's Journal. New York. 1881.
Archives of Ophthalmology (and Otology). New York, Chicago. Current.
Bulletin of the Essex Institute. Salem (Massachusetts). Current.
Chautauqua Farmer. Dunkirk (New York). 1898.
Christian Observer, later *Central Methodist.* Catlettsburg (Kentucky), Louisville. 1931.
Coal Trade Journal. New York. Current.
Chicago Medical Times. 1910.
Chip Basket. New York. 1871.
Christian Quarterly. Cincinnati. 1876.
Counting-House Monitor, later *Bullinger's Monitor Guide.* New York. Current.
De la Salle Monthly, later *Manhattan Monthly.* New York. 1877.
Dental (Practitioner and) Advertiser. Buffalo. 1898.
Educational Journal of Virginia. Richmond. 1891.
Evening Lamp. Chicago. 1909.
Florida Dispatch. Jacksonville. 1910.
Folio. Boston. 1895.
Golden Hours. Cincinnati. 1881.
Heathen Woman's Friend, later *Woman's Missionary Friend.* Boston. Current.
Journal of Social Science. New York. 1909.
Kaleidoscope. New York. 1869.
Ladies' Own Magazine. Indianapolis. 1874.
Life and Light for (Heathen) Women. Boston. 1922.
Little Folks. Chicago. 1877.
Manufacturer and Builder. New York. 1897.
Methodist Advocate. Chattanooga, Knoxville, Jackson (Tennessee). 1931.
Model Farmer, later *Southern Agriculturist.* Corinth (Mississippi), Nashville, etc. Current.
Nebraska Cultivator and Housekeeper. Omaha. 1889.
New Jersey Temperance Gazette. Tom's River (New Jersey), Camden. 1911.
New York Humorist. 1869.
Once a Month. Philadelphia. 1869.
Onward. New York. 1870.
Oregon Agriculturist, later *Willamette Farmer.* Salem, Portland. 1887.
People's Literary Companion. Augusta (Maine). 1907.
Philadelphia Underwriter. 1906.
Pomeroy's Democrat. New York. 1887.
Publishers' Auxiliary. Chicago. Current.
Rural Carolinian. Charleston. 1876.
Rural Southland. New Orleans. 1873.
Van Nostrand's (Eclectic) Engineering Magazine. New York. 1887.

Velocipedist. New York. 1869.
Western Monthly, later *Lakeside Monthly.* Chicago. 1874.
Western Stock Journal. Sigourney (Iowa). 1870.
Working Christian, later *Baptist Courier.* Yorkville (South Carolina), Charleston, Greenville (South Carolina), etc. Current.
Zion's Hope. Lamoni (Iowa), Independence (Missouri). Current.

1870

Advocate of Christian Holiness, later *Christian Witness.* Boston. 1909.
Albany Law Journal. 1908.
American Antiquarian. New York. 1889.
American Cabinet Maker and Upholsterer, later *Furniture (World and) Buyer and Decorator.* New York. Current.
American Chemist. New York. 1877.
American Journal of Syphilography and Dermatology. New York. 1874.
American Protestant. New York, Washington. 1888.
Anthony's Photographic Bulletin. New York. 1902.
Art Review. Chicago. 1872.
Baldwin's Monthly. New York. 1886.
Baptist Teacher. Philadelphia. 1916.
Beecher's Illustrated Magazine. Trenton (New Jersey). 1872.
Bowdoin Scientific Review. Brunswick (Maine). 1872.
California Horticulturist. San Francisco. 1880.
Carpet (and Upholstery) Trade Review. New York. Current.
Catholic Vindicator, later *Catholic (Herald) Citizen.* Milwaukee. Current.
Cherub, later *Illustrated Home Guest.* New York. 1879.
Chicago Magazine of Fashion, etc. 1876.
Christian Union, later *Outlook.* New York. 1935.
Church. Philadelphia. 1886.
Examiner. Chicago. 1871.
Fashion Bazar. New York. 1880.
Index. Toledo (Ohio), Boston. 1886.
Insurance Index. New York. 1935.
Interior, later *Continent.* Chicago. 1926.
Keepapitchinin. New York. 1871.
Literary World. Boston. 1904.
(Live Stock and) Western Farm Journal. Des Moines (Iowa). 1897.
Messenger of Peace. Richmond (Indiana), St. Joseph (Missouri). 1931.
(Michigan) Christian Herald. Detroit. 1910.
National Car (and Locomotive) Builder. New York. 1895.
National Live Stock Journal. Chicago. 1891.
New England Medical Monthly. Danbury (Connecticut), etc. 1912.
New Era. New York. 1876.
New York Genealogical and Biographical Record. Current.
Old and New. Boston. 1875.
Our Monthly. Cincinnati, Philadelphia. 1874.
Pennsylvania Monthly. Philadelphia. 1882.

Petroleum Monthly, later *Monthly Petroleum Trade Report.* Oil City (Pennsylvania). 1882.
Philadelphia Medical Times (and Register). 1903.
Plantation. Atlanta. 1873.
Present Age. New Orleans. 1872.
Proof Sheet. New York. 1891.
Punchinello. New York. 1870.
Rutter's Political Quarterly. Memphis. 1870.
Scribner's Monthly, later *Century Magazine.* New York. 1930.
Simpsonian. Indianola (Iowa). Current.
Sports and Games. Boston. 1874.
Star Journal, later *Saturday Journal.* New York. 1881.
Sugar Bowl and Farm Journal, later *Sugar Planter.* New Iberia (Louisiana), New Orleans. 1910.
Technologist. New York. 1877.
True Woman. Baltimore, Washington. 1873.
Watchman. Washington (North Carolina). 1886.
Wild Oats. New York. 1881.
Woman's Journal, later *Woman Citizen.* Boston, New York. 1931.
Woodhull and Claflin's Weekly. New York. 1876.
World Magazine. Chicago. 1893.
Young Catholic. New York. 1905.
Young Churchman. Milwaukee. 1922.
Young Folks' Monthly. Chicago. 1883.
Young Folks' Rural. Chicago. 1881.

1871

American Brewers' Gazette. New York. 1886.
American Journal of Fabrics and Dry Goods Bulletin, later *Merchant World.* New York. 1888.
American Rural Home. Rochester. 1891.
Apples of Gold. New York. Current.
Bonfort's Wine and Spirit Circular. New York. 1919.
California Mail-Bag. San Francisco. 1878.
Champagne. New York. 1871.
Chicago Pulpit. 1873.
Christian Worker. New Vienna (Ohio). 1894.
Church's Musical Visitor. Cincinnati. 1897.
Church News. St. Louis. 1936.
Coast Review. San Francisco. 1924.
Connecticut School Journal. New Haven. 1874.
Electrotyper. Chicago. 1890.
Columbia Churchman, later *Oregon Churchman.* Vancouver (Washington), Portland. Current.
Dry Goods Reporter. Chicago. 1929.
Equitable Record. New York. 1905.
Frank Leslie's Ladies' Journal. New York. 1881.

Georgia Medical Companion, later *Southern Medical Record*. Atlanta. 1899.
Golden Age. New York. 1875.
Health and Home. Port Chester (New York), Washington, Chicago. 1891.
Illini. Urbana (Illinois). Current.
Illustrated Christian Weekly. 1892.
(Insurance) Herald (-Argus), later *Southern Underwriter*. Atlanta. 1929.
Insurance Law Journal. St. Louis, New York. Current.
Lumberman's Gazette. Chicago. 1898.
(Leffel's Illustrated) Mechanical News. Springfield (Ohio), New York. 1894.
Mackey's National Freemason. Washington. 1874.
Naturalist Advertiser. Salem (Massachusetts). 1875.
Nautical Gazette. New York. Current.
New Northwest. Portland (Oregon). 1890.
New Remedies, later *American Druggist*. New York. Current.
New Varieties. New York. 1875.
Oil City Derrick. Oil City (Pennsylvania). Current.
Oil, Paint and Drug Reporter. New York. Current.
Once a Week, later *Frank Leslie's Journal*. New York. 1881.
Our Home Journal. New Orleans. 1875.
Pacific Rural Press. San Francisco. Current.
People's Monthly. Pittsburgh. 1875.
Photographic Times. New York. 1915.
Printers' Guide. San Francisco. 1890.
Rural Messenger. Petersburg (Virginia). 1882.
School Journal. New York. 1916.
Shaker (and Shakeress), later *Manifesto*. Shakers (New York), East Canterbury (New Hampshire). 1899.
Southern Musical Journal. Savannah (Georgia). 1882.
St. Louis (Ladies') Magazine. 1892(?).
Sunday School Magazine, later *Church School Magazine*. Nashville. Current.
Sunnyside. New York. 1924.
Western Granger and Home Journal. Lafayette (Indiana). 1879.
Whittaker's Milwaukee Magazine. 1877.
Witness. New York. 1920.

1872

American Historical Record, later *Potter's American Monthly*. Philadelphia. 1882.
American Journalist. Philadelphia. 1877.
American Law Record. Cincinnati. 1887.
Arcadian. New York. 1878.
Banker and Tradesman. Boston, Cambridge. Current.
Bee Keepers' Magazine. Chicago. 1889.
Boston Contributor. 1906.

Boston Journal of Commerce. 1908.
Brentano's (Aquatic) Monthly (and Sporting Gazeteer). 1891.
Boston Pulpit. 1872.
Brickbat. New York. 1872.
Carl Pretzel's Pook. Chicago. 1874.
Catholic Review. New York. 1898.
Catholic Union (and Times). Buffalo. Current.
Central Magazine. St. Louis. 1875.
Chicago Ledger, later *Blade and Ledger.* Current.
Clothier and Hatter, later *Clothier and Furnisher.* New York. 1927.
Cocktails. 1872.
Dexter Smith's, Musical, Literary, Dramatic and Art Paper. Boston. 1878.
Fat Contributor's Saturday Night. Cincinnati, New York. 1875.
Fifth Avenue Journal. New York. 1873.
Flower Garden, later *American Garden.* Brooklyn, New York. 1904.
Gleason's Monthly Companion. Boston. 1887.
Grocer. Cincinnati. 1893.
Harkness' Magazine. Wilmington (Delaware). 1877.
Index, later *Standard.* Boston. Current.
Inland Monthly Magazine. St. Louis. 1876.
Jubilee Days. Boston. 1872.
Kansas Churchman. Topeka. 1918(?).
Kansas Magazine. Topeka. 1873.
Ladies' Floral Cabinet. New York. 1887.
Midland Farmer. St. Louis. 1886.
Mining Review. Georgetown (Colorado), Denver. 1877.
Missionary. Richmond. 1889.
National Humane Journal. Chicago. 1917.
North East. Portland (Maine). 1889.
Notre Dame Scholastic. Notre Dame (Indiana). Current.
Our Fireside Friend. Chicago. 1875.
Paleontological Bulletin. Philadelphia. 1885.
Paper Trade Journal. New York. Current.
Popular Science Monthly. New York. Current.
Poultry World. Hartford. 1896.
Publishers' Weekly. New York. Current.
Rocky Mountain Presbyterian. Denver. 1880.
(Rod and Gun and) American Sportsman. West Meriden (Connecticut). 1877.
Saturday Night. Cincinnati. 1885.
Southern Workman. Hampton (Virginia). Current.
Thistle. New York. 1872.
Vox Humana. Chicago. 1899.
Weekly Weather Chronicle. Washington. 1881
Western Star. Boston. 1872.
Woman's Campaign. New York. 1872.
Zell's Monthly Magazine. Philadelphia. 1873.

1873

Acta Columbiana. New York. 1885.
Alliance. Chicago. 1883.
American Medical Journal. St. Louis. 1916.
American Miller. Chicago. Current.
American Progress. New York. 1891.
American Stationer. Brooklyn. 1928.
Brittan's Journal of Spiritual Science. New York. 1874.
Chicago Commercial Advertiser, later *Industrial World.* 1898.
Chronotype. New York. 1874.
Church Union. New York. 1899.
Cincinnati Pioneer. 1885.
Crucible. New York. 1877.
Delineator. New York. 1937.
Domestic Monthly. New York. 1895.
Drovers' Journal (Weekly), later *Goodall's Farmer.* Chicago. 1910.
Forest and Stream. New York. 1930.
Grand Army Gazette. New York. 1900.
Gregg's Dollar Monthly. Hamilton (Illinois). 1877.
Griffin's Journal. Philadelphia. 1900.
Grocer's Criterion. Chicago. 1912.
Grocers' Price Current. Philadelphia. 1886.
Industrial Age. Chicago. 1877.
Insurance Age (-Journal). Boston. 1936.
Insurance Journal. Hartford. 1924.
Journal. Philadelphia. 1885.
Kindergarten Messenger. Cambridge. 1876.
Living Issue. Utica, New York. 1886.
Locomotive Firemen's (and Enginemen's) Magazine. Cincinnati, Peoria
    (Illinois), Cleveland. Current.
Magenta, later *Harvard Crimson.* Cambridge. Current.
Medical Advance. Cincinnati, Chicago, ctc. 1915.
Medical Brief. St. Louis. 1929.
National Labor Tribune. Pittsburgh. Current.
National Presbyterian. Indianapolis. 1902.
Northwestern Miller. Minneapolis. Current.
Oberlin Review. Oberlin (Ohio). Current.
Occident. Chicago. 1895.
Our Banner. New York. 1894.
Our Church Paper. New Market (Virginia). 1907.
Our Home and Fireside Magazine. Portland (Maine). 1888.
Our Living and Our Dead. Newbern (North Carolina), Raleigh. 1876.
Our Rest. Chicago. 1891.
Patron of Husbandry. Columbus (Mississippi). 1883.
Presbyterian at Work. Philadelphia. 1878.

Price Current and Live Stock Record, later *Live-Stock Indicator,* later *Farmer and Stockman.* Kansas City. 1922.
Proceedings of the American Society of Civil Engineers. New York. Current.
Railway Register. St. Louis. 1891.
Republic. Washington. 1878.
Rhodes' Journal of Banking. New York. 1895.
Sanitarian. New York. 1904.
Sewing Machine Journal. New York. 1893.
Southern Planter and Grange. Atlanta. 1880.
Thistleton's Jolly Giant. San Francisco. 1883.
St. Nicholas. New York. Current.
Truth-Seeker. New York. Current.
Western Hotel Reporter. San Francisco. Current.
(Woman's) Home Companion. Cleveland, Springfield (Ohio). Current.

1874

Alabama Baptist. Birmingham. Current.
(American) Baptist Reflector. Nashville, Chattanooga. 1888.
American Fashion Review, later *(American Gentleman and) Sartorial Art Journal.* New York. Current.
American Laboratory. Boston. 1877.
American Medical Weekly, later *Gaillard's Medical Journal,* later *Gaillard's Southern Medicine.* Louisville, New York, Savannah. 1911.
American Poultry Journal. Cedar Rapids (Iowa). Chicago. Current.
Amphion. Detroit. 1885.
Analyst. Des Moines (Iowa). 1883.
Andrew's Bazar. Cincinnati, New York. 1883.
Archives of Dermatology. New York. 1882.
Baptist Messenger, later *Texas Baptist (and Herald).* Paris, Dallas. 1900.
Belles and Beaux. New York. 1874.
Carl Pretzel's National Weekly. Chicago. 1893.
Cash Grocer. Philadelphia. 1894.
Catholic Universe (Bulletin). Cleveland. Current.
Central Law Journal. St. Louis. 1927.
Chicago Grocer. 1903.
Chicago Journal of Nervous and Mental Diseases. Current.
Cincinnati (later *American*) *Grange Bulletin.* 1906.
Cincinnati Quarterly Journal of Science. 1875.
Confectioners' Journal. Philadelphia. Current.
Conference News, later *Pennsylvania Methodist.* Harrisburg. 1906.
Cornell Review. Ithaca (New York). 1886.
Cottage Hearth. Boston. 1894.
Crockery and Glass Journal. New York. Current.
Dirigo Rural. Bangor (Maine). 1887.
Engineer and Surveyor, later *Engineering News (-Record).* Chicago, New York. Current.

Equity. Boston. 1875.
Expositor. New York, Philadelphia, Newark. 1922.
(American) Field (and Stream). Chicago, New York. Current.
Humorist. New York. 1874.
Husbandman. Elmira (New York). 1893.
Insurance Critic. New York. 1926.
Insurance World. Pittsburgh. 1924.
Investigator. Chicago. 1908.
International Review. New York. 1883.
Ladies' Illustrated Newspaper. New York. 1886.
Lithograph. New York. 1874.
Metal Worker, Plumber and Steam Fitter, later *Sanitary and Heating (Engineering) Age.* New York. 1931.
New Jersey (later *New York*) *Eclectic Medical and Surgical Journal.* 1895.
New Orleans Monthly Review. 1876.
Novelist. Chicago. 1881.
Operator. New York. 1885.
Organists' Quarterly Journal and Review. Boston. 1877.
Owl. Chicago. 1876.
Painters' Magazine. New York. 1933.
Pansy. Boston. 1896.
Peck's Sun. La Crosse (Wisconsin), Milwaukee. 1894.
Psyche. Cambridge. Current.
Public Leader. Detroit. 1895.
Pythian Journal. Indianapolis. 1933.
San Francisco Grocer. 1936.
Saturday Evening Herald. Boston. 1908.
School Bulletin and New York State Educational Bulletin. Syracuse. 1920.
Sovereigns of Industry Bulletin. Worcester (Massachusetts). 1880.
Trade Bureau. New York. 1893.
Truth. St. Louis. 1897.
Unitarian Review. Boston. 1891.
United States Tobacco Journal. New York. Current.
Vickery's Fireside Visitor. Augusta (Maine). 1907.
Virginia Medical Monthly. Richmond. Current.
Washington Law Reporter. Current.
Western Manufacturer. Chicago. 1888.
Western Tobacco Journal. New York. Current.
Woman's Temperance Union, later *Union Signal.* Chicago, Evanston (Illinois). Current.
Ye Giglampz. Cincinnati. 1874.

1875

American Art Journal. New York. 1887.
American Journal of Microscopy and Popular Science. New York. 1881.
American Meteorologist. St. Louis. 1877.
Arkansas. Boston. 1875.

Arkansas Farmer. Little Rock. 1895.
Baptist Flag. Fulton (Kentucky). 1925.
Book Exchange Monthly. New York. 1878.
Botanical Bulletin. Crawfordsville (Indiana). 1875.
Boys of New York. New York. 1894.
Brown's Phonographic Monthly (later *Weekly*), later *Shorthand Educator*. New York. 1899.
Bulletin of International Meteorological Observations. Washington. 1889.
California Patron. San Francisco. 1889.
Carpet Trade. Philadelphia. 1890.
Chicago Index. 1891.
Connecticut Farmer, later *New England Farms.* New Haven. 1927.
Fabrics, Fancy Goods and Notions. New York. 1920.
Girls of Today, later *New York Mirror.* 1876.
Golden Rule, later *Christian Endeavor World.* Boston. Current.
Grain and Provision Review. Chicago. 1887.
Grocer. Philadelphia. 1890.
Horse Shoers' Journal. Detroit, Chicago, Indianapolis. 1930.
Hotel World. Chicago, New York. Current.
Jewish Progress. San Francisco. 1900.
Journal of the American Electrical Society. Chicago. 1880.
Kansas Industrialist. Manhattan. Current.
Kentucky Church Chronicle. Louisville. 1889.
Kentucky Livestock Record, later *Thoroughbred Record.* Lexington. Current.
Knights of Honor Reporter. Boston. 1915.
Leader. Boston. 1904.
Library Table. New York. 1879.
Literary News. New York. 1904.
Maine Genealogist and Biographer. Augusta. 1878.
Michigan Christian Advocate. Detroit. Current.
Millstone. Indianapolis. 1892.
Minneapolis Review, later *Northwestern Prohibitionist.* 1890.
National Agriculturist and Working Farmer. New York. 1881.
(New England) Journal of Education. Boston. Current.
New York Dramatic News (and Society Journal). Current.
New York Sportsman. 1892.
Observer. St. Louis. 1900.
(Ornithologist and) Oölogist. Rockville (Rhode Island), Boston. 1893.
Our Fireside Journal. Augusta (Maine). 1880.
Peninsula Methodist. Wilmington (Delaware). 1910.
Philatelic Monthly. New York. 1899.
Presbyterian Journal, later *Westminster.* Philadelphia. 1910.
Rocky Mountain Husbandman. White Springs (Montana), Great Falls (Montana). Current.
Scientific Commercial. Buffalo. 1876.
Scientific Monthly, later *Journal of Science.* Toledo, Chicago. 1882.

Spirit of '76. New Haven. 1877.
Sunny South. Atlanta. 1907.
Temperance Benefit. Easton (Pennsylvania). 1887.
Voice of Angels. Somerville (Massachusetts). 1887.
Wallace's Monthly. New York, Chicago. 1894.
Ware's Valley Monthly. St. Louis. 1876.
Weekly Budget. New Orleans. 1876.
West Shore. Portland, Spokane. 1891.
(Western) Confectioner and Baker. Chicago. 1913.
(Western) Paper Trade. Chicago. 1931.
Wide Awake. New York. 1893.

1876

American Architect. Boston. Current.
American Berkshire Record. Springfield (Illinois). 1923.
American Bookseller. New York. 1893.
American Catholic Quarterly Review. Philadelphia. 1924.
American Dairyman. New York. 1907.
American Socialist. Oneida (New York). 1879.
Appalachia. Boston. 1922.
Babyland. Boston. 1898.
Botanical Gazette. Crawfordsville (Indiana), Chicago, etc. Current.
Bulletin of the Nuttall Ornithological Club, later *Auk.* Cambridge, etc.
    Current.
Casket (and Sunnyside). Rochester, New York. Current.
Centennial Record. Portland (Maine). 1879.
Cincinnati Weekly Law Bulletin (and Ohio Law Journal), later *Ohio Law
    Bulletin.* 1921.
Comic World. New York. 1879.
Connecticut Catholic, later *Catholic Transcript.* Hartford. Current.
Dr. Foote's Health Monthly. New York. 1895.
Frank Leslie's Popular Monthly, later *American Magazine.* New York.
    Current.
Harvard Lampoon. Cambridge. Current.
Home and Farm. Louisville. 1918.
Hotel Gazette. New York. Current.
Library Journal. New York. Current.
Merry Masker. New York. 1876.
Metropolitan Pulpit, later *Homiletic (and Pastoral) Review.* New York.
    Current.
Millinery Trade Review. New York. Current.
Mississippi Valley Lumberman. Minneapolis. Current.
(National Citizen and) Ballot Box. Toledo (Ohio), Syracuse (New York).
    1881.
New York Aquarium Journal. 1877.
New York Illustrated Times. 1884.
North Carolina (later *Southern*) *Farmer.* Raleigh. 1893.

Notices of Recent Publications, later *New England Bibliopolist*. Boston. 1901.
Olive Branch. Utica (New York). 1889.
Our Boys. New York. 1878.
Our Country. New York. 1878.
Our Second Century. Philadelphia. 1886.
Pacific Life. San Francisco. 1885.
Penman's Gazette and Business Educator. New York. 1886.
Railroad Conductors' Brotherhood Monthly. Chicago. 1878.
Railway Age. Chicago, New York. Current.
Rocky Mountain Christian Advocate. Salt Lake City. 1883.
Scientific American Supplement. New York. 1919.
Socialist, later *Labor Standard*. New York, Paterson (New Jersey). 1900.
Southern Historical Monthly. Raleigh (North Carolina). 1876.
Southern Historical Society Papers. Richmond. Current.
Spirit of the Turf. Chicago. 1881.
United States Miller. Milwaukee. 1894.
Washingtonian. Chicago. 1893.
Wasp, later *Wasp News-Letter*. San Francisco. 1935.
Western Brewer, later *Beverage Journal*. Chicago. Current.
Western Magazine, later *Weekly Magazine*. Omaha, Chicago. 1884.
World's Advance-Thought. Salem (Oregon), Portland. 1918.
Y.M.C.A. Watchman, later *Association Men*, later *Young Men*. Chicago, Cleveland, New York. 1932.

1877

Acanthus. Atlanta. 1884.
American Bicycling Journal. Boston. 1879.
American Cricketer. Philadelphia. 1933.
American Exporter. New York. Current.
American Homoeopathist, later *American Physician*. Chicago, New York. 1926.
American Machinist. New York. Current.
American (later *National*) *Stockman* (*and Farmer*). Pittsburgh. 1921.
American Veterinary Review, later *Journal of the American Veterinary Medical Association*. New York, Ithaca. Current.
Argonaut. San Francisco. Current.
Baptist Beacon, later *Pacific Baptist*. Oregon City, Portland, etc. 1920.
Baptist Record. Clinton (Mississippi), Jackson (Mississippi). Current.
Bee Keepers' Guide. Kendallville (Indiana). 1893.
Bentley's Book Buyer, later *Robinson's Epitome of Literature*. New York. 1879.
Book Bulletin. Boston. 1890.
Catholic Times. Rochester. 1881.
Central School Journal. Keokuk (Iowa). 1895.
Engineer of the Pacific. San Francisco. 1880.

Farm and Fireside, later *Country Home*. Springfield (Ohio), New York. Current.

Farm, Field and Fireside, later *National Monthly Farm Press*, later *Better Farming*. Chicago. 1925.

Farm Journal. Philadelphia. Current.

Farmer and Mechanic. Raleigh. 1908.

Farmers' Review. Chicago. 1918.

Field and River. New Brighton (Pennsylvania). 1882.

Frank Leslie's Sunday Magazine. New York. 1889.

Geyer's Stationer. New York. Current.

Good Times. Boston. 1885.

Grange Record. Louisville. ?

Granite Monthly. Concord (New Hampshire). 1930.

Half-Dime Library. New York. 1898.

Hotel Mail. New York. 1897.

Housekeeper. Minneapolis. 1913.

Ice Trade Journal. Philadelphia. 1904.

Iowa Churchman. Davenport. 1923.

Iowa Normal Monthly. Dubuque. 1912.

Kansas City Review of Science and Industry. 1885.

(Kindergarten Messenger and) New Education. Milwaukee. 1882.

L. B. Case's Botanical Index. Richmond (Indiana). 1881.

Labor Balance. Boston. 1879.

Ladies' Home Journal. San Francisco. 1887.

Lady's Bazar. New York. 1886.

Leisure Hours. New York. 1882.

Liberal Freemason. Boston. 1891.

Magazine of American History. New York. 1917.

Maryland Medical Record. Baltimore. 1918.

Minnesota Farmer and Stockman. Minneapolis. 1887.

(National) Firemen's Journal, later *Fire and Water*, later *Fire Engineering*. New York. Current.

Naturalist and Fancier. Grand Rapids (Michigan). 1879.

Naturalists' Leisure Hour. Philadelphia. 1895.

Nebraska Farmer. Lincoln, Omaha. Current.

New England Grocer and Tradesman, later *New England Grocery and Market Magazine*. Boston. Current.

New Preparations, later *Therapeutic Gazette*. Detroit. 1927.

New York Boys' Weekly. New York. 1878.

New York Mining Record. 1892.

Old Times. North Yarmouth (Maine). 1884.

Our Neighborhood, later *Brooklyn Advance*. 1886.

Pacific Printer. San Francisco. 1891.

Penman's Art Journal. New York. 1916.

Pennsylvania Magazine of History and Biography. Philadelphia. Current.

People's Journal. Portland (Maine). 1891.

Play. Chicago. 1883.

Practical Teacher. Chicago. 1885.
Primary Teacher. Boston. 1916.
Puck. New York. 1918.
Racine (later *Wisconsin*) *Agriculturist.* Current.
Radical Review. New Bedford (Massachusetts). 1878.
Retail Grocers' Advocate. New York. 1934.
Scientific Observer. Boston. 1887.
Score. Boston. 1882.
Semi-Tropic California, later *Rural Californian.* Los Angeles. 1914.
Sewing Machine News. 1893.
Shoe and Leather Review. Chicago. 1902.
South Atlantic. Wilmington (North Carolina), Baltimore. 1882.
St. Louis Practical Photographer, later *St. Louis and Canadian Photographer.* 1910.
Supplement to the Popular Science Monthly. New York. 1879.
Treasure Trove. New York. 1893.
Virginia Law Journal. Richmond. 1893.
Warrington's Musical Review. New Orleans. 1886.
Woman's Century, later *Woman's Magazine.* Brattleboro (Vermont). 1890.
Woman's Words. Philadelphia. 1881.
Young Men of America. New York. 1888.

1878

American Antiquarian (and Oriental Journal). Chicago, etc. 1914.
American Inventor, later *World's Progress.* Cincinnati. 1898.
American Journal of Mathematics. Baltimore. Current.
American Kindergarten Magazine. New York. 1887.
American Quarterly Microscopical Journal. New York, Washington. 1902.
Art Interchange. New York. 1904.
Artisan. Cincinnati. 1887.
Baptist Home Mission Monthly. New York. 1909.
Benedict's Fashion Journal. Philadelphia. 1887.
Canning Trade. Baltimore. Current.
Champion of Freedom and Right (later *of Fair Play*). Chicago. 1929.
Chautauqua Herald. Chautauqua (New York). 1880.
Christian Herald. New York. Current.
Church Progress. Marshall (Illinois). 1884.
Council Fire. Washington. 1889.
Dime Library. New York. 1897.
Farm and Hearth. Augusta (Maine). 1887.
Forney's Progress. Philadelphia. 1885.
Frank Leslie's Budget. New York. 1896.
Gospel Messenger. Williamston (North Carolina), etc. 1923.
Grain Cleaner, later *Modern Miller.* Chicago, etc. Current.
Illustrated Scientific News. New York. 1881.
Iowa Farmer, later *Wallace's Farmer.* Cedar Rapids, Des Moines. Current.

Iowa (Farmer's) Tribune, later *Farmer and Breeder*. Des Moines, Sioux City, Sioux Falls (South Dakota). 1929.

Jewish Advocate. New York. 1887.

Kunkel's Musical Review. San Francisco. 1884.

(Laws of) Health. Reading (Pennsylvania), etc. 1887.

Lever. Grand Rapids (Michigan), Chicago. 1898.

Living Church. Chicago, Milwaukee. Current.

Magazine of Art. New York. 1904.

Marine Journal. New York. Current.

Maryland Law Record. Baltimore. 1889.

Mining and Metallurgical Journal. San Francisco, New York. 1901.

Mining and Scientific Review. Denver. 1895.

Missionary Review of the World. Princeton (New Jersey). 1912.

Music Trade Indicator. Chicago. 1930.

Musical Record and Review. Boston. 1903.

National Socialist. New York, Chicago. 1879.

New Orleans Quarterly Review. 1878.

Orchard and Garden. Little Silver (New Jersey). 1892.

Paine Family Records. New York. 1883.

Paleontologist. Cincinnati. 1883.

Paper Mill and Wood Pulp News. Philadelphia, New York. Current.

Pictorial Gallery for Young Folks. Chicago. 1893.

Poultry Monthly. Albany. 1902.

Railway Purchasing Agent, later *Railway Master Mechanic*. Chicago. 1916.

Rideout's Monthly Magazine. New York. 1883.

Rough Notes. Indianapolis. Current.

Science News. Salem (Massachusetts). 1879.

Scientific Man. New York. 1882.

Southern Clinic. Richmond. 1919.

Spice Mill. New York. Current.

St. Louis Grocer. 1904.

Stoves and Hardware Reporter. St. Louis. 1913.

Sunday Afternoon, later *Good Company*. Springfield (Massachusetts). 1881.

Sunday Gazette. Atlanta. 1881.

Teachers' Institute. New York. 1906.

Temperance Cause. Boston. 1930.

Turf, Farm and Home. Waterville (Maine). 1911.

Underwood's United States Counterfeit Reporter. New York. 1931.

Unity. Chicago. Current.

Vick's Illustrated Monthly Magazine. Rochester. 1909.

Watchword (and Truth). Boston. 1921.

Western Sportsman and Live Stock News, later *Western Horseman*. Indianapolis. 1893.

Wide Awake Library. New York. 1891.

Woman's Home Journal. Boston. 1909.

Young New Yorker. 1879.
Young Scientist. New York. 1887.
Zion's Watchman. Albany. 1913.

1879

Afric-American Presbyterian. Wilmington (North Carolina). 1891.
Alabama Historical Reporter. Tuscaloosa. 1885.
American Art Review. Boston. 1881.
American Chemical Journal. Baltimore. 1913.
American Contractor. Chicago. 1930.
American Hairdresser (and Perfumer). New York. Current.
American Hebrew. New York. Current.
American Journal of Otology. Boston. 1822.
American Journal of Photography. Philadelphia. 1900.
American Model Printer. New York. 1884.
American Punch. Boston. 1881.
Andrew's American Queen, later *Town Topics.* 1931.
Antiquarian Papers. Ipswich (Massachusetts). 1885.
Archives of Otology. New York. 1908.
Army and Navy Register. Washington. Current.
Art Amateur. New York. 1903.
Association News. Philadelphia. 1891.
Baptist (Quarterly) Review. Cincinnati, New York. 1890.
Barbers' National Journal. Philadelphia. 1886.
Bicycling World. Boston. 1915.
Boston Budget. 1918.
(Dun and) Bradstreet's (Review), later *Dun's Review.* New York. Current.
Brethren Evangelist. Ashland (Ohio). 1889.
Bullion. New York. 1885.
Butchers' Advocate and Market Journal. New York. Current.
Carpentry and Building, later *Building Age.* New York. 1930.
Carpets, Wall Paper and Curtains. Philadelphia. 1889.
Carriage Journal. Chicago. 1893.
Catholic Book News. New York. 1909(?).
Chromatic Art Magazine. New York. 1883.
Church Kalendar. Westfield (New York). 1890.
Classmate. Cincinnati. Current.
Courier of Medicine. St. Louis. 1907.
(Dental) Items of Interest. Philadelphia, New York. Current.
Dental Luminary. Macon (Georgia). 1893.
Donahoe's Magazine. Boston. 1908.
Economist. Boston, New York. 1888.
Farm Journal and Live Stock Review. Cedar Rapids (Iowa). 1886.
Fireside at Home, later *Ladies' World.* New York. 1918.
Florida Agriculturist. De Land. 1911.

Fonetic Techer. St. Louis. 1879.
Frank Leslie's Chatterbox. New York. 1887.
Game Fanciers' Journal. Battle Creek (Michigan). 1910.
Grocers' Journal. New York. 1905.
Harper's Young People, later *Harper's Round Table.* New York. 1899.
Homoeopathic Journal of Obstetrics, later *Journal of Surgery, Gynecology and Obstetrics.* New York. 1910.
Insurance Salesman. Indianapolis. Current.
Jewish Times. San Francisco. 1924.
Jewish Voice. St. Louis. 1933.
Journal of the American Chemical Society. New York, Washington, Cambridge. Current.
Kansas Methodist. Topeka. 1888.
Library Magazine. New York. 1888.
Literary (and Musical) Review. Chicago. 1880.
Louisville Monthly Magazine. 1880.
Maine Horse Breeders' Monthly. Canton. 1892.
Medical Bulletin of the Jefferson Medical Association. Philadelphia. 1908.
Medical Summary. Lansdale (Pennsylvania). Philadelphia. 1928.
Merchants' Review. New York. 1908.
Milling World and Chronicle of the Grain and Flour Trade. Buffalo. 1898.
Music Trade Journal (later *Review*). New York. Current.
Musical Bulletin. Chicago. 1883.
Musician. Boston. 1894.
National Harness Review. Chicago. 1920.
New Albany Medical Herald. New Albany (Indiana). 1931.
New York (Dramatic) Mirror. 1922.
North Pacific Coast. Tacoma (Washington). 1881.
North Pacific Rural Spirit, later *Western Breeders' Journal.* Portland (Oregon). Current.
Overseer. St. Louis. 1924.
Pacific States Watchman. San Francisco. 1896.
Philadelphia Methodist. 1914.
Physician and Surgeon. Ann Arbor. 1915.
Pottery and Glassware Reporter. Pittsburgh. 1893.
Proceedings of the Engineers' Club of Philadelphia, later *Engineers and Engineering.* 1932.
Queen Bee. Denver. 1896.
Rambler and Dramatic Weekly. New York. 1879.
School of Mines Quarterly. New York. 1915.
Scientific Record. Washington. 1881.
Sewing Machine Advocate. Chicago. 1913.
Song Friend. Chicago. 1894.
Southern Practitioner. Nashville. 1918.
Southwestern Miller. Kansas City. Current.
Spiritual Record. Chicago. 1880.
Textile Colorist. Philadelphia. Current.

Tradesman, later *Southern Hardware and Implement Journal*. Atlanta. Current.
Uncle Sam. New York. 1879.
United Service. Washington. 1905.
Vedette. Washington. 1883.
Voice, later *Werner's (Voice) Magazine*. Albany, New York. 1902.
Western Druggist, later *Drug Bulletin*. Chicago. 1933.
Western Friend. Baxter Springs (Kansas). 1890.
Western Undertaker, later *American Funeral Director*. Grand Rapids, New York. Current.
(Zion's) Watch Tower. Pittsburgh, Brooklyn, etc. Current.

1880

Aegis. Cincinnati. 1886.
Albany Medical Annals. 1922.
American. Philadelphia. 1900.
American Artisan. Chicago. Current.
American Building Association News. Cincinnati. Current.
American Engineer. Chicago. 1889.
American Furniture Gazette. Chicago. 1902.
(American) Hatter (and Furrier). New York. 1935.
American Journal of Philology. Baltimore. Current.
American Tailor and Cutter. New York. 1916.
Anchor and Shield. Paris (Illinois). 1918.
Anti-Polygamy Standard. Salt Lake City. 1883.
Archives of Laryngology. New York. 1883.
Book Keeper, later *American Counting Room*. New York. 1884.
Boston Musical Herald. 1893.
California Architect. San Francisco. 1900.
California Medical Journal. Oakland, San Francisco. 1908.
Californian. San Francisco. 1882.
Chautauquan. New York. 1914.
Chic. New York. 1881.
Chicago (later St. Louis) Medical Review. 1915.
Coin Collector. Philadelphia. 1886.
Criminal Law Magazine and Reporter. Jersey City. 1896.
Dental Headlight. Nashville. 1910.
Dial. Chicago. New York. 1929.
Dunglison's College and Clinical Record. Philadelphia. 1899.
Education. Boston. Current.
Empire State Agriculturist, later *Farm Life*. Rochester. 1897.
Fancy Goods Graphic. New York. 1897.
Farm and Home. Springfield (Massachusetts). 1925.
Farmer's Home. Dayton (Ohio). 1902.
Forest, Forge and Farm. Ilion (New York), Albany. 1886.
Furniture Trade Review. New York. 1932.
Georgia Baptist. Augusta, Macon. 1934.

Golden Days for Boys and Girls. Philadelphia. 1907.
Guernsey County (later *Ohio*) *Teacher.* Cambridge (Ohio). 1935.
Home World. New Haven. 1888.
Illustrated Catholic American. New York. 1896.
Independent Practitioner, later *International Dental Journal.* Buffalo, Philadelphia. 1905.
Journal of United Labor, later *Journal of the Knights of Labor.* Marblehead (Massachusetts), Philadelphia. 1918.
Kansas (City) Medical Index (Lancet). Ft. Scott, Kansas City. 1910.
Kansas Telephone. Manhattan. 1894.
Kentucky Law Reporter. Frankfort. 1908.
Law Journal. St. Louis. 1907.
Little Folks' Reader, later *Our Little Men and Women.* Boston. 1894.
Live-Stock Journal, later *Texas Stock and Farm Journal,* later *National Co-Operator and Farm Journal.* Ft. Worth, Dallas. 1913.
Lucifer. Valley Falls (Kansas), Topeka, Chicago. 1907.
Maine Mining Journal, later *Industrial Journal.* Bangor, Portland. 1918.
Market Basket, later *Rural Farmer.* Philadelphia. 1913.
(Michigan School) Moderator-Topics. Lansing. 1921.
Musical (and Sewing Machine) Courier. New York.
Musical Harp. Berea (Ohio). 1897.
Musical People. Cincinnati. 1884.
Nebraska Congregational News. Lincoln. 1910.
Newport (later *Rhode Island*) *Historical Magazine.* 1887.
Odontographic Journal. Rochester. 1899.
Ohio Poultry Journal, later *American Poultryman,* later *Farm Stock Success.* Springfield. 1908.
Oriental and Biblical Journal. New York. 1880.
Our Little Granger. Cincinnati. 1890.
Pacific Electrian. San Francisco. 1898.
Paper World. Holyoke (Massachusetts), Springfield. 1898.
Pennsylvania Farmer. Mercer (Pennsylvania), Pittsburgh, etc. Current.
Philatelic World. New York. 1891.
Picture and Art Trade, later *Picture and Gift Journal.* Chicago. Current.
Presbyterian Review. New York. 1889.
Ridley's Fashion Magazine. New York. 1890.
School Visitor. Ansonia (Ohio). 1914.
Signal. Chicago. 1883.
South and West. St. Louis. 1886.
Sporting and Theatrical Journal, later *Sporting Review.* Chicago. 1893(?).
St. Louis Drug Market, later *Meyer (Brothers') Druggist.* 1933.
Steam. New York. 1884.
Stoddart's Review. Philadelphia. 1882.
Style. New York. 1894.
Sugar Beet. Philadelphia. 1911.
Texas Farmer. Belton, Dallas, Birmingham (Alabama). Current.
Textile Record of America. Philadelphia. 1903.

Thomas' Musical Journal. Albany. 1894.
Virginias. Staunton (Virginia). 1885.
Watchman. Chicago. 1891.
Western Stationer. Chicago. 1900.
Wheel. New York. 1900.

1881

American Angler. New York. 1900.
(American) Journal of Railway Appliances. New York. 1901.
American Literary Churchman. Baltimore. 1885.
American Merchant. New York. 1887.
American Methodist. Detroit. 1894.
American Register. Washington. 1884.
Appleton's Literary Bulletin. New York. 1890.
Boomerang, later *Republican-Boomerang.* Laramie (Wyoming). Current.
Bowditch's American Florist and Farmer. Boston. 1889.
Boys' Library of Sport, Story and Adventure. New York. 1890.
Breeder's Gazette. Chicago, Spencer (Indiana). Current.
Brick, Tile and Metal Review, later *Manufacturers' Chronicle.* Pittsburgh. 1890.
Carpenter. Philadelphia, New York, Indianapolis. Current.
(Church Progress and) Catholic World. St. Louis. 1929.
Civil Service Record, later *Good Government.* Washington, New York. Current.
Confectioners' Gazette, later *Candy.* New York. Current.
Critic. New York. 1906.
Dakota Farmer. Huron, Aberdeen. Current.
Dramatic Times. New York. 1896.
Dubuque Trade Journal. 1906.
Farm and Garden. Philadelphia. 1888.
Fiction. New York. 1882.
Fireman's Herald, later *Fire Service.* New York. 1927.
Ft. Wayne Journal of the Medical Sciences, later *Journal of the National Association of Railway Surgeons.* 1907.
Furnishing Gazette, later *Haberdasher.* 1931.
Gibson's Monthly Review, later *Clothing Gazette.* New York. 1903.
Glovers' Journal. Gloversville (New York). 1909.
Gospel Trumpet. Moundsville (West Virginia). 1903.
Home and School Visitor. Greenfield (Indiana). 1927.
Horseman. Chicago. 1915.
(Illinois Farmer and) Farmers' Call. Quincy (Illinois). 1924.
Illinois School Journal, later *Public School Journal,* later *School and Home Education.* Normal, Bloomington. 1922.
Indiana Baptist, later *(Indiana) Baptist Outlook.* Indianapolis. 1902.
Journal of the Association of Engineering Societies. New York, Chicago, etc. 1915.

Journal of (the Society of) Biblical Literature (and Exegesis). Middletown (Connecticut), New Haven, etc. Current.
Judge. New York. Current.
Legal Bibliography. 1913.
Liberty. Boston. 1908.
Light for Thinkers. Atlanta (Georgia). 1886.
Lumber World. Buffalo. 1898.
Manufacturers' Gazette. Boston, etc. 1898.
Mascot. New Orleans. 1900.
(Mechanical) Engineer. New York, Cleveland, Chicago. 1908.
Microscope. Ann Arbor (Michigan), Washington. 1897.
Mining Herald, later *Colliery Engineer.* Pottsville (Pennsylvania), Scranton. 1915.
Minnesota Journal of Education, later *(American) Educational Digest,* later *School Executives' Magazine.* St. Paul, Lincoln, etc. Current.
Mississippi Valley (later *Memphis*) *Medical Monthly.* 1922.
Musical Times. Chicago. 1926.
Mutual Underwriter. Green Springs (Ohio), Rochester. Current.
National Real Estate Index. Kansas City. 1890.
New-Church Life. Philadelphia, Bryn Athyn (Pennsylvania). Current.
New Hampshire Journal. Concord. 1898.
Northwestern Farmer, later *(Northwest) Pacific Farmer.* Portland. 1928.
Northwestern Lancet, later *Journal-Lancet.* Minneapolis. Current.
Ohio State Journal of Dental Science, later *Dental Summary.* Toledo. 1925.
Orange County Farmer, later *New York Farmer.* Port Jervis (New York). 1917.
Petroleum Age. Bradford (Pennsylvania). 1888.
Pharmaceutical Record and Market Review. New York. 1893.
Pilgrim. Minneapolis. 1890.
Platonist. Osceola (Missouri). 1888.
Plumbers' Trade Journal. New York. Current.
Presbyterian Home Missionary. New York. 1886.
Record of Christian Work. East Norfield (Massachusetts). 1934.
Schoolmaster, later *Intelligence.* Oak Park (Illinois). 1905.
Shroud. Chicago. 1886.
Southern Lumberman. Nashville. Current.
Texas Medical and Surgical Record, later *Texas Courier-Record of Medicine.* Ft. Worth. 1917.
Texas Siftings. Austin, New York. 1897.
Texas Stockman (and Farmer). San Antonio. 1916.
Thoroughbred Stock Journal. Philadelphia. 1889.
Tidings. Chicago. 1911.
Tobacco World. Philadelphia. Current.
Toilettes. New York. 1914.
United States Monthly Magazine, later *Abbot's Monthly.* Chicago. 1883.
West Virginia School Journal. Wheeling, etc. Current.

(Wilford's) Microcosm. New York. 1893.
Wit and Wisdom. New York. 1881.
(Woman's) Evangel. Dayton (Ohio). 1931.
Young People. Philadelphia. Current.

1882

Adam, later *Catholic Journal of the New South.* Memphis. 1936.
American Canoeist, later *Sail and Paddle.* New York. 1891.
American Chemical Review. Chicago. 1887.
American Elevator and Grain Trade. Chicago. 1930.
American Free Trader. New York. 1884.
American Jeweler. Chicago. 1929.
American Laundry Journal. Troy (New York). 1902.
American Merino. East Troy (Wisconsin). 1884.
American Metal Market. New York. Current.
American Press. New York. Current.
American Silk Journal. New York. Current.
American Woodworker and Mechanical Journal. Cincinnati. 1922.
Archery and Tennis News. New York. 1886.
Arkansas Methodist. Little Rock. Current.
Arkansas Traveler. Little Rock, Chicago. 1916.
Art Student. Boston. 1884.
Baptist Exponent, later *Baptist Commonwealth.* Philadelphia. 1917.
Beadle's Weekly, later *Banner Weekly.* New York. 1897.
Book News (Monthly). Philadelphia. 1918.
Boot and Shoe Recorder. Boston. Current.
Boots and Shoes (Weekly). New York. 1901.
Breeder and Sportsman. San Francisco. 1920.
Brooklyn Chess Chronicle. 1887.
Building, later *Architecture and Building.* New York. 1932.
Caterer and Household Magazine. Philadelphia. 1887.
Christian Herald. Omaha. 1887.
Christian Quarterly Review. Columbia (Missouri). 1889.
Church Building Quarterly. New York. 1909.
Cincinnati College of Music's Courier. 1893.
City and Country. Columbus. 1899.
Columbus Medical Journal. 1916.
Commercial Record. New Haven. Current.
Congregational Iowa. Oskaloosa, Grinnell. 1928.
Decorator and Furnisher. New York. 1898.
Denver (later *Western*) *Medical Times.* 1933.
Drake's Magazine. New York. 1893.
(Duroc) Swine Breeders' Journal. Indianapolis. 1928.
Electrical Review, later *Industrial Engineering,* later *Maintenance Engineering,* later *Factory Management and Maintenance.* Chicago. Current.
(Electrician and) Electrical Engineer. New York. 1899.

(Engineering–) Mechanics. Philadelphia. 1899.
Facts. Boston. 1887.
Farm Implement News. Chicago. Current.
Forward. Philadelphia. Current.
Free Baptist. Minneapolis. 1904.
Freund's Weekly, later *Music and Drama.* New York. 1892.
Glassworker, later *Commoner,* later *American Glass Review.* Pittsburgh.
    Current.
(Golden) Argosy (All-Story). New York. Current.
Good Cheer. Greenfield (Massachusetts). 1888.
Harness Gazette. Rome (New York). 1926.
Hebrew Standard. New York. 1922.
Housewife. New York. 1917.
Indiana Medical Journal. Indianapolis. 1908.
Indicator. Detroit. 1936.
Journal of Banking Law. New York. 1888.
Journal of Cutaneous Diseases. Chicago. 1919.
Labor Enquirer. Denver. 1889.
Leisure. New York. 1883.
Lumber Trade Journal. Chicago, New Orleans. 1931.
Lutheran Church Review. Philadelphia. 1927.
Lutheran Witness. St. Louis. Current.
Manufacturers' Record. Baltimore. Current.
Mascot. New Orleans. 1895.
Mathematical Magazine. Washington. 1910.
Miller's Review. Philadelphia, Atlanta. 1933.
Mission Dayspring. Boston. 1913.
Montana Christian Advocate. Helena. 1889.
Music and Drama. San Francisco. 1901.
Narragansett Historical Register. Hamilton (Rhode Island). 1891.
Northwestern Architect. Minneapolis. 1894.
(Historic Magazine and) Notes and Queries. Manchester (New Hamp-
    shire). 1909.
Ohio Mining Journal. Columbus. 1898.
Old Testament Student, later *Biblical World.* 1920.
(Our) Continent. New York. 1884.
Outing. Albany, Boston, New York. 1923.
Outlook, later *Sabbath Quarterly.* Alfred Center (New York). 1893.
Printer and Publisher, later *National Printer-Journalist.* Indianapolis,
    Milwaukee. Current.
Printing Trade News. New York. 1915.
Punch and Judy. Boston. 1882.
Roller Mill. Buffalo. 1912.
Sanitary Plumber. New York. 1900.
Season. New York. 1896.
Sidereal Messenger. Northfield (Minnesota). 1891.
Southern Bivouac. Louisville. 1887.

Southern Dental Journal (and Luminary). Atlanta. 1900.
St. Louis (later *National*) *Druggist.* 1935.
Sugar Beet News, later *Northwestern Farmer,* later *St. Paul Farmer.*
  Fargo (North Dakota), St. Paul. Current.
Truth. San Francisco. 1884.
Union Printer. New York. 1893.
Universe. San Francisco. 1893.
War Cry. New York. Current.
Western (later *Wisconsin*) *Farmer.* Madison. 1929.
Western Machinist, later *Scientific Machinist.* Cleveland. 1898.
Western Plowman. Moline (Illinois), Chicago. 1900.
Wheelman. Boston. 1883.
Wood Worker. Indianapolis. Current.

1883

American Agriculturist. Wenham (Massachusetts). 1895.
American Horse Breeder. Boston. 1913.
American Journalist. St. Louis. 1885.
Art Age. New York. 1889.
Art Folio. Providence. 1884.
Biographical Magazine. New York. 1885.
Bivouac. Boston. 1885.
Book Notes for the Week. Providence. 1916.
Bookmart. Pittsburgh. 1890.
Breeze. Chicago. 1883.
Building Trader Journal. St. Louis. 1903.
California Maverick. San Francisco. 1886.
Christian Hebrew. New York. 1896.
Confederate Annals. St. Louis. 1883.
Continental Magazine. Baltimore. 1883.
Converted Catholic. New York. 1928.
Cotton Plant. Marion (South Carolina), Columbia. 1904.
Craftsman. Washington. 1891.
Current. Chicago. 1888.
Dio Lewis's Monthly. New York. 1884.
Drug Topics. New York. Current.
Echo. Lafayette (Indiana), Chicago. 1901.
Electric(al) Age. New York. 1910.
Electrical World. New York. Current.
Empire State Workman. New York, Buffalo. 1910.
Étude. Lynchburg (Virginia), Philadelphia. Current.
Fanciers' Gazette. Indianapolis. 1906.
Farm and Ranch. Dallas. Current.
Figaro. New Orleans. 1884.
Florida Baptist. Live Oak. 1887.
Fox's Illustrated Week's Doings. New York. 1884.
Free-Soiler. New York. 1884.

Gilhooley's Etchings. Pittsburgh. 1883.
Gleanings in Bee Culture. Medina (Ohio). Current.
Gospel Messenger. Mount Morris (Illinois), Elgin (Illinois). Current.
Historical Register. Harrisburg. 1884.
Home, Farm and Factory. St. Louis. 1895.
Inland Architect and Builder. Chicago. 1908.
Inland Printer. Chicago. Current.
Insurance (and Insurance Critic). Newark. Current.
Insurance News. Philadelphia. 1926.
Jersey Bulletin (and Dairy World). Chicago. Current.
John Swinton's Paper. New York. 1887.
Journal of the American Medical Association. New York. Current.
Kentucky Stock Farm. Lexington. 1907.
Keynote. New York. 1897.
Keystone. Philadelphia. 1934.
Ladies' Home Journal. Philadelphia. Current.
Lancaster Law Review. Current.
Leather Manufacturer. Boston. Current.
Life. New York. 1936.
Manhattan. New York. 1884.
Medical Herald (and Physio-Therapist). St. Joseph (Missouri), Kansas
    City. 1933.
Medical World. Philadelphia. Current.
Medico-Legal Journal. New York. 1933.
Microscopical Bulletin and Science News. Philadelphia. 1902.
Mission Gleaner. New York. 1917.
Missionary Tidings. Indianapolis. 1918.
Missouri School Journal. Jefferson City. Current.
Modern Age. Buffalo. 1883.
Montana Churchman. Helena, etc. Current.
New Amsterdam Gazette. New York. 1895.
North Carolina Teacher. Raleigh. 1895.
Northwest Magazine. St. Paul. 1903.
Peacemaker. Philadelphia. 1914.
Pickings from Puck. New York. 1923.
Pulpit Treasury. New York. 1907.
Railroad Record and Investment Guide. Philadelphia. 1901.
Rural and Workman. Little Rock. 1891.
Science. Cambridge, New York. Current.
Shakespeariana. New York. 1893.
Southwestern Journal of Education. Nashville. 1895.
Sporting Life. Philadelphia. 1926.
Sports and Pastimes. Boston. 1886.
Summary. Elmira (New York). 1885.
Telegraph (and Telephone) Age. New York. Current.
Telegrapher's Advocate. New York. 1885.
Texas Dental Journal. Dallas. Current.

Texas School Journal. Houston, etc. 1932.
Vindicator, later *American Insurer.* New Orleans. Current.
Water-Gas Journal, later *Progressive Age,* later *Gas Age* (*-Record*). New York. Current.
Western Architect and Builder, later *Building Witness.* Cincinnati. Current.
Western Cyclist. Ovid (Michigan). 1886.
Western Railroader, later *Railroad Brakemen's Journal,* later *Railroad Trainman.* Peoria (Illinois), Cleveland. Current.
Wheelman's Gazette. Springfield (Massachusetts), Indianapolis. 1908.
Woman's Tribune. Beatrice (Nebraska), Washington. 1909.

1884

Alarm. Chicago. 1916.
A.M.E. Church Review. Philadelphia, Nashville. 1936.
American Catholic Historical Researches. Philadelphia. 1912.
American Journal of Ophthalmology. St. Louis. Current.
American Medical Compend. Attica (Ohio), Toledo. 1913.
American Meteorological Journal. Ann Arbor (Michigan), etc. 1896.
American Musician. New York. 1891.
(*American*) *Sheep Breeder* (*and Wool Grower*). Chicago. Current.
American Sportsman. New York. 1890.
Annals of Hygiene. Philadelphia. 1897.
Annals of Mathematics. Williamsburg (Virginia), Cambridge, Princeton. Current.
Archives of Pediatrics. Philadelphia, New York. Current.
Art Union. New York. 1885.
Boston Beacon. 1904.
Carrier Dove. Oakland (California). 1893.
Chautauqua Young Folks' Journal. Boston. 1889.
Chironian. New York. 1918.
Christian Nation. New York. 1929.
Clay Worker. Indianapolis. 1933.
Every Other Saturday. Boston. 1885.
Farm, Stock and Home. Minneapolis. 1929.
Fishing Gazette. New York. Current.
Florida Baptist Witness. De Land, Jacksonville, etc. Current.
Furniture Workers' Journal, later *General Woodworkers' Journal.* Baltimore. 1896.
Galop. Boston. 1900.
Hebraica. Chicago, etc. 1895.
Hotel Register. New York. 1912.
Kansas City Medical Record. 1911.
Literary Life. Cleveland, Chicago, New York. 1903.
Magazine of Western History, later *National Magazine.* Cleveland, New York. 1893.
Maine Historical and Genealogical Recorder. Portland. 1898.

Manufacturing Jeweler. Providence. Current.
Medical Progress. Louisville. 1928.
Milk Reporter. Sussex (New Jersey). 1930.
Missouri and Kansas Farmer. Kansas City. 1920.
National Glass Budget. Pittsburgh. Current.
National Journalist. Chicago. 1888.
(New) Voice. New York, Chicago. 1906.
Northwestern Presbyterian. Minneapolis. 1890.
Official Railway Equipment Register. New York. 1932.
Our Country Home, later *Our Grange Homes.* Greenfield (Massachusetts),
    Boston. 1894.
Poultry Keeper. Quincy (Illinois). Current.
Poultry Raiser, later *American Farmer, Livestock and Poultry Raiser.*
    Chicago. 1911.
Power (-Steam). New York. Current.
Present. Cincinnati. 1886.
Presto (-Times). Chicago. Current.
Railway Conductor's Monthly, later *Railway Conductor.* Elmira (New
    York), Cedar Rapids (Iowa). Current.
Rambler. Chicago. 1886.
Santa Clara Valley, later *Pacific Tree and Vine,* later *California Country
    Journal.* San José, San Francisco. 1913.
(Shoe and) Leather Gazette. St. Louis. 1913.
Stevens Indicator. Hoboken (New Jersey). Current.
Street (later *Electric) Railway Journal,* later *Transit Journal.* Current.
Tid-Bits, later *Time.* New York. 1890.
Transactions (later *Publications*) *of the Modern Language Association.*
    New York, Menasha (Wisconsin), etc. Current.
West American Scientist. San Diego (California). 1919.
(Western) Finance and Trade. San Francisco. 1931.
(Young) Oölogist. Albion (New York). Current.

INDEX

INDEX